SHAKEDOWN

Exposing the Real Jesse Jackson

Kenneth R. Timmerman

Since 1947
REGNERY PUBLISHING, INC.
An Eagle Publishing Company • Washington, DC

Library of Congress Cataloging-in-Publication Data

Timmerman, Kenneth R.
Shakedown : exposing the real Jesse Jackson / Kenneth R. Timmerman.
p. cm.
Includes index.
ISBN 0-89526-108-1
1. Jackson, Jesse, 1941– 2. Jackson, Jesse, 1941– —Ethics.
3. African American civil rights workers—Biography 4. Civil rights workers—
United States—Biography 5. African American politicians—Biography
6. Presidential candidates—United States—Biography. I. Title.
E185.97.J25 T56 2002
973.92'092—dc21

2002000669

First paperback edition 2003
Regnery Publishing, Inc.
An Eagle Publishing Company
One Massachusetts Avenue, NW
Washington, DC 20001

Visit us at www.regnery.com

Distributed to the trade by
National Book Network
4720-A Boston Way
Lanham, MD 20706

Printed on acid-free paper
Manufactured in the United States of America

10 9 8 7 6 5 4 3 2 1

Books are available in quantity for promotional or premium use. Write to Director of Special Sales, Regnery Publishing, Inc., One Massachusetts Avenue, NW, Washington, DC 20001, for information on discounts and terms or call (202) 216-0600.

To the victims of racial brokering,
from the West Coast of America
to the eastern shores of Africa,
this book is dedicated.

CONTENTS

INTRODUCTION

Since *Shakedown* was first published, the story I called the most under-reported scandal of the Clinton administration burst back onto the front pages, as President George W. Bush and his national security advisors debated in July 2003 whether to send U.S. troops to Liberia as part of a multinational peace-keeping force. In keeping with the muted reporting on Jackson's past scandals, not one "mainstream" American news organization reported on Jackson's deep involvement in the Liberian crisis. The liberal bias of most American newsrooms was evident.

As I argued in the first edition of *Shakedown,* the disaster in Liberia and neighboring Sierra Leone was, in part, Jackson's creation. This edition is buttressed with a new chapter containing previously classified documents from the Department of State, which I obtained under the Freedom of Information Act. They provide extraordinary insight into Jackson's unique role in crafting and implementing U.S. policy in Africa at a critical juncture in recent history; we are feeling the consequences of his involvement today.

As President Clinton's special envoy for democracy and human rights in Africa, starting in October 1997, Jackson became the Clinton administration's point man for Africa. He spearheaded Clinton's ten-day African safari in March 1998, which cost taxpayers $42.8 million. He legitimated Liberian strongman Charles Taylor and his protégé, the machete-wielding militia leader in neighboring Sierra Leone, Colonel Foday Sankoh. Without Jackson's active intervention, both leaders were headed toward international isolation and sanction.

At Jackson's prompting, President Clinton made an unprecedented phone call to Charles Taylor from Air Force One while flying over Africa. Until then, Taylor had been virtually shunned by the United States because of his grisly past. Among his many accomplishments were the murder of American Catholic nuns in Liberia and the storming of the U.S. embassy in Monrovia.

The tragic story of Liberia's long, spiraling descent into chaos is chronicled in Chapters 13 and 15 of this book. But the documents released to me by the State Department raise many new questions about Jesse Jackson's willingness to go beyond the prescriptions of U.S. policy, which called on him to put pressure on Taylor and Sankoh to stop the killing and disband the militias. Instead, Jackson encouraged both leaders and sought to entice them to the peace table, helping them attain their military goals by putting pressure on their common adversary, Sierra Leone president Ahmed Tejan Kabbah. Was this a "private" foreign policy, or just a stretch of his State Department negotiating guidelines? Readers can judge for themselves. But the record shows without a doubt that Jackson's policy of appeasement cost thousands of Africans their lives.

The most remarkable event that followed the publication of *Shakedown* in March 2002 was the total silence of Jesse Jackson. Jackson did not simply decline to comment on a book to which he had contributed through several in-depth interviews. There was total radio silence from the Jackson camp in Chicago. For three months, Jackson refused to return reporters' phone calls and declined interview requests from CNN, ABC, FOX News, and others. It was as if he had simply vanished. Throughout his thirty-five-year political career, it was the first time Jackson had ever been silent for so long. Even after the revelation of his "love child" with former staffer Karin Stanford, Jackson disappeared from the media scene for only forty-eight-hours.

I am not privy to whatever back-door deals Jackson may have cut with his friends in the mainstream media to shut down discussion of

Shakedown. Matt Drudge revealed a memo by a CNN producer in Chicago who attempted to convince her network not to allow me onto the airwaves. Despite this pressure, Lou Dobbs, the anchor of CNN's *Moneyline*, invited me onto his show. No follow-up invitations ever came.

Shakedown readers will not be surprised to learn that Jackson, who has smoked cigars and traded kisses with America's enemies, finds it natural to address rallies organized by International ANSWER, which joined Saddam Hussein in opposing the U.S. war to liberate Iraq. For Jackson, such appearances reaffirm his long-standing ties to the hard-left that have consistently gone unreported by the "mainstream" media. Nothing has changed today.

Nor will readers of *Shakedown* be surprised to hear Jesse Jackson denounce President George W. Bush on the war on global terror, tax cuts, or Medicare reform. Jackson's intense partisanship continues to belie the legal structure of his nonprofit corporate empire, which requires that an overwhelming majority of his resources be spent on non-partisan activities.

Since *Shakedown*, Jackson has been increasingly challenged by his donors and by his followers. I witnessed his appearance at what was supposed to be a slam-dunk audience of lefties at Stanford University in April 2003. Jackson was visibly taken aback when a white female student challenged him to defend affirmative action. The student asked him how he could support policies that led to a public perception that black professionals had succeeded because of racial preferences, not talent. She asked him how he could support policies that, in effect, harmed the black community in America. Jackson mumbled a rambling reply that quotas had not seemed to affect the racial balance at Stanford, where affluent whites continued to learn side by side with black, Hispanic, and Asian students. When he had finished ten minutes later, the entire audience was still trying to figure out if he had just insulted them or was being profound.

The most comic fallout from *Shakedown* involved revelations of Jackson's efforts to shake down NASCAR, the wildly popular stock car racing organization. Peter Flaherty, president of the conservative National Legal and Policy Center in Washington, D.C., first exposed Jackson's efforts to pressure NASCAR for the lack of successful black drivers on the stock car circuit. Fearing a Jackson-led boycott effort, NASCAR coughed up $250,000 in sponsorship fees to Jackson's groups in 2001 and 2002, and Jackson dutifully ignored the issue.

Flaherty wrote NASCAR president William C. France on April 3, 2003, asking him to end support for Jackson and his groups because of Jackson's vocal opposition to the U.S.-led war in Iraq. "You have stated that NASCAR fans are the kind of people who go to war and win wars for America," Flaherty wrote. "NASCAR's support for our troops is undercut by your support for Jackson, which includes substantial monetary contributions, at a time when Jackson is leading anti-war protests, even in foreign countries. Disturbingly, Jackson has employed extreme and provocative anti-American rhetoric."

NASCAR responded that its contributions to Jackson were intended to support "diversity," not a political group, but the uproar began. NASCAR fans were outraged to learn of the contributions. Their anger reached new heights when one of Jackson's employees, Charles Farrell, claimed in an interview with CNSNews.com correspondent Marc Morano that NASCAR officials had told him, "there is a perception that stock car racing is a good ole' boy's southern redneck cracker sport." Farrell's blatantly racist comments were never condemned by Jackson or retracted, and sparked a wave of angry letters to the editor from NASCAR fans.

I must give a special word of thanks to Rev. Jesse Lee Peterson in Los Angeles and to David Noebel of the Summit Ministries in Colorado, who together have sent out hundreds of copies of *Shakedown* to black ministers across America. At last count, three copies of the book had been returned, accompanied by angry notes. Hundreds more appear to have reached readers eager to learn the truth.

Jesse Jackson's dedication to racial division in America continues. But, due in part to the revelations contained in *Shakedown*, he is finding it a bit more difficult to get away with the type of outrages he has made his stock in trade for the past thirty-five years.

Bethesda, Maryland, November 3, 2003

ꞩ

The Death of Willie Warfield

We didn't realize he was dead until much later, after the drinks began to flow.

Cool jazz filled the atrium reserved for the May 2001 Rainbow/PUSH gathering of black businessmen and their white snares at the Hyatt Regency in Chicago's brand new McCormick Place Convention Center. The Reverend Jesse Jackson suddenly stood and called us to silence to mourn the passing of Willie Warfield.

Warfield's excess weight and the stressful inequities facing a black businessman in America conspired to do him in at high noon. "High noon—when the sun is eclipsed and people are confounded," the Reverend intoned, his voice rising and gaining rhythm. "We know how to bear crosses," the Reverend continued. "Somebody say 'Amen.'"

A few lone voices in the crowd answered quietly, "Amen."

I was standing next to Jackson in the hallway when Willie Warfield was hauled out on the gurney. The ambulance attendants hovered over Warfield, grappling with a loose sac of serum and plastic tubes and oxygen bottles. They tried to pound life back into his chest. I thought they had succeeded, because Warfield gave audible gasps. But the Reverend turned to an assistant next to him and said: "We'd better find his address, where his family is." Apparently, nobody knew Willie Warfield, and he hadn't come to the confab loaded with identification.

Later that afternoon, dousing the capitalist fervor that gripped his audience, the Reverend called his congregation to prayer. Even the loudmouths in the audience—who had berated their rich black entrepreneurial brothers for "selling out to the corporate boardrooms"—fell silent. "Many of us in this room have more yesterdays than tomorrows," the Reverend said. "This is something of a downer." After asking for our prayers for Willie's family and soul, the Reverend evoked all the extra problems Willie confronted as a black entrepreneur in America. "He was so tense," Jackson said. "I was speaking to him when he died, and he was saying, 'I didn't get the bid, the bid of my dreams,' and he asked me if I could help. I said I would, but it would be tomorrow, after this summit." Jackson shook his head, *mea culpa,* then offered a quick prayer, asking the Lord to "bless our efforts to break through these barriers."

Certainly, it was not his best performance; his audience was not enthused. Soft and hesitant, the Reverend's voice lacked the rhetorical pitches that normally enthralled the troops. Did anybody really believe Jackson had talked to Willie Warfield just before he died? I doubt it. But then again, I'm not sure it mattered. After all the lies of Jesse's life, after the love child and the public chastening, one lie more or one lie less was insignificant.

What mattered was the smell of success. And the banquet room was full of it. Bankers, brokers, headhunters, juice makers, board members, executives of all flavors, venture capitalists, lawyers, and even a deputy director of the Chicago Federal Reserve Bank: all of them black, all of them successful beyond the wildest dreams of their parents, all of them

Americans looking to get richer tomorrow. They were living proof that the successes of black America are making Jackson irrelevant, a sideshow, almost a relic of the past, half-embarrassing and half-cherished by those who are already molding the fortunes and feats of tomorrow's America.

"This is not the America of twenty years ago," a young black entrepreneur told me as we sipped glasses of white wine. "I was born after the freedom riders and the marches of the '60s and '70s. I was brought up to think everything was all right. But I heard today from Johnnie Cochran and the Reverend of the horrible things happening in America today, the Ku Klux Klan dolls in workers' lockers, the racism that still exists in places I've never seen. So I'm beginning to wonder. Maybe everything is not all right."

How long will he wonder? My bet is, once he gets back to work and gets ready to cut his next deal, he'll be wondering much more about how to sock away his earnings tax free. To this black businessman, and to the growing number like him, Jackson is fast becoming something like a Halloween ghoul, good for a scary speech once a year, but not much more.

CHAPTER 1

Manufacturing a Myth

I have a dream that my four children will one day live in a nation where they will not be judged by the color of their skin but by the content of their character.

> —Martin Luther King Jr., August 28, 1963, on the
> steps of the Lincoln Memorial, Washington, D.C.

"HE DIED IN MY ARMS"

The date was April 5, 1968. Just twelve hours after an assassin murdered civil rights leader Martin Luther King Jr. on the balcony of the Lorraine Motel in Memphis, a young black follower announced on the NBC *Today Show* that King had "died in my arms." He had cradled King's head and was "the last person on earth" to whom King had spoken. As proof, he appeared on TV wearing an olive-brown turtleneck sweater that he claimed bore the stains of Dr. King's blood.[1]

The young man was Jesse Jackson, a twenty-six-year-old dropout of the Chicago Theological Seminary, who had insinuated himself into King's entourage three years earlier. His powerful story made for riveting television.

Later that day, Jackson appeared at a rare public session of the Chicago City Council convened by Mayor Richard Daley to commemorate Dr. King. Mayor Daley hoped the memorial service would help calm the anger in Chicago's predominantly black South Side. Once again, wearing the same bloodstained turtleneck and Rap Brown sunglasses, Jackson told the story of King's final moments.

"I come here with a heavy heart because on my chest is the stain of blood from Dr. King's head," Jackson told the audience. "This blood is on the chest and hands of those who would not have welcomed him here yesterday. He went through, literally, a crucifixion. I was there. And I'll be there for the resurrection."[2]

Jackson's tale of cradling the head of the dying Dr. King was repeated four days later in the *Chicago Defender* and in more than a hundred news articles over the next seven years. The only problem with Jackson's cathartic tale: it is false.

Jackson got away with the lie for nearly a decade, and repeated it at every opportunity. One of Jackson's early backers in Chicago, *Playboy* magnate Hugh Hefner, published an in-depth interview with Jackson in the magazine's November 1969 issue, labeling him the "fiery heir apparent to Martin Luther King." The puff piece helped promote Jackson with white liberals, and noted: "The Reverend Jackson's first national exposure came as a result of his closeness to Dr. King. He was talking to King on the porch of the Lorraine Motel in Memphis when the fatal shot was fired, and cradled the dying man in his arms."[3]

On April 6, 1970, to commemorate the second anniversary of King's death, *Time* magazine featured Jackson on its cover. "Jackson was the last man King spoke to before he was shot in Memphis," *Time* wrote. "Jesse ran to the balcony, held King's head, but it was too late."

It wasn't until 1975 that a black reporter from Chicago, Barbara Reynolds, tracked down other members of Dr. King's entourage and published their account of what actually happened in Memphis.[4]

"The only person who cradled Dr. King was [the Reverend Ralph] Abernathy," said Hosea Williams, a top deputy to Dr. King at the Southern Christian Leadership Conference (SCLC) who was present during the shooting. "It's a helluva thing to capitalize on a man's death, especially one you professed to love."

Said Andrew Young, the SCLC executive director who went on to become a United States congressman, U.S. ambassador to the United Nations, and mayor of Atlanta: "The blood, the cradling, were all things I read in the newspaper and they are all mysteries to me."

King's chosen successor as leader of the SCLC, the Reverend Ralph D. Abernathy, said, "I am sure Reverend Jackson would not say to *me* that he cradled Dr. King. I am sure that Reverend Jackson would realize that I was the person who was on the balcony with Dr. King and did not leave his side until he was pronounced dead at St. Joseph's Hospital in Memphis. I am sure that he would not say to *me* that he even came near Dr. King after Doc was shot."

Chicago musician Ben Branch was with Jackson in the courtyard of the motel when the shooting occurred. "My guess is that Jesse smeared the blood on his shirt after getting it off the balcony. But who knows where he got it from? All I can say is that Jesse didn't touch him."

Branch later told WJM television in Chicago that Jackson "disappeared in thin air" after the shots rang out, apparently in fear of the Memphis police officers who rushed to the scene. Another King follower said Jackson hid behind the motel swimming pool. Yet another said that he complained that he was sick and was leaving immediately for Chicago to check into a hospital. "This whole thing's really shot my nerves," Jackson reportedly said.[5]

But wherever he went immediately after the shooting, it was not up to the balcony or to King's room. Andrew Young was the first one to reach King, along with an unidentified white man who grabbed a towel and fitted it over the gaping wound where the right side of King's face had been. The Reverend Abernathy, who had been shaving for dinner in the next room, joined them moments later and shouted down to an aide to call an ambulance.

For many years, Jackson's aides circulated a photograph of Jackson, Dr. King, and the Reverend Abernathy on the Lorraine Motel balcony, which they claimed was taken only minutes before King was shot. Once again, it was a lie. That picture—a posed shot—had been taken a day earlier.[6] When King was assassinated, the scene was different. Reynolds writes: "A photographer for the Public Broadcasting Library, documenting the Poor People's campaign, caught forever in his camera lens all those who were on the balcony seconds after the gun blast. They were pointing in the direction from where the shots were fired, a two-story brick rooming house about 200 feet across the street. Jesse was not identified in photos as being among them."[7]

When the ambulance came, Abernathy and Young accompanied King to the hospital. Twenty minutes later, camera crews from NBC, ABC, and CBS started arriving at the motel. "Jesse called to me from across the lot and said, 'Don't talk to them,'" Branch recalls. "I agreed because I thought he meant none of us were supposed to talk until Abernathy got back from the hospital. So I walked away."

But that wasn't what Jackson had in mind. Hosea Williams recounts what happened next. "I was in my room. I looked out and saw Jesse talking to these TV people. I came out to hear what was being said. I heard Jesse say, 'Yes, I was the last man in the world King spoke to.'" Williams says he was so furious that he climbed over a railing and rushed toward Jackson, until he was restrained by a police officer. "I called Jesse a dirty, stinking, lying so-and-so, or something like that," Williams said. "I had no hang-ups about Jesse talking to the press. That was okay, but why lie?"[8]

When NBC reporter David Burrington came on the air from Memphis later that evening, he added a second layer to the lie Jackson was broadcasting about being the last man with whom King spoke. "The *Reverend* Jesse Jackson of Chicago, one of King's closest aides, was beside him when he was shot while standing on a veranda outside his motel room," Burrington reported.

At the time of the shooting, Jackson was no Reverend. But, says former confidant and speechwriter Hurley Green, "Dr. King told Jesse that everybody who worked in the movement was a minister, so Jesse went to seminary for six months, dropped out, and called himself a minister."[9]

Nor was Jackson on especially good terms with King or other members of the SCLC staff, who mistrusted his ambition, his audacity, and his refusal to be a team player. At the last SCLC staff meeting, one week before he was shot, King expressed his displeasure with Jackson's criticism of his decision to call off a March 28 demonstration in Memphis (which would subsequently degenerate into a riot).[10] Disgusted with Jackson's behavior, King walked out of the room.

Jackson ran after him, trying to continue the discussion. Wheeling around, King said angrily, "Don't you ever pull that kind of thing at one of my meetings." He added, "If you are so interested in doing your own thing that you can't do what the organization is structured to do, go ahead . . . but for God's sake don't bother me."[11]

Just two minutes before he was shot, King spied Jackson in the courtyard of the motel and asked him to put on a tie and join him for dinner. It was the first time he had exchanged pleasantries with Jackson since their angry encounter at the staff meeting a week earlier. "Those in the courtyard knew that the personal invitation was Dr. King's way of making up with Jesse," Reynolds writes.

Like that other monumental overachiever, former president Bill Clinton, Jesse Jackson has long had a troubled relationship with the truth.

It's not as if Jackson needed to stretch the truth. Like Clinton, his accomplishments are many and the mainstream press has lavished attention on him. And yet, from the very start of his career as a national leader, he has consistently bent the facts to fit the glorified self-image he has sought to create: that of Dr. Martin Luther King Jr.'s one true heir.

Don Rose was the publicist for the Chicago-based civil rights coalition, the Coordinating Council of Community Organizations (CCCO), which became Dr. King's center of operations in Chicago during the last two years of his life. He was one of the first people Jackson called when he rushed back to Chicago after King's assassination. According to one account of their conversation, which Rose gave to the *New York Times Magazine* for a July 9, 1972, profile of Jackson, the two "decided that Jackson could be sold to the press as the new King."

Later, during Jackson's second presidential campaign in 1988, Rose told reporters that his account of Jackson conniving to grab King's mantle had been "overblown." They had only discussed Jackson's "terrific potential to become the leader of the movement." But there was "no concerted plan," Rose said.[12]

Jackson called Rose after his weekly Operation Breadbasket meeting, which, on the first Saturday after King's death, was attended by 4,000 people—ten times the normal crowd that came to hear Jackson speak. According to reporter Betty Washington, who watched Jackson's performance that morning, "I felt he was imitating Dr. King. . . . I remember it had some of the people in the audience in hysterics. The way they acted, it was as if King was being reincarnated in that man. It was like he was trying to be King, like something staged."[13]

Jackson drove to various Chicago television stations that afternoon with Rose and aides from Operation Breadbasket. According to one aide, Jackson and Rose calmly talked in the limo about how they could build Jackson's image as the sole heir to King's civil rights throne. "There was a very conscious effort to project Jackson as the figure most closely associated with King, a little like the myth-making that evolved from Memphis. Jesse very seriously and very calculatingly discussed the ingredients and objectives necessary to assume the position of the new leader. The psychological impact of the project and the reaction of the press to Jesse were discussed. . . . The conversation was cut and dried. He would be packaged like any other product."[14]

EARLY LIES

Jackson's lies about Dr. King's assassination were not his first. He has consistently embellished his own upbringing and his early days in the civil rights movement, and has danced around his troubled personal relationship with Dr. King and the movement King left behind, the SCLC.

Born on October 8, 1941, to a sixteen-year-old unwed woman in Greenville, South Carolina, Jackson has often said that he grew up in dire poverty "on the wrong side of the tracks." His adoptive father, Charles Jackson, was a returning World War II soldier who gave Jesse his last name at the age of thirteen, and prided himself on providing for his family. Jackson would later say in a biographical sketch called *Up from the Ghetto* that his father was a janitor and his mother, a maid. "I used to run bootleg liquor, bought hot clothes. I had to steal to survive." The facts were quite different. Jackson's father was a career postal worker, while Jackson's mother worked as a beautician. The Jacksons even had a telephone in the early 1950s, when many whites, as well as blacks, did not. Charles Jackson responded with embarrassment when reporters confronted him with Jackson's tales. "We were never poor. We never wanted for anything. We've never been on welfare, because I was never without a job. We never begged anybody for a dime. And my family never went hungry a day in their lives."[15] They lived modestly, but not in poverty, thanks to his hard work.

Some biographers have speculated that Jackson's uneasy relationship with the truth stems from his having been an illegitimate child. Jackson's biological father, Noah Robinson, was happily married when he fell for the sixteen-year-old girl next door. He was also one of the wealthiest men in Greenville's black community and lived in a large, imposing house with a wrought iron "R" on the chimney. Jackson's middle name, Louis, was that of Robinson's own father, a pastor.

Less than one year after Jackson was born, Robinson's wife gave birth to a son they named Noah R. Robinson Jr. Jackson and his younger half brother attended the same schools, but returned home to separate households every evening. Although Greenville was a sizeable town of 62,000, the black community was small enough to be plagued by small-town gossip, and by the time Jackson was nine he clearly understood that he had two fathers.

Before he died in 1997, Noah Robinson Sr. reminisced with biographer Barbara Reynolds about seeing Jesse as a nine-year-old boy, standing in his backyard, gazing in through the window. "Sometimes I wouldn't see him right away and Noah Junior would tell me he was out there," Robinson said. "No telling how long he could have been there. As soon as I would go to the window and wave, he would wave back and run away." Robinson acknowledged Jackson as his son, but was unable to welcome him openly into his home until Jesse was sixteen.[16]

Jackson has frequently claimed that Old South racism prevented him from pursuing a career as a star athlete. In all-black Sterling High, Jackson played quarterback and pitched on the baseball team. His rival at all-white Greenville High was named Dickie Dietz. Years later, Jackson would say that he and Dietz competed against each other in the summer of 1959 at major league tryouts, and that he struck Dietz out three times. But because of a racist system, Dietz was offered a $95,000 contract with the major leagues, while the scouts only offered Jackson $6,000 and a chance to go to college in the off-season.[17]

But in his inimitable sycophantic style, biographer Marshall Frady acknowledges that Jackson's account "under closer scrutiny, proved a trifle evanescent in some particulars." The problem, as Dietz himself would later tell reporters, was that far from striking him out three times, Jackson "merely hit him once in the back with the ball, hard."[18]

Jackson was no "victim," though he has spent his life developing the cult of victimhood. Compared to many inner city schools today, after thirty-five years of a federal welfare system that has promoted single-parent households and eroded the quality of education, Jackson's all-black high school was a haven of respectability and academic achievement. By the eleventh grade, Jackson was studying French. He won an athletic scholarship directly out of high school to attend the University of Illinois at Urbana-Champaign. As a freshman during the 1959–1960 season he played quarterback briefly, before he was moved to the backfield and then to the line. It was about as far from stardom as one can get, and Jackson wasn't happy.

As Jackson tells the story, even up North in the Big Ten, the long arm of racism reached down to prevent a talented young black man from realizing his dream. "They told me blacks could not be quarterbacks."[19] But once again, facts don't bear him out. University records show that Illinois's starting quarterback that year was Mel Meyers, who also happened to be black. Years later, when Jackson was running for president, his coach at Illinois, Ray Eliot, told the *Los Angeles Times* that Jackson had been placed on academic probation during his second semester.[20] In other words, he faced the choice of leaving the University of Illinois voluntarily or possibly flunking out. The story about not being able to play quarterback because he was black was just an excuse.

After freshman year, Jackson transferred to the predominantly black Agricultural and Technical College of North Carolina at Greensboro. There, a big fish in a small pond, he went on to play quarterback. He met his soon-to-be wife, Jacqueline Lavinia Brown, on campus in 1961. The two were married on New Year's Eve in 1962. Six months later their first child was born, a daughter they named Santita.

Jackson almost missed his daughter's birth. The spring of his senior year, 1963, was the year Dr. Martin Luther King Jr. later immortalized as the "Year of the Negro Revolution"[21] and the year Jackson joined CORE, the Congress on Racial Equality. CORE president James Farmer recruited Jackson and other A&T students to lead a series of demonstrations at segregated theaters and restaurants in downtown Greensboro. He and a column of students sat blocking a busy street in front of the Greensboro municipal building. On June 6, 1963, just weeks before Santita's birth, Jackson was arrested for inciting a riot.

Already, Jackson's proclivity for theatrics was evident. "I know I am going to jail," he told his fellow demonstrators. "I'm going without fear. It's a principle that I have for which I'll go to jail and I'll go to the chain gang if necessary." Of course, as Reynolds points out, "at that time there were no chain gangs in North Carolina." But no matter. Jackson was already playing to the media and found that he liked the attention they readily accorded him. Later he would tell reporters that before he was released from his brief stint in jail, he had found time to sketch out a "Letter from Greensboro Jail" in emulation of King's already famous "Letter from Birmingham Jail." But Jackson apparently never finished it because it was never published.

Fateful Trip to Selma

Jackson graduated in the spring of 1964. With help from the campus chaplain at A&T, he received a scholarship from the Rockefeller Fund for Theological Education to attend the Chicago Theological Seminary (CTS) that fall. According to the chaplain, A. Knighton Stanley, Jackson was not yet committed to the church nor had he discovered a vocation. But he was keenly aware that Martin Luther King and the leaders of his movement were all clerics. "I decided to go to the seminary to learn how to do without the law to change society, change it in deeper ways," Jackson told Frady.

But he hadn't gone to Chicago to study theology. Or at least, not for long. He had gone to acquire a title: Reverend.

CTS was a tiny enclave ensconced in the scholarly atmosphere of the University of Chicago campus, in Chicago's well-bred Hyde Park district. The main administrative building, located in a chapel, evoked an old English baronial home, with its dark stained-glass windows, unadorned stone staircase, and deep oak-paneled library.

Joan Blocher, who attended the seminary in the late 1960s, recalls the atmosphere at the time. "We were all a bunch of draft dodgers," she says. "We were pretty white, pretty male, pretty straight. There were only two blacks in my class, and only one black full-time faculty member."[22]

Campus radicals were everywhere. Stories about University of Chicago "Freedom Workers" and Student Nonviolent Coordinating Committee (SNCC) demonstrations filled the student newspaper. But until March 1965, Jackson stayed home, supplementing his scholarship with part-time work for Chicago's black publishing baron, John Johnson, the founder of *Jet* and *Ebony* magazines. At one point, he attempted to get a political patronage job from Chicago mayor Richard Daley but was rebuffed. It was a snub he would remember for years.[23]

Then Jackson fell in with the Coordinating Council of Community Organizations (CCCO). The group brought together moderate black church leaders and white leftists.

In March 1965, CCCO tapped students and faculty at the Chicago Theological Seminary to drive to Selma, Alabama, to join Dr. Martin Luther King Jr. after "Bloody Sunday," when nonviolent demonstrators had been brutally beaten by Alabama state troopers.

To hear Jackson tell the story, it was entirely his operation. After a sleepless night haunted by television footage of the beatings, Jackson claims he stormed down to the campus cafeteria, clambered atop a table, and began haranguing his fellow students with "a challenge to everybody there. . . . Who was gonna go with me down to Selma? A whole bunch of 'em took off with me down there. All of 'em white, too."[24] In another account, Jackson claimed to have organized "half the student body" in Chicago to drive down to Selma.[25]

But it didn't happen quite that way. Leading the small caravan to Selma was none other than the president of Jackson's school, noted civil rights, and left-wing, activist Dr. Howard Schomer, a white pastor of the United Church of Christ. In a contemporaneous account in the University of Chicago student newspaper, Schomer described in great detail the week with Dr. King in Selma. Schomer mentioned by name several of the twenty-two students who accompanied him but said not a word about Jackson.[26]

THE MENTOR

Schomer's omission may have been intended to shield Jackson from scrutiny by the FBI, which was then engaged in an open feud with Dr. Martin Luther King Jr. and was suspected of carrying out clandestine surveillance of King and other civil rights leaders. In a telephone interview shortly before Schomer's death on June 28, 2001, Karine Schomer says her father had always boasted that he introduced Jackson to Dr. King during the Selma vigil, and had quickly identified Jackson for his leadership potential. "He was the key person who brought Jesse Jackson to CTS and made it possible for him to study there," she says.[27]

What is now clear is that Howard Schomer came to exert a major influence on Jackson's thinking, and tried—unsuccessfully—to mold him into a disciplined scholar as well as an activist. In handwritten notes for a speech profiling Jackson, Schomer recalled Jackson's abysmal academic achievement. "His first long research paper was a disaster. I called him in and said that he must learn to use his reading critically, not to do a scissors and paste job. He must develop the power to gather very large bodies of data into his own mind, organize it in ways that would give him understanding of problems and working hypotheses for their solution. I warned him that these graduate school years were his great opportunity to acquire the discipline of understanding and solving problems. I remember suggesting that if he didn't do so at CTS, he would, by the time he reached age 30, be just one more '[civil rights] activist' capable of making stinging remarks about wrongs which everybody knew were wrong, but with no capacity to right them. He began to listen."[28]

A well-known and well-respected leftist, Schomer transformed CTS during his tenure as president from 1958 through 1966 into a bastion of civil rights and anti–Vietnam War activism. Schomer himself had been jailed for the duration of World War II when the War Department rejected his demand for conscientious objector status.[29] In 1942, according to a three-page biographical sketch provided by Karine Schomer, he volunteered to perform civilian service as a relief worker in Protestant refugee camps in the unoccupied portions of France. His request was denied by the Selective Service. He remained in jail until January 1946.

By 1958, when he took the helm at CTS, Schomer was a committed leftist who had gone on record for denouncing the anti-communist "witch hunt" of the early 1950s led by Senator Joseph McCarthy and the chief counsel of the Senate Governmental Affairs Subcommittee, the future attorney general Robert F. Kennedy. According to his personal papers, which he subsequently turned over to the Harvard Divinity School in Cambridge, Massachusetts, Schomer repeatedly refused to sign the loyalty oath required to obtain a United States passport, because it required him to affirm that he was not a member of the Communist Party.[30]

Well after Jackson dropped out of CTS, the two remained in close contact, and, according to Karine Schomer, in later years Jackson took to addressing her father as "Doc"—the same affectionate title used by Dr. King's supporters to address him. While at CTS, Jackson appears to have been unprepared to embrace or even comprehend the breadth of Schomer's radical leftist economic and political agenda. But in Schomer's teachings one can find the seeds of many of Jackson's subsequent campaigns against corporate America.

Schomer pioneered the left-wing assault on U.S. and multinational corporations for their "antiprogressive" investment policies. In 1971, he initiated a unit at the United Church of Christ headquarters devoted to "corporate social responsibility." By buying small numbers of shares in target companies, Schomer and other leftists gained access to shareholders' meetings where they demanded an end to corporate profits derived from arms production or the U.S. war effort in Vietnam. Jackson does the same thing today. Schomer also sought to end corporate policies he deemed to be discriminatory, and became a major voice in the movement that finally culminated in the 1980s to force corporate disinvestment from South Africa, a goal that was shared by the Soviet Union and its front organizations operating overseas.

The tactic of publicly embarrassing corporations, the hard-core leftist agenda, the meetings with international communist front organizations and terrorist groups: all were ingredients of Jackson's future success. All that was missing from Schomer's approach was the private, behind-the-scenes shakedown. This would be Jackson's main contribution to leftist politics, and it would make Jackson, his family, and their friends very rich.

BRIEF ENCOUNTERS

During his brief stay in Selma in March 1965, the twenty-three-year-old Jesse Jackson did everything he could to worm his way into King's presence. At one point, to the surprise and annoyance of King's staff, he appeared on the steps of Brown Chapel during an all-night vigil and made a speech to the crowd. After repeatedly pestering the Reverend Abernathy, the staff's top lieutenant, Jackson was finally brought in to see King. According to Abernathy's account, King was by no means taken with Jackson or his excited offer, apparently hatched in the midst of their conversation, to organize the civil rights movement in Chicago on Dr. King's behalf. "Doc [King] did not agree with me that we ought to employ this young man on the basis of my experience with him during that short time," Abernathy said.[31]

After a few sleepless nights in Selma, Jackson came down with the flu and was driven back to Chicago by Dr. Schomer and the other CTS students. Altogether, he had been gone from Chicago a total of five days.[32] Dr. King went on to lead the massive voting rights march to Montgomery. Despite occasional claims that he had gone to Montgomery with King, Selma was the closest Jesse Jackson ever got to Montgomery that year.

But already, Jackson had identified an opportunity. King had little awareness of Chicago politics, and had no presence in Jackson's adopted city, although he eagerly sought to take his crusade to the North. So after returning to Chicago from Selma, Jackson appointed himself King's emissary. His first task was to find a church that could serve as a local base for King's controversial SCLC.

One Sunday evening not long afterwards, Jackson tuned into a broadcast by the Reverend Clay Evans of the Fellowship Missionary Baptist Church, whose gospel-singing services were famous in Chicago. A few days later Jackson strolled into Evans's office at 45th and S. Princeton Avenue, and suggested that Evans work with him and Dr. King. "He had on beach sandals and these short cut-off pants," recalled Evans's secretary at the time, Lucille Loman. "He came right in and went straight into the pastor's study. I said to myself, 'Who is this audacious character, where in the world did he come from?' "[33] Loman did not remain offended by Jackson for long, and went to work for him a few years later. Despite periodic falling-outs, she continues to work for him today as the head of PUSH finances.

With his feet up on the Reverend Evans's coffee table, Jackson began to expand on his relationship with Dr. King, despite the fact he had only met him briefly in Selma. The next Sunday, he became a member of Evans's church. Evans was a power broker in Chicago's African-American community as an outspoken leader in the growing civil rights movement—one at odds with Mayor Richard Daley and his lackeys. "Jesse started his career in Chicago with Reverend Evans," recalls Cirilo McSween, a close associate of Dr. King who went on to become Jackson's chief financial backer. "He attached himself to Reverend Evans and the Fellowship Missionary Baptist Church."[34] With Evans, Jackson played up his connections to Dr. King; with King, he played up his ability to serve as a Chicago fixer. Like a Ponzi scheme artist, Jackson would constantly leverage assets he didn't actually possess. And no one thought to call his bluff.

Mayor Daley had organized the black community as an adjunct of the Democratic Party machine, doling out thousands of patronage jobs through the black churches. He didn't want Martin Luther King Jr. showing up in his town to ruin the scheme, and he intended to punish any black pastor allied to King. But the Reverend Evans felt that the tide was turning, and he wanted to be the first to oppose the Daley machine. He invited King to speak from his pulpit in the summer of 1966, dispatching a limousine to O'Hare International Airport to fetch him. At the wheel was Jesse Jackson.[35] As a reward for his efforts in Chicago, King offered Jackson a staff job and a salary of $3,000 per year.

CLASH WITH KING

Jackson based his rise to prominence after King's death on his role as King's trusted lieutenant and heir apparent. In the official biographies put out by Rainbow/PUSH, Jackson still claims that he began at SCLC "as an assistant to Dr. Martin Luther King Jr.," making it sound as if he were working side by side with King at Ebenezer Baptist Church in Atlanta.[36] In fact, as SCLC archives and former associates make clear, King was suspicious of Jackson from the start. The longer the two worked together, the more suspicious King became.

On July 11, 1966, thanks to the introduction to the Reverend Evans, King came to Chicago to lead a massive nonviolent demonstration in Soldier Field, demanding that Mayor Daley end racial discrimination in public housing projects. King called it the Campaign to End Slums, and by all accounts it was a failure that demonstrated to many black leaders that King was out of his element in the North. That summer, temperatures in Chicago rose to one hundred degrees, and a riot erupted when city firemen turned off the fire hydrants in the black ghetto. The headlines the next day read, "Mayor Blames King."

On August 5, King led marchers into Gage Park, a blue-collar suburb on the city's South Side composed mainly of ethnic Lithuanian, Polish, and Italian immigrants. Shortly after he got out of his car to lead the marchers, a stone hit King in the head, and the white mob shouted, "Kill him!" Later that night, King told his wife, Coretta, that the "march was worse than any of those I ever experienced in the deep South, in Mississippi and Alabama. I have never seen as much hatred and hostility on the part of so many people."[37]

Mayor Daley offered a few quick-fix concessions, which included three hundred jobs for blacks as housing project guards. King rejected the proposal. The marches continued, but without success.

Finally, on August 24, Jackson stepped in. Without consulting King, Jackson told the press that the marchers would move into Cicero, an all-white working class suburb best known as the home of Al Capone. Jackson had "seriously overstepped his authority," said PR man Don Rose, who would later advise Jackson on how to model himself as King's heir apparent. "I'm not sure we ever really meant to march into Cicero, at least not then. We knew the move would really shake the mayor into action, so we were batting the threat around for leverage, never saying anything definite about it."

Moving into Cicero would almost certainly have provoked major race riots, and everyone knew this including Jackson, Mayor Daley, and Dr. King. But in his effort to put himself at the head of the movement, the twenty-four-year-old Jackson dared King to call off the march. "If we don't go to Cicero, we can't go back to Mississippi," Jackson was quoted as telling a major Chicago daily. "Some of us live in Mississippi, so by virtue of that logic, we're going into Cicero. Negroes work there but can't live there."

Not to be upstaged by Jackson, King took the bait and replied through the papers the next day. "We're not only going to walk in Cicero, we're going to work there and live there." But privately, movement leaders were angry.[38]

Jackson had escalated the encounter without consulting King or any members of his entourage. But this time he was lucky. Two days before the marchers were supposed to take to the streets, Mayor Daley and King reached an agreement to desegregate public housing, provide mortgages to blacks, and build public swimming pools in the black community. While many black leaders would subsequently decry the compromise as a fiction that never had any concrete effect, King touted it as a success. But it also left him profoundly suspicious of Jesse Jackson's taste for self-promotion.

King returned to Chicago in September for a dinner to raise funds for the grand new church the Reverend Evans planned to build.[39] Jackson was the catalyst who brought the two together. His role in this marriage would enhance his position with both men and launch his career. But Evans would be made to pay for his association with Dr. King by the Daley administration.

NO MORE BOOKS

Jackson has often said that he abandoned his seminary studies six months before graduating because Dr. King called him to work full time. Once again, the facts belie Jackson's claims. Jackson's professors recall that he simply stopped showing up for classes after going to Selma in March 1965. He had been a student less than a year. He even failed to fulfill the requirements for the mandatory course in sermon writing and delivery. When one professor confronted him with his scholarly failings, Jackson reportedly said he didn't need to go to class or complete course requirements. "I'm special," he said.[40]

Jackson did register that fall for classes, according to Sharon Thistlethwaite, the current president of CTS. But in an interview she cited confidentiality when asked to provide any details of Jackson's academic record or even to reveal how many classes he was required to take as a full-time student.[41] (The answer, according to CTS archives consulted by the author, was three one-hour classes per week.) Thistlethwaite had cause for her reserve. Under her direction, CTS finally awarded Jackson his master's degree in divinity in June 2000—thirty-three years after he was officially dropped from the rolls. CTS records, still on file at the Chicago campus, show that Jackson was put on the "reserve" list of the class of 1967, the year he was originally scheduled to graduate. "Students get listed this way when it has become clear they will never graduate," said a CTS archivist.[42]

Although it would appear Jackson had dropped out by early 1966, after a miserable academic performance, the sole requirement the CTS board asked Jackson to fulfill for his year 2000 graduation was an ethics class, which he accomplished by chatting for two hours about abortion and the death penalty with an attractive young African-American professor, Joanne Marie Terrell. She later told associates she found it an "intimidating experience" to be asked to interrogate Jackson.[43]

What Thistlethwaite and other CTS officials failed to mention was that by the time the decision was made to grant Jackson his degree, CTS had a prominent new member on its board of trustees: Jesse Jackson Jr., a Democratic member of Congress from Chicago. The younger Jackson revealed his link to CTS in a mundane financial disclosure form filed with the U.S. House of Representatives Ethics Committee for the year 2000.

But just as Jackson had brokered his tenuous relationship with Dr. King to gain entry to the black churches in Chicago, he used his time at CTS to arrogate unto himself the title "Reverend," which he began using while at Operation Breadbasket almost from the start. "To make himself relevant to the community, which has always given pastors a major role, he cloaked himself behind the title Reverend," says the Reverend Caesar Leflur, a Chicago pastor who has long opposed Jackson. "All the leaders of the civil rights movement were Reverends. Jackson used that position to get followers to accomplish his political agenda."[44]

Dr. King had grown wary of Jackson's penchant for freelancing after the Cicero encounter. Putting Jackson in charge of Operation Breadbasket in Chicago was a way of keeping him at a distance, keeping him under control, while compelling him to assume responsibility for his actions. It turned out to be a job perfectly suited for Jackson's talents.

Operation Breadbasket was the extension of an economic campaign first waged in Philadelphia in the early 1960s by the Reverend Leon Sullivan, which King adapted and sought to expand nationwide. It was based on a simple but far-reaching premise: that black Americans could transform their purchasing power as consumers into political clout, and compel supermarkets, bakeries, and soft drink suppliers—who were present in the black community but employed few blacks—to provide jobs and award contracts to black suppliers.

The Reverend Sullivan had already demonstrated in Philadelphia that black consumer boycotts could be a success. By 1962, he had built a patronage network within the black community, while King was leading civil rights demonstrations in the deep South. He also demonstrated that boycotts could be personally lucrative, as he was subsequently appointed to the board of directors of General Motors. But until Jackson ramped up Operation Breadbasket in Chicago four years later, no one had tried to expand these efforts to other parts of the nation or to use consumer boycotts to help black businesses grow. That was Jackson's innovation, and it was ingenious.

Jackson's partner when he first started at Breadbasket was a white seminary student from CTS, David Wallace, who had been close to CTS president Howard Schomer. Later, two other white CTS alumni, Gary Massoni and Alvin Pitcher, joined them. Using the Reverend Evans's church as a base, Jackson cobbled together a coalition of black ministers and forged them into a powerful tool of economic persuasion.

"I followed Jackson from the very first," says Hurley Green, who became Jackson's ghostwriter for a weekly column in the *Defender*. "In the beginning, he had no office space, and lived with his family in a third floor walkup in South Shore, eating at a picnic table. He couldn't pay his rent, so a bunch of businessmen, including me, helped him out."[45] Getting the business community to support his activities was a technique Jackson would hone and perfect as the years went by until he could convince major multinational corporations to pony up.

"Being with Jesse was like a jamboree," says Green, who went to most of Jackson's Saturday morning meetings once Operation Breadbasket found office space. "When you first meet him, he's energizing. He utters hip phrases, grabs his crotch. White folks flocked to him. They gave him dollars, while black folks gave him coins." But they gave, and in time, Jackson gave in return, establishing his own network of patronage right in Mayor Richard Daley's own backyard.

One of Jackson's early patrons was Cirilo McSween, a Panamanian immigrant who was on the board of the black-owned Independence Bank. "I helped put together a group of people to finance the movement," McSween recalls. Together, they paid all Jackson's expenses, both personal and professional. "Obviously he has to carry himself and dress in a fashion that represents the leader he is," McSween says. "We could not have him as our leader and not supply the appearance and the satisfaction that go with it."[46]

Operation Breadbasket's first target was Country Delight Inc., a local dairy that employed no blacks, but was solidly implanted in black neighborhoods on Chicago's South Side. Jackson asked the Reverend Hiram Crawford to lead the initial confrontation with company officials. It ended in a standoff. The following Sunday, one hundred black preachers took to their pulpits and instructed their congregations to boycott Country Delight products. During the four-day Easter weekend, Country Delight lost more than half a million dollars as black consumers left cartons of milk, butter, and cream to sour on the shelves. Within a matter of days the company called Jackson to capitulate, offering forty-four jobs to blacks. Operation Breadbasket had won its first victory. Word traveled fast through the corporate community. Even before the first black employees could be trained and sent out in the dairy trucks, other dairy companies serving black areas in Chicago called Jackson to negotiate.

Next came the turn of the soft drink suppliers. Jackson and his aides did their homework, and went around to corporate offices armed with charts and diagrams that demonstrated the importance of black consumers, threatening a boycott if the companies didn't pledge to hire more black employees. Before the summer was over, all three major suppliers—Pepsi, Coke, and 7Up—agreed. Jackson was on a roll. But it was one thing to get low-paying service jobs for blacks. It was quite another to force open the doors of the corporate purchasing managers and get them to buy products made by black-owned companies. Jackson was careful to choose targets where he had the leverage to win.

The first was Hi-Lo stores, a white-owned grocery chain that operated primarily in black neighborhoods. After winning an agreement from management to provide 184 new jobs for blacks, including positions as store managers, Jackson pressed a new demand: that Hi-Lo guarantee shelf space for products made by minority-owned businesses.

What products did Jackson push? Those made by the handful of black businessmen who had latched onto his wagon and were paying for his operation. At his Saturday morning meetings Jackson would exhort the crowd to buy Joe Louis Milk and Grove Fresh orange juice, inventing rhyming jingles as he warmed up and engaged the crowd. Before he was done, Hi-Lo not only stocked those products but other black products, such as Archie's Mumbo Barbecue Sauce, Staff of Life Bread, and King Solomon Deodorant.[47]

"He gets dollars from white corporations to help his black buddies who in turn contribute to his organization," says Barbara Reynolds. "Only today, he's more sophisticated than he was thirty years ago."[48] Jackson was providing a very real service for these businessmen, a service worth far more than anything they might spend to advertise their products. If they couldn't get their products onto store shelves, they obviously couldn't sell them. In exchange, they were prepared to reward Jackson personally and handsomely for his services. Jackson became a fee-for-service provider.

George Jones was the owner of Joe Louis Milk, one of the companies Jackson helped in those early days. "If anybody buys Jackson, it must be blacks," Jones said. "Hypothetically, if Jackson needed a home, if his children need special medical attention or a trust fund is required to support his family in the event of death, if his radio broadcast needs sponsors, if he needs automobiles, clothes, anything at all, why not? I don't believe he should suffer just because he is leading the poor. I feel he should live in a decent manner and most of us will try to make that possible."[49]

Jackson's "boycotts for business" approach generated controversy within the civil rights movement itself. The Reverend Hiram Crawford, who was instrumental in energizing the Chicago black clergy to support the Breadbasket boycotts, grew disenchanted with Jackson and accused him of cutting a secret deal with the businessmen behind the back of the black pastors.

"Dr. Martin Luther King and Jesse Jackson were introduced to Black businessmen of Chicago at the old H&H Restaurant on 51st street in 1966," he wrote. "The wound which I received was to discover later that Rev. Jesse Jackson and George Jones of the Joe Louis Milk Co. had been holding private meetings" and that Jackson "had collected pledges" from them in exchange for Breadbasket boycotts. "I brought this to the attention of the general body of Breadbasket and revealed money had been raised without our knowledge or consent." Jackson's behind-the-scenes operation led to "the first split" in the civil rights movement, Crawford wrote. It was not the last time the two men would tangle.[50]

ENTER THE GANGS

Jackson always points to his success in launching a boycott against the national food chain A&P as Operation Breadbasket's shining hour, the event that put it on the map. When Breadbasket took on A&P, its stores were everywhere in America's inner cities, with forty in Chicago alone. In fact, A&P was so pervasive that the company had run afoul of the Sherman Antitrust legislation.[51]

A&P was no easy hit, as Jackson's other targets had been. This was a national chain, and it had deep pockets. Although the black ministers used their pulpits to exhort the faithful to boycott A&P, profits from other parts of the country steeled company management against giving in to Jackson's demands.

For sixteen weeks Jackson's picketers surrounded A&P stores on the South Side of Chicago. But according to Hurley Green, Jackson himself scarcely bothered to get his hands dirty. "Willie Barrow actually led the boycott," recalls Green. "She was out there every day for sixteen weeks. She actually accomplished it, not Jackson." Standing four-feet nine-inches tall and dubbed the "Little Warrior" by Rainbow/PUSH, the Reverend Willie T. Barrow is still working with Jackson today.

But while the media and the black public focused on A&P, Jackson was drawn into the consequences of another success: Breadbasket's successful boycott of Red Rooster.

The Red Rooster food stores were notorious in Chicago for the poor quality of their products and their high prices. The Chicago city authorities, not famous for cracking down on lapses in hygiene, had fined them thirty-two times for flagrant violations of various regulations, from selling spoiled meat to short weighting.[52] Nevertheless, they were unlike Jackson's other targets in that they had black employees, some of them prominent in the chain's management. In July 1968, as Jackson's campaign against Red Rooster intensified, the company's personnel manager, Ron Johnson, a black, lashed out at Jackson for his boycott. "Jesse Jackson is hurting black people," he said. After calling Jackson "an opportunist and a liar," he went on: "He's using the boycott to further enhance his own image and doesn't care one bit about the black community."[53]

But despite this resistance, Red Rooster management eventually caved. The price of Jackson's boycott was unusual: he demanded that the company pad its payroll by hiring twenty-two members of the Black Stone Rangers, the biggest and most violent street gang on the South Side, carrying them on the books with such puffed-up titles as "outside store inspector" and "inside store inspector" and of course, "security guards."[54] Among those hired under Jackson's auspices were members of the Main 21, the ruling body of the Black Stone Rangers. These were the "twenty-one street gang leaders personally selected by [Jeff] Fort" to transmit his orders and exactions to the thousands of gang members spread across Chicago's South Side, federal prosecutors said.[55] "Management trainee positions went to youths awaiting trial for robbery, and security guard jobs went to gang members out on bond on murder and theft charges."[56]

The FBI took note of the extortion racket. In an April 18, 1968, memo from the Chicago field office summing up events during the race riots that followed King's death, Jackson's gangland friends figured prominently. "[T]he Blackstone Rangers, a large and violent Negro youth gang operating on Chicago's south side, were reported by PD sources to be engaged in extortion activities against merchants and business establishments in that area, in an implied or indirect promise of protection of these merchants for contributions and donations to the Rangers." Worried about reprisals as word of the extortion racket leaked out, two black business associations called a hasty press conference on April 16, 1968, to praise the Rangers for helping to keep down violence during the disorders. "These spokesmen did concede, however, that there had undoubtedly been isolated extortions where some individuals had attempted to take advantage of the tense situation in this fashion."[57]

Jackson's close association with a prominent Chicago gang was well known locally,[58] but was rarely reported in the national press. Chicago criminal justice officials vividly recall Jackson's friendship with gang leader Jeff Fort and describe a photograph taken in the late 1960s showing the two together. "Jeff Fort is sitting on his 'throne,' " one official says. "His deputy, Mickey Cogwell—who was later killed on Jeff Fort's orders—sits in a chair to his left. Jesse is seated at Fort's feet, on the floor." Fort appears preoccupied in the picture, but Jesse Jackson—already massaging his public image—has struck a tough Black Power pose, facing the camera directly. Fort may be sitting in the throne, but Jesse Jackson is the Man to reckon with.[59]

"Jeff Fort and the Jester would make the rounds of the small business owners, telling them that if they didn't contribute, 'We'll burn you down,' " another official recalled. "It was a shakedown, pure and simple. They called themselves 'community organizers.' "[60] In those early days, Jackson boasted of his ties to the gangs. "I get a lot of them to go to church. I baptized Jeff Fort at Fellowship Baptist Church," he told one reporter.[61] Jackson's relationship to gang leader Jeff Fort was a key element in his rapid rise to political prominence, and set a pattern for many things to come. Ron Johnson, the black manager who publicly denounced Jackson, later lost his job and watched Red Rooster go bankrupt, thanks in part to the exactions of the Black Stone Rangers.[62] It was Jackson's shakedown method in an early and crude incarnation.

Jackson also used gang members to pad his own events. In 1968, Hurley Green recalls, Breadbasket and other activist groups launched a "hunger campaign" in Illinois and went down to the state legislature in Springfield. "We made demands and the state met every one of them. But Jesse said, no, we have to go down there and get our picture taken. So we took a busload of gang members with us and drove down there from Chicago. They started fighting on the bus, and when we got off they were still fighting. But we got our picture taken holding up the agreement on the steps of the capital. Jesse is always camera conscious."

Among the gang members on the bus was Black Stone Rangers leader Jeff Fort, who had been lionized earlier that year with an invitation from Charles Percy, a United States senator from Illinois, to attend the inauguration of President Nixon in Washington. (Fort declined to attend, sending two of his deputies in his stead.)[63]

Later, the gang changed its name to El Rukn (Arabic for "The Foundation") and its leaders were successfully prosecuted in federal courts for murder, extortion, drug dealing, and racketeering. Top among the new crop of El Rukn leaders who took over from Fort and his "generals" was Jackson's half brother Noah Robinson Jr. "It was Jesse who introduced Noah to Jeff Fort, not the other way around," a Chicago police investigator points out. "It was Jesse who had the gang connections."[64]

"There was one very powerful reason why none of us spoke out more loudly against Jesse for all those years," says one black minister. "It was fear of the long arm of the black mafia that Jesse's half brother controlled." Today as Noah Jr. and gang boss Jeff Fort serve life sentences behind bars for multiple counts of fraud, extortion, and murder-by-hire, this chapter of the Jesse Jackson story can be told for the first time.

CHAPTER 2

⌇

Stepping Out

HASTY ORDINATION

While the death of Dr. Martin Luther King Jr. undoubtedly affected Jackson deeply, it also set him free. With King dead, Jackson could become his own boss. The Reverend Ralph Abernathy, King's hand-picked successor, was still in control of the SCLC. But Jackson rarely reported back to Atlanta and held the mild-mannered Abernathy in contempt, at one point telling friendly biographer Eddie Stone, "I never listen to that nigger."[1]

The successful early boycotts organized by Jackson and his white associates from the Chicago Theological Seminary catapulted Jackson to the head of the line among black leaders in Chicago and allowed him to dole out patronage jobs in increasingly large quantities. At a gala luncheon in Jackson's honor at the New York Sheraton on January 13, 2000,

President Bill Clinton summed up Jackson's early successes: "In just two years, he helped more than three thousand men and women secure good jobs and an income that totaled over $22 million a year."[2] While Clinton's count was grossly exaggerated, some of those jobs went to Jackson's friends in the Black Stone Rangers, or El Rukn, the brutal street gang that ruled Chicago's South Side.[3]

Today, Jackson lays the blame for his long, troubled relationship to the gangs squarely on the doorstep of Dr. King. "When we first came here in 1966 with Dr. King, the idea of the urban gang was a phenomenon we had not known in the South. There was no such thing in Birmingham and Atlanta. Clearly there was an underground movement of gangs that we later found to be very connected to the higher-up Mafia. It was not innocent children, but real, real stuff." Dr. King thought he could redeem them, Jackson says. "People said Dr. King was naive about his capacity to change them. It was in that context—the Black Stone Rangers, the Disciples—that we got to know Jeff [Fort]."[4]

With King dead, Jackson had one more order of business he had to finalize before he could confidently set out on his own. He had to become a real minister. Since he hadn't completed his seminary studies and didn't have a church, there was only one way to go. He needed to find a friend willing to take the heat for conducting a ceremony that broke all the rules and traditions of the Baptist church.

What were those rules? Here's how the Reverend Johnny Hunter, who heads the Life Education and Resource Network (LEARN) in Virginia Beach and is an ordained Baptist minister, described the many long steps a candidate pastor must take before he is accepted into the fold:

"A candidate must be compelled to the ministry. He must be called, and this takes place in an official ceremony in the church when his calling is announced. He must preach a trial sermon under the authority of another pastor." Many candidates drop out after the trial sermon, which is critiqued by other pastors and by church elders. The church governing body then decides if they will grant the candidate minister a temporary license, usually for a two-year trial period. "If after the trial period of being licensed the candidate is walking right and it becomes clear that his calling to the ministry is a true calling, then his pastor and bishops may hold a special ordination service," the Reverend Hunter says.[5]

And that's not all. "The ordination must include the authorizing pastor as well as neighboring pastors who come for the laying on of hands. This is not done independently; it is well organized. Once accomplished and recognized, ordination is eternal, unless the minister falls from grace. It is a lengthy process."

There is no record that Jackson ever fulfilled these requirements, and he certainly never underwent the two-year probation period required by the church. Similarly, there is no record that he ever obtained the temporary minister's license. Once he dropped out of the seminary, Jackson's only qualification was his gift for political rhetoric. But he had a friend who was willing to take the risk of offending his fellow ministers by rushing Jesse Jackson to the head of the class: the Reverend Clay Evans, whom Jackson had introduced to Dr. King two years earlier.

Evans had already annoyed other black clergymen in Chicago by inviting Dr. King to his church and by getting King to attend a fundraiser for his building. He was an iconoclast, an activist, and if he thought the cause was right, he was willing to break the rules. But even the Reverend Evans had to overcome opposition from within his own community, especially from the Reverend Hiram Crawford Sr., who objected that Jackson had not fulfilled the necessary requirements.

Crawford had been a close confidant of Dr. Martin Luther King Jr., and benefited from tremendous moral authority within the civil rights movement. The first time the Reverend Evans informed him he intended to ordain Jackson, Crawford objected, referring to Jackson's recent appearance before the Ministers Alliance. When quizzed on matters of Christian faith, he was asked if he accepted the doctrine of the Virgin Birth. "I'm wrestling with it," Jackson replied.

"My father called up Reverend Evans after this," Crawford's son recalls. "He was furious. He said: 'How can you ordain somebody as a Christian minister who doesn't believe in the Virgin Birth?'" Jackson eventually quit wrestling and told Evans he accepted church doctrine, and the Reverend Crawford lifted his hold.[6]

The Reverend Evans held the ordination service for Jackson on June 30, 1968, at his Fellowship Missionary Baptist Church, then located at 45th and S. Princeton Avenue in Chicago. Also presiding was the Reverend C. L. Franklin, father of Aretha Franklin, the "Queen of Soul," who became a Jackson devotee in future years and whom black scandal sheets frequently suggested had more than just a passing friendship with Jackson.[7] Martita Hines, who keeps the church records, could find no other details on the ceremony because a fire destroyed most of the church records from the 1960s. She remembered Jackson preaching on the day of his ordination, but couldn't remember whether he had given a trial sermon. The existing church records make no mention of one.[8] But one thing is clear: since his ordination, Jackson has never been assigned to a church, nor has he submitted to any religious authority, as fellow Baptist ministers must do. Indeed, says the Reverend Charles Jenkins, the current pastor of Fellowship Missionary Baptist Church in Chicago, Jackson doesn't even come to his church on a regular basis—even though Chicago is Jackson's primary residence. "We see him here every three or four months," Jenkins said in an interview.

Jackson and the Reverend Evans forged an enduring friendship, and worked closely for many years to come. After Dr. King's 1966 visit to the church and Jackson's ordination, the "city's financial doors closed," former church secretary Edith Banks recalls. The Reverend Evans had already acquired land to construct a much larger church at 4543 S. Princeton Avenue but was unable to obtain building permits or a loan to build the new church because of opposition from a black alderman in the pay of Mayor Richard Daley. "Daley was furious at the Reverend Evans for bringing Dr. King to Chicago," Miss Banks said, "and he blocked everything. We sat in the old building next door watching the steel beams laying on the ground for seven years."

In the end, Jackson worked together with the Reverend Evans to put together a coalition that "unlocked the doors to the city," recalls church comptroller Mrs. Walterine Johnson. "Jesse Jackson was the key. He pulled in the bankers and countersigned the loan."[9]

The key banker was Cirilo McSween, who got the Independence Bank of Chicago and a consortium of nonblack banks to lend the Reverend Evans $500,000 to build the new church. Jackson personally guaranteed the loan at a public ceremony captured by a church photographer. Standing just behind him as he signed the papers on December 18, 1971, was actor Sammy Davis Jr. The new church was consecrated two years later. Jesse Jackson had made the Reverend Clay Evans's dream a reality.

JESSE GETS A HOUSE

With three small children and a fourth on the way, the Jacksons needed a proper home. On August 24, 1970, for $49,500, they purchased a fifteen room Tudor house at 6845 S. Constance Avenue where they still live today. The purchaser of record was "Trust 24210," established with the Exchange National Bank of Chicago. An official at the Cook County real estate records office in Chicago explains: "This is a secret land trust, set up to conceal the names of the owners or the people who hold the note. Sometimes the owner will put himself in there, but he does it this way to shroud the true ownership. The only way you can find out who really paid for the house is to call the bank."[10]

The Exchange National Bank is long gone, but Trust 24210 still exists. It is now registered with Chicago's LaSalle Bank. With some difficulty, a bank official located the trust on a computerized index along with the names of the current trustees: Jesse and Jacqueline Jackson. "It's set up in the names of both Jesse and Jacqueline Jackson so that any operation involving the trust—even pulling the paper file, to trace any changes— requires both of their signatures," the official says.[11] There is no way to identify the original trustees without the written approval of both Jacksons, he added.

When the home was purchased, nobody seemed to flinch at the secrecy of the deal or the opulence of the house. Jackson supporters told Barbara Reynolds, one of the few reporters who inquired, that they didn't want their preacher to look poor and so they helped out however they could. Within days of purchasing the house, Trust 24210 turned around and took out a $37,000 mortgage on the property with the black-owned Independence Bank of Chicago, whose vice president, Cirilo McSween, was Jackson's financial advisor and became a founding board member of Operation PUSH. The mortgage bore a fixed rate of 8 percent—a godsend when interest rates skyrocketed later in the decade—and required monthly payments of just $309.48 plus one-twelfth of the yearly real estate taxes on the property.[12] Today the handsome, antique-filled house is carried on the tax roles for a modest $246,000, but it is worth much more. Located only blocks from the badlands of South Stony Island Avenue and the mosque of black Muslim leader Louis Farrakhan, Jackson's neighborhood is an oasis of million-dollar houses with Beverly Hills style lawns and automatic sprinklers, whose quiet streets are blocked off from the ghetto on three sides by cul-de-sacs and concrete barriers. To the south lies 71st Street, a mean street cut in two by railroad tracks. To the west lies Blackstone Avenue, ruled by street gangs who inherited the territory from Jackson's half brother and his Rukn friends after they were jailed. South Constance Avenue is accessible only from the north, where it dead-ends into the golf course at Jackson Park. Today, African sculptures from Jackson's many overseas trips adorn the bay window overlooking the quiet street, and the basketball hoop by the garage no longer has a net. The sculpted garden is protected by an ancient shade tree, blocking the view from the street of the sprawling rear quarters of the house. In the driveway sits a black Lincoln Navigator, while the chimney is adorned with a two-foot "J," just like the "R" on his father's house in Greenville. Even by today's standards it is a large, elegant house. Jackson had no intention of living poorly.

As his subsequent career amply demonstrates, he knew how to get others to pick up the tab for his expenses. It was a lifestyle that had the added advantage of being almost totally opaque. For years, no one really knew how Jackson paid for the expensive private schools where he sent his children, the first class airfare and presidential suites, or the Cadillacs, Lincolns, and SUVs he used as his personal vehicles. With little visible personal wealth, Jackson could continue to pretend to be a humble preacher. "I'm no Father Divine," he liked to say. "I have not amassed a great fortune. I have a modest income. I don't find it necessary to live ostentatiously."[13] But the reality was quite different.

THE BLACK EXPO SCANDAL

Far from Atlanta and Abernathy's control, Jackson ran Operation Breadbasket as a kind of Jesse Inc., devoted to expanding his power and personal glory. What Abernathy and the other members of the SCLC leadership didn't know was that Operation Breadbasket had become Jesse Inc. *in fact*, not just in perception.

The scandal was brought to Abernathy's attention by Angela Parker, a black reporter for the *Chicago Tribune*, and would prompt Abernathy to suspend Jackson from the SCLC. Jackson's treatment of Parker, in turn, set the pattern of how he would almost always respond when challenged, especially when the challenge came from another black.

In 1969, under the SCLC umbrella, Jackson launched Black Expo in Chicago. It was to become a yearly event modeled after professional trade fairs where black companies and their white clients could display their wares to each other and to the general public. Billed as a tremendous success from the start, Black Expo boasted hundreds of thousands of paying visitors each year. As the organizer, Operation Breadbasket also took in money from the exhibitors, with white exhibitors paying several times the average booth rental of black exhibitors.[14]

Under the arrangement with the SCLC, Jackson was to remit 25 percent of the Black Expo proceeds to Atlanta. But the accounts he submitted to Abernathy were spotty at best. For the first year's operation, he remitted $60,000. But in 1970, that amount dropped to a mere $11,000.[15] In 1971, the last year of Jackson's association with the SCLC, the accounting was so poor that even Jackson's supporters began to question his integrity in public.

Jackson claimed that more than 700,000 people visited Black Expo in 1971, where the daily admission fee cost one dollar for adults and fifty cents for children. Another 66,000 people attended six nights of entertainment, paying four dollars each. Almost all of this money was paid in cash. In addition, hundreds of exhibitors paid substantial fees for their stands, many of them upwards of $10,000 each. Yet, Jackson reported just over $500,000 in gross receipts for the entire event—an amount so paltry that Jackson had to trot out Black Expo bookkeepers to a news conference, where reporters hammered them as they tried to explain away the paucity of receipts with elaborate charts.[16]

Jackson himself would later claim that in his generosity he had let in half the visitors for free. Biographer Barbara Reynolds, quoting show promoter International Amphitheatre, expressed serious doubt that any more than twenty thousand people per day had attended, bringing the total attendance to one hundred thousand.[17] But Hermene Hartman, who helped plan the Black Expos, recalls that the events were so popular that they were deluged with visitors. "The ushers and box office got overwhelmed," she told me. "I saw people at the box office literally stuffing their pockets, the money was coming in so fast. They weren't stealing; they just couldn't handle so much money coming in so fast."[18] But that still didn't explain the huge discrepancy between the presumed receipts and the amount Jackson claimed Black Expo had earned when he turned over the accounts to the SCLC. A Chicago judge later slapped a contempt of court motion on Jackson for failing to produce financial records demanded by the promoter, who remained unpaid.[19]

One event that happened has never been told. It involved Jackson's friend Jeff Fort, head of the notorious Chicago street gang, the Black Stone Rangers.

According to Hurley Green, who stopped ghostwriting for Jackson in 1971 to become the editor of the *Chicago Defender*, "Jesse made a deal with the Black Stone Rangers. If they didn't cause trouble for Black Expo, he offered to give them a share of the take." Black Stone Rangers gang members were to be paid to guard the gates, and to keep other gangs away, just as they were put on the payroll of Red Rooster to "prevent" gang assaults. It was an old-fashioned protection racket; not very sophisticated, but effective.

But things didn't work out as planned. When Jackson was counting the cash from the ticket sales, a group of young toughs burst into his office with sawed-off shotguns. "They were members of the Black Stone Rangers," Green says.

Five people were in the room with Jackson when the gang members burst in. One of them was Hermene Hartman, who now publishes *N'Digo* magazine in Chicago. "I wasn't supposed to be in the room," she recalls. "I ran in by accident and saw Jeff Fort and company and said, 'What are you guys doing with these guns?' They had them on Jesse and wouldn't leave. They said, 'You're on our turf, and we take a third.' But Jesse never reacted. He said, 'If you want to sit down and talk, you got to put your guns away.' Eventually they did, but it lasted hours."

Finally someone—Hurley Green thinks it was Calvin Morris, who was then married to Hermene Hartman—turned to Jesse and told him to hand over the money. But Hartman herself is less certain. "They kidnapped Cirilo McSween at one point. He was the treasurer. They took him into an alley, stripped him naked, and had him walk down the street. They may have gotten some money that way, but if so it was appeasement, a life-saver. Pure robbery."

Clearly, dealing with the street gangs was risky business, and even Jackson could get stung. But the worst was yet to come.

By combing through state records, *Chicago Tribune* reporter Angela Parker discovered that on September 29, 1970, Jackson and his friends had incorporated Black Expo as a nonprofit foundation, totally independent of the SCLC, and then as a corporation on September 14, 1971.[20] As a further shield from the SCLC, they established two other corporations that actually managed the show, Black Expo Inc. and Breadbasket Commercial Association.[21] The *Tribune* charged that both moves were made "under the direction of the Rev. Jesse L. Jackson, national director of Breadbasket, without the knowledge or approval of Dr. Abernathy or SCLC's board of directors." On the board of directors of Black Expo Inc. were Jackson's most trusted associates. In addition to the Reverend Clay Evans, the board included Chicago businessmen Celion Henderson,

George Jones, Thomas Todd, and Al Johnson, a Cadillac dealer who was helping to bankroll Jackson's personal lifestyle.[22] Black Expo no longer belonged to the SCLC, as Ralph Abernathy and the SCLC board had always assumed. It belonged to Jesse Louis Jackson and a bunch of his friends, so the SCLC couldn't take it away from them in the event of a clash. Indeed, that appeared to have been Jackson's intent, according to his half brother and business partner Noah Robinson Jr.

"We secretly incorporated BCA [Breadbasket Commercial Association] as a separate entity from Breadbasket," Robinson told Jackson biographer Barbara Reynolds. "We were not pushing the name because we didn't want SCLC to know about it, because Jesse thought he might have to leave and he wanted BCA to be underground, so we could get up and run if we had to. When we decided to make the break out the door, we would have a concerted effort because the businessmen would underwrite the new movement." Abernathy summoned Jackson and Robinson to Atlanta in April 1971 suspecting that something was amiss. "All during the meeting with Abernathy, I heard later, Jesse denied that BCA existed," Robinson told Barbara Reynolds. "Since I have a habit of talking too much, Jesse had made me sit out in the hall, so I wouldn't spill the story."[23]

Parker's editors at the *Tribune* flew her down to Atlanta on November 27, 1971, to show Abernathy the evidence of Jackson's betrayal and get his comment. Abernathy was stunned as he went through the documents. He and other SCLC directors had tolerated Jackson and his personality cult with relative good grace since Dr. King's assassination, under the assumption that for all his flamboyance and independence, Jackson would still play by the rules. This was hard evidence that Jackson had pulled a fast one on them.

"This is most unusual," Abernathy told Parker. "I find it difficult to believe. Although there may not have been any mishandling of funds by this move, if it is still true, it is wrong and should not have been incorporated without approval and knowledge of the board of directors and the SCLC president. . . . If it is true, the Rev. Mr. Jackson had no right to direct the founding of either a foundation or a corporation—no department has that right under the policies of the national organization. It cannot make any legal move without the approval of the president and the board of directors of the national office. We cannot at this time allow a department to get out of line, it can hurt the entire organization."[24]

At first, Abernathy phoned Jackson, summoning him to Atlanta to explain his actions. When Jackson refused, Abernathy and his board flew to Chicago and set up shop in the Marriott Hotel near O'Hare Airport on December 3, 1971. Jackson alerted the press, who came in abundance. Once the news cameras were turning, Jackson supporters packed the hotel lobby carrying picket signs that said, "Don't Get Messy with Jesse," as if Abernathy and the SCLC board were a white lynch mob.[25] Although Jackson showed up with a briefcase full of documents to make his case, Abernathy kept him outside the conference room for three full hours. Twice Jackson attempted to force his way in, but he was tossed out.

Finally, after a long, tense meeting Jackson stormed out into the crowd of reporters. For perhaps the only time in his life, he brushed them off with a curt "no comment." Abernathy emerged shortly afterwards to announce that the SCLC had suspended Jackson for sixty days "for administrative improprieties and repeated acts of violation of organizational policy," and had forbidden him to take part in any SCLC activities during that time. He also pledged that the SCLC board would conduct a detailed investigation of the Black Expo finances.[26]

Jackson, the self-styled heir to Martin Luther King, had been repudiated in public by King's appointed successor and accused by Abernathy of what sounded like embezzlement. For a weaker soul, it would have spelled the end of his career. Indeed, imagine the public outcry if Elizabeth Dole, as president of the Red Cross, had secretly incorporated a company for her personal profit that traded in blood products and then, once exposed by her board, arrogantly denied any wrongdoing? Not only would she never be able to consider running for president; in all likelihood, the feds would have prosecuted her.

But Jackson is nothing if not audacious. He knew that the best defense was a brutal, unforgiving offense. That Saturday, he appeared at the weekly "prayer meeting" of Operation Breadbasket, introduced no longer as an SCLC staff member but as a guest speaker. He denied outright Abernathy's accusation that he had acted without the consent of the SCLC executive board, and to deflect attention he took a swipe at the Internal Revenue Service, which, he said, "has been looking at our books for months. My record needs no defense. We don't owe the IRS anything, but in case we do, we're going to pay."[27] Then he unveiled a tactic he would hone and perfect in the years to come. In its later versions, Jackson's shakedown act could be subtle, persuasive, even compelling, by appealing to the better instincts of white corporate leaders. But here, played out against fellow blacks, it was hardball of the most vicious sort: dirty, ugly, played with a malevolence that spoke of revenge.

Jackson went after Angela Parker, the *Chicago Tribune* reporter who had exposed his corruption to Abernathy. Addressing Parker, who was among the reporters in the room, Jackson said, "Dr. Abernathy is not the problem or the issue. The issue is that last Friday a black woman reporter left Chicago with her mission being to separate great black men. She took a plane from the Tribune Tower to Atlanta. Now you know who your enemy is."[28]

The crowd greeted Parker with "a hail of boos," and Jackson went on for a full fifteen minutes, railing about "the treachery of black women."[29] At one point, Jackson compared Parker to the woman who stabbed Dr. King in New York in the early 1960s, a remark that produced "thunderous applause" from the audience. "I was sitting next to her when she was booed at PUSH and I was praying: I hope this never happens to me," Barbara Reynolds recalls today. "I promised myself then that I'd never tell the truth about Jesse."[30] But she did.

Within hours, pickets arrived to surround Angela Parker's apartment. "And these were not capricious actions by a few of Jackson's followers, momentarily stirred to vengeance by the power of his oratory. This was a planned and sustained program of abuse designed to punish Parker for her apostasy and to make of her an example to other reporters."[31] Like Barbara Reynolds and other black reporters who dared cross Jackson, Parker would be plagued by demonstrations, death threats, and more subtle efforts to destroy her career for years, even after she moved to a new address. "Angela went underground, but they destroyed her life," Reynolds recalls.

It was the Jesse Jackson technique. If a white leader had dared employ such tactics, the press would have pilloried him. But Jackson was given a free ride.

The Split with Abernathy

Jackson didn't waste time plotting his next move. He was a young man in a hurry. Just days after Abernathy had publicly rebuked him, Jackson fired off a contemptuous letter, resigning from the SCLC. "Since the time has come when I cannot any longer give my active service to the organization," Jackson wrote, "I consider sixty days too long for this vital work to be endangered by my leave of absence and hereby submit my resignation effective Friday, December 17, 1971." He signed the letter, "Jesse Louis Jackson, The Country Preacher."[32] It was a curious parting shot given the fact that Jackson had tied himself to the big city and had never had his own pulpit in any church. Once again it was a not-so-subtle attempt to wrap himself in the mantle of Dr. Martin Luther King Jr. Jackson would invoke the "Country Preacher" moniker thirty years later, in January 2001, after it was reported he had fathered an out-of-wedlock child.

Jackson unveiled his SCLC resignation letter at an emotional press conference the next Saturday, attended by 3,000 supporters. "I need air. I need to grow," he said, vowing to begin his own organization. "Whatever its name shall be, we are going to organize and to keep on pushing."[33]

Furious at Jackson's tactics, Abernathy issued a scathing rebuke in the name of the SCLC board. "We will not accept the resignation of the Reverend Jesse L. Jackson until he gives an accounting of hundreds of thousands of dollars and explains the operation of Black Expo. Mr. Jackson must clean his house before he leaves. I never thought it would come to the point that a brother would quit and walk out on the movement started by the late Dr. Martin Luther King Jr., rather than to deal forthrightly with the issues."[34]

Jackson eventually hired an accounting firm, Washington, Pittman & McKeever, to go through the Black Expo '71 books and transfer the SCLC share of the take to Atlanta. But even this most friendly of audits, remitted to the SCLC board the following April, showed several anomalies that were never resolved, including a $100,000 loan from Stax Record Company in Memphis, Tennessee. Stax vice president Al Bell contributed an additional $32,000 to Jackson in 1972 and distributed Jackson's speeches, recorded on the Stax label. It was unclear whether Jackson ever repaid the loan.[35]

With Jackson's resignation, Operation Breadbasket collapsed. Or more accurately, it was transformed from being a branch of the SCLC to becoming Jackson's personal organization. On December 12, the day after he announced his resignation, Jackson called a group of former Breadbasket supporters to the Commodore Hotel in New York to gather public pledges of loyalty and renewed support. Among the crowd were singers Aretha Franklin and Roberta Flack, black politicians Carl Stokes and Richard Hatcher, black reporters and publishers, and even a member of the SCLC board, W. A. Saunders. Also in the crowd were some of Jackson's black business supporters, who jokingly referred to him as "Godfather," including Chicago Cadillac dealer Al Johnson, who provided Jackson luxury vehicles from his dealership free of charge.[36]

On Christmas Day, Jackson announced the birth of his own organization: People United to Save Humanity, PUSH. If Abernathy and the SCLC leadership had thought for an instant that Jackson would go quietly into the night, they were wrong. Instead, he took over the mission, the supporters, even the board members of Operation Breadbasket, without paying so much as a cent for those assets. It was the ultimate in leveraged takeovers. The only asset Breadbasket had left was its name, and even that virtually disappeared from the press after Jackson created PUSH. Abernathy had tried to stand up to Jackson, but the civil rights movement largely ignored Abernathy's protest.

But outside the movement, the appearance of malfeasance attracted federal officials. The Internal Revenue Service scrutinized Jackson's personal financial records as well as those of Operation Breadbasket. Jackson called it "throwing mud around," and claimed the IRS eventually concluded they owed him $842.[37]

Federal prosecutors, Cook County court officers, and criminal justice officials knowledgeable of the investigation tell the author that federal and local officials also probed Operation Breadbasket after Jackson split with the SCLC. They were examining the reported misuse of funds from the SCLC. "We used to joke that we had found the baskets, but the bread was all gone," said a Cook County official knowledgeable of the inquiry. "It wasn't a fishing expedition. Somewhere between $500,000 to $600,000 seemed to have gone missing."[38] Jackson insisted then—and now—that there was no impropriety.

A former senior FBI special agent said he had "a clear recollection" of an investigation, and had heard details from FBI colleagues who participated in the probe. Federal agents from the IRS and the FBI participated in the probe, law enforcement sources tell the author. The investigation was shut down during the early months of the Carter administration. Jackson says today that he can not recall that specific investigation, but there is "a history of the FBI investigating on the one hand and the IRS [being used] as a tool on the other, leaking to the press, to disrupt and discredit" activists such as himself.[39]

Former U.S. attorney Thomas P. Sullivan was sworn in on July 19, 1977. In his initial annual report as U.S. attorney, Sullivan noted: "During 1977, a monthly grand jury sat every day, and five special grand juries met 2 or 3 days a week." The biggest case under investigation at that time involved fraud in minority set-asides awarded by the Metropolitan Sanitary District. It was "the largest bribery scheme successfully prosecuted to date in a federal court," Sullivan wrote.[40]

One of the players in that scheme was Jesse's half brother and Breadbasket business partner Noah Robinson Jr.

BROTHERS TOGETHER

Robinson was always considered the brainy member of the family, the technician, the money manager, whereas Jackson was the mercurial social activist who lived by fast talking. Even before he claimed to have graduated with an MBA from the prestigious Wharton School of the University of

Pennsylvania in 1969, Robinson had set up his own management consulting firm in Philadelphia that was hailed by *Fortune* magazine as "one of the most successfully and enthusiastically supported programs of its kind in the nation."[41] Said brother George Robinson: "Noah was about making as much money as he could possibly make, while Jesse was about helping people. Noah wanted to help himself. And he was very good at it."[42]

But Noah also wanted to help Jesse and reportedly turned down thirty-two job offers, preferring to join Jackson at Operation Breadbasket in 1969. For a short time Robinson took over Operation Breadbasket on behalf of the SCLC after Jackson left, then devoted himself full time to running Breadbasket Commercial Association (BCA), the private company he had set up with Jackson cronies to run Black Expo. Robinson's job was to rake in the contracts, while Jesse prepared the way. As Noah himself put it, "I complement Jesse. He's high profile. I'm low profile; he likes to shout about it, I like to make money."[43]

One of the first people Jackson introduced him to in Chicago was Jeff Fort, capo supremo of the Black Stone Rangers street gang, Chicago police investigators say.[44] Noah Robinson and the street toughs of the Black Stone Rangers gave muscle to the threats of boycott, and negotiated their own "covenants" with businesses promising to create jobs for ghetto youth. Noah's brief association with the SCLC in 1971 gave him legitimacy and helped him to win a $155,000 per year grant from the federal Office of Minority Business Enterprise to train minorities in setting up and operating their own businesses. Jackson's friend Jeff Fort, the gang leader, was later convicted on March 29, 1972, along with other leaders of the Black Stone Ranger's ruling "Main 21" for conspiring to defraud the federal government out of $927,000 they had received through a similar federally funded jobs training program aimed at putting gang members to work.[45]

At one point, after Jackson split from the SCLC, the half brothers appeared to become rivals in a gangland-style turf battle, with Jackson publicly warning Robinson to "back off." At issue were spoils from a juicy municipal contract to build a new library in the South Side. Jackson threatened to close down the construction site with demonstrators until "all the facts" about the contracts were disclosed. Robinson shot back that he would bring in his own street toughs if Jackson showed up. The real reason for the squabble was money. Robinson had cut a deal with the main contractor, a white-owned firm called Ruby Construction, that put him in charge of doling out the minority set-asides to subcontractors who were BCA members. Jackson had been cut out.[46]

Robinson and Jackson frequently crossed paths as they made their rounds of black business owners looking for money in the early 1970s.[47] Fishing in the same small pond had a comic side. For instance, when Jackson wanted to hit up Joe Louis Milk, whose products he regularly touted, he had to fly directly under Robinson's nose, since Joe Louis Milk was now run by Robinson's brother and was headquartered in his BCA office on South Michigan Avenue.[48] For his part, Robinson liked to talk, and it would get him into big trouble later on. "Jesse does have all the prerequisites for success," he said. "He has intelligence, drive, ruthlessness and vindictiveness. And Jesse can be as terrifying as Al Capone." But in the end, Robinson said, he was "a paper tiger who thinks power is made of press releases."[49]

Jackson elevated his call for minority set-asides, which amounted to economic racial quotas, into a philosophical construct he called "The Kingdom Theory." The poorly written essay was part Marx, part Martin Luther King, and part Leon Sullivan, and would have pulled a failing grade from Howard Schomer. But it sounded a theme Jackson returns to even today. "[A]s blacks and non-white, we control, potentially, the margin of profit on most of the consumer items and nearly all the basic consumer items in the nation," he wrote. "If we account for 20 percent of a firm's sales, then that firm must give us 20 percent of its business, 20 percent of its advertising dollar, 20 percent of its banking business, and 20 percent of its jobs."[50] That meant distributorships for blacks, advertisers for black newspapers, and new business for black banks. The recipients of this new business were expected to return Jackson's favor by making hefty financial contributions to PUSH or becoming members of one of its parallel organizations. That was how Jackson's system worked, and it was extremely lucrative.

Jackson publicly acknowledged the quid pro quo relationship with the black business community in Chicago. In response to criticism that he was "tithing" black businessmen in exchange for his services as an intermediary, Jackson said: "Absolutely. It's like a tax. You pay taxes to the government for your services, don't you? . . . We're all family here, but you have to pay to play. You cannot ride to freedom free in Pharaoh's chariot."[51] The "taxes" were collected in various ways: at the collection plate of Operation PUSH, through in-kind contributions to the Jackson family expenses, and through personal visits to local black businesses by Jackson and his friends.

They were also collecting through the boycotts. Retired Chicago police detective Richard Kolovitz remembers one such incident well. "Jesse went down to a Kroger's Grocery at 39th and Giles, just west of King Drive, making his demands. When nothing happened, he sent in the Stones, who formed a picket line outside." The gang members wore a distinctive uniform of black trousers with green, military-style stripes down the side, and red berets. They formed an intimidating presence, effectively scaring customers from entering the store. "The store owner told us that she wrote Jesse a $5,000 check to go away."[52]

Jackson admits to using gang members for the boycotts, but insists they participated in the picket lines "as consumers, citizens, within the law." He vigorously denies using the gangs to shake down store owners. "That would be extortion. That would be illegal. We never did that. It was never necessary to do that." His group was keenly aware of the laws governing consumer boycotts and picketing, he says, because pastors had been jailed for using extortionist tactics. "There's never been a single instance when we've been charged with extortion, except by members of the press," he adds.[53]

Jesse Jackson nearly became a casualty of gang violence, Kolovitz recalls, when Jeff Fort found out he hadn't been "sharing" contributions. "Jesse had become friends with the local Stones leader on 46th Street, Leonard Dickerson (a.k.a. Leonard Sengali)," recalls Kolovitz. "They'd worked together raising money in the neighborhood. When Jeff got out of

Cook County jail in 1969, where he'd been held on a kidnapping charge, he came around looking for money. Jesse told him off." Not long afterwards, Dickerson was driving Jackson to the Stones' clubhouse at 4630 Greenwood, where Jackson had bought an old church. "They were driving east on 47th Street, just east of Drexel, when somebody opened fire on the car," says Kolovitz. Neither Dickerson nor Jackson was hurt in the spray of bullets.

Jackson still recalls the shooting. "It was a very tense period. The post-King period was full of riots ... lots of threats. Civil rights leaders and ministers had to have bodyguards [because of] threats by gang members on their churches."[54] But after that incident, Jackson and Jeff Fort worked more closely together, taking part in each other's events.[55]

Noah Robinson's ambition was to use minority set-asides as the cornerstone for building a commercial empire. By the mid-1970s, success smoothed the rivalry between the brothers. Noah left the politics to Jesse and took care of business.

Robinson branched out into fast food, winning a concession from Kentucky Fried Chicken. As he expanded his empire to include Wendy's and Bojangles, using Jackson's political push as leverage, Robinson plunged deeper into a relationship with Jeff Fort, leader of the Black Stone Rangers street gang, at this point known as the Black P Stone Nation, and later, as El Rukn. Brother George Robinson chalked it up to Noah's big heart. "Noah was the kind of person that liked to help black youths, when they came out of prison, get back into society, but got involved in trying to do things for people that he shouldn't have been doing."[56]

Glen Bone III worked for Jackson as part of his Jackson Action Task Force. "Noah Robinson would show up at the weekly PUSH meetings. Everybody knew he was into drugs and gangs," he recalls.[57] Just how deeply he was involved wouldn't become apparent until later.

JESSE JETSTREAM

Jackson's solo flight with Operation PUSH almost never got off the ground. While he had surrounded himself with serious individuals with serious expertise, such as Northwestern University law professor Thomas Todd, who gave PUSH its name, his own instincts as a leader were still shaky. The early years of Operation PUSH could best be described as a campaign a minute: a frenzy of activity, a dozen directions at once, with scant results other than front-page headlines.

His most glaring failing was his lack of follow-through. When two black employees from Trans World Airlines (TWA) contacted Operation PUSH with complaints of racial prejudice, Jackson announced that he had written to TWA president F. C. Wiser, demanding that he meet with black employees "immediately." Wiser must discuss "policy matters and specific discriminatory treatment in seniority assignments and promotions" with the disgruntled TWA employees, recent hires who were let go during routine layoffs. TWA patiently rebutted Jackson's claims, and that was the end of it. PUSH moved on to other things.[58]

Chicago Daily News columnist Mike Royko dubbed him "Jesse Jetstream" in a scathing parody that was widely quoted years later during Jackson's first run for president:

> At a press conference today, the Reverend Jetstream disclosed his latest plans.
> "I wish to announce at this time," he said, "that I am in orbit. There is no way I can be stopped."
> "What are you running for?" someone asked.
> "I have not decided that yet," the Reverend Jetstream said leaving the room.[59]

In May 1972, Jackson announced that PUSH was investigating ten companies for selling products to black customers while not investing in black communities. He said he had received "a very favorable response" from General Foods Corporation and the Schlitz Brewing Company to PUSH inquiries about hiring and business practices. "We have called together groups of people in twenty cities to discuss either our new relationships with those major companies or boycotts of the same companies," Jackson proclaimed.[60] Avon joined General Foods and Schlitz a year later in making a public show of its existing investments in the black community. Jackson claimed this as a great success, but in fact, none of the companies felt compelled by Jackson's threats to change their behavior. It was Jackson who came around to seeing it their way.[61]

In one sense, Jackson had come too late, and he knew it. For much of Jackson's life, he would be a solution in search of a problem, but never would this facet of his character be more prominent than during the early years following Dr. King's death. "The civil rights movement is over; that mission is accomplished," he told supporters in August 1972 outside Cincinnati, home of his faithful attorney, John Bustamante. "We can live any place we want to live, but we can't afford the house notes. We can buy any car we want, but we can't pay the car notes. We have more rights than we can use—but our problem is economic, our solution is economic, and our goal is economic."[62]

Not long after Jackson announced that PUSH would take on ten major corporations, he came back and multiplied that by ten. His new targets included General Motors, Exxon, Ford Motor Company, Chrysler, and Mobil Oil. It was going to be a nationwide campaign to force companies to invest more in the black community. Jackson publicly estimated that he would provide black entrepreneurs with a bonanza of $5 billion to $6.5 billion. He promised to hold seminars to teach activists how to challenge broadcasting license applications and renewals, and to block those using the airways as a "nonresponsible propaganda tool of vested interests."[63] He never held the seminars; but he paid obsessive attention to how the media reported on his activities, and repeatedly went after black reporters and radio commentators who dared challenge him. "There'll be no voting here," he told his Saturday-morning supporters. "I am anointed, not appointed."[64]

In the summer of 1973, PUSH held a four-day convention in Chicago, in an atmosphere *Chicago Tribune* reporter Edith Herman described as akin to a "gospel meeting." Herman went on:

The audience nodded in agreement, clapped, and cheered as he told them to boycott grocery stores, saying: "No one can do without them. Everyone comes to the grocery store, even the President of the United States."

"Say it again," the audience demanded. "That's right," they yelled. . . .

"Boycott milk to start with," he told the PUSH members from throughout the country. "It is perishable."[65]

Boycotting milk from white-owned dairies in favor of Joe Louis Milk was a far cry from threatening corporate America. But Jackson didn't yet understand corporate power, profits, or what motivated corporate leaders. He was still just a street hustler who derived his power from his ability to mobilize crowds. He later claimed that he had picked the food industry as a target because it was the most vulnerable. "If you are looking for a fight, you don't choose someone who can whip you," he told Edith Herman. "You didn't see me suggesting that we start out with General Motors."[66] Although Herman had reported Jackson's earlier boast that he *was* going after General Motors, she refrained from pointing that out in her article.

MONEY TROUBLES

Scarcely two years on his own, Jackson appeared on the verge of financial collapse. In early November 1973, PUSH board members were shocked to receive bank statements that showed PUSH with only $6,000 in cash. They were especially shocked because Black Expo '73 had been judged such a success, netting $163,195 on gross receipts that topped $642,000. Just days before the crisis became public, Jackson's top deputy, Thomas Todd, resigned as PUSH vice president and as a board member.[67] The remaining board members summoned Jackson to a four-hour meeting on November 9. PUSH faced debts of more than $51,000, including $13,000 for Jackson's personal travels and another $12,000 for his telephone bill. "It is doubtful whether PUSH can survive in the wake of this," one board member said.[68]

Jackson complained that he had expected the revenues from Black Expo to be higher. He vigorously denied he had siphoned off funds for personal use, although PUSH records revealed that Jackson's travel bills alone had amounted to $85,985 during his first year of independent operations.[69] "My annual pay from PUSH is $1," he said. "My income is derived from preaching and lecturing."[70]

It was a curious statement. If Jackson was making money from preaching and lecturing, he was being awfully shy about it, because the first press report of Jackson delivering a sermon dates from 1974, six years after his shotgun ordination and one year after he claimed it was his major source of income.[71] PUSH auditors, however, did uncover that Jackson had brought in $117,434 from PUSH Saturday morning collection plate "offerings" during the organization's first year. For Jackson to claim a percentage of PUSH revenues as remuneration for "preaching" at the same time he claimed he wasn't earning a salary was disingenuous. Since PUSH was then operating as a nonprofit corporation under Section 501(c)(3) of the Internal Revenue code, earmarking collection money for Jackson without paying him a salary amounted to a commingling of public and private funds, a clear violation of the IRS code. Bustamante urged him to change the status of PUSH to a religious organization, which would exempt it from nearly all reporting requirements.[72] "John Bustamante did very good work for the movement," Cirilo McSween recalls. "Every attempt was made not to violate the law."

The PUSH financial woes weren't affecting Jackson's high-flying lifestyle in the slightest. Jackson was netting more than $100,000 annually from speaker's fees, lectures, and commentaries on WBMX-FM radio in Chicago, which were paid into a separate entity known as the Freedman's Bureau.[73]

Jackson didn't always tell those who donated their time to the movement that he was personally profiting from their labor. Hurley Green worked for Jackson as a ghost writer and publicist for nearly three years, writing a weekly column under Jackson's name that appeared in the *Chicago Defender*. He quit when he learned that Jackson was being paid a fee for the column, which he thought was delivered gratis, and pocketing all the money for himself. "Jesse uses people like a lemon," Green says today. "He squeezes all the juice out, then gets another lemon. I've seen him go through lots of people like that."[74]

At a November 13, 1973, press conference at the lavish new PUSH headquarters at 930 E. 50th Street, a deconsecrated Jewish temple on South Drexel Boulevard, Jackson's friends and benefactors circled the wagons. "The Rev. Mr. Jackson has not overspent and we are not critical of his management," said Al Johnson, a PUSH board member who owned the biggest Cadillac concession in the black community and paid many of Jackson's bills personally. "Operation PUSH was born broke," he added. "It has never been news to this board that the organization is now, always has been, and always will be genuinely in need of money, and a lot of it. When you're in the business of fighting racism and poverty, you don't attract a lot of contributors."[75] Johnson said PUSH would have to launch a major fundraising drive, but would most likely fall short by $40,000 to $50,000 of wiping out its debts. "That's not bad, when you consider we started with a $110,000 deficit this year," he added. (According to the auditors, PUSH started that year with a deficit carried over from 1972 of $143,963.)[76]

Beyond the excuses, there were frontal attacks. When respected *Chicago Tribune* columnist Vernon Jarrett had a front-page story exposing the PUSH financial crisis, he became Jackson's target. Jarrett wrote:

> I was verbally bombarded by disciples of the Rev. Mr. Jackson.... Several of my critics were upset over my revealing that black colleges had contributed $13,400 to PUSH Expo. These needy institutions were attracted by PUSH's "Save the Black Colleges" slogan.
>
> Other critics screamed "traitor" because I reported that PUSH was faced with an unpaid air-travel bill of around $13,000 and a $12,000 telephone bill....
>
> Regardless of what the basic story may be, the image created by media—with Rev. Mr. Jackson's approval—is that PUSH is a man

named Jesse and a man named Jesse is PUSH. When white media appears to slow down its coverage of the Rev. Mr. Jackson's activities he often accuses them of racism over his radio program.[77]

Jarrett then added a new revelation by exposing that Jackson had attempted to coerce a payment of $70,000 from Detroit mayoral candidate Coleman Young, in exchange for Jackson's support during a contested Democratic Party primary.[78] Jackson angrily rejected the charge, but a Young campaign aide, Phil Smith, was soon talking to reporters. The exchange had occurred after Jackson gave a speech at Michigan State University. Afterwards, a faculty member reintroduced Jackson to Young, who asked him for his support. According to Young's aide, this was Jackson's pitch: "I've got rings. I've got jewelry. I've got a car. I got a house. I don't need nothing, but my staff has needs and they have to live. And I don't see how my staff could help what you're doing for less than $70,000."[79] Young declined the offer and Jackson withheld his support. When Jackson attempted to jump on Young's bandwagon just days before the general election that November, Young refused to give him a seat at the speaker's table, where guests included the widow of Dr. Martin Luther King Jr. and other luminaries, Jarrett reported.

Jackson would try anything to stay afloat. At one point, during the 1973–74 oil crisis, he embraced a black service station owner on Chicago's South Side named Sam McBride. McBride had gained national notoriety for his scheme to attract business to his Action Shell: he sold last will and testament forms and rabbit foot charms (worth about fifteen cents and twenty-five cents respectively) to customers for as much as $2.00 a piece. In exchange, he offered them two gallons of "free" gasoline. The gimmick quickly came to the attention of the IRS, which shut down McBride's station as part of a campaign to protect consumers from price gouging.

Instead of denouncing McBride for ripping off black consumers, Jackson invited McBride to address the weekly Saturday meeting at PUSH headquarters, where Jackson called him a "victim of the oil monopoly's exploitation."[80] Jackson urged the formation of a new trade association of independent service station operators in Chicago. The association, Jackson said, would wrest concessions from the oil companies. Instead, the idea drew ridicule from the Illinois Gasoline Dealers Association and from black leaders. Jackson defended himself in an editorial that attempted to prove that McBride was a victim "of the energy-crisis hoax." He revealed his motive by noting that McBride had brought "a large number of those independent station operators" with him to the PUSH meeting. Jackson said that he had given them "the platform and the opportunity to tell their story on the Saturday morning broadcast."[81] The PUSH broadcasts on WJPC reached an estimated 100,000 listeners and generated significant advertising revenues. "Tithing" McBride and his friends for his promotional services offered Jackson a potentially generous new source of revenue.

THE JACKSON NEBULA

Whenever problems have surfaced with the finances of his organizations, Jackson typically claimed that he never took care of the petty day-to-day operations of the various groups under his control. When Black Expo finances were challenged in 1970 and 1971, for example, Jackson hid behind his accountants and his board. He has used similar tactics ever since, arguing that he is just the inspiration, not the implementer. "I am a tree shaker, not a jelly maker," Jackson likes to repeat.

Early on, Jackson displayed a talent for organization that most often went unappreciated. He established for-profit political action groups and nonprofit charities, and shifted funds among them as it suited him. Clearly Jackson knew what he was doing by crafting this complex network of companies. He wanted his finances opaque, his donors secure, and his personal income and assets unknowable. Jesse Jackson Inc. was set up with all the creativity of a foreign tax shelter. But it was done for the most part in the United States.

Providing Jackson with key expertise were two close aides: lawyer John Bustamante, who has done the court filings for almost all of Jackson's forty-odd companies over the last thirty years; and financial wizard Cirilo

McSween, who has handled Jackson's personal and corporate accounts. McSween is Jackson's moneyman, banker, and business consultant. He is one of several dozen black businessmen who owe their considerable fortunes at least in part to Jesse Jackson, but who also used their own incipient fortunes to promote Jesse when he needed it most. "I've always had business," McSween recalls today. "Jesse needed me, not the other way around. When he came to me in the beginning with his project, I told him: I'll work with you for three months and that's it, but I'll work day and night. That three months has now become thirty years."[82]

PUSH established right after Jackson's break with the SCLC, began as a nonprofit corporation, which meant that donors could take a tax deduction for all moneys contributed to it. However, as Jackson soon learned, as a nonprofit corporation PUSH was required to report its activities and major donors to the Internal Revenue Service as well as to the state of Illinois, where it was incorporated. Within months of establishing PUSH in Chicago, Jackson asked Bustamante to set up a separate PUSH Foundation in Ohio that could collect additional tax-exempt funds for the Jackson nebula.[83] By incorporating in Ohio, Jackson could keep the origin of these funds secret from Mayor Richard Daley in Chicago, and so prevent him from applying pressure on Jackson's local donors. It was a smart legal trick that required a thorough knowledge of the IRS code and the legal reporting requirements incumbent upon nonprofit organizations.

Jackson's nonprofits were eligible to apply for foundation grants. Thus, in 1972, PUSH received a $750,000 loan from the Ford Foundation to produce an educational film called "Save the Children," the theme of that year's Black Expo, which Jackson now owned free and clear and renamed "PUSH Expo." Jesse Jackson was the star of the show, and used the film as a personal promotional vehicle to reach new audiences across the United States. This type of unabashed self-promotion earned him a new nickname within the black community, "Just-Me" Jackson. When Jackson couldn't repay the debt, the Ford Foundation ultimately forgave it.[84]

In 1973, PUSH Expo sounded a similar theme, "Save the Black Colleges." By this time, Jackson had begun to develop a more systematic approach. One exhibitor who felt the sting of Jackson's shakedown was the venerable United Negro College Fund. Black columnist Vernon Jarrett published a letter by a UNCF board member who blasted Jackson for exploiting the UNCF for purely financial purposes. "I was really appalled when I found out earlier that PUSH, using the slogan 'Save the Black Colleges,' in turn charged those institutions and/or alumni that wanted to participate. Of course the figure you quoted [$13,400 per booth] doesn't represent the additional money spent by staff who came and represented the Black Colleges at Black Expo '73. Please be assured that I am upset because some of my colleagues allowed themselves to be used by PUSH. Does PUSH publish an annual report?"[85] Jackson appears never to have replied. His nonprofits were so late in filing the scanty activity summaries required by the federal and state authorities that during Jackson's 1984 presidential campaign they filed five years' worth of reports at one time.

Jackson continued to portray himself as the defender of the poor. But already his self-serving behavior was beginning to attract negative attention from black community leaders, even in his hometown of Greenville, South Carolina.

In the fall of 1973, Jackson took his "Save Our Children" road show to Greenville to hold a series of fundraisers ostensibly to benefit the Greenville Happy Hearts Park, the first black-run sports club in the South. Jackson claimed he had played at the site as a child. While the Greenville *Piedmont News* pointed out Jackson's ties to the community, they noted: "While he is here to help raise money for Happy Hearts, Jackson's appearance here is also expected to initiate a local PUSH chapter."[86]

In a November 21, 1973, follow-up article, the *Piedmont News* was more pointed in its criticism. "How much did Happy Hearts receive from proceeds of Jesse Jackson Day activities? Advertising stated that all proceeds were to go to the Happy Hearts Club." But according to James A. Carter, the coordinator of the Greenville club, Happy Hearts got cut out of the picture entirely by a greedy Jackson operation. "After expenses, which included paying a motel bill of approximately one thousand dollars for Jackson and around thirty other people," the paper quoted Carter as saying, "PUSH Greenville received one thousand five dollars and nine-teen cents, Happy Hearts received five dollars and thirty cents."[87] Rather than help a local black club, which sponsored his return to Greenville, Jackson took the money for himself.

Jackson transformed the original PUSH into a religious organization in 1974, making it exempt from state and local taxes and users' fees, as well as federal income taxes. More important, the religious exemption meant PUSH did not have to file financial reports with the state, giving it an added layer of obscurity. PUSH became Jackson's "church." He used the Saturday morning services, where he announced his latest political and business projects, as yet another vehicle for raising money by regularly passing a collection plate.

Dozens more companies would be set up in the years to come, starting with Operation PUSH Inc., a for-profit political advocacy group with Jackson as president that Bustamante established in Ohio on May 3, 1976, just in time for Jackson to involve himself in that year's presidential election. It was important to have a for-profit group to serve as a cover for Jackson's openly political work in order to avoid obvious violations of the IRS code, which in theory imposed strict limits on the amount of political or lobbying activity a nonprofit corporation could do using tax-exempt dollars.

ANOTHER PESKY REPORTER

In April 1975, black reporter Barbara Reynolds, whom Jackson had long considered a friend, published her book *Jesse Jackson: The Man, The Movement, The Myth,* which mercilessly exposed some of Jackson's many lies. Her account of how Jackson fabricated the founding myth of his career—that Dr. Martin Luther King Jr. had died in his arms—has never been contradicted. While Reynolds was careful to display no personal animosity toward Jackson, and highlighted his achievements as well as his failings, she refused to display the type of awestruck fawning to which Jackson had become accustomed and believed was his due. She told the truth, and the truth was not flattering to Jesse Jackson.

"On tree-lined Constance Avenue, the leader of poor folks occupies a fifteen-room Romanesque residence," she wrote. "The fifty-five year old home purchased on August 25, 1970, for $49,500 is in a secret land trust, apparently to shield the names of his pals who hold the note."

> Automobiles like his maroon 1974 Lincoln Continental and his wife's red Toyota are often leased or loaned gratis from black automobile dealers, such as Al Johnson Cadillac. Jackson is chauffeured, not just because of his eminence but by popular demand. Speeding tickets and a couple of crashes have labeled the Reverend a bit of a public nuisance.
>
> Other amenities include free landscaping and dinners and banquets catered in his home, as well as many of his image clothes. In his closet among the Brooks Brothers pin stripes are denim suits from Los Angeles' Fred Segals and several shades of browns from Wilson's House of Suede, many of them from fans in the entertainment world.
>
> Personal gratuities, such as these, should be expected for someone so important, but keeping the movement afloat is what counts. Jackson will never be poor, but somehow the movement always is. . . .[88]

The *Chicago Tribune* ran generous excerpts from the book and in a lead editorial on April 29, 1975, asked a key question that has come back to haunt him throughout his career: "Whose interests is Mr. Jackson serving?"

> One searches in vain for evidence that Mr. Jackson has a coherent program for his people, or has the influence in his constituency to see it through.
>
> Mr. Jackson clearly sees himself as the successor of Dr. Martin Luther King Jr. as the leader and spokesman of millions of black Americans. Yet it is strangely unclear just whom he is leading, and in what direction. . . .

As Barbara Reynolds makes clear, there is a curious contrast between Mr. Jackson's fierce posture as a militant and the lack of friction between him and white leaders in business and government. They seem, in fact, to get along remarkably well.... [T]he record does not seem to square with the image of a fighting popular crusader that Mr. Jackson projects so well, and we can only wonder which is closer to the truth. Is Jesse Jackson a media hero, or a real one?[89]

Jackson immediately lashed out at Reynolds. In an interview reproduced in the book's appendix, Jackson warned Reynolds to stop "digging around in my personal life." "No white reporter tells it all and neither should you," Jackson said. "It is crucial that you understand this. For example, one American president died in bed with his girlfriend—a heart attack. That wasn't revealed until many years later.... Remember what happened to that black female *Tribune* reporter [Angela Parker] who busted up our organization? Her drive to gain the world was so strong that she did not know what it meant to lose her soul. You just don't tell it all."

Just in case Reynolds hadn't fully understood the implicit threat, Jackson made clear what he had done to Angela Parker: "Today she can't hold her head up in her own community. Now, I wouldn't want that to happen to you. Boy, am I going to tear you up. I'm going to have a ball helping you to make a fool out of yourself."[90]

Among Jackson's techniques, wrote *Chicago Tribune* columnist Vernon Jarrett, was to "visit the editors of daily newspapers for the implied threat of a picket line or boycott just because their black writers dare to say what their white writers refused to say."[91]

Years later, Reynolds told the sequel of how Jackson made good on his threat. In a 1984 interview with Tony Brown, she described how she was gradually ostracized, then vilified, and finally became the subject of "personal attacks on my life," following the publication of her book. Asked how her book was selling now that Jackson was a presidential candidate, she said it had disappeared from the shelves and the publisher was treating orders and inquiries "like the book was never written." The book had been a bestseller in 1975, but after a few weeks, she told Brown, "I noticed some very strange things happening. . . . Kroch's and Brentano's, which was the largest bookstore in Chicago, they had said was going to have an autograph party, it was going to be displayed in the window. . . . All of a sudden they withdrew all these things."

Comedian and occasional political candidate Dick Gregory told her that she should forget about the book and even her sanity, because she had become the "primary topic of conversations among Chicago blacks."[92] Radio and TV talk shows "wouldn't have me on but would have Jesse on," she says. "I would go across the country to make . . . appearances and I would walk into a television station much like this one and they would say, 'Well, I'm sorry you can't be on unless Jesse's on with you.'"

"Then came the personal attacks on my life," Reynolds says. "Ultimately, because I had fought . . . for black causes, black people in the community did give me police protection."[93] With Jackson's friends in the street gangs, she needed it. "I received death threats from anonymous callers. I had a Chicago policeman with me at my house and wherever I went," she tells me.[94] Finally, Reynolds left Chicago and today lives in the Washington, D.C., area, where she published a new collection of essays entitled, *No, I Won't Shut Up!*[95]

Jackson's next target was the popular black radio host Lucky Cordell. Cordell praised Reynolds's biography on his shows, but soon thereafter got "PUSHed" upstairs to a management slot. According to *Chicago Tribune* media critic Gary Deeb, Cordell's "promotion" was meant to silence him as a Jackson critic.[96] As a reward for getting rid of Cordell, Jackson brought the Saturday morning PUSH broadcast (and its advertising revenues) to WVON.

WHY CAN'T I HAVE A MANSION?

As PUSH finances steadily deteriorated, half brother Noah Robinson seemed to be rolling in dough. His federal grant from the Office of Minority Business Enterprise brought in $155,000 per year, a handsome sum in 1976. Robinson had found creative ways of spending the money. First, he made sure that it paid the rent on the office he maintained with the Breadbasket Commercial Association at 10842 S. Michigan Avenue— a one-story ghetto building he conveniently owned. Next, he awarded himself a comfortable annual salary of $20,000. Under the grant agreement, he was supposed to assist minority businesses in winning government contracts. Many of the businesses he helped were companies he owned directly—with his brothers or his cousin—or through straw men. In effect, he was being paid by the government to grow rich.[97]

When Jackson bumped into his half brother, as he often did on his fundraising tours of black business owners, he couldn't help but notice his success. It gave him ideas. One idea was that he ought to buy a place, a secret place far from Chicago, far from the media, far from prying eyes. In the fall of 1976, he noticed an advertisement for the famed Kellogg family estate, located forty miles north of Chicago on a twenty-five-acre spread outside of Libertyville. The asking price was $295,000, more than six times what his business friends had paid for his fifteen-room Tudor house in Chicago just a few years earlier. The paneling of the mansion was so impressive that a Las Vegas resort bought some of it to adorn an exclusive dining club, the House of Blues Foundation Room.[98] It was no mere cabin on the lake.

Word that Jackson had toured the property and was talking with real estate brokers soon leaked out. In a commentary ending his newscast on WBBM-TV, popular Chicago CBS News anchorman Walter Jacobson said he had asked Jackson if he was considering buying the estate. In reply, an Operation PUSH spokesperson confirmed that the Reverend was "looking for a place to do some writing, to get away... to do some things on his own."

After Jacobson's commentary aired, Jackson phoned the station owners. They had him invited onto Jacobson's show the next evening. Faced with his accuser, in front of a live television audience, Jackson let fly. Jacobson's report was "racially motivated," he charged. It implied that "PUSH is out of money and that as PUSH goes down I go up, which implies something about the handling of the money."

Jackson claimed PUSH was not going broke and was "coming out of debt," and blamed the financial woes on "the great mortality among black businesses." Then Jackson talked about the gangs. He objected to Jacobson's reporting, he said, because he feared "the response of people who can't deal with innuendoes and inferences," who could "jeopardize my life and my organization." He said he was referring to youths he was attempting to influence away from "robbing and raping and hustling and pimping." These were his people, he said, and he had to show them that there was "a truth beyond big houses and big cars."

Jackson, however, never denied the report. "I'm interested in looking at some property. I want to get away. I want to have a hideaway. I need one but I cannot afford one," he acknowledged.

Then came Saturday, the day of Jackson's weekly meeting at PUSH headquarters, broadcast each week over two black radio stations in Chicago. He began by noting the commercial spat between a black-owned cosmetics company, Johnson Beauty Products, and the "white-owned" Revlon. It helped, of course, that owner George Johnson was a major contributor to Operation PUSH.

Jackson accused the Federal Trade Commission of punishing the black-owned company by strictly enforcing product liability warnings while giving Revlon a free pass. He called it the FTC Revlon "conspiracy." Then he launched into what was then a new area of his thinking: the conspiracy of Jews against blacks. Look at how that CBS reporter, Walter Jacobson, had tried to smear him by broadcasting a false report about how he had mishandled funds that belonged to the movement, he said. "What is the kinship of Walter Jacobson and the kinship of Charley Revlon? Same national origin and same race." He then connected Jacobson to Israel's recent sale of SAAR class missile boats to South Africa. "Because the same people, that's his people, are selling gunboats to South Africa to kill black people. That's what the game is."[99]

It was an ugly, bald anti-Semitic statement, but few people paid attention at the time. One who did was *Chicago Tribune* columnist Vernon

Jarrett, who noted: "This is the first time that I have heard Jackson vent his spleen with wild, unsupported charges against a white newsman. Black writers in Chicago are familiar with the Jackson approach when they write anything that he does not approve."

Jackson didn't get his mansion, perhaps in part because of the vigilance of a CBS news reporter. But he learned to identify a new enemy: the Jews.

CHAPTER 3

A Taste of the Green

WELFARE SCHEME

By mid-1975, Jesse Jackson's enterprises had racked up debts of close to $400,000, the PUSH bank accounts had been drained, and there was no money to meet the mortgage on PUSH headquarters. Staff members were forced to work without pay. Jackson survived these dark days thanks to the loyalty of the prominent South Side black entrepreneurs whose businesses he had promoted, who showered him with loans, gifts, and free cash.[1]

Jackson recruited some black ministers to his cause—though not in Chicago, where he still had few friends. One of these ministers, the Reverend Jim Holley of the Little Rock Baptist Church in Detroit, explained how the ministers came to Jackson's aid: "We have a network. I remember when PUSH couldn't make its payroll one time. I had three hours to raise $8,000 and I did it because of the cause." (Years later, when

Jackson was campaigning for president in 1984, Holley said that he and other pastors regularly donated money to help support Jackson's family.)[2]

Jackson's commingling of personal funds with a nonprofit public trust should have triggered audits by the offices of the Illinois and Ohio secretaries of state, but never did. When he ran for president, such commingling should have led to a federal investigation for violations of the Internal Revenue Code and federal election laws. But Jesse was never pursued.

Jackson worked hard for Jimmy Carter's election in 1976. One of the first things Carter's people did to repay him for his efforts was to close down an investigation into Jackson's finances in early 1977, Cook County criminal justice officials and federal prosecutors say. Jackson said he first learned of the probe in 1975 thanks to revelations from the Senate Select Committee on Intelligence Operations, chaired by Democratic senator Frank Church, and was "not at all surprised" that he was a target of a federal investigation. "It's just another example of the harassment used against anyone who disagreed with the policies of the executive branch," he said.[3]

Within months, Jackson saw friendly faces seeded throughout the new administration, and he began to dream a new scheme: Operation PUSH would transform itself into a service provider and cash in on government welfare programs directly. His train had come.

It was so simple that it was brilliant. Overnight, Jackson would turn PUSH debts into centers of profit and double the size of his organization, without spending a dime of his own money. His first venture as a welfare service provider was "PUSH for Excellence." In keeping with the lessons he had learned in Chicago, he registered the new corporation in Ohio in 1977 with his personal lawyer and confidant John Bustamante, far from the prying eyes of *Chicago Tribune* reporters (or so he thought). Not only was it designed to bring in mountains of cash, but it also kept Jackson in the limelight and allowed him to use taxpayer dollars to sign up new voters for the Democratic Party, a neat payback for the Carter people.

PUSH for Excellence—which was quickly shortened to PUSH-Excel—was described by supporters as a motivation and self-help program, aimed at reducing hostility and improving grades among inner city school children. It had, however, no positive impact in those areas, according to federal auditors who examined the program later on. In most schools the auditors evaluated, grades actually went down, as did the amount of time students spent on homework once the students were exposed to Jackson's "motivational" speeches. After three years of study, they concluded: "PUSH-Excel's presence in these schools had little impact on the atmosphere or opportunity dimensions." In most areas studied—absenteeism, motivation, suspensions, in-class behavior, homework , and dropout levels, the very things Jackson proposed to "fix"—the study found "no pattern of change, positive or negative."[4] Even when lower standards of motivational achievement were applied—such as getting kids to join school clubs or organizations, read for pleasure or for information, or even go to movies— the analysis "did not show a general pattern of improvement."[5]

PUSH-Excel helped Jackson to build a national political base at the expense of the U.S. taxpayer. The program got off the ground with a $100,000 grant from the nonprofit Ford Foundation aimed at launching pilot "Excel" programs in Chicago and Kansas City. And Illinois Bell paid Jackson an undisclosed sum to produce an "idea booklet." With grant-writing assistance from the Joe Drown and Piton Foundations, Jackson was soon deluged with tax-free cash: $105,000 from the Lilly Foundation, $30,000 from the Rockefeller Brothers Fund, and $25,000 from the Chicago Community Trust.[6] Then on September 6, 1977, the first big contract came with a $402,000 grant from the Los Angeles Board of Education.[7]

What did Jackson do with all this money? Just like brother Noah, he took care of himself first. He got the L.A. school board to set aside a "personal stipend" of $5,000 to cover his travel between Chicago and Los Angeles. Next, he hired more staff for his own organization, including a $32,000-a-year director, an assistant director at $18,000 per year, plus a dozen "community representatives" who were to be paid $10,000 each.[8] They all might spend some of their time working on PUSH-Excel, but they were Jackson's people, promoting Jackson's agenda, enhancing his visibility. As sympathetic federal evaluators later concluded, "to Jackson and his supporters, EXCEL was more than a crusade or fledgling program—EXCEL was a national movement."[9]

As presented to the Los Angeles school board, the PUSH-Excel program emphasized basic reading skills, writing, and attendance. Students and parents were asked to sign a "moral contract" under which parents pledged to spend time with their children and the student promised to study hard and avoid what Jackson called "the tools of decadence." These included drugs, alcohol, promiscuous sex, violent television shows, and sex-oriented music. In exchange, when the children graduated from high school they would receive a special diploma and a voter registration card. Most important, they would be treated to regular speeches by Jackson in person. He jetted first class from school to school to make his personal mark on a whole generation of black high school children, while making sure they understood which party owned their vote.[10]

Even in Los Angeles, voices were soon heard criticizing the generous yearly grant to PUSH-Excel. School board member Bobbi Fiedler charged that the budget included numerous "boondoggles" and criticized the hiring of Jackson staff members with taxpayer dollars. The *Los Angeles Times* editorialized that the school board should reject the plan, arguing that "there has been no evidence of great achievement" in other cities where Jackson's program was being implemented. Making matters worse, just $229,000 of the grant amount was earmarked for use in Los Angeles schools. The remaining $173,000 went to PUSH headquarters in Chicago, where the organization was deeply in debt.[11] But despite these problems, the board approved the money.

Jackson put his hustler's skills to good use. He got CBS *Sixty Minutes* reporter Dan Rather to do a puff piece profiling PUSH-Excel as the best hope for black inner city schools. After watching the show, Senator Hubert Humphrey called Health, Education, and Welfare Secretary Joseph Califano, urging him to shovel federal government grants at Jackson in support of the program. Califano recorded Humphrey's call (the senator from Minnesota would die within a month) in his memoirs:

In a weak voice, his strength consumed by his battle with cancer, [Humphrey] asked me if I had seen the "Sixty Minutes" program. When I responded, he said, "Well, then you saw what I saw. I want you to talk to Jesse Jackson and help him. He's doing something for those kids. I've talked to him this morning and told him I'll talk to you. Now you get him down to your office and help him. Will you do that for me?" I told him I would.[12]

Califano sent Jackson an initial check for $55,000 on January 5, 1978, only one month after the *Sixty Minutes* segment aired. "There will be substantial future support from HEW," he announced. Once again, most of the money ($45,000) went to finance Jackson's Chicago-based operation, with $20,000 earmarked for Jackson to "evaluate" the PUSH-Excel program. Another $25,000 was spent on a high-profile conference in Washington later that year, showcasing the Reverend Jackson as school reformer. Within months, Califano found a larger pot of cash and shoveled another $400,000 to Jackson from the National Institute of Education.[13]

But even that was just an appetizer for the rich main course. Using federal government money to do his "evaluation," Jackson asked for $4 million to expand the PUSH-Excel programs into thirty cities nationwide. He was aided by Mary Frances Berry, then assistant secretary of education, who appeared with him at a May 1978 conference devoted to his educational "crusade," at Howard University in Washington, D.C.[14]

Eventually, Califano signed off on a $3 million commitment spread over three years. In June 1979, he unblocked a $700,000 down payment (Contract # 300790111).[15] The huge infusion of federal taxpayer cash doubled the size of Operation PUSH, which Jackson claimed was bringing in roughly one million dollars a year on its own.[16] The Reverend Jetstream had finally taken off, his fuel tanks running over with taxpayer gas. Operation Promote Jesse went national.

In his speeches to high school students, Jackson practiced his rhyming slang. "My mind is a pearl," he chanted, asking the kids to repeat after him. "I can learn anything in the world."

"We've got to get the dope out of our veins and hope into our brains."
Or: "You may be in the slums but don't let the slums be in you."

"Nobody can save us from us but us."[17]

He was hip. He was slick. But not everyone was amused. Before long, black educators began criticizing him openly for jeopardizing funding to remedial and black studies programs by focusing on traditional curricula and self-help. Thomas Todd, former PUSH vice president and now a Northwestern University law professor, called PUSH-Excel "a public relations stunt based on rhetoric and nothing more."[18] African-American columnist Clarence Page wrote a scathing account in the *Washington Monthly* entitled "The Mysterious PUSH-Excel," in which he berated the Carter administration for mindlessly acquiescing to yet another Jackson fundraising scheme:

> This benevolence persists even though almost no one can explain what PUSH-Excel really is. The government officials who fund it speak of it in vague generalities. Few of the political reporters covering Jackson's global media events have any direct knowledge of Chicago's ghetto or of programs presumed to be operating there. Even PUSH-Excel officials themselves are hard-pressed to provide a 25-word description of the program's function. PUSH-Excel is so elusive, so amorphous, that it is called a "program" only as a matter of semantic convenience.[19]

While today Jackson gets slammed from the Right, in the late 1970s he was attacked from the Left as an "ally of right-wing, white America."[20] Coretta Scott King thought Jackson was making a mistake to let whites "off the hook" and "relieve them of their guilt. The problems in our society, the problems of black people, are not of their own making . . . it is the way society is structured." Referring to her slain husband, she told *Chicago Tribune* columnist Vernon Jarrett, "It's a cruel jest to ask a man to lift himself by his own bootstraps when he doesn't have any boots." In a direct reference to Jackson and the PUSH-Excel program, Jarrett bemoaned the hesitancy of black professionals in the past "to question certain charlatans and thugs who have been appointed as our leaders. Even black criminals could not be attacked publicly. I hope that day is over forever."[21]

If Jackson had spent the PUSH-Excel money on its intended purpose, all would have been well. He could have shrugged off the criticism from the Left, while using the money doled out by the Carter administration to build a school and community-based network of grassroots supporters, which one federal evaluator called the Jackson "Movement." But Jesse Jackson wasn't terribly interested in the public schools, and his school self-help program "turned out to be mainly paper."[22] Indeed, he flaunted his contempt for the public schools again and again by his own actions.

Special Schools for Special Kids

Jesse Jackson liked the good life and, naturally enough, he wanted it for his own kids. "Dr. King would say we can be materialistic minded without being mindlessly materialistic," he told the left-wing publication *Mother Jones* when asked years later if he had become greedy. "God did not send the children of Israel into the desert without supplies. . . . I fail to understand why we should have any reluctance to have a resource base as one of the fruits of our freedom struggle. It costs to send children to college. It costs to have health insurance. It costs to have a house of your choice. It costs to travel."[23] To travel first class and send your kids to America's most exclusive private schools, as Jackson would do, costs a lot.

Just as Jesse Jackson began painting himself as the prophet of reconstruction for black inner city schools, he got into a spat with a local elementary school principal in Chicago named Kenneth J. Deiml and sought to have him removed from office. Deiml was white, running a predominantly black school, and Jackson was leading a boycott of the school by local parents. As he was preparing to speak against Deiml at a board of education meeting, *Chicago Tribune* reporter Casey Banas caught up with him and popped the question: Where were his children going to school anyway?

Jackson's four school-age children (the oldest was then twelve) attended an exclusive public school in an affluent part of town that was six miles from his home on Chicago's South Side. When asked why his children didn't attend O'Keeffe Elementary, the public school just four blocks from his house, Jackson replied blandly: "I appealed for special consideration." Other parents could struggle, as he put it, with "lousy principals," but not Jesse.[24]

O'Keeffe Elementary was a typical big inner city school, with 1,650 pupils, 99 percent of whom were black. It drew not only from Jackson's upper-class enclave on South Constance, but also from the badlands that surrounded him on three sides. By comparison, the exclusive public school Jackson picked for his children was tiny, with only three hundred pupils, including twelve whites. It was intended to be an islet of achievement for black students, designed on the model of small, well-to-do suburban schools, with a well-equipped library, a good gym, and the city's best teachers. The school board hoped to attract affluent residents of the Lake Meadows area, who had been sending their children to private schools in droves. Because of the education level of the parents and the resources lavished on the school, reading and math scores were at or above national norms in all grades. In contrast, reading scores at O'Keeffe were below the national norms at all grade levels.

The waiver Jackson received to get his children bused to this exclusive school at taxpayer expense, when other residents of the South Side were stuck in rotting classrooms, was nothing short of exceptional. Chicago school superintendent Joseph P. Hannon told the *Tribune* through a spokesman that Jackson had benefited from a "little-known Board of Education policy." Under that policy, a district superintendent could grant a waiver to allow a child to enroll in another school district, but the second district superintendent also had to agree. "This is the only way this could have happened," he said.

When pressed, Jackson said he was committed to public school education for his family. "My children are going to Hyde Park High School," he intoned. "We can no longer run from the challenge of public schools."

He kept his promise—but not for long. His oldest child, Santita, went on to the local public high school, but the experience so discouraged Jackson and his wife, Jacqueline, that they resolved never to commit another child to a failing school. After personally spending several million dollars of taxpayer money on his school improvement scheme, much of it in Chicago, Jackson turned around and sent two of his boys—Jesse Jr. and Yusef—to the most exclusive private school in the country, St. Albans in Washington, D.C. (St. Albans was Al Gore's alma mater, the school where many senators and presidents sent their children.) His youngest, Little Jackie, was dispatched to private finishing schools in New England and Maryland.[25] It was another stunning example of "Me First Jackson."

"POVERTY PIMP"

Throughout my research for this book, numerous black activists, labor leaders, pastors, and columnists dismissed Jackson as someone out of touch with the black community and uninterested in helping improve the standard of living of the poor, but very eager to enrich himself and his cronies. One of Jackson's supporters, a young black entrepreneur, identified his leader's central failing: "You cannot just be brokers and intermediaries who sell blackness to corporate America," he said. "You need to reconnect to the grass roots. As long as you continue to broker for an elite group and don't reconnect, we're going to have problems."[26]

Eddie Slaughter, vice president of the Black Farmers and Agriculturalists Association in Buena Vista, Georgia, puts it best: "Jesse Jackson is a poverty pimp. 'If there ain't nothing in it for me, I'm not going to help.' That's his mentality."[27]

Slaughter had two unforgettable run-ins with Jackson. In 1983, Slaughter headed the NAACP's Georgia chapter. "We wanted Jesse Jackson to do a news conference with us in Oglethorpe, Georgia, for a class action discrimination case we were bringing against Procter and Gamble," Slaughter recalls. "We had a situation where over five years sixty blacks had been fired for their inability to do their job, while over the same time period only one white had been fired in similar circumstances. When we contacted Jackson, he said he wanted $10,000 to come down."

In 1999, Slaughter asked Jackson to help draw attention to the fact that, in record numbers, black farmers were going bankrupt and losing their land to the federal government. Slaughter blamed, in large part, discriminatory loan policies and outright fraud by county supervisors at the U.S. Department of Agriculture. In one particularly egregious case, which I discovered during an *Insight* magazine investigation in August 2001, Georgia farmer William Miller discovered that USDA employee Henry J. McCleod had registered liens against his property for loans he never received, forcing him into bankruptcy when the loans fell due. "We wanted to expose what the USDA was doing to black farmers," Slaughter says. "We wanted a name of Jesse's caliber to give a news conference, to give us the credibility we needed to show this thing was true." Jackson came down—and promptly demanded that the farmers pay him $100,000 for a public appearance. "We couldn't raise $10,000, let alone $100,000," Slaughter said. "He was completely useless to us. Jesse Jackson, Joseph Lowery—they don't lead the people. The media put these people forward, but they are not in line with the people." Jackson's spokesperson, Keiana Peyton, said that Jackson "only charged fees for speaking engagements, not press conferences."[28]

The "poverty pimp" behavior Eddie Slaughter describes was not new. In the late 1960s and early 1970s, when Jackson got his start, black street hustlers and gang leaders such as Jackson's good friend Jeff Fort of the Black Stone Rangers had made it into an art form. Through confrontational tactics, they succeeded in shaking down government bureaucrats until all the benefits of the welfare state came rolling into their hands. In a hilarious 1970 essay, author Tom Wolfe observed that bureaucrats came to rely on what he called the "Ethnic Catering Service" because they didn't have a clue who should get the benefits of federal poverty programs.

> They sat back and waited for you to come rolling in with your certified angry militants, your guaranteed frustrated ghetto youth, looking like a bunch of wild men. Then you had your test con-

frontation. If you were outrageous enough, if you could shake up the bureaucrats so bad that their eyes froze into ice balls and their mouths twisted up into smiles of sheer physical panic, into shit-eating grins, so to speak—then they knew you were the real goods. They knew you were the right studs to give the poverty grants and community organizing jobs to. Otherwise they wouldn't know.[29]

Jackson would practice his own form of mau-mauing the liberal white establishment at his Saturday morning meetings at PUSH headquarters. Whenever a representative from a large Chicago-based company came to speak, he would be subjected to ritual harassment by the audience of several hundred angry blacks, many of them members of the Black Stone Rangers. Over the years, Jackson refined this so that the mere threat of public humiliation would get his corporate targets to pay up. Again, he seized on a script first identified by Tom Wolfe:

> There was one genius in the art of confrontation who had mau-mauing down to what you could term a laboratory science. He had it figured out so he didn't even have to bring his boys down-town in person. He would just show up with a crocus sack full of revolvers, ice picks, fish knives, switchblades, hatchets, black-jacks, gravity knives, straight razors, hand grenades, blow guns, bazookas, Molotov cocktails, tank rippers, unbelievable stuff, and he'd dump it all out on somebody's shiny walnut conference table. He'd say "These are some of the things I took off my boys last night. . . . I don't know, man . . . thirty minutes ago I talked a Panther out of busting up a cop. . . ." And they would lay money on this man's ghetto youth patrol like it was now or never.[30]

While Jackson's approach with Health, Education, and Welfare Secretary Joseph Califano was more sophisticated, it amounted to the same thing. Pay me off, Jackson was saying, and I'll make your problems with angry black urban youth go away.

In the end, he simply dropped the PUSH-Excel program once he "had begun to shift to other issues," the federal evaluators realized to their astonishment.[31] The Reverend Jetstream had buzzed off to new worlds.

BROTHER NOAH GETS INTO THE GAME

Jesse's half brother Noah Robinson was in charge of the angry black urban youth, along with Jesse's friend Jeff Fort, boss of the ever growing Black P Stone Nation.[32] According to an undercover Chicago police intelligence officer, Sergeant Stanley B. Robinson (no relation to Noah), Fort and the Stones had been attempting to muscle into the cocaine and heroin trade on Chicago's West Side when Fort was arrested in 1972 for bilking the federal government out of a welfare grant. "I found out who the big people on the West Side were," Sergeant Robinson says. "They were legitimate businessmen."

The Stones normally operated on the South Side, Jackson's own territory, but on this occasion they murdered six of their West Side rivals and dumped their bodies into the South Branch of the Chicago River and the Sanitary and Ship Canal, according to Sergeant Robinson.[33]

Jackson never succeeded in winning over the businessmen and black pastors of Chicago's West Side, but at least he managed to keep them from openly criticizing him or exposing his own questionable activities. While there is no information to suggest Jackson asked Jeff Fort to use the gangs to pressure his West Side rivals, the gang turf battle had that effect.

Even today, several black pastors tell me, fear of physical retribution has kept Jackson's critics from talking. The Reverend Johnny Hunter of Virginia Beach explains: "No one crossed Jesse because they feared his half brother would put out a hit on them. That's why he is in jail. It's on the public record."[34]

Moreover, it was known in Chicago that gang members harassed black reporters, like Angela Parker and Barbara Reynolds, who dared criticize Jackson and expose his financial malfeasance. "I had covered the Black P Stones, I'd covered corrupt city councilmen, I'd covered drugs," Barbara Reynolds says. "But nothing was as bad as telling the truth about Jesse.

After my book, my life was in danger. They especially went after black journalists. They called it a 'black code.' "[35] Such treatment had a chilling effect on other would-be investigators.

Dino Malcolm, a former member of the rival Gangster Disciples, infiltrated a Black Stone Rangers meeting at the First Presbyterian Church at 64th and Kenwood and describes the scene. "Members started taking seats by the dozens," he wrote. "There was every type of Ranger: Maniacs, Casanovas, Unknowns, Four-Tray, Five-Tray, Six-Tray, Four-Corner, Imperials, Midgets, Spanish, Boss Pimps, Cobras, etc. It took 30 minutes for the 95th Street Gangsters to fall in. Each of them wore a black hat with a red band. There were Stones from the West Side, Cabrini Green projects from out North, and even from Gary [Indiana]. The Rangerettes, female branch of the Stones were next to the last to come in."[36]

One of the leaders, named Angel, "a short, ugly-looking dude in his late 20s," walked down the aisle after they had all filed in, searching for informers. Hefting a baseball bat in one hand, he made new members stand for interrogation. Malcolm recalled:

> He walked over to Jughead and myself and stared into our faces. Angel said, "Represent brothers."
> Both of us hit ourselves in the chest and shouted "Black P. Stone run it" and "Stones forever." Angel walked back up to the altar.
> "That's right. Stones forever."[37]

During the gang wars between the Stones and the Gangster Disciples in the late 1960s and early 1970s, more than two hundred people were killed. According to Chicago police and federal prosecutors, Jackson's friend Jeff Fort continued to lead the Black Stone Rangers by telephone while in jail, where he got religion. Like Malcolm X, he embraced a form of Islam, absurdly calling himself a Moor "directly tied to Morocco." In 1976, after his release from prison, he immediately returned to his gang.

On April 7, 1976, Fort and three friends took seats in the public gallery of a federal courtroom where several gang members were being tried on gun charges. Fort and his entourage wore red turbans, a symbol which designated them as members of the gang's leadership. A paid police informant named Maurice Childress was about to take the witness stand, but when he spied Fort's distinctive headgear he spun around and faced the wall, refusing to testify. Federal judge Prentice H. Marshall dismissed the jury and declared a mistrial the next day. In the commotion, Fort shrugged and told a bystander he was just there "because one of my friends is on trial."[38] The *Chicago Tribune* noted: "Mr. Fort and his followers broke no law in walking into court. Yet their mere presence, and the gang power symbolized by the red turbans, evidently was enough to throw the whole procedure off the rails."[39]

The muscle-bound Fort had a fetish for fancy clothes and fast luxury sedans. In the summer, he wore lemon-yellow trousers and designer T-shirts that showed off his fourteen inch biceps. In the winter, he favored full-length mink coats. After changing the name of the Stones to the more Islamic-sounding El Rukn, he was briefly rearrested after a wild car chase with police up and down Chicago's Lake Shore Drive. The chase began when police noticed a black limousine speeding out of an alleyway. Instead of pulling over as directed, the driver sped off, hid under an underpass and doused his lights, then crossed the divider and headed off in the opposite direction. When the police finally pulled him over, Fort gave a false name and said he had no driver's license. He was also wearing a full-length mink coat (his passenger was wearing fox). Patrolmen Steve Pamon and Alton Brooks found $5,630 in neatly rolled bills and another $326.66 in coins in the car, as well as three more full-length mink coats in the back seat, one apparently new and still in a box. While they were searching, four cars full of gang members pulled up and parked in front and in back of the squad car, raising their hoods as if they had engine trouble. "Then all of these guys got out of their cars with these long fur coats on and their hands in their pockets," Pamon said. "I told my partner, 'We better call for help.'" By the time reinforcements arrived, the officers had been surrounded by a large group of Rukns. They had come "to see about their chief," Officer Alton Brooks said.[40]

Jesse Jackson's close relationship with Jeff Fort and the Black Stone Rangers was well known to Chicago police and the feds, but was rarely reported in the national press. "Jeff Fort portrayed himself as a community organizer," a federal prosecutor says. "Fort came to Jesse's meetings. Jesse showed up at his events."[41] Jackson frequently called on Fort to pad out his demonstrations and boycotts. "Whenever Jesse needed 100, 200, 300 bodies, he'd just call Jeff Fort to send over the muffins and pay them a coupla' bucks each," one law enforcement official who tracked gang activities tells me.[42] Barbara Reynolds recalls Jackson's friend and supporter Hugh Hefner, the *Playboy* magnate, "catering to Jeff Fort and his gang as if they were an avant-garde group, when they were just a bunch of thugs."[43] Noah Robinson's dealings with Fort surfaced during federal court hearings in the late 1980s when he was charged with racketeering, tax evasion, and contract killings.[44]

Robinson's penchant for shady business and cutting legal corners exploded onto the front pages for an entirely different reason, after a 1978 *Chicago Tribune* investigation into fly-by-night businesses he had set up to serve as "front men" for white contractors so they could bid on minority set-aside contracts. The concept of race quotas in government contracting was brand new in America at the time, a creation of the Carter administration. Preferential treatment for minority businesses by reserving a portion of every government contract for them was a key element of Jesse Jackson's agenda. The first local agency to use set-asides was the Metropolitan Sanitary District of Greater Chicago, which began the practice in 1977 with funds provided by the Environmental Protection Agency (EPA). *Tribune* reporters went to Noah Robinson during the initial phase of their investigation "for his expertise in minority businesses" and because he had written several letters to City Hall and to the newspapers denouncing "sham" companies set up by unscrupulous black businessmen as fronts for whites. As their investigation progressed they discovered that his own companies presented the most compelling cases they could find of precisely that fraud.

One of his companies was called the Robinson Group. Corporate documents listed its president as John A. Robinson, Noah's youngest brother.

Thanks to Noah's $155,000 per year grant from the Office of Minority Business Enterprise (OMBE), they got contracts from the Metropolitan Sanitary District of Greater Chicago worth $1.4 million to haul garbage, far in excess of what the company could actually do with its three trucks and ten full-time employees.

"I feel great about helping my brother," Robinson said. "[The OMBE] pays me a fee to help minorities and says nothing about helping my brother. It's true that there is a blurry arrangement between OMBE, [Breadbasket Commercial Association], and the Robinson Group, but I want it to look blurry. That enhances my clout, and I have no reservations about it at all, to help my brother."[45]

He also revealed that the Robinson Group didn't actually do all the work. "Don't let the figures throw you," Noah boasted. "Robinson group isn't really doing $2 million, or whatever it is. You see, the Robinson Group turned around and subbed most of the work out to subcontracts. That's the beauty of the sanitary district. There is no limitation on what you can sub out. We could sub out the entire amount if we wanted." Many of the subcontractors were white-owned businesses, in effect defeating the purpose of the OMBE grant which was aimed at aiding minorities.

One job the Robinson Group did perform, he said, was to provide young gang members and street toughs as security guards. "But these guys don't carry weapons," he said. "These are unarmed security guards we pick up from the unemployment lines. The only requirement is that they have a car and don't fall asleep." The weapons would come later; and they would get Noah Robinson into heaps of trouble with the feds.

Another company, called Renoja Interiors, Ltd., was described as a building contractor. But not even a federal grand jury, which examined its operations in 1978, could figure out who owned it, how many people it employed, or what it actually did. Robinson ran it out of his basement at home, but used the same phone number as the Breadbasket Commercial Association, the outfit he set up with half brother Jesse Jackson in 1971 to run Black Expo. Despite the fly-by-night nature of the operation, Renoja won $1.4 million in government contracts in a joint venture with a white-owned firm called Fisher, Albright & Masters. David Hernandez served as president of Renoja, but was also an employee of Fisher, Albright & Masters. "When he's not on Fisher's payroll, he's on Renoja's payroll," Robinson said. "And sometimes he's on both at once."

The *Tribune* called Hernandez to ask if he really was president of Renoja. "If you want to construe it that way, I suppose I am," he said. "But I don't know anything about Renoja Interiors. If you want to know about Renoja, then you should talk to Noah Robinson, the man who put it together. . . . The way Noah put it together, I do not know any of the functions of Renoja Interiors. I never have."[46]

Robinson ran a third company, called Minority/Majority Construction Company that won $955,400 in minority set-aside contracts with the Chicago sanitary district. Robinson owned 60 percent of the company, with 40 percent held by Frank Paschen Jr., his white partner. Robinson told the *Tribune* that his job was to "monitor the jobs," while Paschen did the work. "That means, I watch government contracts as they appear, as they come up. And if I see one I think we can handle, I call Frank Paschen. So I monitor the jobs as they come along for my 60 percent. After that, Frank takes over, and I step out. So it doesn't take that much time." A Paschen relative, Henry D. Paschen, ran Paschen Contractors, one of Chicago's largest construction companies. With Noah Robinson as its minority front man, Paschen Contractors could bid on contracts normally set aside for minorities.

Jackson was not only aware of his brother's contracting schemes; he honored Noah's white partner Henry Paschen at the seventh annual banquet of the Breadbasket Commercial Association in 1977 with Breadbasket's Affirmative Action Award. (He also presented an award to Clifford DiLorenzo, vice president of the Robinson Group.)[47] Although Noah's scheme contradicted everything Jackson claimed he was trying to accomplish through PUSH boycotts and covenants with local businesses, he never uttered a word of criticism. It was his brother's scheme; it was family.

Robinson's fourth company, Apache Electric, won $3.7 million in government contracts set aside for minority businesses, although it had no electrician's license and was disqualified twice by federal regulators because it didn't meet the requirements of a minority business. Like his other sham companies, Robinson ran it out of the Breadbasket Commercial Association office, which was financed by his federal grant. His partner was a cousin, Winfred Ashmore, who served as president. When Apache applied for one set- aside job from the Metropolitan Atlanta Rapid Transit Authority (MARTA), Robinson listed himself as chairman of the board. "Yes, I signed a document saying I was chairman of the board of Apache," he told the *Tribune*. "But I'm not the chairman of the board of Apache. It isn't true. The people in MARTA don't know that. I lied when I said I was chairman, but there's nothing illegal about it."

Robinson spoke more freely than Jackson, but the two shared the same ethics. They were special. It didn't matter if they told bald-faced lies, or if their actions harmed black businesses and cost jobs to black workers. They were playing race politics and were out to get what the white government owed them. Someone else would pick up the tab.

PUSH Goes National

The more than $3 million in grants from HEW Secretary Califano was only the beginning of the Carter jackpot for Jesse Jackson. The Department of Housing and Urban Development forked over $75,000 on May 19, 1978, so Operation PUSH could "expand its counseling of inner-city families buying or improving homes in Chicago."[48] The idea, said HUD Secretary Patricia Roberts Harris, was to use PUSH to disseminate financial information to black families in Chicago on how to get a mortgage, how to buy a house, and what to do when they defaulted on loans. "It's very hard for black people to accept rebuff and rebuff," said Mrs. Harris, who wasn't going to be mau-maued. Check in hand, Jackson praised her for "her sensitivity and commitment to the inner city" and promised to spend the money quickly. The Commerce Department soon followed suit with $240,000 in federal funds for PUSH-Excel, bringing the total U.S. government commitment to Jackson's education programs to nearly $4 million.

But there was a problem. The PUSH-Excel youth motivation program was going nowhere, at least not visibly. By mid-1979, Jackson had still failed to produce an evaluation to document the effectiveness of his efforts, or show what the taxpayers were getting for their money. Pressed on the issue, Jackson argued that there could be no true test of its effectiveness because "you only know when you fail, when another student can't read or another girl gets pregnant."[49] Just as he had argued to get his children into elite schools, and as a graduate student he had talked his way out of failing grades, he was demanding that the PUSH-Excel programs receive "special consideration." The rules and requirements to which others had to adhere didn't apply to the Reverend Mr. Jackson. Anyone seeking to evaluate the effectiveness of PUSH-Excel was guilty of a bald racist attack. All his programs needed to succeed was more money.

Even the Carter administration began to have second thoughts. In February 1979, Califano quietly instructed the National Institute of Education, an HEW research center, to conduct an audit. Six months later, director Norman Gold kicked the can down the road, saying there wasn't enough data to evaluate the program. "It takes a very long time," he said.[50] But he had amassed reams of statistics, charts, and models, and at first blush the results just didn't look good.

It would take years for the government to catch up with him, but it didn't take Jackson long to figure out how to spend the money. He went on a rapid building program, opening new offices of PUSH all across the country, making allies, distributing cash, and expanding the PUSH constellation of patronage and plums. He focused on large cities with a large black population because that's where the votes were, and winning black votes for the 1980 election was part of the calculus of the Carter people. So Jackson took PUSH-Excel to Detroit, Philadelphia, Cleveland, Memphis, Little Rock, and Indianapolis. But he also set up shop in less likely spots such as Orlando, San Diego, and Rice Lake, Wisconsin, according to corporate filings with state secretaries of state.[51]

Jackson also made a stab at public interest lawsuits, with mixed success. His first case was a high-profile attack against the Federal Bureau of

Investigation and the CIA, filed in tandem with the American Civil Liberties Union and the American Friends Service Committee. It came at a time when the entire U.S. intelligence community was under assault from Senator Frank Church and his investigating committee. The Church hearings focused the klieg lights on bungled foreign assassination plots and a small number of FBI investigations of left-wing subversive groups while ignoring the Bureau's stunning success against the Ku Klux Klan, an effort personally spearheaded by J. Edgar Hoover.[52]

The PUSH/ACLU lawsuit alleged a massive government plot against them that included "physical attacks . . . covert infiltration . . . and disruption of sources of financial support," and sought access to classified government documents and investigative files. After an initial favorable ruling in the U.S. district court in Chicago, which granted them extensive powers of discovery, the case died for lack of evidence.[53] Why? Because there was no government plot. Indeed, in my own more recent search for evidence of FBI surveillance of Operation PUSH, I gained access to thousands of pages of archival material that had been declassified during the Justice Department review of the FBI files that began under Carter. Some of the FBI field office and headquarters reports had been considered so sensitive that the Bureau waited another twenty years before releasing them on orders of President Clinton.

At the central registry held at the National Archives in College Park, Maryland, only two references can be found that specifically relate to Jesse Jackson or Operation PUSH, both dating from January 1972. One report, a cable from the Chicago field office to FBI headquarters in Washington dated January 6, 1972, described an "extremist meeting" at Operation PUSH, "a new group founded by the Rev. Jesse Jackson." The second, dated one week later, detailed Jackson's plans to hold a march on Washington in emulation of the late Dr. King.[54] There were no further counterintelligence reports on Jackson or his group, classified or unclassified, for a very simple reason: the FBI dropped its surveillance of civil rights organizations almost as soon as Hoover died in 1972. "The Church committee wiped out our domestic intelligence programs," says W.

Raymond Wannall, who retired in 1976 as assistant FBI director in charge of counterintelligence programs. "From then on, the FBI couldn't open an investigation unless it involved a criminal violation or a foreign intelligence threat."[55]

Jackson also joined another handful of leftist groups in an attempt to block federal funding of a 1.7-mile commuter rail tunnel that would link the Reading Railroad and the former Penn Central commuter lines in downtown Philadelphia.[56] Jackson and his new allies, who included Friends of the Earth, argued that building a subway tunnel to help commuters reach downtown Philadelphia would "serve predominantly affluent and white citizens" because 90 percent of minority residents in the metro-Philly area lived in the city and therefore didn't ride the commuter rail system. The racist nature of Jackson's complaint was highlighted by the court, which compared it to a 1976 case in which minority plaintiffs challenged HUD grants to a neighboring community for sewer improvements because they would help "a predominantly white, wealthy, exclusionary community."[57] The courts rejected both complaints.

It was a poor choice of lawsuits, but getting into the game of suing the government revealed Jackson's change of strategy. With his bank accounts stuffed with cash from the feds, Jackson now had the means to buy expensive lawyers and new allies to exploit the U.S. legal system to advance allegations of race discrimination. This was a new area of law in the late 1970s. Today, it has become a multibillion dollar industry, with one of Jackson's closest friends—Los Angeles mega-lawyer Johnnie Cochran, of O. J. Simpson fame—leading the charge.

FRIENDS IN HIGH PLACES

Meanwhile, the Carter money kept on coming. In 1979, the U.S. Department of Labor gave PUSH-Excel a $550,000 grant "to give 250 economically disadvantaged Chicago high school students education and training for career positions in business," a rather significant revision of the original PUSH-Excel program.[58] Jackson forged a personal friendship with Labor Secretary Ray Marshall, who came out to PUSH headquarters in Chicago to hand over the check in a public ceremony on May 21, 1979. Marshall, a university professor and civil rights activist, had worked with the interracial Southern Regional Council in Atlanta in the early 1970s to encourage corporations to hire college-educated black women to management positions.[59] Later known as "diversity consulting," the Recruitment and Training Program pioneered by Marshall got the attention of then Georgia governor Jimmy Carter, who was on his board and subsequently appointed him secretary of labor.[60]

Marshall expanded Labor Department involvement in job training and education and centralized federal affirmative action programs into a single Office of Federal Contract Compliance Programs, a mechanism that gave teeth to the type of diversity scheme Jackson would soon pursue. He hired a former colleague from the Southern Regional Council, Lamond Godwin, to head up the National Employment Programs. Godwin was a long-standing personal friend of Jesse Jackson.

In his testimonial to Godwin shortly after his death in November 1998, Jackson called him "the bridge between our Southern Crusade, the presidential campaigns and Wall Street." Godwin had been "a friend and confidant" whom Jackson said he had known virtually all of his adult life.[61] He had also been the man who unlocked the door to millions of dollars in federal grants for Operation PUSH.

Godwin recommended that Labor Secretary Marshall hire another staffer from the Southern Regional Council, a young woman from Mobile, Alabama, and a childhood friend, Alexis Herman. While at the SRC, Herman worked under Godwin and Marshall on a black female diversity project. Marshall expanded her program and merged it with the Recruitment and Training Program in New York City, run by a man who was already a legend within the civil rights movement, Ernest G. Green. As one of the "Little Rock Nine," Green had been among the black students at Central High School whose confrontation with Governor Orval Faubus prompted President Dwight D. Eisenhower to send in 1,200 troops to enforce a court integration order, ending decades of "separate but equal" schools in Arkansas. Marshall tapped Green for the Labor

Department minority development team, making him assistant secretary for employment and training.

Lamond Godwin, Alexis Herman, and Ernest Green. By their own account, they doled out billions of dollars of federal grants to left-wing groups and political cronies over the four years of the Carter administration. They sent money to legal aid groups to finance lawsuits against the government and private businesses; they sent money to women's groups, civil rights organizations, left-wing think tanks, goodie-goodie nonprofits with names like the National Child Labor Committee, labor unions, and community "organizers" such as those parodied by Tom Wolfe for mau-mauing the flak catchers at City Hall. They had so much money to give out and so little time that during the last few months of Carter's term the three shoveled almost three hundred federal contracts and grants out the door worth more than $100 million to cronies, acquaintances, former colleagues—anyone who had supported Carter's failed reelection campaign—with hardly any documentation. A 1981 General Accounting Office study revealed they were pushing money out the window so fast that Green had to send telegrams to recipients telling them to start spending the cash even before the contracts could be signed.[62]

Among the recipients was PUSH-Excel, which received two separate awards in January 1981 worth $522,736 and $1,999,968 (Contract # 99-1-1878-08-36).[63] In an interview with the author, Green insisted they had selected Jackson's group solely on the basis of merit. "These were organizations that were reaching youth, and it was money well spent."[64]

In the end, Jackson's groups received a whopping $6,677,704 in grant awards from the federal government during the Carter administration, most of which federal evaluators found was spent to create the Jackson "movement."[65] Without these federal government subsidies, Jackson would never have been able to open thirty offices around the country, all ostensibly devoted to promoting the PUSH-Excel "message." Without federal tax dollars, Jackson arguably would never have been able to expand his organization beyond Chicago, where he was considered a nuisance and a gadfly. Thanks to Jackson's friends in the Carter administration he built

Carter-Era Grants to PUSH-Excel

HEW/Department of Education[66]	
1978	HEW Secretary Joseph Califano hand-delivered the initial grant award of $55,000 to PUSH-Excel on January 5, 1978, and added $400,000 more later that year.[67] These initial grants were awarded through the National Institute of Education.[68] Total: $455,000
1979	First full year of funding for the PUSH-Excel "National Program to Promote Excellence in Inner City Schools" (Contract # 300790111)[69]: $1,000,000
1980	Second full year of funding (Contract # G0080000212): $1,000,000
1981	Third full year of funding (Contract # G008104755). Original amount: $1,000,000. Reduced amount: $825,000
Total	**$3,280,000**

Department of Labor	
1979	PUSH-Excel won its first of two training grants under CETA (Comprehensive Employment and Training Act) on May 21, 1979 (Contract # 99-8-1878-33-40).[70] Amount: $550,000
1981	On January 1, during the final weeks of the Carter administration, Alexis Herman (head of the Women's Bureau at DoL), Ernest G. Green (assistant secretary), and Lamond Godwin (head of National Employment Programs) doled out additional money to PUSH-Excel.[71] These were for $1,999,968 and $522,736. Both grants were under the same contract (# 99-1-1878-0836) and were to extend over a two-year period.[72] Amount: $2,522,704 In 1982, the Reagan administration canceled the $2 million grant.[73] It is unclear how much of it had already been paid out.
Total	**$3,072,704**

Department of Commerce	
1979	One grant (Contract # 05-10-300001-00), signed September 1, 1979, tasking PUSH-Excel to "develop an operational guide on future IBEOP [Introduction to Business Education Ownership Program]" as an add-on to the ongoing PUSH-Excel programs in the Chicago schools.[74]
Total	$250,000

Housing and Urban Development (HUD)	
1978	Operation PUSH won a grant on May 19, 1978, to expand its counseling of inner city families buying or improving homes in Chicago.[75]
Total	$75,000

Total grant awards: $6,677,704

a national organization, laying the groundwork for his 1984 and 1988 presidential campaigns, and the corporate shakedowns that would follow in the 1990s and beyond.

Jackson repaid the good deeds; after all, that was what patronage was all about. Once President Reagan took office, Green and Herman left government and founded their own company, which specialized in diversity consulting. "One of their first contracts came from Operation PUSH. It was a nifty deal, and it got Green-Herman off to a good start," wrote *American Spectator* reporter Byron York.[76] When I asked Green whether Jackson was "thanking" them for the grants, he flatly denied it.

Green eventually left for Wall Street, where he became managing director at Lehman Brothers, and Alexis renamed her firm A. M. Herman & Associates, but they continued to work together in the diversity business. The relationship they had forged with Jackson while at the Labor Department began to pay big dividends as Jackson launched his assault on corporate America. "When a company—Jackson's targets included Coca-Cola, Burger King, and the Southland Corporation, which owns 7-Eleven stores—gave in and signed a 'covenant' with Jackson, the reverend would suggest that A.M. Herman & Associates be hired to 'monitor' the agreement," York wrote. Ernest Green insists he and Alexis Herman provided value for money. "We demonstrated a service to these organizations. These firms were interested in increasing minority distributors, minority market share. It was a positive business outcome, a bottom line business outcome called profits. You know, the thing that makes the American economy go round." Asked if he and Alexis Herman competitively bid for the Coca-Cola, Burger King, or Southland Corp. contracts, Green demurred. "I am unaware of the process of selection. I don't know if we were competing with other companies."[77]

As Jackson expanded his horizons, he wasn't content with federal grants, thirty new PUSH offices, or just helping his friends. He began commenting in public on everything from the SALT disarmament talks to human rights in Africa. He wanted to become a national leader, an international icon of "freedom" and "justice." As he grew in stature and ambition Jackson found the perfect guide to provide intellectual content and contacts with the international Left in Communist Party activist Hunter Pitts O'Dell. Their relationship is one of the best kept secrets of Jackson's career.

CHAPTER 4

Travels with Yasser

JACK O'DELL

One of the first people Jackson "inherited" from Operation Breadbasket when he split with the SCLC in 1971 was Hunter Pitts "Jack" O'Dell, a trusted advisor to Dr. Martin Luther King in the 1960s and "a secret member of the Communist Party's governing body, the National Committee,"[1] according to former assistant FBI director Ray Wannall. As Jesse Jackson emerged into the national spotlight, O'Dell would repeatedly steer him toward supporting the goals and policies of America's most dangerous enemy, the Soviet Union.

A look at O'Dell's background shows a college dropout, seaman, dock worker, labor union organizer, civil rights activist, drifter. In the 1963 FBI white paper, "Communism and the Negro Movement,"[2] J. Edgar Hoover wrote that O'Dell had worked "for a number of years as a district organizer for the Communist Party in Louisiana," before working his way into the entourage of Dr. Martin Luther King Jr. In 1961, "O'Dell was made administrator of the SCLC's New York office." In June 1962, O'Dell was named an administrative assistant to Dr. King. Stanley David Levison, another close advisor to King—and a key financial operative in the Communist Party, according to the FBI—had insisted that O'Dell get the position. In Hoover's original memo to Attorney General Robert F. Kennedy, he implied that King was fully aware of O'Dell's Communist Party affiliation, but decided to hire him anyway.[3] In fact, says Ray Wannall, it was O'Dell's involvement with King and the Kennedy brothers' fear of communist infiltration of the civil rights movement that kicked the FBI investigation of King into high gear.

Hunter Pitts O'Dell was the genuine article, a hardened Communist Party cadre with roots in the Stalinist era, whose task was to infiltrate, recruit, and organize for the communist cause. He narrowly avoided jail in New Orleans in 1956, confounding the local police and congressional investigators by using two aliases, Ben Jones and John Vesey.[4]

When an investigator from the Senate Internal Security Subcommittee (SISS) went to his apartment in New Orleans in March 1956 to serve him with a subpoena to testify about his alleged Communist Party activities, O'Dell was nowhere to be found. Finally the investigator, William Arens, tried the Holsum Cafeteria where informers had told him O'Dell was working. But again, he had no luck. As Arens found out later, O'Dell had been in the cafeteria at the time, working under the assumed name "Ben Jones." So deep was his cover that he was using a false Social Security number under that name to get paid.[5]

Unable to locate him in person, the committee then requested that the New Orleans Police Department raid O'Dell's boardinghouse room at 2317 Louisiana Avenue, where they struck gold. The papers seized by the police on March 29, 1956, provided a roadmap of Communist Party activities in "the Southland."[6] Just the inventory of documents and books found in O'Dell's room ran eight pages of fine print and contained more than 175 separately inventoried items.[7]

The material they seized included a detailed plan for Communist Party organization in the South for 1955 and 1956, instructing party cadres how to handle party registration, dues payment, mass education, and the distribution of party propaganda. It included internal financial reports showing dues payments by party members, cash on hand, expenses, and income, as well as directives to all national communist parties from the Soviet Communist Party in Moscow. Recruiting new party members was one of O'Dell's main responsibilities, according to these documents. Investigators found numerous lists of potential recruits containing "hundreds of names," including recent college graduates and the parents of soldiers serving in the Korean War, whom the party thought could be approached. In one notebook, O'Dell had jotted down a party directive as a reminder to himself: "Object of security today is to conceal from enemy function of party apparatus. Previously we concealed individual whereabouts as well as function of apparatus."[8] Among the dozens of tracts, publications, and other official Communist Party propaganda, was a January 1953 monograph published by the Communist Party USA (CPUSA) entitled "Stalin's Thought Illuminates Problems of Negro Freedom Struggle."

"The committee identified Hunter Pitts O'Dell as the head of the Communist Party for the South," says Herbert Romerstein, author of *The Venona Secrets* and an expert on Communist Party activity in the United States. "He was not just somebody who was interested in communist literature. He was a party functionary. From his background and from Stanley Levison's involvement in placing him with Martin Luther King Jr., it was clear that he was a party plant."[9]

The documents seized in O'Dell's room show a broad range of Communist Party activities, from recruitment to infiltration of local labor unions, black churches, and civil rights organizations. He was involved with longshoremen negotiating a labor dispute with the Port of New Orleans in 1950–1951, and closely monitored the strike by United Packinghouse Workers of America at the Godchaux sugar plant. The head of the New Orleans police intelligence squad, Sergeant Hubert J. Badeaux, described O'Dell as the Communists' "top man in the State since 1950."[10]

Testimony from former party members as well as O'Dell's own papers gave committee investigators a detailed picture of O'Dell's past. After two years studying pharmacology at Xavier College in New Orleans, he won a seaman's certificate from the U.S. Coast Guard at the age of twenty on July 10, 1943,[11] and joined the Merchant Marine, where he served off and on for seven years. Asked by the committee if he was "a communist marine organizer on the Gulf Coast," O'Dell took the Fifth Amendment, refusing to answer on grounds that whatever he said might incriminate him.[12] As he climbed up the ladder of the party hierarchy, he reportedly "attended a Communist Party leadership school in New York City in 1950 under Al Lannon," a known CPUSA official. In the summer of 1954, the committee claimed he worked at the Spillway-Harding Airfield in Baton Rouge, breaking off to attend the Southern Regional Convention of the CPUSA in New York City on September 24, 1954. He attended another Communist Party leadership seminar in Baton Rouge in 1955.

Hauled before the Senate Subcommittee on Internal Security on April 12, 1956, O'Dell defiantly refused to answer these and other questions about his alleged Communist Party activities, pleading Fifth Amendment protection. When asked about his activities as a communist union organizer he asserted his First Amendment right to freedom of association and refused to answer. Committee investigators then brought out materials seized from his boardinghouse room. At first, he simply denied any knowledge of them. But as the questions grew more precise and it became clear that the committee had obtained damaging materials, he cited Fourth Amendment protection from illegal search and seizure. Finally, when investigators showed that he had abandoned the boardinghouse room—thus voiding the need for a search warrant—he demanded that the committee return his property, admitting that he had "left a library there."[13]

Two years later, on July 29, 1958, the House Un-American Activities Committee also brought him in for questioning.[14] By this time, the committee had already lost its power of intimidation and the anticommunist prosecutions were foundering to challenges from the American Civil Liberties Union and pro-Communist Party lawyers. After repeatedly refusing to answer direct questions, O'Dell lashed back defiantly in this exchange with committee chairman Edwin E. Willis:

Mr. Willis: I order and direct you to answer the simple question: Are you now a member of the Communist Party?

Mr. O'Dell: Since we are not concerned with the subversive activities, as far as oppression of the Negro people is concerned, I have to rely upon all of the immunity that the Constitution of the United States gives me as a Negro, because I am concerned with subversive activities that have kept my people segregated for this long time. So the First and Fifth Amendments, and any other amendment of the Constitution that offers me support and protection from not being persecuted because I am concerned with the oppression of the Negro people.[15]

O'Dell was brought before the committees under the Smith Act of 1940, which classified a whole host of activities on behalf of the Communist Party or its clandestine affiliates as criminally subversive. The committees also operated under the authority of the Internal Security Act of 1950. The act required Communist Party members to register with local law enforcement officials and make the membership lists and accounting books of the party and "communist front organizations" available for inspection.

Following appeals by several top Communist Party leaders, the Supreme Court found in 1951 that the Smith Act did "not violate the First Amendment or other provisions of the Bill of Rights."[16] At issue was the definition of "clear and present danger," the standard used to justify the prosecution of Communist Party members accused of seeking to subvert and eventually overthrow the United States government through violent means. "Obviously, the words cannot mean that before the Government may act, it must wait until the putsch is about to be executed, the plans have been laid and the signal is awaited," the Supreme Court concluded. "If Government is aware that a group aiming at its overthrow is attempting to indoctrinate its members and to commit them to a course whereby they will strike when the leaders feel the circumstances permit, action by the Government is required."[17]

The Communist Party and civil liberties attorneys had successfully challenged that standard before O'Dell was called before the congressional committees.[18] "After the first tier of Communist Party leaders was prosecuted, it became much more difficult to prosecute the second and third tier leaders," Herbert Romerstein told me.[19]

O'Dell's constitutional defense was upheld, and he was never prosecuted or held in contempt for failing to answer questions from Congress, although he was briefly arrested in March 1957 in New Orleans for participating in a subversive organization.[20] The House Un-American Activities Committee subpoenaed him for a third round of questioning on February 3, 1960. The committee had discovered a fellow Communist Party member, Albert Gaillard, who was willing to testify against him. Gaillard said O'Dell called the American South "the revolutionary front," and had sent him on Communist Party assignments.[21] By the time King hired O'Dell in 1962, he had successfully gone underground. A newspaper article that year in the *New Orleans Times-Picayune*—probably the result of orchestrated leaks from the FBI—exposed O'Dell's Communist Party ties and caused King to issue a statement accepting O'Dell's resignation. But as sympathetic King biographer David J. Garrow states, "The resignation...was more fiction than fact, as King's own message and appointment books for late 1962 and the first half of 1963 reflect."[22]

Both Attorney General Robert F. Kennedy and President John F. Kennedy pleaded with King directly that he fire O'Dell and Stanley Levison because they were communists. In June 1963, President Kennedy took King aside during a walk in the Rose Garden and told him, "You've got to get rid of them."[23]

News accounts that same month revealed O'Dell's position in the clandestine apparatus of the Communist Party and stated that he was now working out of the New York office of the SCLC. This caused King to accept O'Dell's resignation for a second time on July 3, 1963. But again King maintained close contact with both O'Dell and Levison and consulted them on key decisions—including the 1963 March on Washington, which many of King's closest advisors were begging him to cancel due to threats of violence.

But violence, according to King's own account in an April 3, 1965, article for *Saturday Review,* was an essential ingredient to social change. Only when demonstrations provoked a violent racist backlash or an armed intervention by the police would the federal government finally, "under mass pressure, initiate measures of immediate intervention and remedial legislation," he wrote.[24] King was specifically referring to the attack by Alabama state troopers against blacks demanding voting rights who attempted to march from Selma to Montgomery, Alabama, that March. Julia Brown, a black Communist Party member who became an FBI informant for nine years, told the Senate Judiciary Committee that King "was the hero of America's Communists. The cells that I was associated with in Cleveland were continually being asked to raise money for Martin Luther King's activities. . . ." Violence was important because it promoted race consciousness and resentment, she said, which in turn helped divide the American people. It was a tactic taken straight from Lenin.[25] With O'Dell's help Jesse Jackson would adopt and transform these tactics, using false accusations of "racism" to polarize Americans, inflame passions, and cash in.

After O'Dell formally left the SCLC, he worked in both Atlanta and New York for the Freedomways Association, a Communist Party front that published a magazine aimed at black intellectuals. *Freedomways* had been founded with active Soviet support, continued to receive secret Soviet subsidies, and was "close" to the CPUSA, according to KGB archivist Vasili Mitrokhin, who defected in the early 1990s bearing crates of Top Secret files on KGB operations in the West. Like other CPUSA publications, *Freedomways* was financed by the Soviets through cutout banks, including the Soviet-owned Banque Commerciale Pour l'Europe du Nord in Paris.[26] In later years, as he came to play an increasingly central role in Jackson's organization, O'Dell maintained his association with *Freedomways*, identifying himself as the magazine's associate editor when attending international conferences sponsored by the World Peace Council, a notorious Soviet front. The editorial position gave O'Dell a convenient cover for his continued work with Dr. King.

Such was the man who became one of Jesse Jackson's most trusted lieutenants.

THE GOLD ROLEX

The internationalist agenda Jackson began to pursue in the 1970s with the advice of O'Dell coincided almost perfectly with the strategic goals of the Soviet Union, which sought through surrogates and agents of influence to weaken America's self-confidence and global influence. But Jackson's agenda turned no heads in post-Watergate America, when everybody seemed to be moving to the left. The fact that Jackson employed a known communist as his international affairs advisor even failed to attract the attention of the FBI. "I can't recall ever being told that O'Dell had gone to work for Jackson," says Wannall.[27]

During his first tentative forays into the foreign policy arena in the early 1970s, Jackson avoided sweeping policy statements, always keeping his eye on the prize: whatever was in it for Jesse. In 1972, he took a small delegation of Chicago businessmen to Monrovia, Liberia, where he announced plans to develop U.S.-Liberian trade by allowing American blacks to acquire dual citizenship. At a November 20, 1972, press conference in Monrovia, Jackson proclaimed: "It is high time for the nearly thirty million American blacks, who have a gross national product of some $42 billion, to start moving from lip service to ship service with Africa, which means black Americans buying products made in Africa, in Liberia in this case, and exchanging a variety of skills with African countries."[28] Of course, Jackson and Operation PUSH wanted to *facilitate* the ship service—and the visa service, and the freight forwarding service as well. But in the end, nothing much resulted from this initiative but warm talk, since none of Jackson's black business friends in Chicago had begun to branch out into foreign trade.

When Jackson returned to Liberia two years later, President William Tolbert presented him with a solid gold Rolex and a request: if Jackson couldn't bring U.S. businesses to Liberia, perhaps at least he could lobby back in Washington to win increased U.S. aid. Jackson took the watch and thanked Tolbert graciously. But once he returned to Chicago he rebuked Tolbert in public, contemptuously holding up the Rolex in its green leather box and its certificate of authenticity as if it were a tawdry bauble. A country that could afford such lavish gifts had no need for aid, he said.[29] Jackson's outburst was calculated; despite the display of disdain he kept the watch, wearing it later when he dressed upscale during his presidential campaign years. The real message he was trying to convey, which only Tolbert's bloody successors Samuel Doe and Charles Taylor would understand, was that you couldn't buy Jesse Jackson with a gold Rolex. It would take much more.

In 1974, Jackson attended a pan-African conference in Dar es Salaam, Tanzania, but sulked when he was upstaged by rival U.S. black leaders. It wasn't until he took a week-long trip to Panama in November 1977 to meet with leftist dictator General Omar Torrijos that Jackson made a serious entry into the foreign policy arena. He was aided, of course, by the fact that President Carter had included him in his massive lobbying campaign to win support for the Panama Canal Treaty in the U.S. Senate. The treaty called for handing over control of the canal to Panama and withdrawing all U.S. troops by December 31, 1999. Carter made it a symbol of a new era of American foreign policy based on respect for human rights and national sovereignty and pulled out all the stops in the battle for ratification. Booting the U.S. out of Panama—which was how Torrijos and his friend Cuban dictator Fidel Castro played it—had become a cause celebre for the Left. Jackson brought Torrijos much needed legitimacy, as did the Senate floor manager, Paul S. Sarbanes of Maryland, who traveled to Panama with a Senate delegation that same fall.

THE PANAMA CANAL

Jackson and the dictator understood each other well. "General Torrijos is the greatest Panamanian leader who ever lived," says Cirilo McSween, Jackson's top financial manager.

A black Panamanian-American, McSween gave Jackson valuable insights into Torrijos's character in addition to setting up the meeting with the dictator. Twelve years Jackson's senior, McSween came to the United States in 1950 to attend the University of Illinois, and would have participated in the 1952 Olympics on the Panamanian track team if it hadn't been for political turmoil back home. After college, he sold insurance for New York Life Insurance Company, becoming the first black to rack up one million dollars in yearly sales. In the mid-1950s, he was invited to join the board of the Independence Bank of Chicago, one of the country's larger black-owned banks, which provided personal loans and mortgages to Jackson and his organizations. "I knew General Torrijos and thought he and Jesse needed to meet," McSween recalls. "Jesse became a national hero in Panama."[30]

Jackson's instant "popularity" was ratified by the paid mobs of the Panamanian caudillo. Jackson echoed President Carter's line by calling the treaty "a matter of human rights for Panama." He wildly predicted that if the United States Senate defeated the treaty "it will be a matter of days before we have to contain Panama militarily [in] another Viet Nam."[31] It was the type of populist rhetoric that came naturally to Jackson's leftist friends and sat well with the pro-Castro Torrijos. "During his presidency the country had democracy even though it was a dictatorship," McSween says. "That might seem paradoxical, but it's not the elections but the behavior of the leadership that counts." Torrijos, he added, was the first Panamanian leader "to have a diversified cabinet" and to provide housing for ordinary citizens. "He was the only Panamanian leader strong enough to win back the canal, Panama's most valuable property."

Back in Chicago, Jackson did his best to drum up support for the treaty. He announced that the weekly PUSH meeting on December 10 would be declared "Panama Day," and revealed that Torrijos had promised to send the chief justice of the Panamanian Supreme Court, Juan

Martino Vasquez, as his personal envoy to PUSH to explain the treaty. Like so many of Jackson's frenetic initiatives, this one went nowhere.

Serious individuals back in Washington, D.C., were alarmed by Carter's treaty. In testimony before the Senate Armed Services Committee in 1978, former chairman of the Joint Chiefs of Staff and chief of Naval Operations Admiral Thomas Moorer warned of the strategic impact giving up the canal would have on U.S. military readiness:

> The defense and use of the Panama Canal is wrapped inextricably with the overall global strategy of the United States and the security of the free world. I submit that if the United States opts to turn over full responsibility for the maintenance and operation of such an important waterway to a very small, resource-poor and unstable country as Panama and then withdraws all U.S. presence, a vacuum will be created which will quickly be filled by proxy or directly by the Soviet Union, as is their practice at every opportunity.[32]

Admiral Moorer also revealed that just four months before Jackson's meeting with Torrijos, a Soviet delegation visited Panama "seeking port and airport concessions and offering economic assistance," a clear sign of direct Soviet interest in the U.S. withdrawal. And despite the Soviet collapse in 1991, Moorer was right: the vacuum created by the U.S. departure from Panama in 1999 did attract an enemy of America, Communist China. But neither Admiral Moorer nor the FBI realized that in pushing the Panama Canal Treaty and other causes that strategically benefited the Soviet Union at the height of the Cold War, Jackson was aided by a one-time Soviet asset, Hunter Pitts O'Dell.

USEFUL IDIOTS

Jackson's support of the international leftist agenda became more pronounced in two subsequent overseas trips in 1979. In July he made a dramatic ten-day journey through South Africa, where he addressed crowds in black townships and encouraged them to launch massive nonviolent protests to topple the white apartheid regime. "If I ask you what's happening in this country, you're probably going to say 'nothing,' but you're wrong. This land is changing hands," he told one audience of Xhosa-speaking tribesmen in Cape Town. Jackson's trip received favorable coverage from the liberal American media. The *New York Times* crooned in support: "Not since the late New York Sen. Robert F. Kennedy visited South Africa in 1966 has a visiting American caused such a stir among blacks and whites."[33] In Soweto, Jackson told thousands of cheering South African blacks that he would be meeting with President Carter when he returned to the United States and would recommend that the U.S. sever cooperation with the South African government "until there are human rights for our people."

But not everyone was duped by Jackson's rhetoric. The Reverend Charles Scarborough, pastor of the Sea Point Congregational Church in Cape Town, took out newspaper advertisements denouncing Jackson as "a political activist with Marxist ties" and criticizing the South African Council of Churches for inviting him.[34] Dr. Nthato Motlana, a Soweto community leader, shrugged off Jackson's visit. "What Rev. Jackson said here was what blacks say now and all the time. He really said nothing new, except in advocating disinvestment which blacks here are precluded by law from doing."[35] On July 20, Jackson treated a squatter community in Crossroads to his usual bombast and lies, claiming that he had grown up "in a shack."

"We even kept the dirt clean—and that is the challenge facing us," Jackson said. "Just because you're in a slum, it doesn't mean the slum must be in you."[36]

Jackson soon discovered that the world of South African black politics was complicated, with rival leaders and political parties vying to set the agenda and take control of the anti-apartheid movement. Like Bill Clinton years later, Jackson thought there was no problem that American goodwill and material incentives could not resolve. He offered to act as host for a "talk about operational unity" with bitter rivals Bishop Desmond Tutu, Chief Gatsha Buthelezi, and Dr. Nthato Motlana. "Leaders must have the capacity to disagree without being disagreeable and to disagree privately and not publicly," he told an audience of Inkatha members loyal to the conservative Chief Buthelezi on July 28, 1979.[37] Swapping the safari suit he wore for most of the trip for a shiny urban guerrilla black leather jacket, Jackson answered attacks that he should have stayed in America. "I am at home here—I was taken from here 350 years ago against my will. I'm a world citizen and injustice anywhere threatens justice everywhere else."[38]

His attitude was a "complete disgrace," replied Dr. Alpheus Zulu, the former bishop of Zululand. "Most blacks in South Africa resent foreigners who attempt to do our thinking for us."[39]

Once back in the United States, Jackson met with President Carter on August 9 and hammered away at disinvestment by U.S. firms, a step bitterly opposed by Buthelezi and other black South African leaders who argued it would rob black workers of their livelihood.[40] But breaking the commercial and financial lifeline to the apartheid regime was a key goal of the international Left and of Soviet-sponsored front groups such as the World Peace Council (WPC), whose involvement in the anti-apartheid movement Jackson applauded in public testimony, a reference that went unnoticed at the time.[41] Jackson told the House International Relations Subcommittee on Africa that he had visited U.S. plants—run by General Motors, Ford, and Mobil Oil—in South Africa. He had quizzed management on how many blacks were employed, how much they were paid, and how closely aligned each company was with the South African government. "The $5.7 billion of direct or indirect investment that U.S. corporations hold in South Africa is an economic pillar for the apartheid regime," he said. He called U.S. economic cooperation with South Africa "a partnership of serious import," which put the U.S. "on a collision course with most of the countries of Africa and with world public opinion." He went on:

> "Is there a role for U.S. private investment in South Africa?" your letter asked me. Not if they are in partnership with the official policy and regime of apartheid and separate development, and are willing hostages to apartheid law and customs. And that is their present posture, as it is the posture of the U.S. government.

Jackson said he had asked President Carter to "instruct the Commerce Department to closely monitor the activities of General Motors, Ford, Caltex, Mobil Oil and IBM in South Africa" to make sure they were enforcing U.S. civil rights laws in their South African plants. This siccing of the federal government on private corporations was a precursor to the blatant corporate shakedowns he would launch in earnest a few years later.

While many well-meaning American leftists felt deeply about the human tragedy of apartheid—including Jackson's old mentor, Howard Schomer, who accompanied him on the trip—there were other equities at stake that went unmentioned in the press. Among them, as I learned during a reporting trip to South Africa in the mid-1980s, was the security cooperation between South Africa and the United States.[42] The South African navy and air force were monitoring the comings and goings of Soviet warships and electronic intelligence-gathering vessels as they rounded the Cape of Good Hope, providing vital intelligence for U.S. decision makers. The cooperation with South Africa became critically important following the deployment of Cuban troops in Angola in 1975, since the Soviets were resupplying both the Cubans and the Marxist regime in Luanda with arms and materiel by sea. In an irony that didn't fit Jackson's limited vision of race-based politics, "white" South Africa was providing extensive military aid to black freedom fighters in Angola led by Jonas Savimbi, and sought to prevent the spread of communism to southwest Africa (later called Namibia). Savimbi explained the geopolitics to me in an interview that appeared in *Newsweek* in 1986. "If Angola becomes a Soviet bastion, southern Africa will become a Soviet condominium. If southern Africa falls within the zone of influence of the Soviet Union, this will have repercussions on the whole African continent, with negative effects on Europe."[43]

Just as they did in Panama, the Soviets identified in South Africa a key U.S. security asset, which they actively sought to destabilize. Inside South Africa, the Soviets were funding and training the South African Communist Party, which provided the muscle for the underground terrorist campaign being waged by the African National Congress (ANC) against their black political opponents, including Chief Buthelezi. The Communists accused members of rival organizations of being government informers and murdered hundreds of fellow blacks in brutal "necklace" burnings, in which an automobile tire doused with gasoline was pulled down over the victim's head, pinning his arms to his side for a slow and excruciating death. The Soviet interest was to set South Africa ablaze, not set blacks free. Indeed, Nelson Mandela stubbornly remained in prison on Roben Island long after the white government was prepared to release him, because he had not yet succeeded in reducing the influence of the Communists within the ANC leadership. (Oliver Tambo, head of the South African Communist Party, had become the top ANC spokesman while Mandela was in jail. Tambo had no interest in Mandela's release.)

Internationally, the Soviets waged an extensive campaign of active measures against the apartheid regime, using every asset at their disposal. In Europe, they relied on the Stalinist Communist Party in France and front groups such as the World Peace Council. In the United States the Soviets' allies were organizations like Operation PUSH that promoted Western disinvestment. Lenin called such supporters "useful idiots." Jackson had become one of them, wittingly or not.

JESSE AND THE JEWS

There were many other arenas around the world where the United States and the Soviet Union clashed through proxies. One of the most volatile was the Middle East. The Soviets were still smarting from the humiliation they had suffered in 1973, when Egyptian president Anwar Sadat kicked out his Soviet military advisors shortly before launching a surprise attack on Israel during Yom Kippur. Yasser Arafat and his Palestine Liberation Organization, ensconced solidly on Israel's northern border in once-free Lebanon, had picked up the slack. The Soviet goal in 1979 was to gain legitimacy for the PLO and join the Middle East peace process through Arafat as a full-fledged partner. Failing that, they intended to wreck the Camp David Accords negotiated by President Carter between Israel and Egypt through a "rejectionist" front of hard-line Arab states and the PLO.

Jesse Jackson charged into this delicate situation with all the finesse of a rogue elephant. Once again, Hunter Pitts O'Dell was his guide.

Most commentators at the time saw a domestic reason for Jackson's public embrace of Arafat and the Palestinian cause. Andrew Young, a former top aide to Dr. Martin Luther King Jr., had been forced to resign as U.S. ambassador to the United Nations on August 15, 1979, after it was disclosed that he had held an unauthorized meeting with Arafat's representative in New York, Zehdi Labib Terzi.

Jackson condemned the presidential pressure that compelled Young's resignation and blasted Carter for caving into the Jews. "So the President has apparently decided to sacrifice Africa, the Third World and black Americans," he fumed. "I think it's tragic."[44] Young's resignation had created "a heightened sense of antagonism between blacks and Jews," he said. "There are a lot of questions that need to be answered." Among them were suggestions that "Israeli spies" had leaked the news of Young's meeting with Terzi to the press as a way of embarrassing him and American blacks.[45] The resignation made relations between blacks and Jews "more tense this night than they've been in 25 years," Jackson said.[46] Although Jews had helped the cause of civil rights in the beginning, Jackson added, "the conflict began when we started our quest for power. Jews were willing to share decency, but not power."[47]

A Gallup survey of black American public opinion did not support Jackson's allegations of a deep "resentment against Jews in the community." Instead, it showed that 78 percent of the nation's blacks considered relations between blacks and Jews to be either "very friendly" or "somewhat friendly." Jackson swept those findings aside: "You have to question which smattering of blacks they talked to. Also, remember, Richard Nixon was extremely popular only 18 months before he was driven from office. These are public opinions that can be molded," Jackson said.[48]

Almost immediately after Young resigned, Dr. Joseph Lowery, who had taken over from the Reverend Ralph Abernathy as head of the Southern Christian Leadership Conference, met with Arafat's Terzi in New York,[49] then took a delegation of churchmen and black political leaders to Beirut to meet with Arafat. Not to be upstaged, Jackson met with Terzi in Washington, D.C., on September 13 and announced he also would go to Beirut to meet with Arafat. "I am convinced that America must move immediately to recognize the PLO as a legitimate organization, an umbrella organization, just as it is recognized by 115 nations around the world," he said.[50]

Behind the scenes, there were other factors involved. First and foremost was money. The fall of the shah of Iran in 1979 spiked oil prices, and Jackson could smell opportunity among the Arabs. His voyage to the troubled Holy Land was a shakedown cruise, which he had planned carefully in advance and would capitalize upon on his return. In a meeting with Arab-American supporters at PUSH headquarters just before his departure, Jackson warned that he could just as easily abandon them as support them. "By October 1, there will be no black leader left willing to come to the aid of the Palestinian cause, if there is not an immediate infusion of funds into the black community from Arab states," he said. Then he tore a page from the book of street gang leader Jeff Fort to illustrate his point: "We will all learn to recite the alphabet without three letters, P-L-O."[51] It was a clever brand of extortion, and Jackson has never denied it.

Among the new supporters who attended the meeting were representatives of the League of Arab States, the Arab-American Congress for Palestine, the Palestine Human Rights Campaign, and the Libyan Embassy, according to the *Christian Science Monitor*.[52] They immediately gave cash to Jackson's PUSH foundation, using the banner of the Association of Arab-American University Graduates to pay for his new Middle East venture.[53]

But geopolitics was involved as well, in ways that may have eluded Jackson's grasp. Helping him lay the groundwork for his first foray into Middle East politics was Hunter Pitts O'Dell.

One of the groups that O'Dell worked with was the Palestine Human Rights Campaign. His name (and PUSH title) appear in the program brochure of a May 1978, National Organizing Conference for Palestinian Human Rights, which sought to build support for what the Left called euphemistically the Palestinian "struggle for self-determination."[54] Arafat and his armed guerrillas had become the new darlings of the Left, much as Castro and Che Guevara had been in the 1960s. Jackson was already using a version of the oft-repeated slogan of his presidential campaigns, but in the late 1970s he gave it a Marxist tinge: "Keep hope *and resistance* alive!" he said.[55]

O'Dell accompanied Jacqueline Jackson and twelve other PLO sympathizers to Beirut in early July 1979 to open a direct channel with Arafat, according to documents obtained from the Howard Schomer archive at the Harvard Divinity School.[56] After returning to the States, they stopped in New York, where they urged Andrew Young to meet with Arafat's UN representative as a way of nudging the United States toward recognition of the PLO.[57] "My wife went to see Andy because she knew Andy," Jackson says. "She said, 'Andy, you cannot morally ignore this issue. You have a moral obligation to at least talk to Terzi.' That's when he was fired."[58]

At the time, the PLO was heavily financed and armed by the Soviet Union and was being used as a Soviet proxy in the Middle East. The PLO occupation of Lebanon, detested by most Lebanese because of the arrogant brutality of Arafat's men, helped destabilize the region while fueling resentment against the United States among radical Arab youth, two clear Soviet goals. Getting American civil rights leaders to drive a wedge between the American Jewish community and the Carter administration neatly advanced those goals. In internal Soviet archives released after the Cold War, the KGB referred to Andrew Young while he was at the UN by the codename LUTHER. Among the archives was this note written by CPUSA leader Gus Hall to his Soviet masters: "Young himself did not know that several of his close friends in Atlanta were covert Communists, and he listened to them. The Party, while observing the required clandestinity, would cautiously exert an influence on Young in the necessary areas."[59]

At the annual PUSH convention that July, shortly after O'Dell and Jackie had returned from Beirut and well before Young had his fateful meeting with Terzi, Jackson called publicly for the creation of a Palestinian state. Sounding a seemingly bizarre note, Jackson added that the Carter administration also should consider nationalizing the oil industry, which he blamed for high oil prices. "The energy corporations must be made accountable to the public," he said. "The urgency of this demand is underscored by the fact that they have consistently placed corporate interests above the national interests in our nation's security."[60] While state-owned industries have universally proved to be an economic, social, and ecological disaster, nationalization was always a key demand of socialist and communist movements, and put Jackson in the company of the radical Left.

PALESTINIAN CAMPS

Jackson's ten-day Middle East trip generated a firestorm of controversy from the moment he landed in Israel on September 24, the eve of the Rosh Hashanah holiday. Rather than cool the flames, as he had pledged before embarking on the journey, Jackson did his best to stoke them. At a press conference held within minutes of landing at Ben Gurion Airport, Jackson criticized Prime Minister Menachem Begin and his Likud government for refusing to meet with him and his nineteen-member delegation, and suggested that racism was behind it.

Blacks represent a "political reality that Israel should not ignore," he said. "We do have seventeen congressmen. We do have fifteen million eligible voters. We are the difference in presidential elections." Noting that Israel received more U.S. aid than "the whole African continent," he warned ominously, "I would hope that Mr. Begin's rejection of us does not indicate that he rejects that which we have to offer. We have tax money to offer, we have votes to offer, we have moral support to offer."

In case the Israelis didn't get the point, he added: "We tend to support people who support us."[61] This was blackmail talk, mau-mauing on an international scale. But unlike the petty flak catchers at City Hall, Prime Minister Begin wasn't impressed.

Jackson then met with Jerusalem mayor Teddy Kolleck from the opposition Labor Party, who took him on a walking tour of the Old City. Kolleck challenged Jackson to visit the Hadassah hospital to meet with fifty Israelis who had been wounded four days earlier during a Palestinian terrorist attack in downtown Jerusalem. When Jackson tried to form a prayer circle around the beds of the victims and pray, visiting relatives "loudly protested the whole idea" and forced Jackson and his entire delegation to leave. Jackson's former mentor Howard Schomer, who accompanied him on the trip, reported on this incident in a detailed and extremely candid memorandum to Dr. Avery Post, president of the United Church of Christ.[62] He also noted that Labor Party Executive Committee chairman Shimon Peres "reduced to tatters" Jackson's arguments in favor of recognizing the PLO and Jackson's contention that Israel's treatment of the Arabs resembled apartheid.

The real trouble began when Jackson went to Israel's Holocaust Memorial, Yad Vashem. Even the normally upbeat Howard Schomer criticized Jackson's "inability... to draw any more penetrating lesson" from the museum than to say he "could now more readily understand the Jewish persecution complex." Jackson observed, "Jews should learn to see that their 'holocaust' was but one among many in history." The six million Jewish victims of Hitler should be compared to "the 60 million Blacks exterminated in the slave ships and pens," Jackson said.[63] Even *Newsweek* reported Jackson's comment that "a persecution complex... almost invariably makes [Jews] overreact to their own suffering, because it was so great. The suffering is atrocious, but really not unique to human history." At another point, he confided to a Jewish member of his entourage: "I am sick and tired of hearing about the Holocaust and having the United States put in the position of a guilt trip."[64] Jackson's insensitivity toward Jews manifested itself in small ways as well. Schomer noted that Jackson had asked him to recruit liberal rabbis to join the delegation, "but the selection of the Jewish holiday period for the visit excluded the acceptance of the people I contacted."

Jackson then traveled to a Palestinian refugee camp outside Jerusalem, where he lapsed into his "country preacher" drawl with a typical disregard for the facts. "I know this camp. When I smell the stench of the open sewers, this is nothing new to me. This is where I grew up."[65] In the West

Bank city of Nablus, Palestinians greeted him with shouts "Jackson! Arafat!" Jackson swooned in high dudgeon in front of a packed hall: "You are very close to your goal of self-determination and a homeland."[66] Schomer noted that Jackson's "warm support for their ideas and readiness to flash the victory sign brought enthusiasm to a peak. He was ultimately carried out of the hall on the shoulders of his hundreds of admirers."[67]

Jackson has always argued that he took a "balanced approach" toward the Middle East, and recognized Israel's right to exist as well as the Palestinian right to self-determination. But his behavior so exasperated the two American Jews—Philip Blazer, publisher of the Los Angeles magazine *Israel Today*, and Raymond Mallel—who had helped organize the Israeli leg of the "peace mission" that they angrily abandoned him as Jackson headed to Jordan via the Allenby Bridge.

Blazer denounced Jackson as a "dangerous man" who was seeking to cash in on the plight of Palestinian refugees to bolster the finances of his own organization.[68] "Jackson came to Israel to look for supportive evidence for conclusions he had already drawn," Blazer said. Jackson attempted to dismiss such critical statements by Blazer and Mallel as "pure sabotage" and claimed the two Jews had "nothing to do" with his delegation. But not even the liberal press corps let Jackson get away with such a facile lie, noting that on the evening of his arrival, Jackson had introduced the two men and specifically commended Blazer for organizing Jewish and black opposition to a pro-Nazi demonstration in Skokie, Illinois, the year before.[69]

Jackson was simply embarrassing to left-wing Jews. Even David Zucker, a leader of the ultra-leftist "Peace Now" movement, whom Schomer arranged for Jackson to meet, gave the country preacher low marks. "He was arrogant, used questionable language, and he had not done his homework," Zucker said.[70]

With Arabs, it was different. Crown Prince Hassan of Jordan flew Jackson on his own helicopter for a tour of the Jordan valley, so he could see for himself the Israeli fortifications and the high state of military tension along the borders. At a state banquet in Amman, the Jordanians commended Jackson for his efforts to legitimize Arafat and the PLO. "They obviously intended also to use us insofar as possible to weaken Washington's support for Israel and resistance to the participation of the PLO in the peace process," Schomer noted candidly.

Flying into Beirut the next morning, Jackson was given a hero's welcome by the PLO, "with scores of children with elaborate florist shop bouquets lining the narrow pathway left by the crowd from the airplane to the street," Schomer wrote. Heading the reception committee was Arafat's brother, head of the Palestinian Red Crescent, who "pil[ed] us into various jeeps and operational cars of the freedom fighters."

Schomer felt let down in Beirut by Jackson's knack for turning every moment of his trip into an instant press conference, while ignoring the "fact-finding" that was supposed to constitute his mission. "Contrary to our express cable request of ten days ago," he wrote United Church of Christ president Dr. Avery Post, "our hosts had made virtually no place in our intense 48-hour schedule for meeting with the Middle East Council of Churches" or any representatives of Lebanon's majority Christian community. (Had Schomer known Lebanon a bit better he wouldn't have been so surprised, since Arafat was at war with Lebanon's Christians and with most of its Muslim communities except for the socialists.)

Splitting from the group to meet Christian clergymen, Schomer asked his wife to accompany Jackson on the twenty-five-mile journey down the coast to Damour to meet Arafat. Elsie Schomer's account fails to mention the fact that Arafat had seized Damour just three years earlier—after his guerrillas herded its Christian inhabitants into the local church and set them afire. But what the Schomers saw in Lebanon cured them of any naiveté they may have brought with them when they first arrived.

"We were put into a bunch of jeeps and weapons' carriers," Mrs. Schomer writes,

> . . . and were driven lickety-split about 40 km south of Beirut. When I say "lickety-split," it was a true scene from *The French Connection*, a terrifying ride which everyone seemed to enjoy as

an example of macho. Arriving in the village above the Mediterranean Sea, we were greeted by children lined up, shouting
PLO slogans and "Yasser Arafat, Yasser Arafat. . . ." The sight of
9-year-old boys carrying guns was unnerving, as was the big
poster in the courtyard where we met afterwards for discussion
and food. The poster was in violent colors with a gun and spear
crossed.

Mrs. Schomer then recounts the meeting with Arafat,

. . . who was disarmingly simple and direct in describing the military situation, his only real concern. I myself asked him why, in
view of his own statement that the Israeli army was unbeatable,
they engaged in terrorist military or paramilitary activities at all.
His reply left me gasping: "Madame, you are a Christian, your
Lord Jesus was a Palestinian, he resisted the Roman occupation,
we can do no less." Our message of non-violence was completely
foreign to his way of thinking.

Howard Schomer then resumes the narrative with a bald assessment of
Arafat's tactics and goals, and Jackson's response:

Arafat would appear to count on Western need for Arab oil and
Western irritation with Begin's intransigence to persuade the West
to stomach [the PLO's] continuing terrorist tactics. The majority
of the Jackson delegation, identifying deeply with the sufferings of
the unfree Palestinians and believing that the PLO liberation
struggle is one with that of Blacks in the U.S. and of colonized
people in other parts of the Third World, resentful of the alleged
power of the American Jewish pro-Israel lobby and desirous of
developing the U.S. black vote as a potent foreign policy factor in
respect to all freedom-and-justice issues, appears to support the
demand that Israel simply withdraw to its pre-1967 frontiers in

return for de facto recognition by the PLO and all Arab states of its right to exist within its 1948–1949 boundaries.

The PLO seems to have little interest in formally recognizing the right of Israel to exist, but great interest in obtaining diplomatic recognition itself. . . .[71]

Schomer concluded his memo by noting that he and his wife "regretfully asked the Rev. Jesse Jackson to make no reference to them or the United Church of Christ in any final report of findings, declaration, or recommendations." It was a stunning disavowal from someone who counted himself a strong Jackson supporter.

Standing side-by-side with Jack O'Dell, Jackson proclaimed Arafat "my friend and the friend of justice and humanity."[72] He told a Lebanese magazine that he considered Arafat's PLO "a government-in-exile [that] will not renounce armed resistance. As a matter of fact, by international law, they have a right to resist occupation."[73] It was a curious way of describing the PLO armed presence in Lebanon, and their battles against Lebanese Christians, who were fellow Arabs. *Newsweek* reported: "Even Jackson's PLO guides were amazed at his tone, but they were grateful for it."[74]

Jackson's trip to the Middle East, and the huge smacking kiss he planted on Yasser Arafat's cheek—captured for posterity by the horde of news photographers he eagerly asked to follow him—created an unmitigated public relations disaster that would dog him for years. His response to the bad publicity was typical: he attacked the messengers, especially the Jews.

His critics in the media were "all Jewish," and had "challenged us without conversation," he claimed. The reason his trip received such negative editorial comment was because "there are no Arabs and no Palestinians writing for a major newspaper or television station downtown." It was not true that he had called Israeli prime minister Menachem Begin "a racist" for refusing to meet with him. He merely "indicated Mr. Begin's racial sensitivity was much too low" and any reporting to the contrary was unfair. It was also untrue that he had gone to the Middle East for personal benefit.

"How absurd would it be for me to go all the way to Israel to get my picture taken," he said. "I went to the Middle East because I cared."

He then singled out by name three Chicago newspaper columnists and one television commentator as being Jews, and complained of the coverage by the *New York Times* and *Time* magazine. Working himself up into a full-blown fit of paranoia, he accused Phillip Blazer, who had helped set up his meetings with the Israeli Left, of being a spy who had come along to "monitor" his activities.[75]

Other black leaders also criticized Jackson's pro-Palestinian stance. Bayard Rustin, a former SCLC aide to Dr. Martin Luther King Jr., blasted Jackson in an editorial for creating a "black-Jewish rift." Blacks actually "have little to complain about" when it came to the circumstances of Andrew Young's departure from the UN, since "Young quit because he was caught breaching the generally accepted code of behavior for diplomats." Instead, Rustin argued, it was time "for more blacks to question efforts by some black leaders to forge new links with the Palestine Liberation Organization. It is time to make it clear that these efforts probably won't help bring about peace in the Middle East—but rather hurt those prospects," as well as the civil rights movement itself.[76]

Rustin criticized the media reporting on Jackson's trip not because it was pro-Israel but because it focused exclusively "on the rhetoric of some black leaders who do not speak for all blacks. Black America is no longer monolithic, and it is a serious mistake—a racist mistake—to assume that any one or two black leaders speak for all." He suggested that Jackson lacked the basic values of tolerance and civilized discourse required of leaders in a democratic society. "If Jesse Jackson or Joseph Lowery of the Southern Christian Leadership Conference or anybody else cannot be criticized in a civil and intelligent manner by Jews, Catholics, journalists, other blacks, union leaders, or whomever, then America has misunderstood the meaning of racial equality, indeed of democratic politics." He told the *Christian Science Monitor*, "Jesse is one of my best friends. But I believe that, in this instance, he is wrong. I don't know what's in Jesse's mind right now, but I don't like what's coming out of his mouth."[77]

To Rustin's annoyance, the media gave Jackson so much coverage that they created an aura of inevitability around his leadership. Herbert Romerstein, who has spent the past fifty years analyzing disinformation and how the public can be influenced through the media, agreed. "The single most important thing the press did for Jackson was to give legitimacy to his claims to represent the black community. Jackson was a leader by virtue of the press."[78]

In terms of global politics, Rustin pointed out, Jackson's "private diplomacy" gave comfort to the pro-Soviet "rejectionist" elements seeking to sabotage the Camp David Accords. Jackson, he wrote, had become "an unwitting ally" to the Soviet-led struggle against Israel.[79] How "unwitting" is open to question. After all, there was money to be had.

SHAKING THE ARAB MONEY TREE

On October 13, 1979, soon after his return from Beirut, Jackson invited 150 Arab businessmen to a closed-door breakfast at PUSH headquarters. Jackson gave them a report on his trip, then hit them up for money, just as he had done before leaving for the trip. This time they coughed up nearly $10,000, according to his own admission.[80] "Our organization has always survived through contributions from all types of people," he said, in an effort to downplay his brand-new Arab connection. "Why is it questioned when Arab people give?"[81]

Jackson noted that one of his fundraisers, former Illinois Democratic Party chairman Marshall Korshak, was Jewish. When contacted by reporters, Korshak acknowledged that he had helped PUSH in the past but added, "I have never been so ill and disgusted as I have been seeing Jesse promote hatred and division between blacks and Jews. I am completely disillusioned with him."[82]

According to Ayoub Talhami, a Palestinian community leader, Jackson outlined "a program for future joint undertakings" between blacks and Arabs and signed up some of the Arabs for PUSH membership at the breakfast. But Jackson also played to the crowd by calling for U.S. recognition of the PLO and criticizing Israeli premier Menachem Begin whose government "itself is engaged in terrorism." Taysir Yunis, the Palestinian director of the Arab Information Center in Chicago that helped set up the fundraising breakfast at PUSH headquarters, said Jackson had given "us a voice in a city where we have not been heard. We don't want to be viewed as terrorists or camel drivers or tent dwellers. We want to be viewed as human beings with rights like anyone else."[83] For Arab-Americans seeking dignity, $8,000 to $10,000 to win the support of an energetic spokesman such as Jackson was a small price to pay.

But there was more. When Jackson ran for president, reporters combed through his financial disclosure reports and discovered that he had established a nonprofit called the PUSH Foundation, which received a donation of $100,000 from the Arab League, the official body of twenty-one Arab nations. Arab League secretary general Clovis Maksoud gave an additional $100,000 to PUSH-Excel during the same time period, 1978-1981. The timing of these contributions was left vague in the reports filed by Jackson's lawyer John Bustamante, but subsequent news accounts reported the checks were signed just two days apart. Another $350,000 was given to the PUSH Foundation by an "anonymous" donor during the same period.[84]

When *New York Times* reporter Jeff Gerth asked him whether the Arab money had influenced him, Jackson replied, "So has white money, and black money, except all of it is the same money and that's the double standard." At one point in the interview, he referred absurdly to the Arab League as an "American organization." Covering for Jackson, lawyer John Bustamante took the fall and said that he had gone to Maksoud in 1981 "and asked him if he could support us. . . . I may have told Reverend Jackson. But I do not recall any discussion." The Arab League check accounted for 80 percent of the money the PUSH Foundation had raised that year, but Jackson claimed he knew nothing about it.[85]

Less than three months after his meeting with Arafat, Jackson's PUSH took a separate $10,000 check from Libyan diplomat Ali El Houderi. The Libyan donation eventually triggered a four-year Justice Department investigation as to whether Jackson was required to register as a Libyan agent under the Foreign Agents Registration Act.[86]

When the *Atlanta Constitution* first broke the story on September 24, 1980, Jackson claimed he "would accept no financial deal from Libya and none has been offered." Pressed for more specifics, he said he had written the Libyan embassy in Washington on behalf of the Wallace Company in Tuskegee, Alabama, a black-owned oil company, and had sent "several letters" to the Libyan government in support of "opening trade routes between that country and black America." But he still denied having received any money from the Libyan government.

His secret ties to Libya were detailed in a classified memo sent on March 31, 1980, from Stansfield Turner, director of Central Intelligence, to Zbigniew Brzezinski, President Carter's national security adviser. The memo reportedly identified a Libyan government effort to influence the administration by funneling cash to Jackson and Billy Carter, the president's brother, and identified Jackson as a "special Libyan oil broker." Billy Carter eventually registered as a Libyan agent on July 14, 1980, after acknowledging he had received a $220,000 payment from the Libyan government on an oil deal.[87] Jackson, typically, confessed nothing and never registered as a foreign agent.

But Jackson's Libyan connection blew up in Carter's face just one week before the 1980 presidential election, when the two were campaigning together through the South. An NBC reporter told Jackson that the FBI was trying to locate him to serve him with a Justice Department subpoena relating to his Libyan dealings. Jackson again denied that he had taken Libyan money, but telephoned an official in the Carter White House. Following his call, White House counsel Lloyd Cutler contacted Deputy Attorney General Charles B. Renfrew and the FBI withdrew the subpoena. Once again, the Carter White House saved Jackson from embarrassing scrutiny.

As Jackson and Carter were flying on Air Force One between campaign stops in St. Louis and Columbia, South Carolina, the press reported that the White House had interfered with a Justice Department investigation.[88] Thus, early on, Jesse Jackson exhibited a quality that would later make Bill Clinton famous: the ability to leave other people holding the bag for his scandals.

CHAPTER 5

Corporate Shakedown

END OF AN ERA

The year 1981 was disastrous for Jesse Jackson. Despite public differences with President Carter over the Middle East, he worked tirelessly for Carter's reelection, neglecting his own business for months. A day before the November 4, 1980, election, former mentor Howard Schomer wrote Jackson a note. It reminded him that his South African church sponsors were still begging him to pay his hotel and local travel expenses from his July 1979 trip. "TOMORROW is it," Schomer wrote. "I trust that you will be able to draw back from national politics a bit, whoever wins, for I know how much PUSH and PUSH-FOR-EXCELLENCE need you."

The champion of the poor had run up a tab of nearly $7,500 in South Africa (over $19,000 in 2001 dollars), and was expecting the victims of apartheid to pay it on his behalf. Joseph Wing, secretary of the United

Congregational Church of Southern Africa, had written numerous letters to Jackson asking to be reimbursed. Frustrated after eighteen months without a reply, Wing asked Schomer to intervene. "It would be very good if the UCCSA could be the perfect host and cover all expenses in connection with Jesse's visit," he wrote on October 24, 1980, "but the inadequate resources of the UCCSA would not stretch that far.... [I]t would be appreciated if you would kindly remind Jesse of the outstanding account in as gentle a manner as possible."[1]

A few months later Schomer made a note at the bottom of yet another reminder from Joseph Wing: "Phoned Jesse 1-1-81, Happy New Year! ... He said he'll get on Joe Wing's bill Monday—remind him." It would take several more reminders for Jackson to come up with the cash, which he sent via Schomer on September 23, 1981, but only after Schomer flew out to Chicago and confronted him in person, insisting he cover his debts.[2] Jackson liked to tell reporters that he lived modestly and had few needs. "I don't carry a billfold. I don't have much need for money."[3] What he meant was that he expected others to pay his bills.

South Africa wasn't the only bill catching up with Jesse. Already in October 1979, just days after his first Middle East trip, Chicago Circuit Court judge Irwin Cohen froze the PUSH payroll account so the public relations firm Burston-Marsteller could collect on a three-year-old bill Jackson had failed to pay. Jackson's reaction to Judge Cohen's ruling was typical but troubling, suggesting a growing anti-Semitic hysteria. He claimed it was linked to "other harassment" he had received from Jews following his meeting with PLO leader Yasser Arafat. "We would hope these expressions of aggression now being put upon us by the Jewish community will stop," he said, vowing to raise the $16,356.56 to pay off the lien.[4] The order came down just as he was meeting with Arab-American businessmen in Chicago and gave him a good pretext for following up with demands for cash, which they fulfilled by donating between $8,000 to $10,000 to Jackson's groups. In 1980, International Amphitheatre, from whom he rented the fairgrounds used for the yearly PUSH-Expo, sued him for failing to pay his debts. Jackson refused to testify but satisfied the claim once the plaintiffs got a court order giving them access to financial records from his corporate and philanthropic empire.[5]

Jackson had good reason for his reluctance to provide documents to the courts, since his financial dealings skirted the fringes of legality. In a 1981 suit filed by another creditor, lawyer John Bustamante was forced to reveal a 1979 fundraising contract issued by PUSH-Excel, Jackson's educational foundation, stipulating that outside fundraising consultants were to be supervised jointly by Jackson and Bustamante. This belied Jackson's claim that he was unaware of efforts to solicit money from the Libyan government, Yasser Arafat, and the Arab League. The contract, whose existence was revealed in 1984 by *New York Times* reporter Jeff Gerth during Jackson's first presidential campaign, showed that the PUSH Foundation had been set up "as a conduit for funds" for PUSH-Excel, a potential violation of the laws governing nonprofits. It also showed that Jackson was using funds from his nonprofits to pay for personal expenses and political travel, an abuse Jackson would repeat with impunity.[6]

But after Ronald Reagan became president, the new administration launched a government-wide search and destroy mission known to insiders as "Defunding the Left." Its goal was to identify federal grants that had been awarded to left-wing organizations and reduce them or cut them off entirely. Favorite targets were pro-Soviet disarmament groups, Planned Parenthood, left-wing trade unions, the National Urban League, the Gray Panthers, the American Civil Liberties Union, the pro-Marxist United States Student Association, and Jesse Jackson's PUSH-Excel. "Is it fair to require taxpayers to finance the political activities of groups whose views they do not share? Most people would say no," conservative activist Richard A. Viguerie wrote in a *New York Times* op-ed. "Yet it has been estimated that, since the 1970s, hundreds of millions of dollars—maybe more than $1 billion—in taxpayers' money have been used each year to support and spread political views that the American people have consistently and overwhelmingly rejected."[7]

Word soon began circulating that Jackson's groups were getting federal grants for the same project from different agencies. The new White House

budget managers quickly put a hold on nearly $100 million in question-
able grants the Department of Labor's Alexis Herman and Ernest Green
had doled out to cronies during the final weeks of the Carter administration. These funds included $2.5 million to PUSH-Excel for a career
development program under the Comprehensive Employment and
Training Act (CETA). Jackson complained that the cut-off was "motivated
by political considerations."[8]

The Reaganauts turned to federal auditors at the General Accounting
Office and the inspectors general at individual agencies. At Commerce,
the green eye shades questioned bookkeeping practices by PUSH-Excel
on a $240,000 grant and demanded a $56,411 repayment. At Education,
they discovered a huge file on PUSH-Excel left behind by the Carter
administration that alleged massive irregularities. "Even the Carter
bureaucrats thought Jesse was crooked," recalls Reagan's Education
Department official Dan Raney. "We cut off the grants but eventually
chose not to prosecute."[9] A performance review of PUSH-Excel had
been commissioned in 1980 from the American Institutes for Research
(AIR), a Department of Education think tank, which concluded that
Jackson's motivational program for troubled inner city schools had failed
to achieve its stated goals. "PUSH-Excel is still predominantly a movement, inspired by the presentations of the Rev. Jesse Jackson," the AIR
report said. "Jackson had failed to translate his charisma into a workable
educational program," it concluded.[10] The program "turned out to be
mainly paper."[11]

Based on the AIR findings, the Reagan administration announced its
intention to reduce the yearly Department of Education grant to PUSH-
Excel from $1 million to $825,000, and withheld payment from March
until September 30, 1981, as additional audits were carried out. On
September 11, 1981, the Department of Education notified Jackson it
would not renew the federal grants for his program because PUSH-Excel
"has refused to permit access to its books by our auditors."[12] Assistant
Secretary Vincent Reed, the former superintendent of the District of
Columbia school system, sent a hand-delivered letter to Jackson advising

him that the group's accounting system was "not adequate to safeguard assets" the federal government had entrusted to it.

Jackson's initial response was sour grapes. "We want to phase out the relationship with the government because the government has been more disruptive than supportive," he said. Government grants "simply give them the platform to try to destroy the program."[13] The last thing he would want was a pack of federal auditors rifling through his books, so he went on the attack.

THE REAGAN AUDITS

The church on Columbus Avenue in Boston's South End was packed. More than two thousand people jammed into Union United Methodist on Sunday, October 4, 1981, where normally six hundred gathered to worship. It was just eleven months after President Reagan's election. Jesse Jackson was the guest speaker, and he was late. The Reverend Charles Stith began the service without him. Nearly two hours later, well past noon, Jackson ascended the pulpit dressed in a white pastoral robe and a green stole and launched a forty minute political harangue. He blasted President Reagan for leading a "right-wing revolution" and called on his audience to do battle with a government he claimed was committed "to the fittest, the whitest and the elitist." He called the Moral Majority organization that helped elect President Reagan the new "white church."

It was not just Reagan's popularity, but the budget cuts that irked Jackson. Jesse's easy, government-sponsored lifestyle was about to end. "I want to speak to what to do when you're cut off," he said. "In the face of this revolution, the water of hope that was in the New Deal, the Fair Deal and the New Frontier...has been replaced by the ashes of despair." Reagan's social austerity had left only "dry bones," not just for the black community but for the needy around the world. "This is not just a local or national struggle," Jackson said. "This is an international struggle." The notion that the civil rights struggle in America was linked to national liberation movements around the world was becoming a regular Jackson theme.

But Jackson was just warming up. "The new nation . . . is of the few, for the few, and by the few," he said. Reagan and his administration "are right-wing ideologues. The new government has turned its back on the people." He then urged the congregation to vote in the upcoming November general election for the Democratic Party candidates for the city council and the school board, who just happened to be sitting in the front pews.

If Jackson was worried about elitism and the concentration of wealth in the hands of the few, his concerns vanished when wealth fell into his own hands. Following the service, the "Country Preacher" was greeted by a uniformed chauffeur wearing white gloves and a white ruffled shirt, who opened the door to the black Fleetwood Cadillac limousine waiting for him outside. The limo took him to a local restaurant and nightclub for a fundraising reception on behalf of the nonpartisan, nonprofit Operation PUSH.[14] Chauffeur-driven limousines were Jackson's preferred means of local transport.

As the Reagan administration auditors dug deeper they found that huge sums of money paid out to Jackson for education projects in the schools had seemingly gone missing, spent without a shred of documentation. Somebody was paying for Jesse Jackson's chauffeur-driven limousines, and increasingly it appeared that the taxpayer was getting stuck with the bill. Lawyer John Bustamante sought to head off the investigations through a preemptive attack, writing Education Secretary Terrell H. Bell to accuse the administration of racially motivated harassment.[15] Jackson's friend Walter Fauntroy, a nonvoting congressman from the District of Columbia, followed up by calling for a GAO investigation of the Reagan administration for wrongly withholding a $1 million Education Department grant to PUSH-Excel.

The initial reply from the acting comptroller general of the United States, available through the Freedom of Information Act, reinforced the bad news. "Education's decision not to award the grant earlier was based primarily on factors relating to the efficient operation of the grant program," the November 2, 1981, letter states. Following the Commerce

Department audit, which found that "none of the expenditures reported by PUSH...was adequately supported by PUSH's records," the Education Department launched its own audit on September 17, 1981.[16]

As the audits proceeded, the news just kept getting worse. Soon, the administration claimed that Jackson had misspent $1.7 million of the $4.9 million in federal grants he had received, not counting the last $2 million in Labor Department money that was blocked before he could get his hands on it. One million dollars had gone to "questionable" expenditures, including unauthorized salaries and travel, while another $736,972 had been spent in ways that were "contrary to Federal laws and regulations"—a polite way of saying "illegally."[17] Jackson apparently had not planned on government audits when he took the grant money during the Carter administration and thought he could continue to treat his various legal entities as one big "Jesse Inc.," transferring money back and forth as his personal needs, travel, and political campaigning required. The Reagan administration eventually demanded that PUSH reimburse the government $1,455,647.[18]

Jackson sought cover by hiring Mary Frances Berry to head PUSH-Excel once she left her grant-giving job as assistant secretary of education under Carter.[19] To make her transformation complete, he put her in charge of closing down the program she had helped to fund. "I've been discouraged," she said in 1982, when the Los Angeles school district abandoned the PUSH-Excel program after spending more than $640,000 on it over two years. "I've learned a lot of things from this." Berry, who went on to head Jackson's campaign to become the "Shadow Senator" for Washington, D.C., in 1990, later distinguished herself by authoring the highly partisan report of the U.S. Civil Rights Commission on alleged "massive" voter intimidation during the November 2000 election in Florida.

JESSE FINDS A NEW SCHEME

With the end of the Carter era grants and strong pressure from the Reagan administration, Jackson needed to find a new scheme to finance his operations. When no new money flowed into PUSH-Excel he simply jettisoned the school programs and revived the tried and true tactics of Operation Breadbasket. So much for his dedication to improving the quality of inner city schools. Jackson was sending his own children to exclusive schools such as St. Albans, so why should he care?

Breadbasket's main drawback was its limited scope and financial benefits. When Jackson had turned to government grants, his base of black business backers in Chicago had been tapped out. He couldn't have squeezed greater contributions from them. But now, in the 1980s, there were thriving black businesses all over the country, and Jackson had rich and powerful new friends. He decided to adapt the Breadbasket techniques to the big leagues and become the broker for black businesses in their dealings with major U.S. corporations. This went way beyond the minority set-asides that were becoming Noah Robinson's specialty. Jackson used his experience with the early boycotts by Operation Breadbasket to pressure large corporations to sign "trade agreements" and "covenants" with PUSH that established racial quotas across the entire spectrum of corporate activities, not just government contracting.

His first target was Coca-Cola. Based in Atlanta, where former UN ambassador Andrew Young was now running for mayor,[20] Coke prided itself as an equal opportunity employer and charitable donor to the majority black community. Coke thought it had nothing to fear from Jackson's threatened boycott. But Jackson was planning to beat Coke with another stick: its business dealings in apartheid South Africa. It was mau-mauing, 1980s style.

"Jesse brings up South Africa and the whole pressure in the negotiation shifts," a longtime PUSH operative told biographer Marshall Frady. "This is one of the areas where they're most vulnerable, because they've got big operations in South Africa."[21] Coca-Cola came to terms in August 1981 and offered distributorships of the patented Coke syrup to blacks. Coke shareholders were furious. A Coke spokesman, Carlton Curtis, said, "There's been a strong reaction in the marketplace that this is outright blackmail, that this is a $30 million give-away plan." But Coke management went along, and soon downplayed the dollar value of the concessions they made to Jackson, claiming they barely reached $11 million and consisted of already planned expenditures.[22] But for Jackson the lesson was clear: public shaming worked better than the threat of boycott and was much less work.

The first to benefit was Jesse's half brother Noah Robinson. Covenant in hand, he won the first black syrup distributorship from Coca-Cola just one month later. Shortly afterwards, Coke also granted a distributorship to Cecil Troy, a major financial backer of Operation PUSH.[23] In March 1982, Jackson signed a similar covenant with Heublein Corporation, a wine and spirits company that owned Kentucky Fried Chicken. Under the deal, Heublein pledged it would spend $360 million over five years with black banks, advertising agencies, and newspapers, and would expand the number of minority franchise owners. Once again Noah Robinson cashed in, using the covenant to lock in a Kentucky Fried Chicken franchise that would become the launching pad for a fast food empire.[24] "I told Jesse, 'If you just do the talking for us—and I handle the financial operations—we can rival the Rockefellers in riches,'" Robinson said.[25]

Cirilo McSween, Jackson's treasurer and early financial supporter, denies receiving any financial assistance from Jackson. "I'm certainly one of his friends, one of his closest friends—and there is no evidence that I ever benefited from Jesse," McSween says today. "I've always had business. He needed me, not the other way around."[26] Nevertheless, in the early 1980s, McSween's Independence Bank of Chicago won several accounts from Burger King as a result of the PUSH covenant, a company spokesman said.[27] And the list went on.

Jackson benefited from the covenants at both ends, not just through his brother and his friends. Heublein spokesman Erik Pierce told the *Washington Post* that Heublein gave $5,000 to Jackson in 1982 to help underwrite the annual PUSH convention, and another $10,000 in November 1983.[28] 7UP and Coca-Cola also made cash contributions to Jackson's groups. Jackson and his new corporate partners were careful to avoid any appearance of impropriety. "We felt the covenant was a smart business decision, a marketing decision at that," said a Burger King spokesman. A 7UP vice president added: "We did not feel at any time extorted, blackmailed, any of those things." But another corporate executive who spoke on condition his name and company not be disclosed paints a very different picture. "It seemed like a shakedown to me. They had lists of people they wanted us to do business with, lists of things they wanted us to do, donations and things like that."[29] Jackson described the covenants as "moving corporate America into the black for the good of America," and denied benefiting personally from the practice.[30]

Other Jackson friends and cronies also prospered as a direct result of the covenants. Among them: Alexis Herman and Ernest Green, the Carter-era Labor Department officials who shoveled so much government money his way. The PUSH covenants created a whole new profession, that of "diversity consultant," and corporations scrambled to find individuals friendly with Jackson who could devise plans he would find acceptable. Green told the *Washington Post* in 1984 that his consulting firm derived 30 percent of its business from contracts with Jackson targets Heublein, Coca-Cola, and Southland Corporation, which owned the 7-Eleven chain. But he quickly added that any suggestion he was profiteering was "hogwash."

Jackson grows defensive when challenged about requiring companies to hire his friends as consultants. "The companies choose the consultant of their choice. We don't appoint them....We recommend a list of them."[31] Ernest Green soon joined the board of directors of Operation PUSH, and, along with Alexis Herman, went to work for Jackson's 1984 presidential campaign. It was Jackson's way to hold close to him those who benefited the most, binding them through dependence and loyalty.

Just as Jackson's school programs benefited from perfect timing during the Carter administration, when the federal government was seeking ways of improving performance and combating violence in predominantly black inner city schools, his new emphasis on winning concessions for black businesses fit well with the entrepreneurial 1980s. According to a U.S. Census Bureau survey, the black business sector was booming. The number of black-owned businesses jumped nationwide by nearly 50 percent during the five years from 1977 to 1982, from 230,000 to 340,000. Gross receipts for black businesses reached $12.4 billion in 1982, a 44 percent gain from just five years earlier. The majority of these firms were either service or retail trade. Auto dealers and service stations accounted for the largest dollar volume with $1.3 billion. Next were "miscellaneous retail firms" with total receipts of $993 million. These were followed by food stores with $883 million in total income, food and drink establishments with $675 million in receipts, and health services with $595 million gross.[32] Jackson would ride the wave.

Ironically, the biggest constraint on the growth of minority businesses was the practice of minority set-asides, or quotas, which made black firms dependent on federal largesse and less able to compete in the private market. In 1980, for example, only one black-owned firm managed to "graduate" to self-sufficiency in the private market.[33] Jackson's "covenants" with large corporations did not seem aimed at growing healthy black businesses, but rather at generating dependence on Operation PUSH by extending the federal set-aside program to the private sector. He became the broker, the intermediary, and he made it clear that he wanted to be paid for his services. This was the fundamental operating principle of Jesse's new scheme. Some considered it illegal.[34]

YOU HAVE TO PAY TO PLAY

To formalize these arrangements, Jackson had lawyer John Bustamante create a new Illinois nonprofit corporation in 1982 called the PUSH International Trade Bureau. Jackson was listed as founder and chairman.[35] Black businessmen who wanted to "ride on Pharaoh's chariot" with Jackson would be invited to join and pay annual dues starting at $500. In return, they would get preferential treatment whenever Jackson negotiated a business covenant. Their firms would be on the list of minority subcontractors provided by Jackson to his corporate targets. It was a neat scheme that allowed Jackson to get paid for his brokerage services while denying any direct payoff. All the money was run through a separate nonprofit organization.

The problems began when Jackson sought to enlarge his circle of benefactors beyond the friends and cronies who understood his method of operation. His new scheme nearly came unraveled when he took his road show to St. Louis and attempted to hit up black businessmen at an August 2, 1982, luncheon.

The *St. Louis Sentinel,* which served the black community, published a scathing editorial about the luncheon three days later entitled "Rev. Jesse Jackson: Minister or Charlatan?" It accused Jackson of taking "a kick-back approach" toward civil rights activism. During the lunch, Jackson revealed that he planned to launch a boycott against St. Louis–based Anheuser-Busch, the nation's largest brewery, that could result in lucrative new contracts for black businesses. But "if you want to play, you have to pay," he told the businessmen.[36] Calling Jackson a "self-proclaimed negotiator for the Black community," the *Sentinel* said Jackson's approach "demonstrates his million dollar commitment to himself" and raised an argument that has haunted Jackson ever since. "By his language, the only Black people that can benefit from Rev. Jackson's dealings are the wealthy and rich, the ones who do not need any economic support. What about the millions of poor and indigent Black families and persons that are responsible for spending billions of dollars with white corporations; are they to profit?"

Jackson's call for donations during the lunch fell on deaf ears, and many of the businessmen were angry that he was targeting Anheuser-Busch. The *Sentinel* said the company "has led the way for 'Corporate America' in attempting to give something back to the Black Community," and accused Jackson of "wheeling and dealings" with corporate America. "Anheuser-Busch was a good corporate citizen," said Michael Williams, co-publisher of the *Sentinel.* "We questioned his motives. We had black business owners who were really offended that Mr. Jackson would want money to go after this company."[37] Jackson's response was to sue the *St. Louis Sentinel* for libel, demanding $3 million in damages.

Bolstered by the *Sentinel's* support, Anheuser-Busch refused to sign a deal with Jackson that summer, and Jackson publicly announced a nationwide boycott of the brewer in October 1982. At a press conference—not in St. Louis, but in Chicago—Jackson ceremoniously held up a can of Budweiser and poured it into the gutter, proclaiming, "This Bud is a dud." He cheered as the fifty young bloods he brought with him poured out four more cases of beer.[38] But the company successfully swept aside his claims of discriminatory hiring practices. If Jackson had done his homework, he would have understood why and spared himself the expense and embarrassment he suffered as a result.

Anheuser-Busch had been sued surprisingly few times in St. Louis and rarely with success. A search of St. Louis district and circuit court records going back twenty-five years shows only a few dozen cases against Anheuser-Busch involving job discrimination, and of these, only a handful involved questions of race. Most of these cases were summarily dismissed by the courts, at times with the plaintiff ordered to pay the company's legal fees. Only once did the court order a mediated settlement for an undisclosed amount, and that wasn't until 1998.[39] The black business community was not eager to help Jackson attack a company that was hiring blacks and providing black subcontractors with good business. "A boycott can be successful only when the target is perceived by almost all blacks and their white friends to be a blatant enemy of black justice," wrote syndicated columnist Carl Rowan. "This boycott smells of Jesse Jackson's ego and of his determination to wreak vengeance on a company that dared to criticize him."[40]

But corporate father August Busch III had no intention of relying on a popularity contest, especially when Jackson had shown a talent for stacking the odds through race-baiting and hate tactics. Just as Jackson was getting ready to muster his troops against Bud, Augie Busch's attorneys filed a preemptive lawsuit in the Twenty-Second Circuit Court in St. Louis. The suit was not against Jackson, but against the Missouri Commission on Human Rights, which had accused the company in May 1982 of "using race as a factor" in evaluating employee performance.

The case involved a black woman named Phyllistine Quinn who worked on the bottling line and who, by her own admission, was frequently late or absent from work. After several reprimands from her supervisor and a week's suspension, she was given a four-week suspension without pay in 1979. She promptly took her case to the Missouri Human Rights Commission, which filed an official complaint against Anheuser-Busch on her behalf. After extensive hearings, the commission found in 1981 that the company had failed to reprimand white employees for similar absenteeism, and ordered Anheuser-Busch to "cease and desist from using race as a factor in its decision to discipline some employees more severely than others." It was a potentially damaging opinion that Jackson would surely exploit once his boycott got underway.

In their countersuit against the Missouri Human Rights Commission, Anheuser-Busch presented detailed employee records showing that many black employees actually benefited from company leniency, and that Ms. Quinn herself had been reinstated with back pay after an earlier suspension. "This evidence shows that Anheuser-Busch was color-blind in its administration of the absentee control policy, and that not just whites, but blacks, too, were favored by its application," the company argued.

But the Missouri Human Rights Commission pressed on, demanding that Anheuser-Busch set up new procedures for evaluating employees to prevent the taint of racism in the future. Pressing the commission's case in court was Missouri attorney general John Ashcroft, who would later be accused of racism during his confirmation hearings as U.S. attorney general in January 2001 by Jackson and members of the Congressional Black Caucus.

The Busch attorneys won a stunning victory on December 21, 1982, when Circuit Court judge George A. Adolf invalidated the claims of racial discrimination against the company, calling them "unsupported by competent and substantial evidence." His opinion, in essence, swept away any factual basis that may have underpinned Jackson's boycott of Anheuser-Busch.[41]

But Jackson was not one to let the facts get in his way. He accused August Busch III of unleashing a smear campaign against him through the *Sentinel*.[42]

ANHEUSER-BUSCH STRIKES BACK

The company had indeed launched a secret effort to undermine the boycott, but in ways Jackson didn't suspect. The company hired a team of private investigators to conduct a thorough background check on Jackson, his family, his finances, and his claim to be the rightful heir to slain civil rights leader Martin Luther King Jr. They collected case files from courts around the country involving Jackson's shaky finances, the frozen PUSH payroll, and his secret fundraising agreements. They discovered the secret payments he had received from the Arab League shortly after he embraced Yasser Arafat in Lebanon. They documented Jackson's multiple residences and opulent lifestyle, including tuition payments for two of his children to attend the exclusive St. Albans school in Washington, D.C.

According to a lawyer who reviewed the file, Anheuser-Busch investigators discovered documents that uncovered a number of Jackson's tactics—tactics that I have exposed in this book, but which were unknown to the public at that time.[43] Among them were documents from the Southern Christian Leadership Conference that alleged Jackson had misappropriated funds from Operation Breadbasket in Chicago in the late 1960s. "The file clearly demonstrated that Jackson was not the favorite son of Dr. Martin Luther King Jr., or his intended heir, but a hustler who fabricated a reputation out of thin air," the lawyer says. "The idea was to show Reverend Jackson the report and make him go away."

By late August 1983, the lawyers had completed a report detailing their findings and asked Jackson to meet them at one of Washington's most powerful law firms. Jackson was apparently led to believe that Anheuser-Busch was prepared to make a peace offer, and began describing the benefits of cutting a deal that would end the boycott. One of the attorneys working for Anheuser-Busch cut him off. "Mr. Jackson, before you go any further, read this." He slid a black legal binder across the conference table to Jackson.

The lawyer pointedly failed to address Jackson as "Reverend." Jackson appeared taken aback by the chilly tone of the meeting and opened the binder warily. As he flipped the pages, he remained silent. "After about fifteen minutes, Jackson slammed the file shut, got up, and walked out without a word," the lawyer said. Jackson announced the end of the PUSH boycott of Anheuser-Busch almost immediately afterwards, in early September 1983. He said that his previous denunciation of Anheuser-Busch "may have been attributable to a failure of communication," an astonishing admission from the usually self-righteous Jackson.[44] Anheuser-Busch's victory was a message to other corporate attorneys: Jackson could be embarrassed if confronted with facts from his own past.

Meanwhile, lawyer Frankie Freeman, defending the *St. Louis Sentinel*, called Jackson's libel action against the paper "a misuse of legal process [that] constitutes an extortion."[45] Freeman struck a sensitive nerve when she demanded that Jackson provide extensive financial documentation on his nonprofit empire in discovery. She wanted "the complete organizational structure" of Operation PUSH, a complete description of its programs, a breakdown of all donors, and the group's books. But most embarrassing of all, she demanded that Jackson "identify all sources and amounts of [personal] income, international, national, state and local."[46] This small black newspaper was about to become the mouse that roared.

When the judge ordered Jackson in September 1983 to provide all information about his finances under oath or face stiff financial penalties and contempt of court charges, Jackson dropped the suit. By then, he had larger ambitions. He wanted to be president of the United States.

CHAPTER 6

Tool of the Left

RUN, JESSE, RUN!

For someone who had never held public office, had no foreign policy experience, and had never demonstrated he could successfully manage a large organization, it was an incredible pretension. Black leaders such as Atlanta mayor Andrew Young, Coretta Scott King, Joseph Lowery of the SCLC, and even his good friend Washington, D.C. delegate Walter Fauntroy, lined up against Jackson in his 1984 presidential bid.[1] "This is not an election to take a chance on," Young said as Jackson crisscrossed the South drumming up support for his candidacy. "I guess I still hope he doesn't do it."

Democratic congressman Mickey Leland of Texas, chairman of the Democratic National Committee's Black Caucus, said many black leaders "don't trust Jesse because of his ego.... We will not be blackmailed into supporting Jesse simply because he is black. We will make a sophisticated political decision about who we will support—black or white."[2] Jackson's swaggering leap into elective politics was even more extraordinary given the little-known fact that he had only recently registered to vote.[3]

The "Southern Crusade" rallies in the summer of 1983 inevitably ended with a preacher's call-and-answer routine that sounded the refrain "Run, Jesse, run!" And while a great deal of ink was spilled on whether America had overcome its long history of racial tension enough to elect a black president, Jesse Jackson the candidate ignited controversy less because of the color of his skin than because of the content of his character. Even his glitzy voter registration drive was criticized by grassroots Democratic Party activists. During a typical four-day swing through Georgia, Jackson went to Plains to see former president Jimmy Carter, granted ten formal press interviews, called two press conferences, and "attracted impromptu media gatherings in churches and airports," the *Washington Post* reported. "Constantly, he invoked Martin Luther King's name." Joseph Madison, who directed voter registration for the NAACP, called Jackson's voter drive "the biggest hoax that's been pulled on black folks that I can think of."[4]

Jackson had two secrets he feared could doom his campaign: his murky financial dealings, and the even murkier criminal dealings of half brother Noah Robinson. "If and when Jackson runs for the Presidency," wrote William Brashler in the *New Republic* in October 1983, "the press and his opponents will dig into his seldom-divulged financial records with a vengeance, and Jackson knows it." Despite the many stories about Jackson's finances, they never managed to seriously damage Jackson's campaign because they never uncovered evidence that Jackson had personally profited from his nonprofit empire. (That evidence was yet to come.) When federal auditors alleged in July and August that he had misspent $1.7 million in grants he had received for PUSH-Excel, Jackson simply swept it aside as a political attack. The evidence, however, indicated that much of the money had gone to pay for his own travel around the country to promote his education program and build his organization.[5] Most polls showed that he had extremely high negatives—well over 60 percent—even among registered Democrats. Those who were going to vote for him followed his banner no matter how serious the allegations of financial improprieties. Jackson was even luckier when it came to half brother Noah. When the press eventually discovered him late in the campaign, he was painted as a successful black entrepreneur whose example showed that intelligence, perseverance, and good business sense were all blacks needed to succeed in today's America.

Jackson's tremendous energy and his verbal pyrotechnics succeeded in diverting attention from these very real scandals by creating a series of mini-crises at every stage of his campaign. Typical of these was his scandalous behavior when Harold Washington was elected the first black mayor of Chicago on April 12, 1983. Washington won after a massive registration drive among black Chicago voters in which Jackson played only a minor role. "Once the people were registered, it was all Washington's campaign, with Jackson making few official appearances," Brashler wrote. But on election night, Jesse showed up at Washington's campaign headquarters to claim the prize. "Jackson grabbed the microphone and started chanting, 'We want it all. Super Bowl! Super Bowl!' It was embarrassing, and Washington's aides scrambled to literally push him off the podium."[6]

One thing Jackson wasn't worried about, however, was his utter devotion to a hard-left agenda. Throughout his first presidential run he referred to America's black population as a "colony" of the American empire, and called his hometown of Greenville, South Carolina, an "occupied zone." His presidential platform, such as it was, called for an initial 25 percent across-the-board cut in defense spending, income redistribution, and accommodation of the Soviet Union. Typical of his views was his only recorded criticism of the Soviet invasion of Afghanistan. Jackson likened Afghanistan's foreign occupants to Israeli settlers in the West Bank, and called on the United States to reduce aid to Israel and to condemn Israel at the United Nations.[7]

HARD-LEFT ADVISORS

Jackson built a record of anti-American activism during President Reagan's first term that disturbed many of his friends in the Democratic Party who felt he was coming dangerously close to a third-party candidacy.

"Many find it difficult to overlook the embrace of Yasser Arafat, the cheerleading for Fidel Castro and the Sandinistas, the appearances before pro-Soviet 'peace' groups, and the presence of veterans of the authoritarian Left among Jackson's closest advisors," wrote Democratic Party activists Penn Kemble and Joshua Muravchik in a research report on Jackson's Rainbow Movement. They quoted Michael Walzer, who noted with dismay in *Dissent*, a left-wing magazine, that Jackson's positions "constitute a more or less coherent world view in which liberal and democratic values have, to put it cautiously, no secure place."[8]

Indeed, Jackson had no qualms about allying himself—repeatedly—with communists or communist front groups. One of the most egregious examples was on June 12, 1982, when Operation PUSH helped sponsor a massive rally organized by the Communist Party USA and the Soviet-backed U.S. Peace Council, calling for the dismantling of the U.S. military. The Communist Party's *Daily World* claimed it attracted more than a million people.[9]

Jackson hired two distinct sets of advisors for his presidential campaign—one set was made up of blacks in highly public positions, the other was far less visible and made up of hard-core radical leftists who were Jackson's "brain trust." Jackson put Lamond Godwin, a black Labor Department official under Carter, in charge of his voter registration drive in the South during the summer of 1983. And he hired Godwin's deputies from the Carter Labor Department, Ernest Green and Alexis Herman. At Labor, these three had funneled $3 million in job training grants to Jackson's groups. All three went on to build substantial personal fortunes, cashing in on the prominence they earned under Jackson's wing and in the Carter administration. Joining the team later were Richard Hatcher, the black mayor of Gary, Indiana, as Jackson's campaign chairman, and Frank Watkins, the PUSH communications director who became the campaign's chief spokesman.

The leaders of the "brain trust" were Jack O'Dell, the former Communist Party functionary who went to work for Jackson in 1971, and Robert Borosage of the Institute for Policy Studies (IPS). The IPS was a hard-left think tank in Washington, D.C., that consistently took a pro-Soviet line during the Cold War.

As an IPS director, Borosage traveled repeatedly to Nicaragua in the early 1980s to support the pro-Soviet Sandinistas and undermine U.S. aid to the Contras. Along with Morton Halperin, a former National Security Council aide who resigned in protest of the Nixon-era bombings of Cambodia, he set up the IPS Center for National Security Studies, which advocated sharply reducing U.S. defense spending and ending the counterintelligence role of the FBI and the CIA. Borosage openly acknowledged that the goal of IPS was to "move the Democratic Party's debate internally to the left by creating an invisible presence in the party."[10]

The IPS frequently hosted trips for left-wing members of Congress to Nicaragua, Cuba, and Grenada, including an infamous 1982 visit by Democratic congressman Ron Dellums and his top aide Barbara Lee to a military airstrip being built in Grenada by Soviet and Cuban advisors.[11] Borosage, O'Dell, and the IPS were identified in a 1979 Heritage Foundation report as founding members of the Coalition for a New Foreign and Military Policy, a pro-Soviet group that included many active members of the CPUSA and publicly advocated Soviet positions. Heritage called it "the most comprehensive organizational manifestation of what some observers call the 'anti-defense lobby' . . . which styles itself as 'an effort to develop a peaceful, non-interventionist and demilitarized U.S. foreign policy.'" The coalition grew out of the anti–Vietnam War movement and focused on, according to Heritage,

> such issues as ending U.S. aid to regimes like those in South Africa and Chile while, at the same time, advocating "normalization of relations" with Vietnam and Cuba coupled with "reconstruction aid" for Indochina; withdrawal of American forces from South Korea; opposition to the B-1 bomber; passage of the so-called Transfer Amendment to convert military spending to "human needs" as part of a general program aimed at a drastic reordering of spending priorities combined with steady reduction

in American military spending; and approval of the strategic arms limitation (SALT II) agreement.[12]

That enumeration constitutes a precise list of the national security and foreign policy positions Jackson defended during his 1984 presidential campaign. As Roger Wilkins, a Borosage colleague at IPS, commented in the radical left monthly *Mother Jones*, Jackson's campaign had attracted "a range of thinkers and activists who found [Jackson] to be an enormously effective vehicle for getting their ideas before the public."[13]

MISSION TO EUROPE

Jackson's advisors knew they needed to correct the image he presented of someone with no foreign policy experience, especially since his few forays overseas had been almost total disasters. On September 7, 1983, Jackson advisor John Bustamante sent a confidential memo to the Jackson campaign team and to two trusted supporters in Congress, representatives John Conyers and Ron Dellums, spelling out the details for a European tour. This and other documents relating to the trip, disclosed here for the first time, provide an unusual inside glimpse of Jackson's PR machine. They also reveal the harsh criticism he encountered from his own advisors for his lack of discipline, and for failing to move beyond his own hype in creating a truly broad-based "rainbow" coalition, the catchword he made famous during his presidential run.

Each participant in the trip was asked to have his bank transfer $3,321.89 to a special account to cover transatlantic travel and hotels. But the U.S. taxpayer picked up part of the tab because Jackson billed the trip as an effort to "inspire American servicemen" to register to vote. "It is Rev. Jackson's intention to eat with the troops on the three days that you will be visiting the Army bases," Bustamante informed the participants. Given that Jackson's campaign platform advocated reducing U.S. deployments overseas and spending less on modern weapons—thus ensuring greater U.S. casualties in the event of war—Jackson's use of crowds of soldiers as a backdrop for staged campaign photo ops was shameless exploitation of the cruelest sort.

The schedule included a private audience with Queen Beatrix of the Netherlands and a half-hour parlay with West German Socialist Party leader Willy Brandt, intended to demonstrate to American voters that Jesse Jackson was not only comfortable but intimate with world leaders.[14] Jackson also met with Democratic Party activists. Dutch field coordinator Rob de Laet added a special reminder to the itinerary that Jackson should be sure to wear the button of Democrats Abroad, because this would encourage expatriates to vote.

Jackson's trip began with a secret meeting in London on September 12, 1983, with South African Communist Party leader Oliver Tambo, who was also vice president of the African National Congress. Tambo "is flying to London solely for this visit," according to the telex itinerary that accompanied Bustamante's memo. Neither Tambo's Communist Party affiliation nor the fact that he was secretly receiving aid from the Soviet Union seemed to bother Jackson, who embraced him enthusiastically.

In Amsterdam, Jackson was hosted for lunch by the Dutch parliament and gave a foreign policy speech at Amsterdam's Free University, where former mentor (and now, campaign advisor) Howard Schomer introduced him to international "peace" activists who opposed the Reagan administration's anti-Soviet military build up. Later, as Jackson went off by limo for a photo-op with Congressman Ron Dellums to visit the grave of a fifteen-year-old boy "assassinated by racists," Schomer met privately with the peace activists who were heartened by Jackson's opposition to the deployment of U.S. cruise and Pershing II missiles in Europe. "You now have a few key friends in the mainstream of the European peace movement, and you have avoided being used by other strands of this movement that may be more interested in either Soviet foreign policy promotion or plain anti-American nationalism," Schomer wrote in a confidential post-trip memo on September 26, 1983.

Schomer may have been overly optimistic. In any case, he went on to note that the Dutch leftists were planning a "hot autumn" campaign against the Euromissiles. These were missiles President Reagan argued were necessary to counter the Soviet SS-20s, recently deployed throughout the

Warsaw Pact, that were aimed at West European capitals. Preventing deployment of the NATO Euromissiles was the foremost strategic goal of the Soviet leadership in 1983. To this end, the KGB waged an extensive campaign to block deployment of the missiles, including clandestine support for the "nuclear freeze" and other "peace" movements, political pressure on European leaders, as well as saber rattling, war scares, and planting extensive disinformation in the European press. Getting Jesse Jackson to sign onto the anti-Euromissile bandwagon was a major accomplishment for Soviet policy. The peace activists were asking Jackson to organize a "great Congress" in the United States the following spring in tandem with another they might organize in Western Europe, with the object of launching a "Third Way—neither U.S.S.R. nor U.S.—movement for justice and peace." Their main question, Schomer wrote, was whether Jackson understood "that capitalism is the underlying cause of the current war peril, and that democratic socialism *is* the Third Way?"[15]

Throughout the weeklong trip Jackson made sure he was accompanied by an extensive press pool, and scheduled a press conference at the end of every day in addition to numerous impromptu press events and photo ops. What good was strutting his stuff through Europe if the American press didn't record his brilliance? On September 14 he flew to Frankfurt and gave two interviews to U.S. armed forces media.[16] Then the U.S. Army flew him on board Huey helicopters to the western approaches of the Fulda Gap, the main invasion route Soviet and Warsaw Pact forces were expected to use should war erupt in Europe, and where the United States and its allies had positioned massive defenses.

Colonel Frederick M. Franks Jr., commander of the Eleventh Armored Cavalry regiment, met his high profile guest with a snapping salute as Jackson's helicopter landed on the tarmac of Sickels Army Airfield at 12:40 that afternoon, and briefed Jackson on the U.S.-Soviet standoff in Germany. Then he took him on a walking tour of forward observation posts so he could see with his own eyes the proximity of Warsaw Pact forces. Later that day, Major General Howard G. Crowell Jr., commander of the Third Infantry Division, treated Jackson and the busload of reporters to an impressive combat demonstration of M-1 tanks and UH-60 helicopters. That evening, Jackson was allowed to speak for fifty-five minutes with soldiers of the Second Regiment of the 64th Armor Battalion and their families about voter registration at Schweinfurt Army Airfield, the ostensible justification for his trip.

The next day U.S. Army Hueys flew Jackson and his party to Heidelberg, where he was briefed on Operation REFORGER (Return of Forces to Germany), the key U.S. war plan in the event of a Soviet invasion. Again, he was given fifty minutes to speak with the troops on voter registration. Although the meetings with the troops were brief, Jackson was greeted enthusiastically and responded in kind, perhaps not realizing that U.S. troops almost always welcomed attention from home, regardless of the political flavor. As Schomer noted later in his postmortem memo, "Those were great meetings on the bases in West Germany. . . . This could mean a lot of votes—for somebody." The trip ended on September 16 in West Berlin, where the U.S. minister for Berlin, Nelson Ledsky, hosted a lunch for Jackson and the forty-two members of his party, which now included local German politicians, left-wing academics, a labor union leader, members of the press, and even representatives of Turkish guest workers living in Germany. After lunch, Jackson held a much photographed walking tour through the city that ended dramatically at the Berlin Wall. In all it was a breathless eight-day extravaganza, an extended photo-op from start to finish.

But despite the generally glowing coverage, reporters grumbled to Schomer about Jackson's habitual tardiness and scatter-brained organization. Schomer made excuses as best he could. In a memo to Jackson, Schomer explained, "I insisted to angry press-men that . . . you are a guy who learns every day, are continually growing, and can proceed from the vocation already mastered, preacher and charismatic speaker, to that of a leader of a nation-wide action-campaign, and eventually of a nation." But what Jackson needed, he said, was to "recruit a Chief Operating Officer." He berated Jackson for the organizational snafus, and reminded him that first year students at Harvard Business School "learn early that tardiness among corporate executives, when important business is to be decided, is simply intolerable. . . . The Harvard MBA student arriving late for a work-team session is automatically failed for that particular session. I remember how Dr. King often kept us all waiting and waiting. You are now entering a circuit where this is not done." Jackson had even shown the effrontery of stiffing West Berlin mayor Richard von Weiszacker, Schomer noted with exasperation. He had been scheduled to meet the mayor for break-fast, but instead had preferred to sleep in at his hotel.

Even worse for his political aspirations was Jackson's failure to craft a truly multiracial "rainbow" coalition. "We sorely needed an articulate Hispanic leader, an outstanding spokesman for the women's movement, Jewish peace worker of note, etc.," Schomer wrote. "And I could not alone adequately symbolize the whole category of 'white males over 40'—without whom the rainbow will never be able to straddle the continent—either the North American or the European." Schomer went on:

> Here is where I have said, and now must write, a tough truth. Your sentences that begin with "we" have got to be inclusive of the top agenda items of other than the U.S. black or the African black communities, or the "Rainbow vision" will evaporate. It just won't do to have your mind not only rooted in, but confined to, the black experience and hope, simply adding an occasional reference to the other locked-out elements of our society. You have got to become steeped in the distinct agendas of each sector of the coalition you hope for, and become their champion also, or they will feel that they are simply being used.[17]

Atlanta Journal cartoonist Gene Basset summed up the problem with a stinging portrait of Jackson dressed as a painter, wielding palette and brush before an easel to paint a rainbow. On the ground before him are a half-dozen cans of paint, all labeled "Black," while stooping to examine the rainbow is Ralph Abernathy, his former boss. "Jesse, have you ever seen a rainbow?" he asks.[18]

In fact, Jackson can't claim to have coined the phrase "rainbow coalition," although he made it famous. Pride of ownership goes to former Massachusetts state representative Mel King, who made an unsuccessful bid for mayor of Boston in 1983 and who used the term "rainbow coalition" to describe his supporters. "Mel described his supporters as a rainbow," former campaign staffer May Louie, now a project manager at the Dudley Street Neighborhood Initiative, recalls. "Jesse began calling it Mel's rainbow of support" after attending a 1983 campaign rally for King in Boston.[19] Compared to Jackson's other antics, the theft of the "rainbow coalition" name was minor larceny of the sort politicians commit every day.

"ENEMY OF THE JEWISH PEOPLE"

After months of tantalizing the press and terrorizing the Democratic Party establishment, which feared he would split the vote, Jackson formally announced his candidacy on November 3, 1983, in front of some two thousand supporters at the Washington, D.C., Convention Center. The campaign rally didn't quite go as planned—in fact, Jackson ran into trouble. Public television broadcaster Jim Lehrer singled out the incident when he reported Jackson's announcement that evening:

> *Lehrer:*   The emotional pleasure of the event was cut cold at two early moments, when two hecklers who identified themselves as members of a militant Jewish group accused Jackson of being anti-Semitic. This was the scene during one of those incidents.
>
> *Mr. Jackson:* That we might serve the ends of justice, and . . .
>
> *Heckler:*   Anti-Semite! [confused shouting] Anti-Semite! [shouting]
>
> *Crowd:*   Run, Jesse, run! Run, Jesse, run! Run, Jesse, run![20]

Jackson's embrace of Yasser Arafat in Lebanon in 1979 was still on the minds of American Jews, as were his comments during that trip that he was "sick and tired of hearing about the Holocaust." Taken aback by his inability to intimidate the white hecklers, who carried signs calling him an "enemy of the Jewish people," Jackson insisted that he was "neither anti-Semitic nor opposed to the right of Israel to exist within secure boundaries." At a press conference in New York, the right-wing Jewish Defense League said it had formed a new coalition, Jews Against Jackson, and was taking out full-page newspaper ads itemizing Jackson's anti-Semitic statements.[21] The ads prominently featured a sinister-looking photograph of Jackson wrapping his arms around a beaming Arafat during his trip to Lebanon. Calling Jackson "a danger to American Jews, the state of Israel, and to America itself," the ads included Jackson comments such as these:

- "When it came to the division of power we did not get from the Jews the slice of cake we deserved . . . the Jews do not share with us control of wealth, broadcasting stations and other centers of power." (Jesse Jackson on CBS's *Sixty Minutes*, September 16, 1979)
- "One who does not think Arafat is a true hero does not read the situation correctly." (Jesse Jackson in Israel, as quoted in Israel's largest newspaper, *Maariv*, September 27, 1979)
- "Arafat is educated, urbane, reasonable. I think his commitment to justice is an absolute one." (Jesse Jackson in *Penthouse* magazine, February 1981)

President Reagan's ambassador to the United Nations, Jeane Kirkpatrick, while not blasting Jackson directly, explained why the United States had a problem with Arafat's PLO. "The United States' dispute with the PLO isn't just about Israel," she told the *New York Times*. "It's about the PLO's role in the world. It isn't just because of Israel that the PLO chooses violence as its instrument of first resort. It approved the Soviet invasion of Afghanistan. It supports violence in Central America. It functions as an important member of the radical Soviet bloc. The Soviets strengthen the PLO and the PLO strengthens the Soviets." The PLO ambassador to the UN, Zehdi Labib Terzi, agreed with Kirkpatrick's characterization.

Describing himself as "philosophically a Marxist," he acknowledged that the PLO supported Soviet goals around the world, from the fight against apartheid to the struggle against the Contras in Nicaragua. "The Soviet Union recognizes that we are a people like other people and that we have a right to our own state," Terzi said. "We get military aid from them." In exchange, the PLO had established close links with pro-Soviet groups in Central America, and provided military training and other forms of assistance to the Sandinistas in Nicaragua and the communist guerrillas in El Salvador. "We naturally sympathize with people who are fighting for their freedom," he said. Calling Jesse Jackson "a friend," Terzi said he "kept in touch" with him regularly through Jack O'Dell.[22]

The Jewish Defense League campaign woke up moderate Jewish leaders who until then had kept silent on Jackson's presidential aspirations. "Jesse Jackson's image in the Jewish community is conditioned by more than his views on the Mideast," Nathan Perlmutter, executive director of the Anti-Defamation League of B'nai B'rith, told the *New York Times*. "Many of us remember that he is the man who is sick and tired of hearing about the Holocaust and that he blamed 'Jewish domination of the media' for some of the news coverage he has gotten. Considering these things, coupled with his embrace of Yasir Arafat, I have no question that Jews, like most groups who have a commonality of interest, will be listening closely to what he says."[23] Rabbi William Berkowitz, head of the American Jewish Heritage Committee, noted that Jackson's "past record is not one that will endear him to the Jewish vote," while Morris Amitay, a director of the powerful America-Israel Public Affairs Committee (AIPAC), said Jackson's embrace of Arafat endangered his "rainbow" coalition. "Normally the kind of support a black would receive [from Jews] won't be there," he added.[24]

Jackson compounded the problem by flying out to Los Angeles two days after his campaign announcement to address the American Arab Antidiscrimination Committee (AAAC), a pro-Palestinian group that was attempting to counterbalance AIPAC as a lobbying force in Congress. Visibly entranced by Jackson's presence and his warm embrace of a

Palestinian state, AAAC executive director James Zogby glowed when he told the press it was the first time a presidential candidate had appeared before the group. Jackson's support for Arafat and his American backers didn't make sense to his campaign staff—at least, not to those he paraded about publicly. When asked to comment why Jackson had gone to Los Angeles, Ernest Green commented wryly: "It wasn't the most politically wise thing to do." He admitted that "professional political campaign strategists would have advised against the appearance."[25] What Green didn't say, however, was that the appearance and indeed Jackson's embrace of Arafat and the Palestinian cause were fully in line with policies previously advocated by Jackson's wife Jacqueline and by the hard-left coterie of advisors led by Robert Borosage and Jack O'Dell, who remained in the background throughout the presidential campaign.

RENDEZVOUS WITH THE KGB

Jackson had initially planned to return to Europe in mid-November to address a disarmament forum in Vienna hosted by the World Peace Council from November 14 to 17, but the firestorm over his candidacy and his problems with Jewish Democrats required his immediate attention. In his stead, he sent O'Dell, who was identified in the final conference *Documents* as the head of the entire thirty-six-member U.S. "delegation."[26] In addition to his title as Director of International Affairs for Operation PUSH, O'Dell was listed as board chairman of Pacifica Radio and Associate Editor of *Freedomways*, a magazine closely tied to the Communist Party. Its editor, Esther Jackson, was the wife of Communist Party leader James Jackson.[27]

The U.S. intelligence community repeatedly warned the U.S. Congress, in public hearings and in private briefings, that the World Peace Council was "a Soviet front organization," a charge rejected by the Left as red-baiting propaganda. World Peace Council chairman Romesh Chandra headed the Indian Communist Party and was a well-known Soviet agent of influence whose activities were being closely monitored by U.S. intelligence agencies. Chandra noted that Jackson "was unable to attend at the last moment" but had "sent a message of support and encouragement which was presented by his personal representative . . . Jack Hunter O'Dell."[28]

The Vienna gathering sought to give an international veneer to the desperate Soviet effort to block the NATO Euromissile deployment. "The World Peace Council was in a separate category from other nuclear freeze organizations," says Herb Romerstein, who tracked Soviet active measures for the Reagan administration. "The WPC was wholly owned and operated by the USSR."[29] That's what made Jackson's association with O'Dell and the Vienna conference so troubling. O'Dell himself was one of seventeen U.S. members of the World Peace Council who "have been identified at various times as members of the CPUSA."[30]

The U.S. attendees were not run-of-the-mill liberals or even nutty pacifists, but represented hard-left groups. After O'Dell and Patricia Louise McGurk from Operation PUSH came Eugene "Gus" Newport, the mayor of Berkeley, California, who was chairman of the U.S. Peace Council, the lead U.S. partner of the WPC. Also participating were Tony Bonilla, the chairman of the National Hispanic Leadership Conference, who had accompanied Jackson on the September trip to U.S. bases in Europe; Barbara Lee, aide to Congressman Ron Dellums (identified in the conference documents as president of the U.S.-Grenada Friendship Society—at a time when Grenada was a Soviet-backed Marxist dictatorship); Ellen Siegel, of Washington Area Jews for an Israeli-Palestinian Peace and the Palestine Aid Society; Dwight Bowman, an advisory board member of D.C. Nuclear Weapons Freeze; Michael Parenti, of the Institute for Policy Studies and the Washington, D.C., Peace Council; Patricia Scott of the U.S. Peace Council; and Harry R. Bridges, who for years headed the International Longshore and Warehouse Union, an organization "which has long been controlled by identified members of the CPUSA." Bridges himself had been "identified many times in sworn testimony as a member of the Communist Party."[31] Patrick Tobin, union vice president and international representative, accompanied him. Tobin's position put him into frequent contact with KGB officers and other members of the World Peace Council.

But the real key to the Vienna conference was the Russians. They included top Soviet propagandist Victor Afanasiev, a Central Committee member and editor in chief of *Pravda*, who was a known KGB disinformation officer,[32] and Yevgeny Maksimovich Primakov. Known to the KGB by his codename, Maxim, Primakov was a specialist in active measures who worked with the International Department of the Soviet Communist Party Central Committee and played an active role in a wide variety of Soviet front organizations around the globe.[33] Primakov went on to head the KGB and was appointed foreign minister, and ultimately prime minister of the Russian Federation. A communist—and later, Russian nationalist—hard-liner, Primakov fiercely opposed U.S. power and cut deals with Third World tyrants such as Saddam Hussein to advance his anti-American agenda. A total of seventeen Soviet officials attended the conference, many of them KGB officers.

Although the U.S. press ignored the Vienna conference and failed to notice Jackson's involvement, his "PUSH-paid foreign policy advisor" Jack O'Dell surfaced in a November 28, 1983, editorial in the *New Republic*. "The politics of Mr. O'Dell will not bear scrutiny," the center-left weekly opined. "He has a long record of public identification with Stalinism, American-style, and he is one of several members of the intimate Jackson circle who are also leaders of the unabashedly pro-Soviet U.S. Peace Council. Obviously Mr. Jackson is not a communist or anything like one, but the presence of such people in key foreign policy roles in his entourage is evidence, at the very least, of very bad political and moral judgment."[34]

Eric Breindel, writing in the same publication a few weeks later, got even more specific. In the meantime, the magazine had gained access to the FBI's COINTEL and COMINFIL material from the investigations of Martin Luther King Jr., including still classified documents that incorporated information from Operation Solo, the most sensitive FBI intelligence coup of the Cold War. O'Dell "had a long public history as a Communist Party organizer; he never repudiated his ties to the party," Breindel wrote. He then accurately predicted that O'Dell's communist ties would never become a campaign issue for Jesse Jackson. "Even today, to note simply that someone was or is a Communist, or that some institution had party ties, is seen in some quarters of liberal opinion and the national media as 'red-baiting.'" Although secret FBI files on Martin Luther King's ties to the Communist Party were released that year during the debate on whether to make his birthday into a national holiday, "the national press demonstrated remarkably little interest," Breindel wrote. This lack of curiosity in the midst of a vitally important debate on the deployment of new nuclear missiles in Europe and the covert Soviet effort to block them had become "a lasting legacy of Senator Joseph R. McCarthy."[35]

Longtime Jackson crony Ernest Green, who now works as an investment banker with Lehman Brothers in New York, scoffs at the FBI investigations. "I knew about the FBI files on Jack. It's history. But remember, I worked for Bayard Rustin in 1963," he told me in an interview. "So in my view any FBI files on Jack would be a badge of courage, not a discredit. Jack O'Dell has known Reverend Jackson for at least forty years. They were fairly close."[36]

One reporter who didn't miss the significance of the once secret FBI files was CNN investigator Pat Clawson. He was intrigued by the work O'Dell was doing for Jackson, and spent seven months in 1983 checking out his past. He'd also worked on Jackson's close personal ties to leaders of the El Rukn street gang, and the questionable business activities of half brother Noah Robinson. "I wanted to bring those stories out," Clawson says in an interview.

Clawson was preparing for a confrontational on-camera interview with O'Dell about his ties to the Communist Party, when CNN pulled the plug on his investigation. "I was told the decision had been made at the highest level of CNN," Clawson tells me. "Burt Reinhart, Ted Kavanau, and [news director] Ed Turner gave the orders to stop my investigation on the pretext that they didn't want to hit blacks and that it was old news. In 1983, at the height of the Cold War, I thought it was big news for an American presidential candidate to have as his top international advisor someone who had been a card-carrying Communist." CNN disagreed.[37]

Ted Kavanau, Clawson's direct boss at the CNN investigative unit, angrily denies that he conveyed the orders to shut down Clawson's investigation, but, in repeated exchanges with the author, could provide no explanation for how or why that investigation was shut down by CNN. Nor in his multiple protests does he once suggest that he stood up to the CNN mass on behalf of Clawson or his story.

Nevertheless, on the November 14, 1983, edition of *Crossfire*, conservative columnist Pat Buchanan popped the question about Jack O'Dell.

Jackson: O'Dell is not a Communist; he is a Catholic and has been involved with Dr. King's organization.

Buchanan: He's not a Communist?

Jackson: Jack O'Dell is not a Communist.

Buchanan: Was he a Communist?

Jackson: Not to my knowledge.[38]

After that brief exchange, Jack O'Dell became a nonissue for the remainder of Jackson's 1984 campaign.

NEW YEAR'S WITH HAFEZ

As the aircraft door swung open in the starlit desert night at Damascus airport on December 31, 1983, Jesse Jackson emerged with his arms outstretched, flashing the V-for-victory salute. Flashbulbs punctuated the dark as Syrian deputy foreign minister Issan al Naeb and U.S. ambassador to Syria Robert P. Pagnelli went to greet him on the tarmac. "My presence shows our interest in this effort," Pagnelli glumly told the press.[39] For three weeks, Pagnelli had been deep in negotiations with the Syrians for the release of navy lieutenant Robert O. Goodman Jr., a black flyer downed over south Lebanon during a bombing mission in support of U.S. peacekeepers who had come under hostile fire from Syrian-backed forces. Now Jackson was about to upstage Pagnelli and his boss, President Reagan.

Behind Jackson, far from the flashbulbs of the press, was his closest advisor, Jack O'Dell, who had set up the trip with Assad's people. Also along for the ride was Mary Tate of the U.S. Peace Council.[40] What were these two pro-Soviet activists doing with Jackson, and why was he cozying up to Hafez al Assad, a top Soviet ally in the Middle East?

All week long, Jackson and his PR team had done their best to embarrass Reagan. "Our problem is the President has a war policy and a weapons policy when what we need is a peace policy," Jackson told the *New York Times* in a rambling interview. Reagan's blind support for Israel and his unjust war in Lebanon were bad for America, he insisted. "The bottom line is more Americans were killed and now Lieutenant Goodman is a prisoner of war, an undeclared war in Syria," he said.[41] Jackson's PR man Don Rose made sure Jackson's efforts to secure Goodman's release dominated the headlines over the Christmas week, suggesting that for all the billions Reagan was spending on defense he was unable to secure the release of "the only American POW in the world."[42] The contrast was clear, and Jackson exploited it to the utmost. The American commander in chief was powerless to do what a simple Country Preacher could accomplish through good will and a sincere dedication to peace. Syrian dictator Hafez al Assad obliged Jackson's passion play, allowing him to meet the imprisoned Goodman later the same day—in the presence of American photographers, to boot! Several days later, Jackson flew home with Goodman on board the U.S. Air Force VC-137 once used by Secretary of State Henry Kissinger. It was only "poetic justice," Jackson claimed, without a hint of irony, that Lieutenant Goodman had grown up in New Hampshire, where Jackson was facing off with his Democratic rivals in the upcoming presidential primary.[43]

The first question Jackson was asked by reporters when he stepped out of the plane back in Washington was who paid his hotel bills in Syria. It turned out that it was the Syrian government. Visibly annoyed, Jackson pledged to repay the $1,140 tab, but President Reagan swept aside the allegations that Jackson had been bought by the Syrians. "You don't quarrel with success," he said, and extended a hero's welcome to both Jackson and Lieutenant Goodman at the White House. (While Jackson was hobnobbing with Assad, actor Charlton Heston was in Beirut giving moral encouragement to U.S. troops now on combat duty, but his mission received scarcely a mention in the U.S. press.)

In hindsight, Jackson's trip to Damascus was predictable, although at the time it was greeted with surprise, skepticism, and disbelief that he had charmed one of the world's most dour dictators. Jackson's hidden agenda—or the fact that he had powerful friends whose purposes he fulfilled, wittingly or not—went unnoticed.

Syria at that time was a key asset in the Soviet strategy to destabilize Israel, force the United States to withdraw from Lebanon, and reduce American presence throughout the Middle East. I witnessed many of these Soviet maneuvers first hand. On April 18, 1983, I was interviewing a former Lebanese president, Camille Chamoun, when a powerful explosion rocked the windows of his East Beirut apartment. I hastily excused myself and hopped in a cab, crossing over the checkpoint into predominantly Muslim West Beirut, following the ambulance sirens to the sparkling Mediterranean coast. As we approached, police blocked the road, and U.S. Marines whose faces were blackened with blood and grime wandered about aimlessly as if stunned. Medics with blood-smeared white smocks and red crescents were hustling stretchers over concrete blocks and bits of smoldering furniture, carrying wounded comrades from the ruins of what had been the U.S. embassy just twenty minutes before. Ambassador Reginald Bartholomew emerged from the ruins a while later, and described how he had been standing at the rear of his seventh floor office when the explosion tore the front of the building off, throwing him to the floor. He eventually inched his way back from the edge and let himself down to the next floor, hand by hand over exposed girders, until he reached an interior staircase that was still intact. It took several years and a highly classified congressional investigation by a retired U.S. Army general to determine that the bomb had been assembled by Iranian-backed Islamic extremists in the basement of the Soviet embassy in Beirut with the help of Syrian intelligence officers.[44] But in the murky intelligence world that was Beirut, the rumors began to fly almost at once that this had been a Soviet-backed Syrian coup, timed to wipe out an entire cadre of CIA operatives who had come to Beirut to meet with the top CIA operations officer for the region, Robert Ames.

I returned to Lebanon in late October 1983, just one week after a second series of murderous attacks wiped out 241 United States Marines stationed near the Beirut International Airport and fifty-six French peacekeeping colleagues at a barracks a few kilometers away. By that point, the Soviets and the Syrians were waging an all-out war to force the United States and its allies to withdraw the multinational peacekeeping force that had allowed Beirut to flourish in ways not seen since Arafat's PLO launched its assault on Lebanon's sovereignty in 1975.

Arafat and Syria's Assad came to blows themselves that year. In June 1983, I was in Damascus when Arafat's convoy limped into town from Lebanon's Bekaa Valley after Arafat had narrowly escaped an assassination attempt. His armor-plated Chevrolet Caprice was riddled with bullet holes. He had been attacked by Syrian-backed PLO rebels, and his driver had been killed. Arafat himself emerged unscathed, and Assad booted him from Damascus that same day. It wasn't the first time the Soviets saw their plans temporarily set back by bloody quarrels among their own clients and proxies. But their primary goal in 1983 and 1984 was to force President Reagan to withdraw the U.S. peacekeepers from Lebanon, and Jesse Jackson fit perfectly into their plans.

In a 1984 study, "To Save the Soul of America" published by the U.S. Peace Council in New York, Geoffrey Jacques explained Jackson's importance to these Soviet efforts. "It is Jesse Jackson's Rainbow Coalition that has brought the issue of peace to the forefront of people's consciousness in many areas the traditional peace movement has failed to reach.... Rev. Jesse Jackson's January trip to Syria may have had its partisan aspects as far as his Presidential candidacy is concerned, but his initiative also strengthened the movement to remove U.S. Marines from Beirut, and helped consolidate a growing resistance to Ronald Reagan's Lebanon policy. With his initiative, Rev. Jackson demonstrated himself to be not only a civil rights leader, but a peace leader as well."[45]

The strategy of joining the international "peace movement" to the domestic civil rights movement was described in great detail in Communist Party literature during the 1950s. What is less known is that it remained a Communist Party and KGB goal well into the 1980s. In a speech to an antiwar and nuclear freeze convention at the Massachusetts Institute of Technology convened by Noam Chomsky in the fall of 1982, Jack O'Dell resuscitated the CPUSA line from the 1950s when he was a clandestine party organizer. "We in PUSH founded our international affairs department in 1976 in response to the events in Soweto.... Fundamentally, our concern is that the dichotomy between foreign policy and domestic policy be ended," he said. "The arms race is directed against the people of the Third World, directly and indirectly. It is also directed against the poorest strata of the working population within the United States and Western Europe." After condemning Israel's war in Lebanon, he called for "unity between the disarmament and non-intervention wings of the peace movement and the coalition that is focusing on anti-racism and human needs work."[46] Jesse Jackson was the leader who brought the two together. The antimilitary rhetoric that marked his 1984 presidential campaign had a familiar ring. It could have been torn directly from the Communist Party playbook by the hand of Jack O'Dell.

Another person whose presence on Jackson's "peace mission" to Damascus went unnoticed would soon be an embarrassment for Jackson. This was Black Muslim leader Louis Farrakhan.[47]

CHAPTER 7

"Hymietown"

JUMBLED FINANCES

Shortly after Jackson's return from Syria, lawyer John Bustamante filed the candidate's first financial disclosure form, which was dissected in the press. Jackson's preliminary income tax return for 1983 showed that he earned $115,000 from speaker's fees and his salary from Operation PUSH. But the campaign failed to disclose how he maintained his opulent lifestyle, his first-class travel, or the origin of the $30,000 certificate of deposit he had placed with First Bank of Cleveland, a bank owned by Bustamante and Jackson's campaign manager, Arnold Pickney.[1] Similarly, no explanation was given of the secret arrangement between Jackson and financial backer Cirilo McSween, whose Independence Bank of Chicago held the mortgages on Jackson's fifteen-room house as well as PUSH headquarters and had received substantial new business from Jackson's shakedown victims. What did come out, to Jackson's anger, was the $200,000 he had received from the twenty-one-nation Arab League following his 1979 embrace of Yasser Arafat, and an additional $350,000 he received two days later from an "anonymous donor," presumably from a related source.[2]

Typical of the confusion was the way those donations were eventually reported: $450,000 to the PUSH Foundation, and $100,000 separately to PUSH-Excel. Bustamante scrambled to bring some order to PUSH finances and record keeping, and filed a jumble of reports with the Ohio and Illinois state authorities that were several years overdue.[3] The reports revealed that the PUSH network "has collected at least $17 million in the past 13 years," including $4.9 million in federal grants, of which $2.1 million "has been improperly accounted for," according to federal auditors.[4] Both the *Washington Post* and the *New York Times* began to explore Jackson's potentially improper practice of soliciting large payoffs from corporations such as Burger King, Heublein, and Coca-Cola after threatening them with consumer boycotts. Noting the PUSH organization's "penchant for secrecy plus an unconventional and ad hoc corporate style," and Jackson's lack of public experience, the *Post* justified its probe by saying his "tenure at PUSH is one of the few litmus tests for gauging his administrative acumen." The results were less than glowing and showed undocumented expenses, commingled accounts, and overlapping organizations. Jackson treated his corporate and nonprofit empire like his personal privy purse. And no records were ever produced publicly on Jackson's "church," recently renamed more modestly People United to *Serve* Humanity. The church owned the building at 930 E. 50th Street that housed Jackson's corporate empire; it collected rents and contributions from undisclosed donors, and made payments and covered expenses, all without a trace.

Jackson tried to explain the jumbled finances of his groups by claiming they were forced "to draw upon a poverty-stricken community for support."[5] In fact, most of the money he used to finance his personal lifestyle and his political activities came from large corporations or federal grants.

The rest came from wealthy cronies, many of whom benefited from Jackson's activities.

One of these was George Johnson, a Chicago magnate and early Jackson supporter who made a fortune in black beauty products, and a founding trustee of the PUSH Foundation.[6] For years Jackson pushed Johnson's products at his Saturday morning meetings. Johnson gave cash to the PUSH Foundation, providing himself with a significant tax break (since the contributions were tax deductible), and giving Jackson a valuable source of funds.

The trust agreement filed with the Ohio state attorney general's office by Bustamante when he set up the PUSH Foundation in 1972 gave PUSH Inc. authority to designate the foundation's trustees should its board become vacant because of death or resignation. The foundation showed an average income during the 1970s of around $500,000. The foundation's 1978 IRS return, the only report still on file with the Ohio attorney general, shows income of $650,000 and assets valued at $114,136, although it does not specify the origin of the money. PUSH Foundation grants for 1978 totaled $506,586 with almost 98 percent of the money going to three PUSH affiliates, presumably to fund Jackson's day-to-day operations.[7] According to Clovis Maksoud of the Arab League, his group donated $200,000 to Jackson on December 9, 1980, for "shipments of food and medicine and other relief" to Africa. But there is no record of Jackson ever engaging in such activities.[8]

Jackson blamed media criticism of his finances on the Jews. Saying that he wanted to "talk black talk," Jackson confided in black reporter Milton Coleman that he was being unfairly treated by the "Hymies" who controlled the media. The worst of all was the *New York Times*, but what could you expect from "Hymietown"? Coleman included Jackson's remarks near the bottom of a long story on Jackson's campaign, but "Hymietown" would jump to the forefront of public controversy.

"Jesse Jackson has Jews on the brain," commented Nathan Perlmutter of the Anti-Defamation League of B'nai B'rith. "The media is critical? It's the Jews' fault. He doesn't like organized labor? It's the Jews' fault."[9] After what seemed like endless hesitation and denial, Jackson traveled to a synagogue in Manchester, New Hampshire, just days before the New Hampshire primary to deliver a mea culpa. It was hardly convincing.

And it got worse. On March 11, Jackson received the public endorsement of Black Muslim preacher Louis Farrakhan. Well known on Chicago's South Side where he had a much larger following than Jackson himself, Farrakhan had been supporting Jackson quietly from the sidelines, making campaign appearances and raising money as Jackson's approved "surrogate." In a vitriolic sermon delivered at his Final Call Temple in Chicago, Farrakhan blasted reporter Milton Coleman as a "Judas" and a "traitor," and according to *Newsweek*'s Steve Strasser, "came within a rhetorical inch of threatening violent retaliation to anyone who imperiled Jackson's campaign."[10]

In one passage of his sermon, Farrakhan remarked that a Jewish critic had compared him to Adolf Hitler, and said this was a curious criticism since Hitler had been "a great man." At a campaign rally with Jackson, Farrakhan warned Jews: "If you harm this brother, it will be the last one you harm." Jackson, standing a few feet away, said nothing.[11] *Newsweek* called Farrakhan "Jackson's Albatross."

Farrakhan muddied the waters further when on May 28, 1984, he traveled to Tripoli to meet with Libyan leader Colonel Muammar Qaddafi. The visit was announced by the official Libyan news agency, JANA. Qaddafi had loaned $3 million to Farrakhan interest-free in the early 1970s to build a mosque and had maintained extensive dealings with him ever since. The timing of Farrakhan's Libya trip raises serious questions about potential foreign funding of a presidential campaign through straw donors, in exchange for political favors. Jackson subsequently condemned the U.S. bombing of Libya in 1986.[12]

As the primary campaign continued with mixed results, Jackson denounced black voters who supported the Democratic front-runner Fritz Mondale as "Uncle Toms," a tactic that further alienated him from his grassroots. A poll conducted during the final lap of the campaign showed Jackson winning just 31 percent of registered black Democrats, with Mondale favored by 53 percent. The reason, said black academic Adolph L. Reed Jr., was that Jackson appealed to "upwardly mobile and upper-income blacks who saw [his campaign] as a means to further individual business or political careers."[13] Reed argued that Jackson's campaign was "fundamentally anti-democratic," and sought to "reconstitute politics in the black community as a conceptually empty, self-aggrandizing zealotry."[14] Elsewhere, he denounced Jackson's approach as a "strategy of racial brokerage . . . removed from arenas of public scrutiny and participation. It endorses instead a principle of decision making via exclusively private negotiations between corporate and advocacy organization elites." The poor who were supposed to benefit from Operation PUSH were used "as the bargaining capital represented in the dubious threat of boycott." Jackson regarded them merely as "the objectified leverage of an extortionist bluff."[15]

BROTHER NOAH, BLACK CAPITALIST

Jackson's problem with the Jews had one positive benefit: it focused media attention away from where he was potentially most vulnerable—his ties to gang leader Jeff Fort and his Rukn partner, Jackson's half brother Noah Robinson.

Fort and El Rukn were pursued relentlessly through 1983 by Cook County state attorney Richard M. Daley, son of the former mayor. In a series of civil cases, Daley sought to repossess office buildings and apartments the Rukn had allegedly acquired through extortion and theft.[16] In one case, Daley alleged that Fort had transferred ownership of the Rukn fortified headquarters at 3947 S. Drexel Boulevard to his brother for $20 to avoid paying $40,061 in real estate back taxes. On November 9, Jeff Fort pleaded guilty to felony charges in Mississippi that resulted from a federal grand jury investigation into his involvement with a Rukn-led Chicago drug ring.[17] Two weeks later, Fort was placed on the FBI's Most Wanted List when he failed to appear for sentencing. "We will consider him to be dangerous," Stanley Morris, director of the U.S. Marshal Service, told reporters in Washington.[18] Luckily for Jackson, no one covering the national campaign ever wrote about his relationship to Jeff Fort and the El Rukn street gang.

By this point, Fort and the Rukn had also forged close ties to Noah Robinson, who, federal prosecutors say, was angling to replace him as ultimate boss of the Rukn.[19] Noah's name surfaced only briefly as the media probed Jackson's finances. The *Washington Post* noted that "the candidate's half-brother, wealthy Chicago businessman Noah Robinson, was granted a fountain distributorship by Coca-Cola a month after the covenant was signed with Operation PUSH in August."[20] But the *Post* let the story drop. The few media mentions of Noah also failed to identify his connections to the Chicago street gangs and glossed over his shady business deals. Noah was a successful black businessman who liked to boast that he would finish the 1980s as a "hundred-million-dollar-man."

Chicago's *Dollars & Sense* magazine profiled Robinson in its August/September issue. "Only 42 years old, Robinson already has contract rights to a total of 61 Wendy's Old Fashioned Hamburgers and Bojangles' Chicken 'n' Biscuits fast food franchises in the New York and Chicago areas, which ranks him as one of America's preeminent fast-food operators," it wrote glowingly. Robinson was "black America's best kept business secret."[21]

As with much that Noah Robinson touched, there was a great deal of hype in that description. His one-story office at 10842 S. Michigan was a rat trap, with the front door opening onto an improvised pool hall, shown in lurid police photographs that later became part of the state's evidence against him.[22] It wasn't really sixty-one fast food restaurants but closer to a dozen, and most were just getting started. His ambitious plans called for opening ten new restaurants every year in Chicago, plus an additional one in New York. "That's a yeoman's task," said Ron Reinke, vice president of sales and development for Wendy's International, which granted him the concession. "Anything over three stores a year takes an extraordinary effort. It would be rare in my estimation to open five stores a year."[23] But Robinson claimed he had plenty of staff. Once his empire began to crumble, it became apparent that many of his "staff" were members of the El Rukn street gang.[24]

But Noah Robinson was on a roll in 1984. He'd survived a federal grand jury probe led by Scott Lassar, the crack financial crimes prosecutor in the U.S. attorney's office in Chicago. Lassar had seized Robinson's files at the Breadbasket Commercial Association, the nonprofit agency he had set up with Jesse more than a decade earlier. Lassar interviewed their current and former employees and subpoenaed Robinson's corporate records.[25] Lassar was guided by a scathing twenty-six-page confidential audit by the Metropolitan Sanitary District of Greater Chicago, which had awarded Robinson millions of dollars in minority set-aside contracts.[26] That report blasted Robinson's "minority" firm as a front for white businesses after examining payroll records and finding that only 10 percent of those employed on the set-aside contracts were actually minorities. The auditors recommended removing Robinson's firm from the list of approved minority contractors, although it had already won twelve subcontracts worth $4.3 million. "The benefits and advantages promised to the minority community are not being realized as was intended," the auditors concluded.[27]

And that was just for starters. When the report was finally released, its devastating conclusion became crystal clear. After examining Robinson's payroll, the auditors found:

- Electrical work subcontracted to the Robinson group was later subcontracted to Tunnel Electric Inc., a "white" contractor, without prior approval
- Trucking services supposedly being performed by Robinson's companies were "being accomplished with the prime contractor's trucks and employees who are temporarily being paid through the Robinson Group"
- Minority employees shown as working on district jobs were "in fact working on other jobs or not working at all"

The report concluded: "All of the employees of the minority joint ventures are employees of the majority (white) contractor. We cannot find work force participation by the minority firms."[28]

U.S. Attorney Thomas Sullivan came to a similar conclusion after a year-long grand jury probe in 1979 when he sent a letter to the director of the Environmental Protection Agency, which was providing money for the minority set-aside contracts. While he found no evidence that Robinson had broken the law, he had serious questions. "It appears that in a substantial number of contracts awarded by the Metropolitan Sanitary District, the set-aside contracts are going to white contractors whose ventures with minorities are a facade," he wrote.[29] During the first two years of the affirmative action program in Chicago, Noah Robinson was estimated to have received fully half of the set-aside contracts. Despite these challenges, the Department of Commerce continued to award the BCA its yearly $153,000 grant.[30]

Not only did Noah beat the auditors and a federal grand jury, he eventually won an additional $33 million in government contracts between 1979 and 1984. Jesse and Noah must have thought they were invulnerable. Noah recruited gang members to help Jackson's campaign and Jackson praised the Rukn publicly for helping get out the vote—and no one blinked.[31] "I complement Jesse," Noah said modestly during the campaign. "He's high profile, I'm low profile; he likes to shout about it, I like to make money."[32] Jesse made a similar comment, contrasting their personalities. "I'm not interested in making money," he said. "Noah is interested in making money because that's what his interest is. . . . It's hard for Noah to relate to my value system, and it's hard for me to relate to his."[33]

Noah put his hand to anything where there was a minority set-aside. At one point, he briefly won a contract to run the cafeterias at the City Colleges of Chicago, but lost it when his sham companies couldn't provide the service.[34] Undaunted, he turned around and tried to win a competitive contract to provide engineering and custodial services to the colleges. When he was underbid he cried racism, but the college was so disgusted by his antics and the gang members who worked for him that it hired elsewhere.[35]

Robinson returned frequently to his hometown of Greenville, South Carolina, as did Jesse Jackson, who purchased a home there for his mother in 1984 for $40,000. Robinson briefly operated the Rolls Royce Car Wash in Greenville, then bought a bar called the Sterling Tiger Lounge. "He was a big guy in Greenville. There was a Robinson building. He owned businesses, real estate. He was a big fish in a small pond and it made him very self-important," says federal prosecutor Victoria J. Peters.[36] It was in Greenville that Noah's house of cards would come crumbling down.

MY FRIEND FIDEL

Jackson visibly gloated at his success as he paced back and forth in the VIP lounge at Havana's Jose Marti Airport with Cuban dictator Fidel Castro. The Country Preacher had just "negotiated" the release of Cuban political prisoners and American detainees, something none of his Democratic rivals for president had done, and now he and Castro were discussing how they would announce the deal. Dressed in his customary military fatigues, Castro pulled out a handmade Cohiba cigar and handed it to Jackson, who waved it about with relish. When a reporter called out that a Baptist minister might not want to actually light it, Jackson snapped back with good humor: "This is not a cigar. This is a peace pipe!" Then he made a show of taking a light from Castro and blowing smoke for all the reporters to see. "Havana has been good to me," he said. "But Washington, here I come."[37]

Jackson began the six-nation, four-day tour in Panama, where he blasted the U.S. administration of the Canal Zone as "the worst dimension of American segregation and South African apartheid."[38] Jackson was hoping that the whirlwind tour through Central America and the Caribbean would win him a seat at the foreign policy table of the Democratic Party once Walter Mondale won the November 1984 election against Reagan.

Traveling to El Salvador, Jackson urged the anticommunist government of President Jose Napoleon Duarte to "negotiate" with communist rebels, but in Managua, Nicaragua, he urged the Sandinistas to smash the anticommunist rebels confronting them. At the Managua airport, he gushed, "We know how long you have fought and suffered in the battle for peace and justice... We know that now, even after having won your revolution, you must still defend the sovereignty and integrity of your nation against those who would invade your borders, mine your harbors, disrupt your economy and murder your citizens." The Marxist Sandinista regime offers "hope" and "charity," he said.[39] In an interview with *Marxism Today*, the organ of the British Communist Party, he called President Reagan a "sponsor" of state terrorism for backing the Contras in Nicaragua.

But the real homecoming was Cuba. Jackson greeted the crowd specially assembled for him on the tarmac at the Havana airport with cries of "Long live Fidel Castro! Long live Che Guevara! Long live Patrice Lumumba!" At the University of Havana, he punched the air with his fist clenched in the Communist Party salute while leading students to chant these same slogans.[40] Castro returned the courtesy, calling Jackson "the most honest, courageous politician I have ever met," a "brilliant man with a great talent, capable of communicating with people, very persuasive, reliable, honest." After the two huddled together for eight hours in the Palace of the Revolution, Jackson told the press that he and Castro "had a lot of common understanding" and "identify with a lot of the same people in Africa and Central America."[41]

To aid his election campaign, Castro handpicked a group of twenty-two Americans for release to Jackson with the same care he devoted to selecting his cigars. Most had been jailed in Cuba on drug charges. *Newsweek* quoted an unnamed Reagan aide: "Castro's got to be going ho ho...he has given us a bunch of drug dealers and hopheads." Just as Jackson was preparing to leave, the Cuban dictator announced he would also free twenty-seven Cuban political prisoners who had family members in the United States, most of whom were nearing the end of twenty-year jail terms.

When Jackson's plane landed at Dulles Airport in Washington, U.S. immigration officials popped his balloon, immediately arresting six of the freed Americans on outstanding federal or state drug warrants. At Jackson's press conference, the one Cuban political prisoner whom he allowed to speak, poet Andres Vargas Gomes, said he was grateful to be free but turned to his liberator. "To go to Cuba to join in a moral offensive with Fidel Castro is more than morally offensive," he said, facing Jackson. "It is a moral offense." Visibly stung by the rebuke, Jackson mumbled something about Vargas's comment being a tribute to "what makes America America . . . the right to express ourselves and different points of view." But the *New York Times* also blasted Jackson in its lead editorial the next day. "These prisoner deals demonstrate no diplomatic skill on Mr. Jackson's part. On the contrary, they confirm his lack of it. How much skill does it take, after all, to flatter the interests and views of another government against those of your own and thus to cadge a favor from a dictator?"[42]

Many years later, the former State Department coordinator of Cuban affairs during the Reagan administration, Kenneth N. Skoug Jr., revealed that Jackson's real motivation behind the prisoner release was to avoid prosecution in the United States, since it was then illegal for Americans to travel to Cuba. Jackson's trip, says Skoug, was "designed to promote his own candidacy for the presidency and to embarrass the Reagan administration. . . . Only when he learned that travel to Cuba was subject to the embargo and would require some humanitarian action to justify his trip did Mr. Jackson agree with the State Department to seek the release of long-term political prisoners."

But Castro at first wouldn't go for it, and only offered common criminals. That's when Jackson disappeared for long closed-door discussions with Castro. "After State Department spokesman John Hughes warned that the release of these people did not qualify as a humanitarian action, Mr. Jackson then persuaded Castro to release twenty-six long-term prisoners of conscience, with the condition that the United States would have to take them all, immediately, in the company of Mr. Jackson."[43]

In addition to Jack O'Dell, who helped set up the trip, Jackson was aided by Jorge Lawton, a former advisor to Chile's Marxist president, Salvador Allende. Lawton had worked for Senator Frank Church during the 1974–75 hearings that exposed worldwide CIA covert operations, which director of Central Intelligence William Colby called the agency's "crown jewels." As Jackson's chief interpreter, Lawton "also participated in conversations between the candidate and representatives of the Salvadoran guerrillas."[44]

Jackson never revealed who financed the trip, but Ernest Green, who helped with logistics, said that total costs could "be in excess of $250,000–$300,000." Jackson campaign aide Eugene Wheeler said supporters had been asked to donate to a separate "humanitarian fund" that was controlled by campaign attorney Edward Coaxum, but never revealed how much the "special fund" raised, who contributed to it, or whether it had been incorporated. Then he dropped what in any other campaign would have been a bombshell: the Cuban and Nicaraguan governments picked up part of the tab.

In Havana, Castro lodged Jackson and his delegation in government guest houses that were "the kind you would find in Beverly Hills.... There was no bill, there were no charges for this. There was no money to pay for this because we were just guests. In Managua," Wheeler added, "it was very much the same, though with less flair."[45]

The reason Wheeler was so quick to admit that Jackson had accepted gratuities from Fidel Castro was a U.S. law that made it a felony for U.S. citizens traveling to Cuba to spend money there. The law allowed Americans to apply for an exemption if the Cuban government paid all the costs. Assistant Treasury Secretary John M. Walker Jr. revealed that Jackson had applied for an exemption on June 20—just days before starting his trip—which was granted with the proviso that his entourage could not "spend a dime" while in Havana.

But there was a catch: laws governing the use of the nearly two million dollars in federal matching funds Jackson had received made it illegal to accept money or other assistance from a foreign government for campaign-related activity. This caused Wheeler to insist, incredibly, that the Cuba and Nicaragua trip was "not considered part of Jackson's campaign for the Democratic presidential nomination," *the Washington Post* noted. But the reporters who covered the trip were the same ones who were covering Jackson's campaign, and the excessive fares they and the Secret Service agents assigned to Jackson paid, "substantially reimbursed" the cost of Jackson's chartered aircraft, Walker said. If Fritz Mondale had taken a trip at the peak of the campaign at the invitation and expense of Communist

China or even a U.S.-ally such as South Korea, it would have generated a media feeding frenzy. When Jesse Jackson did it, it didn't even make the front page.

While Jackson made no bones about his hard-left agenda, he had more problems with Louis Farrakhan, who had been stealing headlines from him during his trip. In another sermon to followers in Chicago, Farrakhan called the creation of the state of Israel an "outlaw act" and termed U.S. support for Israel a "criminal conspiracy." He went on to call Judaism a "gutter religion," a comment that had Democrats cringing because of Farrakhan's open support for Jackson. Farrakhan frequently provided the security detail for Jackson's campaign appearances from his "Fruit of Islam" militia.

Jewish leaders demanded that presumptive Democratic presidential nominee Fritz Mondale "screw up enough courage" to repudiate Jackson if he refused to speak out against Farrakhan.[46] In the end, Jackson had his staff issue a statement characterizing Farrakhan's remarks as "reprehensible and morally indefensible." But he refused repeatedly when questioned directly by reporters to utter the rebuke in person. And at the next Saturday morning PUSH meeting in Chicago, Jackson sat on stage alongside Abdul Akbar Muhammad, Farrakhan's right-hand man, a stunning display of solidarity at a time when Farrakhan's racist and anti-Semitic remarks had become a national scandal.[47]

SHAKING DOWN THE DNC

Jackson's 1984 presidential campaign resembled in key aspects the corporate boycotts and shakedowns he had been practicing for the previous fifteen years. As Walter Mondale moved closer to claiming the nomination that summer, Jackson pouted and Mondale's advisors squirmed. At one point, they were not even sure he would show up at the Democratic National Convention in San Francisco, because he had not been promised a cabinet slot if Mondale won. Eventually Jackson did go, but only when he was told his speech would be scheduled for prime time television. Most commentators agree that the July 17, 1984, speech was the best performance of his life.

Jackson campaign chairman Richard Hatcher, claiming to represent the "black leadership family," presented a detailed list of demands to the Mondale camp if they wanted Jackson's support:

1) Black input on the expenditure of the $30 billion for social programs;

2) A major domestic policy speech on or about Aug. 29 which includes black issues ([Representative Charles] Rangel and [Representative Walter] Fauntroy involved);

3) Senior black policy person—public announcement;

4) One-half of voter registration funds under control of [Jackson advisor and now Mondale staff appointee] Ernie Green for black voter registration programs throughout the nation;

5) Meeting with blacks at invitation of Vice President Mondale (Mondale must attend), Gerry [Ferraro] and all senior staff within next 10 days per Ernie Green;

6) Major foreign policy address that covers all black international concerns; C. Rangel and W. Fauntroy for input;

7) On-going regular base touching with [Mondale campaign advisor Bob] Beckel by Hatcher group.[48]

It was a sweeping array of concessions, more in line with a PUSH-led corporate "covenant" than a political platform, and Jackson intended to hold Mondale's feet to the fire. When Mondale groused in August that Jackson had not given him the public support he had promised, Jackson shot back on ABC's *Good Morning America*: "I'm not really aboard. I'm not part of the inner circle, for example. I'm not part of the policy-making arrangement."[49] Then he unveiled the gloved fist: "Without the black voters voting in great numbers, the Democratic Party cannot win. The black vote has been more loyal to the Democratic Party than the Jewish vote or the labor vote, or any vote." It was the ultimate political shakedown.

Not only did he intend, as his advisors explained, to move the Democratic Party far to the left; he also aspired to recruit Arab-Americans to the party, and with them weaken the party's ties to American Jews and to Israel. That could be a primary reason Jackson never denounced Louis Farrakhan and indeed continued to appear with him and cultivate his support in subsequent years.

Jackson's insistence that Mondale hire campaign aide Ernest Green showed that he had mastered the first rule of politics: place your own people in positions of power. Green would give Jackson intelligence and leverage over Mondale's campaign, which he used to advance his own agenda and his political career. He also made sure that Alexis Herman was brought into the circle of power, and got her named chairwoman of the National Commission on Working Women.[50] Another Jackson friend, Ron Brown—then a Washington lawyer and part-time political operative—was given a slot on the Democratic National Committee, where he could have a say in crafting the rules for the 1988 primaries.

Meanwhile, Chester Davenport, another former top Carter administration appointee not yet associated with Jackson's entourage, was working his way up the corporate and financial ladder. Teaming up with Washington attorneys Keith A. Seay and Stanton D. Anderson, Davenport rescued the floundering Berkley Federal Savings Bank of Norfolk, Virginia, in a deal that would earn him millions. Davenport worked with federal regulators to turn the depositor-owned company into a stock-owned company. Only a few thrifts—black or white—had made such a conversion, but those risking it showed considerable growth. By 1985, Berkley Federal Savings, which had a negative net worth of almost $500,000 when Davenport took over, showed a plus of $1.5 million and had increased its assets by almost 75 percent, to $23.6 million.[51] Jackson targeted Davenport as another black businessman who should contribute to his fortunes. The payback would come years later, but it would be worth the wait.

AN OPPORTUNITY AT COORS

Jackson returned briefly after the Democratic National Convention to Operation PUSH, joining a proposed boycott of the Adolph Coors Company of Golden, Colorado, that was being led by the NAACP and the

AME Church. The nation's fifth largest brewery, Coors was a family-owned business run by staunch conservatives who were major backers of Ronald Reagan and conservative causes. Since 1977, organized labor had led a boycott against Coors following a bitter strike when Coors workers voted the union out. Joseph Coors Sr. was later hauled before a congressional committee when Iran-Contra investigators learned he had donated a $65,000 airplane to "freedom fighters" in Nicaragua.[52] But it wasn't until William Coors—considered a political moderate compared to his brothers—made a careless remark in a 1984 speech to black businessmen in Denver that Jesse Jackson and the NAACP took note of the company. Coors told his audience they should be grateful that slave traders "drag[ged] your ancestors over here in chains" from Africa, since today they had greater freedom in America.[53] The remark caused an uproar in the local papers and caught the attention of the national race brokers, who sniffed an opportunity.

Jackson never said a word about Coors during the campaign, but once it was over he joined an ad hoc National Black Economic Development Coalition led by the NAACP's Fred Rasheed, who for several months had been negotiating a deal with Coors to avert a black consumer boycott. Announced on September 17, the "national incentive covenant" committed the company to spending $325 million over a five-year period to expand opportunities for black employees and increase transactions with black businesses.[54] Coors also committed to involve blacks in the formation of corporate policy "from upper management to the board of directors," and in May 1989 appointed a black director, J. Bruce Llewellyn, when the first nonfamily members were named to the board. Included in the deal were up front "contributions" of $600,000 in cash to the boycott partners, including Operation PUSH.[55] The next year Coors announced it was expanding its sales into the Chicago area and to other Midwestern and Eastern states with heavy minority populations,[56] so the payoff was a small price that packed big returns. And Coors kept up the payments, giving Jackson another $20,000 at a PUSH fundraiser in Chicago in 1987.[57]

Needless to say, organized labor was disappointed at what they called the "defection" by Jackson and the NAACP of their long-standing boycott. The Colorado state AFL-CIO president chalked it up to the Reagan-era "economic climate."[58] One thing that separated Jackson from his hard-left advisors was his willingness to cut deals with management at the expense of organized labor, which he denounced as a "special interest" during the 1984 campaign. "As black leaders' racial agendas become ever more targeted to upper income, upper status black interests—as the focus of the 'fair share agreements' exemplifies—the programmatic basis for unity with the labor movement's social agenda recedes," leftist academic Adolph Reed moaned.[59] Jackson didn't want to kill the goose that laid the golden eggs; he wanted the eggs.

Money Matters

Jackson never really stopped running for president between 1984 and 1988—and that meant a constant need for cash. He continued to hold fundraisers throughout the November 1984 election—not for the Mondale-Ferraro Democratic ticket, but to retire his own campaign debt. Campaign coordinator Arnold Pinkney said that Jackson had spent $3.6 million as of August 1984 and still owed more than $360,000.[60] But an audit by the Federal Election Commission found much higher numbers. Jackson had underreported receipts by $826,000 and expenditures by more than $1 million, the FEC said.[61] When the campaign closed its books on September 30, 1985, total receipts stood at $9,146,402, according to an FEC print-out obtained through the Freedom of Information Act.[62]

At a fundraiser in Chicago only a few weeks after the 1984 Democratic National Convention, Jackson told PUSH members in Chicago he wanted them to "pay the lion's share" of his debts. "I didn't just run for President, PUSH gave me an assignment," he said. "We must pay off our own debt." In his southern preacher's style, he called for anyone in the crowd who would make out a check then and there for $1,000; when no takers stood up, he called for $500, and then $250. Finally, a couple stood up and said they would each write a check. Jackson thanked them, saying (erroneously) it would be matched dollar for dollar by federal funds to make their combined contribution worth $1,000 to the campaign.[63]

Having to deal with federal election regulations that required financial disclosure and limited contributions to $1,000 per person taught Jackson important lessons. He couldn't use campaign money as a slush fund to pay his personal expenses, nor could he just ask his friends to pick up the tab. He had to have a visible means of support. On the advice of attorney John Bustamante he set up a "speaker's bureau" called Personalities International Inc. in August 1984, which he ran out of his house on S. Constance Avenue, but ultimately registered in Delaware, where financial records are protected by the strictest corporate secrecy laws in America. According to the initial financial disclosure form he filed when he announced his second run for president in 1988, Personalities earned him $192,090 between January 1986 and October 6, 1987. He provided no records for earnings before then, and the state of Delaware rejected reporters' inquiries, claiming that the information was confidential. But in October 1986, Jackson gave an indication of how much he expected to earn when he signed a one million dollar per year contract with a Hollywood talent agent called the Agency for the Performing Arts, which guaranteed him that amount as a minimum for speaking engagements, television and radio appearances, as well as a newspaper column. The agency sued Jackson for $10.1 million soon afterwards, alleging he had reneged on the contract.[64] When they demanded access to Jackson's financial records, Jackson settled out of court.

Jackson campaign advisor Arnold Pinkney had less luck. When he returned to private life in Cleveland after the campaign, he became embroiled in a scandal involving municipal contracts, and was eventually given an eighteen-month suspended prison sentence for having an unlawful interest in a contract let out by the Cleveland-Cuyahoga County Port Authority.[65]

RETURN TO VIENNA

At the urging of his foreign affairs advisor Jack O'Dell, Jackson flew to Vienna on January 25, 1985, to address the Third Vienna Dialogue for Disarmament and Detente, an international confab organized under the auspices of the World Peace Council, which the U.S. Information Agency called "the foremost Soviet front."[66]

On the official roster of participants Jack O'Dell was listed as a member of the executive committee of SANE, a hard-left antinuclear advocacy group, in addition to his affiliations to PUSH and *Freedomways*, the magazine closely tied to the Communist Party. The Soviet delegation was led by Radomir Georgievich Bogdanov, identified by the House Select Intelligence Committee in 1982 as a senior KGB disinformation officer. Bogdanov first met World Peace Council chairman Romesh Chandra while posted as KGB *rezident* (station chief) to New Delhi from 1957 to 1967.[67] By the time Jesse Jackson met him in late January 1985, Bogdanov was using a cover position at the "Soviet Academy of Science Institute of U.S. and Canada Studies" to maintain control over the World Peace Council.

Jackson's direct involvement with the World Peace Council has never been reported.[68] In his January 27, 1985, speech in Vienna he warmly congratulated KGB agent of influence Romesh Chandra for his work in favor of "the cause of peace," and displayed detailed knowledge of the World Peace Council and its activities, which he called "our movements for peace and justice."

"The use of fronts, of course, is as old as Lenin," said Dewitt S. Copp, a U.S. Information Agency specialist in Soviet active measures. "Their purpose since the end of World War II has been twofold. One is to advance the Soviet policy line, whatever that line may be, and [two] to do so while attempting to convince noncommunists and Third World audiences that they speak freely and are not under Soviet influence or control." The conference Jackson was attending "was organized and directed covertly by the World Peace Council," he said, with the goal of blocking the deployment of U.S. cruise and Pershing II missiles in Europe, and opposing the U.S. Strategic Defense Initiative.[69]

In his speech, Jackson lashed out at President Reagan's military spending, referring to the Strategic Defense Initiative as "this Star Wars adventure...this madness," and called for "a new international economic order." He went on to describe his 1984 election platform as "a more humane and effective way of conducting public policies," and said it included advocacy of the following points:

- "A pledge by the United States of no first use of nuclear weapons..."
- "The restoration of serious dialogue between the United States and the Soviet Union designed to complete a treaty of comprehensive disarmament"
- "...An end to all covert operations designed to overthrow the government of our neighbor, Nicaragua"
- "Recognition of the right of the Palestinian people to self-determination and state sovereignty as the key to peace in the Middle East..."
- "The normalization of diplomatic, economic, and cultural relations with Cuba"
- "A new Africa policy based upon... an end to U.S. corporate and governmental relations with the racist apartheid regime [in] South Africa... 20 percent real cut in the military budget"[70]

It was a plan worthy of Moscow Central, but delivered by a genuine American politician. Jack O'Dell's SANE paid for Jackson's trip.[71]

Later that same year, Jackson crashed the first summit between President Reagan and the new Soviet Communist Party secretary general, Mikhail Gorbachev, in Geneva. He was granted a private audience by Gorbachev, and received flattering headlines back in Washington.[72] Gorbachev's job before assuming supreme power in Moscow had been as commissar of the Party's so-called administrative organs, where he supervised the entire Soviet intelligence apparatus, including the efforts to co-opt the antinuclear movement.

NOAH'S FIRST STUMBLE

To counter charges of unfairness and racism, the Reagan administration expanded minority set-asides after the 1984 elections, and Jesse Jackson's half brother Noah Robinson saw opportunities everywhere. The emperor of Bojangles and Burger King even bid on a contract for snow removal at the Chicago airports, teaming up with well-connected black businessman Clarence McClain, who was a close friend of Mayor Harold Washington.[73] "There's millions and billions out there for blacks," McClain said, scarcely hiding his greed.[74]

With McClain's political connections and Jesse's clout, Robinson figured he could do anything. With great fanfare he announced that he was setting up a steel company with McClain to compete for minority set-asides on mega-construction projects, including the $138 million dollar "people mover" system at O'Hare International Airport.[75] A deal of that size attracted major league players—Westinghouse Corporation and Matra of France—but they all needed minority partners. Robinson bet heavily on the third bidder, Urban Transportation Development Corporation, Ltd., of Toronto. When it looked as if they would lose, Robinson called in his chits. He called Jesse. At his Saturday morning PUSH meeting on March 30, 1985, Jackson urged the city to reject the low bidder, Matra, because of its business ties to South Africa. He asked Mayor Harold Washington to reject Westinghouse for the same reasons. That left Noah Robinson's Canadian partner the only company left standing. A Jackson spokesman said he hadn't known of Robinson's interest in the bidding until after research had been done on the three companies a month earlier.[76]

With friends in City Hall, and a high-powered half brother who could come through in a pinch, Noah Robinson's goal of building a $100 million business empire appeared within reach. But then the troubles began.

The first incident was so minor he got off after posting $100 bail. It began late one Saturday night when the police noticed his car parked illegally in a crosswalk. As the patrol car approached, the policemen saw Noah rush out of a building. When he saw the police, he dropped a blue handbag on the sidewalk. The police picked it up and found it contained a forty-five-caliber revolver and several pieces of identification. It wasn't a big deal in South Side Chicago. After all, Robinson made the rounds of his fast food restaurants every night, and it wouldn't have been unusual for someone in his position to be armed. He offered no explanation for why he had left the gun behind.[77]

Then on October 18, 1985, police arrested three young men from the South Side for the murder of Officer Michael Ridges, who had been fatally shot during a routine traffic stop the night before. Ridges had pulled over a car in which Allen Falls, age twenty-two, Ira Jackson, twenty-three, and Dwayne M. Coulter, twenty-seven, were riding. While he was examining Falls's driver's license, Coulter pulled a gun and murdered him. Coulter had a history of crime. Convicted of theft in 1977, he jumped bond on a robbery charge in 1982 and was still wanted by the police. He and his companions were Noah Robinson's men. They were Rukns, street bloods. Their arrest brought the police to Noah's door.

Robinson told police all three had worked for him recently but had been fired for various reasons. Coulter, who used the Rukn alias "Makia," had last worked for Digby's Detective and Security Agency, one of the fronts used by the Rukn to provide jobs for the bloods while they gathered strategic intelligence on likely targets for plunder. Robinson said he fired Coulter in May because he left his restaurant job before his shift was over and took food without paying for it. He also told police that Coulter had posed as an Illinois state trooper and had acquired a badge and a trooper's uniform. He described Falls as a "white-collar guy" who had been assistant manager at a Bojangles chicken joint Noah owned at 47th and Prairie until it closed that May.[78]

Noah hadn't ordered the murder, and he cooperated with the police. But his deep ties to the Rukn were about to come out.

CHAPTER 8

⧉

Brother Noah
Goes Down

A MURDER IN GREENVILLE

El Rukn leader Jeff Fort figured he could beat the system. Despite being sent up for thirteen years on charges of cocaine trafficking in the late 1970s, he still controlled several million dollars' worth of real estate and thousands of gang members. And he had powerful friends, among them Jesse Jackson. Even from jail, Fort managed to negotiate loan guarantees to renovate his group's headquarters at 39th and S. Drexel Boulevard on Chicago's South Side. "Jeff Fort was controlling the gang by telephone from prison," recalls Assistant U.S. Attorney Matthew M. Schneider. "He was on the line hours a day, giving them orders down to the most minute detail."[1] Jackson agreed to help his old friend with the renovation project and called Hollywood star Sammy Davis Jr., who eventually provided a loan guarantee just as he had done many years earlier when Jackson called on him to help the Fellowship Missionary Baptist Church.[2]

Noah Robinson also ponied up, and not just with money. In 1984 he wrote Fort's probation officer at the federal prison in Terre Haute, Indiana, calling Fort "a legend, a great champion of the people . . . a natural leader of men."[3]

> [Fort's] sense of concern for others and willingness to challenge perceived injustice by those in authority has resulted in his being characterized by some as a *dangerous* man. But Jeff's not the first man who's been so accused for so acting.
>
> I know of two other men in history who got in big trouble and eventually lost their lives for the same reason.
>
> Martin L. King, Jr.
>
> Jesus Christ.
>
> History now refers to both as dedicated and determined. Whatever else Jeff might be, he is also dedicated and determined.[4]
>
> [Emphasis in original.]

Federal prosecutors would later learn the reasons for Robinson's solicitude. By this time, Noah had "formed an association with the El Rukns" and was making runs to South Carolina, Detroit, and New York to obtain cocaine and heroin for the Rukn. "In fact, Robinson introduced the El Rukns to numerous drug dealers" from whom they "obtained multiple kilograms of cocaine," trial transcripts and federal court documents show.[5]

One of the keys to communicating with his brothers on the outside was Jeff Fort's conversion to Islam. When he changed the name of the Black P Stone Nation to El Rukn after an earlier jail term, Fort called himself "Malik," imam of the bloods, and swapped the gang's distinctive red beret for a North African-style red fez. Now he was suing the government from his Texas jail cell to get the gang recognized as a religious order, the "Moorish Science Temple of America, El Rukn tribe." The advantage of official recognition was that they could then hold private "religious" services in prison without surveillance. That got Cook County prosecutor Richard M. Daley steamed. "If El Rukn is a religious group," he said, "its sacraments are narcotics trafficking, intimidation, terror, and human sacrifice."[6]

Prosecutors suspected that Jeff Fort could also order murder from jail and were investigating him in connection with the shooting death of a Chicago man named Leroy "Hambone" Barber on January 2, 1986. Barber was shot execution style, with a single bullet in the back of the head, after being called to a pay telephone booth outside Bridges Lounge in Greenville, South Carolina. Bridges was in a shopping plaza owned by Noah Robinson Jr., who had become a big man about town.[7]

Robinson and Barber had grown up together in Greenville and were childhood rivals, but Noah's college education and string of semilegitimate businesses in Chicago gave him a sense of superiority he liked to flaunt. In 1980, Barber came to Chicago and worked for Robinson as a janitor at the City Colleges of Chicago, one of many employees Robinson had brought up from South Carolina. "Noah gave them jobs, he housed them in his tenements down on 109th street, he fed them. It was like the old South, living in the company store," recalls one member of the prosecution team.[8]

That December, Barber and an associate robbed Noah at gunpoint of $2,800. Robinson filed a criminal complaint and testified against him at trial. Barber claimed Robinson had concocted the robbery charge to punish him for refusing orders to burn down a building and beat up a creditor.

Noah sent a venomous handwritten screed to Barber in state prison in Joliet, Illinois, which would come back to haunt him later on. Addressed pointedly to "Miss Leroy Barber N20679," the letter provides extraordinary insight into the character of the man who would subsequently claim he had been persecuted for his blood ties to a Democratic Party presidential candidate, Jesse Jackson.

Fat Boy!

Congratulations on your safe arrival to the Joliet "Joy House," the recreational resort for big time DMF's. I trust your stay will be long and enjoyable, perhaps in time you'll evolve from a *gorilla* into a *gayrilla*. You know you've got that cute, shapely round eye (smiles). Do what you got to do, sweetie. Want me to send you some lipstick and powders?

Having presented you proper greetings, I'll get right to my point....

Given the options readily available to me, in terms of courses of action against you for your betrayal (of my trust), treachery (stealing my money at gun point) and assassination set-up (giving Runt the gun to blow me up in my own office), letting the law have you was the kindest, most considerate move that I could have made on you. You didn't deserve to get get away [*sic*] or have a chance to run....[9]

Noah added a chilling touch of nonchalance to his threat:

I said to myself, let him enjoy, splurge, rip-it up, have fun, because you were already gone. No doubt in my mind. Or yours, either. It was just a matter of time. And place. And method.

Barber felt sufficiently threatened by Noah's letter that he turned it over to prison authorities, who placed it in his file and promptly forgot all about it. Only later, when Noah was in the dock for Barber's murder in South Carolina, would prosecutors stumble upon it and have it read aloud to a stunned Noah Robinson. "Noah was cocky going into that trial," recalls a member of the prosecution team. "Then we present this letter. It was a Perry Mason moment. Noah's defense attorney read the letter aloud in court, then threw it at Noah in disgust. 'Is this yours?' Noah actually grips his head in his hands. It's the first time we ever got to him."[10]

When Barber was paroled in 1984, he returned to Chicago and knocked at Noah's door. Incredibly, Noah hired him back, this time to work in one of his fast food restaurants. But their childhood rivalry broke out repeatedly. In November 1985, Noah accused Barber of responsibility for several break-ins that had occurred at one of Robinson's buildings on South Michigan Avenue. In a fit of disgust, Noah told tenant Carolyn

Harris, "It looks like I am just going to have to kill the nigger just like Jeff [Fort] told me a long time ago."[11]

Fearful of Noah's powerful Rukn friends, Barber moved back to Greenville in December 1985. On December 19, Noah drove home for Christmas, and got into a fistfight with Barber the next evening in a pool hall. Prosecutors later convinced multiple juries that Robinson returned to Chicago in a rage, called Jeff Fort in prison, and hired a Rukn hit team to kill Hambone Barber for $10,000. "Noah should have just walked away from Hambone Barber," says federal prosecutor Matthew M. Schneider. After the murder, Fort directed a lieutenant to "give each member of the hit team $500 and a small amount of cocaine," court documents show.[12]

Barber's murder didn't attract much attention at first. It was far from Chicago, and in South Carolina it was dismissed as a drug killing. No one yet drew the connection back to Noah Robinson. But local police and federal prosecutors had their eye on Robinson's shopping plaza because of an ongoing investigation that culminated in the conviction of a Greenville man named Thomas Allen Burnside on drug charges. Burnside owned What's His Name Disco and Mert's Deli, which leased space from Robinson, and was operating a $1 million-a-year heroin ring in Greenville, New York, Boston, and Bridgeport, Connecticut.

Burnside testified in federal court that he had been working as a courier for Robinson since 1983 traveling to New York, Chicago, Greenville, and Connecticut—coincidentally the same places where he was running dope. Police seized Burnside's phone records and found that he had placed nearly two hundred telephone calls to Robinson over an eighteen-month period, including calls to Robinson's unlisted home telephone number in Chicago and to a motel in Albuquerque, New Mexico.

Robinson told investigators that he and Burnside were childhood friends who had lost contact after high school and met again in 1983, when Burnside walked into one of Robinson's restaurants in New York and Robinson offered Burnside a job. A federal judge sentenced Burnside in 1985 to fifty-four years in jail, but he refused to cooperate with prosecutors or disclose who was behind his drug operation. That would come later, through a bizarre incident that would give prosecutors enough evidence to send Robinson and dozens more Rukn members up the river for life.[13]

CONNING QADDAFI

Noah Robinson thought he had all the bases covered. The Bridges Lounge where his killers encountered Hambone Barber was owned by the local sheriff, who was a friend. And Noah was nowhere near the scene of the crime. He called the Greenville police from New Mexico shortly after he "read about" the murder in the papers, and offered details about his fight with Barber two weeks earlier. He claimed he had left Greenville the next day—not staying for Christmas as he had originally planned—and later presented police with a speeding ticket he had received in Arizona on the day of Barber's murder. It was a great alibi, but it didn't wash.

Unknown to Robinson, the feds had a source they were using to close in on him and Jeff Fort: a Rukn "officer mufti" named Anthony Sumner. Police investigators said Sumner began cooperating with them in 1985 during the Burnside case and eventually "helped police pin at least a dozen homicides on the Rukns." His information on the gang's dope-running operation enabled the FBI to go to a federal grand jury and obtain wire-taps on the telephone at Rukn headquarters on Drexel Boulevard,[14] the building "renovated" thanks to loan guarantees arranged by Jesse Jackson and Noah Robinson. The first crime they uncovered was nothing short of bizarre.

President Ronald Reagan and Libyan leader Colonel Muammar Qaddafi were on a collision course in 1986. In April, the United States launched a spectacular long-distance bombing raid against Tripoli that killed one of Qaddafi's adopted children and wounded another, after the U.S. intercepted Libyan communications to a terrorist team in Germany ordering them to plant a bomb at a popular discotheque in West Berlin. A U.S. serviceman died in the La Belle bombing, and President Reagan was determined that the terrorists could "run, but they cannot hide." But when Jeff Fort and his Rukn cronies first contacted Libyan officials that

March, all they knew was that Qaddafi had spoken favorably of Jesse Jackson and given him some money in the late 1970s, and had offered a three-million-dollar loan to black Muslim leader Louis Farrakhan. For Fort and the Rukn gang, Qaddafi was a soft touch.

The federal wiretaps picked up the gang's efforts to contact the Libyan government from the start. By the time the initial indictment was handed down on October 30, 1986, gang members had made forty-two calls or trips as part of a scheme in which they offered to destroy buildings, vehicles, and property belonging to the U.S. government in exchange for $2.5 million.[15] El Rukn members negotiated the deal with Libyan government officials by phone and in face-to-face meetings in Libya, New York, and Panama, said U.S. Attorney Anton R. Valukas. The indictment alleged that Jeff Fort directed the scheme by phone from a federal prison in Bastrop, Texas, where he was serving a thirteen-year sentence on drug charges. In one taped conversation presented to the grand jury, Fort discussed "shooting a commercial airliner out of the sky."

In another call monitored by police, Fort suggested that gang members use the LAW rocket to blow away Chicago police detectives Richard Kolovitz and Daniel Brannigan, but the FBI pooh-poohed the incident. "They wanted terror targets, not just some threat against a cop," Kolovitz recalls.[16]

The gang had good reason to be angry with Kolovitz and Brannigan after they busted a security firm run by Noah and arrested one of Jeff Fort's brothers. As prosecutors later demonstrated at trial, Noah had set up the corporation, Security and Maintenance Services, so he could put Rukn gang members on his payroll as "security guards" and legally issue them handguns.[17]

With the help of an Illinois state police officer who posed as a gem dealer, Kolovitz and Brannigan set up an elaborate sting operation to entrap Robinson and his partner, Rukn "general" Eugene Hunter, who was running the company under an alias. Thinking they were coming to work at a jewelry exhibition, eighteen Rukns showed up at McCormick Place on the morning of June 19, 1986, six of them carrying their guns.[18]

"We had them come into a room one by one, so we can take their identity and their Social Security numbers," recalls Kolovitz. "They thought it was for payroll, but actually we were booking them."

Then the gang members were escorted one by one outside to the loading dock, where a police paddy wagon was waiting. "We thought we'd have a little fun, so we put this big cardboard box over Detective Brannigan and left him on the loading dock. When the gang members came out, he popped up out of the box: 'Surprise!' I'll never forget the look on their face: 'Aw shit, it's Brannigan!' they said." Chicago police and prosecutors still refer to the incident fondly as "Brannigan in a box."

Things got hotter for Noah Robinson and his friends after that. In August 1986, the feds raided El Rukn headquarters and seized nearly "forty weapons, including firearms, grenades, and an inoperative antitank rocket launcher purchased for $1,900 from an undercover FBI agent," prosecutors said.[19] They also arrested two top Rukns, Alan "General Gangster" Knox, and Tramell "Tacu" Davis. What Tramell Davis began to reveal went way beyond a silly scheme to take Colonel Qaddafi for a ride: it went right to the heart of El Rukn's operation, providing the feds with enough information to hand down a forty-six-count indictment against Jeff Fort and other top Rukns for racketeering, conspiracy, and weapons violations.

The day the indictment was unsealed, the feds arrested another Rukn named Charles Knox on charges of impersonating an attorney while visiting Fort in prison. Later, the noose would close on Noah Robinson as well. But before that happened, Robinson's financial house of cards would collapse, a victim of his own lies and machinations.

THE PERMANENT CAMPAIGN

Between the 1984 and 1988 presidential elections, Jesse Jackson was in permanent campaign mode. He was raising money and traveling abroad extensively, to raise his profile and dodge the scandals that continued to dog him back in Chicago.

In 1985, according to *Time* magazine investigative reporters Jonathan Beaty and Sam Gwynne, Jackson was given the "royal treatment" in Paris by top officers of the Bank of Credit and Commerce International, the BCCI. Bank chairman Agha Hassan Abedi ordered his country manager for France, Nazir Chinoy, to "put Jackson up in Abedi's usual suite at the Paris Hilton and paid some $11,000 for his accommodations there and later at the Hotel George V." In return for Abedi's generosity, Chinoy says Jackson asked "if it would be profitable for BCCI branches if the central banks for different countries banked with BCCI," and said he would "take this up with Abedi" when he next visited him in London.[20] BCCI was later shut down for establishing a massive international criminal conspiracy to bribe foreign leaders, broker arms deals, and cheat its depositors.

In August 1986, Jackson toured some of the worst regimes in Africa, cozying up to pro-Soviet or military dictators in Nigeria, Angola, Mozambique, and Zimbabwe. He billed the trip as an "anti-apartheid" campaign, but Jackson had mixed motives, including financial ones. In a dinner at the presidential palace in Luanda, Jackson brought great comfort to Marxist Angolan president Jose Eduardo Dos Santos by calling for the United States to cut off aide to the UNITA freedom fighters led by Dr. Jonas Savimbi who were threatening his regime.

But Dos Santos was hoping for more than just words: he needed help in ending the U.S. embargo on his regime, which put limits on oil drilling technology Angola could purchase from U.S. companies. In his toast that evening, Dos Santos said he was eager to strengthen business ties with the United States, and Jackson immediately offered to help. "We hope that very soon diplomatic ties will follow trade ties," he added.[21] The next day, Jackson visited the northern province of Cabinda, where U.S. oil giant Chevron was operating a joint venture with the Angolan state-owned firm, Sonangol. There, he told oil field workers: "I want to send a message to the American people that if the Angolans are good enough for us to work and trade with, they should be good enough to have diplomatic relations with."[22] Upon his return to the United States Jackson called repeatedly for the administration to end military aid to UNITA and to recognize the Marxist Dos Santos regime, essentially lobbying for the government of Angola. Once again, at a key Cold War flash point where the Reagan administration was trying to roll back Soviet expansionism, Jackson sided with Moscow.

But it was in Nigeria that real money was in play.

Shortly after General Ibrahim Babangida seized power in a military coup in August 1985, Nigerian business magnate Moshood Abiola came to Washington. The Reagan administration was concerned that General Babangida might halt covert U.S. assistance to UNITA that was flowing through Zaire. As an old friend of the general, Abiola said his top priority was going to be fixing the Nigerian economy, not making trouble in the region. While in Washington, he also met with members of the Congressional Black Caucus—and with Jesse Jackson and Ron Brown. "Abiola was funding the Black Caucus," says Dr. Mobolaji E. Aluko, a prominent Nigerian pro-democracy leader. "He and Jackson knew each other because they were both involved in the reparations issue."[23] According to Karin Stanford, who wrote a doctoral thesis on Jackson's "citizen diplomacy" and went on to give birth to an illegitimate child by Jackson, Abiola had donated "$250,000 to a Jackson-backed campaign to build business links between Africans and African Americans."[24]

Abiola was staying at the Four Seasons Hotel, the most modern luxury hotel in Washington, D.C., with its glass-walled spa and breakfast lounge overlooking the bucolic C&O canal in Georgetown. He welcomed Jackson and Ron Brown to his suite to talk business, and agreed to get Jackson an invitation from General Babangida to visit Nigeria.[25] Shortly afterwards—Jackson says it was through the Nigerian embassy in Washington—General Babangida offered to fly Jackson and a delegation across Africa on the general's own Boeing 707, luxuriously fitted out as a presidential ship of state. "Nigeria offered a plane and we gladly accepted," Jackson says.[26]

Jackson traveled, as always, with a large entourage, including several PR people and reporters, but also businessmen, union leaders, academics, and farming officials. Babangida's jet picked them up in New York and flew the whole traveling circus to Africa where they skipped across eight different nations, then back across the Atlantic to New York.

While in Nigeria, Babangida provided Jackson and his friends with luxury accommodations, as did several of the richer countries they visited.[27] Although Babangida's sponsorship was clear to the reporters who covered the trip, no one seemed to find it unusual that an American civil rights leader, traveling in Africa to denounce South Africa's white government as the 1980s version of Hitler's Third Reich, should fly gratis on the presidential aircraft of a military dictator whose human rights record and corruption were regularly denounced by Nigerian pro-democracy groups.

The Nigeria leg of the tour laid the foundation for a long and potentially profitable relationship. But it would take several years to bear fruit. (Ron Brown was the first to cash in, not long afterwards flying to Nigeria with Portuguese businessman Jose Amaro Pintos Ramos, to help him resolve a blocked communications deal with the Nigerian government. Ramos paid Brown $30,000 for his services, and later arranged for a $108,000 loan to Brown's "longtime friend" Lillian Madsen, one of many cloudy deals that prompted congressional investigations during the Clinton years.)[28]

Jackson had been hoping to return to Africa for the installation of Archbishop Desmond Tutu of South Africa on September 7, but complained that the South African government had singled him out with a "restricted visa" that would not allow him to visit churches, speak publicly, or attend antigovernment demonstrations.[29] But the truth was that Jackson was upstaged by Coretta Scott King and dozens of other U.S. civil rights leaders who were among the 1,000 foreign guests invited to attend and who had agreed not to hold public demonstrations against the government. After pouting at the slight, he claimed victory when the U.S. Senate imposed sanctions on South Africa in October.

The Reagan administration continued its probes of Jackson's handling of the Carter-era grants and in 1987 demanded that he reimburse the government more than $1.4 million he allegedly misspent. Government auditors found that he had established thirty regional outposts of his "Movement" during the grant period, and was crisscrossing the country in style.[30] After years of denying any wrongdoing, Jackson attorney John Bustamante agreed to pay $550,000 to settle all claims and set a schedule for the repayments. The dispute helped to put PUSH-Excel nearly out of business. Jackson's educational venture had boasted revenues topping $2.6 million in 1980, but six years later they had dropped to a mere $209,071. The group ended 1986 saddled with $1.5 million in debts, including the money it owed to the government.[31]

Adding to the bleak picture was a review of PUSH accounts released by Henry L. Creel of the Cleveland accounting firm Tony H. Smith Co. in July 1987. Creel announced that the group's high debts and lack of working capital required him as an auditor "to raise the question of whether the group could survive," although he added: "They have had similar financial problems over the years and always survived." Creel found that at the end of 1985, PUSH owed $325,082 to creditors. He filed a copy of his audit report with the Illinois attorney general's office.[32]

Despite Jackson's financial woes, the Democrats and the mainstream press continued to treat him with kid gloves. In a snap profile, the *National Journal* (an inside the Washington, D.C., Beltway publication) said Democrats "fear alienating him and his constituency but also don't want to create the impression they are appeasing him; Jackson continues to keep up the pressure on the Democrats not to turn to the right." As for the press, constantly criticized by Jackson for investigative coverage, it treated him "as the unelected spokesman for black America and the poor," the *Journal* concluded.[33] Black academic Adolph Reed agreed. "The media anointed Jackson's attempt to gain paramountcy as a black spokesperson." Jackson "consistently has sought attention from media representatives, alternating cajolery with charges of victimization by those who have not been properly supportive of his efforts."[34] Good coverage or bad, the single most important thing the press did for Jesse Jackson was to give legitimacy to his claims to represent the black community. Jackson was a leader by virtue of the press.

NOAH'S EMPIRE COLLAPSES

Noah Robinson was not so lucky. When the *Chicago Tribune* started paying attention to his exploits, it usually meant that trouble was just around the corner.

On August 2, 1987, the *Tribune* published a 2,800-word investigation of Robinson's financial troubles, after learning that Assistant U.S. Attorney William Hogan had prevailed upon a federal grand jury to subpoena the corporate business records of no fewer than twenty firms in which Robinson had a financial interest or control.[35] It turned out that the Robinson firms had filed for bankruptcy seven times since 1975, most of them over the past five years. It was a miserable record for a self-styled financial whiz who had predicted in 1984 that his fast-food and construction business empire would generate $35 million in revenue that year.

Court records that no one had bothered to consult until then showed that four firms he had used successively to operate the cafeterias of the Chicago City Colleges from 1978 through 1982 all went bankrupt, passing the contract from one to the next. (The firms were Stanley Ryan & Associates, Food Service Management, Master Food Service Inc., and First Class Cafeterias.) A fifth firm, Immaculate Maintenance, filed for bankruptcy protection on April 30, 1982 when it had amassed tax debts of $650,000 and back wages of $261,260 on a separate contract with the City Colleges. Shortly after filing for protection, Robinson reported that all the firm's records had been stolen from a van. "The van was not stolen," the *Tribune* countered, noting that Robinson's assertion of theft "compounded" the difficulties of the company.

Robinson returned to bankruptcy court in 1987, seeking protection from creditors who claimed he owed them $2.5 million from the six Wendy's restaurants he operated in Chicago. William Goodall, a West Side restaurant owner, had invested in one of the restaurants in the corporate name of Stony Island Management Corp. In a 1984 lawsuit that eventually prompted Robinson to file bankruptcy three years later, Goodall alleged Robinson had "plundered" $300,000 from Stony Island to lease two Cadillacs and cover other personal expenses.

The twenty Robinson companies named in the federal grand jury subpoena were:

- Precision Contractors Inc., a construction firm that won city and state minority set-aside contracts and then subcontracted them to a white-owned firm, Wolverine Marble Co., of Detroit[36]
- El Campeon Jose Luis and Joe Louis Milk Co., two milk companies (El Campeon filed for bankruptcy protection in 1982)
- Renoja Management Co. Inc. (formerly known as Renoja Interiors), which filed for bankruptcy in 1986
- First Class Cafeterias, and Stanley Ryan & Associates, cafeteria operators that filed for bankruptcy
- Rising Sun Ltd., a construction firm sued by several trade unions for unpaid pensions[37]
- Apache Electric Inc., an electrical subcontractor Robinson used extensively for minority set-aside contracts
- Noah Robinson Co. Inc, which Robinson established to own property in his hometown of Greenville, South Carolina
- Robinson Group Inc., an arm of Rising Sun
- Brenico Inc., which owned a fried chicken restaurant in Chicago
- Wendee's of Chicago Inc., which Robinson formed after Renoja filed for bankruptcy protection
- Kuverol Flooring Inc., a floor installation company in which Robinson disclaimed an ownership interest
- Minority-Majority Construction Co., a firm that received the lion's share of the $35 million in minority set-aside contracts Robinson won from the Chicago Metropolitan Sanitary district starting in 1977
- Po-Bean Management Co. Inc., which owned a restaurant in New York City
- Galaxy Products Inc., a wholesaler of cleaning products
- Wen York Inc., a subsidiary that once operated a Wendy's franchise in New York
- Noajangles, another New York restaurant company

- Big John Henry Inc., a company Robinson formed in 1980 and dissolved in May 1986
- A.O. Vaughn & Associates, Ltd, whose president was Alfreda Vaughn, a longtime Robinson employee and business manager[38]

Robinson was indignant when reporters called him for comment on the investigation. "What is significant about my filing for bankruptcy? Texaco has done it. Continental has done it. Why me, and why now? . . . Filing bankruptcy petitions are white American capitalist tools. Do you mind my using it, too?" Once the *Tribune* investigation was released to the wires, he honed his reply and claimed he was a victim of a political trap. "What makes it significant, other than me being Jesse Jackson's brother, me being black and Jesse being the front-runner for the Democratic nomination for president?" he asked the Associated Press.[39]

MURDER BY HIRE

Noah's real trouble began once Tramell Davis began talking to federal investigators in the fall of 1987.

Davis, the top Rukn "general" arrested the year before, claimed that imprisoned gang leader Jeff Fort ordered the January 2, 1986, killing of former Robinson employee Hambone Barber because Barber had been "bothering" Robinson. In a pretrial filing, federal prosecutors Susan Bogart and John Podliska said he would testify for the prosecution on the gang's involvement in drug running, murders, and witness intimidation.

Two of the five Rukns Fort ordered to travel to Greenville to murder Barber were employees of Noah Robinson, Davis said. They were Jackie Clay, who worked for Robinson's construction company, Precision Contractors Inc., and Eugene Hunter, a convicted murderer who ran Security Maintenance Ltd. Inc., the security guard firm busted by Chicago police and Illinois state cops in June 1986. Robinson said that hiring former cons to protect his fast food restaurants and his office was a "Christian thing to do . . . to provide legitimate, bona fide job opportunities for the unemployed who are seriously interested and able to work."[40]

The story that Jesse Jackson's half brother was under investigation in a case of murder-by-hire made the national wires. But as soon as Jackson denied any knowledge of the case and said he had no ties to Noah's business ventures, the story died in less than twenty-four hours. Astonishingly, when the *Los Angeles Times* ran its first full-length portrait of Jackson the presidential candidate that December, not a single word about Noah Robinson appeared in the entire 6,500 word piece—not even the fact that Jackson has a half brother (six of them, actually).[41]

What cracked the case wide open for the feds was a decision by Assistant U.S. Attorney William Hogan to use the powerful Racketeer Influenced and Corrupt Organizations (RICO) statute to go after Noah and the El Rukn gang. RICO provided prosecutors with a "catch-all" clause that allowed them to get at organized-crime families who carefully structured their activities to fall through the loopholes of existing law. "If an individual belonged to a crime family, all the government had to do was demonstrate membership in the family and then prove that the family collectively engaged in criminal acts," says civil rights lawyer Rick Wagner of the Brooklyn, New York, Legal Services Corporation.[42]

In an interview, Hogan said the Rukn were "perfectly suited" for a RICO prosecution. "They were into narcotics, extortion, murder, interstate murder-by-hire. They were as organized as any organized crime group we had ever seen. The only difference was, they were not Italian."

The unique thing about the Rukn was their lifestyle. "They were almost a cult," says Hogan. "They lived together with their families in buildings purchased with narcotics funds. They had members who were carpenters and security guards. The Rukn were the first organized black gang in the United States, and exported their model to Los Angeles and elsewhere in the 1960s."[43]

Hogan ran the investigation of the El Rukn gang through a federal grand jury and tapped the resources of the Chicago police Gang Intelligence Unit. He deputized police sergeants Brannigan and Kolovitz as federal marshals, allowing them to participate in arrests and place wiretaps from South Carolina to Texas. A Greenville, South Carolina, woman named Janice Denice Rosemond was present the night of the killing in Robinson's shopping plaza. In closed-door testimony before the grand jury, she positively identified Rukn general Jackie Clay from a lineup as one of the killers. On the night of December 4, 1987, shortly after her testimony in Chicago, Rosemond was attacked at her home in Greenville by another former Robinson employee, thirty-four-year-old Freddie Elwood Sweeney. He stabbed her four times, but fled because of her screams. Noah had ordered the killing, Sweeney testified.

Sweeney was one of Noah's hired hoods. In trial testimony, he related how Noah had asked him to travel down to Atlanta in the early 1980s to burn down the office of a dope dealer named Billy Taylor, who Noah claimed had sold him watered down marijuana. Noah showed him a briefcase full of cash as an enticement. "Mack, you ain't never seen this much money in your life, have you?" Later, Sweeney said he served as Noah's "bodyguard" when he traveled to Greenville.[44]

In August 1987, Robinson called Sweeney to meet in Greenville, and drove up in a black Lincoln. "Mr. Robinson told me that Nicee [Rosemond] had fingered one of our guys...the guy that killed Hambone," he said at trial. Robinson was hiding the killer at his house in Albuquerque, New Mexico. "He told me, he say he wanted me to kill her. He told me he wanted me to cut that bitch's throat because she fingered one of our guys." Noah promised him $5,000 for the job.

In December, he returned to Greenville and paid Nicee a visit, carrying surgical gloves and a pearl-handled fishing knife with a long blade. Sweeney had known his victim since childhood. Unsuspecting, she invited him upstairs to watch television. A half hour later, he started stabbing her, but she screamed and the knife folded up and cut his hand. "Why didn't you cut her throat?" the prosecutor asked. "I just couldn't cut her throat," he said.[45]

When Sweeney surrendered to police four weeks after the murder all the pieces that would contribute to Noah Robinson's undoing were in place. It would take federal prosecutors another six months to put them together and lay them before a judge.[46]

SKELETONS

Jackson was better prepared during his 1988 presidential campaign to fend off embarrassing questions about his finances and lack of managerial experience than in 1984. When lawyer John Bustamante filed his financial disclosure form in October 1987, it showed that Jackson's annual income had more than doubled in four years, jumping from $115,000 in 1983 to more than $250,000. Almost all the money came from speaker's fees, since he had remained on a "leave of absence" from Operation PUSH (now called the National Rainbow Coalition) since late 1983 and only claimed to have been paid $18,750 by the organization over the past year.

In an urgent fundraising appeal sent to donors during his Africa tour, Jackson painted a depressing picture of America and PUSH finances. "Every basic victory that we have won in the sixties is now being challenged and threatened: voting rights; affirmative action; equal opportunity; and access to higher education.... We need money, now!"[47]

If the PUSH finances were in shambles, Jackson's own business was thriving. His for-profit speaker's bureau, Personalities International Inc., paid him $192,090, but he also declared to have received separate payments totaling $33,000 for other speeches and honoraria.[48]

Some of the money came from political appearances and probably should have been reported to the Federal Election Commission as direct contributions to his campaign and not personal income. "On the campaign trail, Jackson loves to tell how he allied himself with the workingman by standing with the striking meatpackers in Cudahy, Wis., in their hour of turmoil in April 1987," the Associated Press reported during the campaign. "He doesn't mention that he was paid $2,000 plus expenses by the United Food and Commercial Workers Union for making that appearance."[49]

Another paid appearance that generated controversy was a Black History Month address Jackson gave to cadets at West Point that February, where Jackson questioned America's "confidence in military leadership." The lecture caused talk show host Les Kinsolving to question the good judgment of the West Point superintendent for inviting someone who "has publicly saluted communist dictators such as Fidel Castro and Daniel Ortega who are, unquestionably, enemies of the United States."[50]

Jackson also disclosed healthy gains in his personal net worth, with bank accounts and certificates of deposit now worth between $97,000 and $235,000. The source of this new wealth was never disclosed. Real estate records showed that Jackson had purchased two new homes in addition to his fifteen room Tudor house in Chicago: a three story brick mansion in the historic LeDroit Park district of Washington, D.C., purchased from Howard University in 1985 for $100,000, and the house in Greenville, South Carolina, purchased for his mother in 1984 for $40,000.

One entry that should have raised eyebrows was Jackson's declaration that he now owned stock in a company he identified as ICBC Inc. worth between $250,000 and $1 million. The company's real name was Inner City Broadcasting Corporation Inc. It owned the famed Apollo Theater in Harlem, seven radio stations, and part of a cable television company, and was controlled by the chairman of Jackson's campaign finance committee, former Manhattan Borough chairman Percy Sutton. Jackson never explained how he acquired the stock, but Sutton told the London *Sunday Times* in 1988 that it would be worth "in excess of a million dollars" if the company were sold.[51]

It was a financial boon akin to the original mortgage on his house that Barbara Reynolds disclosed had been paid by Jackson's black business friends in Chicago in a "secret land trust" in 1970. Jackson subsequently borrowed against the house whenever he needed cash, in essence using their original payment to secure fresh money for living expenses and luxuries, financial records on file with the Chicago and Washington, D.C., recorders of deeds show. Years later, when Jackson's finances again came under scrutiny because he got caught using funds from his nonprofit empire to pay off a mistress who had borne his illegitimate child in 1999, he claimed the Inner City stock had grown from a $10,000 investment made in 1977 by his wife, Jacqueline.[52]

Another potentially sensitive point that was never probed by the media during the campaign were allegations of Jackson's marital infidelities, which had been rumored since Barbara Reynolds first reported in 1975 that Jackson had had relationships with singers Nancy Wilson and Roberta Flack. In an article in the *Christian Science Monitor* of January 20, 1988, Hattie Clark reported that when Jackson was asked about his relationships with Wilson and Flack, he held up his hand in protest and replied, "That's an inappropriate question." Barbara Reynolds, who in 1988 had become an editor at *USA Today*, commented that Gary Hart's womanizing is "almost a blueprint of what has been the case with Jesse."[53]

In an unsuccessful effort to assuage the fears of Jewish voters, Jackson appointed as campaign manager a white Jewish political operative named Gerald Austin, who had managed two successful campaigns for Ohio Democratic governor Richard F. Celeste.[54] Austin had him walk back his support for PLO leader Yasser Arafat in an interview on CBS's *Face the Nation* when Jackson said that as president he would not meet with Arafat because of the ban on talks with the PLO.[55]

But his heavy reliance on contributions from Arab-Americans, including high profile Arafat supporters, revived the ghosts of 1984 and "Jews Against Jackson." Jewish Democrats got the message when Jackson hired James Zogby, former executive director of the radical pro-Palestinian American Arab Antidiscrimination Committee to head his fundraising efforts with Arab-Americans. In April 1988, Zogby announced proudly that Arab-Americans had kicked in more than $400,000 to Jackson's 1988 campaign. Before Jackson, Zogby claimed that Arab-Americans felt excluded politically. "Jackson brought them into the process and they don't forget that."[56]

Among Jackson's contributors, according to FEC records obtained through the Freedom of Information Act, were people like Hani Masri, scion of a prominent banking family in Jordan who invested heavily in Arafat's Palestinian Authority after the Oslo Peace Accords in 1993 and whose cousin and brother became ministers in Arafat's cabinet. Also contributing was Abdulrahman Alamoudi, who headed the American Muslim Council. This group called for the U.S. to cut off aid to Israel and raised funds for "charitable" organizations in Gaza and the West Bank which were closed down by Arafat in September 1997. These "charitable" organizations were funneling money to the military wing of Hamas, the radical Islamic group which gleefully claimed responsibility for suicide bombings in Israel. Alamoudi, Zogby, Masri and others later became embroiled in the campaign finance scandals of 1996, when they raised close to a million dollars for the DNC and the Clinton-Gore reelection campaign.[57]

Similarly, Jackson's continued reliance on advisors such as Robert Borosage and Jack O'Dell, and his embrace of Cuban dictator Fidel Castro got Jackson in trouble with Democrats, such as former Lyndon Johnson advisor Ben Wattenberg, now a national columnist. Jackson's foreign policy views were far outside the mainstream, Wattenberg said, and represented "the hard left." Wattenberg criticized Jackson's salute of the communist Vietnamese ambassador on the tenth anniversary of the communist victory in Vietnam, and his description of the Sandinistas in Nicaragua as a "moral force."[58]

O'Dell briefly surfaced in December 1987 when he was quoted by TASS correspondent Alexander Pakhomov in a dispatch from Washington stating that President Reagan's commitment to an Intermediate Nuclear Forces (INF) Treaty was really "a victory for the American people" who had "demonstrated their support" for scraping medium-range missiles from Europe. The nuclear freeze movement had shown the administration "it could not discard people's sentiments," TASS quoted O'Dell as saying.[59] In fact, it was Reagan's refusal to give in to Soviet pressure and the KGB-sponsored worldwide disinformation campaign led by the World Peace Council (to which O'Dell belonged) that forced the Soviets to destroy hundreds of deployed SS-20 and earlier generation SS-4 and SS-5 missiles and to allow U.S. intelligence monitors onto their production sites. In exchange, the United States did not deploy the Pershing II and nuclear-tipped cruise missiles in Europe.

Jackson's continued hard-left positions won enthusiastic support from the *People's Daily World*, the Communist Party newspaper in the United States. Jackson said he would be "hesitant" to accept the endorsement of the Communist Party, and complained that raising the issue was "a scurrilous attempt to scar" his campaign. On March 31, 1988, Communist Party leader Gus Hall told the Party paper:

> As a political party we do not endorse candidates of other political parties. Communists as individuals work in the election campaign, even in the campaign of other candidates, not only Communist candidates. I think our members will work for the candidates they think have the most progressive, most advanced positions. At this stage most members of the Party would be working for Jesse Jackson on the basis that he does have an advanced position. But we do not endorse any candidate, including Jesse Jackson.

Hall's veiled support prompted conservative media watchdog Reed Irvine to comment: "For the first time in years, the Communists aren't running a candidate for president. It is clear Jackson is their man, but by not formally endorsing him, they don't generate demands that he repudiate the endorsement."[60]

Morton Kondracke, writing in the liberal *New Republic*, published a detailed critique of Jackson's far-left advisors and positions. Just as he did in 1984, Kondracke wrote, Jackson "says that the United States should make huge unilateral military cuts, stop intervening in Third World revolutions, and trust international institutions to keep the peace. Even if he's dropped public displays of affection, in other words, Jackson still means to make the world safe for Arafat, Castro, and other national liberationists."[61]

Kondracke quoted yet another interview by Jackson advisor Jack O'Dell with a Marxist publication in November 1987: "The Rainbow Coalition is placing America in touch with the world . . . in the way that the Henry Wallace campaign, Paul Robeson, and Dr. W. E. B. DuBois made the supreme effort to do in 1948," O'Dell said. "We are their children. We are keeping the faith."

Kondracke commented: "There is no evidence that the Jackson campaign is Communist influenced as the Wallace campaign was in 1948, but

Jackson does advocate a decisive leftward shift in foreign policy." Daniel Seligman, writing in *Fortune* magazine that same week, sounded a similar note: "In positioning himself on foreign policy and national security issues, Jesse Jackson never seems to take a stand that puts him in opposition to the world Soviet line. Is that serious enough for you?"[62]

Although Jackson won more votes during the primaries than he did in 1984, his policies were out of step with the America of 1988, when Vice President Bush succeeded in embarrassing his Democratic rival, Massachusetts governor Michael Dukakis, by revealing that he was a "card-carrying member" of the American Civil Liberties Union.

One faction within the Democratic Party was very concerned about Jesse Jackson's rise: the successors of U.S. Senator Henry "Scoop" Jackson. In the 1970s, Scoop Jackson was the spiritual father of the Coalition for a Democratic Majority (CDM), a staunchly anticommunist movement, strong on defense and deeply pro-Israel that at one point counted among its members such conservatives as Richard Perle and Jeane Kirkpatrick, who later joined the Reagan administration.

During the 1988 campaign a CDM successor group known as the PAC for a Democratic Future commissioned a research report on the Communist Party ties of Jesse Jackson and his closest advisors. The report, "The Rainbow Movement, Jesse Jackson, and the Future of the Democratic Party," was given to Democratic Party elders and to Jackson, who never responded. It contended that Jackson was a threat to the Democratic Party personally, through his ideology, and through the questionable loyalties of his top advisors.

"The Rainbow Coalition is seen by many of its leaders as a party-within-a-party which seeks a radical transformation of the Democratic Party," the study warned, "making it an instrument for what they describe as a new 'progressive' politics. . . . If the Reverend Jackson and the Rainbow Coalition continue on their present course, their presence inside the Democratic Party may pose difficulties for the party during the 1988 Presidential Campaign and thereafter—difficulties such as those that began in the British Labor Party a decade ago."[63]

The allusion was clear: the Labor Party committed political suicide by espousing pro-Soviet collectivist policies at the height of the Cold War that effectively shut it out of power in Britain for the better part of a generation. If Jackson seized control of the Democratic Party, he would doom any hope Democrats had of becoming the majority party.

The authors of that report, Penn Kemble and Joshua Muravchik, both recall they were charged with "red-baiting" and "McCarthyism" just for raising the issue of Jackson's hard-left advisors and his pro-Soviet policies. "Jackson won support from people who said he represented the poor and the working people," recalls Kemble, who was appointed a deputy director of the U.S. Information Agency by President Clinton. "Our view was that it was a much more complicated picture."

Muravchik, now a resident scholar at the American Enterprise Institute, drew heavily on interviews with Jackson and his advisors that appeared in left-wing journals and scholarly writing, where they praised Soviet policies and Soviet-backed national liberation struggles. "McCarthyism has left a powerful antibody in the bloodstream," he says. "If you say that someone is supporting communist regimes—no matter how careful the proof or judicious the presentation—it gets rejected out of hand as red-baiting."

Kemble emerged from the civil rights and the labor movements, and acknowledges that "many people were unfairly called Communists in the racist politics of that era." Not Jack O'Dell, whose ties to Soviet front organizations were a main subject of their report. "If you raised these issues, you were lumped together with the racists or people on the extreme right. The reporters who covered the campaign regarded any discussion of that sector of the Left—the people who regarded the Soviet Union as misguided progressives, but progressives all the same—as politically incorrect."[64]

Neither author recalls getting a lot of press from the report, although "it was not a secret," Kemble says.

DYNASTY

The 1988 Democratic National Convention in Atlanta was glory time. Jesse had "made it" and was thrust center stage side by side with the party's nominees, Michael Dukakis and Lloyd Bentsen. Their joint appearance before the cameras as the party's ruling triumvirate on July 18, 1988, almost never happened, and came only at the end of a tense three-hour breakfast meeting. Just as in 1984, Jackson had been squabbling with the party bosses over everything from the size of the banners his supporters would be allowed to bring onto the convention floor to the choice of the vice presidential nominee. But this time he was guided by a master negotiator and well-connected political operator, Ron Brown.

Brown later told reporters that Jackson had tried to hire him a year earlier as his campaign manager, but he had refused. "I thought he was annoyed enough with that decision that I probably wouldn't get asked again," he said.[65] But Jackson had learned from 1984 that it wasn't over until the lights dimmed and the cameras switched off. To leverage the maximum concessions from the tough-nosed Dukakis and his team, he needed an intermediary who knew the ropes and could smooth over his own rough edges. Added to Ron Brown's lawyer's skills were impeccable party connections. Not only had he served on the Democratic National Committee as Jackson's surrogate for the past four years, he had successfully managed Ted Kennedy's presidential primary campaign in California in 1980 and had known the prickly Dukakis and his advisors for years.

There is extensive evidence that Michael Dukakis and the Democratic Party bosses tapped Ron Brown as their "emissary" to the Jackson campaign, to keep Jackson under control and from splitting the party.[66] Jackson hired him to "stage-manage" his appearance at the Atlanta convention, and he was worth every penny of his fee. Working with him was Alexis Herman, a 1984 campaign worker, Jackson crony, and former Labor Department official whose consulting firm, Herman & Associates, continued to monitor the minority-hiring "diversity" covenants Jackson had negotiated with companies such as Coca-Cola, Burger King, and Southland Corp.[67]

One of the first concessions Ron Brown won for Jackson was the appointment of son Jesse Jr. as an at-large member of the DNC. This gave Jackson direct, permanent access to the party bosses. And Brown himself left the convention with the top job, getting named as party chairman for the next four years. But the prize Jackson most coveted was prime time television. At 10 P.M. on Tuesday evening, it was "nation-time" for Jesse Jackson.

"Jesse thinks in dynastic terms," says a congressional aide who deals with Jackson frequently. "He groomed one son as a lawyer, another as a businessman. And then there's Jesse Jr., now a U.S. congressman."[68]

That Tuesday evening, Jackson brought his entire family onto the stage of the Omni. First there were the girls: twelve-year-old Jackie Jr., a student at the private Brooks School outside Boston, who charmed reporters by saying, "If I could vote, I'd vote for my dad"; and twenty-five-year-old Santita, who angrily said she'd turned down Harvard after an "overly hostile" interview by admissions officers who grilled her on her father's political views. After a stint working on a congressional staff for her father's friend, Representative Gus Savage (D-Ill.), she strutted her stuff in a backup band for pop singer Roberta Flack.[69]

Then came the sons: twenty-two-year-old Jonathan, getting his MBA from the Kellogg business school at Northwestern University, and seventeen-year-old Yusef, who famously took time off from his eighth grade graduation four years earlier to join Dad with Fidel Castro in Cuba, and had just graduated from the exclusive St. Albans school in Washington, D.C., en route to the University of Virginia on a football scholarship.

But Jackson let everyone know that his favorite was his namesake, Jesse Jr., age twenty-three, who had just graduated from Dad's alma mater, North Carolina A&T, and was headed for law school and ultimately the United States Congress. Jesse Jr. found the cameras just as Dad carefully negotiated the steps to the podium for his prime-time speech to the nation, and effortlessly assumed the mantle as spokesperson for America's First Black Dynasty. "I am sure that the children in the King family are proud to be Kings," he said. "And I'm sure that the children in the Kennedy family are proud to be Kennedys. But we, the children of Jesse and Jacqueline Jackson, are proud to be Jacksons."

It was perfect. The press gobbled it up and replayed the scene again and again. "It is still too early to tell whether a new political dynasty was born last week in Atlanta," gushed *Newsweek*. "But . . . the Jacksons—poised, proud and living antidotes to inner-city despair—clearly embodied the main message of Jesse Sr.'s convention speech: 'Keep hope alive.' "[70]

Inner city despair? Jesse Jackson with his three houses, his flush bank accounts, his first-class travel, his lucrative friendships with foreign dictators, his children in elite prep schools and colleges, was as close to inner city despair as the Beverly Hillbillies were to poverty.

BUSTED!

Noah Robinson was arrested in Greenville, South Carolina, late on Saturday night, June 4, 1988, and charged with being an accessory to a felony, obstruction of justice, intimidating a witness, and criminal conspiracy. Greenville police detective Keith Morton said Robinson was suspected of soliciting and arranging the stabbing of a federal murder witness. When the news hit the wires, Jackson's campaign headquarters was besieged by reporters. But Jackson was nowhere to be found. Campaign advisor Robert Borosage reiterated what Jackson had said in 1987 when Robinson was under investigation for allegedly violating federal bankruptcy laws: "I have no connection with him." Other than that, the Jackson campaign kept silent.

Three days later, federal agents and Chicago police burst into the offices of Precision Contractors Inc., the construction company Noah owned, seizing documents on his various businesses. They also seized $21,000 in cash from Robinson's apartment at 10910 S. Michigan Avenue, which Robinson said came from cash receipts from two Wendy's restaurants he owned. With that evidence they began probing other potentially illegal schemes run by Noah that would lead to a separate federal prosecution for fraud and racketeering. After posting $50,000 in cash as security on a $500,000 bond, Robinson was released. He promptly told reporters that the Chicago police were trying to turn him into "the Billy Carter of the Jesse Jackson campaign."[71]

On August 7, as Jackson was hitting the campaign trail for the Democratic ticket, a South Carolina grand jury indicted Noah for conspiracy, obstruction of justice, and witness intimidation. Robinson was taken back into custody on September 21, but claimed he had a signed statement from a Rukn gang member swearing that Robinson had no knowledge of the plot to murder fellow Rukn Hambone Barber. Once again, Robinson claimed he was a victim of politically motivated prosecutors.[72]

The next day, Greenville County solicitor Joe Watson struck back, saying he intended to seek the death penalty for Robinson because the Barber slaying was "a murder for hire, a murder for monetary gain." Jailed Rukn Tramell Davis, who had become a government witness, told police that Robinson had paid "$10,000 or $12,000" for the hit. Under South Carolina law, prosecutors can seek the death penalty against an individual who hires killers in murder cases.[73] All of a sudden, Noah's trouble with the law took a dramatic new turn, and the press besieged Jackson at every campaign appearance with a new cry: "What about Noah Robinson, Reverend?"

CHAPTER 9

The Statehood Senator

In 1989 Jackson moved to Washington, D.C.—a symbol both of his political ambitions and perhaps of his desire to escape the scandals of his half brother and the attention of Cook County state attorney Richard Daley. He and Jackie moved into an apartment while waiting for workmen to finish lavish renovations on the fourteen-room brick mansion Jackson had purchased at 400 T Street, just south of Howard University.

To keep his political fundraising efforts warm, Jackson set up a new political action committee called "Keep Hope Alive." In direct mail appeals, he painted a picture of America that was radically at odds with the country most Americans knew. "The Reagan years were devastating to us all. For eight years the lights were turned off," he wrote as America was enjoying widespread economic prosperity, job growth, and the end of the Cold War. He argued that the U.S. Supreme Court, which he called derisively the "Ronald Reagan Court," was taking "pick and axe to the

Civil Rights Legacy in an attempt to crush the hopes and dreams of millions of Americans.... We must also prepare for mass demonstrations and litigation."[1] The promise of demonstrations was vague and the prospect of buying lawyers failed to inspire. The little people who might have believed Jackson's pitch had no money, while the black middle and upper classes who had the money found him out of touch with reality. By mid-1989, Keep Hope Alive had raised a scant $280,000, most of which was plowed into direct mail costs to develop national fundraising lists.

Jackson sought help from Ivanhoe Donaldson, a former political strategist for Washington, D.C., mayor Marion Barry; he paid $8,000 to Donaldson's company, Datafax Resources Inc. The former Barry aide had an axe to grind with the mayor, having just gotten out of jail after serving a three-year prison term for stealing $190,000 from the D.C. government (extraordinary, since no one *ever* went to jail for stealing from the D.C. government), and was urging Jackson to run for mayor. Jackson let reporters know he was considering it.[2]

He also let drop in a July 1989 meeting with black broadcasters in Washington that he was thinking of buying a local radio station to promote his National Rainbow Coalition and his own personal political projects. It just so happened that one was for sale. WYCB was the District's only AM radio gospel station, and its current owner had filed for bankruptcy protection, putting it up for auction. For Jackson, it was a perfect fit. "No matter where he goes in the country, he makes it a point to stop in on a gospel radio station for an interview," a Jackson associate said. "He's a minister, and it makes sense for him to do it, plus he likes it."[3]

Jackson's friend and former campaign worker Alexis Herman filed papers in May 1989 with the Federal Communications Commission to buy WYCB-AM for $3.45 million. Although she was working full-time for Ron Brown as chief of staff of the Democratic National Committee and had no prior broadcasting experience, Herman now owned Columbia Community Broadcasting Company, a firm that was negotiating to buy the station. Herman's partner was Gloria Gutierrez, a lawyer who worked for the Rainbow Coalition, was on Jackson's presidential campaign, and went on to work under Ron Brown at the Commerce Department during the Clinton years. Patricia Kinch, a former Jackson public relations specialist, was also on Herman's board. "This is the old crew from PUSH," another former Jackson campaign worker said. "Clearly Alexis Herman got her start through her association with Jesse, but buying WYCB is not a political thing." Herman's attorney, Gerald Kisner, "strongly and strenuously" denied any Jackson involvement in the proposed purchase. "He is not in any way, shape or form in this project," he insisted. Herman's motive in wanting to buy the station, he said, "is like anybody else acquiring a business: to make a profit, make some money. It's the American way." In any event, Broadcast Holdings Inc., rather than Herman, succeeded in buying the station in March 1990.[4]

By October, Jackson had moved his entire organization to Washington, including Rainbow Coalition executive director Joe Johnson and a full-time staff of seventeen. Johnson told reporters that the nonprofit now had an annual budget of $1 million raised through direct mail and contributions from individuals, but he refused to disclose donors. Jackson's assistant and former campaign spokesman Frank Watkins explained coolly: "There's no campaign now."[5] Meanwhile, former Jackson campaign worker Patricia Kinch was holding fundraisers around town to raise money for *Sandino's Daughter*. This was a pro-Sandinista film by hard-left writer Margaret Randall. Randall had renounced her American citizenship in 1967 and had worked in the governments of the Nicaraguan Sandinistas and Castro's Cuba. Jackson attended one of these events in an elegant salon of Washington's Mayflower Hotel, showing that he still had few, if any, qualms about associating with the radical Left.[6]

Executive Director Joe Johnson stayed with Rainbow for scarcely more than a year, but he did well by the association. After leaving Jackson's employ he set up his own consulting and lobbying firm, Johnson & Associates, and in 1994 founded National Corrections and Rehabilitation Corporation. Within two years the company went public and under the name Corrections Corporation of America earned millions in federal and state grants to run prison "education, vocational training, substance abuse treatment and medical care programs."[7] Jackson began pushing precisely these types of programs at this point, after a well-publicized Christmas Day visit to the Cook County jail in 1988 where he urged prisoners to register to vote.[8]

OUTSMARTED BY MARION BARRY

By late October 1989, Jackson was using Rainbow Coalition funds to hire canvassers to poll Washington, D.C., residents. He wanted to identify "hot button" issues if he were to run for mayor.[9] Coincidentally, an opinion poll commissioned by WRC-TV and radio station WKYS found that 54 percent of District residents were dissatisfied with the performance of Mayor Barry, following revelations of his friendship with convicted drug dealer Charles Lewis. The poll found that either Jackson or former D.C. police chief Maurice Turner would defeat Barry in a head-on contest.[10] It was good news for Jackson and it prompted him to step up his fundraising efforts. "We saw Jesse coming, and we were seriously worried," recalls Burton Wheeler, who ran Barry's 1990 reelection campaign.[11]

But Jackson hadn't counted on Marion Barry's political wiles or on the extraordinary clout he continued to wield in Washington. It would take another year and an FBI drug sting, complete with hidden camera video footage of Mayor Barry smoking crack cocaine during an assignation in a local hotel, to apparently end the Washington mayor's political career. One of Barry's anti-Jackson political tricks was working behind the scenes to change the rules governing mayoral candidates. "Mayor Barry knew very well that Jackson earned most of his money by giving speeches," a D.C. election official explains. "So he got the City Council to change the election rules, making it illegal for anyone running for mayor to earn more than $10,000 from honoraria. The cap applied to the candidate and to all members of his immediate family. They called it the Jesse Jackson law."[12] Jackson only learned of the changes after they had been codified in the District's election laws.[13] He was furious, but he was also stuck. "It was either switch gears, or give up his livelihood," the D.C. official says. "That's when Jesse turned around and decided to run for statehood sen-

ator, where the new rules didn't apply. His original intent had been to run
for mayor."

Nobody took Jackson's campaign seriously, starting with Jackson himself. Although it was an elected position, the District of Columbia's statehood senator was merely an unpaid lobbyist, who was expected to walk
congressional halls berating elected officials to "support the petition for
admission of New Columbia to statehood."[14] It was a cause in disfavor
with Republicans and even most Democrats. Given the District's high
crime rate, its immense bureaucracy, its history of cronyism, and its
abysmal public schools—where students unfailingly managed to score
dead last on all national tests despite the highest per pupil expenditure in
the nation—it made for an unattractive potential fifty-first state.

Typical of Jesse Jackson's contempt for the job (and his contempt for
the D.C. election board) was the unabashed illegal financing of his campaign. Whenever he needed money he simply borrowed cash from the
Rainbow Coalition, transferring it to the "Jackson for U.S. Senate" campaign account at the Adams Bank, and called it "loans." Marianne
Coleman Niles, director of the D.C. Office of Campaign Finance, wrote
Jackson's campaign treasurer, the Reverend Beecher H. Hicks, shortly
after Jackson took the first of these payments, to explain that only banks
could loan the campaign money. Anything else was considered a contribution and was limited to $2,000 for the primary and general election
combined. "The receipt of the loan from the National Rainbow Coalition
exceeds the contribution limits by $14,500," her October 26, 1990, letter
states. "It is requested that the excess receipt be refunded within ten days
from the date of this letter." Jackson refused to comply and had Rainbow
send over two more checks to cover last-minute expenses for the
November 1990 elections.

Jackson was eventually forced to reimburse the $33,500 to the
Rainbow Coalition and pay a stiff fine.[15] "Clearly, Jesse should have
known that this type of loan was illegal," the D.C. election board official
says. "It is illegal in any federal campaign, which he knew because he had
just run twice for president." The D.C. Office of Campaign Finance sent

Jackson a total of twenty-one noncompliance notices, including multiple "second notices of non-compliance" before levying the fines.

Depending on the week, Jackson ran his "Shadow Senator" campaign out of his LeDroit Park home, or out of the Rainbow Coalition headquarters at 1110 Vermont Avenue, or from the offices of a variety of accountants and law firms, or even from the house of campaign chairman Mary Frances Berry. (Berry was a longtime friend and former PUSH operative who was appointed chairman of the U.S. Civil Rights Commission by President Clinton.) Jackson won his election, permitting him another avenue to promote himself. And he used the $175,000 he raised for his "statehood fund" to finance his ongoing political activities, with the single largest chunk of the money going to his presidential campaign spokesman Frank Watkins, D.C. board of election documents indicate. After only a handful of letters and public appearances devoted to the cause of D.C. statehood he simply let the issue drop when more interesting targets came his way. The "Shadow Senator" became increasingly just a shadow.

THE NIKE BOYCOTT

While Jackson was in Washington lying low and plotting his next steps, the Reverend Tyrone Crider had been left in charge of Operation PUSH back in Chicago. On August 11, 1990, apparently without consulting Jackson, Crider announced at the weekly PUSH meeting a boycott of athletic sportswear producer Nike Inc. "Don't buy Nike! Don't wear Nike!" Crider called out, unsuccessfully trying to match Jackson's rhetorical heights.[16] The firm deposited no money in black banks, had no blacks on its board of directors, no black corporate vice presidents, and used no black advertising agencies, he argued, but purchases from blacks accounted for 30 percent of Nike's $2.23 billion in revenues. "We want 30 percent of everything!" Crider said.[17]

Then Crider made an astonishing revelation, disclosing that PUSH had decided to go after Nike only after the company had sent PUSH a request for financial records and released to reporters a list of ten questions it wanted answered. Crider called Nike's preemptive move "an affront." But it was Crider who had made a strategic mistake.

Crider first presented his demands to Nike lawyers in Chicago on July 30, fully expecting that the merest hint of a boycott by Jesse Jackson's organization would scare them into a settlement. After all, there was fierce competition in the industry, and the huge sums spent by Nike and its competition to buy mega-stars such as Michael Jordan to build brand awareness had become a sore subject in many black families. Black teenagers were demanding that their parents fork over $130 or even $170 for a pair of Nike Air Jordans. But instead of cowering, Nike came out swinging. Two days after demanding sensitive financial information from PUSH, Nike president Philip Donahue sent a letter to Crider accusing PUSH of plotting the boycott campaign with help from its competitor Reebok. When Nike released the letter they also showed reporters a full-page ad from Reebok in the latest issue of *PUSH* magazine, for which Reebok had paid $5,950. Crider shot back lamely: "Reebok is not financing our fight. We never solicited nor received funds from Reebok."[18] But Crider was further embarrassed when the publisher of *Sporting Goods Intelligence*, a trade newsletter, reported that a Reebok executive had told him that top Reebok and PUSH officials met quietly in June, well before the boycott was announced.[19]

The Nike boycott sounded fishy from the start. Basketball star Michael Jordan, who earned $200,000 a year for his endorsement of Nike shoes, called the boycott "unfair for singling out Nike." When he had walked off the court a year earlier in protest of the NCAA's Proposition 42, which required minimum academic standards for college athletes to maintain their scholarships, the first phone call he received was from Nike chairman Philip H. Knight, who offered his support.[20] Chicago columnist Clarence Page, a longtime critic of PUSH, said he "felt a profound sense of 'déjà vu'" when he first heard of the boycott. "In covering the activities of PUSH for almost a quarter century, I have seen this dance many times before.... Does anyone truly believe any of the concessions PUSH is seeking will make much difference in the lives of very many of the young people who buy

Nike's shoes? Perhaps instead of seeking black jobs in white companies, PUSH could spend more time helping create black-owned companies that can, in turn, put more workers on black community payrolls."[21]

As things went from bad to worse, Jackson felt compelled to step in to refocus the failing campaign. Gently criticizing Michael Jordan and baseball-football star Bo Jackson, who also defended the firm, he said, "Athletes can speak for the shoes, because they wear them. They cannot speak for the corporate policy because they're not a part of that. So to ask them to speak for the corporate policy is . . . a kind of race manipulation."[22] Then he made clear what he really wanted to see result from the public arm wrestling match: the appointment of a black to Nike's corporate board. He even had a candidate: Georgetown basketball coach John Thompson, head coach of the 1988 U.S. Olympic basketball team. *Chicago Tribune* columnist Steve Daley called Jackson "the stag at bay, a politician without an office . . . a negotiator whose Chicago allies have been outmaneuvered by Nike, Inc."[23] His characterization proved to be prophetic.

"Jackson claimed the Nike boycott was about getting jobs for ordinary black people," recalls Glen Bone III, an economist who was working for the Jackson Action Task Force at the time. "Nonsense. It was about getting a friend of Jesse's on the board of directors." When people realized that was all Jackson really wanted, they became cynical.[24]

Jackson's "demand" was a no-brainer for Nike, since coach Thompson was already on the company payroll with a lucrative endorsement contract and had attended the company's last board of directors meeting as a paid consultant. Two days later, Nike chairman Phil Knight announced that the company would name a black to the board, and within twenty-four months name a minority vice president. That was enough for Jackson. But in Chicago, the Reverend Crider called it just a "first step" and said the boycott would go on.[25] When Crider flew out to Portland, Oregon, along with forty PUSH supporters from Chicago to hold a "mass protest rally" in front of Nike headquarters in suburban Beaverton, Oregon, just one hundred people showed up, many of them curiosity seekers. Robert Phillips, president of the Portland NAACP, stated the obvious: "PUSH wasn't happy it could not rally local support." Other black community leaders said the boycott was "ill-conceived" and "lacked leadership," and expressed anger that Crider had flown into their territory without consulting them first.[26]

Jackson was anxiously seeking a graceful way to back down, and asked Georgetown University basketball coach John Thompson if he could broker a fresh meeting with Nike boss Phil Knight. But after a four-hour meeting on August 24 at Thompson's Washington, D.C., office, neither Knight nor Crider would back down.

Jackson joked with reporters and said the meeting had gone well. "I brought a towel and a baseball bat into the meeting, but I never had to use them."[27] But when Crider emerged he said flatly, "Nothing has changed," and at the PUSH weekly meeting the next day he turned up the rhetorical heat. "We're challenging corporate America's apartheid policy," he said. Carried away with his own talk, he went on to compare the failing boycott to the 1955 Montgomery Bus Boycott that launched the nation's civil rights movement.[28] PUSH pickets planned to march in ten cities around the country in front of stores carrying Nike shoes, he announced, even though most outlets were located inside private shopping malls, which banned such activities.

Washington Post columnist William Raspberry summed up the problem with the Nike boycott in an August 29 column that was reprinted in the *Chicago Tribune* the next day. He called it "hocus-pocus."

> The basis for PUSH's demands is the "exploitation" of inner-city youngsters; poor families are spending $100 a pair and more for Nike's athletic shoes, when their meager resources ought to be spent on more important things. The proposed solution is to place more blacks in top management positions, including seats on the board of directors, and buy more advertising from black-owned media outlets.
>
> But if poor black kids are the "victims" of Nike's sales success, how are they helped by helping a handful of black executives to

get better jobs? If low-income black families are being exploited by Nike's aggressive marketing, how is that exploitation reduced by forcing the company to advertise in black outlets, which, presumably, would expose yet more black youngsters to the lure of the shoes?

Like so many of the affirmative-action proposals, it amounts to a bait-and-switch game. The inner-city poor furnish the statistical base for the proposals, but the benefits go primarily to the already well-off.[29]

Jackson saw which way the wind was blowing. After all, this was August 1990. Saddam Hussein had just invaded Kuwait and taken U.S. businessmen and oil workers hostage. Jackson let the Nike boycott lurch alone and in October flew to Baghdad for a much criticized meeting with Saddam Hussein. He eventually succeeded in convincing Hussein to release a handful of American hostages, who flew back to the United States in Jackson's plane. But rather than the hero's welcome he had expected, President Bush gave Jackson the cold shoulder. Even his fellow Democrats roundly denounced him for dealings with the enemy that verged on treason.

BODY WITHOUT A HEAD

PUSH became a leaderless organization without Jackson's energy and charisma. The Nike boycott was not just a political debacle: it chipped away at Jackson's aura of invincibility, exposing Jackson's organization to ridicule.

Jackson had set up some thirty local chapters of PUSH around the county in his grandiose vision of building a nationwide grassroots organization. The most recent of these, in Columbus, Ohio, had gotten way out of control. Jack Harris, the owner of a local radio station and a black newspaper, knew a good thing when he saw it. Jesse Jackson was hitting up Nike to win advertising contracts for black publishers. These just happened to be such Jackson cronies as John Johnson of *Ebony* and Robert Johnson of

Black Entertainment Television. Jack Harris decided he would use the local PUSH chapter in Columbus, Ohio, to spread some of these benefits to himself.

Harris got a friend to send out a letter over the signature of the local PUSH president, the Reverend Andy C. Lewter, naming nine local businesses as targets of a PUSH boycott because they weren't advertising on WCKW radio or in the *Black Communicator* newspaper, both of which Harris owned. The only problem was that the letter had been sent when the Reverend Lewter was out of town. Questioned about it later, Lewter said, "Central Ohio Operation PUSH assumes responsibility for the letter. I am not going to say or do anything that is going to contribute to a public dispute or division within my community."[30] The incident, while minor, was indicative of how the lack of leadership had infected Jackson's organization even at the local level.

At the national level, PUSH was going down fast. On January 22, 1991, PUSH laid off all twelve full-time employees at the Chicago headquarters and admitted it was facing a $200,000 debt.[31] This debt included a $100,000-a-year payment due to the federal government as part of the final settlement brokered by lawyer John Bustamante in 1988, covering federal grant money misspent by the organization a decade earlier.

"Obviously, when you think of PUSH, you think of Jesse Jackson," said the Reverend Jesse Butler of Chicago's United Life Church. "With him gone, what has PUSH been? Where will PUSH go?" The Reverend Willie Barrow, the tough street organizer who had led Jackson's first boycotts by Operation Breadbasket in the late 1960s—and who preceded Tyrone Crider as PUSH executive president for the four years Jackson was running for president—put up a brave front. "The community comes to our rescue, not Reverend Jackson," she said. "If ever there was a time when PUSH is firm and vibrant, it's mostly now."[32]

But the community wasn't there for PUSH anymore, because it had become like a body without a head, without a soul. With Jackson gone, no one came to the Saturday morning services any longer, and PUSH workers hung heavy red ropes across two-thirds of the pews so the smaller number would still look like the crowded congregation of earlier years.[33] But if the visual tricks worked for the news cameras, no miracles were occurring when the Reverend Crider passed the collection plate, and the big corporate donors Jackson had shaken down over the years stayed home. "A lot of the PUSH thing was getting corporations to give them money," Pastor Jesse Butler said. "When Nike said, 'No way,' other corporations also decided they didn't have to give money. There's a lot of black people who are saying, 'Now I'm going to take a look at PUSH, too.' "[34]

In February, Jackson flew in from Washington and tried to breathe some life into his moribund organization. He worked the phones to corporate donors and made the round of old friends, and his earliest supporters. He let them know there would be a change at the top, and that he would not abandon PUSH.[35]

The axe inevitably fell on Tyrone Crider a few weeks later. The new interim president and CEO was the Reverend Henry Williamson of Chicago's Carter Temple C.M.E. Church. Asked if the Nike boycott had anything to do with Crider's departure, the Reverend Williamson put on a brave face. "Of course not. We've seen Nike respond." Added the Reverend Clay Evans, Jackson's original sponsor in Chicago who stayed on as chairman emeritus of the PUSH board, "The Nike boycott has been extremely successful. We just have not taken a high media role with its success. We will be letting people know how successful it has been."[36]

One reason no one at PUSH was trumpeting about its success was because Crider and the handful of protesters he'd taken recently to a Nike shareholders meeting had been "drowned out by boos" when they tried to speak.[37] *Chicago Tribune* columnist Clarence Page, although a stern Jackson critic, grudgingly admitted his importance to the PUSH effort. "PUSH without Jackson is like the Pips without Gladys Knight. Bright and talented, perhaps, but who cares? The heart of PUSH is still beating, but the body is brain-dead."[38]

Two months after Crider's departure, Nike formally announced the appointment of Georgetown University basketball coach John Thompson to its corporate board.[39] It was a fitting honor for Thompson, who had navigated the dispute between two personal friends—Jesse Jackson and Nike chairman Phil Knight—with grace and good humor. But it spelled the end of the PUSH boycott of Nike, and indeed, of PUSH boycotts in general.

Money began flowing back into PUSH coffers as a result of Jackson's renewed fundraising efforts. Old friends such as John Johnson, the publishing magnate who owned *Jet* and *Ebony*, kicked in significant new funds, which were tax deductible when given to Jackson's "church." Other large donations came in from Soft Sheen Products, Johnson Products, and East-Lake Management. Jackson hustled hard and fast and corralled Ford, McDonald's, Coca-Cola, and Burger King to pay top dollar as sponsors of the annual PUSH convention, held that year to piggyback with the Indiana Black Expo in Indianapolis. PUSH interim director Joseph Gardner said additional moneys were coming into PUSH-Excel through sponsorship of the Scottie Pippen Pro Basketball Classic in which more than a dozen NBA stars participated, thanks to Jackson's ties to John Thompson. The event drew thirteen thousand people, Gardner said, and brought in much needed funds for Jackson's now defunct school excellence program, which continued to exist solely to raise money to pay back the federal government for the misspent grants of the Carter era.[40]

The new PUSH executive director, the Reverend Henry Williamson, would eventually claim to have raised one million dollars by the end of the year and to have expanded membership to fifty thousand.[41] And yet other PUSH staffers said Williamson had expanded its membership base to just twenty thousand paid members[42] and had been forced to increase the yearly dues. While the higher membership number was certainly useful with the organization's financial backers and enhanced Jesse's political clout, the smaller number may have been closer to the truth, an inadvertent slip that was never challenged and never corrected.

But Jackson had reached the end of the line with the old ways of the 1960s and 1970s, which in the end made him work hard for his money. When he returned to shake down corporate America in the late 1990s he would have a new enforcer: the most powerful man in the world.

NOAH'S TRIALS

Jackson was understandably distracted during the Nike boycott and had no desire to be seen in Chicago after May 1990, once half brother Noah's first trial began before Judge George M. Marovich.[43] Separate from the narcotics and murder-by-hire conspiracy for which he was initially arrested in Greenville, South Carolina, the case literally fell in the laps of state and federal prosecutors as they sifted through the boxes of files they had seized from Noah's home and office in June 1988.

Among the documents were cash register receipts and calculator tapes from several of the fast food restaurants Noah operated under the business name of Renoja Management Company. Also seized was a second set of books, labeled "Calculator Funds Accounting." The black book ledgers "reflected the daily amount of cash skimmed from August 1985 through April 1988, approximately $10,000 a month," a federal court judge found.[44]

Facing pressure from creditors, Robinson launched a scheme in January 1984 he thought no one would ever notice—to skim a portion of the take from his all-night Wendy's restaurants into his own pocket. "Employees were instructed to turn off the cash registers from 2 A.M. until 6 A.M., and to use a calculator to add up customer sales," the court records state. After a trial period when the proceeds were rung back into the cash register in the morning, Noah and his brother felt secure enough to siphon off the cash. "That money went into a different safe in the manager's office and was picked up by Tony George Robinson [who] then took the money to Noah Robinson's office," the court found.[45] In all, the court estimated Robinson and his brothers skimmed $650,000 from their Chicago restaurants over a five-year period. "The skimmed amount" therefore was not reflected in the "gross receipt figures taken from the cash register tapes," the court concluded.[46]

By skimming a portion of his restaurants' gross proceeds Noah avoided paying royalties to Wendy's and to his franchise partners, as well as a variety of state and federal taxes. This is what constituted the core of the RICO Act charges against him. On July 30, 1990, a jury convicted

Robinson on thirty counts of racketeering, mail fraud, wire fraud, bank-ruptcy fraud, and tax fraud. "We are talking about a straightforward case of theft, a conspiracy fraud led by this man here," Assistant U.S. Attorney Jeff Stone told jurors, pointing to Robinson at the defense table.[47]

Robinson's lawyer, Robert Simone, elicited a typical Robinson in-your-face reply.

Simone:	Did you wind up with any money that didn't go through the register?
Robinson:	No.
Simone:	Did you ever tell anyone that you wanted the cash to avoid paying your obligations?
Robinson:	Not one of the fifty-four counts in this indictment accuses me of being stupid. I didn't need the staff to help me steal my money.[48]

Robinson claimed that IBM employees had instructed him to turn off his cash registers at night while the days' sales were being tallied sepa-rately, but the jury didn't buy it, returning a conviction after just a day and a half of deliberations. On December 21, 1990, Robinson was sentenced to six years in jail and ordered to pay a $125,000 fine as partial restora-tion of unpaid taxes. (He was subsequently ordered to forfeit over $600,000.) Judge Marovich ordered him to serve time consecutively to a ten-year sentence resulting from his 1989 conviction in Greenville, South Carolina, as an accessory to the attempted murder of Janice Rosemond.[49] But much worse was to come.

In 1991, federal prosecutors, looking to dismantle the entire El Rukn leadership, initiated a massive trial involving no fewer than sixty-five defendants. Top among them was Jesse Jackson's half brother Noah Robinson.[50] When U.S. Attorney Anton R. Valukas first announced the indictment, he called it the long awaited "death-blow" to an organization that had flooded Chicago with drugs, committed twenty known murders, and attempted seven others. For nearly a quarter century, he said, El Rukn had engaged in "a systematic program of murder, narcotics distribution, terrorism, robbery, extortion, kidnapping, and obstruction of justice."[51]

This was the same street gang Jesse Jackson had complimented for assisting his 1984 get-out-the-vote drive in Chicago and whose members he had used many times as props for his boycotts and street theater. It was the gang whose leader Jackson boasted he had baptized. Jackson's opponents accused him of using the gangs to intimidate into silence anyone who disagreed with him. His close personal relationship with Rukn leader Jeff Fort was well known in Chicago, but not beyond. It was a very good time for Jackson to stay out of Chicago, even if it meant the near demise of Operation PUSH. Although some members of the prosecution team urged that Jackson be added as a target of the investigation, Valukas rejected their pleas, arguing that prosecuting Jackson under RICO would provoke race riots.[52]

Noah's central role in the Rukn organization became apparent once the trial got underway in July 1991. Federal prosecutors piled on the evidence obtained through FBI wiretaps and testimony by a half dozen top-ranking Rukns who cut deals with the government to avoid the death penalty. "Throughout these investigations," reads an October 28, 1989, file stamped "DEA Sensitive," "Noah Robinson has been identified as the driving force behind these drug distribution organizations, and he has used [El Rukn] to enforce and silence any potential witnesses against him."[53]

Prosecutors say that "Noah saw an opportunity" from Jeff Fort's continuing incarceration. "Noah thought he could dominate the Rukns. They were young, they were punks. He thought he could outfox Jeff Fort, who was controlling the gang by telephone from prison.

"What happened to Noah was such a waste," says prosecutor Matthew M. Schneider. "He was a big black businessman in the city when it meant a lot as a role model and to pump money back into the community. Instead, he became an outlaw."

Part of his outlaw mentality was a pose. "Noah worshipped major crime figures," Schneider says. "During a search of his office on South

Michigan, we found a movie poster from *The Godfather* up on the wall. He worshipped him. He wanted people kissing his ring and coming to him. He wanted to be the godfather of the South Side." Victoria Peters, another prosecutor, adds, "Ever since he was a kid, he idolized mobsters. Clearly he was very talented. But he sees himself at the center of the universe." On the Marlon Brando poster, photographed by police and entered as a state's exhibit, was the caption, "Make him a deal he can't refuse."[54]

At a sentencing hearing on May 20, 1992, Assistant U.S. Attorney Theodore Poulos compared El Rukn to "what Al Capone and the other gangsters were in the 1920s and 1930s. They poured drugs and spilled blood all over the city."[55] He said the convictions had "incapacitated the entire leadership of the El Rukn organization."

The *Washington Post* sent reporter Michael Abramowitz to interview Robinson in jail, noting accurately that "little ink has been expended outside Chicago on Noah Robinson." Understandably, all that interested Robinson during that three-hour interview was what he described as "a gigantic government conspiracy aimed at targeting and bringing down the half brother of a one-time black presidential candidate." Although he used to talk freely about his relationship to Jackson, now he clammed up, refusing to answer most "Jesse" questions.[56]

On August 21, 1992, the hammer came down and Robinson was sentenced to life without parole and fined $6 million for using the Rukns as hit men and teaming with them in a multimillion-dollar heroin and cocaine trafficking scheme. The sentence, boasted Assistant U.S. Attorney William Hogan Jr., ensured that "he will never get out of prison." In a thirteen-page statement Robinson had submitted to the court (one of many legal briefs he researched by himself while in jail), he likened himself to Nelson Mandela and contended that he was a victim of a political and racist conspiracy. But Judge Marvin E. Aspin shot back, "He is a victim of himself." Prosecutor William Hogan noted that Robinson was personally responsible for the Rukns's "turning point" by getting them into the drug business in 1983 to raise money to pay the million-dollar bond for jailed gang leader Jeff Fort.[57]

Hogan described the Rukn trial as a new chapter in the fight against gang violence. "Individual gang members had been prosecuted, and groups of gang members were looked at, but nobody ever looked at the entire organization."[58] The RICO prosecution against the Rukn was a first in the nation and attracted the attention of U.S. attorney general William Barr, who immediately sent Hogan to Los Angeles to launch a racketeering probe of the notorious Crips and Bloods gangs. The court ordered that the Rukn headquarters on Drexel Boulevard—known as "The Fort"—be razed, and a children's playground was built on the site.

As for Noah Robinson, with his Wharton School of Economics degree, his multimillion-dollar business empire, and his entrepreneurial spirit, "he could have been the greatest example," Hogan said. "The tragedy is that he's the worst possible."[59]

MORE ARAB MONEY AND CLINTON

Jackson thought long and hard about running for president a third time, and was now focusing his efforts in Washington, D.C., on building the National Rainbow Coalition into a powerful political operation. He was also raising funds for the Citizenship Education Fund (CEF), a nonprofit he had established in 1983 to run the PUSH-Excel high school voter registration drives. One of the many Arab-American donors from his presidential campaigns, Hani Masri, sent a $50,000 contribution to CEF in 1991, according to the group's tax returns. Masri and ten of his family members gave Jackson $9,500 in 1988, but the federal campaign limits did not apply to donations to Jackson's nonprofit groups. For the Palestinian businessman, it was payback for Jackson's unwavering support of Yasser Arafat, who would stay at Masri's mansion in the Virginia suburbs when he came to Washington, D.C., in later years.

Jackson desperately needed the money. Masri's check was one of only three large donations that Jackson received that year.[60] Masri later founded "Arab Americans for Clinton/Gore '96" with James Zogby, the fundraiser who boasted he had brought in $400,000 from Arab-Americans to Jackson's 1988 campaign, and wrote corporate checks to the DNC and

Democratic Party candidates for more than $160,000 during the 1996 campaign.

Masri, who frequented Clinton coffees at the White House, was rewarded in November 1997 with $60 million in subsidized government loans from the Overseas Private Investment Corporation (OPIC). The loans were for his Virginia-based Capital Investment Management Corporation, which he set up in 1993 to handle investment in Gaza and the West Bank. Masri's contract "was not competitively bid," OPIC spokesman Larry Spinelli tells me.[61]

At the same time he was working his contacts with the Clinton administration, Masri sat on a key Information Ministry subcommittee responsible for reviewing the content of television broadcasts within the Palestinian Authority, a position akin to that of chief censor. One family member, Munib Al-Masri, became deputy chairman of the Palestinian Monetary Authority, as well as a board member of the Arab Bank, the largest private bank in the Palestinian areas. A cousin, Commerce Minister Maher Al-Masri, sat with him on the board of Palestine Development and Investment Ltd. (PADICO), an ostensibly private company partly owned by Arafat's economic advisor, Mohammad Rashid, that was used as a vehicle for controlling virtually all foreign investment in the areas under Arafat's control. Masri's key role in attracting U.S. government investment in PADICO was confirmed to me in person by PADICO general manager Farouk Zuaiter in an interview in his Nablus office in the West Bank.[62] For Arafat and his bankers of the Masri clan, cultivating Jesse Jackson was a wise investment that paid off handsomely in favors during Clinton's presidency.

Masri's fat check was not the only money that would come from Arab sources into Jackson's coffers, both directly and indirectly. Another staunch Arafat-backer during the "dark" days when it was still illegal for U.S. government officials to speak to the PLO was Edward M. Gabriel, a Lebanese-American polemicist and lobbyist. Gabriel raised money for the DNC through a variety of organizations, including his own Arab American Institute. He worked closely with Zogby and with Abdulrahman

Alamoudi of the American Muslim Council, the group that raised money for radical Islamic fundamentalist groups such as Hamas. Ed Gabriel's wife, Kathleen "Buffy" Linehan, was a lobbyist for Philip Morris. Starting in 1990, Jackson began receiving a series of $50,000 checks from Philip Morris. Between 1990 and 1996, Philip Morris gave Jackson a total of $215,000, according to CEF tax returns. It was money well spent. Jackson never once jumped on the antismoking bandwagon that ultimately led to hundred billion-dollar settlements against the tobacco companies.[63]

At a gala lunch sponsored jointly by CEF and the National Rainbow Coalition at the Omni Shoreham hotel in Washington, D.C., on June 7, 1991, Jackson gave every appearance of launching a new bid for the Democratic presidential nomination. In a vicious partisan attack he compared President George Bush to former Alabama governor George Wallace:

> George Wallace stood in the door of the schoolhouse and said no to desegregation—segregation today, segregation tomorrow, segregation forever. He promised white America protection from blacks and drove a wedge of hatred deep into the heart of the nation.
>
> Today, George Bush stands in the door of the White House and says no to quotas, no today, no tomorrow, no forever. He promises to protect white America from blacks and women entering the work force. He promises to protect corporations from lawsuits for discrimination, putting the burden of proof on the victim.[64]

He ended the speech, which offered policy prescriptions for everything from foreign and defense policy to education and drugs, with a clear political appeal familiar to supporters from his last two presidential campaigns. "We didn't inherit 1,300 delegates, we earned them," he said, referring to his performance in the 1988 primaries. "And you know and I know if we got seven million [votes] last time, we're quite capable of getting ten million the next time and 1,800 delegates. We, the people can win! . . . Keep hope alive!"[65]

But Jackson still had his ear to the ground, and with Ron Brown in charge of the Democratic National Committee and former campaign worker Alexis Herman working under him, he soon understood there was a freight train coming down the tracks whose name was Bill Clinton. Jackson could jump on and ride to victory, but he would be foolish to stand in the way. Nevertheless, Jackson couldn't bring himself to endorse Clinton during the primaries. Instead, he invited rival presidential candidate Paul Tsongas to Rainbow functions. Clinton's pro business stance and his willingness to reform welfare were anathema to Jackson's hard-left anticorporate values. The only Jackson advisor who made it to Clinton's inner circle was street-smart New York labor union lawyer, Harold Ickes, who had followed Jackson all through the 1988 campaign. "The left wing has changed its views on some issues," Ickes said, explaining his new loyalty to Clinton. "I think the focus of the country has shifted more toward economic security, economic growth—people are terribly afraid about their economic future—and so has the focus of the so-called liberal wing of the party."[66]

A top aide to the late Ron Brown told me that Hillary Clinton "never forgave" Jackson for his tepid attitude to the Clinton campaign. During the dark days of February 1992, when tapes of Clinton's sex-laced phone calls to Gennifer Flowers came to light and threatened to torpedo his candidacy in New Hampshire, Clinton needed all the help he could get, but Jackson withheld his support. Later, with Clinton safely elected, Hillary still "never forgave him." "She was so furious with Jackson she wouldn't let him set foot on a government aircraft if she could prevent it," Brown's aide said.[67] When Jackson finally invited Clinton to address a Rainbow Coalition lunch in Washington, D.C., in June 1992—just one month before the Democratic convention in New York—he did his best to make Clinton squirm. The night before Clinton's speech, Jackson invited as his special guest the female rap singer Sister Souljah to address the Rainbow gathering. The Clinton war room went on alert, parsing her lyrics. They were awful—apparently endorsing racial murder—and Clinton's advisors were unanimous: If he didn't condemn her, President Bush would hang Sister

Souljah around his neck like a millstone. Having seen how Bush had demolished Michael Dukakis in 1988 with the Willie Horton scandal, Clinton was determined to portray himself as tough on crime and came out in favor of the death penalty for repeat offenders like Willie Horton.

After praising Jackson and winning prolonged applause for mocking Vice President Dan Quayle's embrace of family values ("I'm tired of people with trust funds telling people on food stamps how to live," he drawled), Clinton lashed out at Sister Souljah. He said she had fanned racial flames before and during the recent Los Angeles riots. Her comments were "filled with the kind of racial hatred that you do not honor today and tonight," he said. Then he went further, creating a rift with Jackson that would take years to heal:

> Just listen to this, what she said. She told the *Washington Post* about a month ago, and I quote, "If black people kill black people every day, why not have a week and kill white people? So, you're a gang member and you'd normally kill somebody, why not kill a white person?"
>
> Last year, she said, "You can't call me or any black person anywhere in the world a racist. We don't have the power to do to white people what white people have done to us. And even if we did, we don't have that low down, dirty nature. If there are any good white people, I haven't met them. Where are they?"[68]

Clinton answered Sister Souljah's question with a soul-searching look into the audience: "Right here in this room." He drew only polite applause as Jackson scowled. Later, Jackson would accuse Clinton of a "sneak attack" that reflected "a character flaw." Clinton repaid the favor, telling intimates that Jackson's set-up with Sister Souljah amounted to "dirty, double-crossing back-stabbing."[69]

Clinton was unlike other white politicians Jackson tried to intimidate with his ugly, race-baiting traps. Clinton could play the white liberal guilt card when it suited his purposes, but he knew that Jackson's real audience—at least those who bankrolled Jackson's campaign and his lavish lifestyle—were now stockbrokers and bankers, business owners and lawyers, who themselves had probably winced at Sister Souljah's ghetto crudery. Clinton appealed to them directly, over Jackson's head. It was a perfect example of Clinton's acutely honed political skills, a technique cynical political consultant Dick Morris would later call "triangulation." In one masterful stroke he neutralized a potential Bush attack, won over Jesse's audience by appealing to their better instincts and their shame, and convinced the business world of his courage in standing up to a shakedown artist like Jackson. Harold Ickes finally brokered Jackson's endorsement for the Clinton-Gore ticket a few days before the Democratic National Convention in New York.

But even longtime Jackson ally Julianne Malveaux dismissed it as "tepid support." She noted that the opening night of speeches at the convention "was marred by tension between Reverend Jesse Jackson and candidate Clinton." She went on: "Jackson's lack of enthusiasm for the ticket has been noted by several delegates and pundits, and many African American politicians have used the word 'pragmatic' to describe their support of Governor Clinton."[70]

After the convention, Jackson dropped his reserve and traveled coast to coast on behalf of the Clinton-Gore ticket. He was such an enthusiastic convert to Clinton's cause that Christian Coalition leader Pat Robertson filed a successful complaint against Jackson and the National Rainbow Coalition with the Federal Election Commission. Robertson contended that Jackson had provided illegal in-kind contributions to the Democratic National Committee by covering the costs of a massive voter registration drive in the fall of 1992.[71] Jackson himself boasted of his efforts virtually every day before the November 3 election. "As we travel around the country, we are winning the campaign. There is a tidal wave of hope," Jackson said at one campaign stop, where he appeared side by side with Alexis Herman. Rainbow Coalition workers had staged similar rallies in thirty-five states since Labor Day, he boasted, and had taken six thousand people to the polls in Houston, Texas, to vote early.[72] With his own close advisors Ron Brown and Alexis Herman at the DNC, and Harold Ickes and Ernest Green now folded into the Clinton entourage, Jackson understood that a Clinton victory would mean it was payback time.

But while victory might be close, Jackson remained on his guard. "I know who he is, what he is," he said of Clinton. "There's nothing he won't do. He's immune to shame. Move past all the nice posturing and get really down there in him, you find absolutely nothing . . . nothing but appetite."[73]

CHAPTER 10

My Friend Sani

THE INTERMEDIARY

Looking at Africa from afar, one sees nothing but chaos, famine, war, and poverty. But Africa is full of riches, for those who know where to mine them. They range from copper in the Congo, to diamonds in Sierra Leone, to oil in Nigeria, Angola, and Gabon. And that's not all. In 1999, for instance, Mozambique was the world's fastest-growing economy, with Botswana second and Angola fourth.[1] And of course, there's always the economic and technological powerhouse of South Africa, built up during the apartheid regime.

Jackson understood that there was money to be made when he first met Nigerian billionaire Moshood Abiola in his suite at the Four Seasons Hotel in Washington, D.C., in 1985. Here was a man who had started from scratch in a Third World country, got himself hired as an accountant by a British subsidiary of ITT, and went on to build a colossal fortune. By the time Jackson met him, Abiola's business empire ran from bread-making factories to telecommunications, from Lagos, Nigeria, to Geneva, Switzerland. He was sending his children to Harvard and other top universities—and some reports claimed he had as many as eighteen wives.[2] As a newspaper owner and media magnate, he was actively engaged in Nigeria's political scene. By late 1985, he had become the "go to" guy for anyone wanting to do business with Nigeria's new strongman, General Ibrahim Babangida. Abiola built close personal relationships with Nigeria's military leaders starting in 1969. As a then lowly employee of ITT, he confronted the head of Nigerian Signals Intelligence, Lieutenant Colonel Murtala Mohammad, in front of the army chief of staff and the minister of defense over a long overdue payment for some military communications equipment. "After a prolonged argument," Abiola recalls, Colonel Mohammad agreed to honor the debt to ITT.[3] Colonel Mohammad was promoted, and in 1975 came to power in a bloodless coup. With him came Abiola, now a good friend.

Although General Mohammad was himself assassinated, his successor, General Obasanjo, had been Abiola's classmate as a child and was a fellow Yoruba tribesman from Nigeria's oil-rich southern provinces. By the time Jesse Jackson met Abiola, Major General Babangida had seized power. "Abiola made his first money from contracts with the military," says Dr. Mobolaji E. Aluko, a Howard University professor who heads the Nigerian Democratic Movement. "Babangida ruled from 1985 until 1993, so you can't be a big businessman in Nigeria without dealing with him. There's nothing intrinsically evil about that. What matters is what is actually done."[4]

When General Babangida seized power on August 27, 1985, he cited Nigeria's sluggish economy, "badly affected by the drop in world oil prices over the past three years," as the main reason behind the coup.[5] In fact, world oil prices had been running close to $28 to $30 per barrel until earlier that month, when the Saudis dramatically increased their production, apparently at the request of President Reagan, as a means of driving down world oil prices and crippling the Soviet economy.[6]

What Babangida really meant, and most Nigerians understood, was that previous rulers, including Abiola's childhood friend Obasanjo, fed like hogs at the trough on the oil boom of the 1970s and 1980s. They had squandered billions of dollars on political payoffs, while running up foreign debt of more than $20 billion. Much of the debt was owed to the World Bank, which loved "white elephant" development projects. "The World Bank financed a $4.2 billion natural gas processing plant that was built by Mobil Oil, one of the wealthiest multinational corporations in the world," says a former U.S. government investigator. "The same plant would have cost two billion dollars to build in South Texas. In Nigeria, with lower labor costs, it should have been even cheaper. And of course, no one ever accounted for the missing billions."[7]

The corruption of Africa's leaders—especially Nigeria's—was legendary among World Bank lending officers. "Once, when I was doing a review of our Africa loan portfolio, I asked my colleagues how many good projects we had ever done in Africa," a former Africa regional officer says. "They answered: perhaps a half dozen. Very little of the money ever gets down to the street level. Most of the time, we're just filling up some SOB's Cayman Islands bank account. The money just evaporates."[8] In other words, Africa is a fertile field for Jesse Jackson—and, of course, Africans know what Jackson is after.

"Jackson is not trusted in Nigeria," says pro-democracy advocate Dr. Aluko, who met with Jackson many times and believes he was "out of his depth" in Nigeria's complex political and tribal conflicts. "He just wants to make money from Nigeria and everybody knows this. He feels that Africa is the one place where black Americans should not be locked out of the economic pie. That is his beef. Call it affirmative action in Africa, if you will."[9]

Increasingly, for Jesse Jackson and his sons, the name of the game in Nigeria would be oil.

GENERAL BABANGIDA'S MEN

If Babangida came to power with pledges to clean up corruption and return the nation to civilian rule, once he seized power he bellied up to the bar like all his predecessors. To get an idea of the size of the pickings, consider this: a government probe by Babangida's successor, General

Sani Abacha, found that $12.4 billion in oil revenue went "missing" during Babangida's years in office, from 1985 to 1993.

While that estimate may have been exaggerated for political purposes, everyone who has ever done business in Nigeria, from the World Bankers to the London oil traders, knew that huge amounts of money were disappearing. The missing billions are sometimes referred to as the "Gulf War windfall," the amount of unexpected money that flowed into Nigeria's state coffers as a result of the spike in world oil prices following Saddam Hussein's August 1990 invasion of Kuwait.[10]

Not all of the money wound up in accounts used by Babangida for his personal use, but most of it flowed through the general's fingers and was dispersed to business partners, cronies, and privileged foreigners who jostled each other lining up at the trough. To this day, much of it has never been found. "It wasn't skimming," says human rights activist Mike Fleshman. "It was more like shoveling—and it happened right at the Central Bank. The oil money came in as cash, in phenomenal amounts. And it went right back out to Babangida's friends and cronies."[11]

Fleshman worked for the Africa Fund, an advocacy group founded in 1966 by the American Committee on Africa, and got to know Jackson well as they collaborated on a variety of projects. "Jesse Jackson never denied having an extensive business relationship with General Babangida," Fleshman says. "He told me it wasn't because he had any great love for Babangida, but because of a common interest. 'Remember, Mike, Nigeria is giving absolutely vital assistance to the ANC [the anti-apartheid African National Congress in South Africa],' he used to say. And it was true. They gave financial, military, and diplomatic aid during the most difficult times."

As Jackson quietly went back and forth to Lagos and the new capital Abuja in the late 1980s and early 1990s, he established a working relationship with Babangida and Babangida's men. And so did his sons. In 1990, Abiola held a conference in Nigeria on reparations for slavery. "Jackson sent his son Jonathan to attend the conference," recalls Randall Echols, who handled Abiola's U.S. business and political interests and was a close personal friend. Jonathan soon became Jesse's surrogate for business dealings in Nigeria.

The most valuable commodity Babangida had to sell was oil—and lots of it. Nigeria produces around two million barrels of oil per day, and 60 percent of it is controlled by the Nigerian military, which has ruled the country with only brief periods of civilian government since 1966. "It was absolutely clear Jesse Jackson had business deals with Babangida," Fleshman says. "There's a significant body of evidence that Jackson helped spread oil contracts to his friends and political allies during the Babangida years." And closer to home.

Some of that evidence would come out ever so briefly in an unusual court case in San Francisco, when one of Babangida's men ran afoul of U.S. laws.

As Jackson tells it, he and his sons Jonathan and Jesse Jr. first met Nigerian businessman Pius Ailemen "socially" during his second presidential campaign and never suspected he was engaged in any illegal activities. The relationship developed rapidly, as Ailemen attended the Democratic National Convention in the summer of 1988 as Jackson's guest. U.S. prosecutors in San Francisco were already on Ailemen's trail by that time. They arrested him initially on drug trafficking charges in 1989, but couldn't make the case in court. In 1990, Ailemen was acquitted by a San Francisco jury on drug charges, but received a five-year sentence for falsifying data on a passport application.[12]

During this time he expanded his relationship to the Jacksons, claiming—apparently falsely—that his father was Nigeria's transportation minister. "We've never been able to confirm that part of his story," says Assistant U.S. Attorney Theresa Canepa.[13] But Ailemen did have close ties to the Babangida clan, and court-ordered wiretaps—entered into the public record in January 1994—show that Babangida's wife provided critical assistance to his drug smuggling efforts. "The heroin arrives here in this country through a high government level," one of Ailemen's coconspirators, Ellis Quarshie, told a U.S. undercover agent who had penetrated their drug ring. "Pilots from Nigeria Airways, Kenya Airways, and members of the government are involved." Quarshie told the agent that the "president's wife is in charge of these things," and mentioned that "her name was Babangida."

Only days after Ailemen was released from jail the first time in October 1991, he and Jesse Jr. went to buy a used Alfa Romeo convertible for $13,517.56. To help his friend, Jesse Jr. paid for the car using his own credit card and didn't flinch when Ailemen listed a false name on the purchase agreement. Jesse Jr.'s lawyer acknowledged the transaction, but said her client was unaware of Ailemen's drug trafficking and had not noticed he was using an alias.[14] In the indictments against him, Ailemen used a variety of identities, including Muhammed Popoola, Cyril Adebayo, and Robert Leda Wright.[15]

None of this appeared suspicious to Jesse Jr., who is now a U.S. congressman from Chicago. Federal agents eventually seized the Alfa because it was being used by one of Ailemen's female accomplices for dope runs.[16] It remains unclear if or how Ailemen reimbursed Jesse Jr. for the car. Despite a faxed inquiry and repeated follow-up calls, Jackson's congressional office declined to comment.

HOT WIRETAPS

Jonathan Jackson's ties to Ailemen went even further than Jesse Jr.'s. The 1993 wiretaps on Ailemen's phones showed he telephoned Jonathan frequently in August, September, and October 1993. The calls were to discuss a variety of commercial transactions. This led the Drug Enforcement Agency (DEA) to state in a sworn affidavit to the grand jury that there was "probable cause to believe that Pius Ailemen, Johnathan [sic] Jackson (and others) have committed, are committing, and will continue to commit" federal offenses. The suspected offenses included heroin trafficking, conspiracy, and money laundering.[17] These calls occurred at a time when his father was attempting to get President Clinton to go easy on the Nigerian regime, despite General Babangida's broken promise of handing over power to a newly elected civilian president: Moshood Abiola, Jackson's old friend.

The affidavit stated that "a Jonathan" from Chicago called Ailemen on August 20, 1993, and asked whether a certain person sold "oil." The DEA told the grand jury that its agents "believe that 'oil' is a code for narcotics." The assumption was a blunder for which the federal prosecutors would pay.

Jonathan Jackson made two more calls to Ailemen on September 21, 1993, the DEA reported.

> Ailemen told Johnathan [*sic*] that they would meet in London. Ailemen also stated that the Lagos price is "9" and the London price may be "11". . . . Ailemen told Johnathan that it is "cash and carry." Ailemen informed Johnathan that he would hear from the higher party in the morning. Johnathan then advised Ailemen to call "Killer Mitch."

The DEA went on to claim that the numbers 9 and 11 "could refer to the price of narcotics" and speculated ominously about the true specialty and identity of "Killer Mitch." Jonathan Jackson promptly called reporters and set them to rights. "Those were all oil quotes," he said indignantly. Ailemen "was telling me that people with large letters of credit could pick up oil below wholesale."[18] As for "Killer Mitch," the younger Jackson said he was Lorenzo Mitchell, the sixty-five-year-old family barber, whom Jackson had suggested Ailemen should visit before making an overseas trip.

Once the story broke in San Francisco, Jesse Jackson threatened to sue newspapers that had reported on the publicly available affidavit, which alleged ties between his sons and the Ailemen drug trafficking network. "I have no fear whatsoever that I will be contradicted when I say that Jonathan, Yusef and Jesse [Jr.] are innocent," he said. "We're going on the offensive. We have nothing to hide and everything to reveal. You can not deal in Jonathan' s business as a stockbroker or an international investor if you are a drug suspect. If Yusef is projected across the nation as a drug suspect as he is trying to get into the Harvard School of Business, it interferes with his education."[19]

At the time the allegations surfaced, Jonathan Jackson was twenty-eight and clerking at the Chicago Board of Trade. "I know Mr. Ailemen, but I know nothing of Mr. Ailemen and drugs," the younger Jackson told reporters. "I do not use drugs, and I have never had a professional rela-tionship with Mr. Ailemen. The quote that was made was in reference to oil. Oil is oil. It is not illegal for a black man in America to discuss oil with an African. We were discussing oil prices." Jonathan Jackson appeared to be fuming, but he was also worried. In his attempt to stifle any further report-ing on his connection to Ailemen he played the race card and the political witch hunt card simultaneously. "This is a malicious attempt to destroy me," he said. "I have the right to discuss business and negotiate price. What you see here is a cultural bias that two young blacks can't discuss oil."[20]

Jonathan and Jesse's heated denials that anyone in the family was involved in Ailemen's drug smuggling network put the issue to rest. Jesse Jackson never carried through on his promise that he had "everything to reveal" about his ties to Ailemen, and not a reporter in America picked up on the real news contained in their denials, which was far more interesting than the drug allegations, which were dropped. Jonathan Jackson acknowl-edged that he was negotiating oil deals with a Nigerian businessman. "Yes, it's oil. It's for your heat. It's for your gas," Jonathan repeated. "It is not ille-gal in America for a black man to discuss with an African, oil."[21]

The oil deals, when they came through, would be placed through a London trading house, according to oil analyst Jonathan Bearman, and involve nearly two million barrels of Nigerian crude, paid into offshore accounts, all perfectly legal.[22] In one interview for this book, the elder Jackson flatly denied that he had ever done business with Babangida, but quickly changed the subject when pressed. "Who was that after Babangida? Abacha? I went there in 1994 to get him to recognize the June 12 election, to free what's-his-name." *What's-his-name*, I said, must have been Moshood Abiola. "Right. I had a press conference there on the lawn of the U.S. embassy in Lagos. I saw Abiola during that trip for the last time. After that, he went down."[23]

As for Pius Ailemen, Jackson claimed in a subsequent interview that he "never saw him" during the 1988 campaign—although he acknowledged that Ailemen had come as his personal guest to the Democratic National Convention in 1988. "And so did thousands. He was not a campaign operative. I don't recall the man." He added: "I think he met my son."[24]

"Jesse Jackson was not about democracy in Nigeria," opines Randall Echols, who was Moshood Abiola's paid lobbyist in Washington as well as his personal friend. "He was about cash." Echols knew Jackson well. A longtime supporter, he traveled with Jackson to Cuba and helped arrange some of the private trips Jackson and son Jonathan made to Nigeria. He also tried—without success—to enlist Jackson's support once Abiola was jailed by Babangida's successor, General Sani Abacha.[25]

STIFFED BY CLINTON

When Bill Clinton moved into the White House, Jesse Jackson was looking for ways to cash in. His relationship with the Clintons was not good, but his good friend and former political ally Ron Brown had received a plum appointment as secretary of commerce. (The appointment had actually disappointed Brown. As one of his personal staff told me in confidence, Brown had wanted to be appointed secretary of state because of "all the prestige and all the perks.")

Other friends had also made it to high places. Alexis Herman, who had befriended Jackson during the Carter administration with generous grants to PUSH-Excel and later worked on his campaigns, was appointed director of public liaison at the White House, a position that put her in daily contact with Bill Clinton's vast fundraising network. Minyon Moore, a secretary at PUSH, became political director at the White House. Donna Brazile, from Jackson's first presidential campaign, had lines into both Clinton and Gore from her work as a paid political consultant during the 1992 campaign. Asked about his former campaign aides, Jackson said with characteristic hyperbole: "Some of the folks who were disenfranchised at that time are now running the government."[26] And yet, despite the friends in high places, Jackson was frozen out. It was not a position he found comfortable, or one he intended to endure.

In May 1993, Jackson traveled to Gabon for the annual African-American summit. It was a time of high expectations as far as Nigeria was concerned. General Babangida had aroused the fury of pro-democracy groups in Nigeria by twice delaying his long-promised handover to civilian rule, and was lobbying American political leaders left and right. Newly elected U.S. senator from Illinois Carol Moseley-Braun even skipped the "freshman orientation" class for incoming Democrats in late November 1992 to fly to Nigeria to meet with Babangida and his henchman, on an all-expenses-paid trip with her campaign manager and fiancé, Kgosie Matthews. Moseley-Braun told reporters she was traveling because she had "a huge campaign debt" to pay off. No one asked her why she would go to Nigeria if she needed money. Matthews went on to become a paid lobbyist for the government of Nigeria at the lobbying shop of Washington and Christian.[27]

By the time Jackson arrived in Gabon, preparations for Nigeria's presidential elections were underway. His old friend, Chief Moshood K. O. Abiola, was leading a coalition of pro-democratic parties that had taken a commanding lead in the polls. Despite ominous rumblings that the generals were determined to resist civilian government whatever the cost, Jackson lavished public praise on Babangida for moving "with a steady beat" toward democracy. On June 12, 1993, as the votes were being counted, Abiola was headed to an overwhelming victory in Nigeria's presidential elections, but General Babangida stopped the count and suppressed the results. Despite his years of friendship with Abiola, and his outspoken attempts to identify himself with the cause of freedom and human rights, Jesse Jackson remained silent as the election was hijacked. The generals ultimately appointed an interim "civilian" government to gloss over the transition to a more brutal military regime that seized power in November 1993.

"Jesse Jackson betrayed Abiola at a critical time for human rights and democracy in Nigeria," says Abiola confidant Randall Echols. "Jackson betrayed him even though Abiola won what was internationally recognized as a fair election with 60 percent of the vote. It was a major letdown. Jackson betrayed the Nigerian people and democracy when he embraced the interim government."[28] The interim government of businessman Ernest Shonekan was a scarcely veiled sham, and included many of Babangida's top cronies in cabinet positions. The country seemed on the verge of civil war. Lagos was completely shut down by a three-day general strike, as Nigerian political leaders attempted to persuade Babangida to proclaim the results of the election, without success.

In August, Abiola fled to the United States. He arranged a meeting with President Clinton at the White House. He hoped Clinton would support him as Nigeria's legally elected president. Coming with Abiola to the meeting was his daughter, Hafsat, a freshman at Harvard. "Abiola sent his Learjet up to Boston to pick her up," recalls Mike Fleshman, who spoke to both father and daughter shortly afterwards. It was the perfect occasion for the U.S. government to demonstrate its commitment to Nigeria's democratic elections—but that never happened. Neither Jesse Jackson nor Bill Clinton saw any benefit in taking the lead on an issue that aroused little passion in the polls and generated no significant campaign contributions. "Clinton gave Abiola a big hug and sent him on his way," Fleshman says. "It was the last time Abiola's name was ever mentioned at the White House. The White House dropped him like a hot rock."[29]

In November 1993, the other shoe dropped, as resistance to the military regime in Nigeria intensified. "The generals asked Chief Shonekan to send in the army to quell the disturbances, but he preferred to resign instead," said a foreign businessman close to General Babangida and other senior officers.[30] The way it was announced at the time, interim president Shonekan "invited" Defense Minister General Sani Abacha to take control of the government. Abacha launched a crackdown on pro-democracy activists and Yoruba rebels who were threatening to secede from Nigeria, taking with them the rich oil fields of the south. One day after seizing power, Abacha officially banned all political activity, and within days placed new restrictions on the media.[31]

Jesse Jackson was nowhere to be found as Nigeria's new leader crushed the revolt and, along with it, the dying embers of an African democracy. His attitude won him scorn from Nigerian pro-democracy groups who believed that his main concern was finding a conduit to Nigeria's new ruler, General Sani Abacha.

BACK TO THE MIDDLE EAST

Jackson sought to return to the limelight in any way he could, but with Bill Clinton in the White House he seemed to have lost his golden touch. In April 1994, he announced with great fanfare a new "peace mission" to the Middle East, only months after Yasser Arafat had set up his newly minted Palestinian Authority under U.S. patronage. It was a good opportunity to visit with the powerful family of his old friend and donor Hani Masri, many members of whom were now top advisors to Arafat and in position to award Jackson allies choice contracts as Arafat sought to develop the West Bank and Gaza. Through PADICO, the semi-private Palestinian investment authority, the Masris had a stake in everything from telecommunications to hotels, construction contracts to electric power generation.

To quell criticism that he would once again betray his anti-Israel sentiments, Jackson announced he would spend equal time in Israel and the Palestinian areas. U.S. Jewish leaders said they were "baffled" by Jackson's initiative and predicted they would spot "mischief." They saw Jackson's trip as a transparent attempt "to revive his stalled political career by casting himself as the great peacemaker of the Middle East."[32]

Jackson made headlines during the trip, but not as he had intended. On April 9, an Associated Press photographer caught him in an instant of terror, frozen between stone-throwing Arab teenagers and Israeli soldiers in downtown Hebron. The reality of the Middle East was a bit different from the way he portrayed it to sympathetic crowds back home.

Jackson saw another opportunity in May, when Commerce Secretary Ron Brown led the U.S. delegation for the inauguration of Nelson Mandela, hero of the anti-apartheid movement, as president of South

Africa. The protocol for the trip was as unusual as the participants were prickly. President Clinton designated Secretary Brown as his personal representative because of the tense rivalry between first lady Hillary Rodham Clinton and Vice President Al Gore, both of whom were also on the trip. Others among the forty-four member delegation were Coretta Scott King, Colin Powell, and Benjamin Chavis, who had just beaten Jackson in a back-room competition to become executive director of the NAACP.[33] "None of them were Jesse's favorite friends," a top aide to Brown recalls. "It wasn't a particularly happy time."[34] He didn't have many friends on the ground in South Africa either. "Jesse wasn't particularly welcome in South Africa," a congressional aide who did prep work for the trip recalls. "The ANC in South Africa viewed him as a rank opportunist because of his earlier trips during apartheid."[35] President Clinton added insult to the injuries Jackson was feeling when he appeared at the annual NAACP Legal Defense Fund dinner on May 31, 1994, in Washington. The president praised virtually every African-American leader past and present—except Jesse Jackson.

BETRAYAL

On June 12, 1994, Jackson's old friend Moshood Abiola, whom he had abandoned so faithlessly, emerged from hiding and declared himself president on the first anniversary of Nigeria's quashed election. In a gesture full of bravado, he named cabinet ministers and claimed to represent the only legal government of Nigeria. General Sani Abacha promptly arrested him, sending the country deeper into crisis. Abiola's fellow Yoruba tribesmen in the southern oil fields went on strike on July 4. The Anglo-Dutch producer Shell Oil declared it was losing 400,000 barrels a day to the strikes, roughly 20 percent of Nigeria's daily output, and pulled senior staff and expatriates from the oil fields.[36]

Fearing a disruption of U.S. oil supplies, and not wanting to get personally involved in Africa at a time when news of the genocide in Rwanda (and his own refusal to intervene) was beginning to leak, President Clinton decided to send the Reverend Jesse Jackson on a poison pill mission. If

Jackson succeeded in getting General Abacha to set Abiola free, then Clinton would take the credit. If he failed, then Jackson would bear the blame.

It was a no-win situation, but Jackson was so eager for publicity and some sign of recognition from Clinton that he accepted the mission immediately. "I supported his mission," recalls pro-democracy activist Dr. Aluko. "I met with Jackson for five or six hours before he left, because all hell broke lose in Nigeria when his trip was announced. People said they would stone him if he came, and Jackson was suspicious. We told our friends back in Nigeria they should give him a chance."[37] Dr. Aluko had an interest in seeing Jackson succeed as a liaison, because General Abacha had chosen Aluko's father as an economic advisor.

Jackson received a stormy reception when he landed at Lagos airport in July 1994. "He was greeted with boos and rotten tomatoes," Randall Echols recalls. "How can somebody who advocates civil rights and human rights in America not advocate civil rights and human rights in Africa? Jesse Jackson had a double standard. Once he got to Africa, he embraced the dictator."[38]

Clinton's diplomatic initiative to resolve Nigeria's political paralysis backfired completely, generating anti-American protests in Nigeria by human rights campaigners who blasted Jesse Jackson for his support of Sani Abacha. "Jesse Jackson can make terrific statements, but he has the attention span of a gnat," Aluko himself said. Nobel Prize-winning Nigerian playwright Wole Soyinka complained to Secretary of State Warren Christopher of Jackson's cozy relationship with the Nigerian military. "General Abacha will manipulate a visit by Reverend Jackson toward his strategy to cling to power," he wrote.[39]

Stung by the criticism, Jackson said he had only come to deliver a letter from President Clinton to Abacha, warning him of the consequences if he didn't release Abiola and other jailed human rights advocates. "We're not close to the military government. We are in disagreement with the annulment [of the election]. I do not know all the internal politics that took place," Jackson said lamely in defense of his trip at a press conference on the lawn of the U.S. embassy.[40]

But Nigeria still had oil, and it was an opportune time to size up the new man in town. Recalling that trip, Jackson told me in an interview that he "had no benefit" from his relationship to the Nigerian strongman.[41]

THE FIXER

General Sani Abacha was nothing like Babangida. If Babangida could be subtle, even humorous, Abacha was withdrawn, cold, and prone to solitary decisions. Babangida had a populist streak; Abacha was shy to the point of appearing aloof. While Babangida spread Nigeria's oil wealth to friends and cronies, who allowed some of it to trickle down to their tribes and extended families, Abacha initially tried to crack down on corruption, arresting big bankers who were robbing the country. In 1994, he turned over a portion of Nigeria's oil exports to a Lebanese businessman named Gilbert Chagoury, in an effort to stop the military from siphoning huge amounts of the state revenues into offshore bank accounts.

Born in Nigeria in 1946—when it was still a British colony—Chagoury was raised as a dual-national (Lebanese-British) in the tiny but influential Lebanese community in Lagos. "I became good friends with the children of Dr. Nnamdi Azikiwe, who became the first president of Nigeria, so I have had contacts with political circles in Nigeria all my life," Chagoury tells me in an interview at his office in Paris. "I was the only foreigner who was invited to the presidential palace in 1960 for the official celebration of independence from Britain. I was fourteen years old. We were so poor then I didn't even have a suit and had to buy one."[42]

After working his way up as a car salesman with Nissan in the 1960s, Chagoury built flourmills in Lagos and Kaduna. "I started working at age thirteen, and made my first fortune by the age of twenty-five," he says. "So of course I frequented politicians and helped them. It's what you did. I admire people who take the risk of politics."

During the 1970s, Chagoury met future military ruler Sani Abacha, who was then an army major. As young men, they forged ties that would flourish twenty years later when Abacha came to power in November 1993, vowing to clean up corruption in the military and develop the country. Chagoury built his commercial empire during the 1970s and 1980s and enjoyed close personal relations with Babangida and other top military officers. But with Abacha, it was different. "Sani, this is Gilbert, your brother," Chagoury would say when he remonstrated with Abacha for actions he felt endangered Nigeria's relations with the United States and the West. The two were as close as lips and teeth.

"I recall one time when I brought Abiola to the Pentagon before he returned to Nigeria and was jailed," says Randall Echols. "We telephoned Aso Rock, the presidential residence in Abuja. The man who answered the phone was Gilbert Chagoury. He was Abacha's political and business mentor. Ever since Abacha was a major, Chagoury was there, helping to build him up." His detractors called him Abacha's bagman, an allegation Chagoury shrugs off, saying that the Nigerian government has exonerated him of any wrongdoing.

Although his biggest contracts had been signed when Babangida was president, Chagoury appeared everywhere once Abacha came to power. The family construction company, C & C, helped build Nigeria's new capital in Abuja, constructing a new headquarters for the secret police, a huge government complex that housed several ministries, and the National Assembly building, projects that mobilized thousands of workers and huge construction sites during the Abacha years. Chagoury companies built the Defense Academy in Kaduna, a sprawling complex eleven kilometers on each side, and the Bonny oil export terminal on an island off the Nigerian coast. "We had twenty thousand employees in Nigeria," Chagoury says. "We were the only Nigerian multinational corporation at the time, and this created great jealousies. We competed for business with multinationals from Europe and the United States."

After Abacha's death in 1998, Chagoury agreed to return several million dollars left over from "state security" contracts entrusted to him by the president's office for government purchases that had been completed under budget, and additional money from contracts that were subsquently cancelled. Despite this unusually scrupulous gesture, a Swiss magistrate in Geneva temporarily froze accounts under Chagoury's control that contained more than $100 million. Some of the money, as he explained in a March 9, 2000, court appearance in Switzerland, had been earmarked for classified projects. "I was entrusted with a number of assignments relating to state security. These assignments have always been entrusted to me directly by General Sani Abacha," he testified.[43]

Chagoury describes his role with Abacha as advisor, friend, and confidant. "I wanted to make sure he didn't make blunders that would harm Nigeria," he tells me. It was in this capacity that he came to have dealings with Jesse Jackson.

Chagoury first met Jackson during one of his unannounced trips to Lagos in 1987 or 1988, when a Nigerian tribal leader, Chief Akanda, hosted a champagne reception for Jackson at the Federal Palace Hotel in Lagos. Seventy or eighty top Nigerian military officers attended. "All the important leaders were there," Chagoury recalls. "When Jesse Jackson came to Nigeria, he was somebody. Babangida and others looked up to him as a leader of black Americans. They believed he had influence in America, and could sell their plight to America." But Jackson's influence proved illusory, as did his dedication to the causes he espoused so publicly in America. When Chagoury tried desperately to get Jackson to help work a deal to free political prisoners many years later, he claims the American civil rights leader wouldn't even pick up the phone.

BUYING FRIENDS

Following Jackson's failed July 1994 trip to Nigeria, pressure mounted in the United States to impose an embargo on purchases of Nigerian oil. The human rights situation in Nigeria had dramatically worsened. General Abacha was arresting journalists, human rights activists, and political opponents. In 1995, he arrested former president Olusegun Obasanjo and scores of his associates on charges of plotting a military coup. The State Department sharply condemned Abacha's actions and warned him against executing his rivals. Randall Robinson, a prominent veteran of the anti-apartheid battle who headed the activist group Transafrica, launched an anti-Abacha campaign across America and staged protests in front of the Nigerian embassy in Washington. "The global image of African people is tainted by the disastrous, indefensible conduct of the military leadership" in Nigeria, Robinson said. "I would welcome an oil embargo." Robinson enlisted Jackson and scores of other prominent African-Americans to sign newspaper ads condemning the Abacha regime.[44] But Jackson never came out in favor of sanctions.

Abacha wasn't terribly worried by the fuss. "Abacha felt he had all his bases covered, with U.S. oil companies presumably taking care of Republicans and the Black Caucus taking care of Democrats," a prominent African-American businessman says.[45] Abacha spent several million dollars a year on high-priced Washington lobbyists, including a smooth-talking African-American lawyer named Bob Christian, who entertained members of the Congressional Black Caucus.[46] Their job was to avoid U.S. sanctions on Nigeria, and Jesse Jackson supported them all the way. "The reason I do not favor sanctions is because they affect the poorest people," Jackson told me. "The leaders are insulated from the sanctions. . . . We've built too many walls, and not enough bridges."[47]

Another key lobbyist was Adonis Hoffman, a former staff director for California Democrat Mervyn Dymally, who had served on the House Foreign Affairs Subcommittee on Africa. Hoffman went to work for a variety of think tanks, where he organized public relations trips to Nigeria for members of the Congressional Black Caucus. "Adonis was doing Abacha's PR, and arranged these Potemkin tours of Nigeria for the Black Caucus, to show them what a democratic place Abacha's Nigeria was," says Mike Fleshman.

At one point, the Nigerian embassy in Washington attempted to buy off the NAACP with what amounted to a $20,000 bribe, according to an internal NAACP report. The offer was made after two NAACP board members, Lucy and Wade Henderson, were arrested in June 1995 protesting in front of the Nigerian consulate in New York. "In the aftermath of the protest," the report explained, "the Nigerian government offered a $10,000 contribution to the NAACP at a major fund-raising event held for Mrs. Myrlie Evers-Williams, the chairperson of the NAACP

national board of directors. In making this contribution, the Nigerian government pledged to contribute an additional $10,000 to the NAACP in
the near future." In the end, the board decided to reject the Nigerian government offer "to underscore the immensity of NAACP concerns over the
reports of human rights abuses and the Nigerian government's refusal to
relinquish its military control of the nation," the report concluded.[48]

Similar concerns didn't deter Dorothy Leavell, president of the
National Negro Publishers Association, who led a junket of black journalists to Nigeria that was paid for by Abacha's official Washington, D.C.,
lobbying firm, Symmes, Lehn & Associates.[49] Leavell became the point
person for the Coalition for Fairness to Nigeria, which took out full-page
advertisements in 110 black newspapers across the country in support of
Abacha. "If Jewish Americans can stand [up] for Israel, we can stand up
for Africa," she wrote. "Now is the time to let President Clinton know that
we African-Americans respectfully recommend responsible engagement
with Nigeria and oppose isolation and economic sanctions." Jesse
Jackson used the same argument, accusing white politicians of a "double
standard" when it came to judging unsavory leaders of black Africa.

In November 1995, Abacha outraged official Washington when he
hanged playwright Ken Saro-Wiwa and eight others after a closed military tribunal found them guilty of murdering pro-government tribal chiefs
in the oil-rich Ogoni homeland in southern Nigeria. From then on, the
abuses read like a sad and familiar Third World litany.

In January 1996, Abacha imprisoned the head of Petroleum and
Natural Gas Senior Staff Association and other labor activists, and "routinely detained human rights monitors, journalists, and political opponents for making or publishing critical statements," according to the State
Department. In June 1996, Abacha agents murdered Kudirat Abiola, the
"senior wife" of imprisoned president-elect Moshood Abiola, gunning
her down in broad daylight in her car. Nearly forty thousand people were
in government prisons awaiting trial, an all-time high. "Some have been
detained as long as twelve years without trial," the State Department
reported in its annual compendium of human rights abuses that year.

Calls for an oil embargo intensified in the United States, and even Abacha's friends were having difficulty making his case—with a few significant exceptions.

Less than two months after the brutal murder of Kudirat Abiola, Illinois senator Carol Moseley-Braun was back in Nigeria for a weeklong junket. She was wined and dined by Abacha and his spendthrift wife, Maryam. Senator Moseley-Braun had the indelicacy to visit executed playwright Ken Saro-Wiwa's home village in Ogoniland where she hobnobbed with the military governor, but refused to meet with the families of the eight executed Ogoni activists. Randall Robinson and other African-American leaders condemned her junket. Even Jesse Jackson found her behavior excessive. "It is unfortunate that the senator's trip gives the impression of lending legitimacy to an illegitimate regime in Nigeria," he said.[50] But he would soon change his tune, as he did many times when it came to Nigeria.

"Abacha paid for his public relations and damage control by giving money to the black leadership in America so they would excuse his most dastardly crimes," says Randall Echols. "It was not incidental that large sums of money were sent to the upper echelons of American black leaders just before or just after some of the worst abuses of his regime."

Echols speaks from hard experience in Lagos and Abuja. "I met with Abacha to clear the way for Jesse to see Abiola in prison," he says. "There were massive bribes on the table for the picking. I was offered huge sums of money, if I would just play ball. It was in the millions: there were insider contracts, oil, commodities, cash. . . ." Echols says the only thing Abacha wanted in return for the money was a public statement in support of the Nigerian government aimed squarely at the African-American community in the United States.

Echols goes on, "He wanted me to say that we in America should allow black people to solve their problems among themselves and not get involved." Echols says he shunned the cash. And he continued to highlight Abacha's abuses which was not the approach Jesse Jackson or other black leaders took. "To meet with them does not mean you catch what they've got," Jackson told me, referring to a variety of dictators he has met over the years. "It's the murky business of diplomacy."

Among the most blatant of Abacha's U.S. apologists was the Reverend Henry Lyons, president of the National Baptist Convention, which claimed to represent 8.5 million black Baptists. The Reverend Lyons received secret payments totaling $350,000 from the Nigerian Permanent Mission to the United Nations from April 1996 through February 1997, in exchange for talking up Abacha with other black preachers and the Congressional Black Caucus. Lyons sent delegations of black ministers on junkets to Nigeria even as Abacha was murdering opposition leaders and torturing his opponents in jail. Lyons met with President Clinton in April 1996, and with Hillary Rodham Clinton two months later, and painted a glowing picture of Abacha, the family man, to the Congressional Black Caucus that summer.

"We didn't know what kind of compensation he was receiving, but we knew from what he said that he was working for the government in some kind of way," said Democratic Tennessee congressman Harold Ford Sr., who has since retired. "If he had told us that he was a paid lobbyist for Nigeria, he never would have been allowed to come before the caucus."[51]

In September, Lyons succeeded in getting President Clinton to make a campaign stop at the annual meeting of the National Baptist Convention in Orlando. There, Lyons launched his own panegyric to the Nigerian regime. "It is the contention of this country that due to the 'infighting' in Nigeria, America cannot allow its products and goods to be brought on U.S. soil," he said. "When the Chinese were committing their crimes against humanity, did the flow of money brought by the exchange of goods and services cease in America? . . . The answer is no! Only when it is a black nation, managed by black people, does the nation of America get involved to the point of negative impact on a people. The stoppage of products, goods, and services is hurting Black America and it is killing Nigeria!"[52]

Jesse Jackson would take up this curious argument almost word for word in private meetings with human rights activists and members of the

Congressional Black Caucus. "There's not a position on Abacha he didn't espouse at one time or another," recalls Mike Fleshman. "You name it, he said it. He would come to meetings with us at the Africa Fund and say the most silly things in support of Abacha."[53] As for the Reverend Henry Lyons, he eventually got caught—not because of his illegal lobbying activities, but because his wife set fire to his luxurious $700,000 love nest. Lyons had bought it for his publicist and mistress, Bernice V. Edwards, with the illicit cash. It was a fitting end to the career of a preacher who clearly preferred Mammon to serving God.[54]

CHAGOURY COMES TO WASHINGTON

Chagoury's close ties to Abacha and his love for America prompted him to use his influence on both sides of the Atlantic to heal the growing rift between Nigeria and the Clinton administration, so all parties in the relationship could prosper. In August 1996, he helped organize a trip to Nigeria by U.S. representative Bill Richardson, whom Abacha refused to meet until Chagoury phoned him from Los Angeles and convinced him to change his mind.[55] To gain influence in Washington, Chagoury sought the advice of a political consultant, who recommended that he contribute to a Democratic Party affiliate known as "Vote Now '96." As a foreign national, Chagoury was barred from contributing to the DNC or to Democratic Party causes, but under U.S. law he could give to Vote Now because it was registered as a nonprofit corporation. In September and October 1996, Chagoury sent three checks totaling $460,000 to the group, which in turn funneled the money to Jackson's Citizenship Education Fund for use in the 1996 election campaign. "I didn't know Jesse Jackson yet, but if they had told me the money was going to him, I wouldn't have given it," he says now. The money was sent through a circuitous route of nonprofit shell companies that ran voter registration drives for the DNC in minority communities, ultimately going to Jackson from Project Vote, a unit of Voting for America Inc.

Project Vote, registered in Brooklyn, New York, shares offices with ACORN, a left-wing political action committee and fundraising group affiliated with the Democratic National Committee. The group's website (projectvote.org) boasts that since 1982 it "has registered 2.7 million low-income and minority citizens. . . . In essence, we do what political parties used to do. We reach out into the community, get people talking to one another about real issues, and mobilize a massive voter outreach effort to mobilize voters to the polls." Project Vote lists only three "real" issues on its website. The first, "Enforcing Motor Voter" legislation, is controversial because it has led to massive voter fraud. The second, "Environmental Issues," covers the range "from global warming due to carbon dioxide emissions to arsenic in the water supply." The third is "Reproductive Freedom." Project Vote's parent organization, Voting for America, which is registered in New Orleans, raised $1.3 million in 1996 and gave $820,000 of that money to Jackson's group, according to Citizenship Education Fund tax returns.[56] The money was a windfall at a time when Jackson's finances were still shaky, allowing him to triple the size of CEF in just one year and to provide valuable services for the Clinton-Gore reelection campaign. This in turn helped Jackson patch up his relations with the Clinton White House, a relationship he now understood needed nurturing if he was going to cash in from this Democratic president.[57]

Jackson got other money from foreign sources that year, including a $100,000 cash contribution from a Haitian named Toussaint Hale. This came on the heels of $35,000 Jackson nonprofits had received in 1994 directly from the embassy of Haiti, tapping accounts controlled by President Jean-Bertrand Aristide. This was after Jackson had lobbied Clinton and made numerous public appearances to win U.S. government support for Aristide during his brief exile to the United States. Neither Jackson nor CEF registered with the Department of Justice as a "foreign agent," as this sort of activity should have required. CEF also booked an "anonymous" $25,000 contribution from a source in Jakarta, Indonesia, in 1996. This came at a time when illegal campaign funds were flowing into DNC coffers from the Riady family in Jakarta and their American representative, DNC fundraiser John Huang. Both the Riadys and Huang are ethnic Chinese who were later tied by federal investigators to communist Chinese intelligence organizations.

Chagoury's contributions bought him, his wife, and three of their children entry to a December 21, 1996, dinner at the White House for 250 top DNC donors. "I wanted to take my wife to the White House on her birthday," he says now. Not long after the dinner, at Jackson's urging, Deputy National Security Advisor James B. Steinberg and Susan Rice, then the top National Security Council official for Africa, met with Chagoury "to discuss Abacha's policies on human rights, drugs, and democracy initiatives," the *Washington Post* reported.[58] Steinberg told the *Post* that they had agreed to meet with Chagoury because "this was an ideal way to get a clear message" to Abacha about the U.S. government's displeasure with Nigeria's policies on human rights.

Jackson then tried his shakedown routine on Chagoury. "Jesse invited me to come out to his church in Chicago. I was ready to go," Chagoury recalls with a chuckle. "Luckily a friend told me I was being set up. He said Jesse would stand up in front of the audience and say 'how pleased we are today to have Gilbert Chagoury with us, who has promised to give us this or this amount of money.' And I couldn't have said no, because it would mean losing face."

Oil journalist Jonathan Bearman in London tells reporters that son Jonathan Jackson was awarded contracts on two supertankers, each loaded with 950,000 barrels of Nigerian crude, which he resold to a London oil trader in 1997. "I met the person who let the contracts in Nigeria. I know the person who traded them in London. The documents exist in the books of the NNPC [Nigerian National Petroleum Corporation] in Abuja; I've seen them," Bearman tells me.[59]

At prevailing spot market prices of $23 per barrel in early 1997, the two cargoes would have sold for $43.7 million. The commission would have ranged between eight to ten cents per barrel, netting the trader around $190,000. "If my sons had those deals, they are legitimate businessmen," Jackson says in an interview. "That's their business. But I know nothing about San Francisco Oil or Ragma," companies used for Nigerian spot contracts according to a July 11, 1996, article by Bearman in the London-based *Oil Daily*. "I've never heard of them," Jackson adds.[62] Jonathan Jackson did not return repeated phone messages to his home and office requesting comment.

Court proceedings in London, Geneva, and Abuja have since revealed that the Abacha family siphoned off an estimated $4.3 billion during Abacha's four and a half years in office. This included an astonishing $2.3 billion taken directly in cash from the Central Bank and another $1 billion in contracts awarded to overseas front companies controlled by Abacha's sons Ibrahim and Mohammad and their business manager Abubakar Atiku Bagudu.[63]

Abacha's widow Maryam was stopped at the airport as she was leaving the country for Saudi Arabia a few weeks after the general's death in June 1998 with thirty-eight suitcases stuffed with cash. Son Mohammad told the courts his father gave him $700 million in cash during his last two years in office "in bags and boxes" for transport out of the country. (Just to play it safe, Mohammad said he always kept around $100 million in cash in his house.) In October 2001, Mohammad Abacha and Atiku Bagudu filed suit in Abuja to overturn the seizure of accounts belonging to eight front companies they controlled in Europe: Doraville Properties Limited, Fawnview Limited, Standard Alliance Limited, Rayvelle International S.A., Morgan Procurement Corporation, Harbour Engineering and Construction Limited, Mecosta Securities Inc., and Ridley Group Limited. Any one of these companies could have been used to buy political favors without leaving a trace.

The real disgrace of Jackson's dealings with Abacha occurred shortly before the general's death. It is a story that has never been told before, and that illustrates just how little interest Jackson really had in human rights. But before that would come new developments on the home front.

CHAPTER 11

Dynasty

JESSE JR. GOES TO WASHINGTON

Jesse Jackson's ambition to found a political dynasty got a tremendous boost in late 1995, when an unsuspected opportunity presented itself. The popular two-term congressman from the South Side of Chicago, Mel Reynolds, was indicted on tawdry charges of having sex with a minor, a sixteen-year-old named Beverly Heard. In a Chicago courtroom in August 1995, Heard testified that Reynolds drove his black Cadillac in front of her high school during his initial election campaign in 1992 and picked her up. "He was saying he needed someone to be a receptionist and asked if I modeled," she said. "I was hoping maybe he would have a job offer or some kind of great modeling opportunity."

Within a week, Reynolds initiated a torrid affair with the sixteen-year-old Heard. "Mel and I had a really sick relationship," she told the court three years later. "I would just do whatever he would tell me. I felt more or less like a slave."

Once Reynolds went to Washington, the two conducted a long-distance love affair by phone. And that's where the feds jumped in, placing a court-ordered wiretap on Heard's phone. The wiretaps were crucial to Reynolds's ultimate conviction in August 1995, juror James Limper said, "though a little hairy to listen to." In one exchange, Reynolds asked Heard if he could join her in bed with her lesbian lover, a fictitious fifteen-year-old Catholic schoolgirl Heard called "Theresa." Reynolds begged her for lewd photographs of the girl. "Jesus," he said on one tape, "a Catholic. . . . Did I win the Lotto?"

A twelve-member jury, composed of six blacks and six whites, convicted the sitting congressman on August 24, 1995, of two counts of solicitation of child pornography, three counts of criminal sexual assaults, three counts of aggravated criminal sexual abuse, and four counts of obstruction of justice. Reynolds's days in the United States Congress were over, only halfway into his second two-year term.

The prosecution of Reynolds raised serious questions, which remain unanswered to this day. According to court testimony, Reynolds broke off the affair shortly after going to Washington in January 1993. Heard took a lesbian lover, joined the air force, and was stationed briefly in Puerto Rico. When she left the air force and returned to Chicago, Reynolds sought to resume the affair. Heard got angry and went to the police, and agreed to FBI requests in 1995 to wiretap fresh conversations with Reynolds, which she steered to explicitly sexual topics.

Once Reynolds had been convicted, Jackson openly criticized him for working too closely with the new Republican majority in Congress. "One of our arguments with him was his support of the crime bill," Jackson told reporters. "While we look at his situation, we pray for that family."[1]

Soon after he was sentenced to jail, Reynolds announced he was resigning from Congress. Within hours, Jesse Jackson Jr. announced that he would run in the Democratic primary to be held in November 1995, to fill the vacant congressional seat for the second district of Illinois.

Jesse's dreams of creating the preeminent black family dynasty in America were about to get a great lift.

In the meantime, black newspapers in Chicago ran a vilification campaign against Reynolds. They suddenly discovered that he had been a "big check bouncer" while in Washington, and had waged a vicious personal campaign against his black predecessor, Gus Savage, when he chased him from the seat in 1992. ("Gus Savage, he's crazy: he hates Jews," was the refrain.) To round off Reynolds's bad deeds, the *Chicago Citizen* noted that he had voted for the "three strikes and you're out crime bill" that required mandatory life sentences for three time felons, legislation that was vigorously opposed by Jackson and Operation PUSH.[2] To make his point, just days after Reynolds's conviction in court, Jackson and the Reverend James Meeks, pastor of the popular Salem Baptist Church, marched to the Cook County jail through a summer heat wave to demand prison reform and the release of black convicts. "Invest in schools, not jails," Jackson led protestors in chanting. "What do we want? The Brothers! When do we want them? Now!" Jackson claimed that Reynolds, in voting for the three-strikes bill, was sending an entire generation of black youngsters to jail, while allowing white youths to go free.[3]

On September 9, 1995, Jesse Jackson Jr. officially announced his candidacy for the second congressional district. His father wasted no time in putting resources at his disposal, raising money, promoting his candidacy at the Saturday morning meetings and radio broadcasts, and bringing high-powered backers to Chicago to support him. With strong support from the Clinton White House (and $3,000 in campaign donations from Clinton's friends in the Lippo Group in Indonesia),[4] Jesse Jr. won the Democratic primary in November, and the special election in December 1995. At age thirty, Jesse Jr. became a power broker in his own right. The election also marked the beginning of Bill Clinton's reconciliation with Jackson. Clinton wanted Jackson's support for the 1996 presidential campaign.

Just one year earlier, Jesse Jr. had no official residence in Illinois. He listed his domicile as 240 M Street, SW, in Washington, D.C., a one-bedroom apartment where his wife, Sandra, had lived in the late 1980s.

The couple expanded it by purchasing an adjoining three-bedroom unit in December 1992 for $110,000, according to Washington, D.C., real estate records. In October 1994, he and Sandra got their own foothold in Chicago, buying a large brick house just one hundred feet from the Lake Michigan waterfront at 2559 E. 72nd Street, for $200,000. Once Jesse Jr. went to Congress, they paid off the $150,000 mortgage with the First National Bank of Chicago in just four years. This was a stellar performance given that the couple purchased a nine-bedroom mansion at 2034 O Street, NW, in Washington assessed at $540,000 during the same time period. It helped, of course, that someone else picked up the mortgage on the O Street mansion. The Washington, D.C., real estate records show that a Sybille Saurbrun took out a mortgage on their behalf with the First Union National Bank in Washington, D.C., for an undisclosed sum, which was not reported on Jesse Jr.'s financial disclosure forms to the House Ethics Committee. Despite repeated interview requests and written questions, Congressman Jackson declined through a spokesman to comment.

The young Jacksons appeared to be big spenders. They liked fast cars in addition to multiple residences, and owned numerous BMWs as well as an Isuzu Trooper. After Jesse Jr. went to Congress, the couple maintained a pair of older BMWs (hers, a 1991 BMW 525i, Illinois plates "BLK66"; his, a 735i, Illinois plates "D523242"), and purchased three more. For the congressman there was a 1993 two-door 850Ci coupe with prestige tags ("2CG"), and a 1995 840Ci with vanity plates ("REPZNTN"). The BMW 850 series is the top of the line sports car, boasting a ripping 5.0-liter, 322-horsepower, V-12 engine that listed new in 1993 at a modest $88,720 without options. Even *Chicago Tribune* car editor Jim Mateja found that a bit pricey. "For $88,720, some might expect two bedrooms and a bath, not the two doors and the $3,000 gas-guzzler tax on the '93 BMW 850i we tested," he wrote. The younger Jackson's 1995 840Ci is a slightly more modest version equipped with a 4.4-liter, 32-valve, V-8 engine that listed new for a mere $72,000. Sandra bought a 1995 740i four-door sedan (plates "D723000"), which Mateja called "a carpenter shop/medical center on wheels" that listed for $59,900 new.[5] The young couple had $300,000 in automobiles alone—not exactly chump change, especially for someone who listed his salary at $26,029 per year.

Jesse Jr. and his wife transferred their official domicile back to Chicago just months before the prosecution against Mel Reynolds began. Was it just luck? Or did Jesse Jr. know that something bad was about to happen to Reynolds and that he needed to reside in Chicago officially if he was going to run for his congressional seat? Again, despite repeated attempts to inteview the congressman about this and other matters, Jesse Jr. declined through a spokesman to comment.

On his initial financial disclosure form, Jesse Jr. lists two sources of income for 1995. There is the $26,029 per year salary as "International Organizer" for H.E.R.E., the Hotel Employees and Restaurant Employees Union.[6] Then there is additional income, $24,500, that he earned from the Program Corporation of America in White Plains, New York, a company listed with Dun & Bradstreet as a supplier of "translators & interpreters" run by Alan S. Walker. He also lists unpaid positions with the Keep Hope Alive political action committee and with PUSH.

Jesse Jackson Jr. had an impressive portfolio of mutual funds for someone fresh out of law school, with a limited employment history, and who was only thirty years old. He disclosed that he owned ten mutual funds each worth between $15,000 and $50,000, one fund worth $50,000 to $100,000, and two more funds worth between $1,000 and $15,000. The imprecise valuations were designed by Congress to frustrate political opponents from putting an outrageous dollar figure on wealthy incumbents. Taken together, the spread of Junior's stock portfolio ranged somewhere between $200,000 to $630,000, in addition to the $300,000 in automobiles, and his three residences whose combined value was assessed for tax purposes at more than $700,000.[7] And this was just his personal wealth. Jesse Jr. soon became a congressman reliant on PACs, raising hundreds of thousands of dollars during each election cycle from political action committees and major corporations, money that naturally came with strings attached. Big labor (including H.E.R.E.) was a major donor, but so were trial lawyers, pro-abortion groups, teachers and government employees unions, and a few choice companies whose names resonate from his father's shakedowns both past and present: Anheuser-Busch, Ameritech, BankAmerica, Citicorp, Nike. It was a good haul.

JESSE, KING OF BEER

With one son taken care of, Jackson turned to his younger sons, Jonathan and Yusef. Their destiny was to make money to support the family dynasty, while Junior was put in charge of the clan's political fortunes. Jackson asked old friend and financial supporter Ronald W. Burkle if he would scout opportunities for them. Burkle understood that by "opportunities" Jackson didn't mean a management job with the Dominicks or Food 4 Less supermarkets he owned. Nor was Jackson interested in getting his sons in the real estate business, although Burkle sat on the board of developer Kaufman & Broad, whose cookie-cutter houses were being built in decent middle-class communities around the world. Jackson was looking for something big, something special, something his sons could call their own, something befitting black America's first family.

One year later, at a fundraiser at Burkle's Los Angeles mansion, where Jackson was the featured speaker, Yusef tagged along. Then twenty-six, he happened to sit down beside August Busch IV, son of Jackson's old nemesis Augie Busch III.[8] But the younger Busch was not like his father, and 1996 was not 1982. He hit it off with the younger Jackson, and two years later, when he was looking for a new majority owner of the Budweiser distributorship on Chicago's North Side, he called Burkle back and asked him if he thought Yusef might be interested.

Busch was having problems with the River North distributorship, both financial and racial. African-American employees complained that they were being denied promotions and were threatening to call in Jackson and Operation PUSH if Busch didn't satisfy their demands. The Busch family apparently assumed Jackson could now launch a successful boycott, because of public support from President Clinton, and sought to defuse the situation by winning him over as an ally. They began with a $10,000 contribution to Jackson's Citizenship Education Fund in 1997, and campaign cash to Jesse Jr.[9] But in the end they preferred marriage to seduction, and in 1998 began exploring ways to sell the troubled beer distributorship to Jackson's own sons. In the meantime, Jesse had turned up the heat.

In tandem with the Reverend James Meeks, the powerful pastor of Salem Baptist Church, the fastest growing black church in Chicago, Jackson had been preaching anti-alcohol messages to the faithful in the heart of the River North Budweiser territory. "You had Jesse and Reverend Meeks saying the community needed to be dried up from alcohol, at the same time Jesse's sons were looking to enter the beer business with Anheuser-Busch," recalls former Jackson associate Glen Bone III. "That type of hypocrisy didn't sit well in the community."[10] But it worked like a charm with Augie Busch IV.

River North Sales & Service was one of the most lucrative distributorships Anheuser-Busch had to offer, and properties this good didn't come on the block very often. It included the United Center sports arena—home of the Chicago Bulls and the Blackhawks—and ran from Lake Michigan to Harlem Avenue, seventy-six blocks to the West. All together, the territory covered sixty-two square miles. "Counting the beer drinkers in that territory would be like counting the stars in the sky," *Chicago Tribune* columnist John Kass joked. "And the Jacksons have them as customers." Yusef was awarded 67 percent of River North and Jonathan given 23 percent, with the remaining 10 percent owned by Donald Niestrom Jr., a longtime Anheuser-Busch employee who ran the distributorship before the Jackson boys were awarded it on a silver platter. Neither son had any experience in marketing or management, let alone in the beer business. Yusef, who at twenty-eight became president of River North, was working at the Chicago law firm of Mayer, Brown & Platt, while Jonathan, then thirty-two, was president of the Citizenship Education Fund, his father's fundraising vehicle. Public records showed that the Jacksons used a $6.7 million loan from Nations Bank to purchase River North assets—including a warehouse and other buildings on Goose Island—which had cost Anheuser-Busch $10.5 million to build just seven years earlier. The City of Chicago sweetened the pot with $2.6 million in grants and loans to Anheuser-Busch that appear to have been forgiven in the transfer to the Jacksons.[11]

Once the deal was consummated, Kass crowned Jesse Jackson the "King of Beers."[12] The distributorship sold an estimated $30 million to $40 million of Budweiser and other products a year when Yusef and Jonathan Jackson purchased it on December 1, 1998.[13] They never disclosed where they got the money to buy it, but claimed they had paid a fair price—although industry analysts estimated in 2001 that the business could be flipped for $25 million.[14] It was a sweet deal, and the Jackson sons showed their gratitude by never responding to reporters' questions about the financial assistance Anheuser-Busch provided them to purchase the business. "If Bush can be president, why can't Yusef and Jonathan have a distributorship?" Jesse Jackson told critics indignantly at a meeting of the Chicago Association of Black Journalists in March 2001.[15]

Anheuser-Busch spokesman Carlos Ramirez brushes off reporters' questions. "What's your thesis?" he asks after I fax questions regarding the sale. Unsure I'm hearing him correctly, I ask him to repeat himself. "What's your thesis? Your angle? What's the point of this story?" I reply that it is an inquiry that could potentially be of interest to Anheuser-Busch shareholders. They might want to know how their money had been spent. He promises to get back to me.

Three hours later, he phones back. "We've researched your request and we don't want to participate in your project," Ramirez says. "No one is available to talk to you."[16] He refused to respond to questions regarding the price the Jackson brothers had paid for River North, or whether Anheuser-Busch had subsidized the sale or written down assets on its books. "We choose not to discuss this information," he said. When I object that Anheuser-Busch shareholders had a right to know the answers, he hangs up.

Ramirez had asked an identical question when confronted by *Chicago Tribune* columnist John Kass, who deadpanned his reply in print. "I've been insulted in many creative ways, by mayors, aldermen, criminals, clowns, jokers and other elected officials," Kass wrote. "Readers have had plenty to say, too. But I have never, ever, been asked to display my thesis. Never. You don't show your thesis to strangers. Only a weirdo would ask such a thing. If the Anheuser-Busch guy wasn't on the other end of a phone, long distance, I might have thought about slugging him."[17] Neither Ramirez nor his bosses seemed to have read the Kass column, or if they did, they didn't care what the public thought.

Ron Burkle and August Busch IV weren't done with their favors to Jesse and sons. In the year 2000, they bankrolled Yusef Jackson's Internet venture OneNetNow.com, a website he claimed would "bring more minorities" to the Internet. Paying the bills was Burkle's investment firm, the Yucaipa Companies in Los Angeles. When the Internet bubble burst later that year, OneNetNow.com went bankrupt. Ron Burkle shrugged it off. "I'm a friend of the family," he told reporters.[18] "Family" apparently included Jesse Jackson's mistress Karin Stanford, hired by Yucaipa on a $10,000 per month retainer in January 2001, only days after her illicit relationship and love child with Jackson were exposed in the tabloids.[19] Burkle was already in the know, but had kept his knowledge to himself. In December 1999, when Jackson's mistress was seeking a new home for herself and her baby, Burkle sent her to Kaufman and Broad Mortgage Company to get a loan. A quick call from board member Burkle convinced Kaufman and Broad to lend her $291,950 to buy a $365,000 house on Don Miguel Drive in Los Angeles.[20]

JESSE PLEADS FOR NOAH

In April 1996, Jackson paid a visit to the courtroom of U.S. District Court judge James B. Zagel. Zagel had helped crack the El Rukn drug rings back in the 1980s as chief of the Illinois State Police. In chambers, Jackson asked the judge to allow half brother Noah Robinson to go free on bail.

"It's clear Jesse was trying to help his brother. He came over here to make a plea for mercy for Noah as a family member," says prosecutor Victoria Peters.[21] "He didn't claim to know the facts of the case. He just said it was his brother and he loved him no matter what. He didn't push anything, or try to manipulate anyone. It was not your typical Jesse move. He didn't use it as any kind of platform."

Judge Zagel was unmoved by Jackson's impassioned plea for clemency for his half brother. Noah had already been sentenced once to life in prison for ordering the murder of a former gang member and of the witness who had seen the murder. He had also been convicted for conspiring to murder a former business partner, Robert Aulston, by sending a Rukn hit team to Texas with orders to stalk and kill him during a business trip. Noah's case had been declared a mistrial by an appeals court, thanks to clever lawyering and incredible mishaps that befell the prosecution. The mishaps included revelations that two key prosecution witnesses—former gang members Henry Harris and Harry Evans—were given special favors in jail including sexual visits by female friends and access to illegal drugs. On May 13, 1996, Judge Zagel denied Noah's motion to be released on bail.[22]

Jesse tried again in September, this time in an appearance before the court. Prosecutors Matthew M. Schneider and Victoria J. Peters had argued successfully to the judge that Jackson should not be allowed to testify in open court because his public stature might sway jurors to overlook incriminating evidence. So Jackson presented himself to Judge Zagel when the jury was absent. "He didn't bring a lot of people," Peters and Schneider recall. "It wasn't a big media event. We were a bit surprised that he was so subdued."

But Jesse didn't come alone: he brought Reverend Al Sharpton, a few associates from Operation PUSH, and a handful of reporters. "It wasn't a crowd. But it wasn't exactly humble pie," recalls one of several law enforcement officials I interviewed who was present at the scene.

Judge Zagel recessed for lunch, and prosecutors were wondering whether Jackson intended to make a scene. "I was eating a sandwich, and then I remembered: we still had the picture," one member of the prosecution team recalls.

What picture? he was asked.

The picture. When he described the 1969 photograph, which was hanging on the wall of his office, the prosecutors told him to run to get it.

He reentered the courtroom as Judge Zagel was getting ready to gavel open the session, with Jackson as the first witness. Several reporters were present in the gallery. To reach the stand, Jackson had to pass along the prosecution table. Still puffing from the exertion of running, the official made a display of sliding the 8x10 glossy photograph, face-up, from one end of the prosecution table to the other, where the lead prosecutor caught it and set it straight so Jackson could see it. "Jackson came around our table, he saw *the picture*, and he froze," the official recalls. "His jaw actually dropped. And then he took the stand and forgot he had a brother."

The picture showed Black Stone Rangers leader Jeff Fort and his sidekick, Mickey Cogwell, seated in the throne room of the "Fort" at 39th and E. Drexel Boulevard. At their feet, facing the camera, was Jesse Jackson.

The sparse news accounts of the event didn't mention the photograph, which was hidden from the press gallery, but the reporters couldn't fail to detect Jackson's mood. Jackson was "admittedly nervous" as he described how he and his half brother had worked closely with the gangs in the late 1960s. He said he had spent "considerable time" with Fort. "As a matter of fact, I baptized him during that same period," he offered. Noah's defense lawyers had been hoping Jackson would deploy his eloquence, to demonstrate the innocence of Noah's gang connections. Instead, Jackson focused solely on the events on 1968-69, when Jeff Fort was engaged with Jackson as a "community organizer," and said he had no knowledge of Noah's activities once Jackson had left Breadbasket to start Operation PUSH in 1972. Judge Zagel ruled that his testimony was "too remote in time" to the events of the case, which occurred a good ten years later.[23]

Zagel then turned to Assistant U.S. Attorney Chris Cook. "Any questions, counselor?" Cook shook his head, no, and Jackson rushed from the courtroom without a glance behind him. "I might as well tell Noah to go back in the lockup, because there ain't going to be no fair trial," said Lewis Myers Jr., one of Noah's attorneys. "You cut our legs out," he told Zagel.[24]

Out in the corridor, Jackson's small circle of supporters crowded around him. "We could hear Al Sharpton jabbering away," one official recalls, "wondering if we had that kind of picture on him." Alfreda

Robinson still believes Jackson's testimony would have helped her husband, and proudly recalled Jackson coming back for closing arguments in the case, along with "a number of other ministers."[25]

Jackson claims that his ties to the gangs ended once Jeff Fort was jailed in the early 1970s, well before the "Rukn-type thing" began. "By that time," Jackson says, "I knew nothing about them. They had a building not far from where I was that became a 'religious' organization, and Jeff called himself a 'minister.' The idea was, they used the church as sanctuary. The police saw them as real organized gangsters and infiltrated them. By that time, we had no communication with them."[26]

But Jackson's ties to the Rukn weren't all past tense, officials say. Not long before Noah's retrial, Jackson brought picketers to a parking garage under construction by the Chicago Museum of Science and Industry, to protest the firing of a black-owned scavenger company. Television news cameras broadcast the protest during the day. "When I saw those pictures, I did a double-take," one federal investigator told me. "Behind Jesse were a number of known Rukns, waving picket signs up and down for the cameras."

He identified three of them by name. "There was Alexander Bland, a.k.a. Moshambe, a five-time convicted murderer; Chester Bland, a.k.a. Blood, who was arrested by police holding the fresh brain of his latest victim as he was entering a bar, where he said he planned to drink to his kill; and Henry Timothy, a.k.a. Rahim, a Rukn general." It was like the early 1970s all over again, when by Jackson's own admission the gangs used to man his neighborhood boycotts, "as consumers, as citizens."[27]

"All through the 1970s and the 1980s, the Rukn were the only business in town," Peters and Schneider said. "They controlled the South Side."

"The gangs were always present, always there, not part of the movement but on the movement's fringes," recalls Barbara Reynolds, now an ordained Baptist minister in the Washington, D.C., area. While they engaged in "community organizing" and took government grants, they also engaged in drug running, extortion, and murder.

"In the 1970s, the Rukn . . . were taking antennas off of cars and making zipguns," recall prosecutors Peters and Schneider. "They used crossbows, single bolt action rifles, everything but automatic weapons, which weren't widely available then. But they killed a lot of people all the same. We proved more than a dozen murders at trial." More than two hundred people died as a result of Rukn violence. "They had mishits," Peters says. "They followed the wrong car, killed the wrong person. They hit innocent bystanders all the time."

Such was the group Noah Robinson had sought to command. Such were the men Jesse Jackson believed deserved respect.

CHAPTER 12

Hitting the Big Time

THE TEXACO LAWSUIT

When black employees Bari-Ellen Roberts and Sil Chambers, senior financial analysts, first sued Texaco for discrimination in March 1994, Jesse Jackson was nowhere to be seen. He didn't raise his head two months later, when four more black employees joined the suit, or in October, when the Community Relations Service of the U.S. Department of Justice extended its services as mediator to the parties. Jackson remained silent in February 1995, when the mediation broke down and the disgruntled black employees returned to court. He even held his fire when the U.S. Equal Employment Opportunity Commission sent the court a "right to sue" letter in August 1996, allowing the plaintiffs and their lawyers to expand the scope of their grievances into a class action lawsuit, paving the way for potentially lucrative cash rewards.

What got Jackson's attention—and indeed, the attention of the NAACP and a broad cross section of the civil rights community—were the "Lundwall tapes," which purported to document racist and sexist slurs made by senior Texaco executives. This case had the potential to pay out big dollars to the aggrieved.

Richard A. Lundwall, described by the court as "a fairly senior staffer in Texaco headquarters' finance department, located in Harrison, New York," had a grievance against Texaco. At age fifty-five, "after a lifelong career with Texaco entities, his employment had been terminated," district court justice Charles L. Brieant noted in his opinion on the case. Lundwall initially approached the lawyers who were assisting his fellow employees in their race discrimination suit, asking them if they would sue Texaco on his behalf. When they refused, he said he had important information that would aid their litigation, "disclosing that he had surreptitiously made micro-cassette recording tapes of certain Texaco business meetings" that contained precisely the type of racist slur Ms. Roberts and her co-plaintiffs had complained about but were unable to prove.[1]

When Roberts's attorneys leaked partial transcripts from the tapes to the *New York Times* on November 4, 1996—the day before the presidential elections—Jesse Jackson and the race baiters swung into high gear, alleging a pattern of race discrimination in one of America's premier companies. *New York Times* reporter Kurt Eichenwald painted a lurid scene that his newspaper repeated in follow-up stories over several days. By the time the tapes began circulating, the lawyers claimed to represent fifteen hundred black Texaco managerial and professional employees, out of a total of twenty-four thousand Texaco employees in the United States.[2] Jackson signed onto a statement by a coalition of 180 civil rights groups, demanding that Texaco fire those who uttered the racist slurs and reward their "victims" richly. The amount of potential damages was initially cited as topping $250 million, making it the largest ever discrimination lawsuit based on alleged racist statements alone.[3]

Texaco stock took a hit, and its board of directors was in disarray. Partial transcripts from the tapes, made available by the lawyers, quoted

Texaco treasurer Robert Ulrich and Lundwall in a 1994 conversation where they were allegedly discussing plans to destroy key documents being sought in the case. Ulrich was quoted as saying he would "purge the [expletive] out of these books." Lundwall, the "hero" in the case, was quoted as referring to African-American employees as "black jelly beans," while Ulrich used the epithet "niggers," according to the transcripts.[4] After discussing the interest shown by a black employee in Kwanzaa, a Christmas substitute invented in 1966 by black radical Ron Karenga,[5] Ulrich allegedly turned to his bosom buddy Lundwall dripping with disgust. "I'm still having trouble with Hanukkah," Ulrich was quoted as saying. "Now we have Kwanzaa."[6]

The impact of the leaked transcripts was devastating, and they went unchallenged. Two days later, the chairman and chief executive officer of Texaco Inc., Peter Bijur, called a press conference and issued a full apology, firing those officials appearing in the tapes who still worked for the company and cutting off retirement benefits to those who had left. "I can tell you that the statements on the tapes arouse a deep sense of shock and anger among all the members of the Texaco family and decent people everywhere," he said. "They are statements that represent attitudes we hoped and wished had long ago disappeared entirely from the landscape of our country—and certainly from our company."[7] Liberal commentator Daniel Shore revved up his rhetorical jets, saying the "tapes exposed what you might call a smoking gun of bigotry."[8] Within days, Jackson was encouraging reporters to inflate the potential damages Texaco might incur to $520 million.[9]

On November 12, just as he was preparing for the ritual humiliation of Texaco CEO Peter Bijur in front of assembled black leaders at NAACP headquarters in Baltimore, Jackson said he would launch a national boycott of Texaco. The company, he said, should "regret, repent and seek renewal." Although Bijur had promised significant changes at Texaco, including a substantial payment to black employees, none of that money had been earmarked for Jackson or his organizations. Talking to reporters along with NAACP chairman Kweise Mfume and the Reverend Al

Sharpton, Jackson said Texaco was becoming the "Mark Fuhrman of corporate America," a reference to the detective in the O. J. Simpson case who was accused of using racial epithets.[10] Jackson claimed he had data showing that only a small percentage of Texaco stations were owned by minorities, positive proof that the racial slurs of Texaco employees were the symptom of a veritable swamp of deep racist sentiment. He wanted Texaco's statistics for minority set-asides. He wanted to know who their black business partners were. Mfume said the NAACP was preparing to initiate "a major divestiture campaign aimed at Texaco stock...if a swift agreement is not reached and Texaco is unwilling to address the root causes of the problems."[11]

The only problem for Jackson, Mfume, and Sharpton was the tapes: they were so poorly recorded as to be virtually inaudible. As they went in to meet with Texaco president Bijur, Texaco lawyers were playing electronically enhanced versions of the tapes to reporters that threw doubt that any racist slurs had been uttered at all. Here are the two versions of the critical passage, as transcribed by the plaintiffs and by Texaco's investigator, an electronic media specialist:

Plaintiffs' version:

Lundwall: Now we have two friggin' national anthems.

Ulrich: I'm still having trouble with Hanukkah. Now, we have Kwanzaa.... (Expletive) niggers, they (expletive) all over us with this.

[Texaco] Investigator's version:

Lundwall: We have two friggin' national anthems.

Ulrich: All right.... I'm still struggling with Hanukkah, and now we have Kwanzaa, I mean I lost Christmas, poor St. Nicholas, they (expletive) all over his beard.[12]

When informed of the expert's analysis just before he went into the shakedown meeting with Bijur, Jackson fumed. "I don't care if it's nigger, trigger or bigger," he told reporters. "It's still talking about blacks."[13] In Jesse Jackson's world the truth was far less important than the bottom line, which he fed by alleging a vast white conspiracy aimed at keeping blacks down. "Even proving that the accused did not utter the offending remark turns out to be no defense," commentator Michael Kelly wrote in the *New Republic*. "To be accused of having said the thing is enough. One man's 'nigger' is another man's 'Nicholas.'"[14]

Bijur emerged from the session unscathed, and made a humble statement to the press admitting Texaco's guilt, regardless of what words had actually been spoken on the tapes. "Our goal is to eradicate this kind of thinking wherever and however it is found in our company. And our challenge is to make Texaco a company of limitless opportunity for all men and women," he said. "As I also said in the discussions, it is essential to this urgent mission that Texaco and African-American leaders work together to help solve the problems we face as a company—which, after all, echo the problems faced in society as a whole. Discrimination will be extinguished only if we tackle it together—only if we join in a unified, common effort."[15]

Bijur's commitment was not limited to words. In the coming days, Texaco agreed to set aside $115 million in a special fund for the 1,400 black employees who had joined the class action suit, and to a one-time salary increase of 11 percent for those employees.[16] And there was more. Minority businesses got $1 billion worth of new contracts. These businesses included law firms and advertising agencies with direct ties to Jackson. Blacks got first dibs on new Texaco franchises; the company established a minority hiring quota of 29 percent of all new employees, and launched a massive "re-education" program of white employees to "sensitize" them to minorities.

"It was pure patronage politics," wrote T. J. Rodgers, the CEO of Cypress Semiconductor, the only corporate leader to date who has dared stand up to Jackson's race hustle. "Doesn't it sound just like one of Bill Lerach's shareholder lawsuits, where a high-tech company (wrongly) pays millions of dollars to settle an expensive, time-consuming lawsuit, but admits no wrongdoing? Jackson runs the discrimination-lawsuit business just like Lerach runs the shareholder-lawsuit business."[17]

Bijur did not, however, agree to payments to Jackson, Mfume, Sharpton, or any of the race brokers who had so crudely attempted to twist his arm. When the company did finally announce it was making a $50,000 grant to benefit minority students, it went to a New York foundation called "A Better Chance," and was earmarked for students seeking tutoring and nongovernment school programs aimed at preparing them for college entrance exams. "We view Texaco's support as important in helping us continue to identify and nurture our nation's next generation of business and community leaders," said foundation president Judith B. Griffin upon receiving the check from Texaco.[18] It was a stick in Jesse's eye and there wasn't a thing he could do about it. Texaco's Peter Bijur had outmaneuvered him.

ORIGINS OF THE WALL STREET PROJECT

Jesse had announced his new scheme just a few months earlier in Chicago, at an August 1996 luncheon of what he then called the PUSH "Commercial Division."[19] Flanked by old friend Hermene Hartman of *N'Digo* magazine, Jackson told the small-business owners in his audience it was time to "change the rules of how we do business" with companies that sell into the black community. Rather than the old technique of consumer boycott, Jackson suggested direct negotiations with corporate management. But to stoke the fires, he said he needed to raise one million dollars (he called it a "Business Investment Budget") to develop a first class research department. "We can't be mad, if we don't know what we're missing," he said.

This was the germ for what soon came to be known as the "Wall Street Project." The lunch was a "brainstorming session, a historic moment," Hartman recalls.[20] Jackson's pitch to his supporters was that it was time to separate the men from the boys. "He said he could deliver quality and top echelon people and told us, 'Let's match make, let's go to Wall Street.'

The idea was to use the political arm for the economic arm. That was the impetus," Hartman says. Patching up relations with the Clinton White House had emboldened Jackson, and his recent experience with Texaco had taught him valuable lessons. Thirty years in the making, Jesse's shakedown technique was about to hit the big time.

Former U.S. ambassador Harold Doley Jr., a successful black investment banker who in 1973 became the first black to purchase a seat on the New York Stock Exchange, recalls bringing Jackson to Wall Street.

"We met when Jesse got involved with Texaco, because of my involvement in oil and gas," Doley says in an interview. "Jesse understood that a consumer boycott on Texaco wouldn't be very effective, so I explained to him that he had to do it at the well-head, not at the pump. He said, 'Whadya mean?' and I explained. After that, we became fast friends." What Doley explained was that Jackson had to exert pressure on the corporate CEOs and shame them into benefiting the black community. It helped, he added, that Peter Bijur's father had also been accused of racism by an African-American businessman (and Jackson donor), Reggie Lewis. "After what happened to his father, the last thing Peter Bijur wanted was a black problem."[21]

Jackson called Doley from his car after making a presentation to the 1996 Texaco annual meeting in Westchester, Doley recalls. "He says, 'Doley, I'm hungry, I'm in the neighborhood. Can you feed us?' So he came over and we had dinner. He said he needed help on Wall Street. 'I gotta meet some CEOs, people who can open doors and contribute.' I called some CEOs I knew to meet with Jesse to see what he was talking about. It wasn't as if corporate America or Wall Street was ready to embrace Jackson. One CEO told me he didn't want to meet him, so I asked him to do it as a personal favor. He said, 'I can't bring Jesse Jackson into my office,' so I said, 'Well, then you can meet with him in your house.' We did that and the guy wrote Jesse a $25,000 check on the spot."

I ask Doley, who had served as a top Interior Department official under President Reagan and had deeper ties to Republicans than to Jackson's leftist friends, why he had agreed to help. "Jesse's beguiling. I believed him. He said this was the new Jesse, and that he wanted to reflect the new corporate America. He was saying all the right things, and I believed him. So I introduced him to other CEOs and helped set up the first Wall Street Project conference. Based on my introductions alone, Jesse raised two million dollars in 1997 and 1998."

Only later did Doley begin to believe that Jackson's operation might violate federal racketeering statutes, at which point he consulted a lawyer and distanced himself from Jackson.

THE VIACOM SHAKEDOWN

After Texaco, Viacom was next on Jesse's hit list. On February 18, 1997, Viacom CEO Sumner M. Redstone announced the sale of the Viacom Radio Group to Evergreen Media Corporation of Los Angeles for $1.075 billion in cash. At the same time, Evergreen announced it was merging with Chancellor Broadcasting Company and with the new entity, Chancellor Media Corporation, inheriting ten radio stations in five major markets, including four that served the black community in the Washington, D.C., area.[22]

Redstone was a major DNC donor, and he was confident he had the support of President Bill Clinton. He had just given the DNC a personal check for $25,000 for the 1996 reelection campaign, with Viacom kicking in an additional $269,100 in soft money contributions to Democratic Party candidates,[23] and he didn't foresee any difficulties with federal regulators for the sale. But he hadn't seen Jesse Jackson coming. Rainbow/PUSH lodged a complaint with the Federal Communications Commission that effectively blocked the sale of his radio stations, on the grounds that Viacom was violating a pledge made in 1994 to divest itself of at least one FM and one AM station in the Washington, D.C., market to minorities.[24] When his aides told him what had happened, Redstone was quick to realize he had a problem.

Jackson had tried using the FCC as a tool to exact economic advantages in the past, with little success. Two cases Rainbow/PUSH filed earlier that year were scrapped when the FCC found that Jackson's group "failed to establish petitioner status" to oppose the relicensing of local stations in North Carolina and Tennessee.[25] But with Viacom, Jackson struck a nerve. FCC chairman William Kennard met with Jackson repeatedly, and was sympathetic to his "thesis" that media giants should be required to sell a portion of their stations to minority owners. Sumner Redstone was in a hurry to close the deal to divest the Viacom Radio group, so he decided to meet with Jackson to discuss his price. It was a "mere" two million dollars, a small commission when cast against a one billion dollars deal.[26]

The FCC cast the agreement hammered out behind closed doors between Jackson and Redstone as a "settlement," leaving unexplained what right Jesse Jackson had to insert himself in a commercial transaction between outside parties. Once Sumner Redstone agreed to play ball, Jackson would withdraw his complaint, and Jackson's Rainbow/PUSH Coalition suddenly began praising Sumner Redstone and his company for helping minorities.

The FCC has "greenmail" regulations barring precisely this type of shakedown. Without them, competitors and disgruntled employees would cripple broadcasters with lawsuits out of jealousy and greed at every opportunity, and the broadcasters would get in the habit of simply buying off their opponents. But Jesse Jackson and the Rainbow/PUSH lawyers found a clever work-around. They had Viacom and Chancellor pay the money into a separate account dedicated to "public education and advocacy" ($600,000), and a special conferences fund "to educate the public about the value of minority media entrepreneurship in promoting diversity and First Amendment values" ($880,000). This was later put under the stewardship of former New York mayor David Dinkins and, later, Washington lobbyist Warner Session, both longtime Jackson allies. Session shoveled $680,000 of the Viacom money to Jackson's Citizenship Education Fund to organize two conferences.[27] Another $400,000 was spread to universities to fund "three research studies on minority broadcast ownership," research which Jackson could use for future shakedowns. Jackson received $40,000 directly from Redstone and his partners as partial reimbursement for the

Rainbow/PUSH lawyers. Just $80,000 was set aside for direct assistance to minorities, as scholarship assistance to a Washington, D.C., broadcast training school.[28] Jesse got the cake; the brothers got the crumbs.

Determined not to get blindsided again, Sumner Redstone turned around and dumped additional sums on Jackson in the form of corporate gifts to CEF. According to the contradictory and incomplete records for the nonprofit Citizenship Education Fund, which Jackson accountant Billy R. Owens released to the public on February 26, 2001, Viacom made separate donations of $377,500 and $35,000 to CEF following the withdrawal of Jackson's objection to the Viacom Radio spin-off. Jackson used Rainbow/PUSH for the shakedown with the FCC, and used CEF to bank his rewards.[29]

After the Viacom deal, Jackson hired more lawyers and filed more protests with the FCC, generating what amounted to a multimillion-dollar protection racket. The Telecommunications Act of 1996, which deregulated the industry, led to a wave of mergers as companies restructured and sought to maximize market share. For Jackson, each merger offered up a new victim ripe for the plucking. Next in his gun sights were GTE-Bell Atlantic, SBC-Ameritech, and AT&T's merger with TCI. Jackson sent the FCC voluminous legal briefs, sometimes amounting to hundreds of pages. He found loopholes that allowed him to delay the merger, all the while he met with corporate executives to "negotiate" conditions that would guarantee "diversity" and "access" to minorities. These were 1990s code words for the minority set-asides he and half brother Noah Robinson had made their rallying cry twenty years earlier. The language was more sophisticated, but the intent was the same. Thus, in one letter in a 1997 case involving the auction of wireless telephone licenses, Jackson insisted the FCC carve out a competition-free market share for minority- and female-owned businesses. "The law and the public interest require nothing less," wrote Rainbow/PUSH lawyer Dahlia E. Hayles, and:

> Congress explicitly recognized the significant hurdle that auctions would create for new companies seeking to participate in

spectrum-based businesses. It directed the Commission to fashion a competitive bidding process that would, among other things, promote economic opportunity and competition, avoid excessive concentration of licenses and disseminate licenses among a wide variety of applicants, including small businesses, rural telephone companies, and businesses owned by women and minorities.[30]

If minority- and women-owned businesses found themselves unable to compete, then the federal government should give them assistance, she argued. "The Commission should be working to strengthen the ability of these congressionally-identified designated entities to bid for, and win, wireless licenses." It was not just equal opportunity, but equal results. Just as during the Soviet era, when favored capitalists such as Armand Hammer could count on rich government contracts ladled out through political connections, Jackson wanted the federal government to preselect black businesses for preferential treatment and assistance, and he wanted to be the broker. Jackson undoubtedly realized that if his friends got a piece of the pie, the companies they controlled would then dump cash into his own coffers. Most times, they obliged. Once an agreement was reached and money paid out, Jackson withdrew his protest and went home. His Citizenship Education Fund doubled again in size from 1997 to 1998, when its revenues topped $2 million primarily as a result of shaking down the telecommunications industry. By this time Rainbow/PUSH had reached $3 million in yearly revenues, giving Jackson a $5 million blunt instrument he could heft against corporate America and his political adversaries. The more he protested, the more money came in; the more money he had, the louder he protested.[31]

But one group of companies would not pay. MCI and WorldCom, which announced plans to merge in 1997, steadfastly resisted Jackson's threats, his attempts at intimidation, his calls for a public boycott. Jackson's failure with MCI WorldCom became almost an obsession with him, and he would cite the company repeatedly as a bad actor:

> For nearly a year, the Rainbow Push Coalition has chosen research, education and negotiation over confrontation. We, however, reserve the right to protect the public interest through legislation, agitation and demonstration. Our protest and opposition to MCI WorldCom will continue until an enforceable, specific plan of inclusion is executed.

Just in case that statement was not clear enough, Jackson crossed his *t*'s: "Good people with good intentions along with enforced public policy make good mergers," he said in public testimony on the telecom mergers. "After the closing of their merger, [MCI and WorldCom] have done little to persuade us to change our position."[32] In Jesse Jackson's world, good mergers pay off the agitators, bad mergers don't.

VERY SPECIAL ENVOY

The year 1997 was a banner year for Jesse Jackson—the year he cemented a prosperous new relationship with Bill Clinton. It included mutual confiding of sexual dalliances, sharing big cigars and "prayer time" with the president in the White House, and a presidential "blessing" for Jesse's business ventures. Jesse had finally become an insider, a most valuable player in the power game, and he was about to cash in, big time.

In October 1997, Clinton awarded him a tremendous honor that was not fully appreciated by the public at the time. In a ceremony presided over by Secretary of State Madeleine Albright, Jackson was anointed as the "Special Envoy for the President and Secretary of State for the Promotion of Democracy in Africa." No one really knew what it meant to be a "special envoy" for Africa, because Jackson was the first American ever to hold such a title. But Jackson knew what he wanted, and what he intended to do with the title, the government aircraft, the all-expenses-paid trips, the prestige. He intended to cash in for his friends and for himself, demonstrating to African leaders that he was now the kingmaker, the "go to" man, the one American black leader with the cash and the contracts and the direct line to the president. "Jesse used this position to position himself," says a knowledgeable congressional source. "That was his style: he'd go to Africa as the U.S. representative, then go broker deals for private companies."

Madeleine Albright stood before reporters at the State Department beaming in all her matronly splendor as she introduced Jackson. "Before I became a diplomat and had all my partisan instincts surgically removed, I attended political conventions," she started off, deadpan.

> And I have sat in the audience—as millions of others have sat in living rooms across our country—listening to this man weave out of mere words a quilt of reason, passion, memory and aspiration that has enabled our spirits to soar while guiding us across racial, ethnic, gender and social lines to a heightened sense of kinship with each other.[33]

The words were there; even the rhythms. But somehow, coming from the mouth of Madeleine Albright, the rush of torrid prose did not inspire, it embarrassed. Jackson seized the occasion by lavishing praise on Africa and African leaders, starting with Robert Mugabe. "Africa is rebounding with vitality and promise," Jackson said with a nod to Secretary Albright. "It is producing world-class leadership—Robert Mugabe, President of Zimbabwe who heads the OAU, and President Nelson Mandela are leading growing economies with multicultural, multiracial societies. They bring a quality of leadership to the world community that is healing and redemptive."

Africa hands attending the ceremony—starting with Jackson's nemesis, the freshly confirmed assistant secretary of state Susan Rice—couldn't believe their ears.[34] A confirmed Marxist-Leninist who had crushed private enterprise during years of heavy-handed, undemocratic rule, Mugabe distinguished himself once Jackson became Clinton's Africa envoy by destroying the last vestiges of multiracial entente in Zimbabwe. He sent black mobs to take over white farms, massacre white landowners, and torch their buildings and crops, all in the name of war veterans who for some reason were not paid pensions by Mugabe's socialist state. The situation became so dire that African leaders held a land summit right in Mugabe's own capital, Harare, warning him that the farm seizures were destabilizing the entire region. The king of neighboring Swaziland later put it even more bluntly: "Mugabe has to be stopped."[35] At the time, however, Jesse Jackson showered Mugabe with official U.S. government praise, in yet another example of what Jackson called the "murky business of diplomacy."

There was serious distress among African-American leaders for the continued neglect the Clinton administration demonstrated toward Africa, and many hoped that Jackson's appointment signaled renewed interest in Africa's plight. In 1994, as Tutsis and Hutus were slaughtering each other in Rwanda, Bill Clinton and his administration remained silent. And in Nigeria, despite having dispatched Jackson bearing a letter of protest to General Sani Abacha for jailing opposition leader Moshood Abiola and many others, the Clinton administration bowed to pressure from the oil companies and refused to put pressure on his regime. "Appointing Jesse Jackson as special envoy was Clinton's way of saying to the Congressional Black Caucus that he was handing Africa policy over to them," one congressional staffer says.

Among Black Caucus members, the feeling was slightly more nuanced. "Many of us saw it as a reward to Jesse for not challenging Al Gore for the 2000 Democratic presidential nomination," another staff member says, asking not to be quoted by name. "Jesse would have given Gore a run for his money. Instead, he presented no real opposition to Gore's coronation" as the Democratic Party candidate.

The special envoy position was tailor-made for Jesse Jackson. An ambassadorship or a top government job would have required Senate confirmation, allowing Jackson's many enemies to question him on his finances and his personal business deals. It also would have required intense FBI scrutiny. "The special envoy position carried tremendous prestige but required no background check or security clearance," another congressional staffer says. "That was a great advantage. It was specially created for Jesse and fed his ego. He became *the* representative in Africa of the United States, with more power than any other U.S. government official, except the president."[36]

Given the long list of his failures in Africa, and the bloodshed and suffering that resulted in countries such as Liberia and Sierra Leone, it should come as no surprise that today Jackson backs away from claiming responsibility for the policies he espoused. "It was U.S. *government* policy," he insists with uncharacteristic modesty. "I have taken personal diplomacy trips, but all of these were government trips, to pursue the government's agenda. Of course, I was a part of shaping the agenda."[37]

Jackson used his position to introduce his cronies to African leaders so they could cut deals at the source, to the dismay of several U.S. ambassadors who fired off cables of complaint back to Foggy Bottom. "Jackson was on a plane with Liberian president Charles Taylor and was talking up an Atlanta telecommunications company that belonged to a friend," says a former congressional staffer. He was trying to get Taylor to award his friends a stake in the Liberian state telecom monopoly that was being privatized. After listening to Jackson's pitch, Taylor turned to him: 'Are you speaking to me as President Clinton's Special Envoy for Democracy? Or as the representative of this company?' Taylor was no fool," the former staffer says. "That was Jackson's style. He'd go over there with a trade delegation one day, and as the president's representative the next. He purposefully shifted hats, creating confusion."

House International Relations Committee chairman Congressman Benjamin Gilman, Republican of New York, asked the State Department's legal advisor to clarify the ethics governing special envoys after that incident. "They just shook their heads," a staff assistant says. "Special envoys are part-time positions, and can work a maximum of sixty days per year on government business. The rest of the time they are on their own. You can't tell them not to do other business, but Jesse Jackson would go out of his way to blur the lines to the point the State Department lawyers were tearing out their hair."[38]

In another instance that rankled members of Congress, Jackson traveled to Ghana as Clinton's special envoy. Jackson gave a speech at the Ghana stock exchange promising he would unblock U.S. government funds to upgrade the exchange while simultaneously promoting the venture capital firms of his friends.[39] Jackson was applying his shakedown technique to whole governments, this time in Africa. "Zambia has already been put on notice that a share of its privatization assets should go to Jackson's constituents," one African commentator mourned only two months after Jackson's appointment.[40] The questionable ethics of Jackson's African dealings were never challenged openly in Congress or investigated by any U.S. government agency. The reason was simple. As one Congressional Black Caucus staffer tells me: Jesse Jackson had become a Friend of Bill, so he got whatever he wanted.

At the same time he began focusing on Africa, Jackson took on odd tasks at home for the president and the left wing of the Democratic Party. In December 1997, Jackson mustered an alliance that raised $300,000 to keep an affirmative action case from getting referred to the United States Supreme Court, fearing that it might become a test case that would end racial preferences for minorities. The New Jersey case resulted from the 1989 firing of a white teacher, Sharon Taxman, justified by the Piscataway school board on the grounds of budget restrictions. But Taxman sued and won on appeal in the U.S. Third Circuit Court of Appeals in 1996 when it was revealed that the school district had decided to retain a black colleague named Debra Williams, hired on the same day as Taxman, for reasons of racial diversity. If race had not been an element, it's not clear which teacher would have been fired since both were considered "equally qualified" by the school board.

The school board offered a $430,500 settlement to Taxman on November 20, 1997, in exchange for abandoning her appeal. Opponents of affirmative action saw *Piscataway v. Taxman* as a good test case for the Supreme Court, and were raising money to support further legal action. "I don't know when we'll ever get such a clear set of facts," said Anita K. Blair, executive vice president of the conservative Independent Women's Forum.[41] Jackson quickly jumped in, helping raise $300,000 in four days to pay off Ms. Taxman and her lawyers to make sure the case died.[42] "This last-ditch effort by the pro-preference establishment tells us the end is near for those suppressing fair and equal treatment for all," said affirmative action opponent Ward Connerly. Connerly, a black university regent who successfully defeated affirmative action programs in California, would become one of Jesse's most eloquent opponents.[43]

CALLING BILL CLINTON

Jesse Jackson was coming to Wall Street, he told his followers, because it was "the capitol of capital." He was coming to collect—or as he called it, to "tithe" corporate America. And he had big-time patrons. Jackson's Wall Street Project set up in offices in New York's Trump Tower, allegedly rent free, according to several of my confidential sources. He was being chaperoned by President Clinton, Federal Reserve chairman Alan Greenspan, SEC chairman Arthur Levitt, New York Stock Exchange CEO Richard A. Grasso, Treasury Secretary Robert Rubin, and former Jackson employee Alexis Herman, now secretary of labor. Clinton's backing convinced Wall Street giants like Merrill Lynch, the Travelers Group (parent of the brokerage firm Salomon Smith Barney), and a host of others to cough up $50,000 each, just to have their names displayed on the marquee for the grand opening session of the Wall Street Project. The *Wall Street Journal* estimated that Jackson took in nearly $500,000 in the three weeks before the January 14–16, 1998, session even opened its doors. "And that was before 'requesting' corporations to purchase $500-per-head fundraiser tickets, conference registrations at $350 each, and $1,295 annual subscriptions to his monthly, three-and-a-half page newsletter."[44] In letters of invitation to major corporations, Jackson's fund-raisers made it sound as if Greenspan and Levitt were inviting the very firms they regulated to become contributors to Jackson's new commercial venture. Even before the gates opened, Jackson was obliged to issue a "cure letter" that made it clear the dignitaries were invited guests, not the hosts of his events.[45]

It was an extraordinary coming-out party, crowned not so much by President Clinton's wholehearted endorsement of Jackson and his shakedown techniques during an hour-long speech on January 15, but by the

almost groveling appearance of Donald Trump, Jackson's landlord. Marc
Carnegie of the *American Spectator* describes the scene unforgettably:

> Jackson knows well that it is one thing to get a Bill Clinton or
> Robert Rubin to pop by with a stock speech about breaking walls
> and building bridges and crossing barriers, and quite another
> thing altogether to put some Fat Cat on the stage next to you, and
> make him bow and scrape and show his fealty in public....
> Jackson's chosen target is Donald Trump, a truly delicious and
> inspired choice.... The Donald is one of the few guys who have
> what's known (and revered) on the Street as F—k You Money, the
> immense wealth that allows them to tell anyone, at any time, to go
> pound rocks. He is the man whose dealdom is the stuff of Wall
> Street legend....
>
> So when Trump first steps onto the dais, with his electric hair
> and his electric tie and his extremely electric personal fortune, you
> can feel all that voltage, almost hear it sizzling through the crowd.
> This is a guy they would like to be like, the guy who has actually
> *made* it to the mountain top, the guy who's so rich he owns the
> mountain in the first place. But as Trump sleepwalks through his
> remarks, a curious thing begins to happen.... Even the guys with
> the F—k You Money can't tell Jesse Jackson to go pound rocks
> anymore. The realization seeps in slowly but inexorably, gradually
> filling the room with its terribly clarity: If Donald Trump will
> come and dance for us, then so will everyone else.[46]

It was much more than a dinner and a conference. It was a consecration.
As an added measure of Jackson's newfound power, the New York Stock
Exchange closed the following Monday for the first time ever to honor the
birthday of a private U.S. citizen, Dr. Martin Luther King Jr. Federal
Reserve chairman Alan Greenspan put on a happy face, deploying an argument that I have heard many times at subsequent Jackson conferences and
from corporate flaks across the country. "Discrimination is patently

immoral," Greenspan said, "but it is now increasingly being seen as unprofitable."[47] That was the new wisdom. It appealed to the Street, and it even appealed to Jesse Jackson, who finally realized there was a better path to self-enrichment and the "A" list than ramming his grievance wagon into City Hall and demanding to be heard. In addition to firms already mentioned, those who paid top dollar to cosponsor the event included brokerage giants Credit Suisse; First Boston; Donaldson, Lufkin & Jenrette; Goldman Sachs; Morgan Stanley; PaineWebber; and Prudential Securities, according to Rainbow/PUSH. And then there were the Jackson cronies who were lining up to collect. They included longtime supporters John H. Johnson, owner of *Jet* and *Ebony* magazines, and Percy E. Sutton, the former Manhattan borough president who owned Inner City Broadcasting. Then there was Leo Guzman, whose Hispanic-owned brokerage firm had hitched its wagon to Jackson's diversity gravy train. Maceo K. Sloan, CEO of NCM Capital Management Group, a venture capital firm that was about to benefit handsomely from Jesse's new Wall Street connections. And there was Loida Nicolas Lewis, a Filipina married to Reginald Lewis, reputedly the wealthiest African-American in the country. After her husband's death in 1993, she went from being his personal and corporate cheerleader to the CEO of TLC Beatrice International Holdings Inc., the largest black-owned conglomerate in the United States.[48]

Among Jackson's most influential supporters was Sanford I. Weill, CEO of Travelers Group, which was then planning to merge with Citibank to create the world's largest financial services company, with assets of $698 billion. Not only did Weill contribute cash and considerable prestige to Jackson's venture, he personally invited big-name guests to meet Jackson. "Sandy Weill was on the board of AT&T and the New York Stock Exchange, and got them to come and to contribute as well," recalls former Jackson colleague Harold Doley Jr., who helped organize the first Wall Street Project conference. Sandy Weill wanted something in exchange: Jackson's support for his company's controversial mega-merger with Citibank.

Within the black community, the mega-merger was unpopular. According to various estimates floating around, the new Citicorp faced obligations under the Community Reinvestment Act (CRA) to earmark funds for the development of inner city communities that could reach $450 billion over ten years. And yet, Citicorp was only offering around $115 billion. At one meeting of black businessmen opposed to the merger, "people were writing Jesse checks for $25,000, $50,000—one guy in Tennessee wrote a $300,000 check," says Harold Doley. "Jesse said he had Sandy Weill over a barrel and claimed that he could force Citicorp to add billions of dollars to its CRA obligations. But it turns out Jesse flew in on Sandy Weill's private jet. Blacks got zero out of that merger, whereas Jesse took in $400,000, all of it from blacks."[49]

When Citicorp finally released its seven-hundred-page Community Reinvestment Act proposal, Jackson issued a statement within the hour praising Sandy Weill for his enlightened policies. "I am pleased with the pledge that has been made by Citigroup to make loans and investments totaling $115 billion over the next ten years into these communities," Jackson said.

"That was $330 billion short under the formula established under the Community Reinvestment Act," says Doley. "It takes the African-American community a full year to generate $650 billion, which is the gross domestic product of black Americans. Jesse took half of that off the table in one fell swoop." Left-wing activists, including the Association of Community Organizations for Reform Now (ACORN), a group Jackson had supported in the past, protested the deal to no avail.[50] Jackson's high-level support essentially guaranteed that Sandy Weill would get his way.

When I discuss the Citibank merger with Jackson, he claims that his involvement began when a black woman, whose name he cannot remember, came to him "in tears" saying she was being harassed by Citibank lawyers because she had a copyright claim to the Citicorp name. "She was trembling. She was just a little ant that was going to be crushed," he says. "It was getting embarrassing, and it was all being done behind Sandy's back. So I brought the matter to Sandy's attention and he realized this woman had a case. So they resolved it. I resolved the conflict."

"And he paid you a lot of money for it," I say.

"That's not true, Timmerman. That's a very different issue. In this case, there would have been an ugly street spat. It was a settlement. That's standard business procedure."

"But right after that, he paid you several hundred thousand dollars. It's on the CEF tax forms," I say.

"Listen to me. It was quite legitimate, aboveboard, the whole nine yards," Jackson says. "We have a program to teach economic literacy—the Thousand Churches..."

"It has nothing to do with the Thousand Churches," I say. That was a program he had launched through CEF that sold a series of self-help videos to black pastors for $1,000, which people who had seen the videos said they could buy for $9.50 over the Internet.

"That's your editorial conjecture," Jackson replies. "My point is, our relationships are legitimate and they are aboveboard."[51]

The Wall Street Project was making Jackson's nonprofit empire seriously rich. Corporate donations brought in revenues of $6 million in 1998. Jackson spent much of the money on lawyers, on hotel suites, on first class personal travel, and in maintaining the lifestyle of a prince.[52] Never once did anyone ask him to explain what shaking down Wall Street had to do with the charitable purpose of the Citizenship Education Fund. No one asked what the enrichment of Jesse Jackson had to do with voter registration, or how it benefited the poor, or the underprivileged, or the underserved whom Jackson claimed were his constituency. Instead, says Wall Street Project cofounder Harold Doley Jr., who grew disenchanted with Jackson, "Jesse leveraged several million African-Americans, threatening boycotts, to benefit just fifteen of his friends."[53]

And those friends—Maceo Sloan, Chester Davenport, Percy Sutton, Kevin Ingram, Ron Blaylock, John Rogers, Jim Reynolds, Christopher Williams, John Utendahl—would profit handsomely.

THE NIGERIAN PRISONERS CAPER

As Jackson was celebrating on Wall Street, events in Nigeria were rapidly spiraling out of control. On December 21, 1997, for the second time in two years, high-ranking military officers were arrested on charges of plotting a coup. Lebanese businessman Gilbert Chagoury remembers the events well.

"It was my wife's birthday, and I had just flown in my whole family to New York where we had planned a birthday celebration for her. As we checked into the hotel, they gave me a stack of urgent phone messages from Nigeria, telling me there had just been a coup." After inquiring what had happened, Chagoury made plans to return to Abuja, to counsel his old friend Sani Abacha who was preparing to put the rebel officers to death. Chagoury knew that if Abacha did so, it would create an international outcry and could lead to an embargo on Nigerian oil, a scenario that would spell disaster for the country.

But Abacha was not one who could be swayed by tough talk. "This is a man who fought in the civil war, who took a bullet within a few millimeters from his heart, who went hunting for hippos in a boat, even though he had never learned to swim. He didn't frighten easily," Chagoury says. "Threatening him just wasn't going to work." But now there were two sets of coup plotters in Abacha's jails, and the generals around him were clamoring for action. Adding to the fragility of the situation, Abacha had become ill and was being treated by foreign doctors, and Chagoury was no longer as close to the general as he had once been.

Abacha eventually realized he could turn the situation to his advantage, and decided to release General Obasanjo, General Diya, and President-elect Moshood Abiola, but only if the price was right. He had put together a list of the top forty-three political prisoners in the country, and was ready to do business.

"Sani phoned me in Paris," Chagoury says, "saying he wanted to release the prisoners and that he wanted to involve the Americans. He said, 'Tell Jesse Jackson to come and I will release the prisoners to him.' So I said I would try to get Jesse to come."

Jackson was now the special envoy of the president and the secretary of state for the promotion of democracy in Africa, and he was preparing his first major trip to the continent in his new, official position. It was going to be an extravaganza as only Jesse could plan, with businessmen and cronies and a full complement of reporters, to record his every rhyming profundity. Yet, Nigeria was low on Jesse's list of African priorities, given that the pressure on Abacha was increasing from the Congressional Black Caucus, that he had no real money coming into his organizations from Nigeria, and that Abacha had treated Jackson poorly during his last trip in 1994. "For three days," Chagoury recalls, "I was on the phone trying to get Jesse to come. He said, 'I can't come until I know which prisoners will be released.' So I called Sani to ask him for a list. He said, 'Gilbert, I can't tell you which ones will be released, because Jackson will leak it to the press beforehand. But you can tell him that if I have asked him to come, it is not to release people who are in jail for theft, but to release the people we have been working on.'"

They went back and forth on the phone, with Jackson referring to the State Department for instructions. Despite Chagoury's entreaties, Jackson simply wasn't interested in dealing with Nigeria or stopping there on his African trip. On February 28, 1998, just two weeks after returning from his first major Africa tour, Jackson stood shoulder to shoulder with the Reverend Wyatt Tee Walker at an Africa Fund event in Chicago, calling for stronger U.S. pressure on Abacha to release political prisoners. "Trade . . . without humane values is slavery," he declared.

According to Chagoury, Jackson knew that Abacha was fully prepared to release the prisoners, but that he insisted on releasing them to Jackson. Jackson today says he "cannot recall" what he discussed with Chagoury and only "vaguely" remembers him.[54]

Said Mike Fleshman, who tracked the U.S-Nigerian negotiations closely, "Jesse Jackson was way out of his league in Nigeria." That opinion was shared by Abacha, who scarcely disguised his contempt for Jackson once Chagoury told him what had happened. "Gilbert, I always said that you were pissing on the wrong tree," Chagoury recalls him saying.[55]

After Abacha's death in June 1998, Undersecretary of State Tom Pickering went to Abuja to meet with Abiola, who was still under house arrest but was about to be released. All sources with whom I've consulted agree that Pickering went to Abiola not to pledge U.S. support for his presidency, but to urge him to abandon all claims to the office in exchange for his freedom under the new military leader, General Abubaker. While Abiola might have wanted to oblige, he collapsed on the floor after drinking tea served (and drunk) by Pickering and Assistant Secretary of State Susan Rice. Transported to a hospital, he died ninety minutes later, reportedly of a heart attack. Pickering had the task of announcing Abiola's death to the world media. "Ever since then, we've referred to him as Dr. Thomas Pickering, the renowned heart specialist," one opposition wag joked.

A better joke would have been to call Jackson "a renowned Africa specialist." Jesse would soon have every opportunity to soil his hands with African disasters.

CHAPTER 13

﹏

African Gems

In February 1998, when Jackson made his first major African safari, Liberia and Sierra Leone were joined at the hip through war and death and devastation. Though they had featured some of the most luxurious beaches in the world just twenty years earlier, these beaches were now littered with human skulls. Jackson had a contact there, a man named Romeo Horton, who like many educated Liberians had gone to college in the United States, and traveled between the two countries through the 1960s and 1970s. The disasters started later, in April 1980, when an illiterate Liberian army master sergeant named Samuel Doe seized power from the democratically elected president William Tolbert in a bloody coup.

Doe's overnight rise to power was all the more shocking as the gruesome details of the coup emerged. "I remember waking up in Abijan on April 12, 1980, to hear the announcement of the coup," a former Voice of America reporter tells me. "Along with a few other correspondents, we rented a private plane and flew into Monrovia just in time to witness the first executions on the beach. Samuel Doe cut the liver and heart out of President Tolbert and ritually mutilated them, leaving teeth marks in the flesh. I remember seeing pictures of Tolbert's mutilated liver thumbtacked to the walls of the John F. Kennedy Medical Center in Monrovia later on."[1] The level of hatred of native-born African Liberians against the "Americos" (as the descendants of American slaves who had resettled in Liberia were called) was extraordinary and fueled the wars to come. As one Doe supporter wrote in bitter criticism of Jackson's support for Liberian warlord Charles Taylor and the "Americos,"

> We will not let Rev. Jackson P.U.S.H. us around. Despite what Jackson may think of us, we have the advantage of having lived the Liberian history on which he now preaches to us while he reads from cue cards held up to his face by his P.U.S.H. co-worker named A. Romeo Horton, who is a scion of ex-American slaves. These returned slaves kept us, African Liberians, as field slaves for well over 130 years in the land of our ancestors.[2]

Jesse Jackson says he first met Romeo Horton in the early 1980s, during the reign of Master Sergeant Samuel Doe. "Romeo was in jail. People started reaching out for Liberians they knew, to help them," Jackson says. "He was being kept naked in a jail cell when I and Dr. Benjamin Mays appealed for his release. When he finally came out he came here to Chicago, where we got him a job and a green card."[3] Horton would repay the favor to Jesse Jackson many years later.

"WAR IS A BUSINESS"

One of Master Sergeant Doe's henchmen, Charles Taylor, was put in charge of government purchasing after the "revolution," but soon had a falling out with his boss. Taylor was on a trip to the United States in 1985 when Doe convinced the American authorities to put him in jail and filed extradition papers. Doe charged Taylor with embezzlement—a fancy way of saying he welched on kickbacks. Although Taylor was held in Plymouth, Massachusetts, it was a member of the Newark, New Jersey, municipal council who spoke out against his extradition most effectively. One reason, sources say, was because the councilman had legitimate business dealings with the Liberian government through Taylor.[4] Then Newark councilman Donald Payne is today a Democratic member of Congress from New Jersey.

Taylor's lawyer, Lester Hyman, a Democratic Party operative from Massachusetts, beat back the first set of extradition papers. Before a second set could be filed, Taylor skipped jail. Hyman would be rewarded many years later once Taylor replaced Master Sergeant Doe as Liberia's strongman. In 1998, Taylor asked him to take over the lucrative Liberian shipping and corporate registry from an American group that refused to finance Taylor's civil war.[5]

After Taylor escaped from his U.S. jail he went to Libya, where Libyan intelligence put him through al-Mathabh al-Thauriya al-Alamiya (World Revolutionary Headquarters), "a sort of university for revolutionary guerrillas from all over Africa."[6] Among the many fellow Africans he met and befriended in Colonel Qaddafi's training camp was a former Sierra Leone army corporal named Foday Sankoh, who had recently taken an army radio communications course at Hythe in southern England.[7] Soon, they would become partners in crime who used Jesse Jackson to further their interests.

On Christmas Eve 1989, Charles Taylor invaded Liberia from the neighboring Ivory Coast, launching a civil war that would last eight years. "One of Taylor's first military innovations was his creation of the Small Boys Unit, a battalion of intensely loyal child soldiers who were fed crack cocaine and referred to Taylor as 'our father.' He and his troops were accused of unspeakable atrocities, ritual mutilations, random amputations of children and women, and even cannibalism."[8] Within two years, Taylor had seized 90 percent of Liberia, and a weakened central government called on Nigerian general Ibrahim Babangida to send in troops to hold Taylor's mercenaries at bay. Known as ECOMOG (Economic/Military

Observer Group), the Nigerians failed to prevent the massacre by Taylor's "boys" of five American Catholic nuns.[9] The Nigerians would remain in the country off and on for the rest of the decade.

As Taylor the warlord grew in stature and force, so he grew in greed. His militias helped him grab control of the economy, making him master of Liberia's timber and raw materials trade. Rumor had it he also trafficked in hashish, and brought in $250 million per year through smuggling and legitimate trade.[10] In March 1991, Taylor encouraged his old friend Foday Sankoh to take the war across the border into Sierra Leone. With help from Taylor, the troops—known as the Revolutionary United Front (RUF)—headed straight for the diamond mines. Taylor then appointed Sankoh "governor of Sierra Leone." His soldiers jokingly referred to Sierra Leone as their Kuwait, because it assured them a regular supply of diamonds and cash.[11]

When pressed publicly, Taylor attempted to put distance between himself and Sankoh's RUF. But as Jesse Jackson and U.S. diplomats would report, Sankoh was Charles Taylor's creation. Without Taylor, Sankoh and the RUF would never have existed. Indeed, Jackson says he first encountered Sankoh at a meeting with Charles Taylor.

The civil war in both countries dragged on during the early Clinton years, with incredible slaughter on all sides. In a country of three million, more than 200,000 Liberians were massacred during seven years of fighting, according to the State Department annual human rights report for 1997. Taylor regularly used peace agreements hammered out by the Nigerians or by the Organization of African Unity as an interval to rearm, then start fighting once again. "He learned this from Qaddafi," says Sierra Leone ambassador John Ernest Leigh. "Peace agreements are stepping stones, not an end point." After violating thirteen peace agreements, Taylor felt strong enough to call for elections, making it clear that if he didn't win he would unleash his child-soldiers for another round of mayhem. That's when his gun-toting youngsters swarmed through the streets, chanting what became his unofficial campaign slogan: "He killed my pa. He killed my ma. I'll vote for him."[12] Charles Taylor won more than

75 percent of the vote in the July 18, 1997, ballot, with his nearest opponent, Unity Party candidate Ellen Johnson Sirleaf, getting just 9.6 percent. But his crushing victory fooled no one. The U.S. State Department concluded that the elections were "conducted in an atmosphere of intimidation, as most voters believed that Taylor's forces would resume fighting if Taylor were to lose."[13]

At the same time, elections were organized in Sierra Leone, but under dramatically different conditions. The RUF had been severely weakened by an offensive spearheaded by the private South African security firm Executive Outcomes, which arrived in the country in May 1995 on contract to the government. By early 1996, reports David Pratt, a Canadian member of Parliament who made several fact-finding missions to the region on behalf of the Canadian government, "the RUF had been seriously damaged." The well-planned, professional assault by the South African mercenaries forced Foday Sankoh's guerrillas out of the diamond areas "that had helped to finance their military efforts."[14]

At that point, the United Nations agreed in February 1996 to send in international election monitors and to allow a longtime UN official, Ahmad Tejan Kabbah, to break his contract (which expressly forbade him from political activities) and run for president. According to a former U.S. official, "Kabbah won key precincts with 130 percent and 180 percent of the vote. We know this from a Norwegian aid worker who compiled the vote tallies precinct by precinct." Kabbah then cut a deal with the Nigerians, who became his protectors. Nigerian troops "set up a major heroin transport hub at the Freetown [Sierra Leone] airport to take the heat off of Lagos airport," which had been identified by the U.S. Drug Enforcement Agency as the main drug center in Africa. "This was called restoring democracy," the former official quipped.[15]

In November 1996, "it looked as though the RUF was a spent force," Pratt says. This prompted President Kabbah to join in yet another "peace plan" with Foday Sankoh to agree to terminate the contract with Executive Outcomes three months later.[16] The results were quick and nearly fatal. In May 1997, disgruntled government soldiers known as "sobels" attacked the central jail in Freetown, releasing pro-RUF officers and an estimated six hundred criminals, and seized control of the government. President Kabbah fled into exile in neighboring Guinea, and the coup leaders brought Foday Sankoh and the RUF into their junta.[17] They suspended the constitution, and placed artillery on the hills surrounding Freetown, threatening to bombard markets and schools if citizens rose up to protest the coup or to support Kabbah.

"The RUF quickly took control of the military junta," the State Department reported, resulting in a total breakdown in law and order. The new regime "routinely jailed anti-regime civic leaders and students without judicial process; junta forces killed some detainees; amputated the arms of others; and raped women as punishment for their opposition to the regime. After the coup, the court system ceased to function."[18]

The RUF also seized control of the rich diamond mines in the Kono District and the Tongo Field and shipped raw uncut diamonds across the border to Liberia in military helicopters operated by Taylor's army. Meanwhile, a British mineral company, Commonwealth Gold, signed a ten-year contract with Charles Taylor in Liberia worth up to $7.5 billion, giving the company "exclusive access" to Liberia's mineral resources, such as they were. The company offered to invest $700 million to set up a mining company called Liberesco, jointly owned with the Liberian government but actually controlled by Taylor himself.[19] Liberia became a major exporter of diamonds, although it produced almost no diamonds domestically.

"The moral of this story is that war is a business," said a former U.S. government official. "So you want to connect with whoever can make you a lot of money, no matter who they are. Everybody's playing Africa for business opportunities—the politicians, the diamond traders, the arms dealers."

This was the mess that Madeleine Albright and Bill Clinton handed Jesse Jackson as he was preparing his first trip to Liberia in February 1998.

A FRIEND ON THE GROUND

"I saw him when I got off the plane. I recognized him," Jackson says, recalling his reunion with Romeo Horton in February 1998 on the tarmac of the Monrovia airport.[20] The presence of Jackson's old friend Romeo Horton in the official welcoming party for the U.S. special envoy was no accident. Charles Taylor hadn't thrived during the past eight years of war by lacking street smarts. He had called Horton back to Liberia specifically to brief him on Jesse Jackson, whom Taylor had yet to meet. Taylor was worried Jackson would hector him on human rights and asked Horton what to expect. Thanks to Horton's intercession, the first meeting between the two, on February 12, 1998, in Monrovia, went well. "Instead of meeting an adversary," Taylor "met a friend" in Jesse Jackson, Horton told *New Republic* reporter Ryan Lizza.[21]

The reasons were not hard to find. The Clinton administration, eager to avoid any serious engagement in potential trouble spots around the world, was equally eager to please the Black Caucus, a key block of support in the U.S. Congress. The administration's only real policy concern in Liberia and Sierra Leone was to prevent a humanitarian disaster on the scale of the Rwanda massacres of 1994, which Clinton chose to ignore until it was too late. "Secretary Albright delegated Africa policy to [Congressman Donald] Payne and the Congressional Black Caucus," says Sierra Leone's outspoken ambassador to Washington, John Ernest Leigh.[22]

A House International Affairs Committee staffer who followed Jackson's meetings with Charles Taylor puts it even more bluntly. "The whole effort under Clinton was to mainstream Charles Taylor, and Jesse Jackson had a lot to do with it. Whenever Clinton was asked a question about Liberia, he turned to Jackson and to Donald Payne.[23] Both believed Charles Taylor was the key to resolving the Western African wars, especially if they could prevail upon him to use his influence on RUF commander Foday Sankoh.

In late 1997, exiled President Kabbah of Sierra Leone took the suggestion of the British high commissioner in Sierra Leone, Mr. Peter Penfold, and turned to a private British security firm for help. Sandline International had close ties to Executive Outcomes and to companies such as Branch Energy and Diamond Works, which had earlier been granted concessions to the Sierra Leone diamond field in exchange for security assistance. With the full blessing of Britain's Foreign and

Commonwealth Office, Kabbah contracted with Lieutenant Colonel Tim Spicer, the former British special services officer who headed Sandline, to provide $28 million worth of weapons to help the Sierra Leone army stage a countercoup against Foday Sankoh and the military junta. Spicer considered himself a warrior and a gentleman, and had seen enough of the RUF rebels during earlier trips to Sierra Leone to need no convincing of the rightness of the cause. Spicer wrote an op-ed for the London *Sunday Times* after his involvement in the ill-fated arms deal was stopped by British customs authorities, who had not consulted the Foreign Office. In it, he paints a chilling picture of the RUF:

> The rebels in Sierra Leone used to play a game with the villagers they terrorised; their own sinister version of Russian roulette. A series of grisly "punishments" would be scribbled on bits of paper: cut off hand, cut off head, kill, and the like. The papers were then screwed up and thrown on the ground. If you were one of the villagers unfortunate enough to be forced to choose one, whatever was written on it would be your fate. . . . Suffice it to say that when I heard President Kabbah, a decent man who had pledged to put a stop to all this kind of thing, had been over-thrown, I offered to help.[24]

Shortly after Jackson's first official trip to Monrovia, the Nigerian ECOMOG soldiers liberated Freetown, pushing Foday Sankoh's troops back across the border into Liberia where Taylor welcomed them quietly. In early March 1998, exiled president Kabbah returned. Two weeks later, Bill Clinton was flying overhead and rewarded Taylor with a thirty minute cheer-up call from Air Force One, which he made at Jesse Jackson's request.[25]

CLINTON'S AFRICAN SAFARI

President Clinton's March 22 to April 2 African safari, which cost U.S. taxpayers $42.8 million in transportation costs alone, put on display all the contradictions and competing interests of an administration that was known to its critics for its "rent-a-policy" attitude. Jesse Jackson and many of his friends were along for the ride, and used their proximity to the president to enhance their own stature and, thus, their credibility as brokers and commercial partners for their African hosts. Although Clinton never stopped in Nigeria or Liberia, both countries preoccupied senior administration officials.

Shortly before the president's departure, Assistant Secretary of State for African Affairs Susan Rice told the House International Affairs Committee that the United States found Nigerian dictator Sani Abacha's plans to run as the sole candidate in the August 1998 presidential elections "unacceptable."

> In Nigeria, we are holding General Abacha to his promise to undertake a genuine transition to civilian rule this year. Victory by a military candidate in the forthcoming presidential elections would be unacceptable. The Nigerian people need and deserve a real transition to democracy.... The political environment, as it stands now, is not conducive to free credible elections.[26]

Similar testimony she gave before the U.S. Senate was even stronger. The United States will "never retreat" from its "steadfast support for democratization and universal standards of human rights in Africa," Rice said.[27] She reiterated the administration's refusal to credit Sani Abacha with any progress toward those goals.

But when asked the same question by reporters in South Africa, after several days on Air Force One with Jesse Jackson and members of the Congressional Black Caucus, Clinton disavowed Rice with a sweeping wave of the hand. It was enough, Clinton said, for Abacha to "stand [for election] as a civilian." He went on: "There are many military leaders who have taken over chaotic situations in African countries, but have moved toward democracy. And that can happen in Nigeria; that is, purely and simply, what we want to happen. Sooner, rather than later, I hope."[28]

In most administrations, Rice would have resigned after such a stunning disavowal by her president, but she did not. After that, says former Africa Fund director Mike Fleshman, "they sent Jesse Jackson out to do damage control. He said, 'Nobody should dictate to the Nigerian people who their leaders are.' When I heard that, I just shook my head."[29]

This was also the trip when Clinton made his now famous "apology" for slavery, after touring a slave transport site in Ghana with Jackson. "It was a big emotional day," Jackson commented. The president "simply said it was morally wrong, a source of great shame, and began to focus on remedy and repair, which is what the African leaders want to hear. They're concerned about partnership, repair and reciprocal interest. Frankly I thought that was statement enough on that matter," Jackson told reporters in Kampala.[30] Jackson came just one step short of calling on the West to pay reparations to African nations who sold their own brothers, sisters, and parents into slavery generations ago. Jesse made sure that good friend Ron Burkle, the supermarket and real estate magnate who was helping his sons get the inside track on the Anheuser-Busch distributorship in Chicago, joined the trip and flew in the president's plane.[31] It was the least one could do for a friend.

RECONCILIATION CONFERENCE

In Liberia, Charles Taylor was pushing his pawns. Just as Clinton and Jesse Jackson were leaving Africa, Taylor ordered Foday Sankoh's RUF back into Sierra Leone, where they launched a war against the civilian population called "Operation No Living Thing." According to State Department reports, it included "brutal killings, severe mutilations, and deliberate dismemberments, in a widespread campaign of terror."[32] Amnesty International reported that several thousand civilians were brutally killed or mutilated, while hundreds more were abducted from their villages and forced to join their attackers.[33] While Jesse Jackson was drumming up support for Taylor and his RUF henchmen, the United States was airlifting mutilated victims of RUF butchery to field hospitals run by international aid groups, where they received artificial limbs.[34]

Taylor soon appointed Jesse Jackson's old friend Romeo Horton as chairman of the Special Presidential Banking Commission, to revive the collapsed banking system, a position that reflected Taylor's total confidence in his loyalty. It was also a position that gave Horton access to Liberian government accounts both at home and abroad. That came in handy as Taylor plotted his next step, a media extravaganza aimed at disguising the mayhem his proxies were once again bringing to African civilians. Jesse Jackson hosted the event in Chicago in order to present warlord Charles Taylor as Liberia's savior, rather than as the bloodthirsty tyrant most Liberians knew.

Jackson called it the "reconciliation" conference, and pretends even today that it gave Liberian opposition leaders a chance to meet Charles Taylor face to face (or almost) for the first time. "Many Liberians came from around the country and saw relatives for the first time since the civil war," Jackson says in an interview. "It was indeed a reunion. There were painful exchanges. People were upset with what happened during the war."[35]

But that's not how opposition leaders remember it. "This was just a PR exercise by Charles Taylor," says Harry A. Greaves, a Taylor opponent who helped found the Liberia Action Party with Ellen Johnson Sirleaf. On the invitation Jackson sent out, not a single Liberian opposition leader was listed as a speaker or even as an invited guest. The Liberian government delegation was led by Taylor's wife, Jewel Howard Taylor, and included several government ministers. Taylor himself appeared on a huge video screen on the PUSH stage in Chicago in a real-time satellite audio link-up to address the audience. "Taylor painted himself as a victim of international conspiracy," recalls Harry Greaves. "He was slick. As he portrayed it, Liberia's only problem was that the world misunderstood Charles Taylor."

When opposition leaders in the United States learned that Jackson was planning the conference, they realized they were being played for fools. Siahyonrkon J. K. Nyanseor, chairman of Liberian Democratic Future, complained in writing to President Clinton and Congresswoman Maxine

Waters, then chair of the Congressional Black Caucus. The conference, he wrote, was "nothing more than a scheme designed to promote Taylor and his repressive government," and called the failure to invite any opposition leaders "an affront to all Liberians."[36] The State Department got wind of the dispute, and Deputy Assistant Secretary Howard Jeter called Jackson, who begrudgingly agreed to allow the opposition groups to send a small delegation.[37] But no sooner had the invitations gone out than Jackson aide Yuri Tadesse bluntly told the opposition leaders that they would not be allowed to speak.

"It is disheartening to hear that you didn't care about how African-Liberians feel regarding your so-called Conference on Reconciliation in Chicago," shot back Bodioh Wisseh Siapoe, the chairman of the New York-based Coalition of Progressive Liberians in the Americas (COPLA). He also protested the presence of Jackson friend Romeo Horton, whom he alleged "helped finance the carnage of our people."[38]

"It's morning time in Liberia. It's morning time," Jackson sang, while Liberian security agents video-taped the audience in the hall. "We have come to reconcile our differences. We understand there are those in this hall who label themselves the opposition, or adversaries to the Taylor administration. If there are any adversaries who are not ready to reconcile, please leave the room." Jackson then did Taylor's work for him, demanding that Liberians stop using the Internet to publish information on Taylor's atrocities. "The international community frequents the Internet and takes note of whatever information is disseminated on the Information Superhighway," he said. "So, please stay off the Net."[39]

Jackson then introduced ten Liberian officials, who droned on for hours about the wonderful new country being built by Charles Taylor, and invited the exiles to return home. "But when COPLA was delivering its presentation, time became a factor," Siapoe complains. COPLA's appeal for the creation of an international tribunal to try war criminals was greeted with "thunderous applause" from the audience, Siapoe says—until the PUSH moderator shoved them off the stage. After just five minutes, PUSH deemed they were "out of time."[40]

No one really knows who paid for the April 18–19, 1998, conference, called hastily by Jackson upon his return from the presidential safari on April 2. But if previous PUSH conferences are any gauge, Jackson spent a good $400,000 on the event. "The general perception in the Liberian community was that Jackson was a paid lobbyist for Charles Taylor," says Greaves. Many sources said they believed Romeo Horton transferred money to Jackson to pay for the conference, an allegation Jackson vigorously denies.

"Rainbow/PUSH paid for that conference," Jackson claims. "Taylor paid for his own delegation. People who came from the U.S. paid their own way. It was not a Liberian government-sponsored conference. We got absolutely no money from the government of Liberia." Jackson does acknowledge that Taylor must have paid for the live video feed from Monrovia for the keynote event of the conference, "but it was a two-way thing. We paid the U.S. part," he says.[41]

Jackson was immediately sensitive to charges that Taylor had financed the conference, and attacked the allegations without even being asked about them. He told the conferees: "This is no assignment from our government or consultant's fee [from Liberia]. I do this because I want to see Liberians live again."

But Jackson's protests of innocence reminded Harry Greaves of an earlier incident, when a coalition of Liberian human rights groups pleaded with Jackson to support their cause by appearing at a prayer service at the Washington National Cathedral in 1990.

The group, called LICORE (Liberian Committee for Relief, Resettlement, and Reconstruction) was seeking to raise money to send relief supplies to refugees from the civil war. "We weren't taking sides; we wanted to bring Liberians together," Greaves says. "We went to Jesse because he had just waged a prominent presidential campaign. We asked him to make a speech during the prayer service at the cathedral." After Jackson responded favorably, Greaves recalls meeting with a Jackson aide at the Operation PUSH office in Washington, D.C., a few days before the event. "I met with a director who was handling the arrangements. Our invitations were already going out, featuring Jackson's appearance. At the last minute, he said that Jackson required us to make an up front payment of $50,000 as a speaker's fee."[42] The group could not make the payment, and Jackson cancelled his appearance without another word.

That July, as accusations began to circulate that he was getting financial assistance from Charles Taylor, Jackson appointed a Nigerian woman named Odusola Blessing Johnson to head up a new PUSH chapter in Houston, Texas, known as People United to Save Humanity in Nigeria.[43] Why PUSH needed a chapter devoted to Nigeria, and why Jackson chose to base it in the capital of the U.S. oil industry, is a mystery. Ms. Johnson's PUSH chapter vanished from the Texas corporate registry within months of being established, just as the Nevada-registered front company San Francisco Oil had done the previous year. When I called the Houston office of Rainbow/PUSH in November 2001, I was told that William Paul headed Jackson's effort in Texas and that no one had ever heard of Ms. Johnson.[44] But sources knowledgeable about the Nigerian oil ministry told me that Odusola Blessing Johnson had business ties to a man named Jackson Gaius-Obasecki, the marketing manager of Nigerian National Petroleum Corporation (NNPC). Gauis-Obasecki was responsible for doling out lucrative oil contracts to friends and cronies. On May 29, 1999, the day the newly elected Nigerian president Olusegun Obasanjo was inaugurated, Gaius-Obaseki was promoted to group managing director of NNPC.[45] It was a small world.

"KIDNAPPING" A PRESIDENT

Ask Africans from Sierra Leone or Liberia what they think of Jesse Jackson and one word comes almost immediately to their lips: betrayal. In their case, betrayal has a time, a place, and it has a name: the Lomé Accord.

The road to Lomé was long and bloody. It began while Jackson was hosting Charles Taylor's wife in Chicago, and it would claim thousands more innocent lives. Jackson gets defensive when questioned about the butchery, and tries to pin the blame on others, starting with Assistant Secretary of State Susan Rice and her assistant Howard Jeter.

But Lomé and the selling of U.S. policy was all Jesse Jackson's deal. It was Jackson who bundled Sierre Leone's President Kabbah into a U.S. government aircraft in Accra, Ghana, and then barred the door to his aides. It was Jackson who gave the orders to his pilot to fly to Lomé, where he forced Kabbah to face the butcher Foday Sankoh and negotiate the terms of his surrender. "Until the UN got close to the diamond mines, everything was all right," Jackson argues in a lengthy justification of his actions in Liberia and Sierra Leone. Everything he did, Jackson insists, was "on assignment for the U.S. government."[46] But many are the witnesses who dispute his benevolent portrait of Charles Taylor and Foday Sankoh. As Sankoh's RUF killers were chopping off children's limbs in Freetown, African journalist Tom Kamara wrote, "Rev. Jackson is considered a civil rights leader in America, but in Africa he is a killers' rights leader."[47]

On July 25, 1998, the Nigerian government returned RUF leader Foday Sankoh to Freetown, where President Kabbah declared he would stand trial for treason.[48] Sankoh appeared in handcuffs on Sierra Leone state television three days later, and appealed to his men to respect a new cease-fire with Kabbah's government and the Nigerian ECOMOG troops supporting it.[49] Behind the scenes, however, Jesse Jackson was working to get Sankoh released. One of the more cynical methods available for putting pressure on Kabbah came from Jackson's friend, Charles Taylor.

In September, just five months after the "reconciliation" conference Jackson hosted in Chicago, Taylor's Special Security Service (SSS) went on a killing rampage in an effort to track down and eliminate rival warlord Roosevelt Johnson, an ethnic Krahn, whom Taylor accused of plotting a coup. Here is how the U.S. State Department described the fighting:

> On September 18, security forces in the capital conducted a military assault, codenamed Operation Camp Johnson Road, against Johnson's base. Hundreds of SSS officers and members of the police Special Task Force, joined by scores of irregular former combatants of Taylor's former faction, employed automatic weapons, rocket-propelled grenades, and mortars. Much of the

shooting occurred at nighttime and was indiscriminate. Credible reports indicate that as many as 300 persons, most of them Krahns, many of them women and children, were killed in a seventeen hour battle, and in subsequent house-to-house searches and summary executions by government forces.... Krahn leader Roosevelt Johnson survived the initial attack and sought refuge in a Western embassy on September 19; police opened fire on Johnson and seven supporters in the entryway of the embassy, killing two members of Johnson's party, and wounding other members of his party as well as two embassy employees.[50]

The Western embassy was that of the United States. In an effort to sweep Taylor's thuggery under the table, it was never named in the State Department's human rights reports, nor was the fact that Taylor's forces wounded two U.S. Marine guards during the assault. Among those killed was Madison Wion, whose body was left to rot in the sun while Taylor's government and the U.S. embassy traded diplomatic notes about who was responsible for removing the dead body. Jesse Jackson called Taylor and begged him to call off his troops, the BBC reported, in an effort to play down the incident. In the end, the U.S. capitulated and buried Madison Wion inside the embassy compound, and flew Roosevelt Johnson, who had sought refuge inside the embassy, to Sierra Leone on a U.S. military helicopter.[51] Taylor's men had violated nearly every article of the Geneva convention governing diplomatic relationships between countries, and the U.S. government kept mum. Emboldened by the State Department's willingness (with Jackson's acquiescence) to cover up such abuses, Taylor and his RUF allies accelerated their return to the Sierra Leone diamond mines.

On Friday, October 23, 1998, the Sierra Leone High Court sentenced RUF leader Foday Sankoh to death for treason. Two days later, Sankoh's troops went on a murderous rampage, beheading several men and women and chopping off the arms of others, including children, during an attack on the northern town of Alikalia.[52] On the floor of the U.S. Senate,

Senator Spencer Abraham noted that Sankoh's deputy had "threatened to wipe out the remaining population if Foday Sankoh is tried...including chickens."[53]

Unperturbed by these events, Jackson embarked on another African tour as presidential "special envoy." In Guinea, he met with Taylor and Kabbah and got them to sign the Mano River nonaggression pact, which included a pledge not to allow their territories to be used as a base for attacks on the others. This was yet another empty promise made by Taylor who was even then deeply engaged in rearming the RUF. "Kabbah had just executed some of Sankoh's guys and was going to execute Sankoh," Jackson recalls. "So we appealed to Kabbah not to kill Sankoh."[54] Jackson met again with Kabbah during a five-hour stopover in Freetown to press the case on Sankoh's behalf. "The government must reach out to these RUF in the bush battlefield," he said publicly.[55] In Ghana, after meeting with President Jerry Rawlings, Jackson repeated his call for negotiations with Sankoh, then announced, "We live in the morning of a new day." Given the bloodbath that was about to occur, Jackson's fantasy vision of Africa was chilling.[56]

In January 1999, Foday Sankoh's rebels launched their offensive, marching on the capital Freetown behind a "human shield" of civilians that prevented the Nigerian ECOMOG peacekeepers from launching an effective counterattack. It was an assault of almost epic proportions, with the guerrilla fighters driving the human horde of bedraggled women and children ahead of them as they raped, plundered, pillaged, and murdered everything in their path. "Divided into squads with names like 'Burn House Unit,' 'Cut Hands Commandos,' and 'Kill Man No Blood Unit' (the last group specialized in beating people to death without spilling blood), the RUF burned down houses with their occupants still inside, hacked off limbs, gouged out eyes with knives, raped children, and gunned down scores of people in the streets," writes Ryan Lizza.

"In three weeks, the RUF killed some 6,000 people, most civilians. When the rebels were finally forced from the city by an ECOMOG counterattack, they burned down whole blocks as they left and abducted thousands of children, boys and girls who would become either soldiers or sex slaves."

These were the rebels Jesse Jackson thought could be rehabilitated and transformed into good partners of the United States. In February, as Sierra Leone was still reeling in shock from the murderous assault, the State Department invited RUF spokesman Omrie Golley for talks in Washington, where Howard Jeter, deputy assistant secretary of state for African affairs, had him speak with Kabbah by telephone. Golley also met with New Jersey representative Donald Payne, who wrote to Kabbah urging him to release Sankoh and negotiate with the RUF "without precondition."[57] Reluctantly, Kabbah agreed, releasing Sankoh from jail on April 19. The State Department weighed in with the UN Security Council to lift the travel ban it had imposed on Sankoh. Later that same day, Sankoh flew to Lomé, the capital of Togo, for talks with West African diplomats.[58]

The pressure on Kabbah to release Sankoh couldn't have come at a worse time, says Sierra Leone ambassador John Ernest Leigh. Kabbah had convinced the Nigerian peacekeepers to launch a counterattack that he believes would have demolished the RUF. "Instead, Jesse Jackson and Donald Payne got them to hold their fire." Jackson would accomplish the destruction of the Sierra Leone government by "kidnapping" President Kabbah in Ghana during the fifth African-American summit, and taking him to Lomé, to submit to rebel leader Foday Sankoh.

It was a gala affair, attended by more than five thousand delegates, and Jackson was wearing his hat as the president's special envoy as well as his hat as a deal broker for private business. Along with him was old friend and Rainbow/PUSH supporter Maceo Sloan, CEO of NCM Capital Management Group, a brokerage firm that began as a subsidiary of North Carolina Mutual Life Insurance Co. The six-foot seven-inch Sloan had built a financial empire trading stocks and political influence, and headed his own financial group. Once Nelson Mandela was elected president of South Africa, Sloan moved in by creating New Africa Advisors in Johannesburg and, more recently, the Calvert New Africa Fund. The North Carolina millionaire and Democratic Party contributor cashed in on his political connections by receiving $120 million in guaranteed loans from the Overseas Private Investment Corporation for his New Africa Opportunities Fund. Jackson wisely named him chairman of the Wall Street Project. As a successful businessman Sloan was at home with CEOs and financial reporters. With other black businessmen he established a political action committee in 1995 called Mobilization for Economic Opportunity, intended to "counter some of the anti-affirmative action rhetoric from conservatives."[59] Sloan raised $241,454 during the 1996 election cycle through his PAC. All but $3,500 of it went to Democrats. He gave $25,000 to Jackson's Citizenship Education Fund in 1997.[60]

At the May 1999 Accra Summit, Jackson praised Flight Lieutenant (and President) Jerry Rawlings for his "able leadership" of Ghana's economic recovery. Jackson promised to find U.S. investment partners for Ghana's stock exchange, and singled out for praise the state-owned Ashanti Goldfields Company, which Jackson said was "doing well" on the international market."[61] But in fact, Ashanti's American banker, Goldman Sachs, nearly bankrupted the company later that year by approving huge hedge contracts pegged to falling gold prices. When gold prices rose by $75 an ounce to $325 an ounce, the company faced massive margin calls on its forward sales, making it vulnerable to a foreign purchaser. At one point, in November 1999, Saudi Prince Alwalid bin Talal offered to cover the margin call.[62]

Other Jackson donors invited to the Ghana love fest included Don H. Barden, whose Barden Industries gave Jackson a tax-deductible contribution of $65,000 that year; Alphonso Corney, corporate counsel for Philip Morris, which had given Jackson $230,000 since 1991; John Hatcher, a finance specialist for DaimlerChrysler, which gave Jackson $50,000 in both 1998 and 1999; Joe Stewart, senior vice president of Kellogg Company, whose nonprofit arm, the W. K. Kellogg Foundation, gave Jackson $15,000 that year; LeBaron Taylor, senior corporate affairs vice president for Sony Corp., which had donated $36,000; and Carl Ware, vice president of Coca-Cola, which gave CEF $69,572 that year.[63] Carl Ware returned with Jackson to Nigeria on a separate trip later that month for the inauguration of the newly elected president, Olusegun Obasanjo.

On May 18, 1999, Jackson cornered Sierra Leone President Kabbah in Accra, and told him that he had arranged for him to meet a very special person: Foday Sankoh. Jackson's U.S. government helicopter was fueled and ready at the airport. "Jackson had State Department people, U.S. embassy people from Sierra Leone, his own staff, and Donald Payne's people with him. They were all Charles Taylor people," says Ambassador Leigh. Kabbah's information minister and his finance minister, Dr. James Jonah, were both opposed to signing any deal with Sankoh and had accompanied Kabbah to the airport. "When President Kabbah tried to board the aircraft with two aides, Jackson said there was no more space. This is why we say President Kabbah was kidnapped. Jackson flew him to Lomé, without a single aide." It was a short helicopter ride to neighboring Lomé, just one hundred miles down the West African coast from Accra, but it was like traveling from a bustling metropolis to a secluded vacation village on the beach.

Michel Desaedeleer, a Belgian businessman who has worked in Africa for the past fifteen years, remembers the scene well. "I happened to be in Lomé, at the time, visiting with the U.S. ambassador who was a relative of my wife," he said in an interview. "We all went to the airport: President Eyedama, the entire Togo government, and the ambassador. Jackson landed, the door to his helicopter opened, and we waited. Ten minutes, fifteen minutes, twenty minutes and still nothing."

Finally the U.S. ambassador went up to the door of the helicopter, Desaedeleer says, and peered inside. "There was Jackson, speaking on the telephone to Ted Turner in Atlanta. He said he wasn't going to get out until a CNN film crew arrived." President Eyedama's office had phoned the press, but the only camera crew in Lomé that day was from the Togolese state television network, and that wasn't good enough for Jesse Jackson. "So we waited another forty minutes for another helicopter, which flew in from Accra with a CNN crew," Desaedeleer recalls. "You had the president of Togo and virtually his entire government waiting outside in the heat for an hour. Finally Jackson deplaned, spreading his arms and greeting his African brothers on CNN."[64]

Desaedeleer had been introduced to Foday Sankoh just a few days earlier. "He was still under detention—but in name only. When I arrived at his villa, he was sitting in his boxers, drinking beer on the balcony." The two became fast friends and later, business partners. Sankoh told Desaedeleer what happened at Lomé. "Foday was stupid, but he wasn't cruel," Desaedeleer insists. "He was simple-minded. When Jackson came to Lomé, he gathered all the heads of state around in a circle, got them to join hands, and prayed. He was a showman, and Foday was amazed. He had never prayed before in his life. But when he saw that Jackson could get all those powerful people to bow their heads and hold hands, that convinced him. Ever since that day, he claims to have become a big believer."

The prayers and the pressure tactics paid off, and Kabbah eventually agreed, against his better judgment, to a ceasefire with the RUF. He also agreed to enter negotiations with Foday Sankoh over a power-sharing agreement, which paved the way to the eight-point Peace Accord signed in Lomé on July 7 under U.S. government supervision. Jackson revealed in an interview that he prevailed upon the State Department to supply Sankoh with communications gear, which undoubtedly helped him to coordinate the murderous battles his RUF forces soon would wage against Kabbah's government and UN peacekeepers. "I asked Sankoh to allow the Red Cross to let food through. There were checkpoints our guys couldn't get through," Jackson says. "So our government supplied Sankoh with two-way radios, so he could communicate with his guys in the bushes. We thought this would reduce the killing, and our State Department agreed."

It is unclear how much the communications gear cost that Jackson whisked through the arms supply pipeline to rebel leader Foday Sankoh, or whether Congress was notified of the transfer. But it was "clearly more than just two-way radios," a former U.S. intelligence officer who had served in Africa tells me.

As part of the Lomé Accord, Foday Sankoh, the death row prisoner released from jail at Jesse Jackson's urging, was made vice president of Sierra Leone. But best of all, he was named chairman of the Commission for the Management of Strategic Mineral Resources, the prize he and Charles Taylor had long been seeking. There was one mineral resource in Sierra Leone, and that was diamonds. A few days later he began commercial negotiations with the Belgian businessman, Michel Desaedeleer. "I even gave Foday a check. He just looked at it and asked me, 'What's this?' It was the first bank check he had ever seen," Desaedeleer recalls.

The two signed a sweeping marketing agreement on October 23, 1999, through an offshore company Desaedeleer controlled with an American named John Caldwell. Their British Virgin Islands company, Beca Group Ltd., got a 50 percent share of all commissions on the sale of Sierra Leone diamonds in Belgium and all reconstruction contracts let through Europe and the United States. "It was real business, legitimate, and aboveboard," Desaedeleer says. But it never got off the ground.

Sierra Leone ambassador John Ernest Leigh just shakes his head at the thought of rebel leader Foday Sankoh in charge of the diamond mines. "How can you put a cat to guard a mouse?" he says. "People who should be put in jail were put in the cabinet. That's precisely what Taylor wanted." Foday Sankoh used Sierra Leone diamonds to buy friends, influence, and arms for the RUF, trade that has been well-documented by a United Nations panel headed by Canadian diamond expert, Ian Smillie.[65] The UN panel found that Belgian air force transport planes brought in shipments of weapons for the RUF hidden in crates of Belgian-made fruit juice. Just months after the Lomé Accord was signed, a Ukrainian arms dealer named Leonid Minim flew in sixty-eight tons of weapons for the RUF via Burkina Faso and Liberia, all in exchange for rebel diamonds. To keep everyone happy, Foday Sankoh paid off UN officials in Freetown and his political friends in the United States with raw uncut diamonds, according to U.S. congressional and former intelligence officials. Most of Foday Sankoh's "gifts" were shipped to diamond merchants in Antwerp who funneled the proceeds to shell companies in Vaduz, Liechtenstein, and other offshore havens.

Today, in hindsight, Jackson concedes that "putting Sankoh over the diamonds, that was a bit too generous." But when questioned closely on the Lomé Accord, he back-pedals furiously, trying to distance himself from any responsibility. "It was the U.S. government position," he insists. "I went with the State Department. When we went to Lomé, our government set up the meeting with Foday Sankoh. Our government felt that Sankoh was the one guy who could end the killing."

It was classic Jackson. "When it worked, you're a genius. When it blew up, you're an idiot," he tells me with feigned humility.[66]

It blew up in a big way in less than a year.

CHAPTER 14

A Full-Service Brokerage

SHAKING DOWN THE STREET

In 1999, revenues for Jackson's Citizenship Education Fund (CEF) sky-rocketed to $10 million, a fivefold increase over the previous year. It was a year when everything came together for Jesse Jackson. Fame, fortune, contacts, ability: all combined to generate a wealth of opportunities which he successfully exploited, making himself, his organizations, and selected friends breathtakingly rich. When the CEF monies were combined with another $5 million Jackson now brought in through Rainbow/PUSH, Jesse Inc. had become a fifteen-million-dollar-per-year industry. But that was just the start.

Jackson owes this visible financial success in great part to Bill Clinton, who helped him launch his Wall Street Project in 1998, and to the extraor-dinary pressures brought to bear by Clinton administration federal regu-lators on major U.S. corporations. The 1996 Telecommunications Act, which Clinton pushed vigorously, mandated minority set-asides during mergers and spin-offs. This gave Jackson tremendous leverage. He exploited this in corporate boardrooms across America, far beyond the narrow confines of a single industry. He used the pretext of racial griev-ance to solicit contributions for his organizations, win contracts for his friends, and primetime television appearances for himself.

At the second Wall Street conference in New York in January 1999, Jackson raked in $1.25 million from corporate sponsorships for the black tie gala held on the floor of the New York Stock Exchange.[1] Jackson revealed the extent of his ambitions when he announced a striking deal with AT&T CEO C. Michael Armstrong to seek a minority firm to comanage a billion-dollar bond offering.[2] Rainbow/PUSH had opposed the proposed merger of AT&T with TCI the year before in a series of peti-tions, letters, and public testimony. Despite "strong programs . . . that pro-mote minority and women-owned enterprise," the merger "must still be reviewed closely," Jackson said in testimony before the FCC. Jackson com-plained vaguely of a "questionable employment record" and a "poor level of customer service," but had no specific grievances.[3] Michael Armstrong understood immediately that Jackson was essentially sticking out his hand, hoping for a payoff. Rather than hold up the merger, he obliged. While he was at it, he instructed AT&T to donate $425,000 to CEF. Jackson imme-diately dropped his opposition to the AT&T/TCI merger.

When the bond deal was finally announced, AT&T went one better, naming black-owned investment bank, Blaylock & Partners, as comanager of a record-breaking eight-billion-dollar bond offering in partnership with Merrill Lynch and Salomon Smith Barney. Touted as "the biggest bond deal in history," the inclusion of Ron Blaylock's eight-year-old firm raised questions. "What's this guppy, one of the few minority-owned businesses on Wall Street, doing swimming among these sharks?" *Business Week* wondered. "Turns out that the decision to include Blaylock came straight from AT&T CEO Michael Armstrong himself." Blaylock's share of the loot was estimated at $1.4 million, its biggest deal ever.[4] CEO Ron Blaylock gave Jackson a $30,000 donation soon afterwards, CEF tax records show. This 2.14 percent payment would have been called a finder's fee in any other situation.

Similarly, Raytheon Company, a $19.8 billion manufacturer of electronic systems for missiles, satellites, and air traffic control systems, awarded Jackson friends Maceo Sloan and John W. Rogers a 5 percent share of its pension fund in a deal announced just days before Jackson's Wall Street extravaganza opened its doors that year.[5] Raytheon spokesman David Polk, an African-American who is an avowed Democratic Party activist from Chicago, insists that the firm made a simple business decision. "We are part of the Wall Street Project," he tells me. "We have contributed to their annual events, and we have invested some of our pension funds with minority and women-owned money management firms. Was this a shakedown? No. We were not extorted. This decision came following conversations between Jesse Jackson and our senior leaders."

Black Enterprise magazine estimated that Raytheon turned over management of $800 million in assets to three African-American companies selected by Jackson: NCM Capital Management Group, Ariel Capital Management, and MDL Capital Management. The first two were major contributors to Jackson's nonprofit empire. The third, MDL, while not identified as a Jackson donor in the public record, was a prime recipient of Jackson's help. MDL began in 1992 and by the end of the decade CEO Mark D. Lay boasted that they were managing $1.8 billion in corporate funds, including $200 million from Boeing and undisclosed sums from Sprint, both of which resulted from pressure from Jackson and Rainbow/ PUSH. "Was our choice of money managers color blind? Obviously, our interest was to increase the representation of minority and women-owned firms, and these firms met our criteria," says Raytheon's Polk.[6]

Jackson made no bones about his approach in the keynote speech he delivered to the second Wall Street Project conference on January 14, 1999. A good chunk of the money he was asking big corporations to pay would be used by Rainbow/PUSH to research the "racial divide" in corporate America, so Jackson could better target his fleecing machine. "Of the Fortune 500 companies, 137 have completely segregated boards,"

Jackson said, without anyone batting an eye. "Another 206 companies have only one minority on their boards of directors."[7]

Segregated boards? As Charles Tribett, one of the most prominent black headhunters, told a panel I attended at a Jackson conference in Chicago on May 9, 2001, "Seventy percent of the time we are asked to look for African-American or female board members. They are the first profile the corporations are looking to put on the board. So minorities are on the rise."[8]

Jackson let slip the real secret a few minutes later, when he cited the names of Ronald Blaylock, Maceo Sloan, and John W. Rogers Jr., aspiring billionaires who had become significantly richer thanks to his racial brokerage. "John Rogers has a new relationship with the Chicago Board of Trade," Jackson said. He was right. Rogers, who owned Ariel Capital Management, was a major sponsor who helped bankroll Jackson's Chicago operations. "We think Reverend Jackson is wonderful," says Melody Hopson, an assistant to John Rogers. "We support his work. We see it as the right thing to do. We support all initiatives relating to diversity."[9] But what she won't say is that the key to her boss's "new relationship with the Chicago Board of Trade" was Jonathan Jackson, who continued to hold down a job with the board at the same time he was settling into the beer distribution business, thanks to Dad's influence with Anheuser-Busch. Jesse was brokering deals for a closely knit black elite, and it rankled many black businessmen who never made it into his inner circle—either because they refused to contribute to Jesse Inc. or because they simply weren't big enough to count.

Once his Wall Street extravaganza closed its doors, Jackson flew out to Seattle on January 22 for a press conference with Boeing CEO Phil Condit in front of local news cameras. Boeing had been defending two class action lawsuits brought by black employees, who alleged racial discrimination at Boeing plants. Jackson intervened on their behalf, unbidden by their lawyers, to "negotiate" a fifteen-million-dollar settlement of their grievances. Condit said he was pleased Jackson could come to Seattle, so they could announce the settlement together. (Condit was perhaps best known for his comment, at the height of the Clinton administration Chinagate scandals, that "whenever a Boeing airliner flies to China it is going home.") When divided by the 12,900 black Boeing employees worldwide, the settlement came to $1,162.79 each, just for the color of their skin.[10] Soon afterwards, 1,700 Boeing employees complained that the settlement was too small, but Jackson remained silent. Boeing had reportedly donated $50,000 to Jackson's Citizenship Education Fund, "the first of several gifts."[11] In the coming months, Boeing also steered significant business to minority investment banks, some of whom were Jackson cronies and donors. "This was part of what the lawyers called 'conjunctive relief,'—i.e., policy changes," Boeing spokesman Ken Mercer tells me.[12] Later, Boeing "lent" a corporate diversity officer, Rosalind Crenshaw, to Rainbow/ PUSH on a pro bono basis. While being paid by Boeing, she spent one-quarter of her time on liaison duties, "focusing on employee and supplier diversity issues, and also coordinating Boeing participation for coalition events."[13] Mercer confirmed that the arrangement was still ongoing when we spoke in July 2001.

Viacom, AT&T, Boeing: Jackson was on a roll. In each case, he had intervened successfully during a spin-off, merger, or class action lawsuit and won a quick victory by withdrawing his threat to oppose the deal once he was rewarded. With President Clinton's sponsorship, corporate shake-downs were approved, and Jesse Jackson Inc. was benefiting handsomely.

BROKERAGE BY HIRE

Jackson also displayed the personal touch, hiring out his services when the price was right to individuals needing "special" assistance. Such was the case with high-flying Wall Street broker Kevin Ingram, who turned to Jackson in January 1999 after he was fired by Deutsche Bank from a two-million-dollar-a-year job.

In the twelve short years he had worked on Wall Street, Ingram had become something of a legend, highly respected by his peers, and very rich. After a stellar career at Goldman Sachs, where his powerful patrons included now New Jersey senator Jon Corzine and Clinton treasury secretary Robert Rubin, he moved to Deutsche Bank AG in April 1996 to run its mortgage and asset-backed security group. *Black Enterprise* magazine listed him as one of the top twenty-five African-American "movers and shakers" on Wall Street that year.[14] The German bank soon promoted him to one of the top five slots, and Ingram added a Bentley and a Porsche Turbo to his personal fleet, which included a 1998 Ferrari and a forty-four-foot boat. With the fancy cars came the women. "Kevin always had these tall, incredibly beautiful models on his arms," a coworker recalled. "And they were not bimbos, either—they were five-foot-ten and gorgeous, with brains to boot. And the funny thing is that he was just five-foot-seven. I would always ask him: 'Kevin, how does a guy like you rate all these women?' He looked at me and smiled. 'Hey, man, it's easy—80 percent of my competition is in jail.' "[15]

Then in September 1998, the long-term capital market imploded and shaky Internet investments he had championed collapsed, causing a deep dip in Ingram's portfolio. A whole year's profit was gone in a week. Ingram's boss, Edson Mitchell, asked for his resignation. But Ingram refused. "You are going to have to fire me," he reportedly said. Eventually, Mitchell did fire him. But the generous severance package he offered didn't satisfy Ingram. So he threatened to sue, claiming he had been fired because of his race. Deutsche Bank shot back with a lawsuit claiming that his "work schedule was erratic, that he failed to show up for days at a time and skipped important meetings." They also accused him of cheating on his expense account, "charging for non-business expenses like $45,694 for a canceled wedding."[16] That's when Ingram called Wall Street buddy Ron Blaylock, insiders say, the CEO of financial services firm Blaylock & Partners LLP. One of Jesse Jackson's privileged circle of black brokers, Blaylock called his Uncle Jesse.[17]

Ingram knew he had leverage that Jackson could exploit when the two first talked in early January 1999. Edson Mitchell was in the midst of pulling together a ten-billion-dollar merger between Deutsche Bank and Bankers Trust of potential concern to Congress because it gave a foreign-owned bank control over a major U.S. financial institution. The last thing

Mitchell needed was a racially charged lawsuit backed by Jesse Jackson, so he agreed to negotiate. Jackson upped the ante by unveiling the race-baiting tactics he would use if the bank didn't meet his terms. "When Kevin Ingram was fired it surprised a lot of people," Jackson spokesman Lou Colasuonno said. "Jesse thought that there was more to the situation than performance. His unit was profitable; it seemed as if Deutsche Bank might have had other reasons."[18] It was Jackson's typical shot across the bow, and it worked.

Deutsche Bank chief executive John Ross phoned Ingram and said he wanted to meet Jackson personally to discuss the matter, so Ingram brought Jackson to the bank, much to the surprise of his former colleagues. "Traders were shocked at the sight: Jesse Jackson was on the trading floor. Kevin Ingram's last Deutsche Bank trade, it seemed, would be a monster one," writes Landon Thomas in the *New York Observer*.[19] The meetings continued through March, when Jackson eventually brokered a severance package for Ingram estimated by the press to be worth somewhere between $15 and $20 million, but which Jackson insiders valued at just $6 million.[20] CEF tax returns show Ingram rewarded Jackson with a $50,000 contribution to the Citizenship Education Fund later that year, a mere down payment on what Jackson insiders say was Ingram's pledge—to pay Jackson 10 percent of whatever severance package he negotiated.

Jackson's account of his involvement in Ingram's contract negotiation with Deutsche Bank verges on the surreal. "It's not unusual in a conflict between a company and labor that they would ask for an honest mediator to resolve their conflict short of battle," Jackson tells me in an interview.

"But this was an individual," I reply.

"Hear what I'm saying. In this case, he was making a strong legal case against them. Rather than having a court battle or a street battle, we sat around a common table, to look at a partial resolution. . . . I do a lot of conflict resolution work," Jackson adds. "Lawyers cost much more and take more time and get into longer battles."[21]

If you believe the public story, that contribution was enough to make Jackson drop his allegation that Deutsche Bank had improperly fired Ingram. But aside from Kevin Ingram's $50,000 contribution, there is no public record of either bank making a contribution to any of Jackson's groups.[22]

Jackson claims he had no further involvement with Ingram after the "negotiated" settlement with Deutsche Bank. But Kevin Ingram's story doesn't stop there. On June 12, 2001, agents from the FBI, U.S. Customs, and the Bureau of Alcohol, Tobacco, and Firearms arrested Ingram and two Middle Eastern accomplices in South Florida as they were closing a $32 million deal to purchase Stinger and TOW missiles, parts for Cobra attack helicopters, and other weapons. One of those arrested was Egyptian-born Diaa Badr Mohsen, an entrepreneur and neighbor of Ingram's in Jersey City who had brokered a wide variety of international deals, moving everything from Sierra Leone diamonds, to oil and wheat in Egypt, to a failed telecommunications project in Somalia.[23] The buyer of the weapons, Pakistani national Mohammed Raja Malik, had expressed an interest in purchasing more than two hundred Stinger antiaircraft missiles, and claimed he had direct ties to senior Pakistani military officials, court documents show. That whetted the appetite of U.S. government officials, who decided to "sting" the Stinger buyers. Since the September 11, 2001, attacks on the World Trade Center and Pentagon, federal investigators have been interrogating Ingram, Mohsen, and Malik about possible ties between the ultimate buyers of the weapons in Pakistan and renegade Saudi terrorist Osama bin Laden. "My client was under the impression he was working for military intelligence or the CIA," said Mr. Mohsen's lawyer, Valentin Rodriguez. "His goal was to help the government and maybe find some terrorists along the way. The bin Laden connection is the craziest thing I ever heard."[24] Ingram's lawyer, Richard Lubin, reacted with indignation. "There is absolutely zero connection between Kevin Ingram and anything remotely connected to September 11 [2001]," he said.[25] In his plea bargain with federal prosecutors, Ingram's testimony against his former arms dealing partners was narrowly limited to his knowledge of their involvement in the government sting operation that led to their arrest.

Court records show that the sting began in December 1998, when a Florida diamond dealer named Randy Glass was arrested for fraud and told government investigators about Ingram, Mohsen, and Malik.[26] He claimed he had first met them in Sierra Leone during his diamond trading days. Federal investigators now know that bin Laden dispatched operatives to Liberia to purchase diamonds from Foday Sankoh's RUF and Liberian president Charles Taylor in an effort "to protect [al Qaeda] money by sinking it into gemstones, a commodity that can be easily hidden, holds its value, and remains almost untraceable." The chief broker of RUF diamonds, Ibrahim Bah, was trained by Libya's Colonel Qaddafi and had fought with bin Laden's Arab Afghans in Afghanistan during the 1980s, before joining the Iranian-backed Hezbollah militia to fight the Israelis in southern Lebanon later that decade. "According to intelligence sources and two people who have worked with him, Bah now acts as a conduit between senior RUF commanders and the buyers from both al Qaeda and Hezbollah."

The RUF connection with al Qaeda was cemented in September 1998, when Bah arranged for bin Laden deputy Abdullah Ahmed Abdullah to meet with top RUF commander Sam Bockerie, who was under the political protection of Liberian president Charles Taylor. Bin Laden then dispatched to Liberia top al Qaeda operatives Ahmed Khalfan Ghailani and Fazul Abdullah Mohammed, identified on the FBI's Most Wanted list in November 2001, to give Bockerie $100,000 in cash in exchange for diamonds, the *Washington Post*'s Douglas Farah reported.[27]

Randy Glass, Kevin Ingram, Sam Bockerie, Charles Taylor, and Foday Sankoh: the illicit trade in conflict diamonds flourished under the Lomé Accord Jackson negotiated on behalf of the State Department. "Jesse Jackson does nothing on a pro bono basis," says former associate Harold Doley Jr. What did Jesse get in exchange for Lomé?

Not a penny, says the Reverend. "I never talked with Charles Taylor on the phone or in person without our government present," Jackson tells me. "I never mixed business with pleasure. It was no pleasure going around those countries trying to get hostages out of the bushes. There was no pleasure in that."

THE PEPSICO IPO

In March 1999, PepsiCo CEO Roger Enrico thought he had it made. He was only days away from launching a $2.3 billion initial public stock offering for the Pepsi Bottling Group, when he received a call from Jesse Jackson. Enrico has refused to comment on the exchange, or any of the ensuing events. But Pepsi insiders involved in the IPO said that "Jackson threatened Enrico with a messy public protest, even a boycott, unless he took steps to ensure that the makeup of the Pepsi Bottling Group's IPO syndicate more closely reflected the fact that blacks drink Pepsi too and celebrity endorsers like Ray Charles help sell it."[29] Put simply, Jackson wanted a cut, for himself and for his buddies.

Overruling the advice of his own chief financial officer and the corporate treasurer, Enrico bowed to Jackson's demands and designated a black-owned investment bank named Utendahl Capital Partners as comanager of the offering. It helped that CEO John Utendahl, whose seven-year-old firm had been founded with support from Merrill Lynch, was a good friend of Jesse Jackson and a member in good standing of the PUSH International Trade Bureau. Following Jackson's muscle-bound intervention with Enrico, Utendahl won a coveted spot on the cover of the prospectus, plus a cut of the $19 million management fee.[30] The financial documents released by Jackson's accountant in the spring of 2001 show that Utendahl Capital made a $20,000 payment to Jackson's CEF shortly after it won the PepsiCo contract. In a statement released after Utendahl was selected, Enrico said: "Rev. Jackson makes a very compelling case for minority business interests." But others believe it was Jackson's threats that won the day. As one senior-level investment banker told *Fortune* magazine at the time, "Pepsi capitulated."[31] Pepsi had given $50,000 to Jackson's CEF between 1991–1993, the group's tax returns show, and kicked in an additional $50,000 to the Wall Street Project in 2001.[32]

Young black brokers are flocking to Wall Street and to venture capital (VC) firms across the country. Paul Rice, of the Chicago-based Mesirow Financial, has been in the business for over thirty years. "When I was young and went to VC conferences, I was the only one in the room who looked like me," he told a panel at Jackson's LaSalle Street conference in May 2001. "Today, I can see lots of people who look like me." Not all of Jackson's supporters are happy with his tendency to muscle his way into every business deal by raising the specter of racial cleavage. "Things are not going well for African-American investment bankers," says Leo Guzman of Guzman & Company, a Hispanic-owned firm that got a share of the Pepsi IPO, thanks to Jackson. "There were five or six major firms a few years ago that are no longer in business or barely in business."[33]

Part of the reason may be Jackson's habit of rainmaking for his friends, while doing little to promote better business practices, habits, and training among young black business people. "A lot of people are nervous about tapping into Jesse too much because they know there's a big backlash out there," one black Wall Street financier said. Another minority banker told *Fortune* magazine he was worried about what will happen when Jackson moves on. "You've gotten paid, but you don't have a relationship [with the clients]," he said. "It's not as though they're going to use you the next time, unless they're forced. It's not as though they're going to be a favorable and willing reference. I think going to war is bad for everyone."[34]

But it wasn't bad for Jackson or for his nonprofit empire. And Jackson had no qualms about hitting up his friends for support, or freezing out those who thought they could climb on board Pharaoh's chariot for free. "There's a group of people that are not ever going to be a beneficiary of what [Jackson] has done because they're not paying the piper enough to get there," says the CEO of one minority firm.[35]

TELECOM SHAKEDOWNS

Arguably the most bald-faced shakedown recently conducted by Jackson involved the proposed merger of telecommunications companies SBC Communications Inc. and Ameritech. When the two companies first announced their intention to merge in 1998, Jackson protested to President Clinton and the FCC.[36] At a press conference at PUSH head-quarters, he called the merger "antithetical to basic democratic values" and harmful to low-income customers. "There is an eerie silence from national political leadership as these mergers radically restructure the nation's economy," Jackson said. "In a sense, there is one party with two names or two parties with one assumption feeding from the same trough."[37] Jackson had reverted to the Rainbow Coalition's class warfare image first suggested to him by former Communist Party organizer Jack O'Dell in 1985.[38] Meanwhile, Jackson's "researchers" were gathering information on the two companies, and his lawyers were meeting regularly with company officials, to explore ways for Jackson and his friends to belly up to that same trough.

Rainbow/PUSH filed several motions with the FCC in late 1998, signaling its intent to oppose the merger.[39] In December, Jackson testified at the FCC's "en banc" hearings to raise objections to the whole series of proposed telecommunications mergers that were flowing out of the 1996 Telecommunications Act. "Competition among a small group of companies targeted at a small sector of our society is not real competition," Jackson said. "As the century ends, there are no minority-owned wireline telephone companies, no minority-owned cellular systems, no truly diverse boards of directors, no minority merger advisors on Wall Street, and very few minority-owned cable TV franchises. These facts make a big, ugly statement about America."[40] In one Rainbow/PUSH motion filed with the FCC on December 17, 1998, Jackson lawyer Janice Mathis noted that the "on-going negotiations" with the CEOs and shareholders of SBC and Ameritech had left Jackson "unsatisfied with major elements of the proposed merger."[41] But just four months later, Jackson turned around and praised the SBC/Ameritech deal as being "in the public interest." Later, he went so far as to personally lobby the FCC to reward the new company with privileged market access in Texas at the expense of MCI WorldCom and other competitors because of their enlightened policies to serve minorities.[42]

What happened in the meantime to cause such a dramatic turnaround in Jackson's attitude? For starters, SBC/Ameritech pledged to make a $500,000 contribution to Jackson's nonprofit empire in 1999, the largest single corporate grant he had ever received, whereas WorldCom stubbornly refused to pay up.[43] And then, once GTE purchased half of Ameritech's cellular business in a spin-off required by federal regulators, GTE topped the SBC/Ameritech pledge with two separate grants to Jackson's Citizenship Education Fund totaling $740,000, according to CEF tax returns. At the same time, GTE was seeking to merge with Bell Atlantic (they became Verizon later that year) and by this point understood that it made good business sense to buy Jackson's silence rather than pay its lawyers to fight him. Bell Atlantic added an additional $800,000 in direct payments to CEF that year.[44] Later, Bell Atlantic chairman Ivan Seidenberg announced he was "loaning" two corporate executives free of charge to Rainbow/PUSH, to serve as liaisons with the company and to locate minority financial services firms.[45] Verizon became a lead sponsor of the 2001 Wall Street Project conference, and pledged another $300,000 to pay for Rainbow/PUSH conventions.[46]

These were direct payoffs of stunning proportions, which Jackson explained in shameless terms. By letting contracts go to "minority-owned businesses in the financial services industry," Jackson argued that SBC, Ameritech, GTE, and Bell Atlantic deserved special praise. "The leaders of these companies understand that inclusion is a smart business policy, and we are comfortable in saying that this merger will deliver on those merits."[47]

One minority business owner who directly profited from Jackson's successful "negotiation" with the FCC and GTE was Robert Knowling, the president of a newly formed broadband telecommunications firm named COVAD Communications. Created to take advantage of the 1996 Telecommunications Act, which required the local Bell companies to allow independent service providers to use the telephone networks they had installed, COVAD had no business and no money until December 1997, according to congressional testimony by a corporate vice president.[48] That was when Robert Knowling turned to Jackson, whose high-profile political pressure helped leverage a deal with GTE. "Getting those DSL lines from Bell Atlantic as part of the GTE merger is what put COVAD in business," one telecommunications analyst said.[49] Within three years, thanks in great measure to Jackson's pressure on GTE,

COVAD became "the nation's largest competitive provider of broadband DSL services in the United States," the company claimed. CEO Robert Knowling thanked Jesse with a $250,000 contribution to the Citizenship Education Fund.

Knowling himself was painfully honest in describing his own rise to fortune. Although he had always been an "overachiever," who had been "mentored" by the head of Ameritech because of his talent, Knowling believes he would never have risen if it hadn't been for his race and the benefits of affirmative action. "He didn't give you a shot because you were an African-American," argued Fox News interviewer Neil Cavuto. "He gave you a shot because you were a talented executive."

Knowling replied flatly: "I don't believe that."

> *Knowling:*   I think I've been successful because I understood the double standard that does exist in business.
>
> *Cavuto:*   Are you more inclined at COVAD to hire African-Americans?
>
> *Knowling:*   No, I'm going to hire the best person for the job.
>
> *Cavuto:*   So you don't practice affirmative action.
>
> *Knowling:*   But my perspective is different because I believe that there is talent in a diverse community...
>
> *Cavuto:*   But as an executive and a pretty shrewd one in your own right, you don't necessarily have a racial quota in mind.
>
> *Knowling:*   No, absolutely not.[50]

Another minority businessman who profited handsomely from Jackson's help was Chester Davenport, whose Georgetown Partners employed Jackson's son Jonathan and was a regular financial and political backer of Jackson's causes. The cell phone spin-off championed by Jesse Jackson did not benefit the little guys in Chicago or Los Angeles hoping for the crumbs from a vast expanding market. It benefited someone who was already a very rich man and a political heavy hitter, but who was—most importantly—a Friend of Jesse. As *Fortune* magazine writer David Whitford wrote, "Does helping Davenport become really, really rich, as opposed to merely rich, truly advance the cause of people who need help most?"[51]

Chester Davenport acquired a 7 percent chunk of the Ameritech wireless business for just $60 million, a mere 25 percent of its official value of $228 million. The rest of the purchase price was picked up by his partners at GTE, who co-owned the new company but named Davenport as chairman. This was the price of appeasing federal regulators, who were taking their cues from Jackson and demanded a token minority "participation" in the combined merger and spin-off deal. Davenport was surprisingly blunt about his own role. He acknowledged that he put up just $60 million for the properties and that he created a new company, Davenport Cellular Communications, solely "to do this particular deal." He also admitted that Georgetown Partners, which controlled Davenport Cellular, specialized in acquiring spin-offs under diversity regulations and had "not done wireless before." A GTE spokesman stated that Davenport's new company was little more than a front and would have "no operational responsibility, none." He added that the arrangement was "simply a way that [Davenport] is involved in terms of watching his equity." Davenport said the new company might eventually provide "marketing services to capture demand for underserved ethnic markets with very high market potential." But he made clear to investors in a conference call that "we are obviously in this industry looking to have some diversity of ownership."[52] One week later, Davenport told the *New York Times* bluntly that "he got a piece of the GTE-Ameritech wireless deal because he is black," and claimed his net worth would be "100 times" bigger if he had been white.[53] The SBC/Ameritech and GTE–Bell Atlantic deals were merely the 1990s version of the late 1970s minority set-aside programs that Jesse Jackson's half brother Noah Robinson exploited so well.

Chester Davenport was a skilled operator who understood federal regulation and race-based negotiation, but who also had fine-tuned business instincts. Once he left the Carter administration, where he had been an assistant secretary for transportation, he used his political connections to leverage real estate deals with developer Oliver Carr, who owned properties in and around the Washington, D.C., metropolitan area and needed a minority "face" to win concessions from D.C. mayor Marion Barry. "Carr put up the money and developed the properties, with Chester Davenport providing the political clout," a former top advisor to Davenport tells me.[54]

In the 1980s, Davenport set up a company that built the emissions test centers required in many states under new federal guidelines for passenger vehicles that he had helped write. Davenport then lobbied state governments to adopt rules that required a centralized auto-testing system, rather than allow service stations to conduct smog inspections. His Envirotest Systems Corporation won big contracts in state after state until, by 1994, it had "nailed down virtually all of the centralized testing contracts in the country." To guarantee success, Davenport pulled out all the stops, including direct pressure from his old friend Jesse Jackson, who intervened in late 1993 with Connecticut governor Lowell Weicker "to overturn an underling's decision and impose a centralized testing system on the state."[55] The company that benefited from that decision was Chester Davenport's Envirotest.

Under the Clinton administration, Davenport won the support of the former head of California's Air Resources Board, Mary Nichols, now a top EPA regulator. To force California governor Pete Wilson to adopt the Envirotest Systems solution of centralized smog tests, Nichols imposed economic sanctions on California in January 1994 and threatened to cut off federal highway funds, on the pretext that decentralized smog tests did not meet federal air quality standards.[56] It was a tremendous boon for Davenport and Envirotest, which forecast that its revenues would quadruple from the 1993 level of $88.5 million as a result of the new EPA rules.[57]

During the second Clinton administration, Davenport helped the company identify new opportunities opened up by friendly EPA regulators, who allowed them to corner the market for automobile emission test centers (now required by law) in state after state across the nation. In May

1998, Davenport announced that the EPA had issued "draft guidelines detailing how states can use Envirotest's Remote Sensing to identify clean emissions vehicles and exempt such vehicles from their next regularly scheduled emissions inspection. The EPA estimates that up to 50 percent of vehicles can be tested through Clean-Screening," an Envirotest device then being tested in New York City. In other words, the EPA was issuing regulations specifically tailored to benefit Davenport's company.[58] It was government cronyism taken to a new height.

After starting the business from scratch, Davenport sold Envirotest to Stone Rivet Inc. in 1998 for $580 million, of which between $266 million and $280 million represented the net equity share, a company spokesman tells me.[59] At the very lowest estimate, that represented a twentyfold return on Davenport's original investment. Said Davenport: "Other people want to say that, 'Oh, well, this is somebody who's a minority.' That's fine with me, but that's not the way that I look at it. So I just kind of ignore all that and do what I do and use my talents to the best extent that I can—to add value and to be successful."[60]

FIGHTING BACK

As Jackson expanded the Wall Street Project during 1999, he opened offices around the country that focused on specific industries. The New York office did finance and banking, Detroit did automobiles, Chicago did venture capital, Houston did oil, while Los Angeles focused on the entertainment industry. Wherever he went, Jackson set up conferences—calling them "economic summits"—where he brokered deals, helped cronies, and banked payments, with little or no opposition from the local business community. But when he tried to move into California's Silicon Valley high-tech corridor, considered by many economists as the locomotive driving the economic boom of the 1990s, he ran smack up against the type of stubborn entrepreneur that seemed to have disappeared from the rest of corporate America—Cypress Semiconductors CEO T. J. Rodgers.

On March 2, 1999, Jackson announced he was "moving west" from Chicago and was opening a Silicon Valley chapter of his Wall Street

Project in an effort "to close the digital divide in the high tech industry." Jackson told a small crowd of supporters in Palo Alto that Rainbow/PUSH planned to purchase stock in the top fifty corporations in the Silicon Valley by the end of the week to forge a new relationship with the firms. "As stockholders, we can say okay, Mr. Chairman, who is on our board?" Jackson said. "Who are our top two hundred employees? Who is managing our pension funds and 401k? Who are our attorneys and advertising agencies?"[61] Jackson didn't explain why Rainbow/PUSH was buying the stock when the Wall Street Project was declared to the IRS as a program run by a separate nonprofit corporation, the Citizenship Education Fund. Indeed, in his own mind the various entities of Jesse Jackson Inc. had no separate identity, but were just emanations of his personal crusade, like hands and feet of the same body. This was just another example of how he confounded and commingled Rainbow/PUSH with CEF, trifling with the laws governing noprofit corporations, which required a clear separation. Challenged when CEF was used to make a payoff to Jackson's mistress Karin Stanford in January 2001, Jackson and his lawyers would declare that he had no legal relationship to CEF, did not even sit on its board, and therefore could not be accused of directing payments for personal benefit.

Patrick Reilly of the Capital Research Center explains why this is important:

> Jackson's organizations are often so closely linked that it is difficult to decipher which group is responsible for a particular program. The organizations share board members, employees, facilities, and even programs.... For instance, the Wall Street Project is officially a project of the tax-exempt Citizenship Education Fund. But it is often labeled the Rainbow/PUSH Wall Street Project, even on its own stationery. Because CEF and Rainbow/PUSH share the same headquarters in Chicago, the confusion only worsens....

> The close relationships between Jackson's organizations are also financial. The groups' public filings report several financial

dealings between the groups, raising questions about whether donated funds to a particular group are being used to advance other Jackson organizations. This is an important concern with regard to Jackson's tax-exempt organizations, which are forbidden to use donated funds for non-exempt activities.[62]

Jackson explained his Silicon Valley project in great detail at his Palo Alto press conference. "For those corporations that engaged in one-way trade, the office will first attempt to negotiate with them. If negotiation works, there will be reconciliation. If it fails, the Rainbow/PUSH Coalition will call for demonstrations," Jackson said. "We don't want to slow down the Silicon Valley. We want to enhance it. We want to do them a favor. We want them to expand the market and include us, because inclusion leads to growth."[63] By inclusion, Jackson meant doing business with members of the Rainbow/PUSH International Trade Bureau, which sold memberships to black entrepreneurs with a pledge to help "build bridges" for them to do business with corporate America. Jackson collected money from both partners of these deals, portraying himself as the necessary middleman, spokesman, and broker.

That's when Jackson made the mistake of knocking on T. J. Rodgers's door.

"Jackson came in here the way he has done it elsewhere. It was classic," Rodgers tells me. "He pre-announces he's going to be there. He claims there are prejudice problems he's going to help. He finds something to demonstrate that prejudice. In our case, he used a poorly researched article from the *San Francisco Chronicle*, which is a soppy, left-wing rag, and combined it with Equal Opportunity data from the government to show an under-representation of minorities in Silicon Valley companies relative to their percentage of the population. It was an obvious, stupid fallacy. If they had looked at employment percentages by race—which we did—and compared that to college graduates by race, they'd have seen that we were flat there."[64] Thirty-five percent of Cypress Semiconductor employees were minorities, and every single one of them was a corporate shareholder.

Rodgers knew his company had a terrific record, and he didn't like getting slammed gratuitously.

Despite this, Rodgers says he had a discussion with his board and had all but decided to accept their guidance to lie low. "There are two camps of corporate CEOs," Rodgers says. "There are the camp followers, who want to suck up and be seen on stage with Jesse to show the world that they are liberal broad-minded people. And then there are those who know deep down that he's a fraud, but who crawl under their desks. They take a long hard look at the upside-downside of a relationship with Jesse and decide it's just not worth it to confront him. I had decided to join the under-the-desk dwellers when Jackson came to town. As much as I'd have liked to criticize him, the upside was limited and the downside appeared astronomical, so I agreed with my board. If by speaking out against him I caused our shareholders to lose wealth, it was simply no good."

But then, something happened. "I remember I was driving to work," he says. "I was listening to him talk on the radio and it was totally outrageous. I got angry. Here was a guy who had no idea how Silicon Valley worked. He was coming in here like a New York City mayor, a big city mayor, with a big state approach. It was so insulting to the whole ethic of high tech, which I hold in high regard. I decided then and there not to let him get away with it."

When Rodgers got to work that morning he started making calls. One of the first was to Gerald A. Reynolds, the former president of the Center for New Black Leadership who had served as a legal analyst at the Center for Equal Opportunity from 1995 to 1997. He asked Reynolds why corporate CEOs were so deferential to Jackson, and quoted his reply in an op-ed he wrote that afternoon for the *San Jose Mercury News*. "It's simple," Reynolds said. "Jesse is a race hustler who makes his living shaking down corporations. Whites would rather be accused of being a child molester than a racist. Jesse's got the power to make corporate chieftains cower."[65]

Next, he called Shelby Steele, an African-American scholar at the Hoover Institution at Stanford University. Steele called Jackson an "extortion artist for the grievance elite," and said Jackson's biggest failing was to have corrupted race relations in America. "Martin Luther King told people they had to take on the responsibility—and risk—to win their freedom," Steele told T. J. Rodgers. "Jesse Jackson tells them . . . that they have no responsibility for their situation."

One of the many black leaders and intellectuals who came to Rodgers's defense was Robert Woodson, head of the National Center for Neighborhood Enterprise. He argued that Jackson's tactics don't benefit the black community: they benefit Jackson cronies. "He uses the black community to threaten corporations, but then who benefits? It's not the black community. It's a handful of black businessmen around Jesse Jackson," Woodson told the *Los Angeles Times*. "And what it's really doing is diluting the rich legacy of the civil rights movement. That legacy is now for sale."[66]

T. J. Rodgers says he was hoping to become a member of a unique third group, "who slapped Jesse back over the head with the absurdity of his own position," but the Jackson camp shot back almost immediately. "We can now officially describe Cypress Semiconductor as a white supremacist hate group," said John Templeton of the Coalition for Fair Employment, the group that invited Jackson to Silicon Valley.[67]

When Jackson took off the gloves, something else happened. "I discovered that the threat of being called a racist—assuming that you're not and that your actions speak for themselves—is not that bad. You don't have to fear Jesse Jackson," Rodgers says. He challenged Jackson to a public debate in California but never received a response. "He turned me down four times," Rodgers recalls. "Jackson's argument was that T. J. Rodgers, with 35 percent minority employment, is prejudiced because he should be employing 43 percent minorities. If I were prejudiced, why would I have 35 percent to begin with? It was absurd on the face of it."

Rodgers has since appeared on several TV talk shows, and likes to talk about facing down Jesse Jackson. "My advice to other CEOs? Why don't you grow a pair of balls? Or if you're a female, whatever is the female equivalent. I don't think Jesse Jackson is making a lot of money out here. We pay for value. He provides no value at all."

PERCY SUTTON, VIACOM, AND CBS

On September 22, 1999, Jesse Jackson trooped down to "Blackrock," the CBS corporate headquarters at 51 West 52nd Street, to meet CBS chairman and CEO Mel Karmazin. CBS was then in negotiations with the FCC to get its merger with Viacom approved, and Jackson wanted to get a piece of the pie. If the $36 billion merger went through, it would create the largest media company in the United States. The combined CBS and UPN television networks would reach 41 percent of U.S. households. Under existing FCC rules and regulations, which limited the market share of any one company to 35 percent, the new company would be required to spin off the excess to other owners. Jackson wanted Karmazin to sell Viacom's UPN network to minority-owned companies. If not, he warned, he would go on the attack and demand across-the-board changes in the way the companies were run.

First, he tried honey. "CBS brings to the table money, market infrastructure and know-how," Jackson said. "People of color bring to the table money, market, talent, and location. It has been said that where opportunity meets preparedness, there is great success. We want to be partners, not just media consumers. We want the opportunity to participate in the American dream of media ownership and participation."[68] But he made it abundantly clear that if CBS and Viacom did not see the advantage of selling off UPN to minorities, with appropriate loans and deferred payments, he could take off the gloves.

"Viacom has no person of color on their board," he pointed out. "CBS only has one. Yet, they now want the public to give them an additional position of power." Unless an agreement could be reached, Jackson said, he would also demand firm dollar and percentage quotas for "vendor relationships" with minority firms. He wanted a budget set-aside for black advertising companies. He wanted "opportunities for people of color to provide both professional services and financial services to CBS."[69] Jackson made a similar proposal in meetings with Viacom chairman Sumner Redstone and with FCC chairman William Kennard in Washington, D.C., on September 29, 1999. Kennard, the first African-American chairman of the FCC, became a powerful Jackson ally.

Unlike earlier "negotiations" with corporate CEOs, when he would present a list of "suitable" minority partners (who also happened to be members of the PUSH International Trade Bureau), this time Jackson brought his candidates for purchasing UPN in person to meet Karmazin. They were old cronies: Chester Davenport, who had no experience in television, but who had also no experience in the cell phone industry before Jackson helped him win a share of Ameritech's business; Joe Garcia, executive vice president and CFO of Spanish Broadcasting Systems; and Percy Sutton, the former Manhattan borough president who headed up Jackson's fundraising team during his 1988 presidential campaign. Sutton was also the president of Inner City Broadcasting Corporation, which owned seven radio stations, an interest in a cable television network, and the Apollo Theater in Harlem. Sutton was one of Jackson's earliest backers and a board member of the Citizenship Education Fund. What Jackson didn't say was that his wife owned shares in Sutton's Inner City Broadcasting worth more than one million dollars, and that he would therefore stand to benefit personally from any deal in which Percy Sutton participated.[70]

CEF's tax returns for 1999 show that Viacom got the message and kicked in three contributions totaling $422,500 to CEF that year. The United Paramount Network (UPN) gave an additional $50,000. But these weren't the only direct benefits that flowed to Jackson and his friends. Later that year, Jackson intervened again with the FCC to block the merger of Clear Channel Communications and AMFM Inc., arguing that minorities should be allowed to purchase radio stations in major cities as a condition of the deal. "Sutton's Inner City bought nine of those stations," the *Chicago Sun-Times* reported.[71] Once the spin-off deal was signed, Jackson lifted his objections and the Clear Channel merger sailed through the FCC in just eight months.[72]

In a complaint filed with the Internal Revenue Service against the Citizenship Education Fund on February 28, 2001, the National Legal and Policy Center cited these deals as clear violations of law. "CEF appears to be providing business services and facilitating transactions for a fee, which, if true, would seem to be a non-exempt purpose." Furthermore, NLPC president Peter Flaherty said, "CEF may have also violated the private inurement and private benefit doctrines insofar as the funds from the nonprofit have been used for private personal ends."[73]

Jackson took his traveling extravaganza to Hollywood on October 7, where he held a fundraiser at the Regent Beverly Wilshire Hotel with actor Warren Beatty, recording giant Quincy Jones, and food mogul Ron Burkle who had helped Jesse's sons Jonathan and Yusef win the Anheuser-Busch beer distributorship for Chicago. Jackson said the fundraiser was intended to help his group's efforts to "stop the rising tide of racism and unfair practices in employment, education, criminal justice, telecommunications, housing and economic development."[74] If the tide of racism was rising, it was because Jackson was in the water paddling as hard as he could.

THE BOTTOM LINE

On January 20, 2000, Jesse Jackson was the featured speaker at the Martin Luther King Jr. "Celebration 2000" dinner at the Sheraton San Marcos hotel in Chandler, Arizona. Town elders were seeking "someone high profile," they said, to dispel negative publicity stemming from roundups of illegal immigrants and undocumented foreign workers, which led to race discrimination lawsuits. It was a worthy cause, and Jackson was happy to lend his talents to easing racial tensions—for a fee. He sent the Chandler Human Relations Commission a contract for $25,000. The town fathers said they expected about three hundred people at the dinner, and would sell tickets for fifty dollars each. To make up the shortfall, they went to corporate donors, who were more than willing to fund Jackson's lifestyle without contributing directly to his organizations. Intel kicked in $30,000. [75] Consider: Jackson makes scores of similarly paid speaking engagements every year. Only rarely does Jackson's income from these events emerge to public view.

Jackson prided himself on "leveraging" concessions from corporate America in highly public forms. He called it "tithing." Once he launched the Wall Street Project, he abandoned the pretext of seeking gains for ordinary folks, and set his sights on getting contracts for friends and cronies in the business world. While press coverage of the first Wall Street conference in January 1998 noted that corporate sponsors were made to pay $50,000 for the honor of their association with Jackson, it was only later, once the CEF tax returns were released to the public in February 2001, that the mainstream media got a glimpse of how Jackson had refined his technique. Among those who caved in to Jackson's methods was the host of the first Wall Street conference, Travelers Group CEO Sanford I. Weill. Jackson praised the "diversity plan" Weill announced when Travelers merged with Citigroup in 1998. Weill had in fact arranged payments to Jackson of $100,000 from Travelers and another $150,000 from Citigroup, well beyond the sponsorship fee.

Jackson collected $10 million for the Citizenship Education Fund in 1999, the vast majority of it from major corporations. We've seen how Jackson collected the money, and we've seen why companies donated: to avoid costly and embarrassing boycotts and demonstrations by Jackson and his allies. As the vehicle for this extraordinarily successful fundraising, Jackson used a tax-exempt corporation. Under the Internal Revenue code, tax exemption can be claimed by corporations which do not seek to make a profit, do not sell business services, and have a clear educational, charitable, or religious purpose. Tax-exempt corporations are prohibited from partisan political activities, and can only use a small portion of their revenues for lobbying purposes. Violations of any of these conditions can lead the IRS to revoke a corporation's tax-exempt status and levy stiff penalties.

In the independent auditor's report and financial statements for 1999, auditor Velma Butler very carefully describes the nature of CEF activities to reinforce its adherence to the law. The following is her complete description, with no deletions:

Note 1 - Nature of the Organization

The Citizenship Education Fund (CEF) was established as a nonprofit organization in 1984. Its purpose is the education of voters and the promotion of full participation in the electoral process. CEF seeks to empower citizens through the effective use of public policy advocacy. To accomplish its objective, CEF provides voter participation services, electoral training workshops and youth leadership development projects. CEF conducts research, collects data on non-partisan related initiatives, and organizes seminars and public awareness campaigns on a variety of public policy issues.[76]

Butler's description essentially paraphrases the language prepared by CEF lawyer John Bustamante in the corporation's tax return, where he described the organization's tax exempt purpose as "educating voters," and the primary program dedicated to "issues related to youth and youth development."[77] Despite this, CEF spent just $50,000 on its primary exempt purpose, a Voter Registration Institute, and just $503,232 on "youth and youth development." Where did the other $9.5 million go?

The tax returns provide more questions than answers: $1,346,164 went for Jesse Jackson's travel. Another $1,307,393 was paid to consultants, whose tasks are not specified. It now appears that a portion of this money was paid to Jackson's mistress, Karin Stanford. CEF spent $1,140,285 on conferences, $300,000 on management and consulting services, $82,500 on Rainbow/PUSH rent (primarily, for the privilege of sharing Jackson's main office at PUSH headquarters on 930 East 50th Street in Chicago), $422,627 on expenses, $48,451 on an "auto expense," and another $223,296 on, well, "Miscellaneous." As for Jackson's much touted "research," which came up with all the examples of corporate America's "rising tide of racism," that required expenditures of just $15,699.

The bulk of the money simply went into a dark hole, and appears to have been used to finance Jackson's corporate shakedowns. Here is how the accountants broke it down:

- Wall Street/LaSalle Street projects: $2,126,002
- SBC Ameritech Project: $500,000

- Viacom project: $302,499
- AT&T project: $283,336
- Bell Atlantic project: $250,000
- GTE project: $125,000
- California project: $188,937
- Detroit project: $165,892
- International project: $97,134
- Atlanta project: $21,303[78]

In addition to this, CEF claims it spent $577,138 for its annual conference (presumably, the January 1999 Wall Street Project conference in New York). Why that money was listed separately from the Wall Street Project money is unclear. Even more vague is what expenditures were made for these various "projects" that had nothing to do with CEF's tax-exempt purpose. Neither Jackson himself, nor his accountants, nor his lawyers have ever offered a clear explanation. Was the $125,000 Jackson's CEF put into its "GTE Project" spent on behalf of Chester Davenport, who was the prime beneficiary of Jackson's efforts to gain minority participation in the Ameritech cellular phone spin-off? What about the $500,000 spent on the "SBC Ameritech project"? Where did that go? For lawyers? Even with all this unaccounted spending, CEF ended the year with more than $3.5 million in cash, a sizeable war chest in preparation for the 2000 elections, where Jackson engaged full throttle on behalf of the Democratic Party ticket.

Rainbow/PUSH raised another $5 million in 1999, for which the accounting is even more vague. Expenditures included $1,211,167 for salaries, another $1,187,975 for travel and conferences (lumped together), $330,962 in rent, and $803,922 for office expenses. Between CEF and Rainbow/PUSH, Jackson's groups spent $2.5 million that year on travel alone. According to the chief financial officer, Billy R. Owens, "all air travel for staff, except for Rev. Jackson, is booked as coach fares. Rev. Jackson's travel is charged to Rainbow and CEF depending on the purpose of the travel. He usually travels with one person."[79]

Despite the questionable accounting and lack of transparency, the Illinois secretary of state declared that Jackson's groups were in "full compliance" with the law and refused to launch an audit. "Corporations have a fiduciary responsibility to their shareholders," black syndicated columnist Deroy Murdock tells me. "But these corporate contributions are going down a Bermuda Triangle. There is no accountability to the shareholders."

Deroy Murdock believes Jackson "could be such a force for good" if he would harness his talents to help black teens or black entrepreneurs, instead of just helping his friends:

> In New York City, for instance, we've got private black commuter vans that charge $1.00 for door to door service to take people to work, when the city buses charge $1.50. Mayor Guiliani has been trying to get more permits for these guys to increase their business, but the city bus drivers unions oppose it. They are mostly black. If Jesse Jackson were to hold a rally and browbeat the city council to allow them to get more permits for this private commuter van service, it would make life much easier for black folks trying to get to work. But it'll never happen. Instead, you dial 911 for Uncle Jesse if you're a black criminal and you want someone to make excuses for your crimes. Jesse Jackson runs a black enrichment and fraud operation that benefits himself, his spider web of organizations, his business associates, and his relatives.[80]

Only one man can stop him, Deroy Murdock believes. And that is Ohio secretary of state Kenneth Blackwell, a popular black Republican who was touted as a possible vice presidential candidate in 2000. Blackwell's hook? "All Jackson's organizations are registered in the state of Ohio," Murdock says. "If Ken Blackwell wants to, he can dismantle them."

CHAPTER 15

⟳

Special Envoy of Black Business

Jackson held his third Wall Street Project conference in January 2000, promoting a new book he had published with his son Congressman Jesse L. Jackson Jr., which was aimed at readers unschooled in basic economic principles. He billed the book as a guide "to teach people how to get out of debt and invest in the future rather than banking on winning the lottery." But the example Jackson himself set was closer to winning the lottery than the patient, hard work of the long-term investor. At the Wall Street conference he once again trotted out big names and large corporations, who each paid $50,000 or more to sponsor the event. Among them were AT&T chairman Michael Armstrong, Bell Atlantic chairman Ivan Seidenberg, and Citigroup chairman Sanford Weill—all of whom Jackson had shaken down at merger time—as well as a politically bruised President Bill Clinton, whom Jackson had supported unfailingly during the impeachment debacle.

The keynote speaker was Time Warner president Richard D. Parsons, a big CEF contributor. Time Warner ought to have presented a tempting target for Jackson's merger shakedown racket. In September 1995, the group merged with Ted Turner's CNN, creating a $19 billion media conglomerate. Only nine days before Parson's January 19 appearance at the Wall Street Project lunch, Time Warner chief executive officer Gerald Levin and America Online Inc. CEO Steve Case announced in New York that they were negotiating a $109 billion merger, the largest ever in U.S. history. But a search of Jackson's own statements, Rainbow/PUSH press releases, and Lexis-Nexis show that Jackson never uttered a word of criticism of the group or ever demanded that they sell off local cable companies or other assets to minority businesses to break down the alleged "digital divide." The title of Jackson's how-to book gives one possible explanation for this surprising acquiescence: "It's About the Money."[1] Since 1991, Time Warner had kicked in more than $250,000 to Jackson's group, according to the group's tax returns. If it was protection money, it was well spent.

Jackson also leaned on his friend the president. The unfaithful Jackson and the unfaithful Clinton became soul mates during their 1998 illicit sexual affairs with Karin Stanford and Monica Lewinsky, respectively. And Clinton had already given Jackson a terrific boost through his patronage of the Wall Street Project. Now Jesse had another favor he wanted: U.S. government patronage of an Africa trade mission so he could take his best friends and most loyal supporters to meet with African heads of state.

THE FEBRUARY 2000 TRADE MISSION TO AFRICA

Getting the U.S. government to sponsor private trade missions had become common during the Clinton presidency, but it was also an open door to corrupt relationships. Clinton's late secretary of commerce, Ron Brown, had been accused by several congressional committees, as well as by the watchdog group Judicial Watch, of "selling" seats on trade missions to business executives in exchange for hefty donations to the Democratic National Committee. Jackson's February 2000 Africa trade mission was even murkier, since he was not a "real" U.S. government official but a special presidential envoy, which was legally an unpaid, honorary title. Jackson milked the title and the prestige for all it was worth. "Clinton turned Jesse and the Congressional Black Caucus loose in Africa to do business deals," a retired intelligence officer who closely follows Africa tells me. "This was a payoff for their support during the impeachment trial."[2]

Jackson was so sure of Clinton's backing he didn't even bother to ask politely for U.S. government support—he demanded it. In an imperious December 8, 1999, letter to Commerce Secretary William M. Daley, obtained through the Freedom of Information Act, Jackson said he was writing "to inform you of my plans to lead a minority trade mission" to Africa just two months hence, from February 5 to 16, 2000. "I am counting on your direct support and the tremendous resources of your department," he wrote, before detailing exactly what he expected Daley to provide in terms of pre-trip and on-the-ground assistance:

1) "Information Research on Telecommunications, Media, and Information Technology sectors"
2) "Company Matchmaking (i.e., providing a list of potential in-country companies; identifying potential joint ventures)"
3) "Logistics & Support"[3]

It was breathtakingly arrogant. If any other business or civic leader had sent a similar note to a cabinet secretary, it's hard to imagine them receiving a civil reply. The very short time frame required Daley to give immediate marching orders to the International Trade Administration (ITA) and the Foreign Commercial Service (FCS), which managed overseas Commerce Department employees, sending them scurrying to do Jackson's bidding. Official guidance for U.S. companies warns them that it requires three to four months of advance planning to schedule such events.

Jackson said that the trade mission "will follow-up on discussions held with [Nigeria's] President Obasanjo, [Ghana's] President Rawlings and [South Africa's] President Mbeki during their recent visits to the United

States." But the discussions Jackson had with these leaders were supposed to be held in his capacity as President Clinton's special envoy to Africa, not as a middleman for private U.S. companies. Jackson didn't even seek to disguise the total commingling of his private and public roles in this or other correspondence with the Clinton administration; he just assumed—correctly—that the entire bureaucracy of the United States government would be placed at his disposal, virtually free of charge.

"[W]e must seize and build on these immediate opportunities to create mutually prosperous markets for U.S.-Nigerian business. I know you agree that we must do all we can to support small and minority businesses, and to address roadblock issues to bilateral commercial development." These were the words Jackson used to dress up his government-assisted self-enrichment scheme.

Some embassies openly complained of Jackson's imperiousness. "Preparations for the Mission began about four weeks before the event date when an advance team came from the United States to discuss ground-support issues and clarify specific areas of interests," wrote a commercial officer at the U.S. embassy in Lagos. "This short notice, however, made event planning difficult and put much pressure on [Commercial Service]—Nigeria and the whole Embassy."[4]

The U.S. ambassador to Nigeria, William H. Twaddell, sent a curt note back to Jackson, asking him to do his homework better. "I need to bring to your attention the fact that the Embassy in Lagos and Embassy Office in Abuja are already preparing for a U.S. Department of Agriculture Trade Mission scheduled for Feb. 3–4, 2000. That event will obviously command most of our personnel." He also pointed out that "February 5–6 suggested in your letter as the beginning of the mission are weekend days which are not suitable for a productive program in Nigeria."[5] It didn't take a rocket scientist to read a calendar, but apparently Jackson and his staff hadn't done so. The aide Jackson put in charge of advance planning, former Ron Brown staffer Charlotte Kea, didn't inspire much confidence in the U.S. government officials she encountered, starting with her former colleagues at Commerce. After meeting with Kea in Washington to discuss the trip, the deputy director of the Commerce Department's Office of International Operations noted in a January 5, 2000, e-mail sent to all the U.S. embassies involved in the Jackson trip that Kea's experience working on Ron Brown trade missions had not served her well. "I doubt that Charlotte knows anything about how trade missions are arranged, what goes into a budget, etc., so please don't be afraid to lay everything out very clearly," she wrote.[6]

Jackson's wish lists soon became more extravagant. His advance team, meeting with the top U.S. embassy official in Abuja, Charles N. Patterson Jr., requested that the U.S. embassy in Nigeria "provide diplomatic rates to members of the Investment Mission" (denied) and a "security vehicle" for Jackson (approved). They also requested that the embassy public affairs people provide a photographer, but said they would pay for it.[7] In Lagos, they sent U.S. embassy officer Anayo Agu scurrying about to the EKO Hotel to sign a banquet contract for fifty guests[8] as if he were a hired hand.

Although the contract clearly stated that the Rainbow/PUSH coalition was sponsoring the event, it listed Mr. Miguel Pardo de Zela, the commercial counselor at the U.S. embassy, as the Rainbow/PUSH local representative.

PAYOFFS IN ACCRA

As he left Chicago on this latest African escapade, Jackson proclaimed that he was on a mission to "bridge the digital divide in Africa," a statement that was absurd on its face.[9] According to the Federal Communications Commission figures he cited at virtually every whistle-stop, only fourteen million phone lines existed for Africa's 739 million people. Jackson claimed this presented "tremendous growth potential for U.S. business," especially for information technology and broadband telephony.[10] What Jackson seemed to forget was that before Africans could benefit from computers, Internet service, and telephones, they needed more basic things such as electricity, clean water, and rudimentary health services. But once again, Jackson's goal was not to help the poor. It was to enrich himself and his friends, using his prestige as "special envoy" to cash in on potentially lucrative government contracts. "Because of Jackson's connections [in

Africa] we stand a good chance of developing some positive business part-
nerships and making some inroads we might never have had access to on
our own," said Charles Johnson of United Communications Systems, one
of the trade mission participants.[11]

After an all-night flight from New York, the group arrived at 6 A.M. at
Kotoka International Airport in Accra, Ghana, on February 6, 2000.
Jackson had planned a press conference in the VIP lounge, but instead
was met "planeside and taken directly to the hotel" by U.S. ambassador
Kathryn Dee Robinson and members of the embassy staff, who realized
that even Jackson could not inspire the press at the crack of dawn on a
Sunday morning.[12] After lunch and a tour of Accra (including a stop at
the grave of W. E. B. Dubois), Jackson's merry band was given the rest of
the day off, an inauspicious beginning.

The U.S. embassy staffs were working overtime to help Jackson set up
appointments with government ministries and other top officials, and
much of the planning was done on the wing. As a full day of business
meetings began on Monday at Accra's La Palm Hotel, Commercial
Officer Johnny Brown took Jackson aside "to emphasize to Rev. Jackson
and the delegation the readiness of the USDOC [Department of
Commerce] to work with this delegation" in securing telecom contracts.
Brown brought in a staffer from the U.S. government Export-Import
Bank and suggested that EXIM, which provided political risk insurance
and export credit guarantees, might also be willing to help.

Jackson immediately seized on these confidences. At the next opportunity, he singled out the U.S. bureaucrats for praise and announced to
the conference: "The USDOC and EXIM is with us in our efforts here."

As Brown reported back to Washington, Jackson's claim to have active
U.S. government support "seemed to give his delegation more credibility
with the local participants." It was a tactic he would refine and repeat
throughout the trip.[13]

While most of the business participants who paid $10,000 each to join
Jackson for the trip were hoping to get the inside track on government
telecommunications contracts, lawyer Tricia Hoffler, of the Florida law

firm of Willie E. Gary, insisted that the embassy set up private meetings for her so she could promote her firm's services in launching a massive liability suit against U.S. tobacco companies. Johnny Brown reported back to Washington: "With hesitation and much effort, I managed to get an appointment with the Director of Public Health for the following day (Tuesday) which the lawyer failed to keep in favor of going to a meeting with the first lady of Ghana. (Life's little hiccups—I guess)."[14]

Gloria Gary, also on the trip, ran a property management firm named "Gary Enterprises" out of her husband's law offices in Stuart, Florida. The Gary, Parenti law firm made $5,000 contributions to Jackson's Citizenship Education Fund in 1994 and again in 1997. Willie Gary has become one of America's wealthiest lawyers thanks to race-based class action lawsuits against Coca-Cola, Office Depot, and most recently, Disney, a case he pursued in partnership with another Jackson pal, Johnnie Cochran.[15] He has a five-billion-dollar class action lawsuit for racial discrimination pending against Microsoft.

While Willie Gary's wife and partner were trolling for business, Jackson was working his own contacts behind the scenes. On Tuesday, he took the group for a ninety-minute "courtesy call" to "the Castle," to meet with Flight Lieutenant Jerry John Rawlings, Ghana's self-appointed president. Afterwards, they met separately with Rawlings's wife, Nana Konadu Rawlings, who headed a notorious political party known as the 31st December Women's Movement. Party officials worked out of a splendid palace in the Ridge suburb of Accra, surrounded by foreign embassies, which they had seized from the private owners of the Dakmak family in 1986. She made it clear that if certain urgent needs of the movement were fulfilled, she would be happy to slip in a friendly word to her husband on behalf of Jackson's business friends. One of the vehicles Mrs. Rawlings used to collect such payments was a holding company called CARIDEM, which engaged in joint ventures with foreign businesses.[16] Jackson agreed to make a $60,000 donation, which he later said was actually two separate $30,000 "grants" from businessmen, one to build day-care centers and the second "to encourage female-owned small businesses" in Ghana.[17]

In his eagerness to pay off the president's wife, Jackson went one step further, by making it appear that the money was a direct subsidy to Mrs. Rawlings's political party from the U.S. government. His actions were so egregious that the first secretary at the U.S. embassy in Accra, Stephanie Sullivan, was ordered by Ambassador Robinson to send a "cure" letter to Samuel Odoi-Sykes, chairman of the ruling New Patriotic Party (the parent of Mrs. Rawlings's group), denying any U.S. government involvement. "Ambassador Robinson received your letter of 23 February, and has asked me to reply on her behalf," Sullivan began. "I wish to clarify the circumstances surrounding Reverend Jesse Jackson's donation to the 31st December Women's Movement." She continued:

> During Rev. Jesse Jackson's February visit to Ghana, he was acting in a private capacity as director of the Rainbow/PUSH Coalition and not in his capacity as U.S. Special Envoy for Promotion of Democracy in Africa. As such, the donation to the 31st December Women's Movement was not a U.S. Government donation, but rather that of a private organization.
>
> Reverend Jackson has a long history of working for democracy and human rights throughout the world, and throughout Africa. Consequently, the Embassy assisted in facilitating his trip, although Rev. Jackson did not head an official U.S. Government delegation.
>
> In this important election year for Ghana, we at the Embassy, and our counterparts in Washington, DC, are committed to encouraging free and fair elections, and will be observing the proceedings closely. However, we will not contribute funds to any political party in order to "level the playing field" or interfere in local politics.[18]

It was an extraordinary admission, which showed just how far Jackson pushed the envelope in using his U.S. government "hat" to conduct private business. On the last day of the group's stay in Accra, as they were gathering with U.S. embassy officials to check out of their rooms, a convoy of four-wheel-drive vehicles screeched to a halt in front of the hotel. Out stepped Flight Lieutenant Jerry Rawlings, Ghana's president. "To the surprise of the delegation...Rawlings and Jackson got into the Chevy Suburban, driven by Rawlings, and led the delegation to the airport, where he stayed until the delegation's chartered aircraft disappeared from view into the harmattan skies of Ghana," commercial officer Johnny Brown e-mailed Washington. It was Rawlings's extraordinary way of saying, "Thank you, done deal."

On February 8, with Jackson set to arrive in Nigeria after three days in Ghana, Mr. Pardo of the U.S. embassy in Lagos arranged with Dr. Ola Balogun, a Nigerian musician, to bring his "IROKO" singers and dancers to the Meridien Eko Hotel for the entertainment of the Reverend Jackson and his guests. Dr. Balogun showed up with nineteen musicians, six dancers, eight technicians and directors, a driver, and two public relations officers, an extravaganza more worthy of a visiting Roman consul than a U.S. trade delegation.[19] But that was in keeping with Jackson's style. A postmortem sent from commercial officer Anayo Agu in Lagos noted that the group's schedule of business meetings "was severely strained by frequent changes arising from over-extensive lunch activities and ceremonial engagements that had no direct business value to the Mission objectives."[20]

Wherever he went on the three-nation tour, Jackson introduced his friends as "chief executive officers," and claimed they had come to make billion dollar investments in Africa.[21] At one point, he told reporters in Nigeria they were ready to invest $3 billion in Nigerian telecommunications, and additional sums in the information technology sector. "The latest investment plan was unveiled in Lagos last week Wednesday by a US trade delegation led by Jesse Jackson, the special envoy of US President Bill Clinton," Nigerian journalist Kingsley Kubeyinje reported. The promised investment was "good news for Nigeria" after years of U.S. ostracism, and was a direct result of the end of military rule, he wrote. "Jackson said the investment was aimed at improving relations with Nigeria." That comment was circled by an unnamed U.S. embassy official who clipped the article and sent it back to Washington with the annotation: "Never knew business to make an investment to do this only."[22]

And that was not the only misrepresentation that Jackson left behind. He told African journalists, as Kubeyinje faithfully reported, that he was "the special envoy of US President Bill Clinton," encouraging them to believe that the business delegation was in fact a U.S. government gesture of support for the regimes they visited. The U.S. embassy in Lagos noted Jackson's misrepresentation in a postevent memo: "Most Nigerians who participated in programmed events perceived the Mission as a U.S. government endorsement of Nigeria's on-going transition-to-democracy," when in fact the embassy and the Commerce Department were clearly aware that Jackson had come under the Rainbow/PUSH umbrella.[23] In addition, many of the "CEOs" who accompanied him and paid $10,000 each for the favor, were not CEOs at all. One of these was Jesse Jackson's own son Jonathan, who was identified repeatedly in Rainbow/PUSH lists of "confirmed business participants" as representing Georgetown Partners, the investment firm of Jackson's friend Chester Davenport.[24] When questioned subsequently, both Jacksons denied that Jonathan went to Africa representing Davenport.

Far more important, however, were the legitimate businessmen who went on the trip in hopes that they could benefit from Jesse Jackson's other hat as a U.S. government envoy. Among them were:

- Jim Reynolds of Loop Capital Markets, a Chicago investment bank. Reynolds boasted in April 2001 that his firm had become "the number one underwriter of public securities . . . in this city and state. We've been in business approximately three years." He attributed his firm's meteoric rise to Jesse Jackson. "A significant part of the access that we've enjoyed . . . has only been made possible through the tireless efforts of Reverend Jackson."[25]
- Maceo Sloan, the Jackson patron who ran large investment portfolios for NCM. He joined the trip to promote a venture called New Africa Advisers, an investment manager and securities brokerage firm. This

was after Jackson had intervened to save Sloan's business with Dreyfus, which had sent him a formal letter announcing their intention to sever his contract as a money manager, according to a former Wall Street Project colleague.[26]

- Texas state senator Rodney Ellis, whose APEX Securities Inc. was virtually unknown except for one key calling card: a claim to have "presented SBC in the privatization of the telecom system in South Africa."[27]

- Paul Longhenry, the personal representative of Jackson crony Ron Burkle and his Yucaipa Company, who had never done business before in Africa and was "interested in exploratory meetings."

- Stephen C. Mack, president of AIC Technologies Inc. of Chicago, a $600,000-a-year firm billed as "a full-service communications technology company which performs all aspects of telephone sales and installations."

- Angelina Knowling, wife of broadband COVAD Communications CEO Robert Knowling, who contributed $250,000 to CEF in 1999 after Jesse squeezed GTE to give COVAD access to GTE's local lines so they could offer DSL service. This business transformed the company from a zero revenue start-up in 1996, to an enterprise worth several hundred million dollars four years later, and Robert Knowling was no doubt pleased to express his gratitude for Jackson's help.[28]

- Crowning them all was Percy Sutton, the former Manhattan borough president, CEF board member and Jackson business partner, who came seeking telecom investment opportunities. Sutton's African Continental Telecommunications Limited (ACTEL) was trying to interest the Nigerians in buying state-of-the-art satellite-based telecommunications services. Sutton told Congress in public testimony that he, his wife, and their company, Inner City Broadcasting Corporation, "personally have invested more than sixteen million dollars" in ACTEL. Jesse Jackson and his wife held a million-dollar investment stake in Inner City Broadcasting, and so stood to gain materially in a significant fashion if Percy Sutton succeeded in winning a major contract in Africa.[29] This clearly raised the question of personal inurement, which was illegal under the IRS code for directors or principals of a nonprofit corporation.

Exactly how much Jackson's business junket cost U.S. taxpayers is unclear, but a few indications emerge from the documents released by the Commerce Department.

The "Gold Key" business service the three U.S. embassies provided Jackson and the twenty business leaders who accompanied him is usually billed between $1,350 and $2,500 per company and is only available "within 3–4 months of confirmed request," according to the Foreign Commerce Service guide provided to Jackson. Normally, each of the twenty companies accompanying Jackson should have been billed between $27,000 and $50,000 for each of the three capitals where the Foreign Commercial Service officers arranged business meetings, receptions, and other contacts for them. But according to embassy cables and Department of Commerce records, Rainbow/PUSH was only billed $5,350 for the Nigerian leg and $10,000 for South Africa. Assuming the Ghanaian leg was also billed at $10,000 (a generous assumption), that means Jackson and his friends received free commercial services worth between $56,000 to $100,000.

In addition, some twenty U.S. government officials traveled with the Rainbow/PUSH delegation. The U.S taxpayer picked up the tab for their airfare, hotels, meals, and incidentals, at an estimated cost of $8,000 each. Cost: $160,000.

Above and beyond the "Gold Key" service, U.S. embassy personnel handled Jackson's hotel reservations, and hired coaches, limousines, and security guards for Jackson; U.S. ambassadors hosted receptions and dinners at their official residences that ranged from a modest fifty guests in Ghana, to a gala hosted by U.S. ambassador Delano E. Lewis at "Hill House" in Johannesburg to which 582 guests were invited.[30] Estimated cost to the taxpayers: $100,000.

In one case, the Foreign Commercial Service in Johannesburg got stuck one year later with an unpaid bill for a breakfast meeting for

Jackson's group with the local Chamber of Commerce, at the cost to the taxpayers of $1,420.[31]

All these lavish freebies cost the taxpayers some $350,000, according to government documents. In addition, at each stop Jackson immobilized the embassy, the ambassador, his residence, and much of the entire embassy staff before and during his visit. He demanded constant attention as he shifted schedule, juggled appointments, and staged impromptu press events.

In all, it was a junket worthy of a Friend of Bill. And it was part of Bill Clinton's way of keeping Jesse happy and out of the 2000 presidential race.

BLOOD IN THE DIAMOND FIELDS

On Thursday, May 4, 2000, the deal Jackson had negotiated for his friend Charles Taylor and Sierra Leone rebel leader Foday Sankoh collapsed when Sankoh's guerrilla fighters took 208 peacekeepers hostage. Sankoh's fighters had seized the mostly Zambian peacekeepers deep in the bush after several days of clashes, as UN forces attempted to move toward Sierra Leone's Kono and Tongo diamond fields, which Sankoh's Revolutionary United Front (RUF) fighters had occupied with Jesse Jackson's help one year earlier. Communications were bad, and for several days only sketchy reports of the fighting emerged. But by Monday, UN surveillance aircraft spotted the rebels on the road, kicking up dust as their convoy of thirteen hijacked armored personnel carriers hurtled toward Freetown, the capital of Sierra Leone.[32] A half-dozen peacekeepers had been murdered, according to preliminary reports. Within a week, Sankoh's RUF had captured five hundred peacekeepers, stolen their weapons and vehicles, and appeared poised to reignite the country's bloody civil war.

Under the Lomé Accord, which Jackson brokered, Sankoh had been released from jail and brought into the Sierra Leone government as a vice president. He was also put in charge of the country's lucrative diamond mines. Following the agreement, formally signed in July 1999, Liberia's diamond exports skyrocketed, although the country had virtually no diamonds of its own. "During 1999 alone, Taylor illegally exported six million carats of 'blood diamonds,' pocketing $300 million," Sierra Leone ambassador John Ernest Leigh told members of the Congressional Black Caucus in a scolding letter after they tried to intervene on behalf of Foday Sankoh and Charles Taylor.[33] RUF commanders regularly carried the diamonds across the border from Sierra Leone to Liberia, where they were met by Liberian military helicopters and flown to Monrovia to hand them over to Charles Taylor in exchange for arms, a traffic well documented by a United Nations panel of experts.[34] Taylor paid off the arms dealers and his friends, including heads of state and foreign diplomats.

Sometimes, Taylor didn't want to be bothered handling the diamonds himself and dispatched a diamond dealer named Ibrahim Bah, a former guerrilla fighter from neighboring Burkina Faso he had met in Colonel Qaddafi's military training camps. "Ibrahim was the brains of the RUF. He was the real commander," said a diamond trader who dealt extensively with Taylor and the RUF.[35]

"Ibrahim Bah was one of the conduits used by Taylor for getting diamonds to his foreign friends in exchange for their political support. He wasn't the only one, but he was probably the smartest." Bah was identified in the UN Experts Panel report as "General" Ibrahim Bah (a.k.a. "Bald"), a Burkinabe who "handles much of the financial, diamond and weapons transactions between the RUF, Liberia and Burkina Faso."[36] Bah personally took the diamonds from the Kono District in Sierra Leone to Charles Taylor in Monrovia, as did Sankoh aide Issa Sesay, who succeeded him as leader of the RUF.

Bah had authentic, legally issued passports from seven countries, including five that had awarded him diplomatic status, and was a dedicated follower of Libya's Colonel Qaddafi. "Officially, everybody is against the RUF and Charles Taylor," the diamond trader said. "But behind the scenes they all support them. That's why Ibrahim Bah can travel wherever he wants," despite a UN travel ban that went into effect on May 7, 2001.[37] "They'll just arrange for him to get five more passports, with five new names," he added. The *Washington Post* reported in

November 2001 that Bah also sold diamonds to buyers from Osama bin Laden's al Qaeda organization and to the Lebanese Hezbollah, which is backed by the government of Iran and has committed numerous terrorist atrocities against the United States. Bin Laden reportedly liked buying diamonds because he feared U.S. efforts to freeze his assets around the world. "Diamonds don't set off alarms at airports, they can't be sniffed by dogs, they are easy to hide, and are highly convertible to cash. It makes perfect sense," an American official says.[38]

But the RUF attack on the UN peacekeepers was quickly unraveling this cozy arrangement between Taylor, Sankoh, and their international backers. On May 8, 2000, an angry crowd stormed Sankoh's villa in Freetown. Sankoh fled before he could be seized, but when the crowd rushed inside his villa they discovered thousands of pages of documents detailing his black market diamond trade. Those documents, says Ambassador Leigh, are now with Sierra Leone attorney general Solomon Berewa and include ledgers of more than two thousand diamonds mined by the RUF during their short ten months in government. These diamonds were simply taken off the government's books and sold privately by Foday Sankoh, Charles Taylor, and their friends. The ledgers reportedly also include the names of those who bought them, but have not yet been made public.[39]

Sankoh's villa overlooking the capital was dedicated to the cult of the lion, symbol of power and majesty. Images of lions were pasted to the walls. In public appearances, Sankoh wore blue robes embroidered with lions, and carried a walking stick carved to look like a lion's jaws. This was a man who mixed the ferocity of a tribal warlord with a childlike ignorance of modern ways. "Once, I gave Foday $100,000 in cash," a former business partner tells me. "I came to visit him at his villa with Ibrahim Bah. When we got inside we found Foday, buck naked, dancing around the money, which he had dumped out into a pile on the floor."[40]

Among the document trove found at the villa was correspondence between Foday Sankoh and foreign businessmen who had come to Freetown to negotiate diamond and investment deals with him. Chudi

Izegbu, president of the Integrated Group of Companies of McLean, Virginia, was one of these American hopefuls. According to these documents, Izegbu chartered an aircraft in Abijan and flew to Freetown to meet Sankoh in November 1999, where they discussed "a range of investment possibilities for the Integrated Group." Izegbu suggested they use an offshore company to handle the money, called Integrated Mining, registered in the Cayman Islands. "They discussed possible investments in civilian aircraft services, petroleum imports and a major investment in the Koidu diamond kimberlites," a UN panel of experts found, after getting an initial glimpse of the Sankoh documents. "Subsequently, Izegbu and Sankoh exchanged correspondence about negotiations and discussions currently going on in the interest of the RUFP," the party's diamond mining company. "And they exchanged text messages in a code which would allow them to disguise names—words like 'diamonds' and 'gold,' and expressions such as 'everything is OK,' and 'things are bad.' In December 1999, Sankoh ordered fourteen vehicles from Izegbu with the logo of the RUF Party painted on the side of each."[41]

Another American hopeful was Damian Gagnon, of Lazare Kaplan International (LKI). His chairman, Maurice Tempelsman, wrote after the meeting with Sankoh that Gagnon had reported "a commonality of views between you and this company on the possibilities of LKI reentering the Sierra Leone diamond business in a manner beneficial to all the people of that country as well as our company."[42]

An April 2000 letter, sent by Belgian businessman Michel Desaedeleer on behalf of his U.S. Trading and Investment Company, addresses Sankoh as "The Leader," and suggests ways for Sankoh to get all the diamonds mined in Kono rather than just 10 percent. Instead of allowing Charles Taylor and the Liberians to siphon off the rest, Desaedeleer proposed that his Belgian partner "Charles" hire a private jet to take the diamonds out directly from Kono, avoiding "the Lebanese" and Monrovia. "We cannot trust those people," he wrote.[43]

JACKSON JUMPS IN

As stories of wounded peacekeepers escaping from the RUF guerrillas began to trickle out, an alarmed UN secretary general Kofi Annan warned that the attacks could imperil *all* UN peacekeeping operations in Africa and called for help. President Clinton responded by summoning Jesse Jackson, his Special Envoy for Democracy in Africa, and the man who arguably had a better rapport with Sankoh and Taylor than anyone in (or near) the U.S. government.

Jackson jumped right in, perhaps without fully realizing how heated the situation had become. In a Washington, D.C., press conference on Friday, May 12, broadcast by the Voice of America throughout Africa, Jackson announced that he was departing for a new and urgent peacekeeping mission to the region, and that he would rely on his good relationship with Foday Sankoh and Charles Taylor to get the UN hostages released. "There is blood on everybody's hands and no clean hands," Jackson said when challenged why he sought to "negotiate" with Taylor and the RUF. "If Charles Taylor can talk to the [RUF] commanders and they hear that, that would be positive. It would be different if he were encouraging fighting but he is not." Then Jackson made a blunder that would make him an object of ridicule and scorn across Africa: he compared guerrilla leader Foday Sankoh to Nelson Mandela, the former African National Congress leader and president of South Africa. "Sankoh should be coaxed back into the political equation," he told reporters. "The voice of the RUF in Sierra Leone is Foday Sankoh's voice and his voice would be a positive one. . . . The support that he needs to turn the RUF into a political organization is deserved." Apparently he did not know that the RUF was already registered in Sierra Leone as a political party. "One of the things I would want to do early on is to seek not only the whereabouts of Foday Sankoh but to assure him of some port of safety," Jackson added.[44]

On Tuesday, May 16, Jackson was all set to take off for Sierra Leone when an urgent message came into the State Department, warning that Jackson could be physically assaulted should he attempt to land. Foreign Minister Sama Banya even went on state radio in Freetown, urging

Jackson to stay away. "When people in Freetown heard Jesse Jackson's statement comparing Foday Sankoh to Nelson Mandela, they were up in arms," recalls Sierra Leone ambassador John Ernest Leigh. "Comparing Nelson Mandela to a guy who was ripping arms off of babies was the biggest insult to Africa you could think of. Jesse Jackson destroyed the credibility of the United States."[45] Sierra Leone pro-democracy activists warned Jackson, "Our people will greet your presence in our country with contempt, and we'll encourage them to mount massive demonstrations in protest." During a conference call to leaders in Freetown just before leaving Washington, Jackson tried to retract his earlier statements but was openly attacked as an RUF "collaborator."[46]

Jackson's flying circus took off on May 17. State Department spokesman Richard Boucher said Jackson was traveling "at the request of President Clinton" and would visit "Nigeria, Liberia, Mali, Guinea, and Sierra Leone, security conditions permitting."[47] After briefly consulting with President Obasanjo in Nigeria, Jackson realized that his attempts to retract his statements in support of Foday Sankoh had antagonized rebel leaders while not appeasing the government. So instead of flying directly to Sierra Leone he sought refuge with old friend Charles Taylor in Monrovia, Liberia. Fighting had broken out all over Sierra Leone, the UN had lost control, and neither the government nor the rebels could guarantee Jackson's safety. A local militia leader in Freetown had captured Foday Sankoh and paraded him about naked in the streets before turning him over to government troops. Everyone was in a bloodthirsty mood. It was a unique moment in U.S. diplomacy for an American presidential envoy to abandon a peace mission because he had helped incite all parties in the conflict to mayhem. Jackson accomplished this through his own unique blend of incompetence, arrogance, and bluster. As Jackson explains it today, "Everything was going all right until the UN got close to the diamond mines. That's when Foday Sankoh cracked down on the UN."

Charles Taylor welcomed Jackson warmly to Liberia, inviting him to spend a wild night at the presidential mansion in Monrovia, promising to "treat him like a king." Several current and former U.S. government officials described "the panic" that seized the U.S. embassy in Liberia that evening, as they frantically sought to dissuade Jackson from accepting Taylor's invitation. "We had seen what went on at Taylor's mansion in the past—drugs, diamonds, women, you name it. We were afraid Taylor was seeking to compromise Jackson and wanted to avoid that." In the end, Jackson spent the night at the U.S. ambassador's residence in Monrovia, after the U.S. embassy hastily organized a press conference for him.[48]

The next day, Jackson returned to the president's mansion where Charles Taylor introduced him to RUF commander Sam Bockerie, also known as Mosquito. "Bockerie saluted Charles Taylor as his commander," one U.S. official told me. "There were no ifs, ands, or buts about it: Charles Taylor was the effective commander of the RUF."[49] Jackson puts it slightly more diplomatically. "We knew Foday Sankoh was the only one who knew the players well enough to get the UN guys out. When we met with Taylor, this guy Mosquito, who was Foday Sankoh's guy, he was there, and so we asked about that. Taylor agreed to help get the UN troops out. We had no capacity to get them out. [Nigerian president] Obasanjo had no capacity to get them out. So they all agreed that we should appeal to Taylor to do that." When Taylor gave the order to Bockerie, the rebels finally released the UN hostages and "Taylor got congratulations," Jackson explained.

Behind the scenes, diamond dealer and RUF strategist Ibrahim Bah was negotiating with Jackson from Ouagadougou, capital of nearby Burkina Faso, according to an aide to rebel commander Issa Sesay. "We drafted a twelve-point proposal and faxed it to Ibrahim," the aide says, "and he faxed it immediately to Taylor and Jackson in Monrovia. There was a price for releasing the hostages. Everyone needed to get paid off."[50]

Part of the "congratulations" Taylor received was U.S. protection from international sanctions. Once the UN hostages were released by the RUF in Sierra Leone, the British government submitted a draft resolution to the United Nations Security Council to ban the trade in conflict diamonds. At the urging of Jesse Jackson, Donald Payne, and members of the Congressional Black Caucus, the United States opposed it and allowed Taylor to continue his diamond trafficking. Although Jackson flew home claiming victory once the RUF started releasing hostages, the fighting in Sierra Leone intensified, prompting Amnesty International, Partnership Africa-Canada, and other groups to urge the UN Security Council to ban "conflict diamonds" and impose sanctions on the government of RUF sponsor and commander Charles Taylor. But once again, at the insistence of Jesse Jackson and members of the Congressional Black Caucus, nothing happened.

That all changed once President George W. Bush took office. On March 7, 2001, the U.S. voted in favor of UN Security Council Resolution 1343, which imposed an international travel ban on top Liberian officials and banned the trade in conflict diamonds. Shortly afterwards, the president issued an executive order to implement it without waiting for legislation.[51]

A Failed Deal

Emperors and warlords from Alexander the Great to Napoleon all understood one thing: to wage war successfully they needed both men and money. The French call it "le nerf de la guerre"—the sinews of war. Without constant financing, armies collapse like rag dolls, potentates fall like cards. It's one of the oldest lessons of warfare, but sometimes it takes new and horrible scenes of butchery for the world to wake up and do something about it. One particularly gruesome advertisement developed by groups seeking an international embargo on conflict diamonds featured a Sierra Leonean boy displaying the stubs where his hands had been hacked off by RUF machetes. The caption reads: "Is your diamond worth this?"

Jackson and American government officials, including Howard Jeter, a deputy assistant secretary of state who traveled with Jackson, and Tom Melrose, the U.S. ambassador to Sierra Leone, "strong-armed the Sierra Leone government into signing a terrible agreement that rewarded Foday Sankoh and the RUF and allowed them to retain control over the diamond-producing areas," says Liberian opposition leader Harry Greaves. "This was the very reason they were fighting this war. By giving them the financial wherewithal to continue their campaign of death and destruction, you take away any incentive to stop the fighting. That's why sanctions on Liberia and conflict diamonds are necessary."[52]

Sierra Leone ambassador John Ernest Leigh agreed. "The whole world has since accepted the plain fact that the war in Sierra Leone is instigated from abroad by diamond merchants intent on plundering Sierra Leone's natural wealth, while their local collaborators use phony talk of good governance reforms as propaganda for waging war to loot."[53] Thousands more children died as a result of the U.S. government's refusal to crack down on Charles Taylor and the RUF in May 2000. The deal Jackson cut solved the immediate crisis, but it allowed Taylor through his RUF proxies to maintain control over the diamond fields, which provided them with the "sinews of war."

When I explain what Jackson had done in Liberia, his longtime friend and supporter Hermene Hartman agrees that it was "not a pretty story." So why did Jackson do it? "Jesse is a minister and sometimes he is blind," she says. "He's looking for the good and truly believes he can convert. When he says he can go to Liberia or Afghanistan and we can sit down and talk, he truly believes that. He could be talking to a butcher and not understand he's a butcher. He'd have to see him chop somebody's leg off."[54]

Was Jackson's support for the murderous regime of Charles Taylor as simple as that? When Jackson negotiated the release of the UN peacekeepers, Taylor revealed himself as commander of the RUF, which distinguished itself from other rebel groups in Africa by its penchant for chopping off the hands and feet of fellow Sierra Leoneans. And yet Jackson essentially legitimized both Taylor and the RUF. If Jackson supported such murderers through ignorance, arrogance, or even just a blind conviction that he could find solutions which had eluded everyone else through the sheer force of his personality, then he deserves to be forever banned from the public policy arena as a dangerous fool. As Sierra Leone's ambassador, John Ernest Leigh, wrote to the Congressional Black Caucus in August 2000, anyone who "is still not sure that the violence in

Sierra Leone is about diamonds and who controls them ... has no business making policy recommendations to the Administration."[55]

But what if there was something more venal involved—a payoff in diamonds or cash? That is a question I have asked dozens of sources over the past year. These sources include former U.S. intelligence officers stationed in the region while Jackson was special envoy, former U.S. diplomats, foreign government officials, current U.S. officials, diamond traders, intermediaries, and others who had personal dealings with Charles Taylor, Foday Sankoh, and Jesse Jackson. Almost all offered their own anecdotes of Jackson's questionable behavior in Africa. Most had heard that Charles Taylor regularly offered small black bags of hot rocks as payment to his friends and business partners—a practice well documented by the UN panel of experts. But no one could provide evidence that Jackson had personally benefited.

Public records on file with the Justice Department show that Charles Taylor has spent millions of dollars on Washington, D.C., lobbyists, who in turn contribute to political fundraisers and make donations to non-profit groups. Ambassador Leigh claims that "the $3 to $4 million Taylor spends annually in the United States to buy political support gets spread around. To whom, we do not know."

Jackson denies categorically that he had any financial relationship with Charles Taylor or Foday Sankoh, and insists that he was operating solely as a U.S. government envoy. But his actions did not always suit that strict definition, as when he asked Charles Taylor during negotiations over the UN hostages about his plans to privatize the state-owned telephone company. "Taylor turned to him and asked if he was inquiring as a businessman, or as special envoy of the president of the United States," a U.S. official who witnessed the exchange tells me. "Taylor might be brutal, but he is no fool."

Even today, Jackson drifts off into mumbo-jumbo whenever I ask him about diamonds and sanctions on Liberia, and his rhymed slogans and sharp images turn into mush. "Africa is not manufacturing any guns or polishing any diamonds. So any serious crackdown on the diamond trade must be on the diamond-runners and the gun-runners, and we know they're running straight to Europe," he says. "Instead of building walls, we need to build bridges. The reason I do not favor sanctions is because they affect the poorest people. The leaders are insulated from the sanctions."

But many Liberians dispute this, even today as the United Nations is contemplating new sanctions on Liberian timber, one of the last resources to be plundered by Charles Taylor. "With or without timber, people are suffering," says Liberian opposition leader Gayah Fahnbulleh. "They are destitute, impoverished. So sanctions on timber will make no difference to the plight of ordinary Liberians. But they will mean the end of Charles Taylor, because all the money goes to Taylor and his inner circle."[56]

Jackson rushed home from Africa to attend a May 22, 2000, state dinner at the White House for visiting South African president Thabo M. Mbeki. In a harbinger of things to come, Jackson's wife, who accompanied him, was identified on the guest list as "Ms. Jacqueline Lavinia," her maiden name. Jackson's friends now admit that the couple was under "tremendous strain" as a result of Jackson's love affair with one of his staff assistants, Karin Stanford, whose illegitimate child with Jackson was just turning one year old. With so many people in the know, the real surprise was that Jackson managed to keep this affair under wraps for so long.

CHAPTER 16

Election 2000

WHAT IF YOU'RE BLACK AND YOU DON'T PAY?

Ask Eddie Edwards, a black broadcaster who owns WCWB-TV in Pittsburgh, Pennsylvania, and six other stations around the country, what he thinks of Jesse Jackson. "Unlike some white broadcasters," he says, "I'm not giving in to these people. They can call me an Uncle Tom because that's their way. I am not going to be intimidated."[1]

As a black entrepreneur who refused to pay his "tithe," Eddie Edwards has been singled out for punishment by Jesse Jackson. Dating back to 1997, when Edwards first applied to sell his TV stations to Sinclair Broadcasting, Rainbow/PUSH has filed a series of petitions with the FCC opposing the sale, on the grounds that Edwards is already a business associate of Sinclair Broadcasting and that his Glencairn Ltd. "hasn't acted like a station group controlled by a black CEO." When the National Association of Black Owned Broadcasters (NABOB) joined forces with

Jackson, Edwards doubled their ire by founding the competing Black Broadcasters Alliance.

Jackson's opposition to Eddie Edwards and Sinclair was unrelenting. Rainbow/PUSH filed petitions in January 2000 against the sale of stations owned by Edwards in Baltimore, Pittsburgh, San Antonio, Columbus, Milwaukee, Raleigh, Birmingham, and Greenville. When Eddie Edwards and Sinclair still refused to alter their plans, Rainbow/PUSH asked the FCC to revoke their broadcast licenses.

Jackson was clearly using Rainbow/PUSH to exploit racial preferences built into the 1996 Telecommunications Act and other legislation by getting corporations to steer business to his friends while donating large sums to his nonprofit empire. "Good" companies, like Bell Atlantic, loaned corporate officers to Rainbow/PUSH at no charge, made hefty cash contributions, and sponsored Jackson events. "Bad" companies had their mergers blocked, their products boycotted, and their owners castigated as racists. There was little or no difference in the way these corporations treated minorities or invested in minority communities. A primary difference was how they treated Jesse Jackson and his friends. Jackson went to war against anyone who refused to play ball.

In April 2000, Jackson testified yet again before the FCC to oppose MCI WorldCom, which had never contributed to his groups or kowtowed to his demands. This time, the issue was the proposed merger with Sprint. "The proposed merger will result in higher prices to low-income consumers and will harm immigrant and minority consumers of international long distance services," Jackson claimed. "I have maps that show that even in Chicago, my hometown, MCI WorldCom's network has significantly expanded in the wealthy North Side and west suburbs since the merger, yet there has not been a single strand of fiber laid to serve the city's primarily minority and low-income South Side neighborhoods," Jackson continued. "This is economic apartheid."[2]

Derrick Collins told a panel at a Jackson "economic summit" that his Chicago-based Polestar Capital Partners in Chicago was providing venture capital to young African-American entrepreneurs to bridge the so-called digital divide. "But you have to find folks on the other side who want to jump over. If they want to jump over, they'll find a way to jump."[3] His point, and that of several other black businessmen addressing city planners and investors, was very simple: companies will invest where there is a market, but don't expect them to sink money into losing ventures and survive.

While these are very real issues, it's much less clear that Jackson is truly dedicated to serving the black community or black businesses. Certainly, he is seeking to pressure companies into making contributions to his nonprofit empire. In an affidavit filed on behalf of Sinclair Broadcasting with the FCC on December 15, 2000, Sinclair vice president Mark E. Hyman describes an extraordinary session with FCC chairman William Kennard and the head of the FCC Mass Media Bureau, Roy Stewart. "The Chairman insisted that Sinclair look toward minorities other than Eddie Edwards in order to receive credit for a minority incubator program," he wrote. "He then asked rhetorically, 'Can Eddie Edwards stand up on his own?' and followed it up with 'When will you set Eddie free?' "

After meeting with Kennard, the Sinclair team was ushered into Roy Stewart's office down the hall for continued discussions. Stewart was in charge of broadcasting mergers, and enjoyed making powerful corporate executives tremble. "As we walked in," Hyman writes in his affidavit, "Mr. Stewart started the discussion by stating, 'If you repeat anything that I say here, I will f—ing deny it. This chairman is serious. This is really important to him. You give him what he wants on this minority issue or he will make you hurt. He has a large responsibility as the first African-American chairman. Not a week goes by that someone from the African-American community doesn't call him to ask what he is doing for blacks. It is an awful lot of pressure and he is feeling it. He's made it clear that if you don't give him what he wants that he will make it really painful for you."[4]

The only problem was, Eddie Edwards *was* black; he just wasn't an ally of Jesse Jackson. He wanted to get out of television so he could buy radio stations being auctioned off at the time by Clear Channel Communications, but was barred by Jackson's opposition.

While Eddie Edwards was still agonizing over the sale of six local television stations, Jackson friend and donor Sumner Redstone announced that his Viacom Inc. (the merged entity that combined CBS and Viacom) was acquiring BET Holdings II for three billion dollars in stock and assumed debt. BET was a privately held company, whose majority stockholder was Jackson friend and donor Robert L. Johnson. Viacom claimed that its flagship property, Black Entertainment Television, reached 62.4 million households in the United States.[5] Despite the clear possibility of competitive and market access questions, the FCC did not question the acquisition and Jesse Jackson never uttered a word in protest. All three parties—CBS, Viacom, and BET—had long been Jackson donors, so whatever they did was okay. But if Sinclair sought to buy out black-owned stations from Eddie Edwards, racism must be involved. It was an irony that went completely unremarked upon by the mainstream press.

Sinclair attorney Martin R. Leader requested that FCC chairman William Kennard recuse himself from the proceedings because of his close personal ties to Jackson, who was a litigant in the case. It was a stunning and direct accusation of malfeasance. Kennard's statements "indicate to any disinterested observer that you have a bias against Sinclair and that you prejudged the facts and law regarding the primary charge in the pleadings filed on behalf of Rainbow/PUSH coalition. . . ." Sinclair's policy, he said, was to sell "to the highest bidder, regardless of its race, color or creed," and because of this its FCC applications "have been languishing for years." He added: "It has not gone unnoticed that companies which have made dispositions to minorities have had their applications granted."[6] Kennard was reportedly so furious when he received the letter that he marched down the hallway to the offices of his fellow commissioners to see if they had received copies of it.

Although Michael Powell replaced Kennard once George W. Bush took office, Jackson's friend Roy Stewart remains in charge of media mergers and has simply put Sinclair's request at the bottom of the pile. "They've made no decision; they've simply ignored us," a Sinclair attorney said.

A millionaire many times over, Jackson's friend Bob Johnson became even richer thanks to BET's lucrative merger with Viacom. He also adopted many of the worst habits of the nouveau riche. Looking for an appropriate sixteenth birthday gift in September 2001 for his daughter Paige, Johnson stopped by the local Mercedes dealer near the family's Salamander Farm in The Plains, Virginia, and picked her up a silver SLK 230 roadster for a tidy $48,000 (without options). Mom was away, but when she came home she put her foot down. "I didn't think this car was appropriate for a 16-year-old," she told a *Washington Post* "Style" reporter. "I wanted her to have a car that was a lot safer." So Mom donated the brand-new Mercedes convertible to charity, taking a hefty tax deduction. Paige told the *Post* she understood. "It's for a good cause," she said. "The Mercedes is a very safe car. It was just too small." So instead, she got off her champion steeplechase steed Just Dreamin' and climbed in the BMW sport utility that Daddy bought her instead. The new car "is also very safe—and more roomy," she said. "I really needed a bigger car for horse shows anyway."[7]

Such was America at the start of the twenty-first century, a country Jackson told an audience at Louis Farrakhan's Million Man March that has a "structural malfunction" and is split into "two Americas: one-half slave and one-half free."

TRAWLING THE RACIAL DIVIDE

"If it means we have to hold our noses and take castor oil, do it," Jackson told a crowd of skeptical black Democrats in Los Angeles on August 15, 2000, urging them to vote for Vice President Al Gore. Jackson was scheduled to address the Democratic National Convention just a few hours later, but his troops were not happy. "So Mr. Excitement is not running for president. This is about pragmatism."[8]

Jackson had good need for pragmatism. His stint as Africa envoy was ending in flames, and his efforts over the past year to fan the dying embers of America's race wars made him appear a figure of ridicule more than a prophet. In Decatur, Illinois, Jackson had stormed into the local high school leading a five-thousand-person mob in support of seven teenage boys who had been suspended after starting a fight during a football game. "The fight was less violent than a hockey match," he declaimed, to the consternation of parents and the local school board. Six months and several lawsuits later, Macon County judge James Hendrian took the unusual step of banning Jackson and his supporters from three Decatur high schools during daylight hours. Jackson was coming under fire from other black leaders, who accused him of becoming the apologist for the reckless behavior of black teens. When three of the seven suspended students were jailed for robbery after beating an acquaintance and stealing $120 in cash, Jackson became strangely silent. Decatur was not one of his finer moments.[9]

Similarly, in his quest for dramatic events that would widen the racial divide to the benefit of the Democratic Party, Jackson seized on the shooting death of twenty-one-year-old Guinean immigrant Amadou Diallo by New York City cops. The four policemen were searching for a suspected rapist when they came across Diallo. He reached for something inside his jacket. The police thought he was reaching for a handgun and opened fire, hitting him with nineteen bullets. The object he was reaching for turned out to be his wallet. A New York State Supreme Court jury composed of seven white women, one white man, and four black women exonerated the officers in February 2000 on grounds they had legitimately feared their lives were in danger. Jackson called the jury's decision "a gross miscarriage of justice," and accused New York City mayor Rudy Giuliani, who was then the leading candidate for New York's U.S. Senate seat, of encouraging police brutality and racial profiling.[10] (First Lady Hillary Rodham Clinton eventually won the seat, after Giuliani dropped out of the race for health reasons.)

Jackson thought he had found a juicier opportunity to paint Republicans as heartless racists when Texas governor George W. Bush took time off the campaign trail in June to return home for the execution of convicted murderer Gary Graham. The thirty-six-year-old Graham had confessed to going on a week-long criminal rampage when he was seventeen, in which he shot two people, one fatally, and raped a woman. But as his execution date approached, Graham called on Jesse Jackson and other civil rights leaders and claimed he was innocent. A last minute plea to stay the execution went all the way to the U.S. Supreme Court, where it was denied. Once the Texas Board of Pardons and Paroles voted overwhelmingly against any reprieve or delay, Bush could not under Texas law stop the execution. But the Texas governor went further. "I support the Board's decision. Mr. Graham has been granted full and fair access to state and federal courts, including the United States Supreme Court," Bush said. "May God bless the victims and the families of the victims. And may God bless Mr. Graham."[11]

Jackson marched on the prison where the execution was to take place. Marching with him were Bianca Jagger, the Reverend Al Sharpton, and Democratic congresswoman Sheila Jackson Lee. Afterwards, a dry-eyed Jackson said on CNN, "I wept uncontrollably when I entered the front door of this place." At a memorial service Jackson offered a eulogy to the convicted murderer. "Texas can't kill the spirit," he said. "We're here tonight because our brother lives. He has multiplied through us.... We must pick up the baton where Shaka has left it." In his final moments, Graham had adopted black separatism and started calling himself Shaka Sankofa, hoping to politicize his crimes. According to a *San Antonio Express-News* account of the service, "Hundreds of fists thrust into the air amid the declaration, 'March on, black people, march on.' " The Reverend Jesse Lee Peterson commented on the display:

> It's worth trying to imagine how the press would have portrayed this event had the racial roles been reversed. What if Graham had been a white career criminal who had been tried, convicted, and executed for exactly the same crimes? What if he had joined the Aryan Brotherhood in prison, rather than becoming a black militant? What if instead of the clenched-fist "Black Power" salute, the mourners had thrust stiff-fingered neo-Nazi salutes amid cries of "March on, white people, march on"? Is there any doubt that

such an event would have been denounced in the mass media as a celebration of racist rage, rather than a solemn funeral? . . . Jesse Jackson wants to continue to judge us by our color. He is really just a David Duke in black skin.[12]

Jesse Jackson's calls for a nationwide moratorium on capital punishment won no votes for the Democratic ticket in Texas. Meanwhile, in North Carolina and Georgia black farmers finally gave up trying to win Jackson's support to collect on a class action settlement against the Department of Agriculture. Instead, they began campaigning on behalf of the Bush-Cheney ticket. "We'd asked for Jesse's help but he was demanding $100,000 just to do a press conference," the vice president of the Black Farmers and Agriculturalists Association, Eddie Slaughter, tells me. "That's when we labeled him the poverty pimp, because we've got to stay in poverty so he can make a living."[13]

Al Gore came to visit Jackson a few weeks before the Democratic National Convention, to make sure he had Jackson's support. Gore knew it was going to be a close race, and he wanted more from Jackson than just lip service. "Gore strategists are counting on Mr. Jackson to play a big role in the campaign, boosting turnout among minorities and assuring liberals in general that Mr. Gore is on their side," the Associated Press reported on the meeting. "He can play a major role bringing people together," said Donna Brazile, a former Jackson aide who was now Gore's campaign manager. "I anticipate that he'll be there a lot."[14]

Gore wanted to send Jackson out on the stump, and offered to pay him to hustle votes in the black community.[15] But there was more than just money involved: Gore offered Jackson a high-profile public role as a surrogate at presidential campaign rallies across the country. Jackson himself could run for president that way, all expenses paid, without having to expose himself to media scrutiny. What a chance to seize the limelight. He would have been foolish to refuse.

Gore's strategy was to paint Bush as a racist. Campaign workers distributed pro-Gore leaflets in New Jersey showing Bush's face superimposed on a Confederate flag. Democratic strategists knew they could only win by making the race card "part and parcel of the Gore campaign," black columnist Walter Williams reported.[16]

Jackson kicked off his new role during a primetime speech at the Democratic National Convention in Los Angeles, where he reminded fellow Democrats of the other national convention that had just nominated Texas governor George W. Bush and Dick Cheney. "Two weeks ago, in Philadelphia, the nation was treated to a staged show—smoke, mirrors, hired acts the Republicans called inclusion. That was the inclusion illusion," Jackson said, his voice dripping with scorn. The Democratic Party was "the real deal. . . . America's working families are here, headed by a Southern Baptist and an Orthodox Jew. This is America's dream team, the Democratic Party."[17]

No one questioned how Jackson could refer to Al Gore as the head of a "working family" or seemed to care. Jackson was doing what politicians have always done at election time, tossing red meat to the party faithful. But for someone who headed a nonprofit empire, dedicated to nonpartisan voter education, his baldly partisan approach mocked about a dozen federal statutes.

Campaign 2000 was just beginning, and Jackson was only warming up. After a Labor Day parade with Gore in Pittsburgh, he was out on the campaign trail day in and day out. Not once did he fail to exhort his listeners to vote for the Democratic presidential ticket; not once did he fail to label the Republicans as racists, seeking to turn back the clock to a darker period of American history. In Richmond, Virginia, campaigning side by side with embattled U.S. senator Chuck Robb, Jackson reminded his audience that the Republicans were the "party of exclusion." The Democrats, he said, are "the all-Americans team," while Republicans were "the some-Americans team."[18] Later that month, Jackson led a six-city Ohio bus tour, pegged as a voter registration drive. At every stop, Jackson exhorted his audience to vote for the Gore-Lieberman ticket.[19]

He frequently asserted that Governor Bush was a supporter of racial lynching. He quoted the daughter of James Byrd Jr., a black man from

Jasper, Texas, who was beaten, chained, and dragged three miles to his death. "When Governor George W. Bush refused to support hate-crimes legislation, it was like my father was killed all over again," she said in an NAACP-paid ad broadcast across the nation. What had actually happened was that a Texas jury had convicted three men of Byrd's murder and sentenced two of them to death. Governor Bush affirmed the verdict, noting that a person could only be put to death once, whether a hate crime had been committed or not. Jackson's message appeared to be that if you're a white racist, you should be executed at least twice; but if you're a black racist, like Gary Graham, you should be pardoned, honored, and extolled.

By the time October rolled around, it was hard to distinguish Jackson's election bandwagon from that of the Democratic candidates themselves. On October 4, he delivered his "nonpartisan" message to students at Northwestern University in Evanston, Illinois. From October 7 through 10, he was off on a ten-city "voter registration drive" in Florida. The very next day, he headed for West Virginia and Eastern Kentucky with labor leaders on behalf of the Gore-Lieberman ticket. From October 20 through 24, Jackson made a four-day whistle-stop tour through Wisconsin, hitting the University of Wisconsin and the Gateway Technical College in Racine. Then he was off to Minnesota for a rally in Minneapolis. On the 27th, he made a second swing through Iowa with a keynote speech at the University of Iowa along with comedian (and DNC activist) Al Franken. On the 28th and 29th he was back in Florida to attack the Bush-Cheney team at an NAACP banquet in Fort Pierce, and for follow-on appearances in Fernandina and Jacksonville. On the 30th, he jetted to the West Coast for rallies at Oregon University campuses at Eugene and Corvallis. On Halloween, he was in Red Square at the University of Washington in Seattle, all expenses paid by the DNC. It was a breathless performance, from coast to coast, exhorting voters to get to the polls to defeat the Republicans.[20]

At the Rainier Beach Community Center on the morning of November 1, Jackson said it all. "This campaign is about what you stand for," he preached. "We who live must save the dream because it's under attack.

November 7th is a kind of judgment day. All we stand for is threatened."[21] Jackson kept up the pace right through the last minutes of Election Day, when he was dispatched by a frantic Gore team to coax voters to the polls in swing communities in several battleground states. He ended the day in Philadelphia, long considered by Gore strategists the key to the national election. "Stay out of the bushes!" was one of his favorite "nonpartisan" refrains.

In all, Jesse Jackson gave more than 150 speeches at cities across the nation on behalf of the Democratic ticket and in coordination with the Democratic National Committee.[22] The DNC funneled money to Jackson's Keep Hope Alive political action committee at several points during the campaign to reimburse him for travel and campaign expenses. More money was paid directly to other Jackson organizations. It didn't much matter, since the PAC, CEF, and all of Jackson's organizations shared offices, staff, and expenses with Rainbow/PUSH. Altogether, the DNC reimbursed Jackson entities a total of $450,000 for Jackson's travel during the campaign, according to Federal Election Commission (FEC) reports and corporate tax returns.[23] In addition, his nonpartisan non-profit empire acknowledged spending $614,419 for Jackson's personal travel during the campaign season, with another $1,314,922 spent on travel of other Rainbow/PUSH and CEF staff, money that was never declared as a coordinated expense by the DNC. And that is only what they actually did acknowledge.[24]

The American Conservative Union filed a complaint against Jackson with the FEC alleging that this constituted "prima facie evidence that the voter registration and get-out-the-vote activities were partisan" and there-fore in direct violation of federal election laws. "Imagine if the head of the National Rifle Association went in a corporate jet paid for by RNC soft money to campaign on behalf of George W. Bush," said ACU lawyer Cleta Mitchell. "This is illegal."[25] The American Conservative Union and the National Legal and Policy Center filed separate complaints with the IRS, demanding an audit of Jackson's nonprofit empire for massive violations of its tax-exempt status. But the damage, of course, had already been done.

GORE, AT ANY COST

On election day, Jackson worker bee Alice Tregay was phoning funeral directors in Chicago—not to line up dead people to vote, but to borrow the funeral directors' limousines. As head of the Rainbow/PUSH's get-out-the-vote drive for Chicago, Tregay had been marshalling volunteers to pass out Democratic Party leaflets at black churches, knock on doors, and drive sound trucks through South Side neighborhoods, urging people to vote for Gore. But borrowing the hearses was a real brainstorm. "We're letting all the nursing homes know they should call if residents need transportation and would like a ride in a limousine," Tregay said.[26] She coordinated her efforts in Chicago with the NAACP, which had earmarked a record $9 million for its pro-Gore "Operation Big Vote" campaign. A single "anonymous" donor was alleged to have financed the "operation."[27] The DNC refused to disclose how much it was spending to turn out the black vote, but indicated it would probably top the $3 million it spent in 1996.[28] Jackson's nonprofit groups spent more than $14 million in 2000, according to the group's own financial records, when Jackson was working feverishly in support of the Democratic ticket.

But November 7 was only the beginning. Once Al Gore decided to contest the outcome of the election, he coordinated almost daily with Jesse Jackson in hopes of unleashing a massive outpouring of "rage" in black communities across America. In rally after rally in Florida and elsewhere, Jackson's anti-Republican rhetoric was incendiary. Toward the end, it verged on the seditious.

Jackson began his radical assault on American democracy within hours of the first Florida recount, which reconfirmed the Bush victory. Following the script provided by Gore's media handlers, Jackson focused on Haitian-Americans who "were denied assistance in the voting booth" that they supposedly needed because they couldn't understand basic voting instructions. Jackson's insult was aimed at naturalized Americans who had passed a citizenship test demonstrating a basic proficiency in the English language. Jackson argued they should have been provided ballots in Creole and French.[29]

Jackson quickly changed tactic, as did Gore, and alleged massive voter intimidation by Florida governor Jeb Bush, including police roadblocks that purportedly prevented black Floridians from voting. It made no difference that the U.S. Civil Rights Commission, chaired by Jackson's former campaign manager, the ever so partisan Mary Frances Berry, could not find a single black Floridian who actually failed to vote because of police traffic controls. Jackson's charges of racism, voter intimidation, and manipulation grew more strident as Al Gore's chances of winning the Florida recounts diminished.

Jackson brought his troops to Washington on December 1, the day of the first Supreme Court hearings, where they faced off angrily with pro-Bush demonstrators. "Racist! Fascist!" Jesse's people shouted, shoving anyone who attempted to cross their lines, including reporters. The Republicans countered with a fifteen minute unbroken torrent of boos when Gore lawyer Warren Christopher descended the Supreme Court steps and tried to address waiting television cameras. Seeing a network call sign, they began chanting: "Concede on NBC! Concede on CNN!"[30]

Jackson was back in Washington, D.C., as the Supreme Court began hearing oral arguments in *Bush v. Gore* on December 11. "Even if this court rules against counting our vote, it will simply create a civil rights explosion," he warned. "People will not surrender to this tyranny." And again: "The people will not stand by and accept this with surrender."[31] Jackson's inflammatory words were dangerously close to a call for insurrection.

The court heard final oral arguments on December 12, but Jackson had not been chastened. Standing outside the Supreme Court building, Jackson told reporters, "We will take to the streets right now, we will delegitimize Bush, discredit him, do whatever it takes, but never accept him." He called the reports of large numbers of spoiled ballots filled out by black voters as "a bold attempt to take from people their franchise.... I can live under Bush winning, I can't live under Bush stealing."[32]

Jackson's apocalyptic assertions had no basis in fact, but that did not deter his efforts to fan the flames of race hatred, paranoia, and political unrest. These were the tactics of the radical Left for whom, as David

Horowitz paraphrased the famed German philosopher von Clausewitz, "politics is war conducted by other means. It is this attitude that inspires the viciousness of left-wing politics, the desire to destroy the opposition entirely, to eliminate adversaries from the field of battle. It is also the perspective that creates the reckless disregard radicals have for institutions and traditions."[33] Gore deployed Jackson, "the nation's most-tolerated racial arsonist," Horowitz wrote, to show that "Bush Republicans are crypto-slave drivers and Nazis."[34]

On December 8, *USA Today* reported "the most widely reported incidents on Election Day have turned out on closer inspection to be unfounded." The famous "roadblock" near Tallahassee was a routine check for faulty auto equipment that stopped a total of 150 drivers and gave eighteen warnings or citations, six to minorities, twelve to whites. Another roadblock turned out to be police responding to a burglary call near a polling place in a black neighborhood, media reporter John Leo noted. One man was stopped for questioning, then sent on his way.[35]

Jackson and his allies claimed "a clear pattern of suppressing the votes of African-Americans." But an analysis of spoiled votes from all of Florida's precincts, conducted for minority members of the U.S. Civil Rights Commission by Yale University scholar John R. Lott Jr., found that the reality was just the opposite. "If spoiled ballots do indicate disenfranchisement, then the new data show that, by a dramatic margin, the group most victimized in the Florida voting was African-American Republicans," Lott wrote. In fact, black Republicans were "in excess of 50 times more likely than the average African-American to have had a ballot declared invalid." Lott found similar data among white voters, where Republicans were much more likely than Democrats to have their ballots tossed out. "We found that the overall rate of spoiled ballots was 14% higher when the county election supervisor was a Democrat, and 31% higher when the supervisor was an African-American Democrat." Lott concluded, "If there were intentional victims in Florida, they were targeted not because of race but because of party."[36]

But facts did not deter Jesse Jackson. Al Gore called Jackson the very day the Supreme Court halted the election recounts in Florida, wondering if the decision "could be parlayed into some sort of massive outcry from the black community, providing political cover for one last assault on Bush," *Washington Times* reporter Bill Sammon wrote in *At Any Cost*, his riveting account of the postelection battles.[37] Jackson foresaw a dim political future for himself under a Republican administration, and implored Gore to "use every means available" to fight on.

Jackson appeared in Tallahassee the next day, telling diehard Democrat supporters he would fight to the end. "As long as Americans' right to vote has been denied, there are foreign particles of undemocracy in the wound," he said. During the "nonpartisan" protest, Jackson walked arm in arm with top DNC fundraiser Terry McAuliffe, who was wearing a Gore-Lieberman T-shirt and was elected DNC chairman shortly afterwards. Jackson proclaimed, "The election was essentially taken and stolen," and vowed to take his protests to the streets of Washington on Inauguration Day.[38] At one point, he warned openly of riots in the streets: "When the right ingredients are present, and the fuse is lit, an explosion happens."[39]

This extraordinary rhetoric, at a time when Americans of both parties had accepted the verdict of the nation's highest court, went far beyond the merely partisan: it exposed Jackson's ideological roots in the radical Left. Commentator David Poe, who edits *Frontpage* magazine, drew a parallel to Jerry Rubin, the former 1960s radical who now admits to using blatant lies to tear America apart. "We put the myth out there that America was in chaos," Rubin explained. "America was not in chaos. When 100,000 people marched on the Pentagon in 1967, we put out the myth that America was divided in two. America was not divided in two. But we put the myth out there and what happened, by '69, 1970, America *was* divided in two." Jesse Jackson was trying to do the same thing in December 2000, by promoting the myth that Bush stole the election, that black voters were disenfranchised, and that America was on the brink of revolution.[40] It was a very old story, learned from revolutionaries from Lenin to Hitler: the bigger the lie, the bigger the chance people would believe it.

On January 15, 2001, Jackson announced he was planning a "week of outrage" that would culminate with "massive" marches in Tallahassee and

Washington, D.C., to coincide with the presidential inauguration. "This election has exposed in Florida—and across the nation—systemic discrimination against poor voters of color," Jackson insisted. There was absolutely no factual basis for this claim either; on the contrary, the black vote in Florida surged by more than 50 percent over the previous election, with 93 percent of it going to Gore. But truth did not discourage Jackson. Posters reminiscent of the revolutionary art of the 1960s appeared on lampposts in black neighborhoods all over Washington, showing a black man wearing a white bandana and proclaiming January 20, 2001, a "Day of Rage." Jackson drummed into his followers that the Bush presidency was "illegitimate," and vowed to make America "ungovernable." The International Action Center in New York, which was coordinating the marches, said it hoped to bring one million protesters to Washington. This was the same group that violently opposed the World Trade Organization in Seattle, and had become the repository for hard-left radicals since the end of the Cold War. They were—and are—professional anti-American protestors, and they were looking for a cause and a leader who could spark new life into their movement.

THE LOVE CHILD

And then, something happened. The movement's High Priest was taken out, removed from the scene by a scandal of his own making that rocked Jackson's supporters and caused the Democratic Party acute embarrassment. On January 17, 2001, when he realized the *National Enquirer* was about to publish the results of a seven-week-investigation into his private life, Jackson announced that he had fathered a baby girl out of wedlock with staffer Karin Stanford in 1998 and would be "taking some time off to revive my spirit and reconnect with my family before I return to my public ministry." He never showed up for the inauguration—nor did many of the protestors, who numbered a scant eight thousand or so (and whom the D.C. police prevented from carrying out their threats of violence).

Jackson's attitude toward his personal behavior mirrored his public disregard for the truth. As the *National Enquirer* revealed, Jackson's sexual escapades had been widely rumored for years. The wonder was not that Jackson finally got caught, but why it took so long. Jackson was so arrogant in his belief that the media would give him special consideration that he even brought his pregnant mistress to meet Bill Clinton in the White House, at the very height of Clinton's own sex scandals with White House intern Monica Lewinsky. The *Enquirer* published a December 3, 1998, White House photograph with a smiling Jackson standing next to Karin Stanford and Clinton in the Oval Office to commemorate that event.[41]

The *Enquirer* mentioned elliptically that Stanford had run a DNA test to determine paternity, because she had been seeing other men at the same time as Jackson. In a later version of the story, the *Enquirer* reported that Karin Stanford had put a condom in her freezer after an evening of sex with the Reverend, and later compared its DNA with DNA taken from her child.[42] Even liberal columnists such as the *Boston Globe*'s Tom Oliphant admitted that Jackson's status as a "religious figure and not just a political figure ... who has talked to all of us about morality and sin as well as appropriations," made the exposé of his private life a "legitimate" subject of public discussion.[43] "It really damages the Rev. Jackson's credibility as a role model for young people, among other things," said Clarence Page, a columnist for the *Chicago Tribune*.[44] Jackson's wife reportedly "pointed a gun at Jesse in their Chicago home and had to be restrained as she suffered a breakdown" following the initial revelations of the affair in the press.[45]

Longtime Jackson friend Hermene Hartman expresses the obvious when she tells me that Jackson's extramarital affairs had made no one happy. "But I've seen him resist women in droves," she adds. Jackson's treasurer, Cirilo McSween, who has been with him since the late 1960s, urges me to use a unique moral criterion for judging his friend. "He's a minister, and ministers are to set an example of love and caring and sharing, of being loyal. He has admitted it. He has expressed his responsibility. He is providing for it. His family is aware of it. I think that his response is appropriate and is worth taking into account. The question is, has Jesse been a responsible father?"[46] Jackson's board convened just two days after he revealed the affair and expressed its full confidence in him. "He's the best we have," said board member McSween.[47]

Potentially more damaging for Jackson than his moral lapse were revelations that he had used his nonprofit empire to pay "hush money" to Karin Stanford, who gave birth to their child in May 1999 but had never spoken about it before. In the first version of the story, picked up by the *New York Post*, Stanford acknowledged she had been paid $40,000 to "relocate" to Los Angeles by the nonprofit Citizenship Education Fund, and that she had been put on a $10,000 per month retainer by the Yucaipa Company, owned by Jackson friend and donor, Ron Burkle. It's unclear if Stanford ever performed any work for Burkle, since she could not be reached at his office, had no voice mail, and never returned repeated phone messages other reporters and I left with the Yucaipa receptionist. Ron Burkle was also on the board of directors of developer Kaufman and Broad, and helped Stanford obtain a $291,950 mortgage from their real estate branch to purchase her new house on Don Miguel Drive in the Baldwin Hills district of Los Angeles.[48]

In an op-ed written several months later, Hermene Hartman dumped on Karin Stanford for suing Jackson to double the estimated $168,000 per year in support payments she was receiving from Jackson and his cronies. "Jackson was wrong to engage in an illicit affair.... But," she wrote, "this story is as old as man. A woman seduces a man, the more famous, the better. The famous man falls into the trap. The woman has a baby. The woman seeks revenge with the revelation because the married man doesn't pay her off. He may pay her to keep her quiet. He may pay to hide her. She may stalk and strike to embarrass the popular man. She brings him down with the dark secret." Karin Stanford's behavior, she argued, "revealed the character of a low woman."[49]

Jesse's friends and former employees were beginning to talk to the press, and try as he might to circle the wagons, embarrassing new details of his secret love life and his multiple families began to leak out. Karin Stanford told CBS News reporter Connie Chung she had been hoping to set up as Jackson's wife at his stately Washington, D.C., mansion—the three-story brick home his real wife, Jackie, had so elegantly restored in the historic LeDroit Park district near Howard University. And then there were less credible reports of a fifteen-year-old illegitimate son by another woman which, if true, would have placed the affair in 1986 or 1987, at precisely the time the national press first aired suggestions that Jackson's personal life might not bear up to the scrutiny of a national political campaign. Confronted point-blank about that rumor, Jackson tells me, "I have no other children."

One of Jackson's former limousine drivers, who became a source to at least one national scandal sheet, told scurrilous tales of ferrying the Reverend about in Chicago several times a week to meet privately with different women, including a top employee of a Chicago loop venture capital firm. When asked about those reports, Jackson said he did "not choose to dignify" them with a response.[50]

I never seriously pursued such rumors during my own investigation because I felt the real scandal of Jesse Jackson's career was his public behavior, which rarely has been analyzed without apology and until now has never been fully documented. From the very start, Jesse Jackson claimed to serve others; and it became clear that, from the start, the first person he served was himself.

THE PARDONS

Jesse's personal life was a mess, but he still had one important item of business to conclude with President Bill Clinton. At ten o'clock on the morning of January 20, 2001—just two hours before he left office—Clinton signed 177 controversial pardons and commutations. Most of them never went through the Justice Department's pardon office, which was legally tasked with contacting prosecutors to inquire if they had objections.

Jackson asked Clinton to grant clemency to three friends. Top on the list was Dorothy Rivers, a well-known Chicago social activist who was sentenced to five years and ten months in prison in 1996, following a forty-count indictment that detailed how she defrauded the homeless of $5 million in government grants. Court records show that Rivers bought six fur coats, including a $35,000 sable, with money that was earmarked to build shelters for homeless families and pregnant teens. She embezzled grant money from her Chicago Mental Health Foundation to buy an $800 purse, a $3,500 dress, a Mercedes-Benz car and business investments for her son, and spent $125,000 on party decorations, invitations, flowers, and alcohol for political fundraisers.[51] When challenged why he asked for her pardon, Jackson retorted, "She ain't shot nobody. She ain't dealt in drugs. She ain't [running] a house of prostitution. . . . She's a good person who overspent a grant or so." The charge had personal resonance for him, since he also had been accused of overspending government grants and under President Reagan had reimbursed the government more than half a million dollars. The Justice Department subsequently revealed that no clemency application had ever been filed for Ms. Rivers; Jackson made the request directly to Clinton as a personal favor. Clinton agreed. Four months after her pardon, Jackson put Ms. Rivers on the board of directors of Rainbow/PUSH Coalition, corporate filings show.[52]

Next came John Bustamante, the Cleveland, Ohio, lawyer responsible for setting up the complex web of Jackson's nonprofit empire. Bustamante, now seventy, pleaded guilty in 1993 to a federal charge of defrauding an insurance company, after a federal judge threw out his 1991 conviction on five felony fraud charges. As in Ms. Rivers's case, there was no clemency application on file with the Justice Department on his behalf, so Jackson appealed directly to the president. Clinton agreed.

The third person was former Illinois congressman Mel Reynolds, convicted in 1995 on felony charges of soliciting sex with a minor. Clinton, impeached for lying under oath about his own sexual escapades, sprung Reynolds from jail, and Jackson promptly hired him as a highly paid consultant on prison reform. "This is a first in American politics," syndicated columnist Deroy Murdock tells me. "An ex-congressman who had sex with a subordinate won clemency from a president who had sex with a subordinate, then was hired by a clergyman who had sex with a subordinate. How more insulting to the nation's intelligence can you be?"[53] Under federal law, Reynolds is required to provide his home address to the police, so concerned neighbors can find out when convicted sex offenders move in next door. As this book went to press, a mugshot of Reynolds—with his date of birth and home address—was posted to a public website of convicted sex offenders maintained by the Illinois State Police.[54]

Jackson requested one more pardon, for half brother Noah Robinson Jr. Noah was in the midst of preparing for his third full-blown appeal of his multiple life sentences for murder-by-hire, racketeering, and drug trafficking.[55] This is the only request from Jesse Jackson that Clinton turned down. Justice Department sources believe that Noah, in a perverse way, sabotaged his own pardon by having filed a voluminous petition for commutation with the pardon office some months before Clinton left office. "It would have been awfully hard to say we hadn't been aware of Noah's request for presidential clemency," one official in Washington said. Prosecutors in Chicago said that Noah's request had been filed in time for them to object formally to clemency well before Clinton left office. "The pardon office asked us to comment, and we did. We objected."[56]

Jackson helped manage to free an embezzler, a defrauder, and a sex criminal, following which the embezzler and the sex criminal joined Jackson Inc. But even he couldn't spring his half brother from jail.

CHAPTER 17

Life After Clinton

APPROPRIATING A CHURCH

Jesse's period of "contrition" didn't last long. The day after the presidential inauguration in Washington, D.C., Jackson made his public reappearance at the pulpit of Salem Baptist Church, pastoral home of his biggest new ally in Chicago, the Reverend James Meeks. "Reverend," said Meeks, "we want you to know something today: Not only do we love you, not only do we care for you . . . we can't afford to lose you." Turning to the congregation, he introduced his friend: "We need you, we want you, we love you, Reverend Jesse Jackson."

Jackson spoke briefly, and he brought down the house. Turning to his wife, who was sitting in the front pew, he became emotional. "After thirty-eight years and five children later, Jackie, we're still here. I love you so much." The congregation stood and cheered.

It didn't take long for the not-so-contrite Jackson to find his political feet. "Yesterday, the winds shifted," he said, referring to the inaugural, "so it's a new stage in our challenge."[1]

Jackson's quick return caused commentator Deroy Murdock to deride "the church of instant forgiveness." Jackson "would have stayed off the national stage longer had he simply twisted his ankle playing tennis."[2] The next day Jackson attended a lunch held in his honor in Chicago, and the following week he was back in New York for the third annual conference of his Wall Street shakedown.

But try as he might, the scandal just wouldn't wash away. While in New York, Jackson called on the Reverend Wyatt Tee Walker to convene a prayer service for him at the Canaan Baptist Church of Christ, one of the largest and most influential congregations in Harlem. The Reverend Walker agreed, but pointed out that he would be absent on January 23, the day Jackson planned to be in town. Graciously, he invited him to join the congregation anyway for a "*Service of Penance*...to help with your restitution."

But Jackson did much more than that. Instead of humbly joining the congregants in prayer, he transformed the service into a political revival meeting. Walker had entrusted his church to the Reverend Al Sharpton, to make sure Jackson kept his promise not to allow the news media to attend the service. But when Walker phoned ten minutes before the service actually began, a Sharpton aide told him that the press was "already in the church."

Jackson was working the room like a politician, and he had brought along handpicked political buddies, including mayoral contenders Alan Hevesi and Fernando Ferrer, and Congressman Charles Rangel. Jackson told the three hundred people in the church that the most important issue since the presidential election was voter access, the right to vote, and the right to be counted. "He did not repent," a Sharpton aide later told the *Village Voice*. "He did not apologize. He made a political speech. He never referred, even remotely, to the scandal."[3]

The Reverend Walker sent a scathing letter to Jackson afterwards. "I am grieved and hurt that you violated the format of the service that you requested be held at my church," he began. "Al Sharpton reported to me that you forced him to allow the public officials to speak when I had specifically agreed that only clergy would speak because I feared that it would become a fiasco in my absence," he added. Walker accused Jackson of transforming the service, which was broadcast live, into a "circus … [that] reinforced the image in the general community that people of African ancestry have little sense of morality. How crass of Charlie Rangel, in light of your fathering a child outside of your marriage, declaring again and again from my pulpit, 'Get over it!' "

It got worse. Walker then compared him to the Reverend Henry Lyons, the disgraced former head of the National Baptist Convention whose extramarital affairs combined with embezzlement of church funds landed him in jail. "The bottom line, in my view, is that you cannot help yourself," the Reverend Walker wrote. "Your addiction to the need of media attention seems to be fatal and you have fallen into the practice of using people for your advantage and personal aggrandizement. … I fear that you have damaged your credibility beyond repair." Just in case Jackson didn't get his point, he spelled out an icy farewell: "Please know that your relationship with me and Canaan cannot be repaired until you make a public or written apology."[4]

"AM I MAKIN' SENSE TO Y'ALL?"

The ballroom at the McCormick Place Hyatt Regency hotel in Chicago was bristling with corporate top brass. There was Jamie Dimon, the CEO of Bank One; David J. Vitale, president and CEO of the Chicago Board of Trade; Thomas M. Patrick, president of Peoples Energy; and David W. Bernauer, president of Walgreens. Dozens of Fortune 500 companies sent senior executives, and William C. Hunter, a vice president at the Federal Reserve Bank of Chicago, showed up. Despite the corporate big guns, and record receipts for Jackson's nonprofit empire, the fourth annual

LaSalle Street conference came and went like a tree falling in the forest with no one to hear.[5]

Even Johnnie Cochran, of O. J. Simpson fame, failed to generate a single inch of print in the Chicago papers. He announced a series of new class action lawsuits alleging discrimination against America's largest companies, potentially worth billions of dollars to the plaintiffs and huge fees for himself. "Jim Crow is dead. But his son, James Crow, Esquire, is still very much alive," Cochran warned at the May 9 lunch. The allusion to lawyers provoked nervous titters: perhaps Cochran was talking about himself? But still, not a single flashbulb flashed or video camera whirred, except for that of Beverly Swanagan, Jackson's own staff photographer. Jackson scowled.

Not even the death of fifty-seven-year-old Chicago businessman Willie Warfield, who collapsed on the floor of the Regency ballroom after the May 9 lunch, got more than a few lines in the press the next morning. Jackson was so upset with the lack of press coverage that he personally phoned the managing editors of Chicago's two top dailies early that morning to complain. "And what did they do?" he told his audience. "They sent a metro reporter! We're here to discuss business and they send a metro reporter!" With that, he launched into a tortured sports analogy about how you wouldn't send a metro reporter to cover a basketball game. Jackson had his worker bees pass out petitions to every table at lunch, asking the several hundred attendees to sign a protest to be faxed to the local newspapers that same afternoon.

The irony is, the LaSalle Street conference of May 9 and 10, 2001, *was* news, but not in the way Jackson intended. It was news because the effort to erase the boundaries of race in corporate America has succeeded beyond Jackson's worst nightmare. Indeed, it has succeeded to the point of making Jackson and his racial brokerage irrelevant.

What I found most intriguing at the LaSalle Street conference were the conflicting messages coming from Jesse Jackson and his partisans on the one hand, and from his audience on the other. Jackson and his PUSH friends were preaching quotas, affirmative action, and government intervention. But black businessmen—both successful and aspiring—were singing another tune; they were talking about quality, opportunities, and competition.

Robert Blackwell is a former IBM executive who did so well he branded his own name, Blackwell Consulting. "I'm sixty-three and I've been black every day of that time. But don't linger on that for thirty seconds," he told aspiring young entrepreneurs. "Get your product or your services together, and you'll do all right. There are a lot of people out there who are fair-minded, and once they realize that you've got a product or that you're capable, they'll give you a shot." He added, "Nobody ever promised you a job. Nobody ever promised you would make a lot of money. You've got to make it on your own."

Gerald Fernandez was so successful in attracting minority suppliers to General Mills that he convinced the food giant to sponsor a new effort, the MultiCultural Foodservice and Hospitality Alliance (MFHA), to foster business deals between minority suppliers and major producers in the food and beverage industry. "We need to start thinking about adding value, and stop thinking like minorities," he said.

Sandra Rand, who managed Supplier Diversity for United Airlines, offered plain common sense: "The economic fat times are over that allowed for minority set-asides," she said. "If a business is going to compete today, they'll have to bring real value to the table."

Jamie Dimon, the CEO of Bank One, explained that big corporations like his own were doing much better at hiring qualified minority employees than ever before, but were not doing well enough to keep them. "After five or seven or nine years," he said, "minorities are still on the porch looking in." Corporate America had to do a better job at identifying qualified minority employees and promoting them, he said.

Jackson wouldn't have any of it. "People tighten up when you use the term 'meritocracy,' Jamie. It means something different on the other side of the track. You can only have a meritocracy on an even playing field. You need to have a *creative meritocracy* to make sure it's the same distance to all bases for all players." America is still mired in "economic apartheid,"

Jackson said. "We have an opportunity crisis, a perspective crisis. Am I makin' sense to y'all?"

But clearly Jackson makes less and less sense to black corporate leaders, and leaves younger black businessmen wondering what planet he is from. But for the scare-muffins who still dominate many Fortune 500 companies, it has become cheaper to toss bones to Jesse than to contest him in the court of public opinion.

And Jackson still has diehard supporters. "Reverend Jackson was responsible for getting our soldiers out of Syria," says Cliff Kelly, of WVON talk radio. "He was responsible for getting our soldiers out of Serbia. And he was responsible for getting our twenty-four fliers back from the Chinese." This was a particularly tortured piece of logic about Jackson's public offer a few weeks earlier to President Bush to negotiate the return of the U.S. crew of an unarmed military surveillance aircraft, forced to land in Communist China after its propeller was shorn off by a daredevil Chinese jet fighter pilot in international air space. "As soon as Jesse Jackson said he was going over to China, the administration started saying 'We're sorry, we're sorry.' That's how much they didn't want Jesse going over to China. . . . The Chinese did the right thing with that plane," he concluded.

Another close Jackson colleague is Dr. Julianne Malveaux, a far-left economist. Speaking to luncheon guests shortly before Willie Warfield collapsed, she evoked the conventional wisdom underlying Jackson's boycott strategies. "What if we decided that we weren't going to buy from the companies that exploit us? That we weren't going to buy from the folks that cannot hire us? That we weren't going to buy from folks who somehow can't find any of us that are 'qualified' to sit on their boards? We need to begin to flex our economic muscles."

Then she evoked the recently released data from the 2000 U.S. Census, which showed that the percentage of blacks in America was declining proportionate to Latinos and Asian-Americans. "The fact is, the population gains do not matter except for this: there are fewer white folks. That's the arithmetic. That's what's important." The racist message was still lurking within the leadership of the movement Jackson claimed to head, and he did nothing to discourage it.

Lon Jones, who moderated a business panel on behalf of PUSH, revived the idea of "set-asides." "You know the price," he told business owners. "Negotiate with a black contractor, don't make him compete. You'll save money all around. Pick a job that's appropriate and negotiate with a qualified black contractor."

Jackson maintained the lists of who was "qualified," but increasingly his top names had become so rich they hardly needed him anymore. People like investors Chester Davenport, Percy Sutton, John Rodgers, Jim Reynolds, and Maceo Sloan; lawyers Johnnie Cochran, James Montgomery, and Willie Gary; CEOs Bob Knowling and Bob Johnson— and dozens more.

"We have an opportunity crisis, a perspective crisis," Jackson insisted. "We have reached the fourth stage of our crisis. . . . Am I makin' sense to y'all?"

The chief crisis for Jackson was the lack of press coverage that made him "feel diminished" and that brought out the increasingly desperate huckster in the Reverend.

"If you are too cheap to write a check for $250 for our gala tomorrow night on the floor of the Chicago Mercantile Exchange, come anyway," he says.

"They're public companies. We IS public!

"The loot is ours, too!

"The only deficit we have is a dream deficit. Let's dream again!

"Somebody say 'Amen'!

"Am I makin' sense to y'all?"

BILLION-DOLLAR MAN

Johnnie Cochran felt right at home with the dark suits of the men and the Sunday hats and dresses of the older women. "I'm in the justice business," he said to wild applause. He told a harrowing story of discrimination in the locker rooms and boardrooms of some of America's biggest and most successful corporations.

Stuffed in their lockers, in an aircraft assembly plant in Marietta, Georgia, Cochran said, black employees found black dolls with nooses around their necks. "Cards are being left on black employees' plates in the lunch room that say 'Greetings from the KKK.' This is the year 2001 in America, and it's happening everywhere," Cochran told a shocked audience at Jackson's gala business lunch in May. "It's happening in Georgia, it's happening in California, it's happening in Maryland."

At least, Johnnie Cochran *claims* it is happening.

"Two weeks ago we held a press conference," Cochran said, "to protest racist behavior at the Southern Power Company. They'd found thirteen nooses on black dolls in employee lockers. They found pictures of people in KKK uniforms where it was written, 'I'm dreaming of a white Christmas.' This is what's happening right now."

Johnnie Cochran has found his new O. J., only this one has pockets as deep as the American Taxpayer. During the Clinton years, an aggressive Justice Department Civil Rights division encouraged minorities to sue their employers for every imaginable slight they might have suffered at the hands of fellow employees. Some of the alleged offenses were real; others were imagined. But in the envenomed atmosphere these suits created, mega-lawyer Johnnie Cochran found a lucrative new trade.

The first step is to find an employee with a story to tell. It doesn't need to be confirmed, but it must resonate with the victim classes. Next comes a class action lawsuit for racial discrimination, which appeals to others who suffered similar indignations. The key third step is to subpoena the financial records of the company. "Once we get the corporate records we begin to see this great disparity in pay," Cochran said. "Twenty percent more for whites. The difference is, the person has a different skin color." Such disparities could be in violation of federal statutes, giving Cochran a new hook for a class action lawsuit, regardless of whether a court found the initial allegations of racism convincing. It's a business that has made Cochran flush with success.

A $1.5 billion race discrimination lawsuit against Coca-Cola he launched with Jackson's help in June 2000 has just won a $192 million settlement. It is the largest-ever settlement under the 1964 Civil Rights Act. "We've got to hit 'em in the pocketbook," Cochran says. "Sometimes they make changes—not because it's the right thing to do, but because it costs them."

Coke's contributions of record to the Citizenship Education Fund—$25,000 in 1994, $15,000 in 1996, and $69,572 in 1999—apparently fell beneath Jackson's pay scale. Pepsi's contributions were on a par, but the rival bottler ponied up significantly more when Jackson convinced CEO Roger Enrico to include Jackson crony John Utendahl in bond offerings tied to the company's March 1999 initial public offering. Over the advice of his own chief financial officer, Enrico gave Utendahl Capital Partners a spot on the cover of the prospectus and a cut of the $19 million management fees. Utendahl then kicked in new contributions to Jackson's CEF.

Fortune magazine wrote in 1997 that Merrill Lynch effectively controlled Utendahl through a 20 percent capital share in the company and $12 million in subordinated debt, and was "using Utendahl to reel in the business of companies that want minority participation in their deals."[6] It was a modern-day version of the minority set-asides exploited by Jackson's half brother Noah Robinson in the 1970s. Jackson didn't mind, because he got his share.

Jesse Jackson sponsored a "ride for justice" to the 2000 Coca-Cola annual shareholders meeting after eight Coke employees complained they were not receiving equal pay. But the real kicker was getting McDonald's to squeeze Coke from behind. Johnnie Cochran and Willie Gary threatened to put together a national boycott with Jesse Jackson in the lead that would target McDonald's for selling Coke. "McDonald's is Coke's single largest customer," a Coke insider told me. "When McDonald's told us there was no way they could have thousands of people picketing their restaurants, we knew we had to fold our cards." The threat of pulling McDonald's business was given instant credibility because Cirilo McSween—the president of the 327-member Black McDonald's

Owners/Operators Association (BMOA), whose franchisees controlled 800 restaurants with more than one billion dollars in annual sales—sat on Jackson's board and was one of his earliest and most steadfast supporters.[7]

Other Jackson allies got smaller crumbs from Johnnie Cochran's Coca-Cola litigation. U.S. District Court judge Richard Story selected former secretary of labor (and Jackson campaign worker) Alexis Herman to head a special task force charged with reviewing pay, promotion, and performance evaluation practices at Coke. It was similar to the type of arrangement she had won after leaving the Carter administration in 1981, when she teamed up with Ernie Green to become Jackson's preferred "diversity consultant." Also selected for the panel was Bill Lann Lee, the assistant attorney general whose recess appointment by President Clinton to head the Justice Department's Civil Rights division had ignited a firestorm on Capitol Hill. Compensation of task force members wasn't announced, but it was patterned after a similar court-ordered body that doled out the Texaco antidiscrimination settlement. There, the head of the task force was paid $125,000, while other members received $75,000. It was cushy pay for a part-time job.[8]

Johnnie Cochran revealed he was planning a similar discrimination suit against Microsoft that could involve upwards of one billion dollars in liability for the software giant. "They have less than 1,000 black employees out of 40,000 and blacks aren't getting the same benefits," Cochran said. "If you're black, they'll give you a loan, but if you're white, they'll give you a jumbo loan. . . . Some of these white folks get one-million-dollar bonuses."

There's a "concrete ceiling" in corporate America, Cochran claimed, that prevents blacks from getting ahead as he has done. "Racism is alive and well in the United States. Don't tell me things are all right. They're all right on the surface—they're always all right on the surface. But America is in denial. I call this America's 51st state: the state of denial."

Johnnie Cochran and Jesse Jackson need each other today more than ever before. "It ought to make good economic sense for these corporations to understand," Cochran told Jackson's audience. "We've got to be ready to boycott these companies, hit 'em in the pocketbook, whatever we got to do. You've got to make good economic sense for them to open themselves." Jackson threatens to boycott, as he did that summer with Toyota over a print ad he found offensive; and Cochran and his lawyer friends fill their pocketbooks.

According to executives at one company the duo tried to shake down, Cochran is on the prowl for local lawyers with grievance cases, then he attaches himself to the lawsuit. "The local lawyers do the heavy lifting, while Johnnie Cochran gets the headlines and the cash," an executive tells me.[9]

Atlanta lawyers Josie Alexander and Hezekiah Sistrunk Jr. filed a series of grievance complaints in 2000 on behalf of current and former Lockheed Martin employees who alleged they had been demoted, or did not receive equal pay with white employees. The U.S. Equal Employment Opportunity Commission picked up the allegations, and issued findings alleging "reasonable cause to believe that discrimination occurred." Johnnie Cochran smelled pay dirt and joined the cases.

On the eighteen-page biography Cochran likes to circulate at meetings of the American Bar Association, he "lists everything from a soap opera appearance to being named one of the most glamorous men in history," according to a Reuters report.[10] Part of Cochran's high-profile role is to rally members of the Congressional Black Caucus in support of his various class action suits. In the Lockheed case, he turned to Georgia Democrat Cynthia McKinney, who viciously and repeatedly attacked the company for alleged racist practices.

But Cochran also loses, if companies play their cards right. Lockheed lawyers William H. Boice and Daniel Piar defended the case relentlessly, proving in detail that the allegations were either misstated or simply untrue. One former employee who Cochran alleged was fired because of racial discrimination admitted he had left the company voluntarily to take a government job. He even told Lockheed that leaving "was beneficial to him because, among other reasons, he could count his time with the Air Force toward retirement in his new position, and he was familiar with the government system."[11] Ultimately, in August 2001, an Atlanta judge threw the case out of court by refusing to certify the class.

Florida lawyer Willie Gary was a big contributor to Jackson's organizations and represented Jackson in the lawsuit filed in April 2001, by his former mistress, Karin Stanford, who was seeking expanded child support payments. It was payback for Jackson's help in setting up the corporations he had sued. Gary got a chunk of the $192 million Coca-Cola windfall, and became so emboldened that he launched several high-profile class action lawsuits on his own. Standing in front of his cream-colored Rolls Royce outside his Spanish-style office complex in South Florida, Gary likes to call himself "The Giant Killer."

"Meet one of the greatest lawyers of all time," the promotional video clip on his website boasts. Willie Gary flies about in a customized Boeing 737-300 corporate jet presumptuously called "Wings of Justice." Gary boasts of the plane's double bed, its conference room, its marble and mahogany bathroom (with the French Florentine gold mirror and shower). A giant "G" is painted on the tail. The designer has interwoven the scales of justice with Gary's initial into a decorative motif used in carpets, paneling, and other features throughout the aircraft. Willie Gary sponsors a celebrity golf tournament and even funds a nonprofit foundation with the proceeds of his cases. The *Palm Beach Post* believes a more fitting title for him might be "Billion-Dollar Man."[12]

Like Johnnie Cochran, Willie Gary works openly with Jesse Jackson; but the two also might cooperate behind the scenes, when a corporate victim has not ponied up sufficiently to the cause. Consider the case of Office Depot. In 1995, Jackson urged black consumers to boycott Office Depot products, alleging that the company discriminated against black employees. Shortly afterwards, Office Depot contributed an undisclosed amount to Jackson's birthday fund, the annual "celebrations" he likes to hold at either the Four Seasons Hotel in Washington, D.C., or at the Beverly Hilton in Los Angeles. Jackson went away.[13]

In February 2001, Willie Gary announced he was joining Johnnie Cochran's billion-dollar lawsuit against Microsoft, but intended to up the ante by demanding $5 billion in damages. Shortly afterwards, he said he would file suit against Office Depot. "I can tell you, this is bigger than

Microsoft," he gushed. "The numbers are so much greater in terms of the people—100 times bigger." Office Depot was running scared. "We take this allegation of discrimination very seriously," Office Depot vice president Eileen Dunn said.[14]

Six months later it was all over. The Delray Beach, Florida, company paid. Exactly how much will never be known, because they signed a confidentiality agreement with Willie Gary that prevents disclosure. Office Depot issued a statement on August 23, 2001, detailing a "plan" to rectify the race discrimination it denied even existed at the company. Among the steps it was taking in response to the suit were "diversity training for all workers; developing a career mentoring program for all employees, including minorities; creating a new executive position to head a Workforce Diversity Office established this year and recruiting more interns from black colleges and universities." Gary said he was pleased with the changes, and withdrew the suit. "The company took our clients' complaints seriously and moved quickly to ensure that its people and workplace policies and practices respect all employees for their unique perspectives, contributions, beliefs and cultural heritage," he said.[15]

Fear of being called a racist continues to make major corporations tremble when Jackson approaches. In May 2001, Jackson began "negotiating" with corporate brass at Toyota Motor Sales USA, after he took offense at an advertising campaign that featured a postcard with a close-up picture of a black face. Etched on a front tooth was a Toyota SUV. Toyota said the ad, designed by the international agency Saatchi & Saatchi, was part of a "buzz" campaign which relied on using postcards distributed to hip urban nightspots and coffee houses and was not directed at any ethnic audience. "The only thing missing is the watermelon," Jackson sneered.[16]

On May 23, he met in Torrance, California, with Don Esmond and Doug West, both Toyota senior vice presidents. "Jackson expressed his concerns about advertising and diversity," Toyota spokesperson Tracy Underwood said. "There was a second meeting in Torrance on June 20, and we have continued to update him since. He expressed concerns that our board was not diverse. We told him that since our parent company is in Japan, getting it more diverse would probably mean getting an American on the board," she deadpanned. "It's a unique challenge."[17]

Toyota then received a proposal from diversity consultant Greg Calhoun, a Jackson friend who had accompanied him on his February 2000 Africa tour. Calhoun demanded an up-front payment of $1 million to fix the problem, but Toyota refused. Calhoun sued Toyota for breach of contract in an Alabama court, while Jackson increased the noise level and threatened a boycott.[18] On the eve of his annual PUSH convention in August, Jackson called off the boycott, claiming victory when a Toyota "diversity" plan was announced that set quotas for increasing the number of minority dealerships. The real sweeteners came later.

One week after Jackson dropped his boycott threat, Toyota instructed Goldman Sachs to "write two Jackson cronies into a $300 million equity offering," says Ken Boehm, a former federal prosecutor who now heads the National Legal and Policy Center (NLPC), a nonprofit group that has been investigating Jackson's activities.[19] They were Williams Capital Group, and Blaylock & Partners, both based in Manhattan.

Williams Capital Group was created in 1994 by Jackson friend Christopher Williams, a former Lehman Brothers vice president whose underwriting successes included Jackson shakedown victims GTE and AT&T and a host of smaller telecom spin-offs created as a result of the 1996 Telecommunications Act.

Blaylock & Partners, also a new firm, was established by Jackson friend Ron Blaylock and had signed dozens of new bond offerings thanks to Jackson's intervention. Blaylock was a close personal friend of Kevin Ingram, the disgraced Goldman Sachs and Deutsche Bank trader who is now doing time after pleading guilty in a federal district court in Florida to money-laundering charges. Blaylock, Ingram, and Christopher Williams were all major contributors to Jackson's nonprofit empire and members of Jackson's International Trade Bureau. "They should teach Jesse Jackson's network and tactics in business school," the NPLC's Ken Boehm says.

BREAKING AWAY

Harold Doley Jr. is one of the wealthiest black men in America. Founder of Doley Securities Inc., a brokerage business based in New Orleans, in 1973 he became the first black man to purchase a seat on the New York Stock Exchange. "When Jesse came to me in 1996," Doley recalls, "Rainbow/PUSH had fewer than twenty employees. At the end of 2000, it had 102 employees. Almost all of that expansion came out of the Wall Street Project."[20] He thinks the Toyota deal was an outrage. "Jesse leveraged several million African-Americans, threatening a boycott, just to benefit a few of his friends."

At first, Doley agreed with Jackson's goals and his methods. But before long, he began to have misgivings and consulted his lawyers. The problem, he realized, came from the way Jackson was using his leverage with legislators at both the state and federal level to benefit himself and his friends directly. "Willie Sutton said you rob banks because that's where the money was," Doley says. "Jesse came to Wall Street because that was his avenue to the pension fund money."

Jackson quickly understood that the way brokers made money on Wall Street was on a transaction by transaction basis, through commissions. "So he focused on transactional Wall Street," Doley says. "And that led him straight to the pension funds."

Under the guise of minority empowerment, Jackson sought legislation to require a percentage of the nation's pension funds to be brokered or managed by minority-run funds. In Ohio, legislators agreed on a 10 percent quota. But in March 2001, Jackson got Illinois state representative Todd Stroger to introduce legislation setting a 25 percent minority quota for all state or public service pension funds.

Stroger stood to benefit personally from his own bill, since he was an employee of a minority-owned brokerage firm, SBK Brooks, which was a contributor to Jackson's Wall Street Project. Tying the loop tighter was Stroger's father, John Stroger, president of the Cook County Board of Commissioners. John Stroger headed the finance committee that recommended pension fund managers to the Illinois Teachers Retirement System. In 1984 and again in 1988, he was on the finance committee of Jackson's presidential campaigns. Despite these close personal and professional ties to Jackson and the legislation he was pushing, no one publicly suggested that the Strogers or Jackson had a conflict of interest.

As Doley got more deeply involved in Jackson's Wall Street Project, he liked what he saw less and less. "I saw a lot of things happen that troubled me, and I confronted him about it." Eventually, Doley also consulted his attorneys. "I was concerned that what is going on here may be illegal," he says. His attorneys told him to get out.

The problem was that few black pension fund managers were professionally qualified to manage such vast sums of money, so Jackson came in with a short list of his friends. "Jesse went to the large money managers and said, give my partners 10 to 15 percent of your business, and by the way, pay them . . . more on commissions than what the Street normally receives," Doley says. "In exchange for steering that business to his friends, Jesse wants 10 percent off the top. Jesse calls it 'tithing.' He has become a Civil Rights Entrepreneur. What you've got is Jesse's own civil rights movement that is benefiting less than three hundred people. It's really less than fifty, but if I say that, people won't believe it."

Doley wouldn't mind if Jackson's broker friends competed fairly. "Jesse has carved out a different niche where you don't have to be competitive. You just have to partner with him." Doley claims that minority firms who don't charge the exorbitant commissions and don't partner with Jackson are getting cut out. "Jesse goes in and says I'm not recommending anybody, but here's a list of my partners."

Doley estimates that Jackson's pension fund shakedown alone generates $170 million a year in commissions for Jackson's friends, who in turn make significant contributions to Jackson's nonprofits. "Every pensioner in America is subsidizing Jesse Jackson, though they don't realize it," Doley says. The biggest beneficiaries are people like Ron Blaylock, John Utendahl, and Maceo Sloan. "Jesse's got seven or eight investment bankers, five or six money managers, and seven or eight brokers. He calls them 'partners.' This is better than a dot com business, because there's no risk," Doley says.

Jackson claims that Blaylock, Utendahl, Kevin Ingram, Jim Reynolds, John Rodgers, and the others on his short list were being "systematically excluded" by Wall Street despite their multimillion-dollar jobs. "These guys were not members of our organization when we started. They joined a movement to level the playing field."[21]

Jackson ally Hermene Hartman disputes Doley's terms, but not the practices he describes. "I take issue with the term racketeering," she says, referring to a description that Doley has used. "The Wall Street Project is directing, recommending, identifying professional people.... It's like if someone phoned you and asked you to suggest five advertising agencies. Are you directing? Or just going off of your Rolodex? The truth is that Jesse was recommending ten—probably only ten companies that had world-class competence. He identified them, recommended them—but not for money."

The accusations remind Hartman of the early days at Operation Breadbasket in Chicago. "I remember when we helped businessmen get hair care products onto the shelf. Jesse was instrumental in getting products placed at Walgreens, Dominicks, Jewel. He was accused of profiteering, but what did he get out of it? He got some growth for some companies. They gave him donations, which seemed apropos. But it was never a percentage, never 10 percent. It's the American way."[22]

Consider Harold Doley's response. "People say, 'Look, we don't do business with you because you're competitive, we do business with you because you're a minority.' That's un-American."[23]

Roy Innis, chairman and CEO of the Congress of Racial Equality (CORE) believes Jackson has done tremendous harm to the black community. "His shakedown of corporate America is destructive. It takes resources away from legitimate programs. It sends a bad message to young black people. It suggests that the way you deal with corporate America is through extortionist techniques."[24]

Starr Parker, president of the Los Angeles–based Coalition on Urban Renewal and Education (CURE), is too young to remember America's segregated past, although her father attended Sterling High School in Greenville, South Carolina, where Jackson was schooled. "When Martin Luther King was killed we were in Japan," she recalls. "My father was in the military. It wasn't until later, when we came back to the States, that I became race-conscious. When I was growing up Jesse Jackson was a spokesman for the radical Left, especially the elite and the hangers-on who were trying to push the civil rights movement toward socialism. Jesse Jackson is not a natural leader; he appointed himself."[25]

CHAPTER 18

﹏

Shakedown Man

HIJACKING AMERICA'S GRIEF

"Friends, it costs to get free," Jackson was saying. "Friends, I need your money. If you'll volunteer today to give $100 or more, please stand up. . . ."

It was four days after the slaughter of September 11 and Americans across the nation were numb with shock. I took one of the first flights to leave the Washington, D.C., area after the terrorist attacks. As we waited in the predawn light at the gate for fellow passengers to clear the security checks at Baltimore-Washington International Airport we were still numb, as if we couldn't quite wake up from a bad dream. We felt like explorers about to embark on an unknown journey. When we finally lifted off, an hour late, there were fewer than thirty passengers on our Boeing 757 bound for Chicago Midway Airport, and we looked each other over several times before boarding the plane.

Buses were parked outside Operation PUSH headquarters on South Drexel Boulevard when I arrived, including a van from the Red Cross. The cavernous hall was packed. Up on stage, Jackson was calling on people to give blood. But rather than have them go outside to the Red Cross van, he asked us to fill out an Operation PUSH recruitment card. He promised that if blood were needed for the victims, we would receive a call.

Something was missing, I thought, as I surveyed the scene on the stage, where Jackson was seated next to the Reverend Willie Barrow and to two Muslim clerics. The choir was singing, the organ was playing, and the gospel band was warming up. Behind Jackson, as he got up to speak, was a bigger-than-life photo of Martin Luther King Jr., and behind me, looking straight down at Jackson from the rear wall of this movie-theater-of-a-building was another giant portrait, his own. There were many white faces in the crowd, but they were not the faces of Jackson's left-wing intellectual friends. These were working-class faces, tough, grizzled faces, men and women with rough hands and thick necks. On their laps they carried banners saying Local 15 IBEW, the International Brotherhood of Electrical Workers, each festooned with an American flag. That was it: these patriotic workers were the only ones in the hall who were carrying the flag. Up on Jackson's stage, there were no flags, no red-white-and-blue ribbons, no sign of mourning, or of rallying, for America. Up on Jackson's stage, Old Glory was not welcome.

It didn't take Jackson long to warm to the theme he would hammer home throughout the morning. "We saw the Twin Towers of capitalism come crashing down. We saw the Pentagon buried beneath the rubble. In the face of that, the reaction has been scapegoating." The nation's leaders, he said, have unfairly singled out Muslims as the perpetrators for the evil deeds of September 11. "It is not fair to stereotype Arabs and Muslim Americans. Hitler did racial profiling of the Jewish people and it was wrong. In Oklahoma City, they said they were looking for a Middle Eastern terrorist, and they found out it was the Middle West. They said black kids had all these guns and drugs, that they did crack cocaine. They said we'd be a lot safer if we just locked up all them black kids. Then

Columbine came. So we know that stereotyping people for their race and religion is wrong."

Jackson invited two leaders from the 350,000-strong Muslim community of the greater Chicago area to speak on his platform. As he introduced Dr. Ahmed Umar Abdallah of the Council of Islamic Organizations of Greater Chicago, Jackson sounded an indictment of America: "We say to our Muslim brothers, we share your pain. It was you today, but before sundown, it's the rest of us." He acted as though the great threat to America—and the great tragedy to be remembered—was not terrorism and the events of September 11, but the potential for racist vigilantism among his fellow Americans. Uncle Jesse's hijacking of America's agony had begun.

Dr. Abdallah noted that in just four days since the September 11 bombings there had been 217 "documented cases of anti-Muslim violence and hate crimes." Indeed, as I arrived in Chicago that morning, the Chicago police announced that a mosque had been ransacked overnight at 63rd and Holman, not far from Operation PUSH. But Dr. Abdallah rose beyond the racialist rhetoric. "Terrorism has no denomination. Terrorists have no religion. Terrorists have agendas," he said. "Islam regards terrorism as a cowardly and predatory act against God and man." It was a stunning indictment from a Muslim cleric. His fellow Islamic cleric Azhar Usman offered Koranic prayers in Arabic, and condemned those who carried out Tuesday's attacks. "What makes this tragedy so despicable is that people commit these atrocities in the name of God. As a Muslim I say to you: any human being who can support these attacks has lost their humanity."

But Jackson had no such words of condemnation for the terrorists, nor did he have words of mourning, words of comfort, or words of love to offer his audience. He displayed little emotion or care for the victims. Rather, he poured fire and brimstone on America's leaders for their arrogance in a typical, blame-America-first tirade.

"Colin Powell, we are told, was talking about multilateralism and reaching out to others," Jackson said. "The next thing we know, *Time* magazine reports that he has been pushed to the side. . . . Man could build some bridges, cure some sick, feed some children. Man could make some friends."

Much better than deploying American troops to root out the organizations that carried out the attacks and strike the countries that support them, Jackson said, was to "launch the fight for the redistribution of resources. One hundred million people will have AIDS in five years. We should use our strength for that."

His scripture for the day was from the book of Job, and his message was the evils of American arrogance. "At high noon when the sun is in eclipse, chickens squawk (oh, yeah!), hogs wallow (that's right!), and people look up in desperation.... We've heard a lot of angry talk since Tuesday... antigay and lesbian talk... talk about hit somebody somewhere.... That is a traumatized gutter and cultural reaction," Jackson said, making perfect sense to himself.

"Bin Laden had been an American ally," Jackson said, repeating a vicious myth. "We trained him. We gave him free weapons. And now the attack dog has bitten the master. We say we're going to bomb the places where bin Laden's people get their training. But they got their training from us."

Testimony from participants in the Afghan war against the Soviet Union says otherwise. According to three former directors of Pakistan's Inter-Service Intelligence, the ISI, whom I interviewed personally during a trip to Pakistan in 1998, neither the U.S. nor Pakistan ever trained the so-called Afghan-Arabs or provided weapons to them. Those who want to rewrite the Afghan-American victory over the Soviets—the key battle that ended the Cold War—into a defeat have propagated this myth, nostalgic as they apparently are for the days of Soviet communism. The actual facts are that bin Laden and his acolytes grafted themselves onto the radical Abu Sayyaf faction of the Afghan mujahideen but refused to come into contact with the handful of CIA trainers actually stationed in Pakistan, who supervised from afar the training of the Afghan mujahideen fighters. Indeed, the CIA "trainers" never actually trained Afghan mujahideen fighters at all, according to Brigadier General Ahmad

Youssef, who headed the liaison effort between the United States and Pakistani intelligence throughout almost the entire decade of war. The Americans trained the Pakistanis, who in turn trained the Afghan mujahideen.

But Jesse Jackson, like other demagogues, has a troubled relationship with the truth, even a complete lack of interest in it. He invents, then embroiders, embellishes, and expands, and few ever have the courage to expose him.

"Members of our organization, some of them perished in the bombings," he said with dry eyes. Having heard him stretch the truth in a similar way in April, when he claimed Willie Warfield, a Chicago businessman who was rushed out on an ambulance gurney with a heart attack had "died at my feet," I was curious. I had forged a journalist's relationship with Barbara Olson during the Bush-Gore standoff in Florida after the November 2000 election and found her to be a refreshing antidote to politics as usual in Washington. I had met her and her husband, Ted Olson, now the solicitor general of the United States, many times over the previous six years while working as a reporter for the *American Spectator*, but had never spoken to her at length until the Florida recount follies. Barbara Olson was one of God's angels. This was immediately apparent as I listened to her recount her tales of political combat in Florida with flair, humor, originality, and a total lack of spite. And it was immediately apparent when I heard the story of her last-minute cell phone calls to her husband from the doomed plane that was crashed into the Pentagon on September 11. I had not been able to think of Barbara Olson those past four days without tears welling in my eyes; and I hardly knew her. And here the Reverend Jackson said he had "lost" several members of his organization; and yet, the statement was uttered cold, without emotion, just staking a claim.

I put the question to him later in his own media center in front of local television cameras. I said I was curious to know the names of the people in his organization who had been killed, and any details he might be able to provide.

Jackson: I can't recall; I can't right now. There are family reasons. There were several members of the Davis Group—Kevin Davis out of Baltimore. There were fifty-two staffers on the forty-fourth floor, fifty-one got out. One of them has not been found. He went back in to save somebody.

Author: Could you give us the name of that person?

Jackson: [mumbles] I can't mention their names, because of their families.... Chris Williams got out safely. People like [Ron] Blaylock and [John] Utendahl who worked in the financial district. One thing that has happened is that now the environmental impact is setting in, on the water, the air. It's going to require a massive economic reconstruction in Manhattan, an economic formula.

Author: So you did *not* have staff members who perished? Or you *did?*

Jackson: No, they weren't actually our staff members. They were members of our organization. Our staff is here and in Washington, in other buildings. But our International Trade group members—and for the first two years of the Wall Street Project, we were on the top floor of the Trade Center, so we frequented that building. We knew a lot of people who worked there.

You can almost see him ducking and weaving, searching the tiny crowd for another journalist who will break in to help him change the subject.

One more word about Local 15 of the IBEW. Until that week, Jackson had ignored the plight of the 1,100 union members who had been locked out of work since August 31, after a debilitating two-month strike against Midwest Generation, the local subsidiary of power giant Edison International of California. That week, faced with the prospect of hundreds of empty seats in his cavernous "church" on South Drexel Boulevard, Jackson cut a deal.

"Several of our members suggested we try to get Reverend Jackson to support our cause," union leader Joe Walker tells me outside on the steps. "So on Monday, we met with Mark Allen at Operation PUSH and showed him documents and explained our grievances. Reverend Jackson never actually met with us, but we sent messages back and forth." The next day, September 11, Jackson called back. "Reverend Jackson asked us to bring our people, and said that he would support our cause."

The plight of the union workers turned macabre the day after the bombings, when one of their members committed suicide. "From talking with his wife and his friends," Walker said, "I think he just gave up hope that he would be able to provide for his family." But Jackson, who has never been a union man and in fact clashed with blue-collar workers during his two presidential campaigns, ignored the plight of Local 15 until he saw the benefit before the cameras. His Saturday morning meetings at Operation PUSH had been running on empty, and he knew the cameras would be out today, after September 11, and he needed to pack the hall.

"How many of your people came here today on these buses?" I asked Walker's co-organizer, John O'Reilly.

"We brought about 250 union members here today," said O'Reilly.

Jackson may have hijacked the union members, and if he had carried through on his pledge to bring equal numbers of PUSH supporters to a union demonstration the following week, Joe Walker and John O'Reilly would have been happy. Instead, Jackson became embroiled in his own lies about an invitation from the Taliban to "negotiate" terms with the United States, which the Taliban said Jackson had solicited himself.

I took a drive around Chicago's South Side that afternoon. There were no flags, no red-white-and-blue ribbons, no sign of mourning at Jackson's home on South Constance Avenue, nor across the street at son Jonathan's house, although several neighbors had flags in their windows. Across town by Lake Michigan at the sprawling house of Jesse Jr., no flags flew either.

Jesse Jr., the Democratic congressman from Illinois, is being groomed to follow in his father's footsteps. He is the politician in the family and has shown himself to be fiercely partisan. At a "Wake Up Democrats! Take Back the Country" conference in Los Angeles on June 24, 2001, he brought down the house with a rousing condemnation of America's federal system of government. He said that the nation's greatest problem is "a separate and unequal system" of "fifty separate and unequal states and 3,067 separate and unequal counties [that] must be rooted out root and branch."

"The enemy here is the Tenth Amendment, the unenumerated rights," which permits inequalities to exist, he said. Jesse Jr.—like his father—believes the only solution is a much stronger central government for "one America." He proposed a constitutional amendment guaranteeing every American "a right to health care of equal high quality [and] a public education of equal high quality." Such an amendment would allow anyone in America, citizen or not, to sue in federal court in order to secure that health care and education. To mounting applause, he shouted, "We ought to have a constitutional right to fairness!"

Of course, as any high school student who has read the Constitution knows, the amendment specifying the unenumerated rights belonging to the people is the Ninth. The Tenth Amendment reserves the rights not delegated by the people to the federal government for the states and the people, respectively. In his mangling of the facts, Jesse Jr. was following in his father's footsteps.

REPUDIATION DAY

Jesse Lee Peterson grew up on a former plantation near Tuskegee, Alabama, and by the time he was a teenager hated whites. "I was a young man, and I had a lot of anger," he says. "I didn't have my father around to teach me. I listened to people like Jesse Jackson, who told me that my problems weren't my fault: it was racism. It was because of slavery. It was because the white man didn't want me to move forward."

Peterson recalls hearing Jackson as an eighteen-year-old in Crenshaw High School in Los Angeles, where he had moved with an uncle and an aunt. Jackson was a visiting speaker at the high school, and he was trying out a version of the PUSH-Excel "motivational" speech he would dispense around the country at government expense in the 1970s. The message was all about race, power, and the evils of the white man; and especially the evils of the Republican Party. "He was saying the Republican Party was the party of the rich white male," Peterson recalls, "and the Democrats were the party of the people. I didn't realize the partisan message at the time, because it was the type of thing black people were hearing everywhere behind closed doors. We've been brainwashed by the civil rights movement for the past forty to fifty years. The people we trusted the most are the ones who are keeping us down and lying to us most."[1]

At the age of thirty-nine, in 1988, Peterson underwent a conversion, after he had reached a dead end in a life of drugs, welfare, and hate. "I forgave my father and mother for not doing the right thing, for not caring for me as a child," he says. "And then I realized it wasn't white Americans, either, who were responsible for my problems and I stopped hating them as well. All of a sudden I was free, and felt at peace. I found purpose in life. I began to see that no one can hold you back if you have high moral character. It's warfare between good and evil, not black and white."

Peterson gradually rebuilt his own life, and went on to become a black pastor and successful radio/television talk show host. He believes Jesse Jackson is a "black racist and an apostle of dictatorship. He offers no genuine hope for Americans of goodwill, black or white." As the founder of the Brotherhood Organization of a New Destiny (BOND) and as an incredibly charismatic leader in his own right, Peterson held his "Third Annual National Day of Repudiation of Jesse Jackson" on Dr. Martin Luther King Jr.'s birthday in 2002, in Los Angeles. Peterson vows to continue holding annual protests against Jackson until the black community "repudiates" him. "I could have a long job ahead of me," he jokes, "but I hope not."

The idea of his annual event, Peterson explains, is "to show the contrast between Dr. King's dream and Jesse Jackson's nightmare. Dr. King had a dream that you could be judged on the content of your character not the color of your skin, whereas Jesse Jackson has made sure we're judged by color and not character. Most blacks are suffering not because of color but from lack of character. We've been brainwashed all these years to think it's racism."

Peterson calls Jackson, Louis Farrakhan, and Kweisi Mfume of the NAACP the CEOs of "the race industry," a tremendously profitable business financed by government and liberal foundations "that seeks to control the black community for personal gain." Increasingly, under Jesse Jackson's leadership, multinational corporations have financed these race industry titans. The corporations think it is cheaper to buy protection than to demand a fair and honest hearing of their corporate practices. But they might be ignoring the potential groundswell of popular support that could greet corporations that would stand up to the race hustlers.

"We are more divided today than ever before in history because of so-called civil rights leaders like Jesse Jackson," Peterson says. "This man hungers and thirsts after power. It means everything to him. This is why he has no shame about keeping black Americans down, to acquire power and wealth for himself.

"White Americans have not understood the brainwashing taking place behind closed doors in black churches, black schools, black community organizations, and black families. I've been called *Uncle Tom* and *nigger* so many times—by blacks—that I'm thinking of changing my middle name."

Until the black community repudiates Jesse Jackson, Peterson fears, the major corporations will continue to finance his nonprofit empire, out of fear of being painted as "racists." And until the corporations cut off funding, Jackson will continue to shake down businesses and victimize black Americans.

As the Reverend Jackson should know, the Gospel says that the truth will set us free. Black Americans deserve to be freed from the shakedown artists who plunder in their name. And all it really takes is the courage to speak the truth to shakedown power.

CHAPTER 19

The War That Jesse Made

After *Shakedown* was first published, the State Department sent me a box of documents relating to Jackson's three years as President Clinton's special envoy for Africa, which they had declassified after my Freedom of Information Act request. This chapter lays out the incredible story the documents tell.

When Jackson first traveled to meet with Liberian strongman Charles Taylor in Monrovia on February 11, 1998, Taylor was living in virtual isolation. The United States and the international community shunned him after his election as president following a campaign riddled with intimidation. But instead of lecturing Taylor on human rights and democracy—as per his instructions—Jackson embraced the Liberian strongman, as the State Department after-action memos show. Upon meeting Taylor in the presidential palace, Jackson gushed that returning to Monrovia was "an emotional homecoming." [1]

A subsequent cable, dated April 29, 1998, provides more detail. "During his twenty-four hours in Liberia, Rev. Jackson met several times privately with President Taylor, and appeared to establish a strong personal bond with him," the U.S. embassy in Monrovia reported. "After Jesse Jackson's visit, President Taylor went out of his way to stress that Liberia is America's best friend in Africa, and that it was time to improve the bilateral relationship—a 180 degree change in direction from the public posture of the Taylor government before the Jackson visit."[2]

What actually transpired during Jackson's "private" sessions with Taylor, when aides and embassy officials were asked to leave the room, has been a subject of controversy ever since. None of the documents released to me indicates that Jackson ever discussed those talks with his State Department handlers.

On May 20, after taking part in a summit in Monrovia between Taylor and Sierra Leone president Ahmed Tejan Kabbah, Jackson urged Taylor to issue a joint communiqué with Kabbah, in which the two leaders would pledge to work together to end the rebellion by the Revolutionary United Front (RUF) in Sierra Leone. Taylor was reluctant, especially since he and Kabbah had made a similar public pledge just weeks earlier at an African summit in Nigeria. But he made it clear that, in exchange for spotlighting Jackson's visit in this way, he wanted Jackson's help in lifting international sanctions against his government. He also sought an end to charges by the United States that he was running guns and diamonds for the rebels. "We are not supporting the RUF," Taylor insisted to an incredulous Howard Jeter, the American deputy assistant secretary of state. Jeter had accompanied Jackson to Monrovia and had not pushed for the communiqué. "We are under the gun from the international community and we won't get any assistance until this issue is resolved."[3] Jackson appeared to take Taylor at his word, and joyously presided over the public signing of the joint communiqué later that day at Taylor's residence in Congo Town, playing the familiar role of publicity hound.

Five days later, Nigeria released Colonel Foday Sankoh from custody and quietly shipped him to Sierra Leone, where he was arrested and charged with treason. In reprisal, RUF and ex-junta forces seized a district capital in the northwest, "and were reported by missionaries as threatening to kill everyone unless Foday Sankoh is released from custody," a background note prepared for assistant secretary of state Susan E. Rice reported.[4] President Kabbah remained firm in his intent to prosecute Sankoh, and continued to believe that he could definitively beat the RUF with help from Nigerian peacekeepers.[5] But that didn't fit with Jackson's plans.

The RUF thrived on its on-again, off-again control of Sierra Leone's rich diamond mines. When Sankoh was ultimately sentenced to death by the Sierra Leone high court for treason, Jackson pressured President Kabbah to lift the death sentence, arguing that it was better to negotiate with an enemy rather than kill him. This went directly against repeated State Department guidance, which warned Jackson against accommodation with the RUF leadership.

"You should also urge Kabbah to face the difficult issue of national reconciliation," a briefing document prepared by Rice for Jackson instructed. "The international community has made it clear that RUF leaders responsible for the atrocities should be brought to justice. However, the bulk of the RUF's fighting force is made up of teenagers and young adults kidnapped from their villages as children, and then drugged, brainwashed, and forced into fighting…Given its brutality and previous bad faith, we will continue to insist that the RUF would have to announce publicly (and its actions reflect this statement) that there will be no further killing or mutilating of the civilian population before we would encourage negotiations."[6] In an interview, Rice corroborated the documents with her own recollections. "[Howard] Jeter and I and the White House all pressed firmly with Jackson to give no quarter to Taylor, Sankoh, or any of the other scumbags," she told me.[7]

Jackson's closeness to Charles Taylor and Foday Sankoh caused him repeatedly to either ignore or go beyond the written and verbal instructions he received from the State Department, the record clearly shows. In September, when Taylor's Special Security Service (SSS) opened fire on the U.S. embassy in Monrovia, the State Department asked Jackson to deliver a sharply worded reprimand to Taylor by phone.[8] No record of what Jackson actually said was released, but in November 1998, during the Mano River summit in Guinea, he again treated Taylor as a statesman, despite clear instructions from Rice and other State Department briefers to deal harshly with him. In public, Jackson continued to babble rhetoric left over from the 1960s.

"Liberia can never be free until Sierra Leone is free," he told members of Sierra Leone's Representatives of Civil Society and the Press in Freetown on November 13, 1998. "Guinea can never be free until Sierra Leone is free of the war. Guinea Bissau cannot be free; Ivory Coast cannot be secure; Senegal cannot be secure; Nigeria cannot be secure. In a real sense, none of us are secure until all of us are secure."[9] In a performance meant to be uplifting but devoid of substance, Jackson ended with a scarcely veiled reference to the pressure he was putting on Kabbah to release Sankoh from prison. "Because we accept the imperative to include all of God's children and leave none behind, that must become the operative word as you seek to look at the tougher choices of reconciliation and repatriation to include all and leave none behind...Even the lost sheep must find a place because the Good Shepherd cannot rest until the last sheep is back in the fold. Thank you very much."[10]

In January 1999, Sankoh's troops went on another killing spree, and launched an offensive that brought them into the streets of Freetown (see page 313). After a month of hard fighting, with many casualties on both sides, a reinforced West African peacekeeping force led by Nigeria managed to drive the rebels out of the capital and fight them to stalemate. The conflict could have ended there, had it not been for Jackson's active intervention.

Here the State Department records are nothing less than astounding. In the talking points he received for a February 10, 1999, telephone call to RUF representative Omrie Golley, Jackson was told to be blunt. Among the points he was supposed to make: "The RUF has repeatedly told us it wants peace in Sierra Leone…The RUF's recent actions make us wonder if the RUF is really interested in peace." Jackson was told to express sadness over the RUF attack against Malian peacekeepers in Port Loko. "Golley may claim the Malians had attacked RUF positions—it is not true," his briefers wrote. State also instructed Jackson to tell Golley that he had read the recent UN human rights reports on RUF atrocities and that "the RUF must stop this senseless violence."[11]

In the heavily redacted transcript of Jackson's actual conversation with Golley, however, nothing like this appears. Instead, Jackson begins by saying he is "anxious to do whatever [is necessary] to get peace," then delivers concession after concession. "I want [to] focus on outcome rather than [the] process of getting there. I urge all parties to get beyond process and get to [the negotiating] table. I want to talk to RUF leadership as soon as I can. [The] U.S. stands ready to urge negotiations over confrontation."

Golley was understandably pleased. He thanked Jackson and said he had been "heartened by your words" during Jackson's sermonizing in Sierra Leone. Golley played Jackson like a violin, and it worked. "[We] seek your help and guidance. Only social and political settlements will solve [the] problem.…We were forced to use force."[12] At the end, the State Department duty officer who transcribed the call notes that Golley's "voice [was] breaking" as he gushed his thanks to Jackson for helping to legitimize Sankoh's Revolutionary United Front.

But that wasn't government policy, as far as Susan Rice recalls, nor as the written record shows. Quite to the contrary.

In a cable stamped "secret," summarizing that conversation and the talks Jackson held with Sierra Leone president Kabbah the same day, it is clear that Jackson was pressuring Kabbah to launch negotiations with Sankoh and the RUF leadership at any cost. "Jackson told Kabbah that in wartime it is important to take extraordinary steps for peace." Kabbah related he had just learned from ambassador Howard Jeter about Jackson's stunning offer to Golley. "Kabbah said that Golley had mentioned the possibility of sharing power with the RUF, something that

Kabbah dismissed as contrary" to earlier agreements. "Kabbah said that power-sharing had failed in Angola and had not worked well in South Africa...[and] pointed out that the RUF had been specifically invited to take part in the last elections, but refused. 'They were only interested in killing us,'"[13]

I have provided several eyewitness accounts of how Jackson muscled Kabbah into precipitous negotiations with Sankoh in Lomé, Togo, on May 18, 1999 (see Chapter 13). The State Department record supplements these personal recollections with some startling new facts.

- The State Department had never instructed Jackson to negotiate an extended ceasefire, nor expected him to do so

- Jackson's detailed instructions for the meetings in Lomé reveal that his objectives were "to encourage Kabbah and Sankoh to start direct talks...to urge both parties to commit to cease hostilities for the duration of the Lomé talks," and "to urge Kabbah to commit to release Sankoh as part of a peace agreement" validated and approved by the UN-backed peacekeeping force.[14] (In fact, Kabbah had released Sankoh at the end of March and had allowed him to travel to Lomé in April to confer with RUF commanders about ending hostilities.)

Susan Rice, who wrote the briefing documents for Jackson, clearly recalls, "We had not expected or planned that an agreement would be achieved in that time frame or that Jackson would have a role in it."[15]

Even clearer evidence that Jackson had exceeded his instructions, negotiating an international agreement that engaged the authority of the United States without having been authorized to do so, can be seen in the cable sent back to Washington, D.C., from the U.S. embassy in Lomé. Witnessing the agreement, which was signed by both Kabbah and Sankoh, were President Gnassingbe Eyadema of Togo; Francis G. Okelo, the special representative of Kofi Annan, the secretary-general of the UN; Adwoa Coleman, the representative of the Organization of African Unity; and Jesse Jackson, U.S. special envoy for the promotion of democracy in Africa. No other American official signed the ceasefire agreement. Jackson, alone and apparently beyond supervision, had signed an international treaty document in the name of the United States government all by himself.[16]

In his interview with me on the subject, Jackson placed the blame for the failed agreement on his State Department handlers ("It was the U.S. government position. I went with the State Department..."; see page 319.) The documentary record proves him wrong.

The kicker, of course, came later, when Jackson pressured Kabbah not only to issue a full and complete pardon to Sankoh—again, well beyond the instructions he received from State—but also to make Sankoh vice president in a coalition government and put him in charge of the newly created Commission for the Management of Strategic Resources, which oversaw the diamond mines. In fact, the RUF already controlled the mines, and Sankoh at first saw no reason to take on official responsibility for Sierra Leone's diamond exports when he already had his hand on them. Jackson changed his mind. "Rev. Jackson encouraged Sankoh to take the lead on the resources commission," a subsequent cable states.[17]

The notion of a complete pardon for Sankoh was first raised by Jackson in a telephone call to Sankoh on June 12, 1999. It appears nowhere in the detailed talking points prepared for Jackson ahead of time by the Department of State (see the Appendix).

Jackson started off by telling Sankoh, a man of limited intelligence, who had first learned to pray just three weeks earlier with Jackson in Lomé, that "I think and pray for you every night." He offered "congratulations" to Sankoh for bringing the peace talks around—and this at a time when RUF militiamen were breaking the ceasefire Jackson had arranged on a daily basis. "We can get the thing on track," Jackson said. "The key in this process is you." He must have thought he was talking to an eight-year-old

American schoolchild, brought up to believe he could climb mountains if only he had enough self-esteem. "In Lomé, you said can't nobody free you because your mind is already free. Like Mandela was in jail."

Sankoh remained concerned that if he returned to Sierra Leone, he might go back to jail, and eventually even face his court-ordered death sentence. That's when Jackson played his ace—without telling the State Department ahead of time. "That's just talk," Jackson reassured Sankoh. "You focus on what is real. You are going to be free and pardoned. Focus on what is real."[18] A senior State Department official involved in the talks insisted that there had never been instructions for Jackson to tell Sankoh he'd be pardoned. "That would have been off message," the official said. And yet, that's exactly what Jackson did.

On November 30, 1999, after a series of RUF attacks and hostage-taking against UN peacekeepers in Sierra Leone, the State Department handed Jackson tough talking points for further discussion with Sankoh. "There are strong indications that you have no intention of fully disarming the RUF and that you are caching arms in Liberia," the briefing document states. "Many believe that you are planning an attack on Freetown. The illegal mining and export of diamonds continues in RUF controlled eastern Sierra Leone with profits going to the RUF, not the people you claim to want to lead and represent." The memo went on: "Commence work on Minerals Commission and stop illegal mining and export of diamonds."[19] There is no record of Jackson having delivered this tough message. But, thanks to the RUF exports, Liberia claimed $300 million in diamond exports that year.

By March 31, 2000, the situation in Sierra Leone that Jackson had helped to create had badly deteriorated. Sankoh had not lived up to his commitments to disarm the RUF; there were almost daily skirmishes between the RUF and UN peacekeepers; and Liberian president Taylor was continuing to provide safe haven, training, and weapons to the rebels, in preparation for a new offensive. Susan Rice prepared Jackson for another series of phone calls to Kabbah, Sankoh, and Taylor with a tough message to all of them: "There is no time to lose." Rice wrote that Jackson should remind Sankoh that he remained accountable for the behavior of his men in the bush. "I hope you will remind your troops that there is no amnesty for crimes and atrocities committed after the signing of the Lomé Accord last July. The international community will not tolerate further atrocities. Release all abductees, particularly the women and children, and work with the Government and NGOs to see them reintegrated into society."[20] There is no record of what Jackson actually said to Taylor, Sankoh, or Kabbah.

WHAT'S IN IT FOR JESSE

In April 2000, Jackson asked to meet with Secretary of State Madeleine Albright. On Jackson's agenda was how the State Department could help him promote the business of his friends in Africa once he completed his term as a special envoy. After a brief discussion of how Jackson could be useful in the Liberia–Sierra Leone crisis, Susan Rice laid it out in black and white in a briefing memo for Albright:

> "Reverend Jackson has other ideas that he will likely raise. We welcome his wish to be involved in our HIV/AIDS initiative, perhaps by spearheading a publicity campaign in Africa, and in connection with the Durban meeting in July. Earlier this year, he led a trade mission to Ghana and Nigeria. He will want to discuss his interest in promoting American business, particularly telecommunications. In May, he will attend a business conference in the Silicon Valley with Hewlett-Packard, Kaiser, Motorola and others. He has ties to Enron."[21]

By May 2000, the fighting in Sierra Leone took on crisis proportions after Sankoh's guerrillas murdered UN peacekeepers and took five hundred of them hostage. The State Department knew that Taylor was providing safe haven to the RUF, and yet Jackson phoned Taylor on May 4,

2000, to reassure him. "One could argue that it's not your business because you're not involved…The State Department assumes you will play a positive role."[22] That simply wasn't true.

Three days later, Jackson called to encourage Taylor again. "Brother Taylor, word is coming through that you are playing a constructive role. Two or three wire service stories. Congratulations! Your public leadership is important." Jackson then gushed about the "importance of you talking sense" to Sankoh and the RUF. "This could be Dr. Taylor's finest hour!" Jackson said pointedly to Howard Jeter, who was on the call and was not a Taylor fan, "This side should publicly acknowledge what Charles Taylor is doing."[23]

Jackson had more kind words for Taylor when he arrived at Robertsfield International Airport in Liberia on May 19, in the midst of the hostage crisis Taylor had helped orchestrate. "President Taylor has been doing a commendable job negotiating for the release of the hostages," Jackson said. "All the hostages should be freed, and freed now. There is no basis for delay. There is no basis for negotiation." After this absurdity, he went on to make a backhanded apology for slavery. "At least in slavery, while we were hurt, our bodies were kept whole for work. But in this fratricidal war in Sierra Leone it is worse than slavery, for it's fratricide, it's genocide, it's maiming the innocent."[24]

The State Department noted that Taylor requested a "one-on-one with Jackson," which lasted about thirty minutes. At the end of the group meeting, Taylor summoned RUF protégé Sam Bockarie, a bush commander whose troops had taken the UN troops hostage in Sierra Leone's diamond mining district.[25] All pretence of Taylor's innocence in the kidnappings vanished.

Jackson made one last phone call, on May 21, 2000, to President Kabbah of Sierra Leone, after having spoken with President Alpha Umar Konare of Mali. "Do you believe that Lomé minus Sankoh can go forward?" Jackson asked. "No problem! Those who do not agree with Foday Sankoh are my friends," Kabbah said. "Very solid," Jackson replied. "That is Konare's view. RUF minus Sankoh."[26]

And then, Jackson simply lost interest in the fate of Nigerian and Malian peacekeepers, and African children who were getting massacred, mutilated, and raped in the bush. Another Bush loomed on the horizon. Africa would have to wait until another day for the mercurial Jackson, who now cast his remarkable talents and energies into a U.S. election campaign.

Jackson has never faced hard questions about his role in the troubles of Sierra Leone and Liberia. Now that the UN-backed High Court for Sierra Leone has indicted Charles Taylor and many of his RUF cronies for war crimes, it's time those questions were asked.

APPENDIX

Many of the photographs and documents* on the following pages have never before been seen by the public. Except where otherwise noted, they have been selected from the author's extensive personal collection.

---

* Language used by Noah Robinson in some of these documents may be offensive to some.

PATRIOTISM, JESSE JACKSON STYLE

No flags or patriotic banners are found at Jackson's PUSH meeting held September 15, 2001, just four days after the terrorist attack on the United States. But there was room for a gigantic portrait of himself.

Jesse criticized Americans' pained reaction: "We saw the Twin Towers of capitalism come crashing down. We saw the Pentagon buried beneath the rubble. In the face of that, the reaction has been scapegoating!"

JESSE AND THE DICTATORS

GAMMA PRESS

Cigars with Castro...

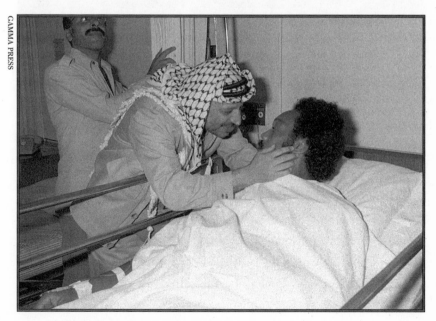

GAMMA PRESS

...and the kiss of life from Yasser Arafat.

JESSE'S NOT-SO-INNOCENT BEGINNINGS

Jesse Jackson (left) and his half-brother Noah Robinson (holding plaque).

Jesse Jackson (left) introduced Robinson to his pal Jeff Fort (seated in throne), leader of Chicago's violent Black P Stone Nation street gang. After he was imprisoned for cocaine trafficking, Fort changed the name to El Rukn, Arabic for "The Foundation," and sought official recognition as a religious organization so his gang could meet in jail.

INSIDE EL RUKN'S SECRET CRIME WORLD

"If El Rukn is a religious group, its sacraments are narcotics trafficking, intimidation, terror, and human sacrifice." —Cook County prosecutor Richard M. Daley

A Chicago police surveillance photo of El Rukn temple.

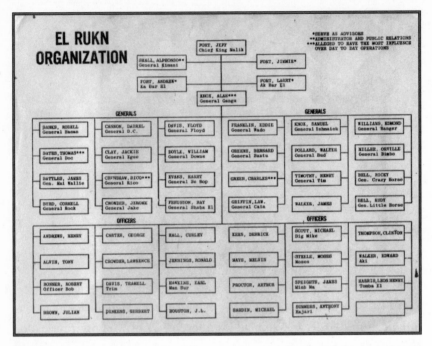

Jesse Jackson's street gang buddies were as organized and dangerous as a Mafia crime family.

CODE NAMES USED BY SUBJECTS

REFLECTION	PICTURE, PHOTO
TOE TO TOE	FACE TO FACE, TALK
BODACIOUS	WISE ASS
HEEL	POLICE
HEEL STATION	POLICE STATION
BIG HEEL	~~POLICE~~/FED'S
COCKTAILS	MARIJUANA: ROACH
FERFECT	MARIJUANA
STERN	COCAINE
BLONDIE	*Sgt* ~~DET~~ DAN BRANNIGAN CPD
LUMBERJACK	DET RICH KOLOVITZ CPD
CALENDAR	ONE YEAR ~~MONTH~~
GREY BICYCLE	POLICE CAR
RENTAL BIKE	RENTAL CAR
BIKE	CAR
LOVE	1/~~100/1000~~ (LOVE LEFT = 100/ LOVE RIGHT = 1000)
TRUTH	2/~~200/2000~~ (TRUTH LEFT = 200/ TRUTH RIGHT = 2000)
PEACE	3/~~300/3000~~ (PEACE LEFT = 300/ PEACE RIGHT = 3000)
FREEDOM	4/~~400/4000~~ (FREEDOM LEFT = 400/ FREEDOM RIGHT= 4000)
JUSTICE	5/~~500/5000~~ (JUSTICE LEFT = 500/ JUSTICE RIGHT = 5000)
GRAPE	10
HALF GRAPE	5
MECCA	CHICAGO
LLOW	~~ROOM~~- House- Apartment
BLANKET	~~HOUSE~~/82nd Marshfield - Dianes house
LOCAL YOKEL	SMALL TOWN POLICE
EMIR	EL RUKN GENERAL
COLOR	MONEY
ALL THE PRINCIPLES	5/~~500/5000~~ (ALL THE PRINCIPLES LEFT = 500/ ALL THE PRINCIPLES RIGHT = 5000)
TANGERINE	$30.00
ORANGE	$50.00
SEED	$1.00
PERRY MASON	LAWYER
DOUBLE BREASTED	PROSECUTOR STATE/FEDERAL
MEDINA	MILWAUKEE
STEER	HEROIN
HUE	MONEY
DRIVE IN	DOPE HOUSE
TIME NEVER WAS	7
MASALIK's	EL RUKN MEMBERS
CREATION	~~ONE DAY~~ One Week
BODY SLAM	SHOOTING OR BEATING
LAST SUNSET	YESTERDAY
LAW DEMONSTRATION	TRIAL/HEARING

MOST CONVERSATIONS ARE PRECEDED BY THE PHRASE "IN THE SCIENCE OF"

Chicago police cracked El Rukn's code of drug jargon and arrested dozens of the gang's members. Forty-six counts of racketeering, conspiracy, and weapons violations were brought against them.

Jackson's Half Brother: A Case Study in Criminology

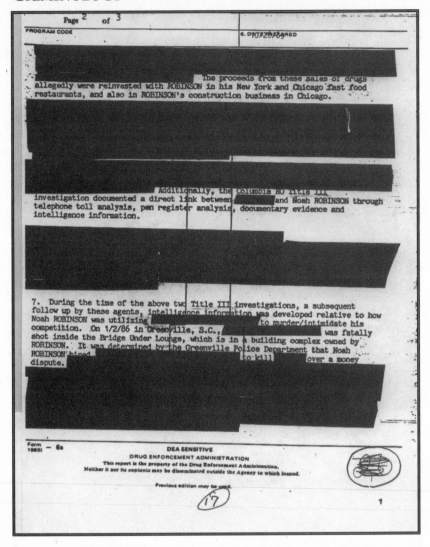

Page 2 of 3

PROGRAM CODE

6. DATE PREPARED

The proceeds from these sales of drugs allegedly were reinvested with ROBINSON in his New York and Chicago fast food restaurants, and also in ROBINSON's construction business in Chicago.

Additionally, the Columbia RO Title III investigation documented a direct link between ___ and Noah ROBINSON through telephone toll analysis, pen register analysis, documentary evidence and intelligence information.

7. During the time of the above two Title III investigations, a subsequent follow up by these agents, intelligence information was developed relative to how Noah ROBINSON was utilizing ___ to murder/intimidate his competition. On 1/2/86 in Greenville, S.C., ___ was fatally shot inside the Bridge Under Lounge, which is in a building complex owned by ROBINSON. It was determined by the Greenville Police Department that Noah ROBINSON hired ___ to kill ___ over a money dispute.

Form 1980) — 6a

DEA SENSITIVE
DRUG ENFORCEMENT ADMINISTRATION
This report is the property of the Drug Enforcement Administration.
Neither it nor its contents may be disseminated outside the Agency to which loaned.

Previous edition may be used.

17

1

Despite his middle-class background and Wharton education, Jackson's half brother and shakedown partner Noah Robinson became the leader of a drug ring, as shown by internal memos from the Drug Enforcement Agency (featured on this and the following page).

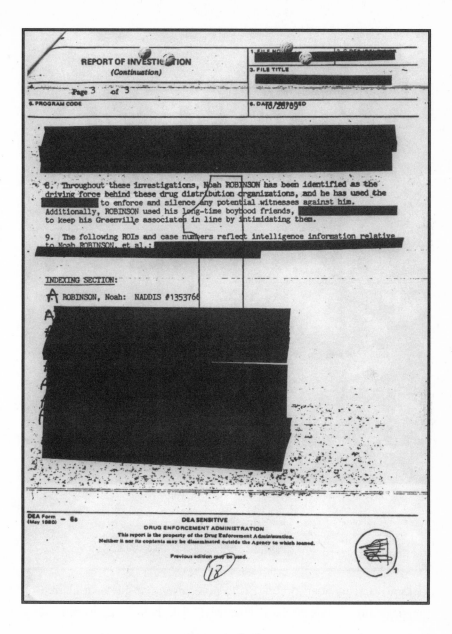

REPORT OF INVESTIGATION
(Continuation)

Page 3 of 3

1. FILE NO. 2. G-DEP IDENT.

3. FILE TITLE

5. PROGRAM CODE

6. DATE 10/26/89

8. Throughout these investigations, Noah ROBINSON has been identified as the driving force behind these drug distribution organizations, and he has used the ▮▮▮▮▮▮ to enforce and silence any potential witnesses against him. Additionally, ROBINSON used his long-time boyhood friends, ▮▮▮▮▮▮ to keep his Greenville associates in line by intimidating them.

9. The following ROIs and case numbers reflect intelligence information relative to Noah ROBINSON, et al.:

INDEXING SECTION:

A ROBINSON, Noah: NADDIS #1353766

THE "REVEREND" JACKSON'S BEST PUPIL

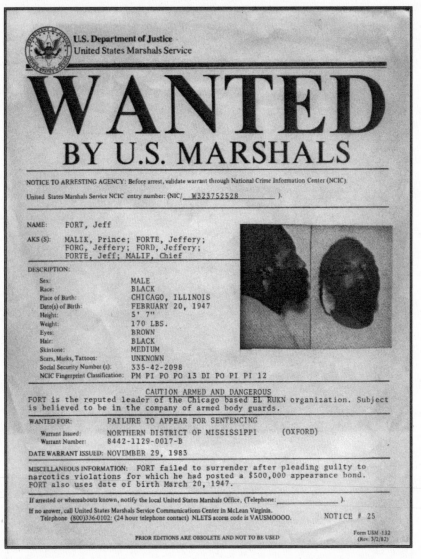

Jackson—a seminarian dropout who never even had his own church or congregation—claims to have "baptized" Jeff Fort in their early days together. Perhaps Fort should have sought the services of a real "Reverend."

NEVER PUT ANYTHING IN WRITING

Given the options' readily available to me, in terms of courses of action against you for your betrayal (of my trust), treachery (stealing my money at gun point) and assassination set up (giving Hunt the gun to blow me up in my own office), telling the law have you was the kindest, most considerate move that I could have made on you. You didn't deserve to get getaway or have a chance to run. Since the day you took off, I wasn't particularly mad at you, maybe disappointed, for a simultaneous cold/chilling and warm/exhilarating (good feeling) feeling came over me. You would be the example, you would answer by the rules of Bones' law. So, I said to myself, let him enjoy, splurge, rip-it-up, have fun, because you were already gone. No doubt in my mind. Or yours either. It was just a matter of time. And place. And method.

Noah Robinson sent this death threat to the imprisoned Leroy Barber, who then turned it over to authorities. Years later, when Noah made good on his threat to have Barber killed, prosecutors produced the letter and convinced the court to lock up Jackson's half brother for life.

Racial Healing Runs in the Family

> **Noah R Robinson**
>
> "Turd "McMahan,
>
> So that you KNOW AND SWEAT OVER whats' coming. Everytime you CROSS the line of the law, I'm going to have my lawyers strike lightning in your ASS. And you ain't got much ass! You Irish cracker cops think you're above the law of the land, you make and play by your own rules. School now begins. Listen up: The one principal flaw that I've detected is that all of you — Brannigan, O'Callaghan, Fitzmaurice, Wolf, etc — ARE dumb as hell and seek to compensate by being dirty as hell. I've been studying and observing you punks. You guys are your own worse enemy. Your combined I.Q. amounts to your shoe size. Fuck with me again, anytime!!

Just as Jesse brandished his prejudice against Jews in his infamous "Hymietown" interview, his half brother and partner Noah Robinson wasn't shy about using racial slurs. In this correspondence he calls a white police officer a "cracker," among other things.

UNCLASSIFIED

RELEASED IN FULL

<u>Rev. Jackson call to RUF Representative Omrie Golley</u>

- The RUF has repeatedly told us it wants peace in Sierra Leone. We have supported your calls for a dialogue with the Government.

- The RUF's recent actions make us wonder if the RUF is realy interested in peace. The RUF had built up some credibility with the international community. That credibility may now be lost.

- I am saddened by the recent RUF attack on Port Loko. The Malian ECOMOG contingent had never taken any offensive action against you. (Note: Golley may claim the Malians had attacked RUF positions--it is not true.)

- Only a few days before this attack against the Malians, you were considering the possibility that Malian troops could monitor a ceasefire. That possibility is now dead.

- I have also read the recent UN Human Rights Report on the atrocities committed by the RUF in Songo and Masiaka. The RUF must stop this senseless violence.

- We want the peace process to succeed as much as you do. It is essential that the RUF act now to show that it is serious about peace.

- For the Lome talks to be successful, the RUF should take the following steps:

  1. Agree to begin dialogue with the Government immediately and without preconditions. You can talk about Sankoh's release after you and the Government sit down at the negotiating table.

  2. Release ALL hostages, including children, women, and captured soldiers. (UNICEF has cataloged more than 3000 children kidnapped by the RUF since January.)

  3. Open the roads to humanitarian relief.

  4. Declare an immediate end to attacks against civilians and hostile action against ECOMOG. And stick to it.

UNITED STATES DEPARTMENT OF STATE
REVIEW AUTHORITY: HARRY R. MELONE
DATE/CASE ID: 5 OCT 2001 200004266

UNCLASSIFIED

Here's what the State Department instructed Jackson to say...

UNCLASSIFIED

Jackson-Golley:

JJ: anxious to do whatever do get peace

G: Grateful for US role. Remember your trip to Sierra Leone.
Heartened by your words. This is a political and social problem
rooted in failure of governance. Politicans haven't taken care
of young and disadvantage. Our movement had to start a struggle
that let us to this point. HJ particulrly helpful. Hope for
peace. Mindful of kabbah approach. Seek your help and
guidance. Only social and political settlemetn will solve
problem. Military force would sovle anything. We were forced
to use force.

JJ: most difficult mile is last mile. Glad taylor made staement
today urge stop to killing glad kabah made his offer sundat. I
want focus on outcome rather than process of getting there. I
urge all parties to get beyond process and get to table. I want
to talk to ruf leadership as soon as I can. Us stands ready to
urge negotiations over confrontation. Too many lives lost. At
point of mutual recognition.

G: pleased. Will pass words on immediately
Can be sure I will do all I can

JJ: ruf leadership in states few weeks ago. Couldn't meet.
Talked with kabbah urged to spare fs (in conakry) meeting with
leadership core inlud fs is right thing to do

G: (voice breaking) grateful for usg help.

UNCLASSIFIED

...and here's the transcript of what Jackson actually said.

UNCLASSIFIED

RELEASED IN FULL

Rev. Jackson call to RUF Leader Sankoh, Sat June 12, 7:15 a.m.

REV. JACKSON: think and pray for yo~ ~~~~~ ~~~~~
Following talks daily
Congratulations for bringing them b.
Can't afford to miss this time
Good news from Yugoslavia,...
But every time make peace, they men
happening in Togo
Today in Chicago organizing relief
Want you to know your role is real

SANKOH: my question (release) is not a precondition, but very important to be addressed now. Government cannot keep on promising without doing anything. Just mere words. Means if I don't sign peace accord I won't be free. I should be free before I sign any documents.

REV. JACKSON: MELROSE is in Lome. You can trust him. You should get the word to him. We can get the thing on track. The key in this process is you. In Lome, you said can't nobody free you because your mind is already free. Like Mandela was in jail. Don't worry about it. World will know that yours is the biggest role. You will be free when this is over.

Sankoh: ok. I'm not worried much about my release. Know god will take care of me with your intervention. I trust in god.

REV. JACKSON: there is momentum and focus on SL. Every time mention Kosovo, mention SL at the same time and your role in making peace. If you make it happen there will be a big payoff

Sankoh: ok thank you very much. Will do all to succeed. There is no turning back. Hope you will continue to pray for us.

REV. JACKSON: also talked to Obasanjo. He is aware of process. Thinks positively about you. Wants to rebuild his own country and wants peace in Sierra Leone. You are key to making this happen. Don't worry you are going to be free. World will make it happen.

Sankoh: ok. My freedom not a precondition. In hands of god. Government is saying do process of law. No freedom unless sign a document.

REV. JACKSON: that's just talk. You focus on what is real. You are going to be free and pardoned. Focus on what is real.

Sankoh: you're a man of god. Trust you.

REV. JACKSON: let's say a prayer. If you need something, let Melrose know.

UNITED STATES DEPARTMENT OF STATE
REVIEW AUTHORITY: HARRY R. MELONE
DATE/CASE ID: 12 OCT 2001 200004266

UNCLASSIFIED

Jackson pumps up rebel leader Foday Sankoh.

UNCLASSIFIED

TelCon May 7, 2000
9:00 PM EST

RELEASED IN PART
B1, 1.5(B), 1.5(D)

Rev. Jackson - President Taylor of Liberia
(DAS Jeter on call, McIlvaine notetaker)

Rev.J: Brother Taylor, word is coming through that you are playing a constructive role. Two or three wire service stories. Congratulations! Your public leadership is important. Your reading on the situation in Sierra Leone?

CT (a little groggy at first, then very focussed. it was one in the morning his time):

B1

Rev. J: Are you going to Conakry (MRU Summit Monday)?

CT: Yes, I'll be there.

Rev. J: The importance of you talking sense to them. This could be Dr. Taylor's finest hour!

HJ: You have a critical role to play. This is not only a crisis for Sierra Leone, it is a crisis for the region and for the international community because of the UN involvement.

CT: I am trying to do a lot of things.

Rev. J: How can we help?

UNITED STATES DEPARTMENT OF STATE
CLASSIFIED BY DEPT. OF STATE, F. MACHAK, DAS, A/RPS
REVIEW AUTHORITY: HARRY R. MELONE
DATE/CASE ID: 7 NOV 2001 200004266
CLASSIFICATION: CONFIDENTIAL REASON: 1.6(6)
DECLASSIFY AFTER: 7 MAY 2020

UNCLASSIFIED

A conversation between Jackson and chum Charles Taylor.

Notes

Introduction

1 Jesse Lee Peterson, *From Rage to Responsibility* (St. Paul: Paragon House, 2000), 14, 26.
2 Jesse Lee Peterson, "Jesse Jackson: Problem Profiteer," *New American*, 14 August 2000.
3 Louis R. Harlan, ed., *The Autobiographical Writings*, vol. 1 of *The Booker T. Washington Papers* (Urbana: The University of Illinois Press, 1972), 430.
4 Barbara Reynolds, *Jesse Jackson: The Man, The Movement, The Myth* (Washington, D.C.: JFJ Association Publishers), 1975. Reprint, 1985, under the title *Jesse Jackson: America's David*. All page citations are to the reprint edition.

Chapter 1: Manufacturing a Myth

1 Marshall Frady, *Jesse: The Life and Pilgrimage of Jesse Jackson* (New York: Random House, 1996), 229.
2 "Aide of Dr. King Vows to Try to Restore Calm to Chicago," *Chicago Tribune*, 6 April 1968; Frady, *Jesse: The Life*, 229. See Reynolds, *Jesse Jackson*, 278, for a photo of Jackson in sunglasses and turtleneck addressing the city council.
3 Reynolds, *Jesse Jackson*, 82.
4 Ibid., 81–97.
5 Frady, *Jesse: The Life*, 229.

6   When the picture first appeared, it was correctly identified. "Memphis Approves a Memorial Parade; Clergy and Teachers Assail Mayor," *New York Times*, 6 April 1968; See also, Reynolds, *Jesse Jackson*, 86.

7   Reynolds, *Jesse Jackson*, 88.

8   Ibid., 89.

9   Hurley Green, interview by the author, 10 May 2001.

10 The 28 March 1968 events are recounted in *Report of the Department of Justice Task Force to Review the FBI Martin Luther King, Jr. Security and Assassination Investigations*, 11 January 1977, 18 (declassified 29 September 1997).

11 Hurley Green interview; Reynolds, *Jesse Jackson*, 86. A fuller account of this fateful meeting can be found in David J. Garrow, *Bearing the Cross: Martin Luther King, Jr., and the Southern Christian Leadership Conference* (New York: William Morrow & Co., 1986), 616.

12 Rita Beamish, "Candidate Close-up: Jackson's Evolution from Confronter to Mediator," Associated Press, 8 May 1988.

13 Reynolds, *Jesse Jackson*, 96–97.

14 Ibid., 97.

15 Thomas Landess and Richard Quinn, *Jesse Jackson and the Politics of Race* (Ottowa, Ill.: Jameson Books, 1985), 8.

16 Reynolds, *Jesse Jackson*, 23–24. Robinson died on 28 January 1997.

17 Gail Sheehey, "Jackson's Lifelong Quest for Legitimacy," *Vanity Fair* profile reprinted in the *Chicago Tribune*, 12 June 1988, C1. See also Reynolds, *Jesse Jackson*, 36.

18 Frady, *Jesse: The Life*, 126.

19 Ibid., 139.

20 Gaylord Shaw, "A Clash Within: The Mixed Blessings of Rev. Jackson," *Los Angeles Times*, 16 December 1987, A1.

21 Martin Luther King Jr., *Why We Can't Wait* (New York: Harper & Row, 1964).

22 Joan Blocher, interview by the author, 11 May 2001.

23 Hurley Green interview; Frady, *Jesse: The Life*, 187.

24 Frady, *Jesse: The Life*, 189.

25 Reynolds, *Jesse Jackson*, 54.

26 "Faculty Members Describe Selma Situation," *Maroon*, 2 April 1965, 1 (University of Chicago student newspaper obtained from the University of Chicago library).

27 Karine Schomer, interview by the author, 11 June 2001. Her father's commitment to the civil rights movement was such that he had taken her and her brother by train for the 28 August 1963 March on Washington, where they heard King deliver his now famous "I Have a Dream" speech.

28 Four-page handwritten document, undated; "Jesse Jackson: Notes on an Intellectual Profile," Howard Schomer archive, Harvard Divinity School. Collection bMS 555/1, Box 45, Folder 14. Hereafter Schomer archive.

29 Schomer archive, Boxes 21–22. Schomer filed for conscientious objector status in 1940, well before his ordination as a minister with the United Church of Christ the following year.

30 Schomer archive, bMS 551/1, Box 32: "Refusal of Communist Oath for Passport, 1958 and 1963."

31 Reynolds, *Jesse Jackson*, 55.

32 Frady, *Jesse: The Life*, 193.

33 Ibid., 195.

34 Cirilo McSween, interview by the author.

35 Reynolds, *Jesse Jackson*, 57. Frady, *Jesse: The Life*, 199, says Jackson became, at age twenty-four, the youngest of King's staff, "some six months after his expedition down to Selma."

36 Quote from Jackson biography on the Rainbow/PUSH website: www.rainbowpush.org. Accessed May 2001.

37 Reynolds, *Jesse Jackson*, 61.

38 David J. Garrow, *The FBI and Martin Luther King, Jr.: From "Solo" to Memphis* (New York: W. W. Norton & Company, 1981), 501. Reynolds, *Jesse Jackson*, 57–65; Landess and Quinn, *Jesse Jackson*, 27.

39 *Fellowship Missionary Baptist Church Historical Synopsis*, May 2000.

40 Frady, *Jesse: The Life*, 205.

41 Sharon Thistlethwaite, interview by the author, 1 June 2001.

42 Interview by the author, CTS, Chicago, 11 May 2001.

43 Ibid.

44 Caesar Leflur, interview by the author.

45 Hurley Green interview.

46 McSween interview.

47 Landess and Quinn, *Jesse Jackson*, 42–44.

48 Barbara Reynolds, interview by the author, 24 September 2001.

49 Reynolds, *Jesse Jackson*, 157.

50 Private communication, undated, Reverend Hiram Crawford Sr., made available to the author by his son, Dr. Hiram Crawford Jr., and his widow, Eleanor Crawford.

51 Landess and Quinn, *Jesse Jackson*, 45.

52 Ibid., 44.

53 Reynolds, *Jesse Jackson*, 142.

54 Ibid. The gang was initially named after the territory it controlled at South 64th Street and Blackstone Avenue. Fort referred to the gang as the "Black Stone" Rangers; later, the Black P Stone Rangers or Black P Stone Nation.

55 Government parole memorandum, dated 15 September 1997, *Re: Noah Robinson* (Docket 89 CR 908-31), Victoria J. Peters and Matthew M. Schneider, Assistant U.S. Attorneys for the Northern District of Illinois.

56 Reynolds, *Jesse Jackson*, 142–143.

57 *Racial Disturbance Following Assassination of Martin Luther King, Jr., Chicago, Illinois, beginning April 4, 1968,* Report from the FBI Chicago Field Office to Headquarters, 18 April 1968; cf. Michael Friedly with David Gallen, *Martin Luther King, Jr.: The FBI File* (New York: Carroll & Graf Publishers Inc., 1993), 586–587.

58 Interviews with Jackson friends Hermene Hartman and Cirilo McSween; Caesar Leflur,

Reverend Johnny Hunter; Hiram Crawford Jr.; former Jackson employee Glen Bone III; Chicago police investigators; federal prosecutors; and others.

59   Sources in Chicago provided the author with a copy of this picture.

60   Interview, Chicago criminal justice official.

61   Russ Ewing, "Jesse Jackson: Penthouse Interview," *Penthouse*, April 1973, 110.

62   Landess and Quinn, *Jesse Jackson*, 45.

63   Chicago criminal justice officials, interview by the author; see also Tom Brune and James Ylisela Jr., "The Making of Jeff Fort," *Chicago* magazine, November 1988, 205. Noah Robinson mentioned the Springfield march in his 1984 letter to Fort's parole officer. See Leanita McClain, "Jeff Fort Can't Be 'Rewritten,'" *Chicago Tribune Sunday*, 24 April 1984.

64   The main court cases involving Noah Robinson Jr. are 89 CR 907 and 89 CR 908, with numerous appeals subsequently filed, tried, and lost, including 98-3014 and 98-3015. Southern District of Illinois court records, Federal Court building, 219 S. Dearborn, Chicago, Ill., 20th floor.

CHAPTER 2: STEPPING OUT

1   Landess and Quinn, *Jesse Jackson*, 52. An uncritical account: Eddie Stone, *Jesse Jackson* (Los Angeles: Holloway House, 1979, 1984 revised).

2   "President Clinton's Speech to the Wall Street Project Luncheon," 13 January 2000, *White House Briefing*, Federal News Service.

3   The $22 million figure would appear to be the combined assets of the two then-existing black banks in Chicago, which grew from $5 million to $22 million during those early years of Operation Breadbasket (Landess and Quinn, *Jesse Jackson*, 46). Many of the jobs Jackson claimed he forced white-owned companies to set aside for blacks were never actually created.

4   Jesse Jackson, interview by the author, 21 December 2001.

5   The Reverend Johnny Hunter, interview by the author, 12 June 2001. The pastor of Jackson's church, the Reverend Charles Jenkins, provided an identical account in a separate interview in Chicago, 16 September 2001.

6   Interview with Dr. Hiram Crawford Jr. and with Eleanor Crawford, 7 December, 2001. Hiram Crawford Jr. served as his father's driver during the 1960s and was personally privy to this and other clashes between his father and Jackson.

7   Reverend Franklin was shot dead by gang members during a burglary of his Detroit home in 1979.

8   Martita Hines, interview by the author, 16 September 2001.

9   Edith Banks and Walterine Johnson, interviews by the author, 16 September 2001.

10   Cook County real estate records clerk, interview by the author, Chicago.

11   LaSalle Bank official, interview by the author.

12   Documents 21 272 546 and 21 272 547, with the Cook County Register of Deeds. McSween is still on the board of the Independence Bank. McSween interview, 19 September 2001.

13   Ewing, "Jesse Jackson: Penthouse Interview," 108.

14 Hurley Green interview; businessmen at the LaSalle Street Project conference in Chicago, interview by the author, May 2001.

15 Reynolds, *Jesse Jackson*, 327; Landess and Quinn, *Jesse Jackson*, 52–53.

16 Landess and Quinn, *Jesse Jackson*, 53; Reynolds, *Jesse Jackson*, 327–332.

17 Reynolds, *Jesse Jackson*, 331.

18 Hermene Hartman, interview by the author, 22 October 2001.

19 Landess and Quinn, *Jesse Jackson*, 81; cf. Jeff Gerth, "Questions Arise on Jackson Group's Finances," *New York Times*, 29 January 1984, 1.

20 Angela Parker, "SCLC Sets Chicago Unit Probe," *Chicago Tribune*, 28 November 1971, 1. Parker subsequently discovered that Jackson's failure to register the foundation with the Illinois state attorney general's office or the Internal Revenue Service, as required by law, led the state to dissolve the foundation on 15 November 1971. Angela Parker, "Learn Black Expo Skipped Legal Filing," *Chicago Tribune*, 2 December 1971, 1.

21 Reynolds, *Jesse Jackson*, 169–170, 349.

22 Parker, "Learn Black Expo Skipped Legal Filing."

23 Reynolds, *Jesse Jackson*, 324.

24 Parker, "SCLC Sets Chicago Unit Probe." See also Reynolds, *Jesse Jackson*, 326, and Landess and Quinn, *Jesse Jackson*, 54.

25 Reynolds, *Jesse Jackson*, 347; Landess and Quinn, *Jesse Jackson*, 55.

26 Angela Parker, "Rev. Jackson Suspended from Breadbasket Duties," *Chicago Tribune*, 4 December 1971.

27 Angela Parker, "Jackson Defends Goals; Rips Reporter in Breadbasket Talk," *Chicago Tribune*, 5 December 1971, 4. See also the accounts of Reynolds, *Jesse Jackson*, 348; Landess and Quinn, *Jesse Jackson*, 62.

28 Ibid.

29 Reynolds, *Jesse Jackson*, 382.

30 Barbara Reynolds interview.

31 Landess and Quinn, *Jesse Jackson*, 56.

32 The letter, dated 12 December 1971, is quoted in full by Reynolds, *Jesse Jackson*, 351.

33 Angela Parker, "He Charges Suspension Ties Hands," *Chicago Tribune*, 12 December 1971.

34 Reynolds, *Jesse Jackson*, 353–354. Abernathy's letter was dated 16 December 1971.

35 Reynolds, *Jesse Jackson*, 155–156. Reynolds reproduced the complete auditor's report of Black Expo '71 in the appendix of her book, 455–461.

36 Barbara Reynolds, quoted in Landess and Quinn, *Jesse Jackson*, 64.

37 Ewing, "Jesse Jackson: Penthouse Interview," 108.

38 Confidential source, Cook County official.

39 Jesse Jackson interview, 21 December 2001.

40 "Thomas P. Sullivan, "Report for 1977: United States Attorney, Northern District of Illinois," 1.

41 Cited by Reynolds, *Jesse Jackson*, 170.

42 Frady, *Jesse: The Life,* 122.

43 "SCLC Directors Give Robinson Top Breadbasket Post," *Chicago Tribune*, 19 March

1972, 3; Herb Greenberg, "Noah of Fast Food: Too Much to Swallow?" *Chicago Tribune*, 12 February 1984.

44 Chicago police gang unit investigators, interview by the author, 14 December 2001.

45 Philip Wattley and Steven Pratt, "Convictions Not Expected to Hamper P Stones," *Chicago Tribune,* 31 March 1972.

46 "Kin Warns Jesse on Work Pact," *Chicago Tribune*, 6 August 1973, 1.

47 "SCLC Directors," *Chicago Tribune*.

48 Robert Unger and William Mullen, "Minority Contracts: A Family Affair," *Chicago Tribune*, 11 September 1978, 1.

49 Frady, *Jesse: The Life,* 123; see also Tom Morganthau, "What Makes Jesse Run?" *Newsweek*, 14 November 1983.

50 Reynolds, *Jesse Jackson*, 171. Reynolds published "The Kingdom Theory" in its entirety in the appendix to her book. A detailed discussion of Jackson's theory can be found in Landess and Quinn, *Jesse Jackson*, 36–40.

51 Frady, *Jesse: The Life,* 260.

52 Retired Chicago police detective Sergeant Richard Kolovitz, interview by the author, 19 December 2001. Other Chicago police officers and federal prosecutors confirmed the accuracy of his recollection.

53 Jesse Jackson interview, 21 December 2001.

54 Ibid.

55 Kolovitz interview.

56 Frady, *Jesse: The Life,* 124.

57 Glen Bone III, interview by the author, 13 July 2001.

58 Clarence Page, "Airline Accused of Discrimination by Black Employees," *Chicago Tribune*, 2 January 1972.

59 Mike Royko, *Chicago Daily News*, 24 May 1971, quoted in Reynolds, *Jesse Jackson*, 238–241.

60 Luci Horton, "PUSH Sets Jobs for Blacks Drive," *Chicago Tribune Sunday*, 21 May 1972, 5.

61 Vince Butler, "Avon in Pact with PUSH," *Chicago Tribune*, 12 July 1973. "A meaningful opportunity of our business comes from black and other nonwhite consumers," Avon president David W. Mitchell told reporters. "We believe an equal proportion of the benefits of that business should flow back to black and other nonwhite employees, suppliers, and the communities in which they live."

62 Luci Horton, "New Thrust: Economic Power. PUSH Mushrooms Under Jesse," *Chicago Tribune*, 9 August 1972, 2.

63 Edith Herman, "PUSH Seeks Black Economic Power," *Chicago Tribune*, 26 July 1973.

64 Quoted in Reynolds, *Jesse Jackson*, 292.

65 Edith Herman, "Jesse Preaches Dollar Power at PUSH Parley," *Chicago Tribune*, 27 July 1973, 2.

66 Ibid.

67 Vernon Jarrett, "PUSH Problems Need Deeper Look," *Chicago Tribune*, 18 November 1973; Reynolds, *Jesse Jackson*, 306.

68 Vernon Jarrett, "PUSH Faces Cash Crisis," *Chicago Tribune*, 10 November 1973, 1.

69 *Audit Report of People United to Save Humanity, by Washington, Pittman and McKeever*, 31 December 1972; quoted in Reynolds, *Jesse Jackson*, 465.

70 Jarrett, "PUSH Faces Cash Crisis."

71 Even this sermon, on the story of Nicodemus, was a commentary on contemporary politics, not religion. Jackson was hosted by the St. Stephen AME Church on 2000 W. Washington Blvd. in Chicago. Athelia Knight, "Jesse Mixes Politics, Religion," *Chicago Tribune*, 22 July 1974. Knight reported that it was the first time since June 1968 Jackson had preached a sermon in a church.

72 Landess and Quinn, *Jesse Jackson*, 68.

73 Reynolds, *Jesse Jackson*, 345.

74 Hurley Green interview.

75 Stanley Ziemba, "PUSH Suffering But Not Near Ruin, Board Says," *Chicago Tribune*, 14 November 1973, 10.

76 Reynolds, *Jesse Jackson*, 466.

77 Jarrett, "PUSH Problems Need Deeper Look."

78 Ibid.

79 Reynolds, *Jesse Jackson*, 344.

80 Alan Merridew and Jack Fuller, "Black Gas Station Operators Urged to Fight 'Oil Monopoly,'" *Chicago Tribune*, 6 January 1974.

81 Jesse L. Jackson, "The Legacy of Sam McBride: How One Enemy of Consumers Became an Ally," *Chicago Tribune*, 27 January 1974.

82 McSween interview.

83 PUSH Foundation was incorporated on 21 March 1972 by Bustamante using his law office address, 33 Public Square, in Cleveland. However, both Illinois and Ohio authorities sent it noncompliance notices in May 1974.

84 Landess and Quinn, *Jesse Jackson*, 70–72. On the forgiven debt: Susan J. Smith, "PUSH-Excel Investigated," Associated Press, 25 April 1982.

85 Quoted in Landess and Quinn, *Jesse Jackson*, 71.

86 Ibid.

87 Ibid.

88 Reynolds, *Jesse Jackson*, 155.

89 "The Jesse Jackson Puzzle," *Chicago Tribune*, 29 April 1975.

90 Reynolds, *Jesse Jackson*, 406.

91 "Jarrett Defends Criticisms," *Chicago Tribune*, 23 November 1973; Landess and Quinn, *Jesse Jackson*, 60.

92 Landess and Quinn, *Jesse Jackson*, 58.

93 Ibid., 262.

94 Barbara Reynolds interview.

95 Barbara Reynolds, *No, I Won't Shut Up* (Temple Hills, Md.: JFJ Publishing, 1998).

96 Gary Deeb, "Was Cordell Kicked Upstairs? Or PUSHed?" *Chicago Tribune*, 29 October 1975.

97 Unger and Mullen, "Minority Contracts: A Family Affair."

98   http://www.hob.com/venues/clubvenues/lasvegas/foundationroom.asp.

99   Vernon Jarrett, "Jackson Versus the Anchorman," *Chicago Tribune*, 5 September 1976, Sec. 2, 6.

CHAPTER 3: A TASTE OF THE GREEN

1   Clarence Page, "Rev. Jackson: Does Reach Exceed His Grasp?" *Chicago Tribune*, 9 September 1979.

2   William C. Hidlay, "Candidate Close-up (part 2): Speaking for the Poor Made Jackson Comfortable," Associated Press, 30 April 1988.

3   Arthur Siddon, "Big Names Targets of IRS Spying," *Chicago Tribune*, 3 October 1975.

4   S. R. Murray, C. A. Murray, F. E. Gragg, L. M. Kumi, and P. A. Parham, *The National Evaluation of the PUSH for Excellence Project*. Washington: American Institutes for Research, March 1982. AIR_78602, FR. ED 240 225, 87. The American Institutes for Research was a nonprofit research agency closely affiliated with the Department of Health, Education, and Welfare (later, the Department of Education).

5   Ibid., 94.

6   Ibid., 20.

7   According to PUSH-Excel financial statements, the Los Angeles city grant was "the inception of financial transactions in the accounts of PUSH-Excel. Earlier moneys for PUSH-Excel programs were funneled directly into Operation PUSH. "PUSH For Excellence Inc., Notes to Financial Statements for the year ended 31 December 1993 and 1992," IRS Form 990 on file with the State of Illinois Attorney General, received 3 June 1994.

8   Michael Coakley, "Jesse's L.A. School Program Puts Him on California Map," *Chicago Tribune*, 18 September 1977, 18.

9   Murray et al., *The National Evaluation*, 22.

10   Ibid.

11   Landess and Quinn, *Jesse Jackson*, 75.

12   J. A. Califano Jr., *Governing America* (New York: Simon & Schuster, 1981), 294.

13   Murray et al., *The National Evaluation*, 24.

14   Ibid., 26.

15   Ibid., 34; Freedom of Information Act.

16   James Coates, "Jackson's Student PUSH Wins HEW Grant, Praise," *Chicago Tribune*, 6 January 1978.

17   Landess and Quinn, *Jesse Jackson*, 73–74; Shaw, "A Clash Within."

18   Landess and Quinn, *Jesse Jackson*, 78.

19   Quoted in Landess and Quinn, *Jesse Jackson*, 78.

20   Thomas Todd, quoted in William Brashler, "Dr. J: He Has a Scheme," *New Republic*, 17 October 1983.

21   Vernon Jarrett, "It's Time to Ask Pointed Questions," *Chicago Tribune*, 22 January 1978.

22   Murray et al., *The National Evaluation*, 101–105.

23   Douglas Foster, "Jesse Jackson: A Populist on Wall Street?" *Mother Jones*, March 2000.

24   Casey Banas, "Jesse's Children Sent Six Miles to Class," *Chicago Tribune*, 21 December 1975, 5.

25   Frady, *Jesse: The Life*, 156.

26   Author's notes and audio tape from the Rainbow/PUSH coalition LaSalle Street confer-
     ence, 9 May 2001.

27   Eddie Slaughter, interview by the author, 13 July 2001.

28   Kenneth R. Timmerman, "Farming While Black," *Insight* magazine, 3 September 2001.

29   Tom Wolfe, *Radical Chic and Mau-mauing the Flak Catchers* (New York: Farrar, Straus
     & Giroux, 1970), 98.

30   Ibid.

31   Murray et al., *The National Evaluation*, 34.

32   The "P" stood for "Peace, prosperity, people, and power," according to the gang, which
     published an occasional newsletter called "Stone Black Press." See also Brune and
     Ylisela, "The Making of Jeff Fort."

33   David Young, "Gang Tied to Drug Deaths," *Chicago Tribune*, 23 August 1972.

34   Reverend Johnny Hunter, interview by the author, 28 April 2001.

35   Barbara Reynolds interview.

36   Dino Malcolm, "Where Being Just One of the 'Gang' Is a Deadly Game," *Chicago
     Tribune*, 27 August 1979, 5.

37   Ibid.

38   R. Richard Ciccone, "Jeff Fort's 'Nation': Allah Gets a Chief Priest," *Chicago Tribune*,
     11 April 1976.

39   "A Problem with the P Stones," *Chicago Tribune* editorial, 13 April 1976. In a bizarre
     interview with *Chicago Tribune* reporter R. Richard Ciccone (see "Jeff Fort's 'Nation'),
     Fort tried to explain his new vision of the world. "There was a misconception about the
     Stones," he said. "The world called us Black Stones and viewed us as rejected people.
     In the years to come, the world will see that nation resurrected. The world will see the
     Stones unfold like the budding of a flower."

         Now that he had discovered Islam, Fort said, he planned to move from gang leader
     to priest. "We now understand the symbolic meaning of the Stones as the cornerstone of
     the holy Kaaba in the city of Mecca. It is the Black Stone what will be the headstone of
     the future." The Kaaba is a black meteorite believed by Muslims to have been given to
     Ishmael by the angel Gabriel, and is housed in the courtyard of the Great Mosque.
     Muslims around the world face toward the Kaaba during their five daily prayers. But
     when the Black Stone Rangers first appeared in the 1960s they took their name from
     Blackstone Avenue where many of them lived, which is just a few blocks east of Jesse
     Jackson's house. By the time Fort went to jail in 1972, their numbers had swelled to
     nearly 8,000 members.

40   Jerry Thornton, "Gang Leader, 6 Fur-Clad Followers are Arrested after High-Speed
     Chase," *Chicago Tribune*, 13 December 1980.

41   Federal prosecutors in Chicago, interview by the author.

42   Interview with confidential Chicago source.

43   Barbara Reynolds interview.

44   See 89-CR 907 and 91-1039, the original criminal convictions, and subsequent appeals,
     91-3150 and 92-4041. Robinson's direct involvement with the Black Stone Rangers/El

Rukn gang is summarized in the appeals court decision handed down on 13 September 1999, Docket No. 98-3014 and 98-3015, of 89-CR-908, a companion to Robinson's initial criminal case.

45 Unger and Mullen, "Minority Contracts: A Family Affair."

46 Ibid.

47 David Axelrod, "Black Business Needs Boost, Jackson Says," *Chicago Tribune*, 21 May 1977, Sec. N1, 4.

48 Barbara Reynolds, "PUSH Gets HUD Grant of $75,000," *Chicago Tribune*, 20 May 1978, Sec. 2, 11.

49 Clarence Page, "Rev. Jackson: Does Reach Exceed His Grasp?" *Chicago Tribune*, 9 September 1979, 1.

50 Ibid.

51 I was aided in sketching out the Jackson corporate nebula by Terry Scanlon, Andrew Walker, and Patrick Reilly of the Capital Research Center in Washington, D.C.

52 W. Raymond Wannall, interview by the author, 31 July 2001; see also, W. Raymond Wannall, "Setting Straight the FBI's Counterintelligence Effort," *World & I* (Washington Times Group), January 1987, 167–177.

53 75 C 3295, *ACLU et al. v. City of Chicago, et al.*; ruling by Judge Alfred Y. Kirriand, 26 May 1976. Defendants included FBI director Clarence Kelley, the FBI Special Agent in Charge for Chicago, Richard G. Held, and James Schlesinger, the Director of Central Intelligence.

54 Case file 146-1-51-25110; cables dated 6 January 1972 and 15 January 1972.

55 W. Raymond Wannall interview.

56 *Philadelphia Council of Neighborhood Organizations v. William T. Coleman, Jr., Secretary of Transportation of the United States*, Civil Action 77-180, U.S. District Court for the Eastern District of Pennsylvania; judgment dated 12 September 1977.

57 *Evans v. Lynn*, 537 F.2d 571 (2d Cir.1976), certr. denied; at 595; concurring opinion by Judge Mansfield.

58 Grant Contract # 99-8-1878-33-40. FOIA correspondence with the U.S. Department of Labor, May 1984, provided to the author by the Conservative Caucus Foundation Inc.

59 Michael Wines, "Friends Helped Labor Nominee Move Up, Then Almost Brought Her Down," *New York Times*, 12 April 1997, A16.

60 For Marshall's official biography, see: "U.S. DOL – Ray Marshall," on the Internet at www.dol.gov/dol/asp/public/programs/history/marshall.htm.

61 From Jackson's speech opening the Second Annual Wall Street Project conference, 14 January 1999; http://www.rainbowpush.org/speeches/wallstreetproject.html. Godwin died at the age of fifty-six of a heart attack on 15 November 1998, while playing golf at the exclusive Druid Hills Golf Club in Atlanta.

62 Byron York, "The Alexis Nexus," *American Spectator*, March 1997.

63 FOIA correspondence with the U.S. Department of Labor, provided by the Conservative Caucus Foundation Inc. to the author.

64 HEW was split, effective 4 May 1980, into two newly created agencies, the Department of Education and the Department of Health and Human Services, HHS.

65   Coates, "Jackson's Student PUSH wins HEW Grant, Praise."

66   Murray et al., *The National Evaluation*, 24.

67   Comptroller General of the United States to the Hon. Walter E. Fauntroy, letter, 2 November 1981. Obtained by the author under the Freedom of Information Act. Earlier FOIA correspondence with various government departments by the Conservative Caucus Foundation showed this grant to be worth $700,000.

68   FOIA correspondence with the U.S. Department of Labor, May 1984, provided by the Conservative Caucus Foundation Inc. to the author.

69   York, "The Alexis Nexus"; see also Wines, "Friends Helped Labor Nominee."

70   FOIA correspondence with the U.S. Department of Labor, May 1984, provided by the Conservative Caucus Foundation Inc. to the author.

71   Ibid.

72   "Notice of Award," dated 12 September 1979. FOIA correspondence between the Department of Commerce and the Conservative Caucus Foundation Inc., 21 December 1981.

73   Reynolds, "PUSH Gets HUD Grant of $75,000."

74   Ernest Green, interview by the author, 13 September 2001.

75   Murray et al., *The National Evaluation*, 105.

76   York, "The Alexis Nexus."

77   Ernest Green interview.

CHAPTER 4: TRAVELS WITH YASSER

1   Ray Wannall, "Unrelenting Assaults Against Hoover," *Washington Times*, 1 August 1999.

2   "Communism and the Negro Movement—A Current Analysis," FBI white paper dated 16 October 1963. Stamped Top Secret (declassified on 28 November 1997). Office of Professional Responsibility; FBI Martin Luther King Task Force Records; NN3-60-93-003; Record Group 60, National Archives II, College Park, Md. Hereafter OPR Files.

3   Director, FBI, to Attorney General Robert Kennedy, memo, *Martin Luther King, Jr., Security Matter-C*, 25 June 1962. "Levison told Hunter Pitts O'Dell on 20 June 1962, that in a recent conversation with King, King said he was thinking of getting another administrative assistant. When Levison recommended O'Dell for the job, King said he liked the suggestion, adding, 'No matter what a man was, if he could stand up now and say he is not connected, then as far as I am concerned, he is eligible to work for me.' It is noted that O'Dell was elected under a pseudonym to the National Committee of the CPUSA, at the 17th National Convention of the CPUSA, in December, 1959," Hoover concluded. Quoted in Friendly and Gallen, *Martin Luther King*, 128.

4   United States Senate Internal Security Subcommittee (hereafter SISS), *Scope of Soviet Activity in the United States, Part 12*. Testimony of Benjamin Mandel, Research Director, 6 April 1956, 674.

5   SISS, *Scope of Soviet Activity, Part 12*. Testimony of Hunter Pitts O'Dell, 12 April 1956, 756.

6   See House Un-American Activities Committee (hereafter HUAC), *Investigation of Communist Propaganda in the United States—Part 4: "Foreign Propaganda—Entry and*

Dissemination in New Orleans, La. Area." Testimony of Sergeant Hubert J. Badeaux, agent in charge, division of intelligence affairs, New Orleans Police Department, 14 February 1957, 108.

7   SISS, *Scope of Soviet Activity, Part 12*, 687–694.

8   Ibid., 677.

9   Herbert Romerstein, interview by the author, 11 July 2001.

10 Ibid.

11 SISS, *Scope of Soviet Activity, Part 12*. Exhibit No. 225-C, 774.

12 SISS, *Scope of Soviet Activity, Part 12*, 763.

13 Ibid., 761.

14 HUAC, *Communist Infiltration and Activities in the South*, testimony of Hunter Pitts O'Dell, 29 July 1958, 2712-2; Hearing in Atlanta, Georgia, Hon. Francis E. Walter (chairman) presiding.

15 Ibid., 2716.

16 U.S. Supreme Court, *Dennis v. United States*, 341 U.S. 494 (1951); 341 U.S. 494 *Dennis et al. v. United States*, Certiorari to the United States Court of Appeals for the Second Circuit; No. 336; Argued 4 December 1950. Ruling 4 June 1951.

17 Ibid.

18 Chief among the lawyers was Elizabeth Gurley Flynn, one of the original founders of the ACLU. Convicted and jailed under the Smith Act in the second tier trial of 1953, she won on appeal in the landmark 1957 *Yates v. United States* decision by the Supreme Court that effectively put an end to the anti-communist trials. See: Mari Jo Buhle, Paul Buhle, and Dan Georgakas, eds. *Encyclopedia of the American Left.* (New York: Oxford University Press, 1998), entry for Michael Steven Smith.

19 Romerstein interview.

20 Friedly and Gallen, *Martin Luther King*, 25.

21 HUAC, *Communist Training Operations, Part 2. Communist Activities and Propaganda Among Youth Groups*; 3 February 1960, 1376.

22 David J. Garrow, *The FBI and Martin Luther King, Jr.: From "Solo" to Memphis* (New York: W.W. Norton & Company, 1981), 50.

23 Friedly with Gallen, *Martin Luther King, Jr.: The FBI File.* The original source for the Kennedy quote was Arthur Schlesinger, *Robert Kennedy and His Times* (New York: Ballantine Books, 1978), 384.

24 Quoted by Congressman Larry P. McDonald, *Testimony before the House Census and Population Subcommittee on Rev. Martin Luther King, Jr. Holiday Legislation*, 23 February 1982; and again, in similar testimony before the Senate Judiciary Committee, 27 March 1979.

25 Ibid., statement of Julia Brown; see also printed materials she submitted for the record, which included a copy of a check dated 7 March 1963 from an official Communist Party front, the Southern Conference Education Fund, to Dr. Martin Luther King.

26 Christopher Andrew and Vasili Mitrokhin, *The Sword and the Shield: The Mitrokhin Archive* (New York: Basic Books, 1999), 626–627, note 79. Congressman John M. Ashbrook detailed the funding mechanism for CPUSA publications and reproduced a

$20,000 check from the Chase Manhattan Bank in New York which he said originated with the Soviet-owned bank in Paris, in "The King-USSR Connection: How the Soviets Funded American Communists," *Human Events*, 10 October 1981, reproduced in *Congressional Record*, 7 October 1981, extension of remarks by Hon. Larry McDonald, 4691.

27 Wannall interview.

28 Reynolds, *Jesse Jackson*, 281.

29 Tom Kamara, "Can Clinton Administration 'Africa Guru,' Rev. Jackson, Help?" *Perspective* (Smyrna, Georgia), 18 May 2000.

30 Cirilo McSween interview. For background on McSween's career, see Rick Atkinson and Kevin Klose, "The Financial House Jackson Built with PUSH," *Washington Post*, 27 January 1984, A1.

31 "PUSH Sets Drive for Canal Pacts," *Chicago Tribune*, 3 December 1977.

32 Senate Foreign Relations Committee, Testimony by Admiral Thomas H. Moorer, USN (Ret.) Tuesday, 16 June 1998. Moorer was appointed Chairman of the Joint Chiefs by President Nixon in July 1970. The 1978 quote is contained in his 1998 testimony.

33 "S. Africa's Blacks Jail Jesse Jackson," New York Times News Service, *Chicago Tribune*, 25 July 1979, 6.

34 "Church Slams Invitation to Jackson," *Citizen* (Cape Town), 23 July 1979; from the Schomer archive bMS 551/45 (15).

35 Ameen Akhalwaya, "Jackson's Visa: The Cabinet Decided," *Mail*, 2 August 1979; from the Schomer archive bMS 551/45 (15).

36 "Church Slams Invitation to Jackson."

37 "Black Leaders Must Work Together," *Zululand Star*, 2 August 1979. See also "Jesse's Plan," *Sunday Times*, nd; Schomer archive.

38 "Black Leaders Must Work Together."

39 John Saar, "Jesse Jackson Takes on Pretoria," *Newsweek*, U.S. edition, 13 August 1979, 36.

40 Ibid.

41 House Committee on International Relations, Subcommittee on Africa, Testimony of Jesse L. Jackson, 6 September 1979, 2. Herb Romerstein, who headed a unit of the United States Information Agency devoted to Soviet disinformation and front organizations, provided extensive declassified information during the Reagan years on the Soviet-backed international "peace" movement and the WPC.

42 Kenneth R. Timmerman, "L'Armee de l'Air Sud Africaine Face au Defi Sovietique," *Aviation Magazine*, Paris, 1 January 1985. See also "Only One Source of the Threat: An Interview with General J. J. Geldehuys, CSADF," *Defense and Armament* 47, Paris, January 1985.

43 Kenneth R. Timmerman, "South African Realities," *Newsweek*, 17 November 1986, 56.

44 Angus Deming, "The Andrew Young Affair," *Newsweek*, 27 August 1979, U.S. edition, 14.

45 William N. Oatis, Associated Press, 16 August 1979.

46 "Andrew Young Resigns as U.S. Ambassador to UN" *Facts on File, World News Digest*, 17 August 1979, 605 A1.

47   William Claiborne, "Begin Reportedly Decides to Snub Jesse Jackson," *Washington Post*, 19 September 1979.

48   Christopher Swan, "Jesse Jackson, A Man with PUSH," *Christian Science Monitor*, 25 September 1979.

49   "Black Leaders Seek Palestinian Ties," *Chicago Tribune*, 20 August 1979.

50   Mike Robinson, Associated Press, 13 September 1979.

51   *Washington Post*, 11 October 1979; Marie Syrkin, "The Media and Jesse Jackson," *Midstream Magazine*, February–March 1988, 33.

52   Swan, "Jesse Jackson, A Man with PUSH."

53   Nathaniel Sheppard, "Arab Group Gives Jackson $10,000," *New York Times*, 17 October 1979.

54   Manning Marable, "Jackson and the Rise of the Rainbow Coalition," *New Left Review*, January–February 1985, 29.

55   Swan, "Jesse Jackson, A Man with PUSH."

56   "Jesse Jackson Peace Mission in Israel, Jordan and Lebanon," Memo to Dr. Avery Post, President of the United Church of Christ, 1 October 1979. Schomer archive, bMS 551/45 (12), General correspondence 1979 to September 1983.

57   Frady, *Jesse: The Life*, 165.

58   Jesse Jackson interview, 21 December 2001.

59   Andrew and Mitrokhin, *The Sword and the Shield*, 290.

60   Monroe Anderson, "Nationalization an Option for Energy, says Jackson," *Chicago Tribune*, 11 July 1979.

61   William Claiborne, "Jesse Jackson Warns Israel of Black Influence," *Washington Post*, 24 September 1979.

62   "Jesse Jackson Peace Mission in Israel," Schomer archive.

63   Ibid.

64   Angus Deming, "Jackson! Arafat!" *Newsweek*, U.S. edition, 8 October 1979, 50.

65   Ibid.

66   Ibid.

67   "Jesse Jackson Peace Mission in Israel," Schomer archive.

68   William Claiborne, "2 Jews Quit Jackson's Group; Jews Accompanying Jackson Assail Black Leader's Aims," Washington Post Foreign Service, 26 September 1979.

69   Ibid.

70   Deming, "Jackson! Arafat!"

71   "Jesse Jackson Peace Mission in Israel," Schomer archive.

72   *On Principle*, 22 August 1983. This and the following citation were among those assembled in an internal memorandum for the PAC for a Democratic Future authored by researchers Penn Kemble, Joseph Ryan, and Joshua Muravchik, "The Rainbow Movement, Jesse Jackson, and the Future of the Democratic Party," 12 July 1988.

73   Micheline Hazou, "Jackson: The PLO Has a Right to Armed Resistance," *Monday Morning (Beirut)*; nd.

74   Deming, "Jackson! Arafat!"

75   Monroe Anderson, "Jackson Attacks U.S. Media Jews," *Chicago Tribune*, 7 October 1979.

76 Bayard Rustin, "Do Blacks Have Anything to Gain from Ties to the PLO?" *Chicago Tribune*, 14 October 1979.

77 Swan, "Jesse Jackson, A Man with PUSH."

78 Romerstein interview.

79 Rustin, "Do Blacks Have Anything to Gain."

80 Monroe Anderson, "Arabs Pledge $10,000 to Jesse," *Chicago Tribune*, 17 October 1979.

81 Clarence Page, "Jackson 'Gives Us Voice,' City's Palestinians Say," *Chicago Tribune*, 28 October 1979, 6.

82 Anderson, "Arabs Pledge $10,000 to Jesse."

83 Ibid.

84 Jeff Gerth, "Questions Arise on Jackson Group's Finances." See also Kemble, Ryan, and Muravchik, "The Rainbow Movement, Jesse Jackson, and the Future of the Democratic Party."

85 Gerth, "Questions Arise on Jackson Group's Finances."

86 Ibid. See also Atkinson and Klose, "The Financial House Jackson Built," who reported that Jackson referred to the Libyan check four years later as the "only PUSH money from overseas."

87 "CIA Considered Jesse Jackson a Libyan Agent, Newspaper Says," Associated Press, 24 September 1980.

88 Charles R. Babcock, "Jackson Calls White House; FBI Drops Letter Delivery," *Washington Post*, 31 October 1980; "FBI Calls Off Letter Delivery to Jackson," Associated Press, 31 October 1980.

CHAPTER 5: CORPORATE SHAKEDOWN

1 Joseph Wing, Secretary of the United Congregational Church of Southern Africa, in Braamfontein, Johannesburg, to Howard Schomer, 24 October 1980, Schomer archive, bMS 551/45 (12).

2 Howard Schomer to Joseph Wing, 23 September 1981, Schomer archive, ibid.

3 Atkinson and Klose, "The Financial House Jackson Built with PUSH."

4 Clarence Page and Monroe Anderson, "PUSH Payroll Funds Frozen in Debt Suit," *Chicago Tribune*, 18 October 1979.

5 Gerth, "Questions Arise on Jackson Group's Finances."

6 Ibid.

7 Richard A. Viguerie, "Defund the Left," *New York Times*, 11 August 1982.

8 Tom Morganthau, "Jesse Jackson's Troubles," *Newsweek*, U.S. edition, 20 July 1981, 29.

9 Dan Raney, interview by the author, 7 March 2001.

10 Morganthau, "Jesse Jackson's Troubles."

11 Shaw, "A Clash Within."

12 Spencer Rich, "U.S. Cancels Grant to Jackson's PUSH," *Washington Post*, 12 September 1981.

13 Morganthau, "Jesse Jackson's Troubles."

14 See Margery Eagan, "Jackson Slams 'Elitist' Right," *Boston Herald American*, 5 October 1981; and Kevin B. Blackstone, "Jesse Jackson Condemns 'Right-Wing Revolution,'

Boston Globe, 5 October 1981, 1. Both accounts describe Jackson's chauffeur-driven limousine.

15 Gerth, "Questions Arise on Jackson Group's Finances."

16 Letter from the Acting Comptroller General of the United States to the Hon. Walter E. Fauntroy, 2 November 1981, B-204905. Obtained under the Freedom of Information Act.

17 Lois Romano, "Dept of Education Audit Finds Missing Money," *Washington Post*, 31 July 1983, H1; "Two Jesse Jackson Groups Misused $1.7 million, U.S. Auditors Say," *New York Times* (Associated Press), 20 August 1983, 12.

18 Accuracy in Media, Report #2, 2001.

19 Susan J. Smith, "PUSH for Excellence: Mixed Results After Six Years," Associated Press, 25 April 1982.

.20 Young was elected on 6 October 1981.

21 Frady, *Jesse: The Life*, 279. In addition, Frady points out that Jackson had a trump card: Bill Cosby, a Coca-Cola image-maker on national television ads, who agreed to back him in boycotting Coke if they didn't sign the covenant.

22 Reginald Stuart, "Coca-Cola Revises Cost of Black Pact," *New York Times*, 15 August 1981.

23 Atkinson and Klose, "The Financial House Jackson Built."

24 Morganthau, "What Makes Jesse Run?"

25 Sheehey, "Jackson's Lifelong Quest for Legitimacy." The Robinson quote is buried deep in this psycho-babble "probe" of Jackson's character, and is properly singled out and highlighted by Reed Irvine, "Jesse Jackson's Skeletons," *AIM Report*, Accuracy in Media, 8 April 1988.

26 McSween interview.

27 Reed Irvine, "Jesse Jackson's Skeletons."

28 Atkinson and Klose, "The Financial House Jackson Built."

29 Shaw, "A Clash Within."

30 Ibid.

31 Ibid.

32 Randolph E. Schmid, "Black-Owned Businesses Up 47 Percent," Associated Press, 10 October 1985, quoted in the January 1990 Heritage Foundation report by Joseph Perkins, *A Conservative Agenda for Black Americans*. See especially Chapter 6, "Creating a Climate for Black Business," which provides an excellent overview of the history of black enterprise in America. While not mentioning Jackson or Operation PUSH, the report puts Jackson's boycott strategy into perspective.

33 Perkins, *A Conservative Agenda for Black Americans*.

34 On 28 February 2001, the conservative National Legal and Policy Center filed a complaint with the IRS calling for an investigation of Jackson's organizations for violating their tax-exempt status by charging for similar business services.

35 Gerth, "Questions Arise on Jackson Group's Finances."

36 See 82-1338-C(3), *Rev. Jesse L. Jackson et al. v. St. Louis Sentinel*, Complaint for libel filed on behalf of Reverend Jesse L. Jackson and Operation PUSH Inc., 20 August 1982. Jackson never disputed the fact that he had made these comments at the lunch.

37 Steve Miller and Jerry Seper, "Jackson's Income Triggers Questions: Minister Says Money Not His Objective," *Washington Times*, 26 February 2001, A1.

38 John Kass, "Jackson's Role as King of Beers: Whassup?" *Chicago Tribune*, 6 February 2001, 3.

39 *Coleman v. Anheuser-Busch Inc.*; Docket 4:96CV02511, Eastern District of Missouri. The judge issued a gag order ruling protecting the company from public disclosure of the nature of the discriminatory acts alleged by requiring any description to be "treated as Confidential Communications" and not filed in the docket.

40 Quoted in Linda Johnson, "Black Groups Oppose PUSH Boycott," *Policy Networks* 2 (December 1982), 11 (a monthly report from the Foundation for Public Affairs).

41 State of Missouri *ex rel Phyllistine Quinn v. Anheuser Busch, Inc.*, Case No. E-1/79-0017 before the Missouri Commission on Human Rights.

42 Jerry Seper, "Jackson Sons Enjoy Success with Suds," *Washington Times*, 26 February 2001.

43 Multiple interviews between December 2000 and July 2001 with a corporate lawyer, who requested anonymity.

44 Atkinson and Klose, "The Financial House Jackson Built."

45 *Rev. Jesse L. Jackson et al. v. St. Louis Sentinel*, 82-1338-C(3). Memorandum in support of defendants' request for leave of court to file defendants' first amended answer and counter claim, 29 August 1983, 3–5.

46 Ibid., First set of interrogatories of defendants, 22 March 1983, 3–5.

CHAPTER 6: TOOL OF THE LEFT

1   Brashler, "Dr. J: He Has a Scheme," provides good context of the political climate leading up to Jackson's 1984 presidential run.

2   Lois Romano, "Jesse Jackson: His Charismatic Crusade for the Voters At the End of the Rainbow Coalition," *Washington Post*, 31 July 1983, Style section, H1.

3   Adolph L. Reed Jr., *The Jesse Jackson Phenomenon* (New Haven: Yale University Press, 1986), 2.

4   Romano, "Jesse Jackson: His Charismatic Crusade."

5   See Romano, "Dept. of Education Audit Finds Missing Money," and "Two Jesse Jackson Groups Misused $1.7 Million, U.S. Auditors Say."

6   Brashler, "Dr. J: He Has a Scheme."

7   "Israel on W. Bank; Russia in Afghanistan," *Jerusalem Post*, 4 April 1980.

8   Kemble, Ryan, and Muravchik, "The Rainbow Movement, Jesse Jackson, and the Future of the Democratic Party."

9   Romulo Fajardo, "Mass Peace Rallies Across the Country," *Daily World*, 15 June 1982. See also John Rees, "Disarmament Rally," *Information Digest*, 14 May 1982.

10 William F. Jasper, "The Clinton Administration's Terrorism Connections," *New American* 12 (25 November 1996), 24. See also S. Steven Powell, *Covert Cadre: Inside the Institute for Policy Studies* (Ottawa Ill.: Green Hill Publishers, 1987).

11 Dellums's one-week visit, April 9–15, 1982, began with a three-day weekend devoted to "resting," then official meetings with New Jewel Party leaders. See "Minutes of the

Political Bureau meeting, April 7, 1982," Document 77, in Michael Ledeen and Herbert Romerstein, *Grenada Documents: An Overview and Selection,* Department of State, Washington, D.C., September 1984. The U.S. seized seven tons of official documents during the 1983 invasion of Grenada.

12 William T. Poole, "The Anti-Defense Lobby: Part III. Coalition for a New Foreign and Military Policy," *Institution Analysis,* No. 12, December 1979, The Heritage Foundation.

13 Roger Wilkins, "The Natural," *Mother Jones,* August 1984, as quoted by Reed, 115.

14 Schomer archive, bMS 551/45 (12) General correspondence, 1979 to September 1983. Recipients included Jacqueline Jackson, Antonio Bonilla, Dr. Howard Schomer, David Williams, Mario Obldo, St. Clair Booker, Camille Cosby, Lamond Godwin, Wyatt T. Walker, Frank Watkins, and Jack Reiley.

15 Memorandum from Howard Schomer to Reverend Jesse Jackson, 30 September 1983, "Requests of the Interchurch Peace Council of the Netherlands," Schomer archive, ibid.

16 Department of the Army, Headquarters, U.S. Army, Europe, and Seventh Army, "Itinerary, 13 Sept. 1983," Attention AEAGS-SSD; Schomer archive, ibid.

17 Schomer memorandum, 26 September 1983.

18 Schomer archive, nd. Appended with the 1983 Europe trip material.

19 Yawu Miller, "Rainbow Veterans Keep Vision Alive," *Bay State Banner,* 15 June 2000.

20 "Jesse Jackson Declares Candidacy," *MacNeil/Lehrer NewsHour,* Thursday Transcript #2114, 3 November 1983.

21 "Jackson Issues Denial Of Being Anti-Semitic," *New York Times,* 3 November 1983, B15.

22 Jane Rosen, "The PLO's Influential Voice at the UN," *New York Times Magazine,* 16 September 1984.

23 Ronald Smothers, "Arabs, Jackson, and Jews: New Page of Tense Relations," *New York Times,* 7 November 1983, A12.

24 Sharon Cohen, "Jackson's Mideast Policies Trouble Jewish Community," Associated Press, 11 November 1983.

25 Smothers, "Arabs, Jackson, and Jews."

26 Romesh Chandra, "The Second Vienna Dialogue: Outstanding Event in Humanity's Efforts to Prevent Nuclear War," introductory essay, in *Documents of the 2nd Vienna Dialogue;* International Conference for Disarmament and Detente, Vienna, 14–17 November 1983, published by the International Liaison Forum of Peace Forces Helsinki office, undated. I am indebted to Herbert Romerstein for this and other documents relating to the World Peace Council, which he obtained while serving at the United States Information Agency during the Reagan administration where he focused on the Soviet disinformation campaign.

27 "Is Jesse Jackson Advisor a Communist?" *Human Events,* 3 December 1983, 4.

28 Chandra, "The Second Vienna Dialogue: Outstanding Event in Humanity's Efforts to Prevent Nuclear War," introductory essay, in *Documents of the 2nd Vienna Dialogue.*

29 Herbert Romerstein interview.

30 Poole, "The Anti-Defense Lobby."

31 Ibid., quoting from the 1970 Annual Report of the House Internal Security Committee.

32   Alvin A. Snyder, *Warriors of Disinformation: American Propaganda, Soviet Lies, and the Winning of the Cold War* (New York: Arcade Publishing, 1995).

33   Herbert Romerstein interview.

34   Editorial, "Jackson Jumps In," *New Republic*, 28 November 1983, 9.

35   Eric Breindel, "King's Communist Associates," *New Republic*, 30 January 1984, 14.

36   Ernest Green interview.

37   Former CNN reporter, interview by the author, 27 September 2001.

38   "Is Jesse Jackson Advisor a Communist? Candidate says no," *Human Events*, 3 December 1983; excerpts from transcript of CNN's *Crossfire* of 14 November 1983.

39   Quote and description from Tom Morganthau, "Appointment in Damascus," *Newsweek*, 9 January 1984, 20.

40   On the presence of Mary Tate, see Jesse Lee Peterson, "Problem Profiteer."

41   Ronald Smothers, "An Interview with the Rev. Jesse Jackson," *New York Times*, 28 December 1973, 18.

42   Sharon Cohen, "Jackson in Media Spotlight Again with Journey to Syria," Associated Press, 31 December 1983.

43   Tom Morganthau, "Jesse Wins a 'Syria Primary,' " *Newsweek*, 16 January 1984, 5.

44   Congressional staff, interviews by the author.

45   Geoffrey Jacques, "To Save the Soul of America: Black Leadership of the U.S. Peace Movement," U.S. Peace Council, New York, 1984, 1, 15. I am indebted to Herb Romerstein for having brought this invaluable document to my attention.

46   Speech by Jack O'Dell at "The Deadly Connection, Nuclear War and US Intervention," MIT, Fall of 1982; reproduced in *Equity* (Grand Rapids, Michigan: Institute for Global Education, 1983), 11–12.

47   John Rees, "Farrakhan and Libya," *Information Digest*, 22 June 1984, 197.

CHAPTER 7: "HYMIETOWN"

1   The main articles dissecting Jackson's finances at the time were Rick Atkinson and Kevin Klose, "The Financial House Jackson Built," Gerth, "Questions Arise on Jackson Group's Finances," and a follow-up piece by Gerth, "Arab League Made a Second Donation to a Jackson Group," *New York Times*, 30 January 1984, A1.

2   Kemble, Ryan, and Muravchik, "The Rainbow Movement, Jesse Jackson, and the Future of the Democratic Party."

3   In all, Bustamante filed six years of reports for Operation PUSH in 1984, after failing to file any reports since PUSH was officially incorporated in 1977. Ray Gibson, "PUSH Fails Its Own Audit," *Chicago Tribune*, 5 July 1987.

4   Atkinson and Klose, "The Financial House Jackson Built."

5   Ibid.

6   The other two trustees listed in the original incorporation documents were Marcus Alexis and James Buckner.

7   The three affiliates were identified as Operation PUSH, the Operation PUSH-Excel Fund, and the Operation PUSH Economic Development Fund, of which only the first existed as a separately incorporated entity. See Patrick J. Reilly, "Jesse Jackson's Empire:

Questions About Accounting and Accountability," *Organization Trends,* April 2001. I am indebted to Patrick Reilly, Terry Scanlon, and Andrew Walker at the Capital Research Center in Washington, D.C., for giving me access to the excellent research they did on Jackson's corporate empire.

8 Gerth, "Arab League Made a Second Donation to a Jackson Group."

9 Steve Strasser, "Jesse Jackson and the Jews," *Newsweek,* 5 March 1984, 26.

10 Ibid.

11 Shaw, "A Clash Within."

12 "JANA: Farrakhan Meets with Qaddafi," *Washington Post,* 6 June 1984. Qaddafi addressed Farrakhan's annual convention in Chicago by satellite in 1985, urging black soldiers in the U.S. military to desert and join black American civilians to fight against "your racist oppressors" and establish a separate nation. "This imperialist country must be destroyed," he said. "Otherwise the nation of blacks will be destroyed, Islam will be destroyed, the state of Red Indians will be destroyed. We are ready to give you arms because your cause is just." Juan Williams, "Desert Military, Blacks Urged," *Washington Post,* 25 February 1985. For Jackson's condemnation of the U.S. bombing raid against Libya, see Paul Taylor, "U.S. Bombing of Libya Assailed by Jackson," *Washington Post,* 19 April 1986.

13 Reed, *The Jesse Jackson Phenomenon.* Reed reported the poll results on page 16. His book provides an insightful critique from the left of Jackson's campaign.

14 Ibid., 36, 38.

15 Ibid., 69–70.

16 See, for instance, Charles Mount, "El Rukns Sued for Back Tax," *Chicago Tribune,* 13 September 1983; and Charles Mount, "El Rukn Sale of Building Is Challenged," *Chicago Tribune,* 13 October 1983.

17 Marianne Taylor, "Jeff Fort Pleads Guilty in Drug Case," *Chicago Tribune,* 10 November 1983.

18 "Gang Leader Jeff Fort on U.S. Most-Wanted List," *Chicago Tribune,* 1 December 1983.

19 Interview with federal prosecutors, Chicago, and with Chicago police detectives.

20 Atkinson and Klose, "The Financial House Jackson Built."

21 "Dollars-&-Sense-2 Presents Profile of Millionaire Noah Robinson Jr.," *Business Wire,* 8 August 1984; press release from *Dollars & Sense* magazine, Chicago.

22 The author wishes to thank the Chicago Police Department for allowing me to view many of the Government Exhibits used in Noah's subsequent trials.

23 Greenberg, "Noah of Fast Food: Too Much to Swallow?"

24 Affidavit for search warrant by Chicago police detective Daniel R. Iranian, filed 5 June 1988, with U.S. District Court for the Northern District of Illinois. See also Larry Close and Fran Spielman, "Sting Snaps on El Rukns," *Chicago Sun-Times,* 20 June 1986; and Rudolph Unger, "Rukn Security Service Gets Stung," *Chicago Tribune,* 20 June 1986. The Rukn security guards arrested in this particular sting were Noah's employees.

25 William Crawford Jr. and Monroe Anderson, "Noah Robinson's Dealings Probed," *Chicago Tribune,* 11 January 1979.

26 The report, entitled "Tunnel Electric-Apache Electric Co. Joint Venture Compliance with Affirmative Action Requirements," was conducted by deputy comptroller William P. Kessler at the request of the head of the district's affirmative action programs, James Braxton. Dated 26 April 1979, it was first revealed by William Crawford Jr. and Monroe Anderson, "Noah Robinson-Linked Firm Hit in Bias Report," *Chicago Tribune*, 18 May 1979.

27 William Crawford Jr. and Monroe Anderson, "Sanitary District Blasts Noah Robinson's Hiring," *Chicago Tribune*, 10 June 1979, sec. 5, 3.

28 William Crawford Jr., "Sanitary District Minority Hiring Plan Abused: Audit," *Chicago Tribune*, 9 May 1980, 3.

29 Dean Baquet, "Minority Firm Hiring Nourishes Well-Fed Few," *Chicago Tribune*, 28 April 1985. Sullivan was U.S. attorney for the Northern District of Illinois from July 1977 through April 1981.

30 The program began in 1977. The DoC grant was renewed in May 1979.

31 "Apologize, Jesse," lead editorial, *Chicago Sun-Times*, 12 February 1984; see also E. R. Shipp, "Chicago Gang Sues to Be Recognized as Religion," *New York Times*, 27 December 1985, A14.

32 Greenberg, "Noah of Fast Food: Too Much to Swallow?"

33 Atkinson and Klose, "The Financial House Jackson Built."

34 Ibid.

35 "Colleges Seek Own Custodians," *Chicago Tribune*, 9 December 1981.

36 Assistant U.S. Attorney Victoria J. Peters, interview by the author.

37 The description of Jackson and Castro and the account of his press conference with Vargas is drawn from Mark Starr, "Jesse Jackson Goes to Cuba," *Newsweek*, 9 July 1984, 16.

38 "Jesse Comes Out of the Closet," *Human Events*, 14 July 1984.

39 Ibid.

40 Charles Lachman, "Jackson Rally Cry: Long Live Castro!" *New York Post*, 28 June 1984, 7; Daniel Seligman and William Bellis, "An Eye on the Rainbow: Jesse's World," *Fortune*, 25 April 1988, 321.

41 "Jesse Comes Out of the Closet."

42 "Mr. Jackson's Prisoner Dealing," *New York Times*, 6 July 1984, A22.

43 Kenneth N. Skoug Jr., "Jesse Jackson's Journey to Cuba," *Washington Post*, 28 April 2001, "Letters to the Editor," A20.

44 "Jesse Comes Out of the Closet."

45 Rick Atkinson, "Cuba, Nicaragua Paid Some Expenses of Jackson's Latin Trip," *Washington Post*, 30 June 1984, A10.

46 Starr, "Jesse Jackson Goes to Cuba."

47 Ibid.

48 Fay S. Joyce, "Leaders of Blacks Debate Conditions on Aid to Mondale," *New York Times*, 29 August 1984, as quoted in Reed, *The Jesse Jackson Phenomenon*, 81–82.

49 ABC *Good Morning America*, 16 August 1984, as quoted in "Campaign Notes," *New York Times*, 17 August 1984, 10.

50 Thomas Riehle and Deborah Galembo, "Washington's Movers and Shakers," *National Journal*, 2 June 1984.

51 Gordon Borrell, "The Rebirth of Berkley Savings," *Black Enterprise*, June 1986, 168. Davenport had been an assistant secretary of transportation under Carter.

52 Bella Stumbo, "Brewing Controversy; Coors Clan: Doing It Their Way," *Los Angeles Times*, 18 September 1988, 1.

53 James Coates, "Will Coors Swallow the Union Label?" *Chicago Tribune*, 11 December 1988, 3.

54 Glen Fowler, "Civil Rights Groups and Coors Reach $325 Million Business Accord," *New York Times*, 19 September 1984, 18.

55 Lisa Collins, "Llewellyn Joins Coors Directors," *USA Today*, 12 May 1989, 2B.

56 Coates, "Will Coors Swallow the Union Label?"

57 William C. Hidlay, "Candidate Close-up: Jackson Left PUSH with Debts and Auditors' Questions," Associated Press, 21 April 1988.

58 Reed, *The Jesse Jackson Phenomenon*, 86.

59 Ibid.

60 "Jackson Is Still in Debt, His Campaign Reports," *New York Times*, 6 August 1984, 14.

61 Steve Miller and Jerry Seper, "Jackson's Income Triggers Questions," *Washington Times*, 26 February 2001.

62 "1983–1984 Candidate Index of Supporting Documents, Jesse Jackson for President," Federal Election Commission report, compiled at request of the author, 18 June 2001.

63 "Jackson Seeks Donations," UPI, 11 August 1984.

64 *Agency for Performing Arts v. Jesse Jackson*, Case #WEC 108096, Los Angeles County Superior Civil Court, Santa Monica, Calif. Cf. Hidlay, "Candidate Close-up (part 2): Speaking for the Poor Made Jackson Comfortable."

65 "Jesse Jackson's Ex-Aide Gets Suspended Sentence," *Chicago Tribune*, 6 July 1985.

66 Statement of Dewitt S. Copp, policy officer on Soviet disinformation, U.S. Information Agency, in "Soviet Active Measures," hearings before the Subcommittee on European Affairs of the Senate Foreign Relations Committee, 12–13 September 1985, 108–109.

67 Herb Romerstein interview; for more on Bogdanov, see also Oleg Gordievsky and Christopher Andrew, *KGB: The Inside Story* (New York: HarperCollins, 1990), 503.

68 A few conservative commentators elliptically referred to Jackson's January 1985 speech in Vienna during the 1988 presidential campaign. I am indebted to Herb Romerstein for providing me with copies of the World Peace Council materials, including Jackson's speech.

69 Statement of Dewitt S. Copp.

70 Reverend Jesse L. Jackson, "An Address to the Third Vienna Dialogue," Vienna, Austria, 27 January 1985; 13 pages.

71 Hidlay, "Candidate Close-up (part 2): Speaking for the Poor Made Jackson Comfortable."

72 For an informed perspective of the U.S. coverage, see Reed Irvine, "Notes from the Editor's Cuff: Jackson Meets with Gorbachev, Fails to Press on Soviet Jews," *Accuracy in Media*, 15 December 1985.

73 Dean Baquet and James Strong, "Snow Contracts Cause Flurry of Deals; Contractors Scrambled for Minority Partners," *Chicago Tribune*, 15 November 1985, C1.

74   John Kass and Dean Baquet, "Mayor's Friend Seeks City Minority Contracts," *Chicago Tribune*, 1 November 1985, C1. McClain had been forced to resign from City Hall two years earlier under a cloud of suspicion for self-dealing.

75   Ibid.

76   George Papajohn and Dean Baquet, "Jackson Cites South Africa Ties, Urges City Reject O'Hare Bids," *Chicago Tribune*, 31 March 1985, 4.

77   "Jesse Jackson Relative Charged," *Chicago Tribune*, 24 December 1984.

78   Ray Gibson and Andy Knott, "Murder Charges Filed Against 2 More in Killing of Deputy," *Chicago Tribune*, 19 October 1985, 5.

CHAPTER 8: BROTHER NOAH GOES DOWN

1   Interview, Assistant U.S. Attorney Matthew Schneider, Chicago.

2   Shipp, "Chicago Gang Sues to Be Recognized as Religion." For Jackson's ties to Sammy Davis Jr., I am indebted to Fellowship Missionary Baptist church officials Martita Hines and Walterine Johnson.

3   Maurice Possley and Ray Gibson, "Businessman's Ties to El Rukns Put Him in Middle of Federal Probe," *Chicago Tribune*, 21 October 1987, 1.

4   See in particular the Second Supplemental Report, *Re: Robinson, Noah,* Docket No. 89CR 908-31, submitted on 15 September 1997 to the U.S. Probation Office by Assistant U.S. Attorneys Victoria J. Peters and Matthew M. Schneider (hereafter "Probation Memo").

5   Ibid., 7.

6   Shipp, "Chicago Gang Sues to Be Recognized as Religion."

7   "Probation Memo," 14. Possley and Gibson, "Businessman's Ties to El Rukns Put Him in Middle of Federal Probe."

8   Interview with a former assistant U.S. attorney, Chicago.

9   Manuscript letter, dated March 19, 1982, from Noah Robinson to Leroy Barber. Author's private collection.

10   Interview, confidential source.

11   "Probation Memo," 12–13.

12   Ibid., 13–14; interview with federal prosecutors Matthew M. Schneider and Victoria J. Peters, September 19, 2001.

13   The account of the Burnside case is drawn from Possley and Gibson, "Businessman's Ties to El Rukns Put Him in Middle of Federal Probe."

14   Interviews with law enforcement officials in Chicago. See also Liz Sly, "Fort, Rukns Hit Hard by Verdicts," *Chicago Tribune*, 29 November 1987, 1.

15   "Gang Charged in Libyan Plot," UPI, 31 October 1986. The amount of the payment only came out during trial. See below.

16   Richard Kolovitz interview.

17   "The El Rukn's purpose in operating a security agency whose employees were authorized to carry weapons was, of course, to strengthen the gang's position in the endless turf wars in the course of which the murders with which these defendants were charged were committed," Appeals Judge Kanne wrote in his opinion. *USA v. Jeff Boyd et al.,* 7th

Circuit, 98-2035 in appeal of 89 CR 908. First Opinion dated April 3, 2000. This scheme was also described in detail in a separate case from the Rukn trials: *USA v. Eddie L. Franklin and J. L. Houston*, U.S. State Court of Appeals for the 7th Circuit, 98-3014 and 98-3015, in appeal of 89 CR 908. Final Opinion dated November 22, 1999.

18 Cose and Spielman, "Sting Snaps on El Rukns."

19 Interview with Assistant U.S. Attorneys Matthew M. Schneider and Victoria J. Peters, Chicago.

20 Jonathan Beaty and S. C. Gwynne, *The Outlaw Bank* (New York: Random House, 1993), 176–177.

21 Reported by the official Angolan News agency Angop on August 17, 1986 ("U.S. Policy Is Entree at Jackson Dinner in Angola," *Chicago Tribune*, 18 August 1986).

22 *Chicago Tribune*, August 18, 1986, sec. 1, 6, as quoted in Karin L. Stanford, *Beyond the Boundaries: Reverend Jesse Jackson in International Affairs* (Albany, NY: State University of New York Press, 1997), 152.

23 Dr. Mobolaji E. Aluko, interview by the author, 4, 7 September 2001.

24 Stanford, *Beyond the Boundaries*, 176.

25 Confidential oil industry source.

26 Jesse Jackson, interview by the author, 21 December 2001.

27 Rogers Worthington, "Rainbow of Speculation Marks Jackson's Return," *Chicago Tribune*, 21 September 1986, 1. See also Stanford, *Beyond the Boundaries*, 149–150.

28 "Clouds Over the White House," Hon. Dan Burton (R-Ind.), floor speech, U.S. House of Representatives, 28 February 1995; $30,000: Brown's trip to Nigeria with Ramos is recounted by *New York Times* reporter Steven A. Holmes in his biography, *Ron Brown: An Uncommon Life* (New York: John Wiley and Sons, 2000), 256.

29 "S. Africans Limiting Jackson," *Chicago Tribune*, 5 September 1986, 5.

30 Murray et al., *The National Evaluation*, 102.

31 Hidlay, "Candidate Close-up: Jackson Left PUSH with Debts and Auditors' Questions."

32 Gibson, "PUSH Fails Its Own Audit."

33 "Getting On the List," *National Journal*, 14 June 1986, Vol. 18, No. 24, 1456.

34 Reed, *The Jesse Jackson Phenomenon*, 108.

35 Ray Gibson and Maurice Possley, "A Trail to Bankruptcy: Millionaire Noah Robinson's Firms Frequently Seek Refuge," *Chicago Tribune*, 2 August 1987, C1.

36 Maurice Possley and Ray Gibson, "Noah Robinson Enigma Grows," *Chicago Tribune*, 12 June 1988, 1.

37 *Laborers Pension et al. v. Rising Sun*, 1:82cv03658, and *Cement Masons Pension Fund 502 v. Rising Sun*, 1:82cv03822.

38 List compiled by Gibson and Possley, "A Trail to Bankruptcy," supplemented by court filings.

39 "Report of Bankruptcy Probe Is 'Political,' Jackson Half-Brother Says," Associated Press, 2 August 1987.

40 Possley and Gibson, "Businessman's Ties to El Rukns Put Him in Middle of Federal Probe."

41 Shaw, "A Clash Within." Jackson's half brothers were Noah, George, and John Robinson on his father's side, and Charles, George, and Tony Jackson from his mother's marriage to his adoptive father, Charles Jackson.

42 Margo Nash, "Racketeering Law New Weapon Against Slumlords," Met Council "Tenant/Inquilino," December 1996, http://www.tenant.net/Tengroup/Metcounc/ Dec96/ricolaw.html. RICO was part of the Organized Crime Control Act of 1970. 18 U.S.C. 1961–1968.

43 Assistant U.S. Attorney William Hogan, interview by the author, 18, 19 December 2001.

44 Northern District of Illinois, 89-CR-908, Testimony of Freddie Sweeney, August 19, 1996, 6549, 6554, 6583.

45 Ibid., 6592–6593, 6599–6600.

46 Ray Gibson and Maurice Possley, "Suspect in Stabbing Surrenders," *Chicago Tribune*, 6 January 1988, 3.

47 National Rainbow Coalition letter to donors, August 26, 1986.

48 Shaw, "A Clash Within." On PUSH finances, see also Michael Oreskes, "Jackson Rights Group Drowning in Debt," *New York Times*, 4 July 1987.

49 Hidlay, "Candidate Close-up (part 2): Speaking for the Poor Made Jackson Comfortable."

50 Lester Kinsolving, "Jackson Blasts Pentagon—At West Point," *Washington Inquirer*, 3 April 1987.

51 Irvine, "Jesse Jackson's Skeletons," *AIM Report*, Accuracy in Media, 8 April 1988.

52 " 'Fund-raiser' Extraordinaire," *Washington Times*, lead editorial, 1 April 2001.

53 Quoted by Irvine, "Jesse Jackson's Skeletons."

54 "Managing Potential Presidents: Sketches of Key Campaign Staff," *New York Times*, 17 April 1988, A32.

55 "Jackson Retains Support of Arab-American Voters," Associated Press, *Chicago Tribune*, 27 April 1988, 5.

56 Ibid.

57 Kenneth R. Timmerman, "Al Gore's Arab Money Man," *American Spectator*, November 1997.

58 Irvine, "Jesse Jackson's Skeletons."

59 Alexander Pakhomov, "Soviet-US Treaty—O'Dell," TASS (Official Soviet News Agency), 24 December 1987.

60 Reed Irvine, "Jesse Jackson's Skeletons."

61 Morton Kondracke, "Jesse's World: President Jackson's Foreign Policy," *New Republic*, 25 April 1988, 11.

62 Daniel Seligman, "Keeping Up: Jesse's World," *Fortune*, 25 April 1988, 321.

63 Kemble, Ryan, and Muravchik, "The Rainbow Movement, Jesse Jackson, and the Future of the Democratic Party."

64 Joshua Muravchik and Penn Kemble, interviews by the author, 21–23 November 2001.

65 Jacqueline Trescott, "Ron Brown, In the Crucible: Jackson's Right Hand and His Atlanta Challenge," *Washington Post*, 20 July 1988, C1.

66 See the account of the convention in Holmes, *Ron Brown: An Uncommon Life,* 143–159.

67   See Vincent McCraw, "Jackson Expresses Interest in Buying Radio Station Here," *Washington Times*, 25 July 1989, B1.

68   Congressional aide, interview by the author.

69   Frady, *Jesse: The Life*, 156.

70   Eloise Salholz, "Proud to Be Jacksons," *Newsweek*, 1 August 1988.

71   "Federal Agents Seize $21,000 from Jackson's Half-Brother," Associated Press, 7 June 1988.

72   Ray Gibson, "Noah Robinson Seized in Employee's Slaying," *Chicago Tribune*, 21 September 1988, 1.

73   Ray Gibson, "Robinson Prosecutor to Ask Death," *Chicago Tribune*, 22 September 1988, 1.

CHAPTER 9: THE STATEHOOD SENATOR

1   October 1989 fundraising letter from Keep Hope Alive, signed by Jackson.

2   Tom Sherwood, "Vast Network Keeps Jackson's Hopes Alive," *Washington Post*, 29 October 1989, D1.

3   McCraw, "Jackson Expresses Interest in Buying Radio Station Here."

4   Broadcast Holdings resold it eight years later for $3.8 million to Radio One Inc., the largest African-American radio network in the U.S.

5   Sherwood, "Vast Network Keeps Jackson's Hopes Alive."

6   Joyce Price, "Jesse Jackson Stars at a Fundraiser for pro-Sandinista Film," *Washington Times*, 4 December 1989.

7   Corrections Corporation of America, Form DEF 14A, 28 March 1996.

8   Blair Kamin, "Inmates Get Message of Hope, Votes," *Chicago Tribune*, 26 December 1988, 1.

9   Sherwood, "Vast Network Keeps Jackson's Hopes Alive."

10   "Washington Briefly," *Orange County Register*, 24 October 1989, 9.

11   Burton Wheeler, interview by the author, 26 July 2001.

12   Election official, interview by the author.

13   D.C. Code 1-1462.

14   Act 8-191, "Representatives and Senators Term of Office, Duties, and Use of Private Funds for Public Purpose Amendment Act of 1990," enacted 13 April 1990.

15   D.C. Board of Elections, Docket #90-20.

16   Jack Houston. "Operation PUSH calls for National Boycott of Nike," *Chicago Tribune*, 12 August 1990, 3.

17   Todd Barrett, "When Games Turn Nasty," *Newsweek*, 27 August 1990, 44.

18   Ibid.

19   Eric Harrison, "Black Group Extends Nike Boycott," *Los Angeles Times*, 19 August 1990, 4.

20   Ibid.

21   Clarence Page, "Boycott Won't Provide Long-Term Solution," *St. Louis Post-Dispatch*, 10 August 1990, 3.

22 Gwen Ifill, "Jackson Asks Defenders of Nike to Think Again," *Washington Post*, 17 August 1990, F1.

23 Steve Daley, "Barry, Nike Issues Expose Jackson's Leadership Gap," *Chicago Tribune*, 19 August 1990, 7.

24 Glen Bone III interview.

25 Harrison, "Black Group Extends Nike Boycott."

26 "PUSH Fails to Win Support from Portland Black Groups," Associated Press, 22 August 1990.

27 Steve Daley, "PUSH, Nike Talk, but Boycott Still On," *Chicago Tribune*, 25 August 1990, 1.

28 Blair Kamin, "PUSH Targets Stores Selling Nike Products," *Chicago Tribune*, 28 August 1990, 3.

29 William Raspberry "PUSH vs. Nike: Serious Issues and Hocus-Pocus," *Washington Post*, 30 August 1990.

30 William Jackson, "PUSH Backs Off Boycott of Nine Firms," *Business First-Columbus*, 24 December 1990, 1.

31 "Operation PUSH Facing Financial Woes, Lays Off Employees," Associated Press, 25 January 1991.

32 Cliff Edwards, "Operation PUSH Out of Money, Wrecked by Divisions," Associated Press, 4 February 1991.

33 Glen Bone III interview.

34 Edwards, "Operation PUSH Out of Money."

35 Jerry Thornton, "PUSH Out of Red, Looks to Future," *Chicago Tribune*, 27 September 1991, 3.

36 Thomas Hardy, "PUSH Officials Say Nike Boycott Wasn't a Mistake," *Chicago Tribune*, 18 March 1991, 1.

37 Ibid.

38 Clarence Page, "PUSH Struggles to Find Ways and Means to Carry On," *Chicago Tribune*, 29 March 1991, 17.

39 Mark Asher, "Thompson Put on Nike Board," *Washington Post*, 22 May 1991, D3.

40 Thornton, "PUSH Out of Red."

41 Lynne Reaves, "Old Dream Still Alive for PUSH's New Leader," *Washington Times*, 17 March 1992, 3.

42 Sharman Stein and Frank James, "Operation PUSH Stumbles Upon Fork in the Road," *Chicago Tribune*, 21 December 1992, 1.

43 *United States of America v. Noah Robinson et al.*, U.S. District Court, Northern District of Illinois; 89 CR 907.

44 U.S. Court of 7th Circuit, Documents 91-1039 and 91-1040/91-2803, 91-3150 and 91-4041: "Appeal from U.S. District Court 89 CR 907," judgment dated 13 October 1993.

45 Ibid.

46 Judge Marovich, "Memorandum Opinion and Order of Forfeiture," 89 CR 907, 15 March 1991.

47 John Gorman, "Robinson Is Portrayed as Schemer," *Chicago Tribune*, 11 July 1990, 3.

48 Trial transcript, 23 July 1990. See also John Gorman, "Robinson Tells Court He Didn't Skim Money," *Chicago Tribune*, 24 July 1990, 5.

49 "Robinson Convicted on Felony Charge," Associated Press, 28 January 1989.

50 *United States of America v. Andrews et al.*, U.S. District Court, Eastern District of Illinois, 89 CR 908.

51 Eric Harrison, "Eight-State Raid Aims 'Death-blow' at Notorious Chicago Gang," *Los Angeles Times*, 28 October 1989, 2.

52 Interviews with three members of the team that investigated and prosecuted Noah Robinson under the RICO statutes.

53 Drug Enforcement Administration, "Report of Investigation re: Intelligence Information re: Noah Robinson's Distribution Organization," 28 October 1989. Case file #1353766.

54 Interview with Matthew M. Schneider and Victoria J. Peters, Chicago, 19 September 2001, and subsequent interviews with other members of the prosecution team.

55 Matt O'Connor, "Four El Rukn 'Generals' Get Life," *Chicago Tribune*, 27 May 27 1992, 6.

56 Michael Abramowitz, "Noah Robinson, in the Shadow of the Rainbow," *Washington Post*, 30 July 1992, C1.

57 Rosalind Rossi, "Life Term, Huge Fine, for Noah Robinson," *Chicago Sun-Times*, 22 August 1991, 1.

58 Rosalind Rossi, "How the Law Was at War with El Rukns," *Chicago Sun-Times*, 24 August 1992, 1.

59 Rossi, "Life Term, Huge Fine, for Noah Robinson."

60 The second was a $125,000 check from Boston Celtics star Reggie Lewis. The third is discussed below.

61 Larry Spinelli, interview by the author, 14 October 1999.

62 Farouk Zuaiter, interview by the author, Nablus (West Bank), 6 November 1999.

63 For more on Ed Gabriel, Jim Zogby, Alamoudi, and the DNC, see Timmerman, "Al Gore's Arab Money Man."

64 Federal News Service, Transcript, 7 June 1991.

65 "Remarks of Reverend Jesse Jackson to the Rainbow Coalition and Citizen Education Fund Conference, The Omni Shoreham Hotel, Washington, D.C.," Federal News Service, 7 June 1991.

66 Lloyd Grove, "The Man Behind the Curtain: Convention Manager Harold Ickes, from Left Wing to Democratic Center Stage," *Washington Post*, 14 July 1992, C1.

67 Brown aide, interview by the author.

68 "Address by Governor Bill Clinton at a Rainbow Coalition Luncheon, Sheraton Hotel, Washington, D.C.," Federal News Service, 13 June 1992.

69 Jill Lawrence, "Jackson: Politician, Spiritual Pillar," *USA Today*, 20 August 1998, 6A.

70 Julianne Malveaux, "Fewer Black Delegates in 1992 than in 1988," *Sun Reporter*, 15 July 1992, 1.

71 Maralee Schwartz, "Tax Exempt Swap Claimed," *Washington Post*, 24 October 1992.

72 Quinton Robinson, "Jackson Encouraged by Voter Enthusiasm," *Commercial Appeal* (Memphis), 29 October 1992, A7.

73 Jessica Wehrman, "Jackson Grabs Limelight in Presidential Crisis; New Role Is Pastor for the First Family," *Washington Times*, 31 August 1998, A6.

CHAPTER 10: MY FRIEND SANI

1   Rosalind McLymont, "Africa's Economic Renaissance," *Network Journal*, January 2001.

2   Chido Nwangwu, "Abiola's Sudden Death and the Ghost of Things to Come in Nigeria," *USAAfrica Online*, 7 July 1998.

3   Abiola described his early work for ITT and the military in great detail in his autobiographical account, *Legend of Our Time: The Thoughts of MKO Abiola*, eds. Yemi Ogunbiyi and Chidi Amuta (Lagos: Tanus Communications Limited, 1993).

4   Mobolaji E. Aluko interview.

5   *African Defense* (Paris, France), no. 61 (September 1985) 24.

6   Author Peter Schweizer argues convincingly that the Saudis took the step of dramatically increasing their oil production and thus causing world oil prices to increase in response to U.S. urging, with the triple goal of limiting Iran's oil revenues, helping the U.S. economy, and most importantly, crippling the Soviet economy. Peter Schweizer, *Victory: The Reagan Administration's Secret Strategy That Hastened the Collapse of the Soviet Union* (New York: Atlantic Monthly Press, 1994), 242–243.

7   Former U.S. government investigator, interview by the author.

8   Former World Bank Africa regional officer, interview by the author.

9   Mobolaji E. Aluko interview.

10 According to one broker, who felt the $12.2 billion figure was wide of the mark, Nigeria's 60 percent ownership share of the two million barrels per day it pumped netted the Treasury $13.1 billion at the peak price of $40 per barrel. From that amount, between 3 and 5 percent was paid back in fees to the companies extracting the oil.

11 Mike Fleshman, interview by the author, 6 September 2001.

12 *United States of America v. Ailemen*, 89 CR 585, Northern District of California.

13 Theresa Canepa, Assistant U.S. Attorney (Northern District of California), interview by the author, 24 September 2001.

14 *Newsday*, 3 April 1995, A14.

15 *United States of America v. Ailemen*, 89 CR 585. Popoola and Adebayo were names of Nigerian tribes.

16 Theresa Canepa interview.

17 Extension of Affidavit of DEA Special Agent Robert J. Silano, dated 8 November 1993, *United States of America v. Ailemen et al.*, 94 CR 0003, Northern District of California.

18 Susan Ferriss and Seth Rosenfeld, "Jesse's Son Named in Drug Case," *San Francisco Examiner*, 23 January 1994, B1.

19 Billy Montgomery, "Jackson Family to Seek Legal Action Over Drug Allegations," *Chicago Citizen*, 30 January 1994.

20 Ibid.

21 Dennis Schatzman, "Jesse Jackson's Son Denies Drug Charges," *Los Angeles Sentinel*, 24 February 1994.

22 Jonathan Bearman, interviews by the author, 3, 7, 25 September 2001.

23 Jesse Jackson interview, 16 October 2001. For more, see Chapter Eleven.

24 Jesse Jackson interview, 21 December 2001.

25 Randall Echols, interview by the author, 10 September 2001.

26 Douglas Foster, "Jesse Jackson: A Populist on Wall Street?" *Mother Jones*, 1 March 2000.

27 Mary Jacoby, "Furor Over Moseley-Braun's Trip," *Chicago Tribune*, 21 August 1996, 1.

28 Randall Echols interview.

29 Mike Fleshman interview.

30 Confidential source, interview by the author.

31 U.S. State Department, Human Rights Report, 1996.

32 Jeffrey Goldberg, "Jackson Jets To Jerusalem In Peace Push," *Forward*, 8 April 1994.

33 "Chavis-Jackson Competition:" Professional staffer of the House International Relations Committee, interview by the author.

34 Senior U.S. Department of Commerce official, interview by the author.

35 House International Relations Committee professional staffer, interview by the author.

36 "Nigeria on the Brink," *Economist*, 6 August 1994, 33.

37 Mobolaji E. Aluko interview.

38 Randall Echols interview.

39 Kenneth Noble, "Rights Groups in Nigeria Fault Jackson," *New York Times*, 24 July 1994.

40 Sonja Ross, "Jesse Jackson Seeks to Ease Tensions in Nigeria," Associated Press, 24 July 1994.

41 Jesse Jackson interview, 16 October 2001.

42 Gilbert Chagoury, interview by the author, 16 October 2001.

43 Ademola Adegbamigbe, "The Crude Pirate," *News* (Lagos), 28 July 2000.

44 Jim Lobe, "Nigeria-U.S.: African-American Group Urges Embargo Against Regime," Inter Press Service, 16 March 1995.

45 Confidential source, interview by the author.

46 Foreign Agents Registration Act (FARA) biannual reports, 1996–1998, Department of Justice.

48 Rose Umoren, "Nigeria: Causing Black Americans Grief," Inter Press Service, 28 August 1995.

49 Ron Nixon, "Divide and Confuse: Selling Nigeria to American Blacks," *Nation*, 15 July 1996.

50 Jacoby, "Furor Over Moseley-Braun's Trip."

51 David Barstow, Mike Wilson, and Monica Davey, "Nigeria Sent Cash to Lyons Fund," *St. Petersburg Times*," 25 November 1997.

52 Ibid.

53 Mike Fleshman interview.

54 For over a year the *St. Petersburg Times* maintained a daily "Lyons Watch" on its front page. Much of that archive, including the stories on his lobbying activities for General Abacha, is still available online at www.sptimes.com/News2/lyons/archive.html.

55   Gilbert Chagoury interview.

56   Citizenship Education Foundation, 1996 Form 990.

57   CEF income went from $360,211 in 1995, to $1,466,803 in the 1996 election year, according to the group's income tax returns. For the first time since its founding in the early 1980s, CEF listed "Get Out The Vote" events as its major activity, spending $979,337 on this and other voter registration efforts—69 percent of its total expenditures for the year.

58   Charles R. Babcock and Susan Schmidt, "Voters Group Donor Got DNC Perk," *Washington Post*, 22 November 1997, A1.

59   Jonathan Bearman, conversations with the author.

60   Case # 96-44579, Northern District of California, Oakland, filed 4 June 1996.

61   Articles of Incorporation, San Francisco Oil Company Inc., State of Nevada, C175.97, filed 7 January 1997.

62   Jesse Jackson interview, 16 October 2001.

63   Ibrahim died in a plane crash in 1996, and was replaced in the business by a younger brother, Abba, who along with Mohammad Abacha controlled the accounts. See, inter alia, "Nigeria: Court Halts Moves by Government to Recover Looted Funds by Late General," *Vanguard* (Nigeria), 7 October 2001; "Money-laundering: The Nigeria Connect," *Guardian* (London), 4 October 2001, 10; Ross Hawkins, "UK Rebuffs Nigeria," *Scotsman*, 10 December 2000, 7; "Son of Late Nigerian Ruler Charged with Corruption," Agence France Presse, 26 September 2000; and David Pallister and Peter Capella, "British Banks Set to Freeze Dictator's Millions," *Guardian* (London), 8 July 2000.

CHAPTER 11: DYNASTY

1   Sunya Walls, "Rev. Jackson Marches for Prison Reform," *Chicago Tribune*, 31 August 1995.

2   Kay Bourne, "When Will We Listen to our Own? Mel Reynolds' Problems First Exposed," *Chicago Citizen*, 31 August 1995.

3   Walls, "Rev. Jackson Marches for Prison Reform."

4   Marc Cooper, Ron Edmonds, "Somewhere Over the Rainbow: Jesse Jackson's Journey to 2000," *Nation*, 24 August 1998, 11, 13–17.

5   Illinois Motor Vehicle agency records.

6   H.E.R.E. was run by Edward Hanley, a long-standing Jackson friend who was forced to step down as the union's president in 1998 on charges of corruption. A federal report released that year revealed "an undemocratic union where funds were lavished on Mr. Hanley and his family to support a luxurious lifestyle." The union allegedly maintained "a fleet of leased cars, many of them Cadillacs, at more than $500,000 a year. They were used by top union bosses and their family members, as well as 'consultants' and officials with no apparent duties," the report said.

     The union also owned a $2.5 million jet that "cost hundreds of thousands a year to maintain," and made huge donations to nonprofit organizations. (See Shu Shin Luh and John Carpenter, "Union Boss Dies," *Chicago Sun-Times*, 9 January 2000.) Those contributions were made both directly and by putting employees of those organizations on the union payroll and providing them with salary and health benefits.

7   Curiously, the Chicago property was assessed at just $34,000, despite the fact the Jacksons had paid $200,000 to purchase it in 1994.

8   Sabrina L. Miller and E. A. Torriero, "Jackson Contacts Cultivated Beer Deal," *Chicago Tribune*, 8 April 2001, 1. Burkle refused to comment on his relationship with Jesse Jackson or son Jonathan, but said through a spokesman that he "will let the published reports stand."

9   Citizenship Education Fund tax returns for 1997, and Federal Election commission reports.

10 Glen Bone III interview.

11 Tim Novak and Chuck Neubauer, "Jackson Sons Quiet on Hiring," *Chicago Sun-Times*, 4 February 2001, 4.

12 Kass, "Jackson's Role as King of Beers: Whassup?"

13 Tim Jones, "Jacksons are poised to work with Busch," *Chicago Tribune*, 18 November 1998, 1.

14 Miller and Torriero, "Jackson Contacts Cultivated Beer Deal."

15 Ibid.

16 Carlos Ramirez, interview by the author, 13 June 2001.

17 Kass, "Jackson's Role as King of Beers: Whassup?"

18 Monica Dave and Ray Gibson, "Rich Pal Comes Through for Jackson," *Chicago Tribune*, 4 February 2001, 1.

19 Abdon M. Pallasch, Tim Novak and Chuck Neubauer, "Jackson and PUSH Pull Funds From All Over," *Chicago Sun-Times*, 21 January 2001, 20.

20 Dave and Gibson, "Rich Pal Comes Through for Jackson."

21 Victoria Peters interview.

22 Docket entry 4439, 89 CR 908.

23 The photograph and other details: interview with Chicago police detectives and other law enforcement officials present at the September 16, 1996, hearing. Press accounts: Matt O'Connor, "Jesse Jackson Testimony for Half-Brother Is Barred," *Chicago Tribune*, 17 September 1996; and Michael Gillis, "Jackson Is Rejected as Witness for Half-Brother," *Chicago Sun-Times*, 17 September 1996.

24 O'Connor, "Jesse Jackson Testimony for Half-Brother Is Barred."

25 Alfreda Robinson, interview by the author, 19 December 2001.

26 Jesse Jackson interview, 21 December 2001.

27 Ibid.

CHAPTER 12: HITTING THE BIG TIME

1   Order by Judge Charles L. Brieant, *Roberts v. Texaco*, U.S. District Court, Southern District of New York, 94 Civ. 2015 (CLB), 29 July 1997.

2   "Texaco Execs Discuss Lawsuit," *Los Angeles Sentinel*, 7 November 1996.

3   "Civil Rights Group Urges U.S. to Join in Texaco Bias Suit," *Minneapolis Star Tribune*, 6 November 1996, 26A.

4   Sharon Walsh, "Texaco Alleged to Order Data Shredding," *Washington Post*, 5 November 1996, A1. See also Jim Fitzgerald, "Tape Recorder Could Be Smoking Gun in Texaco Discrimination Case," Associated Press, 4 November 1996; Thomas S. Mulligan, "Texaco Faces Criminal Probe, Sources Say," *Los Angeles Times*, 5 November 1996, A1.

5   Ann Coulter, "Kwanzaa: Holiday from the FBI," United Press Syndicate, 1 January 2001. "Coincidentally," Coulter writes in this stinging critique of Kwanzaa, "the seven principles of Kwanzaa are the very same seven principles of the Symbionese Liberation Army, another charming invention of the Least-Great Generation." Coulter called Karenga a "black radical stooge of the FBI."

6   Fitzgerald, "Tape Recorder Could Be Smoking Gun in Texaco Discrimination Case."

7   Statement by Peter I. Bijur, 6 November 1996.

8   Daniel Shore, "Blowing the Whistle," *New Leader*, 4 November 1996, 4.

9   "Analysis Finds No Racial Slur on Records of Texaco Officials," *Minneapolis Star Tribune*, 12 November 1996, 4.

10   Del Jones, "Texaco Under Siege: Oil Giant Argues Tapes Didn't Contain Racial Slur," *USA Today*, 12 November 1996, 1B.

11   Ian Simpson, "Texaco Officers Sued by Shareholders Over Tapes," Reuters Business Report, 14 November 1996.

12   "Analysis Finds No Racial Slur on Records of Texaco Officials," *Minneapolis Star Tribune*.

13   Ibid.

14   Michael Kelly, "The Script," TRB column, *New Republic*, 9 December 1996.

15   Statement by Peter I. Bijur, 12 November 1996.

16   "Texaco Announces Settlement in Class Action Lawsuit," Texaco press release, 15 November 1996. In the final settlement, the district court awarded nearly $20 million to the lawyers out of the $115 million settlement, and distributed $82 million to the plaintiffs, with modest incentive awards to the lead plaintiffs, ranging from $85,000 to $2,500.

17   T. J. Rodgers, "Valley Should Stand Up to Jackson's Divisive Tactics," *San Jose Mercury News*, 14 March 1999.

18   "Texaco Foundation gives $50,000 to 'A Better Chance,'" press release, 25 June 1997.

19   Corrie Reed, "PUSH Commercial Division: Jackson challenges black businesses," *Michigan Citizen*, 31 August 1996. It has also been known at various times as the Trade Bureau, or the International Trade Bureau.

20   Hermene Hartman interview.

21   Harold Doley Jr., interview by the author, 4 November 2001.

22   Viacom press release, 18 February 1997.

23   Federal Elections Commission database.

24   FCC ruling, dated 27 June 1997, by Roy J. Steward, Chief, Mass Media bureau.

25   See, *inter alia*, "Re: Applications of WDOD of Chattanooga, Inc.," FCC ruling dated 12 May 1997, File Nos. BR-960401F4.

26   Eric Slater and Myron Levin, "When Jackson Presses, Funds Tend to Follow," *Los Angeles Times*, 13 March 2001, 1.

27 Ibid.

28 FCC ruling, dated 27 June 1997.

29 Rainbow/PUSH was allowed under IRS rules to engage in political activities, whereas CEF could not. "Financial Report to Donors, Citizenship Education Fund, Inc., Rainbow Push Coalition, Inc, Rev. Jesse L. Jackson, Sr., Founder & CEO," prepared by Billy R. Owens, Chief Financial Officer, 26 February 2001. The CEF financial report listed $500,000 in expenses for the "Viacom Project," which was not mentioned elsewhere in the CEF tax return or otherwise detailed. Even the official title of this unusual release of donor information was inaccurate, as were many of the details it pretended to reveal. Jackson held no official title with CEF. In all the tax documents released by Owens, Jesse's son Jonathan was listed as board president, while Jesse had no official position.

30 Dahlia E. Hayles, "Reply Comments of the Rainbow/PUSH Coalition," WT docket 97-82, 30 June 2000, available electronically from the FCC website.

31 The National Rainbow Coalition and Operation PUSH formally merged on 1 January 1997 "for accounting purposes," corporate records show. This left the Rainbow/PUSH Coalition, CEF, and People United to Save Humanity, Jackson's "church." Jackson's accountants said People United raised around $1 million per year by passing collection plates on Saturday mornings and "special programs," but refused to provide any breakdown of income or expense.

32 "Testimony of the Rev. Jesse L. Jackson, Sr. . . . before the Federal Communications Commissions En Banc Hearing," 14 December 1998, 5–6. FCC case 97-211 (MCI/Worldcom merger) and 98-178, which includes a 452-page public hearing convened by Jackson in Chicago on 15–16 March 1998 on the SBC/Ameritech and MCI/Worldcom mergers.

33 Remarks by Secretary of State Madeleine K. Albright at swearing-in ceremony for Reverend Jackson as Special Envoy to Africa, Department of State dispatch, 10 October 1997.

34 A National Security Council staffer and protégé of Madeleine Albright, Rice was confirmed by the Senate on 9 October 1997 and officially replaced Assistant Secretary for African Affairs George Moose on 22 October 1997.

35 "African Leaders Warn Mugabe," *Independent*, 11 September 2001, 11. See also Peter Hawthorne, "The Law of the Land: Zimbabwe Turns Up the Heat on White Farmers, and the Economy Cools," *Time International*, 3 September 2001, 37.

36 Interviews by the author with Republican and Democratic staffers working for members of the House International Relations Committee.

37 Jesse Jackson interview, 16 October 2001.

38 Former congressional staff member; current staff members; members of the Congressional Black Caucus; and African-American businessmen. Interviews by the author.

39 Several congressional staff members, interviews by the author.

40 Simon Barber, "Jackson Makes Big Business Streetwise," *Business Day* (South Africa), 20 January 1998, 11.

41 "New Jersey Preference Case Settled," Facts on File, *World News Digest*, 4 December 1997.

42 Abby Goodnough, "Financial Details Are Revealed in Affirmative Action Settlement," *New York Times*, 6 December 1997, B5.

43 "New Jersey Preference Case Settled."

44 Marc Carnegie, "Jesse Shakes Down Wall Street," *American Spectator*, April 1998.

45 Barber, "Jackson Makes Big Business."

46 Carnegie, "Jesse Shakes Down Wall Street."

47 Kimberly Seals McDonald, "FED and SEC Say Bias Is Bad for Business," *New York Post*, 17 January 1998, 16.

48 Regina Balane, "Loida Nicolas Lewis: From Cheerleader to Coach," *Philippine Post Magazine*, undated: http://www.philpost.com/0800pages/loida0800.html.

49 Harold Doley Jr. interview.

50 Patricia Lemiell, "Community Groups Take Sides on Citicorp-Travelers Merger," Associated Press, 25 June 1998. See also "Citigroup's $115B Under Fire: Pledge to Communities Disappointing to Some," *Newsday*, 5 May 1998, A55; Robert Weissman, "Make Way for Unibank," Vol. 266, *Nation*, 4 May 1998, 6–7; Lawrence A. Kudlow, "Mega-Risk: In the New World of Finance, Everything Is Getting Bigger—Potentially Including Americans' Tax Bill," *National Review*, 2 June 1998, 36.

51 Jesse Jackson interview, 21 December 2001.

52 Among the expenditures, Rainbow/PUSH and CEF audits showed that combined, the organizations spent $770,000 on travel-related expenses in 1998 and another $1.2 million in fundraising activities, including "conferences."

53 Harold Doley Jr. interview.

54 Jesse Jackson interview, 21 December 2001.

55 A military tribunal condemned General Diya and his fellow officers to death on charges of treason in April 1998, but the sentence was never carried out. See the State Department's Human Rights Report for 1998.

CHAPTER 13: AFRICAN GEMS

1 Former Clinton administration official and Voice of America reporter, interview by the author.

2 Tarty Teh, "Liberia Is Being P.U.S.H.ed by Rev. Jesse Jackson," *Perspective* (Smyrna, Georgia), 26 May 2000.

3 Jesse Jackson interview, 16 October 2001.

4 Sierra Leone's ambassador to the United States, John Ernest Leigh, interview by the author, 13 September 2001.

5 The American group, International Registries Inc., sued their successor, the Liberian International Ship and Corporate Registry LLC (LISCR) in the Supreme Court of the State of New York, seeking damages resulting from the takeover and accused Taylor of using the registry as a personal slush fund. A UN Experts Panel found in October 2001 that LISCR made four payments in 2000 to "nongovernment" accounts to purchase arms and transportation services, apparently for Charles Taylor. LISCR manager Yoram

Cohen told me in an interview that when he discovered the arms payments, he turned over documents to the UN and installed controls so that type of payment would not recur. See Kenneth R. Timmerman, "Severing Liberia's Sinews of War," *Insight* magazine, 18 November 2001.

6   Ryan Lizza, "Sierra Leone, The Last Clinton Betrayal," *New Republic*, 24 July 2000.

7   "Out of the Bush: Sierra Leone," *Economist*, 6 May 1995.

8   Lizza, "Sierra Leone, The Last Clinton Betrayal."

9   Tom Kamara, "Taylor's Millions Target U.S. Politicians," *Perspective* (Smyrna, Georgia), 19 September 2000.

10   Lizza, "Sierra Leone, The Last Clinton Betrayal."

11   Ibid. Another partner in the creation of the RUF in 1991 was Blaise Compaore, now president of Burkina Faso. See the excellent *Washington Post* series on Liberia and Sierra Leone by Douglas Farah in January 2001.

12   Lizza, "Sierra Leone, The Last Clinton Betrayal."

13   U.S. State Department, Human Rights Report, 1998.

14   David Pratt, M.P., Report to Canada's Minister of Foreign Affairs, "Sierra Leone: Danger and Opportunity in a Regional Conflict," 27 July 2000. Hereafter Pratt Report.

15   Former U.S. official, interview by the author.

16   Pratt Report, 46. An offshoot of the South African company, known as LifeGuard, was left behind temporarily to protect the diamond areas.

17   Sankoh's relationship to the Abacha regime in Nigeria remains unclear. Nigerian ECOMOG troops reportedly "captured" Sankoh in Freetown shortly before May 1997 and held him for over a year, but Sankoh repeatedly denied he was under arrest and periodically issued public statements.

18   U.S. State Department, 1997 Human Rights Report on Sierra Leone.

19   Star Radio: Liberian Daily News Bulletin (a service financed by the U.S. Agency for International Development), Africa News Service, 21 November 1997.

20   Jesse Jackson interview, 16 October 2001.

21   Lizza, "Sierra Leone, The Last Clinton Betrayal."

22   John Ernest Leigh interview.

23   Interview with HIRC staffer.

24   Tim Spicer, "Why We Can Help Where Governments Fear to Tread," *Sunday Times* (London), 24 May 1998. Details of Spicer's ill-fated dealings with the Foreign and Commonwealth Office were revealed in a four-page letter from his solicitor, S. J. Berwin, to British foreign minister Robin Cook, dated 22 April 1998 and subsequently released by the British government as part of a white paper investigation of the incident.

25   Lizza, "Sierra Leone, The Last Clinton Betrayal."

26   Susan Rice, testimony before the House International Relations Committee, 17 March 1998.

27   Susan Rice, testimony before the Senate Foreign Relations Committee, 12 March 1998.

28   White House transcripts, 27 March 1998 press conference with South African president Nelson Mandela. Available from: http://clinton4.nara.gov/Africa/19980327-9979.html.

29   Mike Fleshman interview.

30   "Top U.S. Officials Brief Journalists In Kampala," White House transcripts, 26 March 1998.

31   Dave and Gibson, "Rich Pal Comes Through for Jackson."

32   U.S. State Department, Human Rights Report, 1998.

33   Amnesty International report, November 1998, quoted by Pratt Report, 48.

34   Secretary of State for African Affairs Susan Rice, "Prospects for Peace in Sierra Leone," testimony before the House International Affairs Subcommittee for Africa, 23 March 1999.

35   Jesse Jackson interview, 16 October 2001.

36   Letter dated 10 April 1998, made available by the Liberian Democratic Future, Smyrna, Georgia.

37   Interview with Unity Party chairman Gayah Fahnbulleh. Jeter was subsequently named Ambassador to Nigeria, but Republicans in the Senate put his confirmation on hold. Al Gore ultimately rammed through his confirmation during the unprecedented three-day period in January 2001 when Democrats briefly held a majority in the Senate with Gore casting the tie-breaking vote. This was before Vermont Republican James Jeffords left the Republican Party and tipped Senate control to the Democrats.

38   Bodioh Wisseh Siapoe, "The Chicago Conference on Reconciliation: Public Relations Ploy or Reality," COPLA press release, nd. Available from: http://theperspective.org.

39   Liberian opposition leaders attending the conference, interviews by the author.

40   Ibid.

41   Jesse Jackson interview, 16 October 2001.

42   Harry Greaves, interview by the author, 4 July 2001.

43   Harris County public records. Corporate registry number 0240854; Microfilm 227810234.

44   Telephone inquiry by the author to Rainbow/PUSH headquarters, Houston, Texas, 1 November 2001.

45   "Cleaning Up Oil," *Africa Confidential*, 22 October 1999.

46   Jesse Jackson interview, 16 October 2001.

47   Kamara, "Can Clinton Administration 'Africa Guru,' Rev. Jackson, Help Sierra Leone as He Links Sankoh to Mandela?"

48   Christo Johnson, "Nigeria Returns Sierra Leone Rebel Leader Sankoh," Reuters, 25 July 1998.

49   Christo Johnson, "West African Force Calls Sierra Leone Truce," Reuters, 28 July 1998.

50   U.S. State Department, 1998 Human Rights Report for Liberia.

51   BBC World Service, 25 September 1998; Teh, "Liberia Is Being P.U.S.H.ed by Rev. Jesse Jackson." See also Sumowuoi Pewu, "An Opposition of Carpetbaggers and Inner-Circle Acolytes," *Perspective* (Smyrna, Georgia), 9 July 1999.

52   "Leone Rebels Behead, Chop Arms from Townspeople," Reuters, 25 October 1998.

53   Statement by Senator Spencer Abraham, 21 October 1998, Congressional Record, S12945.

54 Jesse Jackson interview, 16 October 2001.

55 "Jesse Jackson Calls for Peace in Sierra Leone," BBC World Service, 13 November 1998. See also Lizza, "Sierra Leone, The Last Clinton Betrayal," which succinctly sums up the ensuing events.

56 In an unusual display of reticence, Jackson's Rainbow/PUSH coalition issued but one press release related to this trip, an account of three visits he paid while in Guinea to Stokely Carmichael, the former head of the Student Nonviolent Coordinating Committee (SNCC), who now called himself Kwame Toure and was dying of cancer. Carmichael, who invented the "black power" fist-salute, had "unleashed a new level of consciousness" in America, Jackson said (RPC press release dated 15 November 1998).

57 Lizza, "Sierra Leone, The Last Clinton Betrayal."

58 "Rebel Leader Freed for Talks," BBC World Service, 19 April 1999.

59 Mark Lowery, "The Rise of the Black Professional Class," *Black Enterprise*, 31 August 1995.

60 FEC records. The only Republican recipients were J. C. Watts, who received $1,000, and Joe Rodgers, who got $2,500.

61 Panafrican News Agency (PANA), 17 May 1999.

62 Chris McGreal, "Gold Crisis Exposes Seam of Suspicion," *Guardian* (London), 4 November 1999; South African Broadcasting System, Evening Report, 12 February 2000. This was the same prince who offered New York mayor Rudy Giuliani $10 million for the victims of the September 11 attacks, which Guiliani turned down, because of the Saudi's criticism of U.S. policy toward Israel.

63 Press release, "Fifth African-American Summit in Ghana," 13 May 1999; contribution amounts from CEF and Rainbow/PUSH tax returns and financial audits obtained and compiled by the author.

64 Michel Desaedeleer, interview by the author, 9 November 2001.

65 Report of the Panel of Experts, Appointed Pursuant to UN Security Council Resolution 1306 (2000), Paragraph 19, in Relation to Sierra Leone; December 2000.

66 Jesse Jackson interview, 16 October 2001.

CHAPTER 14: A FULL-SERVICE BROKERAGE

1 David Whitford, "Jesse Shakes the Money Tree," *Fortune*, 21 June 1999.

2 JAXfax, 19 January 1999.

3 "Testimony of the Rev. Jesse L. Jackson Sr. before the Federal Communications Commission's En Banc Hearing," 14 December 1998, 5–6. FCC case 97-211.

4 Joan Oleck, "Up Front: Street Talk: A Minority Firm Hits the Major Leagues," *Business Week*, 19 April 1999, 6.

5 Raytheon corporate press release, dated 12 January 1999. See also Cliff Hocker, "Minority Firms Tapped to Oversee $800 Million Assets," *Black Enterprise*, 30 May 2000.

6 David Polk of Raytheon, interview by the author, 3 July 2001.

7 Text of Jackson speech provided by Rainbow/PUSH, 14 January 1999.

8 Charles Tribett, comments at the LaSalle Street Conference, 9 May 2001.

9   Melody Hopson, interview by the author, 4 October 2001.

10   *Williams v. Boeing*, U.S. District Court, in the Western District of Washington, Docket C98761C. The consent decree, entered on 25 January 1999, spread the money in several categories, with $3.77 million going to 264 named plaintiffs according to several formulae, $3.53 million to "the remaining approximately 20,000 class members," and the rest going to "systems changes, training consultants," legal fees and other expenses (Boeing Company, Form 10-K for 1998, filed 5 March 1999, 11). In the final consent decree, Boeing included payments to former employees as well, thus accounting for the higher number of members of the class.

11   Reilly, "Jesse Jackson's Empire."

12   Boeing spokesman, interview by the author, 3 July 2001.

13   "Boeing Names Rep. to Rainbow/PUSH Coalition," *Ethnic News Watch*, 19 April 2000.

14   Landon Thomas Jr., "Ex-Goldman Trader Stung in Arms Plot, Shocks Colleagues," *New York Observer*, 2 July 2001; David Voreacos, "Rev. Jesse's Arms Dealer Pal," *St. Louis Post-Dispatch* (Bloomberg News), 29 September 2001.

15   Thomas, "Ex-Goldman Trader Stung in Arms Plot."

16   Leslie Wayne, "From Riches to Relative Rags," *New York Times*, 27 October 2001, C1.

17   Confidential source, interview by the author, 3 November 2001.

18   Thomas, "Ex-Goldman Trader Stung in Arms Plot."

19   Landon Thomas Jr., "Rev. Jesse Knows What? Kevin Ingram Pal Questioned about Bin Laden," *New York Observer*, 1 October 2001.

20   Confidential source, interview by the author, 3 November 2001.

21   Jesse Jackson interview, 21 December 2001.

22   Sources close to Jackson claim Ingram's contribution to Jackson was "closer to $100,000," and may have included a separate check to Rainbow/PUSH, which was not disclosed.

23   Thomas, "Rev. Jesse Knows What?"

24   Ibid.

25   Wayne, "From Riches to Relative Rags."

26   Ibid.

27   Douglas Farah, "Al Qaeda Cash Tied to Diamond Trade," *Washington Post*, 2 November 2001, A1.

28   Jesse Jackson interview, 16 October 2001.

29   Whitford, "Jesse Shakes the Money Tree."

30   Ibid.

31   Ibid.

32   Reilly, "Jesse Jackson's Empire."

33   Ibid.

34   Ibid.

35   Ibid.

36   Lead editorial, " 'Fund-raiser' Extraordinaire," *Washington Times*, 1 April 2001.

37   Rainbow/PUSH press release dated 12 May 1998.

38   Internal memorandum by Jack O'Dell to Jesse Jackson, quoted in *In These Times,* 8–14 May 1985, 3. See Chapter Eight.

39 FCC Proceeding 98-141.

40 En Banc testimony, 3.

41 FCC Proceeding 98-141; Rainbow/PUSH withdrawal notice dated 17 December 1998.

42 Letter from Jesse L. Jackson to Magalie Roman Salas, Esq., Secretary, FCC, dated 26 April 2000, Re: Application of SBC Communications Inc. FCC Docket 00-65. See also Noah D. Oppenheim, "Follow the Money: The Jesse Jackson Story," *Weekly Standard*, 2 April 2001.

43 Data drawn from CEF tax returns released in April 2001.

44 CEF tax returns, released in April 2001. The GTE–Bell Atlantic merger, and Jackson's objections to it, was docketed as FCC Proceeding 98-184.

45 Chinta Strausberg, "Wall Street Conference Ends on High Note," *Chicago Defender*, 19 January 2000.

46 Rod Dreher, "How Jesse's PUSH Is Pulling in $$$," *New York Post*, 4 February 2001.

47 "Rainbow/PUSH Supports GTE Bell Atlantic Merger," Rainbow/PUSH press release, 17 May 1999.

48 Prepared statement of Mr. Dhruv Khanna, Executive Vice President and General Counsel, COVAD Communications, on the Tauzin-Dingell bill (HR 2420), 27 July 2000.

49 Corporate lawyer, interview by the author, 6 November 2001.

50 Robert Knowling, interview by Neal Cavuto, *Cavuto Business Report*, Fox News Channel, 17 January 2000.

51 Whitford, "Jesse Shakes the Money Tree."

52 "GTE and Partner Pay $3.27 Billion for Ameritech Wireless Properties," *Communications Daily*, 6 April 1999.

53 Washington Telecom Newswire, *New York Times,* 12 April 1999, C1.

54 Former senior advisor to Davenport, interview by the author, 12 July 2001.

55 Dan Walters, "Smog Tests Blow Out a Cloud of Politics," *Fresno Bee*, 15 January 1994. The deal was finalized in April 1994. Cf. "State Signs Pact for Updated Auto Emissions Tests," *Hartford Courant*, 19 April 1994.

56 Ibid.

57 "Envirotest Systems Hopes to Benefit from EPA's Strict I/M Rules," *Clean Air Network Online Today*, 8 March 1994.

58 "Envirotest Says EPA Takes Important Step to Enable Commercialization of Company's Remote Sensing Technology in 1998," *PR Newswire*, Envirotest press release, 12 May 1998.

59 Robert Siegfried, of Kekst & Co., 30 October 2001. The $580 million sale figure was reported by Hampton Pearson, "Chester Davenport to Become One of the Top 15 Minority Business Owners in the Country," *CNBC Business Center*, 12 April 1999. *Black Enterprise* reported in August 1999 that the sale was worth $266 million, while *Fortune* reported on 21 June 1999 that it was worth $280 million. The difference between these figures was corporate debt, Siegfried said.

60 Pearson, "Chester Davenport to Become One of the Top 15 Minority Business Owners in the Country."

61 "Rev. Jackson Seeks to Close the Digital Divide in the Silicon Valley," Rainbow/PUSH press release, 2 March 1999.

62 Reilly, "Jesse Jackson's Empire."

63 "Rev. Jackson Seeks to Close the Digital Divide in the Silicon Valley."

64 T. J. Rodgers, CEO of Cypress Semiconductor, interview by the author, 18 October 2001.

65 Rodgers, "Valley Should Stand Up to Jackson's Divisive Tactics." Reynolds was named by President Bush to be assistant secretary of education for civil rights in July 2001. His nomination was opposed by Democratic senator Ted Kennedy.

66 Slater and Levin, "When Jackson Presses, Funds Tend to Follow."

67 Ben Stocking and Jack Fisher, "Jackson's Group May Target Firm: Remarks by Cypress Semiconductor CEO Anger Civil Rights Activists," *San Jose Mercury News*, 4 March 1999.

68 "Jackson Continues to Question Proposed Viacom-CBS Merger," Rainbow/PUSH press release, 22 September 1999.

69 Ibid.

70 See Chapter Eight. See also Chuch Neubauer and Abdon M. Pallasch, "Jackson's Protests Benefit His Family, Friends," *Chicago Sun-Times*, 4 February 2001; "Jesse Jackson's Skeletons," *AIM Report*, Accuracy in Media, 8 April 1988.

71 Ibid.

72 *Shareholders of AMFM, Inc.,* FCC 00-296, released 1 September 2000.

73 "Jesse Jackson Financial Disclosure Called 'Inadequate': Group That Filed IRS Complaint Wants 'Real' Audit," National Legal and Policy Center press release, 8 March 2001. The NLPC complaint is available online at: www.nlpc.org.

74 "Rainbow/PUSH Coalition Raises Money for 'Wall Street West' and 'Silicon Valley Project,'" Rainbow/PUSH press release, 7 October 1999.

75 Chris Fiscus, "Jackson to Speak at Chandler Event," *Arizona Republic*, 9 December 1999.

76 "Notes to Financial States for the Year Ended December 31, 1999," Independent Auditors' Report, Velma Butler Company, Ltd., CPA, Chicago, Illinois, 6.

77 Form 990, Statement 4, Primary Exempt Purpose.

78 Ibid.

79 Letter from CFO Billy R. Owens to Donors of Citizenship Education Fund Wall Street Project, 26 February 2001.

80 Deroy Murdock, interview by the author, 16 June 2001.

CHAPTER 15: SPECIAL ENVOY OF BLACK BUSINESS

1 Jesse L. Jackson Sr. and Jesse L. Jackson Jr., *It's About the Money: The Fourth Movement of the Freedom Symphony: How to Build Wealth, Get Access to Capital, and Achieve Your Financial Dreams* (New York: Times Books, 2000). Times Books is not affiliated with Time Warner, but is owned by Random House, itself owned by the German Bertelsmann group.

2 Former U.S. intelligence officer, interview by the author, 21 December 2000.

3   Letter from Jesse Jackson to the Honorable William Daley, Secretary of Commerce, dated 8 December 1999. Freedom of Information Act request CRRIF 01-405, interim document release. Hereafter 2 October 2001 FOIA release.

4   Memo from Miguel Pardo de Zela, Senior Commercial Officer, U.S. embassy, Lagos, Nigeria, to U.S. Foreign Commercial Service, "Trade Event Report: Rainbow/PUSH Coalition investment and trade mission to Africa," 29 February 2000.

5   U.S. Ambassador Twadell to Jesse Jackson, letter dated 17 December 1999.

6   JeNelle Matheson, Deputy Director of OIO/ANESA (Department of Commerce, Office of International Operations), e-mail to U.S. embassies in Nigeria, Ghana, and South Africa, 5 January 2000.

7   Charles N. Patterson Jr., Principal Officer, U.S. embassy, Nigeria, Abuja office, to Ambassador Twaddell/DCM Serpa, embassy, Lagos, fax, re: "Meeting with Reps of Rainbow/PUSH Coalition Investment Mission Representatives," 20 January 2000.

8   EKO Hotel Banquet/Function Contract No. 1463, 4 February 2000.

9   "Rev. Jackson to Lead Trade Mission to Africa," Rainbow/PUSH press release, 2 February 2000.

10   Rainbow/PUSH brochure, "Investment and Trade Mission to Sub-Saharan Africa," 5–16 February 2000; letter to participants from Reverend Jesse L. Jackson Sr.

11   James Hill, "Jackson Leads Investors on Africa Trade Mission," *Chicago Tribune*, 5 February 2000, 10.

12   Johnny Brown, Regional Senior Commercial Officer, U.S. embassy, Abidjan, Cote d'Ivoire, e-mail to JeNelle Matheson, USFCS, Washington, D.C., "Jesse Jackson Trade Mission," dated 15 February 2000.

13   Ibid.

14   Ibid. In the company profiles provided by Rainbow/PUSH to the U.S. embassy in Ghana, Ms. Hoffler was identified as the representative of "MBC Network," identified initially as a telecom company but later as the "multi-million"-dollar law firm of Gary, Williams, Parenti, Finney, Lewis, McManus, Watson & Sperando of Stuart, Florida.

15   Morley Safer, "Lawyer from Small Florida Town Takes on Giant Corporations," CBS, *60 Minutes*, 18 March 2001.

16   "31st DWM & Dakmak Family in Tug of War," *Accra Mail*, 19 April 2001.

17   Paul Salopek, "Minority-Owned U.S. Firms Can Help S. Africa, Jackson Says," *Chicago Tribune*, 16 February 2000, 8.

18   Stephanie Sullivan to S. A. Odoi-Sykes (undated; 2 October 2001 FOIA release).

19   Correspondence from Dr. Ola Balogun to Mr. Miguel Pardo, U.S. embassy, Lagos, dated 8 February 2000.

20   "Trade Event Report," drafted by Anayo Agu; sent by Miguel Pardo de Zela to Kevin Brenna and JeNelle Matheson, USFCS, 29 February 2000.

21   Cf. *inter alia*, "Jackson Says South Africa Is Ideal for Business Opportunities," South African Broadcasting System, *Evening Report*, 12 February 2000.

22   "US Firms Plan Up to $3bn in Nigerian Investments," undated Nigerian news article; 2 October 2001 FOIA release.

23   "Trade Event Report."

24   "Rainbow/PUSH Coalition Africa Trade Mission, Company Profile: List of Confirmed Business Participants," and subsequent revisions provided to U.S. embassies in Ghana, Nigeria, and South Africa; 2 October 2001 FOIA release.

25   Oppenheim, "Follow the Money."

26   Harold Doley, former deputy chairman of the Wall Street Project and chairman of Doley Securities, interview by the author, 4 November 2001.

27   "Rainbow/PUSH Coalition Africa Trade Mission."

28   See "Prepared Statement of Mr. Dhruv Khanna, Executive Vice President and General Counsel, COVAD Communications, on the Tauzin-Dingell bill (HR 2420)," 27 July 2000.

29   Closing the loop was the fact that ACTEL was being financed by Lehman Brothers, where another Jackson crony and friend of Bill Clinton, Ernest Green, was now a senior partner. Green also chaired the African Development Foundation, and told me that Jackson had "made a real contribution to how the United States relates to sub-Saharan Africa." Ernest Green interview, 13 September 2001.

30   Guest list obtained through the Freedom of Information Act, Department of Commerce/ITA, second FOIA release, 29 October 2001.

31   Memorandum for Claire B. Mansberg, Chief, Acquisition Management Division, National Oceanic and Atmospheric Administration, undated. Subject: "Unauthorized Commitment." Source: second Commerce Department FOIA release, 29 October 2001.

32   "Sierra Leone Rebels Take 208 Peacekeepers Hostage: Annan Says Attacks May Derail U.N. Mission in Africa," *Dallas Morning News*, 6 May 2000, 8A (New York Times News Service). The State Department had already condemned the attacks on 3 May 2000, when fewer than two dozen peacekeepers had been abducted.

33   Letter from Sierra Leone ambassador John Ernest Leigh to Representative Corrine Brown, Second Vice President, Congressional Black Caucus, 3 August 2000, provided to the author. The UN Experts Report notes that "[e]stimates of the volume of diamonds mined by the RUF vary widely, from as little as $25 million per annum to as much as $125 million. De Beers has estimated that the total was likely $70 million in 1999." The experts noted, however, that there have been "no reliable statistics for at least two decades," 79.

34   Experts report, December 2000, 82–90 and elsewhere.

35   Confidential source, interviews by the author.

36   UN Experts report, December 2000, 198. See also 73–74.

37   UN Sanctions Committee statement, 7 May 2001.

38   Douglas Farah, "Al Qaeda Cash Tied to Diamond Trade," *Washington Post*, 2 November 2001, A1.

39   Sankoh operated the diamond mines as "RUFP Mining Ltd," according to the UN Experts report, 78.

40   European businessman, confidential interview by the author.

41   UN Experts report, 94.

42   Ibid., 95.

43   Ibid., 96.

44 For complimentary accounts of Jackson's press conference, see Douglas Farah, "Army Presses Sierra Leone Rebels: Troops Advance Despite U.N. Push For a Cease-Fire," *Washington Post*, 16 May 2000, A14; and Kamara, "Can Clinton Administration 'Africa Guru,' Rev. Jackson, Help?" Both accounts paraphrase the comparison Jackson made between Mandela and Foday Sankoh. On Monday, 15 May 2000, Jackson attempted to reel back his statements in an interview with Reuters, which only reconfirmed his earlier comments. Jonathan Wright, "Sankoh Solely Responsible, U.S. Envoy Says," Reuters, 15 May 2000.

45 John Ernest Leigh interview.

46 Lizza, "Sierra Leone, the Last Clinton Betrayal."

47 Press statement by State Department spokesman Richard Boucher, 17 May 2000.

48 The U.S. embassy was being run by a deputy chief of mission since there was no U.S. ambassador at the time. Press conference: Teh, "Liberia Is Being P.U.S.H.ed by Rev. Jesse Jackson."

49 House International Affairs Committee professional staff member, interview by the author, 19 June 2001.

50 Confidential source, interview by the author.

51 To implement the UN ban, President Bush on 23 May 2001 invoked the International Emergency Economic Powers Act and signed an executive order "that prohibits the importation into the United States of all rough diamonds from Liberia, whether or not such diamonds originated in Liberia."

52 Harry Greaves interview.

53 Letter from Ambassador Leigh to Representative Brown.

54 Hermene Hartman interview.

55 Letter from Ambassador Leigh to Representative Brown.

56 See also Timmerman, "Severing Liberia's Sinews of War."

CHAPTER 16: ELECTION 2000

1 "Black Broadcaster Trapped in Race Dispute," *Media Week*, 4 June 2001.

2 Rainbow/PUSH press release, 5 April 2000.

3 Author's notes of panel presentations, LaSalle Street conference, 9 May 2001.

4 "Declaration of Mark E. Hyman," appended to "Request for Recusal from Application Proceedings," filed by Sinclair Broadcasting, 15 December 2000; FCC File No. BTCCT-19991116BDN, Sinclair Acquisition X Inc. et al.

5 "Viacom to Acquire BET Holdings," Viacom Inc. press release, 3 November 2000.

6 Request for Recusal from Application Proceedings," letter from Martin R. Leader to FCC Chairman William E. Kennard, dated 15 December 2000; author's archives.

7 Lloyd Grove, "The Johnson Family's Conspicuous Donation," *Washington Post*, "The Reliable Source," 13 November 2001, C3.

8 Kevin Sack, "Like His Father, Jesse Jackson Jr. Raises Voice for the Left," *New York Times*, 15 August 2000.

9 See: Bob Wing and Terry Keleher, "Zero Tolerance: An Interview with Jesse Jackson on Race and School Discipline," *ColorLines Magazine* (Oakland, CA), Spring 2000; and

"3 Teens in Battle Over Expulsion Held in Robbery," *Atlanta Constitution*, "Nation in Brief," 14 September 2000.The initial brawl occurred on 17 September 1999. The court order banning Jackson went into effect on 29 March 2000.

10   Lynn Duke, "Jury Acquits 4 NY officers," *Washington Post*, 26 February 2000, A1; "Statement of Rev. Jesse L. Jackson Sr. on the Verdict in the Shooting Death of Amadou Diallo," 25 February 2000.

11   "Texas Executes Graham for 1981 Murder Despite His Pleas of Innocence; Jesse Jackson: 'I Wept Uncontrollably,'" CNN, 23 June 2000.

12   Jesse Lee Peterson, "Problem Profiteer."

13   Eddie Slaughter interview. For more details on the plight of America's black farmers, see Timmerman, "Farming While Black."

14   "Gore Seeks to Reassure his Minority Supporters," *Washington Times* (Associated Press), 27 July 2000, A12.

15   "ACU Calls for Investigation of Rev. Jackson and Affiliated Organizations," Complaint to Federal Election Commission chairman Danny McDonald, 13 March 2001; Exhibits 30 through 39.

16   Walter Williams, "Racial Rope-a-Dope," syndicated column, *Jewish World Review*, 20 December 2000.

17   "The Reverend Jesse Jackson Delivers Remarks at Democratic National Convention," Washington Transcript Service, 15 August 2000.

18   Larry O'Dell, "Robb Stumps State's Black Vote with Help from Jesse Jackson," *Washington Times*, 18 September 2000, C3.

19   ACU complaint, exhibits 68–69.

20   ACU complaint, exhibits 14–70. State by state campaign appearances were also compiled by George Washington University political science students: http://gwu.edu/~action/states/kydet.htm.

21   ACU complaint, exhibits 64–65. See also Matt Nagle, "Melissa Etheridge, Jesse Jackson Rally Support for Gore in Seattle," *Seattle Gay News*, 3 November 2000.

22   ACU complaint, exhibits 71–81.

23   ACU complaint.

24   Billy R. Owens, Chief Financial Officer, "Financial Report to Donors," Citizenship Education Fund Inc., Rainbow/PUSH Coalition Inc., 26 February 2001.

25   Cleta Mitchell, interview by the author, 29 March 2001.

26   Mary Leonard, "Visits, E-mail, Even Morticians to Get Out the Vote," *Boston Globe*, 6 November 2000, A1.

27   Kathleen Kenna, "Money Talks," *Toronto Star*, 5 November 2000. See also Joseph H. Brown, "Plantation Politics Goes National," *Tampa Tribune*, Commentary, 5 November 2000.

28   Will Lester, "Democrats Start Big Push for Black Vote," Associated Press, 22 October 2000.

29   "Jackson Holds Media Availability on the Florida Election Recount," Washington Transcript Service, 9 November 2000.

30   Author's notes from the demonstration.

31 "Predictions of Unrest, Victory Abound After Court Hearing," Agence France Presse, 11 December 2000.

32 Donald Lambro, "Democrats Won't Knock Jackson," *Washington Times*, 13 December 2000.

33 David Horowitz, "The Politics of Race," in *Hating Whitey and Other Progressive Causes* (Dallas: Spence Publishing, 1999), 85.

34 David Horowitz, "Al Gore Has Poisoned the Body Politic for Generations to Come," *Jewish World Review*, 5 December 2000.

35 John Leo, "Racial Rhetoric That Ignores the Facts," *Washington Times*, 13 December 2000.

36 John R. Lott Jr. and James K. Glassman, "GOP Was the Real Victim in Fla. Vote," *Los Angeles Times*, 12 November 2001, commentary.

37 Bill Sammon, *At Any Cost: How Al Gore Tried to Steal the Election* (Washington: Regnery Publishing, 2001), 262.

38 Steve Miller, "Jackson Fires Up Tallahassee Rally Outside Capitol," *Washington Times*, 14 December 2000.

39 "Reverend Jesse Jackson Criticizes Supreme Court Decision: Jackson Reiterates, Clarifies Prediction of 'Civil Rights Explosion,'" Rainbow/PUSH coalition statement, 13 December 2000.

40 David Poe, "Jesse's War Plan," *FrontPage Magazine*, 18 December 2000.

41 "Jesse Jackson's Love Child," *National Enquirer*, 18 January 2001.

42 "Jesse's Mistress Tells All," *National Enquirer*, 10 April 2001.

43 Howard Kurtz, "Tabloid News Again Floods the Mainstream," *Washington Post*, 19 January 2001, C1.

44 "Jackson Admits Affair: Civil Rights Leader Acknowledges Fathering a Child Out of Wedlock," ABC News, 18 January 2001.

45 "Jesse's Mistress Tells All."

46 Separate interviews with Hermene Hartman and Cirilo McSween.

47 Robert G. Herguth and Lynn Sweet, "Civil Rights Group Still Supports Jackson," *Chicago Sun-Times*, 20 January 2001, 1.

48 Dave and Gibson, "Rich Pal Comes Through for Jackson."

49 Hermene D. Hartman, "What Karin Stanford Didn't Tell Connie Chung about the Jackson Affair," Publisher's page, *N'Digo* (Chicago, IL), 23 August 2001.

50 Jesse Jackson interview, 21 December 2001.

51 "Dorothy Rivers Indicted for $5 Million Government Fraud," U.S. Department of Justice, Assistant U.S. Attorney's Office for the Northern District of Illinois, press release dated 25 April 1996.

52 "Two Jackson Pals Won Clemency," *Chicago Tribune*, 11 March 2001. See also "Jesse Jackson's Pals Got Last-Minute Clinton Pardons," Judicial Watch press release, 1 March 2001.

53 Deroy Murdock interview. See also Murdock's column, "When It's Time to Exit," *Washington Times*, 12 February 2001, A14.

54 The website showed Reynolds residing at 1515 W. Monroe Street, Chicago, 60607. See: http://samnet.isp.state.il.us/ispso2/sex_offenders/index.asp.

55 *United States of America v. Boyd et al.*, U.S. Court of Appeals (7th Cir.), 98-2035; Judge Posner ordered the new trial in an opinion dated 3 April 2000.

56 Justice Department official in Washington and federal prosecutors in Chicago, interviews by the author.

CHAPTER 17: LIFE AFTER CLINTON

1   "Affair Doesn't Keep Jackson Quiet," Associated Press, 21 January 2001.

2   Deroy Murdock, "Jesse Jackson's Church of Instant Forgiveness," *Liberzine.com*, 5 February 2001.

3   Peter Noel, "The 'Wrongs' of 'Mr. Civil Rights,' " *Village Voice*, 2 May 2001.

4   Reverend Wyatt Tee Walker to Jesse Jackson, 1 February 2001.

5   This section and the next are based on my notes from the conference.

6   David Whitford, "The New Black Power," *Fortune*, 4 August 1997, 47.

7   J. Coyden Palmer, "Black Entrepreneurs Help the Needy," *Chicago Citizen*, 2 December 1999. Coke insider: Confidential source, interviews by the author, 1 and 27 November 2001.

8   Henry Unger, "Judge Instructs Coke Task Force," *Atlanta Journal-Constitution*, 22 August 2001, D3.

9   Corporate executive, interview by the author, 18 October 2001.

10 "Newsmakers," *St. Louis Post-Dispatch* (Reuters), 9 August 1999, A2.

11 Answer from defendants, dated 26 June 2000, in 1:00-CV-1182-ODE, *Reid et al. v. Lockheed Martin Aeronautics Company*; District Court for the Northern District of Georgia, Atlanta Division, 45. See also a parallel case filed at the same time, *Yarbrough v. Lockheed*, 1:00-CV-1183-ODE.

12 Photographs of Gary with the Rolls and the aircraft can be viewed on his law office website along with a streaming video of his greatest accomplishments, http://www.williegary.com. "Trial Lawyer Gary Can Be Called 'Billion-Dollar Man,' " *Palm Beach Post*, 25 June 2001.

13 Patrick Reilly, "Corporate Donations to Jackson Network," Capital Research Center, April 2001.

14 "Office Depot Denies Race Bias Allegations," Reuters Business Report, 28 February 2001.

15 Paul Owers, "Office Depot, Gary Resolve Bias Claims," *Palm Beach Post*, 24 August 2001.

16 Steve Miller, "Toyota to Devote Billions to Jackson Diversity Demands," *Washington Times*, 9 August 2001.

17 Toyota spokesperson Tracy Underwood, interview by the author, 31 July 2001.

18 Steve Miller, "Toyota Faces Jackson's Deadline," *Washington Times*, 31 July 2001.

19 Ken Boehm, interview by the author, 2 November 2001.

20 Harold J. Doley Jr., interviews by the author, 2–4 November 2001. See also Marc Morano, "Jesse Jackson Accused of 'Racketeering' by Top Black Businessman," *CNSNews.com*, 22 October 2001.

21 Jesse Jackson interview, 21 December 2001.

22 Hermene Hartman interview.

23 This particular quote is from an excellent article on Jackson's shakedown of the pension fund business by Robin Goldwyn Blumenthal, "Quid Pro Quota?" *Barron's*, 21 May 2001.

24 Roy Innis, interview by the author, 1 October 2001.

25 Starr Parker, interview by the author, 13 July 2001.

CHAPTER 18: SHAKEDOWN MAN

1 Reverend Jesse Lee Peterson, interview by the author, 15 November 2001. See also Peterson's autobiographical account, *From Rage to Responsibility*.

CHAPTER 19: THE WAR THAT JESSE MADE

1 U.S. embassy, Monrovia, to Department of State, 1 February 1998; Monrovia 583; document D1.

2 U.S. embassy, Monrovia, to U.S. Information Agency (USIA), 29 April 1998; Monrovia 1554; document A256.

3 U.S. embassy, Monrovia, to Secretary of State, Washington, D.C., 28 July 1998; Monrovia 2737; document A138.

4 Background note, drafted by Africa desk officer Michael Thomas, 29 July 1998, as part of briefing memorandum for assistant secretary Susan E. Rice from deputy assistant secretary Howard F. Jeter, in preparation for Rice's meeting with Kabbah in Washington, D.C., on 30 July 1998; documents 139A and 139, respectively.

5 U.S. embassy, Monrovia, to Secretary of State, Washington, D.C., 28 July 1998; Monrovia 2737; document A138. "...Kabbah did not embrace the view that a military victory would not bring lasting peace to Sierra Leone."

6 Briefing memorandum from assistant secretary of state Susan E. Rice to special envoy Jesse Jackson, 5 November 1998. Secret; document 151.

7 Interview with Susan E. Rice, now at the Brookings Institution, 17 July 17 2003.

8 "Talking Points for Rev. Jackson Conversation with President Taylor 21 September 1998"; document A270.

9 Transcript of meeting of Jesse Jackson and Representatives of Civil Society and the Press, USIS Library, Sierra Leone, 13 November 1998; document A153.

10 Ibid.

11 "Rev. Jackson call to RUF Representative Omrie Golley," undated, document A15.

12 Jackson-Golley transcript, five pages, undated; document A16.

13 "Sierra Leone: Rev. Jackson talks to President Kabbah and RUF Representative Omrie Golley," State Department Cable 26809, 12 February 1999; document A18

14 "Briefing Memorandum for Jackson-Kabbah-Sankoh meeting," drafted by Susan Rice, 17 May 1999; State Department cable 90957; document A42.

15 Susan Rice interview, 17 July 2003.

16   U.S. embassy, Lomé, to Secretary of State, Washington, D.C., 18 May 1999; Lomé 1619; document A48. The State Department first received a copy of the actual agreement, with the signatures of the participants and witnesses, not from Jackson or from U.S. diplomats in the region, but from the embassy of Togo in Washington, D.C. (document A56A.)

17   "Rev. Jackson's June 30 Phone Call to Foday Sankoh," 2 July 1999, Ref 7-1658; (document A94.)

18   "Rev. Jackson call to RUF Leader Foday Sankoh," State Department briefing document A83, undated; "Rev. Jackson call to RUF Leader Sankoh, Sat. June 12, 7:15 a.m.," State Department transcript of conversation; document A85.

19   "Talking Points for Reverend Jackson-Foday Sankoh Telecon: The Price of Failure," undated, released in full; document A131.

20   Talking points, 31 March 2000; no serial; document A167. The second draft, document A168A, includes Rice's admonishment to Sankoh.

21   "Briefing Memorandum from Susan Rice to Secretary of State Madeleine in preparation for her meeting with Jackson," 10 April 2000; document A169. When the Enron scandal erupted in early 2002, Jackson initially denied he had ties to the corporation until cornered by CNSNews.com correspondent Marc Morano. Jackson was accompanying a busload of former Enron employees to Washington, D.C., so they could complain to Congress about the loss of their retirement funds when Morano asked him about the Enron contributions. "Whatever it was, it was miniscule," he told Morano. Jackson insisted there was no reason for him to return the money because it was "irrelevant to the magnitude of this issue." (Marc Morano, "Jackson Admits Contributions from Enron," CNSNews.com, 31 January 2002). Indeed, I have seen no instance where Jackson returned any contributions to his organizations, even from convicted felons such as Kevin Ingram.

22   "Telecon between President Charles Taylor and Reverend Jesse Jackson," 4 May 2000; document A171

23   "Telecon May 7, 2000, Rev. Jackson to President Taylor of Liberia"; document A172.

24   U.S. embassy, Monrovia, to Secretary of State, Washington, D.C.; Monrovia 1586, 22 May 2000; document A191.

25   "S/E Jackson's May 19 meetings with Charles Taylor," US embassy, London, to Secretary of State, Washington, D.C., 23 May 2000; document A192. The cable bears the notation "cleared by DAS Jeter," and appears to have been filed by Howard Jeter during a stopover in London.

26   "Reverend Jackson to President Kabbah Telecon 5-21," 21 May 2000, no serial; document A190.

ACKNOWLEDGMENTS

Thanks to the many people who scoured their memories, their archives, and donated their time to helping me research this book.

In Chicago, special thanks to Glen Bone III; the Reverend Charles Jenkins of Fellowship Missionary Baptist Church and church staff Martita Hines, Celeste West, Bill Brown, Beverly Tatum, Walterine Johnson; the Reverend Caesar Leflur; Cirilo McSween; Hermene Hartman; current and former U.S. attorneys William Hogan, Tom Sullivan, Samuel K. Skinner, and Assistant U.S. Attorneys Matthew M. Schneider and Victoria J. Peters; Sergeant Dan Brannigan and Sergeant Richard Kolovitz of the Chicago Police Department; the staff of the Cook County district court archives division, who helped me research old court cases; Joan Blocher at the Chicago Theological Seminary; Hurley Green; Mike Anguiana; Joseph A. Morris, of the law firm Morris, Rathnau & De La Rosa; and to the dedicated public servants of Chicago's criminal justice system who helped unearth long-buried documents from the public record and shared their personal recollections with me.

In Washington, D.C.: Terry Scanlon, Patrick Reilly, and Andrew Walker of the Capital Research Center, who gave me access to their terrific research on Jackson's organizations; Howard Phillips of the Conservative Caucus Foundation and his able assistants Louise Lovelace and Gisella Tello, who searched archives and dug up invaluable information on federal funding for Jackson's organizations during the Carter and Reagan administrations; Jim Holmes of the Institute of World Politics, who manages one of the most extensive libraries of national security documents in Washington, D.C.; Scott Stanley, my editor at *Insight* magazine, for his pithy wisdom, wealth of experience, and prodigious memory; and Herb Romerstein, W. Raymond Wannall, William Schulz, Telly Lovelace, J. Randall Echols, Ambassador John Ernest Leigh, Richard Falknor, Gayah Fahnbulleh, Mobolaji E. Aluko, C. Boyden Gray, Ken Boehm, Michael Leader, Cleta Mitchell, Donatella Lurch, and many others who have asked not to be named who shared insights and information.

And elsewhere: Karine Schomer, who steered me to the archives of her now deceased father, Dr. Howard Schomer, and Francis O'Donnell, Curator, Manuscripts and Archives Office of the Andover-Harvard Theological Library of Harvard Divinity School, for permission to quote from the Howard Schomer Papers, 1928–1998; Deroy Murdock, Starr Parker, the Reverend Johnny Hunter, the Reverend Jesse Lee Peterson, Roy Innis, Eddie Slaughter, Mike Fleshman, Harold Doley, Michel Desaedeleer; Jonathan Bearman and Patrick Smith in London; Gilbert Chagoury in Paris; Pat Clawson of Radio America; Theresa Canepa and Debbie Husnick, with the U.S. attorney's office in San Francisco.

A special thanks to my publisher, Al Regnery, whose personal interest in this project provided added insights; our dedicated team of editors headed by Harry Crocker, who helped give shape to this manuscript and save me from unfortunate errors, and Bernadette Malone, who worked night and day with me to incorporate last-minute changes; the meticulous eye of Robert Lystad of Baker and Hostetler; and to my wife, Christina, and our five children, who tolerated a new member of the household for the better part of a year.

INDEX